THE SELECTED ESSAYS OF
SEAN O'FAOLAIN

The Selected Essays
of Sean O'Faolain

Edited by
BRAD KENT

McGill-Queen's University Press
Montreal & Kingston · London · Chicago

© McGill-Queen's University Press 2016

ISBN 978-0-7735-4776-6 (cloth)
ISBN 978-0-7735-4777-3 (paper)
ISBN 978-0-7735-4861-9 (ePDF)
ISBN 978-0-7735-4862-6 (ePUB)

Legal deposit fourth quarter 2016
Bibliothèque nationale du Québec

Printed in Canada on acid-free paper that is 100% ancient forest free
(100% post-consumer recycled), processed chlorine free

This book has been published with the help of a grant from the Canadian
Federation for the Humanities and Social Sciences, through the Awards to
Scholarly Publications Program, using funds provided by the Social Sciences
and Humanities Research Council of Canada.

McGill-Queen's University Press acknowledges the support of the Canada
Council for the Arts for our publishing program. We also acknowledge the
financial support of the Government of Canada through the Canada Book
Fund for our publishing activities.

Library and Archives Canada Cataloguing in Publication

O'Faoláin, Seán, 1900–1991
    [Essays. Selections]
    The selected essays of Sean O'Faolain/edited by Brad Kent.

    Includes bibliographical references and index.
    Issued in print and electronic formats.
    ISBN 978-0-7735-4776-6 (cloth). – ISBN 978-0-7735-4777-3 (paper). –
    ISBN 978-0-7735-4861-9 (ePDF). – ISBN 978-0-7735-4862-6 (ePUB)

    I. Kent, Brad, 1973–, editor II. Title. III. Title: Essays. Selections.

    PR6029.F3A6 2016   824'.912   C2016-904278-2
                                                C2016-904279-0

This book was typeset by Marquis Interscript in 10.5/13 Sabon.

For Anne, Ryan, and Zoé

Contents

Acknowledgments

One of the pleasures of preparing this volume of Sean O'Faolain's essays has been my acquaintance with the many wonderful people who helped me during my research and who contributed to the realisation of this project in one way or another. Most of the work was carried out during the 2013–14 academic year, while I was visiting professor in the School of English at Trinity College Dublin. For their very warm hospitality and intellectual camaraderie, I would like to thank Paul Delaney, Nicky Grene, Chris Morash, and Eve Patten. Jennifer Daly and Ben Murnane, the graduate students who ran the School of English seminar series at Trinity, were likewise kind in asking me to present my research on O'Faolain. During my time in Dublin I was fortunate to make my way back to Northern Ireland, some sixteen years after I moved away. For giving me the occasion to return to my old stomping grounds and to present an abridged version of the introduction, I am grateful to the School of English at Queen's University Belfast, and in particular to Eamonn Hughes, Gail McConnell, and Sinead Sturgeon. I also owe a longstanding debt to Ron Rudin, who over the years encouraged my interest in O'Faolain and was always ready to have a long chat about him.

In collecting and transcribing the essays, I was aided by Joseph Dubé and Mark Lepitre, two excellent and reliable research assistants who always had something interesting to say about what they had read.

The greatest pleasure of preparing this project with McGill-Queen's University Press has been that I have made the acquaintance of Mark Abley, who has been unstinting in his support and is as fine an editor as one could find.

This manuscript would never have seen the light of day had it not been for Julia O'Faolain, Sean's daughter and an excellent author in her own right. Like her father, she deserves more recognition by scholars and the general public, both in Ireland and beyond. I thank her wholeheartedly for having faith in me and my ability to edit Sean's essays – and for the wine, chocolates, and good conversation.

Of course, none of this would have been possible without my family, Anne, Ryan, and Zoé, who have followed me every step of the way – and whom I gladly follow in turn.

Introduction

ON POLEMICAL ESSAYS AND
THE PUBLIC INTELLECTUAL

Sean O'Faolain authored some of the most sensitive, trenchant, and provocative essays ever to be published by an Irish writer. Scholars of all
stripes seeking a quotable, contrary, and intelligent voice have long mined
them as invaluable sources, and his essays are often included in antholo-
gies alongside what is considered to be the best and most representative
of Irish writing.[1] In more recent years, work on the essays has come to
rival study of O'Faolain's short stories, for which he was internationally
renowned throughout his lifetime.[2] This volume – the first significant collection of his essays – has been assembled in the hope of sparking further
re-evaluation of O'Faolain's writing, his place in Irish history, and his
relevance to the contemporary world.

Born at the turn of the twentieth century, in many ways Sean O'Faolain
was moulded by the turbulent times of his country. Raised in Cork by a
piously Catholic mother and a father who served loyally in the Royal
Irish Constabulary, he was the youngest of three brothers whose career
paths reflected the forces that battled for his generation's allegiances: one
became a priest, the other a British civil servant, and he a rebel-artist.
Swept up in his youth by Ireland's romantic struggle toward national
sovereignty after the 1916 Easter Rising, he immersed himself in the Irish
language, hibernicised his birth name, John Whelan, to Sean O'Faolain,
and worked as a bomb-maker and propagandist in the IRA's war against
government forces. In the mid-1920s, when the business of the newly
independent Irish government was the sober and comparatively dull task
of managing the country, the Catholic Church and the bourgeoisie began

to exert their power. In this climate, a good number of idealistic youths and former revolutionaries became disillusioned and took up their pens to express their anger, their sense of betrayal, and their fading dreams. O'Faolain's essays need to be considered against this backdrop of disillusionment, but what constantly shines through them is a hope for reform, even if it is reform by increment. Each essay is born of a need to instigate debate, to intervene in a larger conversation already under way, or to make a plea for greater recognition of what he deems to be a neglected or misunderstood subject.

One account persists that O'Faolain turned away from fiction towards the end of the 1930s and began to be politically engaged in his writing, preferring in his middle years the polemics of the essay. This narrative is supported by O'Faolain's editorship of *The Bell* from the moment that the monthly periodical was founded in 1940. But by this time he had already refined his public voice through more than a decade of essay-writing that is too often obscured by *The Bell*'s well-earned reputation as the mid-century Irish counter-cultural journal of record and by the yeoman's work O'Faolain did as its editor and chief essayist. Although his fiction and biographies are readily acknowledged as noteworthy in their own right, his earlier essays often get short shrift. Yet the range and prestige of the journals in which he published them indicate the regard that some of the English-speaking world's leading editors had for the young writer. "The Cruelty and Beauty of Words," which opens this collection and offers one of the earliest commentaries on what would become James Joyce's *Finnegans Wake*, was published in *The Virginia Quarterly Review* in 1928; with some minor changes, it appeared under the title "Style and the Limitations of Speech" in T.S. Eliot's *Criterion*. O'Faolain published a number of articles in both of these reviews, as well as in other respected venues such as the New York–based liberal Catholic *Commonweal*, *The Yale Review*, Rolfe Arnold Scott-James's *The London Mercury and Bookman*, Cyril Connolly's *Horizon*, the Fabian-founded *New Statesman and Nation*, H.L. Mencken's *The American Mercury*, and, closer to home, Æ's *Irish Statesman*, Seumas O'Sullivan's *Dublin Magazine*, and *Ireland To-Day*. Many of these were to become direct models for *The Bell* and, in the case of the latter three, they nurtured a ready stock of established contributors who were committed in various ways to O'Faolain's aesthetic and political project.[3]

To consider a collaborative effort like *The Bell* as a one-man show might appear to be folly, but there never was much question as to whose personality and outlook stamped it with an identity.[4] O'Faolain's razor-sharp editorials provided contributors, subscribers, and even detractors with a lodestar, a regular sense of direction that was needed after the *Irish Statesman* folded in 1930 and *Ireland To-Day* in 1938. In his introductory piece, "This is Your Magazine," O'Faolain famously set out his objectives in manifesto form. As a title, he says, *The Bell* was chosen because it had a minimum of associations and was not symbolic of Ireland in any sense. Moreover, unlike its precursors, the new publication did not flag its provenance: it would be of and for Ireland, and yet also of and for the modern world. Its liberal and progressive bent was to counter the isolationism arising from the disastrous years of the economic tariff war with Britain and the neutrality of the country as World War II raged. Although its ethos was an amalgamation of many of those journals for which O'Faolain had published essays in the past, it was also fittingly linked through its name to another foreign source: *Kolokol*. This London-based nineteenth-century Russian journal, whose name translates as *The Bell*, went against the grain in advocating for political reforms that would expand democratic rights and increase standards of living for peasants in a starkly stratified and autocratic country.[5] Such awareness of and openness to outside forces were essential to bring to bear on *The Bell*. "We are absolutely inclusive," O'Faolain booms in emphatic conclusion to his opening editorial, in invitation as much as provocation: "Whoever you are, then, O reader, Gentile or Jew, Protestant or Catholic, priest or layman, Big House or Small House – THE BELL is yours."[6]

This call to readers was intended to give them a sense of ownership, to attract and endear them to the journal. It was furthermore meant to stir the public to action, to incite them to contribute to the contents of the magazine and to engage with the views it offered in a much broader critical sense, one that would go beyond its pages and instigate positive reform in the wider society. Such interaction is essential for polemical essays, for without it they simply fall flat, leaving the audience unmoved.

In the corpus of Michel de Montaigne – who established the genre of the essay in 1580 – readers are confronted with a much different type of writing than is found in O'Faolain's essays. After Montaigne, the essay developed in two distinct directions: the informal mode of Montaigne, which is personal, descriptive, and reflective; and the formal mode of writers such as O'Faolain, which tends to be more expansive, rigidly organised, and impersonal.[7] At the same time, both types of essays share certain conventions: the essay is a highly malleable genre, is of indeterminate length, and is undergirded and shaped by personality, the stated or implicit authorial "I" that speaks directly to the reader and imposes a viewpoint.[8]

This intimacy affords the essayist an opportunity to pull the reader in closer, to convince him or her that there is something of merit in what is being said. The name of the genre comes from the French *essai*, meaning "an attempt." But it is rather a succession of attempts: a first attempt to articulate one's thoughts to one's self and a second attempt to communicate those thoughts to others.

Despite the essay's pedigree and prevalence in literary history, it has been marginalised in academia, where the novel, poetry, and drama reign. Not surprisingly, then, it is also under-theorised. This is particularly troubling considering that so many canonical writers have contributed so much to the form. In the British literary tradition alone, there is a respected and diverse lineage from the sixteenth century through to modern times, stretching from Bacon to Jonathan Swift, Richard Steele, Joseph Addison, Samuel Johnson, Mary Wollstonecraft, Charles Lamb, William Hazlitt, Thomas Carlyle, Matthew Arnold, Bernard Shaw, Joseph Conrad, Virginia Woolf, Aldous Huxley, and George Orwell. Rather than seeing the essays of these authors as something apart from their "literature," we should regard them as literary works of another register; this needs to be recognised in studies of O'Faolain's oeuvre as well.

Not being bound to the same strictness of convention that polices other genres, the essay enjoys the virtue of a relative lack of limitations. Carl H. Klaus has shown that writers throughout the ages have regarded the essay's formlessness as allowing a broad range of thought and style, and that this formlessness translates into freer content.[9] Similarly, Theodor Adorno claims that "the essay's innermost formal law is heresy. Through violations of the orthodoxy of thought, something in the object becomes visible which it is orthodoxy's secret and objective aim to keep invisible."[10] This resistance to definition, coupled with the genre's ability to illuminate, is in part what György Lukács drives at in his claim that "were one to compare the forms of literature with sunlight refracted in a prism, the writings of the essayists would be the ultra-violet rays."[11]

As Adorno's formulation suggests, the didactic potential, revolutionary capacity, and immediacy of the essay have long made it a medium of expression for public intellectuals like Sean O'Faolain. In one of the most celebrated texts on the subject, *La Trahison des clercs* (1927), Julien Benda defines intellectuals as "all those whose activity essentially is *not* the pursuit of practical aims, all those who seek their joy in the practice of an art or a science or metaphysical speculation, in short, in the possession of non-material advantages."[12] As the title of his book implies, Benda was writing against those whom he considered had betrayed their society.

They had done so in siding with the offices of power and, in turn, had shirked their duty to pursue knowledge and truth in order "to please the bourgeoisie, who are the creators of fame and the source of honors."[13]

Instead, Benda asserts that the public intellectual should operate in the interests of the people, that is, those who are outside the halls of influence and power. In *Representations of the Intellectual* (1994), Edward Said, like Benda before him, emphasises the importance of the ethical impulse, the "special duty to address the constituted and authorized powers of one's own society, which are accountable to its citizenry, particularly when those powers are exercised in a manifestly disproportionate and immoral war, or in deliberate programs of discrimination, repression, and collective cruelty."[14] This is not a smug belief in the innate superiority of the public intellectual as one who has the right to speak on behalf of other people, but rather a recognition that the public individual must use his or her abilities in the service of those who lack the occasion or the ability to express their plight. In other words, it is a plea for selflessness and, indeed, self-sacrifice to forward a moral cause. Coupled with this service is an obligation to instruct, to make people aware of injustices, abuses, and wrongheadedness.

Given the obstinacy and bravery of the public intellectual in confronting popular opinion and the official narrative of the State, it is no small wonder that O'Faolain's writings are peppered throughout with references to Irish rebels. From the political and military sphere we encounter in O'Faolain's essays Hugh O'Neill, Wolfe Tone, Daniel O'Connell, Charles Stewart Parnell, and Roger Casement, and in the literary sphere Thomas Davis, Bernard Shaw, W.B. Yeats, Æ, James Joyce, Sean O'Casey, and Liam O'Flaherty. What is most striking in this rather brief and entirely male list is the disparity of personalities and beliefs, which attests to O'Faolain's ability to esteem the contrariness and visionary qualities, if not the actual politics or aesthetics, of each of these public figures. In a moving essay on Roger Casement that reveals O'Faolain's powers as a biographer, he warns: "[I]t is the penalty of fame that men become symbols, whether for good or ill. One passes no final judgment on Casement because one knows that all human beings read these symbols out of the past, according to their own ambitions, their own desires, their own hopes or their own fears as to what life ought or ought not to be."[15] There is a suggestion here that he might be speaking about himself, both as one who made symbols of others and as one who had become a symbol himself.

The rebels that O'Faolain held up for his audience were important not only for what they had done, but also for how they measured up to the leaders of mid-century Ireland. His contemporaries – Daniel Corkery and Eamon de Valera in particular – might have been rebels in the past, but they had ossified with the passage of time and in the proximity of power. In O'Faolain's view, they were in turn ossifying Irish life by wiping out its vitality, praising a mythical golden past instead of ameliorating the present, and fear-mongering about the dangers of alien influences. In the case of Corkery, O'Faolain found himself rebelling against a former mentor and friend, the man whose guidance and teaching of the Irish language had facilitated O'Faolain's move away from his childhood loyalty to the beloved Empire of his policeman father, a loyalty that was propagated in *Boy's Own*, *Gem*, and *The Magnet*, the British magazines he had read so devotedly in his youth. The break in his relationship with Corkery was the result of a genuine difference in opinion, but it was hastened and worsened in 1931 when Corkery was awarded the chair in English at University College Cork, with O'Faolain placing second.[16] O'Faolain took especial exception to Corkery's *Synge and Anglo-Irish Literature* (1931), which he felt denigrated Irish literature written in English. In Corkery's words, Anglo-Irish literature "shows itself scornful of the judgement of this country, such as it may be, shows itself indeed utterly provincial in its overwrought desire to be assessed and spoken well of by the critics of another people. It is therefore not normal, for a normal literature while welcoming the criticism of outsiders neither lives nor dies by such criticism. It abides the judgement of its own people, and by that judgement lives or dies. If this literature then be not a normal literature it is not a national literature, for normal and national are synonymous in literary criticism."[17]

This brutal conflation of "national" and "normal" led O'Faolain to align Corkery with the exclusivist policies of Nazism as early as 1936. O'Faolain's fear was that Corkery had come to "influence our political evangels considerably: all that is behind our system of education in the modern Ireland, much that enthuses and supports all our more fervent politics, has come out of his books and his lecturings."[18] For O'Faolain, Corkery was one of those who had betrayed his status as an intellectual. Writing at almost exactly the mid-point between the publication of Corkery's two influential studies, *The Hidden Ireland* (1924) and *Synge and Anglo-Irish Literature*, Benda remarks: "Germany, by creating for herself the nationalist 'clerk' and thereby acquiring the additional strength we know she has acquired, made this species of 'clerk' necessary to all other countries."[19] Like O'Faolain, Benda is critical of the desire of such men "to relate the form of their own minds to a form of the *national* mind, which they naturally brandish against other national forms of mind."[20] And he similarly dismisses those novelists and playwrights who inject nationalist values into their works: "[I]nstead of making their heroes feel and act in conformity with a true observation of human nature, they make them do so as the passion of the authors requires."[21]

Following his 1936 article, O'Faolain appears to have actively decided to devote his attention to those who ran the nationalist State and had come to institutionalise Corkery's views, most notably the Taoiseach, or Irish Prime Minister, Eamon de Valera. This move put O'Faolain into conflict with another former comrade of the revolutionary period. His turn is most readily evidenced in his two biographies of the man, the flattering *The Life Story of Eamon de Valera*, which, published in 1933, reflected the hope for a more progressive society after de Valera's victory in the general election of 1932, and the more critical *De Valera*, which was published in 1939 as a revision of and an apology for the first. According to O'Faolain, de Valera had sold out his republican ideals and been swallowed up by what he refers to in "The Stuffed Shirts" as the middle-class putsch of the post-independence era. And this putsch did not simply mean the bourgeois gombeen men, but all that they had brought with their rise to power: the unfettered control of Irish society by the Catholic Church and the exalted place of what he refers to as the lunatics, that is, the exclusive nationalists of the Gaelic Athletic Association and the Gaelic League, among others.

With such stark lines drawn in the sand, the most divisive issue that O'Faolain repeatedly dissects in his polemical essays is official nationalism and its implications for national identity. For example, in "Our Nasty Novelists," in riposte to those who, like Corkery, suggest that readers should reject works not "typical" of the race, O'Faolain humorously remarks: "There is no such person as a typical Englishman, or a typical Irishman. The infinite variety of human nature rejects such an intellectual abstraction for what it is, and literature illustrates the depths of its folly. Thus, Hamlet can hardly be a typical Englishman (or Dane) except to those who believe that all Englishmen (or Danes) believe in ghosts, behave outrageously to women, kill their uncles and their uncle's employees, and spend their spare time mooning about in graveyards."[22] He takes this up a year later in "That Typical Irishman," diagnosing that "this narrow differentiation comes, no doubt, from the fact that our knowledge of our own history is still incomplete, and that a great part of Irish history as it is written is such a refraction of the facts that our books of history are not so much lenses – through which we see more clearly that which happened

– as prisms through which we see coloured distortions of what happened."[23] In effect, because of the paucity of the historical record, propaganda and illusions substitute for fact and it is once again left for the intellectual to challenge such interpretations.

Thus, O'Faolain's visionary rebels were Janus-faced, looking towards Europe for inspiration while remaining firmly concerned with Irish affairs. Take Hugh O'Neill who, O'Faolain argued, had been a leading man at Europe's courts, and Wolfe Tone, the apostle of French secular Republicanism who had fought for a non-sectarian country; or, in the literary sphere, Joyce, who could write of nothing but Ireland while being influenced by the continent in all manner of aesthetic concerns, and Yeats, equally inspired by French symbolist poets and Irish peasant folktales. O'Faolain writes repeatedly about how Ireland had become a stagnant backwater that had failed to be caught up in the current of world events and the stream of intellectual developments, blaming a mix of isolationism, xenophobia, and chauvinism. In his essays and biographies, he maintains that Ireland has always advanced and been a beacon to the world when it has participated actively in it. Acculturation is the natural way towards progress, infusing society with new ideas and models, while hermetically sealing a society in the narrow interests of one group is the fastest way to ensure its decline. In "Ireland and the Modern World," O'Faolain turns abroad to illustrate his point: "France, in the 16th century, was influenced powerfully by the Italian Renaissance, and by the German Reformation. In the 17th century she was influenced by the Catholic revival from Rome. In the eighteenth century she was influenced by the English revolution of 1648 and the history of the American colonies. It was from England that Voltaire and Montesquieu derived the formulas of religious toleration and political liberty that they propagated at home."[24] If even France – for O'Faolain the pinnacle of all that is most advanced in culture, politics, and science – regularly adopts the best that other countries have to offer, what choice does Ireland have if it is to move forward?

Taking his cue from these precursors, O'Faolain often looks abroad in his essays for models against which he can diagnose problems and prescribe reforms for Irish life. The British Arts Council, for example, offers the Irish a guide to effectively promote their own culture and politics abroad.[25] Similarly, he discusses the Rowell–Sirois Report – a comprehensive inquiry into federal–provincial relations in Canada – to point to lessons that could be illuminating for those attempting to negotiate relations between Ireland North and South.[26] In "Books and a Live People," he compares publishing practices in Ireland with those in such similarly small European states as Denmark, Sweden, and Finland to show ways that the country might better nurture and support native talent. Likewise, in "The Dilemma of Irish Letters," Henry James's study of Nathaniel Hawthorne's New England becomes the point of entry into O'Faolain's theorisation of the failure of the novel and the rise of the short story as the predominant literary form in mid-century Ireland. O'Faolain via James introduces the concept of Ireland as a thin society: one defined by "a general jelly-like mass of friendly egalitarianism which is as comfortable as it is indeterminate and where hammered-out convictions and ideas are so few or so elementary as to suggest a quite unperplexed and uninquisitive communal mind."[27] And in "That Typical Irishman," O'Faolain praises French historian Charles Seignobos's landmark *Histoire sincère de la Nation française* (1933) – which was to provide the intellectual guide to O'Faolain's *The Irish* (1947) – for outlining "a long, complex, formative story of the life and growth and consolidation of a free people, and only after he had carefully indicated the many varieties (Gascon, Fleming, Norman, etc.) that exist inside the general bracket of their ultimate syntheses."[28]

It was out of this same curiosity about the greater world that O'Faolain would, in the late 1940s, turn towards travel writing more consistently, especially with the publication of *A Summer in Italy* (1949) and *An Autumn in Italy* (1953). As in his essay "The Irish and the Latins," he desires to show his people other modes of living, to make them recognise that they have better choices available to them. He saw in Italy a Catholic country that was more progressive and tolerant, more in touch and at ease with the sensual and sexual aspects of life that Irish Catholicism had attempted to cauterise from its adherents. His daughter Julia, who lived in France and Italy as a student abroad, suggests that his motives went even further than seeking out a positive model: he was performing an auto-exorcism of sorts, "trying to get rid of Ireland through Italy."[29]

It is no wonder, then, that O'Faolain saves his most fiery rhetoric for those who close themselves and – what's worse – their fellow citizens from the world beyond Ireland's borders. Allusions, metaphors, analogies, and similes are all employed with the deft skill of a man of letters. Many of these become aphoristic phrases that have the ring of truth about them. Such showmanship is essential: public intellectuals must surprise the audience, be memorable and authoritative at once, and jolt them with words just as they do with their ideas. Fittingly, the first essay that O'Faolain published after he had stepped down as editor of *The Bell* and taken stock of his six-year tenure there was on Bernard Shaw's prefaces to his plays.[30] O'Faolain notes that Shaw shocks with a wit that forces the reader to examine received ideas and question common assumptions. After pages of praise, it is difficult to read his conclusion that Shaw's "only frailty is that he likes too much to astonish" without recognising the tinge of envy behind the statement.[31] And yet O'Faolain holds his own beside Shaw, as is most evident in his comments on exclusive nationalists. He writes: "They are trying to squeeze us, as the feet of Chinese women used to be squeezed, into an ideological shoe. And some have not the slightest objection to mutilating us in the process."[32] Of the state's policies to revive the Gaelic language: "We have choked the Irish cat with Gaelic butter ... For it is greatly to be feared that the so-called revivalists – vivisectionists would be more like it – have done irreparable harm to the Language. The very sight and mention of Gaelic is now what the sight of butter would be to the half-choked cat."[33] In "Autoantiamericanism," he criticises Irish isolationism, ironically adopting Winston Churchill's metaphor: "[W]e are snoring gently behind the Green curtain that we have been rigging up for the last thirty years – Thought-proof, World-proof, Life-proof."[34] This strategy of appropriating the effective terms of other polemicists to suit his needs was practised with some regularity. For example, Lilliput, Jonathan Swift's island where the small stature of its inhabitants reflects their small-mindedness, is a repeated reference for O'Faolain. It is the title of one of his short stories in *Midsummer Night Madness*, in which it refers to the mentality of his native provincial town of Cork; in his essays, though, Lilliput comes to represent all of Ireland.[35]

Not surprisingly, the rhetorical language is heightened around those particular contemporary figures that O'Faolain held responsible for Irish insularity. Eamon de Valera comes in for the harshest treatment in this regard. His 1945 essay on the Taoiseach reveals the degree to which O'Faolain had gone beyond disillusion in his hopes for Irish republicanism. Despite the two biographies that he had written of the man, O'Faolain now believed that he was not worthy of such a study: "Indeed I can only think of two kinds of books about Mr. de Valera that might grip one to the end, and both would really be prolonged essays – a murderous attack or a comic satire."[36] In a provocative moment, considering his own support of de Valera's position in the early 1920s, O'Faolain says: "The whole of the Civil War period must force every normally percipient observer to agree that when Mr. de Valera's devotees present him as an utterly honest man they are quite right if they mean honest according to his lights, but that those searchlights which he turns on his heart have some very well-timed blackouts."[37] His humour here is the result of his need to vent his frustration, as it is when he takes the time to criticise both the rhetoric of M.J. MacManus, a later de Valera biographer, and de Valera himself: "It is not information to list a man's qualities: one must measure the quality of his qualities. Mr. MacManus by not bothering to do this is so foolish as to compare Mr. de Valera to Abraham Lincoln, presumably because each came from the equivalent of a log-cabin and reached the equivalent of a White House, each could amuse himself solving problems in Euclid, each had to do with a Civil War, each is tall, each has two eyes and two legs and two hands, and unless something is done to make it possible for artists to live in Ireland it may yet be possible to say that each was assassinated by a mad actor."[38]

Humour is quite possibly the most unacknowledged aspect of O'Faolain's writing. Yet his essays testify to his warm and sometimes devastating wit. The examples abound. Bemoaning the state of Irish writing and reading, he says: "Of all the people in Ireland who even have heard of James Joyce, how many have even read a line of him? I remember my long debate with a commercial traveller about *Ulysses* which ended when I found that he thought the author was George Bernard Joyce."[39] O'Faolain admits to having the following reaction when a dinner companion at the Gresham Hotel asked whether the place corresponded to a notably luxurious London establishment: "I looked around, in astonishment, at the good folk up from the country. 'No,' I sighed. 'It corresponds to the Garden of Eden. Except that they are all dressed.' And I thought to myself that they certainly have not eaten of the apple of knowledge."[40] Such barbs and jokes do not water down the critique; rather, they add spice, rendering it more palatable and more memorable for his audience; in turn, they keep people returning for further helpings.

As his phrase "the apple of knowledge" suggests, one of the policies that drew O'Faolain's sustained ire was censorship. The role of the intellectual can be rather Mephistophilean in this regard: getting people to partake in knowledge that is branded as dangerous and prohibited by the authorities. A certain amount of his interest in the subject was undoubtedly born of his personal experience. While he was studying for his MA at Harvard, "Banned in Boston" was fast becoming a national catchphrase in the United States for the pains that serious literature faced in a city controlled by a puritanical ethos informed in part by Irish Catholicism. Writing in 1928, the relatively unknown O'Faolain warned Ireland of the attendant dangers of restrictive legislation as the Censorship of Publications Bill was discussed in the Irish parliament. His article "Censorship in America" was featured in the *Irish Statesman* as part of a series of essays on the subject by such luminaries as Yeats, Shaw, and Æ. Publishing in this venue alongside these names announced O'Faolain's arrival on the Irish scene as a young spokesman for artistic freedom. Although some scholars have claimed that literary censorship had little effect on Irish writers, this is a callous underestimation of the very real professional and personal toll that seeing their work banned took on authors; in effect, it wiped out their major, natural audience, and thus curbed their ability to live by their pens, while provoking no small amount of resentment, frustration, and outright anger, not to mention making them into social pariahs.[41] O'Faolain recounts being notified of the proscription of *Midsummer Night Madness* in Ireland in 1932 just as he was basking in its positive reviews: "Outwardly I laughed at the news. In my heart I felt infuriated and humiliated. Above all I felt frightened at the thought that I was soon to return to live with these stupid, boorish, dispirited people who publicly disowned and insulted me."[42]

The banning of his second novel, *Bird Alone*, triggered a similar reaction in 1936. Fellow writer Frank O'Connor led a protest campaign, registering his shock and astonishment at the banning and the injustice of his close friend being found guilty without trial: "I admit that by adopting the profession of literature O'Faolain has put himself outside the pale of decent society, and shown himself unworthy of our great Gaelic heritage of intolerance and illiteracy; but does not the law go too far in denying him the rights accorded to a murderer?"[43] Compelled to respond after O'Connor's letter instigated a flurry of sympathetic responses, O'Faolain defended himself, Austin Clarke, and Francis Hackett – two other Irish writers who had recently suffered the same fate. He claimed that, through censorship, the state took away choice and responsibility from the people and thus infantilised them. Standing against the censors were the cosmopolitan intellectuals who, O'Faolain claimed, "are the sole bulwark between the national character and the disintegrating influences of the Censorial mind. But in so far as their influence is limited by the Censorship, the country hears them only by chance, and at random, and we are witnessing the extraordinary spectacle – though perhaps not so extraordinary in the Europe of today – of a country deliberately deprived of its own intellectuals by (in our case) a junta of misguided, however well-meaning, Gaelic Revivalists and Catholic Actionists."[44] If censorship sought to stifle debate, to prevent the circulation of certain ideas and modes of thought, it was the role of the intellectual to challenge the authorities by openly questioning the practice.

Living in a society in which the Catholic Church dictated policy to politicians not only from behind closed doors but from the pulpits and in regular decrees, O'Faolain was also preoccupied with religion. Tom Inglis, a sociologist of religion in modern Ireland, notes: "The strength of the institutional faith was such that Irish Catholics did not experience, think about or question religion for themselves. There was a close correspondence between the official doctrine of the Church and the way Catholics read, understood and acted in the world religiously. The unquestioning centre of their religious habitus, the orthodoxy, corresponded to the orthodoxy of the institutional Church."[45] One of the earliest examples of O'Faolain's fortitude in the face of such apparently immutable opposition to critique is his essay "The University Question." Written in response to Archbishop McQuaid's declaration in his Lenten Regulations on 7 February 1944 that no Catholic should attend the traditionally Protestant Trinity College Dublin, O'Faolain was one of only a few individuals who dared to openly question the dictate. Indeed, McQuaid had warned: "Any Catholic who disobeys this law is guilty of mortal sin and while he persists in disobedience is unworthy to receive the Sacraments."[46] The divisive effect of this pronouncement galled O'Faolain: "One cannot … touch Religion without touching Politics and affecting Society. We cannot, to give a homely example, tell our children not to mix with our neighbours' children on religious grounds, and at the same time expect our neighbours to believe that we have no personal objection to them. Irish Protestants would have to be angels, not human beings, not to feel a sub-implication that there is something sinister about their creed, and their society."[47] O'Faolain believed that the university that would be able to accommodate the widest spectrum of beliefs and open exchanges would be the one to lead Ireland in the future.

One of his concluding remarks in "The University Question" is ominous. He wonders: "In this Ireland the question to be decided is whether we have *any* lay leaders or rulers: Of what kind? With what aim? With what image of life?"[48] Seven years later, in 1951, the Mother and Child Scheme – a proposed government programme to install a small measure of universal health care – failed when the Church hierarchy came out against it; the government and opposition parties cowered and rescinded the measure. Dr. Noël Browne, the Minister for Health at the time who had crafted the proposal and midwifed it through committees, was forced to resign. Browne later wrote in his memoirs that the hierarchy had struck because it sought to maintain its control of women by keeping them ignorant regarding sexual knowledge, contraception, and abortion, while defending its wealthy constituents who would have had to subsidise the scheme.[49] In his essay "The Dáil and the Bishops," O'Faolain argued that the crisis revealed that Irish society was ruled by two parliaments: the democratic-ally elected one of the people and the cloistered authoritarian one of the Church. What made this dysfunctional situation worse was that the second dictated to the first. And what gave it the power to do so was what O'Faolain memorably labelled "the weapon of the Sacraments."[50] Essentially, the Church could intimidate any remotely pious people by threatening to refuse them access to religious rites. O'Faolain understood the power of this weapon, having been excommunicated when he joined the IRA in his youth, and his article predictably argues for the need to establish the separation of Church and State. However, his originality lies not in warning the people of the dangers of allowing the Church to control the material and political realm, but in pointing out that the Church itself runs serious risks to its spiritual authority when it tries and is not able to alleviate such social diseases as infant mortality and poverty. Although the essay may seem tame by today's standards, the audacity of telling the Church that it should know its proper place cannot be underestimated.

In some cases, O'Faolain's reputation appears to have drawn more attention than the articles themselves perhaps merited or would have received otherwise. This ability to attract people's notice is of course the goal of the public intellectual, but it also highlights the attendant risk of the personality drowning out the message. When a writer has by and large defined his outlook and established nemeses, any comment or view-point will provoke knee-jerk reactions – from those in favour as much as those in opposition – and *ad hominem* attacks. One such example was O'Faolain's "Love Among the Irish," which appeared in *Life* magazine on the week of St. Patrick's Day in 1953 and just three days after "The Irish and the Latins" was published in *Commonweal*. A mainly American readership approaching 17 March might have been expecting some senti-mental shamrockery nonsense, especially as it was the year after John Ford's *The Quiet Man* (1952) had taken movie theatres by storm, but O'Faolain desired to enlighten these people with the realities of contem-porary Ireland. The *Life* article began as O'Faolain's contribution to a forum on "The Vanishing Irish" that was organised by a priest at the University of Notre Dame. While exile and emigration had marked Irish history since the Famine in the 1840s, according to O'Faolain the more damning reason for the decline in Irish population stemmed from sexual relations – or the lack thereof. He provides a range of reasons to explain this situation, including late marriages that are the result of the delayed transfer of land to the next generation, the lack of birth control, terrible social services, costly housing, and abominable rural conditions. When the *Irish Press* – the newspaper founded by de Valera – got wind of the article, it issued a scathing editorial. True to form, O'Faolain refused to back down and wrote a long and damning letter in response.

Noting that he used census figures to support his claims for the drop in the Irish population, O'Faolain criticised the paper's argument that the Irish have no fear of being a dying people because there are more than 20 million of them scattered around the world. Such figures, he argued, have nothing to do with the population of Ireland. "Unless indeed," he impishly added, "the Editor of THE IRISH PRESS has some plan for asking families of Irish descent abroad to beget a child apiece to send home to Ireland in the hope that our dual-purpose cows will take care of them? Such nonsense! Such contempt for the intelligence of your readers!" In the end, he claimed that he did not "give tuppence" that the editor had misrepresented his article by portraying him as merely complaining about divorce and birth control being forbidden. "But I do care very much," he countered, "that you should be so recklessly unfair to the public ... This thing is a national cancer and you have no right to cover it up with plasters of pseudo-patriotic propaganda. For God and Ireland's sake stop acting like a kid in a crowd hopping around and meouwling, 'Oh, me sore toe! Oh, me sore toe!' every time an Irish writer is moved to tell you the truth. If you want to bring this matter out into the open I am ready to debate it with you publicly, in the Mansion House, or over the Radio. Or throw your columns open to it like a man and face the facts of life, not kill them. You know what Bacon said about the people who kill the truth? That they are cowards before men – but take a risk before God."[51] The flair of this conclusion illustrates the intellectual's prizing of truth, the assertion of the primacy of facts in the interests of the broader society, the importance of calling forth respected predecessors to make a point (in this case Bacon), and the willingness to engage in public debate.

While such immediate controversies did much to make a name for him, they have tended to obscure his analysis of Irish writing, which was a consistent subject of interest for him.[52] O'Faolain read the state of the country's literature in conjunction with his understanding of its social and political structure to become one of Ireland's most engaging and acute literary critics. The Danish writer Signe Toksvig noted after one of her meetings with O'Faolain in 1933 that he got "quite school mastery and oracular" when discussing the Irish novel.[53] There is indeed a blend of didacticism and authoritative finality in many of his statements, such as when he writes in 1949 that "the two outstanding marks of Irish literature to-day are exile and lack of originality" and in later years that the problem with Irish literature is that it had become the story of an author in search of six characters.[54] The blame for the unoriginality and flight of Irish authors lay not with the writers themselves, but with the thin society of de Valera's "dreary Eden," as O'Faolain called it. He suggested that its narrowness and absence of dynamism had led Lord Dunsany and James Stephens to write fantasy, drawn Austin Clarke to the mediaeval period, and forced Liam O'Flaherty to pen, with one exception, historical novels after 1932. In such a country, only the short story could thrive in realist prose, and realism was desperately needed in this period to reflect the people and dissect the variety of social malaises that blighted the land. Gone was the revolutionary fervour of the pre-independence years. Gone, too, was Yeats: for O'Faolain, his passing was the passing of an age and the death of a native intellectual life. The massive achievement of Yeats and those of his time – Joyce, Synge, Shaw, O'Casey – cast a considerable shadow across the literature of the post-independence period; O'Faolain and his contemporaries, he acknowledged, were doomed to fail to measure up against the stature of their great predecessors. Yet O'Faolain sought to combat hopelessness and cynicism in his essays, histories, and travel writings. Significantly, however, although he produced several fine collections of short stories from this time on, he did not publish a novel between *Come Back to Erin* in 1940 and *And Again?* in 1979.

In line with his admiration of past rebels who kept one eye trained on Europe and the other on Ireland, O'Faolain and the best writers of his generation likewise looked abroad for inspiration while writing of their own people. The most important influences for these short story realists were the Russians Chekhov, Turgenev, and Dostoevsky, and the French de Maupassant and Flaubert, all of whom wrote wonderfully coruscating, biting vignettes of provincial life. Joyce was also a model, but it was the more grounded naturalist of *Dubliners* and *A Portrait of the Artist as a Young Man*, not the high modernist of *Ulysses* and *Finnegans Wake*, whom they admired nonetheless. This is no coincidence. Edward Said points out that Turgenev's *Fathers and Sons*, Flaubert's *Sentimental Education*, and Joyce's *Portrait* are all engaged with representing the modern young intellectual: their protagonists pull away or live apart from their society (Bazarov, Dedalus) or they are co-opted and betray it (Moreau).[55] There is a distinct connection to be made, then, between the prose of these Irish, Russian, and French authors and their reformist impulses. Such threading of form and politics weaves throughout O'Faolain's writings, and while he theorises at length on realism and naturalism, his essays have no sustained discussion of surrealism, fantasy, science fiction, or modernism.[56]

Despite such lacunae, one should be struck by the breadth of O'Faolain's interests and references in the essays collected here. They traverse all spheres of Irish life and of the world beyond, from the renowned to the obscure, the contemporary to the ancient. A quick perusal of the notes and the index to this volume will give the reader a healthy idea of O'Faolain's range of knowledge. It will also reveal that he was decidedly less active as a polemicist after the 1950s.

O'Faolain's near abandonment of the polemical essay can be understood as the product of several factors. Many of the liberalising forces that O'Faolain had argued in favour of began to have some currency in Ireland by the late 1950s: the Censorship Board was less conservative, though it would be a far stretch to call it liberal until the 1970s; new economic policies opened the country to outside markets; the Catholic Church undertook small measures of reform that issued from the Second Vatican Council of 1962–65; and Ireland gained membership to the United Nations in 1955 and to the European Economic Community – the forerunner of the European Union – in 1973. In the 1960s and 1970s, traditional Irish society was further challenged by such internal demographic shifts as urbanisation, the civil rights, student, and women's movements, and the eruption of the Troubles in Northern Ireland. O'Faolain also began to accept jobs at leading institutions in both Ireland and the United States, and if he did not betray Irish society by working in the interests of the powerful, he was to some extent co-opted. However, he did not simply accept these jobs with a sense of entitlement. For example, he viewed his time as director of the Arts Council of Ireland from 1956 to 1959 as an opportunity to increase the public's aesthetic standards and was pugnacious in his constant efforts to secure its independence from government interference.[57] In accepting lectureships at such prestigious American universities as Princeton, Wesleyan, Northwestern, and Boston College, he taught creative writing to a future generation; at Princeton he also penned one of his most important works of literary criticism, *The Vanishing Hero: Studies in Novelists of the Twenties* (1956), a penetrating examination of modern literature through the works of Aldous Huxley, Evelyn Waugh, Graham Greene, William Faulkner, Ernest Hemingway, Elizabeth Bowen, Virginia Woolf, and James Joyce. But while O'Faolain continued to produce the odd cultural essay, his journalism in the 1960s turned, rather, to the better-paid work of writing for glossy magazines, notably travel features for *Holiday*. O'Faolain's move away from the polemical essay should also be considered from the point of view of his own nature: it is the signature of any artist to change over time, to move restlessly from one genre or form to another, to create, in effect, marked periods in his or her development. And age itself might have played a part: as the fire in the belly for the good fight dimmed, so grew the desire to pass the flame to a new generation.

In looking back at O'Faolain's essays, it is useful to compare them with some of his contemporary revolutionary comrades to measure just how radical his critique was. Peadar O'Donnell, a more staunchly left-wing Republican, is particularly important in this regard, since he founded *The Bell* and was the one who hired O'Faolain as editor;[58] he also took over the reins when O'Faolain resigned in 1946 and continued to publish him in the pages of *The Bell* long afterwards. Further afield are Hubert Butler and Elizabeth Bowen. These close friends of O'Faolain's wrote from the perspective of the déclassé Anglo-Irish Protestants who had found it increasingly difficult to identify with Ireland, their beloved native country that had come to be dominated by a parochial Catholic faith and a hostile nationalism. Butler was primarily an essayist, and although he was not so well known in his time, his skills were admired enough that O'Faolain commissioned articles by him for *The Bell*. Bowen, too, wrote for *The Bell*, and in many ways O'Faolain, who was her lover for a time, shaped her thoughts on Ireland.[59]

In a broader international context, it would be productive to consider O'Faolain and his Irish colleagues as aligned with a cohort of British writers who were likewise born around 1900. Cyril Connolly, George Orwell, V.S. Pritchett, and Arthur Koestler were each in his own right a compelling essayist. Although from an earlier generation, E.M. Forster – whom O'Faolain cited as an influence – could be grouped with these younger men, as he developed into a notable essayist at the same time that they did. All of them came in to their own as writers from the late 1920s to the 1940s in a world that was increasingly torn apart by warring ideologies and militant patriotism. The rise of totalitarian fascist and communist regimes on the continent and similarly inclined movements in Ireland and Britain – such as Eoin O'Duffy's Blueshirts and Oswald Mosley's British Union of Fascists in the 1930s; the pro-Axis Craobh na hAiséirghe and its political wing Ailtirí na hAiséirghe in the 1940s – were of grave concern.[60] All of these writers were attuned to and concerned about the repercussions of such politics, and in particular the threats that they posed to the place of the individual and freedom of expression in society. It is against this larger backdrop that one can best understand the alarmism in O'Faolain's writings and his denunciation of the authoritarian impulses of the Church, State, and official nationalism in Ireland.

Although O'Faolain's essays and criticism have kept his reputation alive and made him an imposing figure in accounts of twentieth-century Ireland, it was his fiction that drew the most critical attention in the earliest studies of his work. Benedict Kiely, in the first major survey and analysis of post-independence Irish writing, *Modern Irish Fiction: A Critique* (1950), discusses O'Faolain in a chapter entitled "Rebels" – along with Frank O'Connor, Liam O'Flaherty, James Joyce, and, rather provocatively, Daniel Corkery. Successive studies have taken up this rebellious note, but O'Faolain's non-fiction has gone on to attract greater attention. In the first monograph devoted to him, *Sean O'Faolain: A Critical Introduction* (1967), Maurice Harmon opens with chapters on O'Faolain's biographies of Daniel O'Connell, Hugh O'Neill, and Eamon de Valera to illuminate how O'Faolain's reading of the past is essential to understanding his views of contemporary Ireland; this model has been replicated in later studies.[61] Appearing on the heels of Harmon's study, Paul A. Doyle's *Sean O'Faolain* (1968) includes an entire chapter on *The Bell*, serving notice for future critics to attend to the essays as well as the books. Situating O'Faolain in the tradition of the best eighteenth-century pampleteers, Doyle notes that O'Faolain was "a voice for acceleration."[62] The term "acceleration" is taken to mean here a hastening of Ireland's maturation from a cultural backwater to an open, pluralistic society. This viewpoint has come to dominate the argument in studies of O'Faolain's essays.[63]

Since the closing years of the twentieth century, O'Faolain's reception has been tied to prevailing currents within the field of Irish Studies, which was revivified and bitterly divided by the revisionist debates.[64] These debates hinged on the earlier ones instigated by O'Faolain in *The Bell* and the work undertaken in *Irish Historical Studies*, a journal founded in 1938 to bring more rigorous international standards and scientific methodology to bear on the discipline of history as it was practised in Ireland. Characterised as "revisionist" because, in a broad sense, they revised, or challenged, the accounts of official nationalism, these publications shifted the perspective of the Irish from one of victimisation and finding fault with the legacies of British governance to one of taking responsibility for the present, holding the Irish government and fellow citizens to task for ill-conceived and ill-implemented policies, and viewing the failures of contemporary Ireland as the result of native traditions that were not able to adapt to modern conditions. Yet O'Faolain's work as historian, biographer, and literary critic did not adhere to the strict academic codes of *Irish Historical Studies*: although much of his insight was generated from a culling of facts, he did not scrupulously detail his sources and he relied upon his skills as a writer of fiction to fill in the blanks and to develop gripping narratives.

In the sense of revisionism that has been applied to O'Faolain's work, Doyle's notion of "acceleration" means modernisation writ large, and the context of his diminishing polemical output after the 1950s is indicative of how his position in the field of Irish Studies is somewhat ambiguous. Although O'Faolain is celebrated for taking on the more negative aspects of Irish nationalism, his modernist rhetoric can be viewed as sometimes impatiently sloughing off native traditions at the expense of anything of value that they might have possessed. Furthermore, attacks on the protectionist aspects of nationalism helped to pave the way, wittingly or not, for the rampant consumerism and arch-capitalism that has increasingly marked Irish society since the 1960s. This is certainly the guiding principle behind Luke Gibbons's inclusion of O'Faolain's article "The Gaelic Cult" in his section on revisionism and cultural criticism in *The Field Day Anthology of Irish Writing* to serve as a counterpoint to Terence Brown's inclusion of O'Faolain's "The Stuffed Shirts" in his section on provincialism and censorship. Indeed, the perspectives of these two editors do well to illustrate the competing visions of O'Faolain.

The opening paragraphs of Brown's essay could very well have been penned by O'Faolain himself, describing the dominant nationalism as the combination of "a restrictive catholicism ... and a limited vision of Gaelic tradition ... that lent legitimacy to the new political order." Brown asserts that, taken as a whole, O'Faolain's editorials form "a body of biting, pungent, commonsensical, clearly argued realistic analyses of current Irish society," in contradisctinction to the "myopic view" found in the "narrowly intense studies" of the "able polemicist" Daniel Corkery. Indeed, Brown claims, "O'Faoláin performed a vital function in maintaining the sense of ideological alternatives." Aside from the important countering "realistic" vision of Ireland that he furthered, Brown suggests that the legacy of O'Faolain's essays also lies in their collective "challenge to the Irish tendency to see only in lyric poetry, fiction and drama the expression of a creative imagination."[65]

Whereas Brown entirely lauds O'Faolain, Gibbons repeatedly castigates him, holding him aloft as the forefather of revisionism. Most notable among O'Faolain's stratagems is the one-two punch of undermining the tradition on which the Gaelic cult is founded by arguing that it is both of recent origin and racialist in practice. From Gibbons's point of view, O'Faolain's critique is wholly dismissive of nationalism, seeing only the more extreme insular forms and failing to recognise its more enlightened strands in Irish culture. O'Faolain's writings are emblematic of what Gibbons claims is "the often simple-minded historical pieties that revisionist critics and historians attribute to nationalism" and are intended to pull Ireland towards a liberal, fully modernised society.[66] Gibbons draws the reader's attention to O'Faolain's exclusion of Sean Lemass from his criticism of the governing party, a detail that is not explained but that assumes knowledge of Lemass's work as the Minister for Industry and Commerce throughout much of the 1930s, 1940s, and 1950s. In this role, Lemass was responsible for the Tariff War with Britain from 1933 to 1938, just as he was for gradually liberalising the Irish economy after its resolution. Gibbons also appears to expect that the reader make the leap from 1944, the date of O'Faolain's article, to a decade and a half later: in 1959, Lemass, having succeeded de Valera as Taoiseach, introduced the First Programme for Economic Expansion, which would effectively open up Ireland to foreign direct investment and set the template for its full entry into the global economy.

In this light, O'Faolain's criticism in "Autoantiamericanism" of those wary of the influx of American capital becomes representative not of one who fights against power, but of one who defends it.[67] This was certainly the opinion of Hubert Butler, who, like others who responded to the essay, saw the Marshall Plan as necessarily tying the Irish to Cold War militarism and believed that it was naive to expect that no quid pro quo was involved. These critics demonstrated that the United States, like anyone else, had always expected a return on its investment and, in fact, had threatened to withdraw financial support from countries that did not align themselves with American foreign policy, thus causing them to eventually fall into line. Butler lamented O'Faolain's blindness to such facts in his haste to critique anything that resembled isolationism. In doing so, he had effectively damaged himself: "Sean O'Faolain is normally the least traitorous of clerks," Butler wrote, "so it is disquieting to find him perverting Benda's famous phrase, '*la trahison des clercs*,' to endorse a war-policy that would have horrified the French philosopher."[68] O'Faolain had, he believed, come to adopt the dichotomous perspective wherein the world would now be neatly divided along the axis of capitalism versus communism and had come to defend the policies of a state with visions of imperial glory and might.

In these terms, O'Faolain's liberalism becomes more problematic, its ramifications more complex. His open hostility to left-wing politics might suggest that he was against social welfare measures that are still noticeably absent in Ireland. But in "Autoantimericanism" he justifies – however awkwardly – his defence of foreign investment in the Calabria region of

Italy as having empowered the impoverished locals; in some respects, this mirrored what the land acts of the early twentieth century did for the Irish peasantry. And, while adhering to a liberal project of modernisation, he also included several documentary articles in *The Bell* to highlight the conditions of those who were marginalised and suggested ways that society could better serve them.[69] Moreover, although he was against the tyranny of the State and could at times be blinded to the more nefarious impact of transnational capitalism, he was not in favour of complete deregulation, believing that it was possible for the government to positively intervene in the economy and other sectors of society. And more recent studies have posited that he was not anti-nationalist, instead arguing that his views are rather liberal-nationalist.[70] Such tensions in O'Faolain's rhetoric have contributed to his contested status in Irish Studies when it comes to defining his legacy. But, paradoxically, these tensions are often passed over by critics who prefer a more easily definable figure.[71]

Regardless, O'Faolain's relevance should be evident to an Ireland that is dealing with the residue of the issues he confronted in his own day. Having enjoyed the riches of the Celtic Tiger's boom years, the country has struggled through an austerity program to ostensibly repair the deleterious effects of a poorly regulated economy and kleptocratic politics; the gap between rich and poor continues to increase; Ireland's place in Europe, and specifically the European Union, is regularly debated; the power of the Church has collapsed in the wake of scandals and reports on the systemic abuses of those in its care; the influx of immigrants who have sought a better life find that, despite the fact Irish people are increasingly well travelled, the old racisms survive, making it difficult to adapt to a multicultural society that does not do enough to integrate its most vulnerable new members; and Irish letters still stand in the shadow of the Literary Revival, while a number of its most important figures continue to live outside the country's borders.

It is hoped that the writings collected here will be regarded as essential artefacts of Ireland's intellectual heritage. However, as it should now be clear, they should not simply be seen as museum pieces, fit only for affording a view into another time. O'Faolain was the leading Irish public intellectual of his day, and from these pages we can better grasp some of the modes of thought that have shaped the making of contemporary Ireland and the world far beyond its borders.

NOTES

1 See, for example, Seamus Deane, ed., *The Field Day Anthology of Irish Writing*, vol. 3 (Derry: Field Day Publications, 1991); and David Pierce,

ed., *Irish Writing in the Twentieth Century: A Reader* (Cork: Cork University Press, 2000).

2 Some of the more recent work on the essays includes Bryan Fanning, "Out of the Mist: *The Bell* 1940–45," in *The Quest for Modern Ireland: The Battle of Ideas, 1912–1986* (Dublin: Irish Academic Press, 2008), 41–66; and Mark McNally, "Countering the Hegemony of the Irish National Canon: The Modernist Rhetoric of Seán O'Faoláin (1938–50)," *Nations and Nationalism* 15, no. 3 (2009): 524–44. For a recent study of O'Faolain's fiction, see Paul Delaney, "Changing Times: Frank O'Connor and Seán O'Faoláin," in *A Companion to Irish Literature*, vol. 2, ed. Julia Wright (Chichester: Wiley-Blackwell, 2010), 145–58.

3 For an excellent critical survey of Irish periodical culture in the post-independence period, see Frank Shovlin, *The Irish Literary Periodical, 1923–1958* (Oxford: Clarendon Press, 2003).

4 For a more holistic approach to analysing *The Bell*, see Kelly Mathews, *The Bell Magazine and the Representation of Irish Identity* (Dublin: Four Courts, 2012).

5 Richard Bonaccorso, *Sean O'Faolain's Irish Vision* (Albany, NY: State University of New York Press, 1987), 71.

6 "This is Your Magazine," 126.

7 Marc Lits, *L'Essai* (Bruxelles: Didier Hatier, 1994), 14.

8 Good introductory works on the essay include Robert Vigneault, *L'écriture de l'essai* (Montreal: Hexagone, 1994); Yolaine Tremblay, *L'essai: Unicité du genre, pluralité des textes* (Ste-Foy, QC: Le Griffon d'argile, 1994); and Lits, *L'Essai*. For a brief survey of the developments and tendencies of the essay in England, Canada (in both English and French), the United States, Germany, Spain, Latin America, and France, see Richard M. Chadbourne, "A Puzzling Literary Genre: Comparative Views of the Essay," *Comparative Literary Studies* 20, no. 2 (Summer 1983), 133–53.

9 Carl H. Klaus, "Essayists on the Essay," in *Literary Nonfiction: Theory, Criticism, Pedagogy*, ed. Chris Anderson (Carbondale, IL: Southern Illinois University Press, 1989), 164.

10 Theodor W. Adorno, "The Essay as Form," *Notes on Literature*, vol. 1, ed. Rolf Tiedemann, trans. Shierry Weber Nicholsen (New York: Columbia University Press, 1991), 23.

11 György Lukács, "On the Nature and Form of the Essay: A Letter to Leo Popper," in *Soul and Form*, ed. John T. Sanders and Katie Terezakis, trans. Anna Bostok (New York: Columbia University Press, 2010), 22.

12 Julien Benda, *The Treason of the Intellectuals*, trans. Richard Aldington (New York: W.W. Norton, 1969), 43.

13 Ibid., 164.

14 Edward W. Said, *Representations of the Intellectual: The 1993 Reith Lectures* (London: Vintage, 1994), 72–3.

15 "Roger Casement," 66.

16 Maurice Harmon, *Sean O'Faolain: A Life* (London: Constable, 1994), 90–5.

17 Daniel Corkery, *Synge and Anglo-Irish Literature: A Study* (New York: Russell & Russell, 1965), 3.

18 "Daniel Corkery," 88.

19 Benda, *The Treason of the Intellectuals*, 58.

20 Ibid., 61.

21 Ibid., 70.

22 "Our Nasty Novelists," 160.

23 "That Typical Irishman," 183–4.

24 "Ireland and the Modern World," 199.

25 "One World: An Irish Council."

26 "One World."

27 "The Dilemma of Irish Letters," 398.

28 "That Typical Irishman," 180.

29 Julia O'Faolain, "The Man Who Stayed," *Irish Review* 26 (Autumn 2000), 5. For a revealing first-hand account of her father, see Julia O'Faolain, *Trespassers: A Memoir* (London: Faber and Faber, 2013).

30 For a study of how Shaw served as a model for O'Faolain, see Brad Kent, "Bernard Shaw, Sean O'Faolain, and the Irish Public Intellectual," *Irish University Review*. Forthcoming.

31 "Shaw's Prefaces," 371.

32 "That Typical Irishman.," 181.

33 "Gaelic – the Truth," 194.

34 "Autoantiamericanism," 421.

35 See, for example, "Ireland and the Modern World" and "The Strange Case of Sean O'Casey."

36 "Eamon de Valera," 313.

37 Ibid., 315.

38 Ibid., 316.

39 "Our Nasty Novelists," 164.

40 "The Dilemma of Irish Letters," 400.

41 For an account of Irish censorship that downplays its effects as well as the grosser abuses of the post-independence state, see Gabriel Fallon, *An Age of Innocence: Irish Culture, 1930–1960* (New York: St. Martin's Press, 1998).

42 Sean O'Faolain, *Vive Moi!* (Boston: Little Brown, 1964), 340.

43 *Irish Times*, 21 September 1936.

44 "The Dangers of Censorship," 95.

45 Tom Inglis, *Moral Monopoly: The Rise and Fall of the Catholic Church in Modern Ireland* (Dublin: University College Dublin Press, 1998), 21.

46 John Clooney, *John Charles McQuaid: Ruler of Catholic Ireland* (Syracuse, NY: Syracuse University Press, 2000), 167.

47 "The University Question," 263.

48 Ibid., 267.

49 Noël Browne, *Against the Tide* (Dublin: Gill and Macmillan, 1986), 161.

50 "The Dáil and the Bishops," 434.

51 *Irish Press*, 2 April 1953.

52 This trend has more recently been bucked. For two studies of O'Faolain's literary criticism, see Mark Quigley, "Sean O'Faoláin and the End of Republican Realism," in *Empire's Wake: Postcolonial Irish Writing and the Politics of Modern Literary Form* (New York: Fordham University Press, 2013), 65–121; and Joe Cleary, "Distress Signals: Sean O'Faolain and the Fate of Twentieth-Century Irish Literature," *Field Day Review* 5 (2009): 49–73.

53 *Signe Toksvig's Irish Diaries, 1926–1937*, ed. Lis Pihl (Dublin: Lilliput, 1994), 257.

54 "The Dilemma of Irish Letters," 392.

55 Said, *Representations of the Intellectual*, 11.

56 The creative writing published in *The Bell* reflects his preferences, with a preponderance of the former and an absence of the latter forms.

57 Brian P. Kennedy, "Better sureshot than scattergun: Eamon de Valera, Seán Ó Faoláin and arts policy," in *De Valera's Irelands*, ed. Gabriel Doherty and Dermot Keogh (Cork: Mercier Press, 2003), 115–31.

58 Donal Ó Drisceoil, *Peadar O'Donnell* (Cork: Cork University Press, 2001), 110.

59 Eibhear Walshe, "'The Indefinite Ghosts of the Past': Elizabeth Bowen and Ireland," in *Elizabeth Bowen's Selected Irish Writings*, ed. Eibhear Walshe (Cork: Cork University Press, 2011), 7–11.

60 The Irish names translate, respectively, as the Branch of the Resurrection and the Masons of the Resurrection. See O'Faolain's mention of this movement in "That Typical Irishman."

61 For a recent example that sheds new light on O'Faolain's work, see Paul Delaney, *Seán O'Faoláin: Literature, Inheritance and the 1930s* (Dublin: Irish Academic Press, 2014).

62 Paul A. Doyle, *Sean O'Faolain* (New York: Twayne Publishers, 1968), 124. This lineage owes some debt to John V. Kelleher's essay, 'Seán O'Faoláin,' *Altantic Monthly* 199 (May 1957): 70–5.

63 See, for example, Lawrence McCaffrey, "Sean O'Faolain and Irish Identity," *New Hibernia Review* 9, no. 4 (2005): 144–56. In Richard Bonaccorso's *Sean O'Faolain's Irish Vision*, a significant chapter on

O'Faolain's critical writings appears before those on his fiction. While this placement is useful for illuminating O'Faolain's views and applying them to his fictional writing, it also gives the critical writings precedence.

64 See Ciaran Brady, ed., *Interpreting Irish History: The Debate on Historical Revisionism, 1938–1994* (Dublin: Irish Academic Press, 1994); D.G. Boyce and Alan O'Day, eds. *The Making of Modern Irish History: Revisionism and the Revisionist Controversy* (London: Routledge, 1996); and Kevin Whelan, "The Revisionist Debate in Ireland," *boundary 2,* no. 31, vol. 1 (Spring 2004): 179–205.

65 Terence Brown, "The Counter Revival: Provincialism and Censorship 1930–65," *The Field Day Anthology of Irish Writing,* vol. 3, ed. Seamus Deane (Derry: Field Day Productions, 1991), 89ff.

66 Luke Gibbons, "Challenging the Canon: Revisionism and Cultural Criticism," *The Field Day Anthology of Irish Writing,* vol. 3 (Derry: Field Day Productions, 1991), 565.

67 For an article that considers the economic aspect of O'Faolain's writings in a comparative context, see Brad Kent, "Sean O'Faolain and Pierre Elliott Trudeau's Midcentury Critiques of Nationalism," *New Hibernia Review* 12, no. 1 (Spring 2008): 128–45.

68 "Four Comments," *The Bell* 17, no. 2 (May 1951), 12.

69 For more on this feature of *The Bell* and its legacy in Irish journalism, see Mark O'Brien, "Other Voices: *The Bell* and Documentary Journalism," in *Periodicals and Journalism in Twentieth-Century Ireland: Writing Against the Grain,* ed. Mark O'Brien and Felix M. Larkin (Dublin: Four Courts Press, 2014), 158–72. See also Bill Kirwan, "The Social Policy of *The Bell*," *Administration* 37, no. 2 (1989): 99–118.

70 Aligned with these more recent reassessments of O'Faolain's views, Niall Carson, examining O'Faolain's BBC broadcasts in comparison with his articles in *The Bell,* illustrates that O'Faolain could at times construct arguments that were favourable to Corkery's when addressing a British public. Niall Carson, "The Barbaric Note: Seán O'Faoláin's early years at the BBC," *Irish University Review* 43, no. 2 (Autumn/Winter 2013): 398–413.

71 For a riposte to such critical tendencies, see Mark S. Quigley, "Modernization's Lost Pasts: Sean O'Faolain, *The Bell,* and Irish Modernization Before Lemass," *New Hibernia Review* 18, no. 4 (Winter 2014): 44–67. Quigley posits that O'Faolain moved to the right in the late 1940s and that most critics fail to account for this shift in his politics, seeing O'Faolain as either left wing or right wing in his polemical writings throughout his lifetime.

Editorial Practice

Having been published in three countries, in numerous periodicals, and over the course of almost fifty years, the essays included in this collection had a wide range of textual disparities. Brought together here, they have been standardised to the Irish-English that O'Faolain employed while he was editor at *The Bell*. Even under his own editorial watch his spelling sometimes changed from essay to essay; I have thus taken the more common forms of words and names with variant spellings: for example, "businessman" as opposed to "business-man" and "de Valera" instead of "De Valera." O'Faolain's own name appears both with and without accents in author credits; I have kept the accentless form that he used while working at *The Bell*. Likewise, some typographical variation has been rendered uniform; for example, O'Faolain inconsistently uses italics and quotation marks in signifying the titles of books, plays, short stories, and poems. I have also deleted superfluous quotation marks around lengthy cited passages that he had already indented and set aside from the body of the main text. In some cases, O'Faolain used archaic words and spellings, but the regularity with which he employed them demands that they be kept; thus readers will find "to-day" instead of "today" and "shew" instead of "show." Similarly, he always spelled Chekhov without the second "h," so that it appears as Chekov, and Joyce's protagonist appears as Stephen Daedalus, not Dedalus; such personal ticks have been maintained. The ellipses and section breaks in the essays were all made either by O'Faolain or by the editors of the journals in which the essays appeared. Nothing has been abridged. Likely because of the nature of journal publishing — the tight deadlines, the over-stretched staff, the many hands involved in the production of the final texts – typographical errors appeared in some of the essays when they were first published; these have been silently corrected.

This collection includes fifty-five of the more than one hundred and fifty essays that O'Faolain published over the course of his life. The selection of texts was determined by several factors. Most importantly, the purpose of the book is to bring O'Faolain's writings to a wide audience and, in the same spirit, to demonstrate the range of his thinking. This range is reflected in the variety of subjects that he wrote upon and will be found in the essays collected here. Yet readers should find themes that connect many of these subjects and that give the book some cohesion beyond the fact of having a single author; a number of these themes are treated in the introduction, but more can be found and indeed should be pursued as avenues for further study.

By placing the essays in chronological order, this book allows readers to trace the movement of O'Faolain's mind and his preoccupation with certain subjects over time. This also creates provocative juxtapositions and links between successive essays, such as those on Roger Casement and the need to revamp Ireland; on Sean O'Casey and nationalism; on the place of religion in Irish society and the issue of partition; and on Bernard Shaw and Wolfe Tone. The essays have been divided into three phases: (1) those written in the years before *The Bell* was established; (2) those written while O'Faolain was the editor and chief essayist of *The Bell*; and (3) those written while he was editor emeritus and in his twilight years. It is interesting to note, in this way, the development in his rhetoric, style, and outlook over the years, and the subjects that preoccupied him at specific moments.

The majority of the essays included here first appeared in *The Bell*, which accounts for the importance of this journal in Irish history and in O'Faolain's career. A worthy volume could focus solely on the essays that O'Faolain published in *The Bell*, of which there are around eighty. However, this would necessarily place limits on how O'Faolain is regarded as an essayist. It would, for one, confine us to writings that appeared from 1940 to 1954 and were addressed to one particular readership.

O'Faolain reworked a number of his ideas in essays that were published in different periodicals, sometimes simply reproducing the same piece, sometimes changing how the issues are cast while keeping entire passages the same; these variants are mentioned in the notes for readers interested in pursuing such lines of inquiry. At times, O'Faolain's essays take essential ideas from one piece, but move them in other directions to make a different argument or to respond to a changing context. These repetitions allow readers to see how he worked through material over time and attest to the immediacy of the essays: while they reveal his core beliefs, the ephemeral nature of the genre allows him to revisit, revise, and clarify earlier points.

Some readers might find that certain notes are not necessary, in that they merely reproduce general knowledge. However, what is evident for one person is not necessarily so for another. I have tried not to make assumptions about the readership of this collection. O'Faolain is a major figure in the interdisciplinary field of Irish Studies, and what might be common knowledge for a student of literature might not be so for a student of history, film, theatre, theology, or political science. There might also be undergraduate students who are coming to O'Faolain and his era for the first time, either in a course or through this book; the notes should help guide them without the need for side excursions to reference works and, I hope, will remove any feeling that they are interlopers lacking insider knowledge. As well, advanced scholars beyond the field of Irish Studies might have next to no knowledge of Irish matters. And there is also a recuperative effort here: I have provided explanations for a number of references to indisputably arcane subjects that are all but lost to recorded history and that will not be recognised even by many experts in the field of Irish Studies.

The editorial practice that has guided the work on the texts is meant to capture the spirit of the public intellectual that animates O'Faolain's writing: to speak to and for a particular audience, and yet to say something that goes well beyond any borders; to be of a moment and yet to stand the test of time.

Suggested Thematic Groupings

Although this collection is ordered chronologically, some readers might be interested in tracking a particular theme as O'Faolain engages with it over time. Most of the titles of his essays are fairly straightforward, but in order to assist with such work I have included below some possible categories. These themes are drawn from those that I mention in the introduction and that tend to dominate research on his essays. As nationalism and national identity form the backbone of the vast majority of his essays, I have not included a list of those that address these subjects as doing so would come close to simply replicating the table of contents.

Further study and changing contexts will undoubtedly drive the creation of other perspectives through which to read O'Faolain's work. Indeed, readers are heartily invited to discover new ways of discussing and understanding the essays, to pull at some of the untouched threads that weave through his public discourse and that have contributed to the larger fabric of Irish, European, and world civilisation.

CENSORSHIP
Censorship in America
The Dangers of Censorship
Our Nasty Novelists
The Mart of Ideas
The Senate and Censorship

LANGUAGE
The Cruelty and Beauty of Words
The Gaelic League
Gaelic – The Truth
On Translating from the Irish

POLITICAL FIGURES
Roger Casement
Eamon de Valera
Rebel by Vocation [on Wolfe Tone]

RELIGION
The Modern Novel: A Catholic Point of View
The University Question
Toryism in Trinity
Religious Art
The Dáil and the Bishops
On a Recent Incident at the International Affairs Association

WRITERS
Dickens and Thackeray
Daniel Corkery
Don Quixote O'Flaherty
Æ and W.B.
Jack B. Yeats
Frederick Robert Higgins
The Strange Case of Sean O'Casey
All Things Considered – 2 [on Eoin MacNeill]
Shaw's Prefaces
A Portrait of the Artist as an Old Man [on Sean O'Faolain himself]

WRITING
The Cruelty and Beauty of Words
Literary Provincialism
The Modern Novel: A Catholic Point of View
Ah, Wisha! The Irish Novel
Ulster
Our Nasty Novelists
Books and a Live People
Romance and Realism
On Translating from the Irish
The Dilemma of Irish Letters
Fifty Years of Irish Writing

Essays: 1928–39

The Cruelty and Beauty of Words[1]

We are too often so arrogant as to think that language is a christening at which man is present as priest, father, godfather, and sponsor while all the helpless phenomena of life wait patiently for the label whereby we shall know them when we speak of them to one another. The truth is that in language Nature and Man have enriched life together: one may well say, Nature, when the philologists tell us that every thought we express has to be indicated by a sensual image – as when we speak of *insipid* poetry, music of *depth*, and so on. But even if we could not perceive this in almost every sentence we utter we cannot fail to see that every natural sound, and colour, stem and branch is as much the bestower, in language, as we: each natural object informs our aged symbol that is but its shadow and its sound. Thus the beauty of a beautiful word like *conched* is not merely the beauty of letters set side by side, not merely the beauty of liquid sound, but its beauty is a shell's re-entrant curve, one of the most beautiful of all natural lines.

But our words are informed by more than that: they bear on their backs riches piling up by as often as there are days and nights and dawns for every symbol to gather fresh nuances of meaning from all that their reality undergoes in the varied mind. As often as there are gradations of light and differences in the human heart, so often will the word – or let it be a flower-word like *cup, petal, bell* – gather overtones of meaning and lay them fresh upon the countless other overtones that these simple words have gathered in time in our human experience of them, so flooding

1 "The Cruelty and Beauty of Words" appeared in *The Virginia Quarterly Review* 4, no. 2 (April 1928): 208–25. It later appeared as "Style and the Limitations of Speech," *Criterion* 8 (September 1928): 67–87.

themselves out with those thousand multifarious mingling resonances lost in one rich sound that the artist, coming fresh upon the word, no more dare use it without careful premeditation than he dare drink from an array of cups where poison and wine are poured without distinguishing mark. No word but carries the fragrance of a thousand years, no word but is heavy with the sweet and sweat of a thousand hearts, and no word but swells with every passing tick of life.

And these are but simple words, primitive sense-images from the most primitive stage of civilisation when life seemed bounded by the eyes. And they are but single-root words reverberating without internal harmony. Since their birth we have striven outward from the shell of flesh that binded us when the world was red from the womb: as our needs grew our words were stretched and developed, they were further enriched by such cunning oblique application and figurative use that they are gone far from their original sense and we call them new words thinking of their new meanings. Words have been developed by combination and composition, developed by analogical use, so that the artist who feels wealth beneath his fingers in such words as *wave* or *cow* or *man* or *box* or *dust* cannot but pause timorous before words luxuriant because of their history, words that have travelled the barbarous sands of the Orient, words spicy from the East, dewy with the mountain spew of the Celtic world, hoary from being bandied from tongue to tongue in synagogue and temple, barnacled by the seas of the world – *arrogant, lavish, spice, chasuble, cinnamon, pepper, emerald, sapphire, lapidary, grape, necromancer, wizardry, incantation, haggard, chisel, coward, admonition, chamber, incarnadine, plum, cithern, pear, parsley, caravan, ink, pen, basilisk, morris, damask, charioteer*. The penman might be forgiven for thinking his materials too rich to hold. And as if they were not thus rich enough for any man the poet makes them thrice rich in their last voyage out from the womb of nature: he lays his hands upon them. It is true that he could never give the primal reality – he is not God – but he adds a wealth that one may consider more than equal to nature's, a magic that she too can give, but gives largely because of the preparation of men by poetry. The poet takes the body of nature that words yield to him in all its sensuous, naked beauty and as if it were not beautiful enough pours on it the magic of the moon. We know all these words – *light, air, sea, lake, wind,* and *rain,* and *elm, willow, wave, trees* – we have all experienced them in a thousand ways, but when the poet ends we may experience them, and lastingly, as never before: the poet adds something that is not in the mind of man:

in such a night as this
When the sweet wind did gently kiss the trees
And they did make no noise ...

In such a night
Stood Dido with a willow in her hand
Upon the wild sea-banks, and waft her love
To come again to Carthage.[2]

They are the same words, but forgotten as words:

The sullen wind was soon awake,
It tore the elmtops down for spite
And did its worst to vex the lake.[3]

The result urges us to speak of the craft of writing – technique – style, of which we must speak later on as the sole release from words: for the moment it might seem as if language were too rich for the artist's use. And yet there are some who give us pause when they cry out (or behave as if they would cry out) – how poor, stale, impoverished, fossilised is this imposition men call speech – how inadequate for human needs!

One must admit that there have always been signs of this dissatisfaction – Shakespeare's racking of language in his rage; Carlyle; even the goodhumoured protest of Lewis Carroll's Jabberwocky talk[4] – but nowadays there is complete rebellion. One's mind naturally reverts to James Joyce who in his latest work "in progress" has written many pages in this

2 These lines are spoken by Lorenzo to Jessica in act V, scene i, lines 1–3 and 9–12 of *The Merchant of Venice* (1596–97), by William Shakespeare (1564–1616).
3 From the poem "Porphyria's Lover" (1836), lines 2–4, by Robert Browning (1812–1889).
4 Thomas Carlyle (1795–1881) was a prominent and influential essayist, historian, and reformist of his day. Lewis Carroll (1832–1898), né Charles Lutwidge Dodgson, was the author of *Alice's Adventures in Wonderland* (1865) and its sequel *Through the Looking-Glass* (1871); "Jabberwocky" is a nonsense poem that appears in the latter work.

manner, and may do more in that manner before he publishes his work[5] in book-form.[6]

> In the name of Anem this earl on the kopje a parth a lone who the joebiggar be he? Forshapen his pigmaid hoagshead, shroonk his plodsfoot. Me seemeth a dragon man ... He is almonthst on the kiep fief by here, is Comestipple Sacksoun, be it junipery or febrowery, marracks or alebrill or the ramping riots of pouriose and froriose. What a quhare soort of a mahan. It is evident the michindaddy. He can prapsposterus the pillory way to Hirculos pillar. Scuse us, chorley guy! You tollerday donsk? N. You tolkatiff scowegian? Nn. You spigotty anglease? Nnn. You phonio saxo? Nnnn. Clear all so! 'Tis a Jute. Let us swop hats and excheck a few strong verbs weak oach eather yapyazzard abast the blooty creeks.

We are not in the habit of hearing very much from this artist either about his meanings or his intentions but we can know at least that this is intended to be language and that these are presumably words; furthermore in writing thus Mr. Joyce has rejected valid English, and, one may conclude, for but one possible reason – that normal speech is insufficient for his needs. Nothing but necessity can bring language into being and nothing but necessity can justify its overthrow.

The average layman, on hearing such a plaint, would be inclined to give an answer similar to Dr. Johnson's when confronted with Berkleyan doubts as to existence – he would get up and talk.[7] If an earnest man and one anxious to perceive, if he could, the difficulties of the artist he would talk on the most intricate and exact science he knew, and would most likely finish by admitting sorrowfully that language does indeed at times

---

5 O'Faolain's note: transition: April, 1927, and following months, Shakespeare and Company, Paris. [Editor's note: transition was a Paris-based journal devoted to avant-garde art. It was published from 1927 to 1938. At this time, O'Faolain would have been reading Joyce's work as it appeared in the journal.]

6 The Irish writer James Joyce (1882–1941) was the author of Dubliners (1914), A Portrait of the Artist as a Young Man (1916), and Ulysses (1922). The fragment was taken from his work-in-progress, which was later published as Finnegans Wake (1939).

7 Samuel Johnson (1709–1784), also known as Dr. Johnson, was Britain's leading intellectual and man of letters of the eighteenth century. George Berkeley (1685–1753) was an eminent Irish philosopher.

present problems to our demand for complete and exact appellations for various phenomena. Thus while preparing this essay I had a chemist protest to me against the inadequacy and inaccuracy of the common phrase referring to "the arrangement of electrons clustering around the nucleus": yet even he, I felt, would not agree that the English language had therein been weighed and found wanting – the right word was somewhere if he only knew where to search for it or how to form it from little roots. It is after all only the philosopher and the artist who might be expected to find that language as it stands does not suffice – the one, because he, though expected rather to analyse than protest against life, would feel how nearly bounded by language is conceptual thought; the other, because as he will shew us, and as we might well expect in any case from everything that is born of life, there are real limitations to the eloquence of words. These are mainly two – despite the overteeming richness of what we do possess our vocabulary is not of our manufacture and it is limited: and meanwhile, liberty to invent, and add to, and replace is absolutely denied us – denied us, as it would seem, for all time.

Without this racking of words of which I have made mention to suggest that speech is not always satisfying to the artist, more than one country presents the illustration of a people expressing itself at different periods in ways so far divergent that we are inevitably driven in the end to examine the matter of the influence of language as the most satisfactory explanation for several reasons. Language does not explain everything in such cases as the difference between the mediaeval verse of Ireland – say to 1300 – and the verse that was written in the period to about 1600, and the far different verse written between then and 1850. But consider that problem as we may, and make as many interesting generalisations as we will, the influence of a dissolving language – among those other influences which it does not in any way invalidate by being of all of them the most ineluctable – impresses itself profoundly on us as being the most positive and (for being so well documented) the most securely founded as well. Or consider the more familiar transformation which overtook English literature after c. 1300, when the Saxon gloom that is a byeword among critics of the period was swallowed up by any casual couplet you may pick from the *Canterbury Tales*,[8] no more than the spice or the salt that a cook dashes in a sweet cake. With the exception of certain fleeting impressions in poems like the "Be Domes Daege," the "Havelok," the "Owl and the Nightingale," and the romances (best typified by *Sir Gawain and the*

8 *The Canterbury Tales* (1387–1400), by Geoffrey Chaucer (c. 1342/43–1400).

Green Knight) there had been no warning of that transformation in the verse previous.[9] It is not suggested that language began to change before the eyes of men and that they found their thoughts changing shape like a woman's waist in a corset as a result, but though we take the easy course of leaving the problem in mid-air we may point out the one significant fact: for all the gentle influences from France and Italy, for all the troubadour songs, the fragrant stoups of lyric from Normandy and Castile,[10] for all the power of chivalric fashions and of virginity raised on an altar taming the passion of hard men, for all the fragrant airs from where Boccaccio and Petrarch were writing luscious bawdiness[11] – despite all such preparation for the Wyatts, Surreys, Raleighs, for Shakespeare,[12] for the anonymi who sang of Lenten coming with love in turn – had the English tongue not softened out to limber length for song, dropping its trochaic stutter, becoming rhythmical, becoming light with many tiny dancing words hitherto unused, he would have had to stumble in the chains who so lightly could sing in and around 1625:

> Merry Margaret,
>   As midsummer flower,
>   Gentle as falcon
>   Or hawk of the tower:
> With solace and gladness
> Much mirth and no madness
> All good and no badness,

9 "Be Domes Daege" is a poem whose translation from the Latin to Old English is ascribed to Saint Bede the Venerable (672/73–735); "The Lay of Havelok the Dane," written c. 1300, is a Middle English romance composed in a Lincolnshire dialect; "The Owl and the Nightingale" is a Middle English poem composed in the twelfth or thirteenth century; *Sir Gawain and the Green Knight*, an Arthurian tale of chivalry, is also a Middle English poem, composed in the second half of the fourteenth century.

10 A stoup is a cask or a jar. It is now considered a literary archaism. O'Faolain likely chose it for its resonances with a time long past.

11 Giovanni Boccaccio (1313–1375) and Francesco Petrarca (1304–1374), both Italian poets and scholars, set the foundations for the Renaissance.

12 Sir Thomas Wyatt (1503–1542) and Henry Howard (1517–1547), the Earl of Surrey, introduced Italian styles and metres into English literature, including the sonnet and terza rima verse form; Sir Walter Raleigh (1554–1618) was an English explorer and writer who was eventually executed for treason. The former two were particularly influential on Shakespeare's use of the sonnet.

So joyously,
So maidenly,
So womanly
Her demeaning in every thing,
Far, far passing,
That I can indite,
Or suffice to write
Of Merry Margaret,
As midsummer flower,
Gentle as falcon
Or hawk of the tower.
As patient and still,
And as full of good will
As fair Isaphill.
Coliander,
Sweet Pomander,
Good Cassander:
Steadfast of thought,
Wellmade, wellwrought,
Far may be sought,
Ere that ye can find,
So courteous, so kind
As Merry Margaret
This midsummer flower,
Gentle as falcon
Or hawk of the tower.[13]

It would have been a physical impossibility for him, John Skelton, to write, for Raleigh to write, for Shakespeare to write, as they did all write, had they lived in Cynewulf's day – as impossible for them as for Cynewulf to write this lyric, passion as he might, and think how he might: he might have uttered his high regard for a woman but one has but to read any of the alliterative verse of his day to realise how far, far removed his poem would be from this tripping form.[14] He could not have moulded language to his thought – this is my point – for it is not given to any one man

13 "To Mistress Margaret Hussey" (1523), by John Skelton (1460–1529), a Tudor poet and satirist. O'Faolain quotes a version in which the spelling has been modernised.
14 Cynewulf was a ninth-century poet who wrote in Old English.

to do that, but only to time and nations. Of course such an imposition did not occur to Skelton or Wyatt or Surrey or Shakespeare, a fact from which we might like to draw the great consolation of supposing that when men have certain thoughts to express, language will always be found to have readied itself for their expression beforehand. Yet who will dare say that no Skelton struggled with inarticulateness in Cynewulf's day and who can refrain from wondering what Cynewulf might not have said if he were born about the year 1600!

Therefore the vital question (which we do not propose to answer here) is whether the thought of man is like a wind bending the tops of the boughs of speech, or whether language is like a great layer of stone that impresses its substance and its texture on the flowers of human idea that fall between there and lie there through the ages. One would like to believe that men weave language as a weaver weaves his sally-rods – that it is the sonneteer who coaxes words into the lap of his thought, not words that coax the sonneteer into their web. As it is we can make but one observation in complete security, to-wit, that every artist is at his birth confronted by an imposed speech. He becomes aware of the continuity of language as soon as he begins writing and give him but the shadow of a desire to be independent of his predecessors and you sow in him discontent with his materials – which are in the poet's case but words: they were not made by him, or chosen by him, he must become antagonistic to this continuity that is the first and most vital characteristic of all language. Yet it is this continuity – this alltime-spirit as opposed to the time-spirit, the *zeitgeist* – that makes words so rich and overteeming, and here we find the artist declaring that this quality that makes words so rich and full of nuance is exactly the quality that makes of language an imposition that counters his free expression at every step. Thus a man like Joyce would appear to be like an heir who chafes at a will because of the qualifications it contains. But there are qualifications to the whole of the phenomenon of existence and it seems a desperate thing that a man should thus rebel against what is not merely inevitable but inexorable.

This unrest in the face of the inexorable is of our time. We have reached a point of painful self-awareness. Our historical-critical sense has become so developed that we have been able to trace with great minuteness and some exactness the actual mechanism of the rise of genius and the development of periods of great art, and we can even detect around us in our own day many of the influences that are moulding our destiny in art: we predict what our trend is, more disturbing still we declare what our trend *should be*, with the result that we behave rather as we think we should behave, than according to any inevitable natural urge: art coming like leaves to a tree seems more difficult than it was in Keats' day.[15] Under such circumstances continuity in art does not stand in our regard: it is opposed by an individual ambition, an individual attitude to traditions, an assertion of the *moi*. The virility of the moment may be like a river in its heavier, lower reaches thrusting away in an unexpected direction: or it may be like a river flooding over the levees and frustrating itself. It is thus part of the *zeitgeist* that men should thrust back the gift of the external mother even though it be riches that they refuse. It would seem wiser that in this matter of language they should behave as they do in the case of many another inexorable law in other fields, for language is like sleeping and breathing and growing and loving. Might it not affright any man to consider that the centuries may have been preparing the way for him alone and that a frustration of their work is not merely a frustration of the design in Life, but a frustration of all that he is in himself who is part of it.

It remains to consider the limitations of vocabulary as it stands. Language has been like a caravanserai collecting wealth as it crossed the plains of time.[16] And does it still collect? The layman thinking of electricity would say it does: the artist, thinking of the cows in the field, of the wooden box upon his table, of the wind that hums in the pines, of *is not* and *was not* and *will not* and of the fact that there is nothing to express in one word both *is, was,* and *will be* would say, no; language is traditionalised and whatever changes occur are not organic, and speech is no longer able to mould language into a new freshness. The artist would see that the vast mass of literature which is being printed today and which imposes itself on him constantly is the real power in the forming of the personality of words. And the language of books is static. Today books are more powerful in the matter of changing language than speech is: organically it can never change one iota more. The forces which are responsible for change in language are held at bay by the forces that crystallise it, so that English is nowadays not merely imposed on us at birth but it has in itself the paralysis which halts its own continuity, which denies not alone to the artist but to all men the power of affecting it except by the most meagre changes and additions. The artificial of literature has grown too powerful for the natural of men's conversation.

15 John Keats (1795–1821) was a major English Romantic poet.
16 A "caravanserai" refers both to an inn where caravans stop to rest and to a group of people travelling together in a caravan.

Consider the position: literature was once the tribunal that gave a tardy sanction to the usages of speech; it was the last tribunal but one – the last being the handbooks of the grammarians. Nowadays the usage which we heed, and heed more consciously and widely than we ever heeded the usages of the spoken word, is within the tribunal itself. It would appear that the suppleness of language is doomed unless we demand of literature that it do what it has denied to the spoken word, unless we give to the pen that tolerance we formerly gave to the tongue alone. To effect this, all standards of literary criticism must change and the philologist direct his attention away from the dialects of peasants and discuss the dialects of the literary innovator; the whole science of etymology would have to change; for the past would have but little to do with the present, and all the derivations that men memorise from the *Oxford English Dictionary* could be of no interest when dealing with a form of language that held no promise of continuing to behave according to rule. We university men would be flung on our natural wits without a learned journal to help them out, or to help out the lack of them that some taunt us with today. It is a nightmare of confusion too dreadful to contemplate!

When we regard the state of English after the Romantics had done with it, its precision all gone, overloaded with analogy of all sorts, strained to its utmost limit – witness its awful state in Carlyle's hands – without incisiveness, diffuse, vague, roguish for having had to say so many different things with the same symbols, we cannot wonder that the writer should say in our time – Ah, but it was well for the men who saw first the resemblance to a crane's bill in the colour of the geranium and then named it so:[17] it was well for those for whom the daisy was still the eye of day: for whom attention still held its visual image of a stretched mind; then words were vivid, living things, near to the reality, making immediate impress on the mind. But words are but symbols to us and we use a hundred props, a hundred helps to revivify them by extending their meanings in bizarre ways far beyond their original connotations: these props we call figures of speech, sometimes we call them the adornments of speech: in fact they are but the necessary encumbrances of speech added to it because we cannot add words indefinitely, and because our words grow weary from use and need new blood: not being able to add new blood we add more words. Poor wisdom indeed: it is like adding as many again to an army of wounded men when they cannot be replaced by fresh fighters.

17 The name of the cranesbill geranium likely does not refer to its colour, but rather to its elongated shape, which resembles the bird's appendage.

A simple example will indicate the nature of the limitations of the vocabulary we possess: take the matter of the names of specific designs, as in rugs – Ghiordes, Baluchistan, Kurdhistan, Mille-Fleurs, Bokhara, and so on;[18] these all call up an immediate image in the mind of a trader in rugs, he knows the design I mean at once. But as I raise my eyes from this page I see many other designs for which there is no name and for which there never can be a name. I see the trees beyond the tennis-courts, I see the varied *patterns* in the grass – to use painters' jargon – and trees and courts and grass, each and all together make as evident a design as the scattered flowers on a Mille-Fleurs rug. Move my eyes an inch and it is new and strange, wave the wind a breathful and the design is transformed, shine the sun on the tips of the leaves and the whole pattern of light and shade becomes different. The fact is that language was made for communication among masses of men and these exciting and most beautiful individual experiences must go unrecorded, unspoken because the masses found them too unimportant to have invented for their recording any form of communication other than actual imitation on canvas in colour.

An example to indicate the limitations of vocabulary again; Carlyle of all people declaring against the hollow backs and weak chests of words. In his notebooks he has this amusing and quite correct entry – amusing because it should be Carlyle who makes it:

All language but that concerning sensual objects is or has been figurative. Prodigious influence of metaphors! Never saw into it until lately. A truly useful and philosophical work would be a good *Essay on Metaphors*. Some day I will write one.[19]

I cannot forbear to quote the entry immediately preceding this for he would not have written in the fashion of it if he had actually done his "Essay on Metaphors," nor had cause to feel so keenly the tyranny of his speech.

18 Ghiordes, also spelled Gördes, is a town in Turkey; Baluchistan is a region in southeastern Iran; Kurdhistan, often spelled without the "h," is a region straddling eastern Turkey, northern Iraq, western Iran, and northern parts of Syria and Armenia; Mille-Fleurs, which directly translated means "thousand flowers," is a style of French rug so named for its floral backgrounds; Bokhara, now spelled Bukhara, is a city in south-central Uzbekistan.
19 This and the next quotation are from *Two Note Books of Thomas Carlyle from 23rd March 1822 to 16th May 1832* (1898).

An institution, a law of any kind, may become a *deserted* edifice; the walls standing, no life going on within, but that of bats, owls, and unclean creatures. It will then be pulled down if it stand interrupting any thoroughfare: if it do not so stand, people may leave it alone till a grove of natural wood grow round it; and no eye but that of the adventurous antiquarian may know of its existence, such a tangle of *brush* is to be struggled through before it can be come at and viewed.

At the end of which sentence one might well need to go back to the opening to assure oneself that it is really all about Laws and not *Buildings!* It was Locke who said: "words interpose themselves so much between our understandings and truth that like the medium through which visible objects pass their obscurity and disorder cast a mist before our eyes and impose upon our understandings."[20] (What ailed Carlyle was simply that he saw everything as a visual picture.) The fact is that we are the inheritors of a very little store of concepts embodied in words, and that we are separated forever now from the source whence more might come. Never more can we name the simple flowers that stir the heart's core, never again name the light that comes stealing down from the sky at dawn, never again the light poured down across the waves from a sea-moon: that primitive poetry of wordbuilding is denied us in the case of all the things we would most love to make live again by a fresh name. And the primitive philosophy of wordbuilding is not to be ours again, that which enabled the Greeks to declare a doctrine in one word as in the case of *apathy*, which shews the history of the intellectual prejudice of a race in the gradations whereby *miscreant* that once meant nothing worse than unbeliever became dyed with a passion and hate that have clung; or English *quintessential* derived from Aristotle and Empedocles.[21] Old Archbishop Trench found the revelation of our moral decline in euphemisms like *fille-de-joie*, and *love-child*:[22] he might continue to bewail the tendency today when we call adultery and suicide a *lovepact*, or hesitate to speak of *murder* – replacing

20 English philosopher John Locke (1632–1704), from *An Essay Concerning Human Understanding* (1689).
21 The Greek philosopher Aristotle (384–322 BCE) regarded Empedocles (490–430 BCE) as the inventor of rhetoric.
22 Richard Chenevix Trench (1807–1886) was Archbishop of Dublin. His "On Some Deficiencies in Our English Dictionaries" (1857) spurred the Philological Society to begin work on what would become the *Oxford English Dictionary*. A *fille de joie* is a prostitute.

the honest word by some rogue like *tragedy* that tends to weaken the force not merely of itself but of what it replaces.

Carlyle saw the bitterness of our state in being thus separate forever from the wellsprings of language: how to circumvent the tyranny of that state he did not know – and "circumvent" is the exact word to use, for we must in fact express our thought not so much in words as by means of words. George Moore says the thing well: "In the beginning a language is pure like spring water: it can be drunk from the well – that is to say from popular speech. But as the spring trickles into a rivulet and then into a river it has to be filtered and after long use the language has to be filtered too. The filter is the personal taste of the writer. We call the filter 'style.'"²³

It is our sole release from the limitations of words – it opens to the writer the wide width of the skies.

Style is the admission of the inadequacy of our materials; it adds humility to art, remediaevalising the artist arrogant since a Renaissance that bounded the spirit it thought to free when it denied that there were any bonds at all to the flesh. Style adds a gentle wisdom to art, adds subtlety and suggestiveness and a sophistication that is never weary: it gives the silver of a Monet evening for the hideous opaque scarlet of a Turner.²⁴ But because our Western minds are antagonistic to the indirect – how slowly we have come to see the wisdom of the Chinese love of line rather than mass – we do not take kindly to the freedom of style: and above all the Saxon mind has been slow to take the narrow path.

The Saxon mind has and always did have such a jovial downright way of doing things – Turner is so characteristic of this, Turner facing the sun and painting it (for which presumption may God forgive him and all the galleries that house him for our pain); Carlyle is typical of it; Dickens wringing his emotions dry; even Hardy the most unsubtle of English novelists.²⁵ What style England has learnt she probably got for the most part from the French – they who gave England "method" according to Taine,²⁶ using here as he so often did the wrong word – though England

---

23 Irish writer George Moore (1852–1933), from his plea to teach the Irish language on literary grounds.

24 Claude Monet (1840–1926) was the initiator and leader of impressionist painting. J.M.W. Turner (1775–1851) was an English Romantic landscape painter.

25 English novelists Charles Dickens (1812–1870) and Thomas Hardy (1840–1928).

26 Hippolyte Taine (1828–1893) was an important French historian and literary critic who adapted the scientific method to the study of the humanities.

might have even more easily learnt style from the Irish Mediaevalists if
she had not always been so proud and stiffnecked about Ireland, Spenser
alone among her poets even guessing that the Celt knew more about writing than he ever learnt.[27] Where the French wore their passion down to a
filigree of refinement, and the Irish in a like manner chastened their even
fiercer passion by imposing on it monastically ingenious forms, the Saxon
blurted his passion right out: and where he has been successful – we think
sadly of the many times he has not – he has perhaps achieved as much
success as either. But the fact remains that, but for the brief race of
the metaphysical poets, style never sold a poor English poem until Swinburne's day,[28] whereas style was always selling perfectly worthless verse
for the Irish and the French, and sells it yet: now style is become the
important thing for all, kept alive in the English language for the most
part by the Anglo-Irish writers, and the result may well be that content is
only galling its kibes.[29]

As far as words are concerned style presents but one main problem to
our consideration – that of the principle of selection. It is a query that
naturally arises when we find ourselves sifting at the one time for words
of quite various purpose and personality. Thus in Joyce whose maltreat-
ment of language largely prompted this study I find at the same period, in
the same volume a predilection for lightsome and delicate words, homely
words, and sonorous Miltonian words so that all these lie side by side –
one might almost say – within the same covers: girdle, eucharistic, dawn-
ing, hymn, incense, crucifix, light, fragrance, unrest, dung, snot, bile,
arrogant, lavishlimbed, all without the least discord but on the contrary
as most people who have read the *Portrait of the Artist as a Young Man*
will agree with very beautiful results.[30]

This has a great deal to do with design of course: one has but to attempt
to compose a sentence containing the words "dung" and "fragrance" to
see how much a matter of design it is when two such words can lie together
in complete harmony. As clearly it is not a matter of meaning alone, for

---

27 Edmund Spenser (1552/3–1599) was an English poet and author of *The Faerie
Queene* (1590–6).
28 Algernon Charles Swinburne (1837–1909), English critic and poet known for
his innovative style.
29 To gall on kibes means to walk on feet that have sores. It is also an expression
that refers to someone being irritated or annoyed.
30 "Miltonian" describes that which is typical of the English writer John Milton
(1608–1674), who is best known for his epic poem *Paradise Lost* (1667).

dung is but animal ordure and fragrance a word usually reserved for the most delicate of odours, and the layman would see no fitness in their use together. The continuity of speech has however been at work here, and without its aid design alone would not be powerful enough to make such words sound together without harsh discord. The cruder word has been given numerous connotations, overtones, associations that are capable of awakening the most pleasant thoughts – the coming of the Springtime when the fields are made rich for the new seed, the cattle at the pools at evening trampling their own mire, the beauty that painters have made of old byres and of sodden straw and the sun sucking up the steam from its gold after heavy rains, a thought of peasants in their heavy clothes trampling the bedding in the dusk of stone stables where their beasts wait patiently and humbly for the voice that will cry them out to new labour. This is the alltime-spirit of words in which they find a clear and definite part allotted them for the fashioning of the *sprachgefühl* of their tongue;[31] this is their constant character as opposed to the temporary character wherewith the spirit of the age endows them. It is this constant character that the writer needs to determine with the greatest care for unless he senses it correctly he is using English on his own authority alone, enriching it with his own personality alone, using it without reference to the multitudinous associations in the minds of his readers – ahistoric English.

On the other hand "words are not exact signs for definite and unchanging conceptions ... Circumstances and a people's thought alone determine whether in (a word's) commonest use it shall include all those conceptions or a few of them, or shall be confined to a single one."[32] That is to say that words have their temporary value as well as their constant values in the *sprachgefühl*; which temporary value it is important for the writer to note, though it will impress itself on him more forcibly in any case, as it is for him to take account of the ultimate significance of his word. The foreign translator is more inclined to overlook the latter than the former for he would be better acquainted with the value of words in literature than in the life of his day: the native writer more often fails in assessing the alltime-spirit of words than in using words in discord with their momentary values.

31 *Sprachgefühl* is a German term, meaning the character or nature of a language.
32 This is a slightly inaccurate quote taken from *Words and their Ways in English Speech* (London: Macmillan & Co., 1901); the book was co-authored by Harvard professors James Bradstreet Greenough (1833–1901) and George Lyman Kittredge (1860–1941).

These two forces it is that govern the selection of words as they govern their ultimate and immediate values. The artist cannot ignore either – the *sprachgefühl* or all-time-character, or the *zeitgeist* or momentary character. The word *virtue* may serve again to illustrate this. It is a word that has had many connotations for it has had a long history and many vicissitudes have overtaken it in its progress through the winding ways of man's brain. It had the sense of physical courage and martial power in the days of the Romans who associated it with its root-word *vir*:[33] even in their day it was developing a wider application and carried into French a moral value: it came into English when its moral value was more regarded than its physical by the intellectual idea, and it developed there an ethical sense: yet it has been applied in a degraded way to mere *objets d'art* that possess some "virtue," and we find Trench railing at the Italians for reducing its metal to the base use of "virtuoso," "one skilled in the appreciation of painting, music, and sculpture; for these, the ornamental fringe of a people's life, can never, without loss of all manliness of character, be its main texture and woof – not to say that excellence in them," says he, "has been too often dissociated from all true virtue and moral worth."[34] It has come to be applied, far from its original sense, to the special quality of chastity in woman, and in our cynical and precise age we hesitate to use it at all, so little precision does it now possess. *Virtue* may in time regain its lost values, but for the day no artist but must pause and most likely pass by with prudent care a word so harshly treated both by the past and the present. It is an example of a word between whose ultimate and immediate connotations any writer might find difficulty in keeping harmony. Yet between these two formative influences there is a point of rest where the artist may handle speech in security: a point between the eternal coming-on and going-off of the values of language, and in this quiet valley the writer must work. He must do justice to the past of his people, to the labour of the forces in life that have brought speech to its present point, whether rich or poor, cruel or beautiful, or all of these things – a little inconsistent, the layman might complain, or add that life is very much like that anyway.

Here lies the condemnation of such language as Joyce's. It is not merely ahistoric – not merely the shadow of an animal that never was, the

33 The Latin word *vir* on its own means "man," but it also connotes "a true man" or a soldier.
34 Trench, *On the Study of Words* (1851), the work that made his name as a philologist.

outline of a tree that never grew, for even then we might trace it to some basic reality distorted and confused – but it comes from nowhere, goes nowhere, is not part of life at all. It has one reality only – the reality of the round and round of children's scrawls in their first copybooks, zany circles of nothing. It may be that Joyce wishes these meaningless scrawls to have a place in his design and if so nobody will grudge him his will of them. But we cannot be expected to understand them as language for they are as near nothing as anything can be on this earth.

Yet who cannot sympathize with this rebellion? It would seem that Joyce does not realise, however, that in language we are countering one of those primal impositions that give to life its inexorable character: he must see that in language there is an individuality which we must counter at every step, much as an actor must counter his own character to express ideas at variance with it. But a man who has had the great courage to accept so many of life's inexorable laws does unwisely to push a puppet in the actor's place; that offers us no release. It is a puppet without as much as the shape of a human being, and suggests the idea of a human organism for but one reason, that it has usurped the place of one.

Censorship in America[1]

A censorship law raises exactly the type of social problem which annotates the compromise on which society is founded – the inevitable compromise between the ideal of the individual and the need of the masses for ordered community-living. The mass of people and the more conservative among the few sometimes forget that society, as well as having a constant factual element in its structure – a *status quo* – also suffers constant flux as a result of the abstractions of the philosophers among it; it has, like the earth, an outer core of stability and an inner heart of molten movement. Few people, however, abstract about their own world in this way, but those who do, and whom we call leaders of the people when their reforms are approved and enemies of the people if they are not, become thereby more than mere individuals: they are the inheritors of those who have given society whatever lasting character it possesses and become an everlasting part of its history, the acknowledged interpreters of their social world – no longer just one point of the infinite number of points in the straight line between the ideal and the necessity which any society must be. This individual element comes to the surface definitely in the formation of laws for the preservation or cleansing of its moral self. The point is of importance – for in the final judgment it is one man or two who become the measure of his people's culture and civilisation. The police in such a case will do no more than enforce the law which one man has drawn up, enforce it at the initiation frequently of one individual, and cases actionable under it will be finally judged by the individual mind alone and the mass of people will not interfere at all in such a problem. Here a

---

1 "Censorship in America" appeared in *The Irish Statesman* (6 October 1928): 86–8.

superintendent of police has said to me that the police are censors in every-thing from larceny to murder, but he failed to recognise an essential differ-ence in the case of literature. There is very little doubt in any man's mind as to what constitutes robbery or arson or homicide, and for the most part the business of a judge is merely to say whether or not such and such an overt act complained of actually did take place: rarely is it a matter of measuring the people's reactions to the defendant, their hates or fears – his act is mostly without complications – though one might well say when writing from Boston that the case of the radicals Sacco and Vanzetti exe-cuted here a year ago this September falls into that category.[2] But in the case of a man's writings, it is not so much the author as the people who are arraigned: their desires, cultural, social, religious, educational – their his-tory, in brief, is in court with the author. It is a problem akin to a problem in language or logic, in which the materials for the examination of the case are also themselves the materials under examination: the people in arraign-ing their own literary output arraign themselves; in calling on an individ-ual to pass judgment on the fitness of a piece of literature they call on him to judge also their own fitness to receive it. If they are not in that measur-ing their own history and civilisation, they are certainly measuring the cultural part of it, which to many must be the only part by which a nation may be judged to have succeeded or failed in justifying its existence. How many men in Ireland to-day might be considered fitted to go down in his-tory as judges of what did or did not accord with the aims of their people? As true interpreters of the civilisation of their century?

This is one thought suggested by an examination of the manner in which censorship is effected in the city of Boston to-day.[3] Another has to do with the apparent unfitness of private reforming bodies for the same task. It is natural that such bodies should be unwilling to discuss the

2 Nicola Sacco (1891–1927) and Bartolomeo Vanzetti (1888–1927), Italian immigrants and professed anarchists, were accused and tried in the robbery and murder of two men in South Braintree, Massachusetts, on 15 April 1920. Their case, which drew international condemnation and mass protests, including bombings in New York City and Philadelphia, was viewed to have been prejudicial. Because much evidence suggested that neither Sacco nor Vanzetti were involved in the crime, many believed that they were convicted, rather, for their political beliefs. The two men were executed on 23 August 1927. On the fiftieth anniversary of their deaths, Governor Michael S. Dukakis issued a statement that Sacco and Vanzetti had been treated unjustly and that no stigma should be attached to their names.
3 Boston was renowned at the time for its censorship.

problem for long from this point of view. Even in Ireland, where we are scarcely a race of Roundheads and there is so much of frank delight in nature – and human-nature – in our monkish literature which recalls the spirit of Assisi that few are likely to aver that for them all the beauty of the world is of no consequence beside the immortality of a soul – as I have heard said here, a country with a rabid Puritan tradition still strong – such bodies must nevertheless have next to no conception of the traditions and aims of the national culture – it being their chief business, and rightly so, to concern themselves with the affairs of another Kingdom.[4] That has been my experience, at any rate in this country, where I have interviewed the heads of one or two such organisations. The Watch and Ward Society of New England is not likely to discuss whether, in the words of a Superior Court, the definition of an immoral book, Shakespeare, or Murray's Dictionary, or even the Bible, is not quite liable "to excite in the minds of those susceptible to such influences impure thoughts."[5] For such bodies sufficient for the day is the evil thereof – the evil of other days they would not attempt to amend.

The great objection to censorship is that once begun it becomes difficult to stop. It is not at all clear to me why Boston has stopped short at Shakespeare and Balzac,[6] but it seems quite logical, on the other hand, for the police to have arrested last week in this city a university professor for stating in public that "if Sacco and Vanzetti were anarchists so were Socrates and Christ" – the charge being blasphemy, and the Act under

4 A Roundhead was an adherent to the Parliamentary Party during the English Civil War (1642–51). They were so named because they wore their hair cropped closely to their heads, as opposed to wearing it in more fashionable and luxurious curls. Many of these men were Puritans. Saint Francis of Assisi (1181/2–1226), who founded the Franciscan orders of friars, devoted himself to administering to the poor. He considered all creatures his "brothers" and "sisters" and was considered to have a particularly strong relationship with the natural world: some stories exist of him preaching to the birds.

5 The New England Watch and Ward Society was founded in 1879. It was modelled on the New York Society for the Suppression of Vice. The group's power was such that books were expurgated for special Boston editions and local libraries kept certain books under lock and key. Murray's Dictionary is the early title for what would later become known as the Oxford English Dictionary. Sir James Murray (1837–1915) spearheaded and worked on the project for more than three decades.

6 Honoré de Balzac (1799–1850) was a French realist novelist; his work is generally regarded as essential to the development of the genre.

which he was charged being a two hundred year old Act that once carried the death penalty.[7]

The situation here illustrates these three points adequately, and is analogous to that of Ireland in so far as it has arisen out of imported material.

There is not a sole censor in Boston; there are many censors – far too many; no single State could produce so many wise judges – and as a result Boston is one of the most censored cities in the United States, and the most mocked at for that reason by all the rest. New York, whose theatres now function under the shadow of a threat of a two years' closure for an indecent production, laughs loudest of all: the individual element in New York is of a different and more liberal type, and the punishments for misdemeanour, though severe, are only inflicted when absolutely necessary. A show like the New York production *Diamond Lil,* or *The Front Page* – a newspaper play where everybody calls everybody else a son of a bitch or a bastard, or worse – is not likely to see the boards of any Boston theatre without severe cuts in the script, while the thought of importing a burlesque like Mr. Earl Carroll's *Vanities* would probably throw the censor into a violent fury.[8] Barefoot dances are supposed to be forbidden in Boston, where all danseuses must wear tights (though I have seen Ruth St. Denis and her troupe brave the regulation successfully).[9]

The importation of books is regulated under a law which reads as follows:

Whoever imports, prints, publishes, sells or distributes a book, pamphlet, ballad, printed paper or other thing containing obscene,

7 The Professor in question was Horace M. Kallen (1882–1974), a philosopher who was, at the time of the incident, a faculty member of the New School of Social Research in New York. The phrase was reportedly spoken at a Boston meeting to commemorate the anniversary of Sacco's and Vanzetti's executions. Socrates (470–399 BCE) was an influential Greek philosopher; like Sacco, Vanzetti, and Jesus Christ, Socrates was executed.

8 *Diamond Lil* (1928) is a play by actress and author Mae West (1893–1980). *The Front Page* (1928) is a play written by Ben Hecht (1894–1964) and Charles MacArthur (1895–1956) that was later adapted to film, most notably as *His Girl Friday* (1940). Earl Carroll (1893–1948) was the director and producer of *Earl Carroll's Vanities* (1922–48), popular shows featuring songs, dances, and beautifully costumed women.

9 Ruth St. Denis (1879–1968) was an important and innovative choreographer in contemporary American dance.

indecent, or impure language, or manifestly tending to corrupt the morals of youth, or an obscene, indecent or impure print, picture, figure, image or description, manifestly tending to corrupt the morals of youth or introduces into a family, school or place of education, or buys, procures, receives or has in his possession any such book, pamphlet, ballad, printed paper, obscene, indecent or impure print, picture, figure, image or other thing, either for the purpose of sale, exhibition, loan, or circulation, or with intent to introduce the same into a family, school or place of education, shall be punished by imprisonment for not more than two years and by a fine of not less than one hundred dollars or not more than one thousand dollars.[10]

Now this law as it stands contains some obvious injustices. The vendor – a clerk, maybe – is punished, not the author or the publisher, and the punishment is excessive: not only does the bookseller condemned under this law suffer a serious fine with possible imprisonment, but he suffers even more by the unpleasant publicity attached to his trial, and, worst of all, he gets, in addition, a criminal record. The Boston booksellers have given up fighting cases under this statute – in a city where the local justices are for the most part anything but reading men, and, in addition, Irish and Catholic, convictions are inevitable. Instead – after some convictions had taught them a sad lesson – they made an agreement with the police and with the body most prominent in initiating prosecutions – the New England Watch and Ward Society – an old organisation and highly regarded by such people as the late President Eliot of Harvard[11] – whereby upon notice from the police that a book had been complained of and was found actionable by them, the Booksellers' Association ordered the silent withdrawal of the book from their members' shelves – which was done, it need hardly be said, with the least possible grace in the world. In passing, one may note here the influence of the individual element. Of some sixty books suppressed in one year, only three were complained of by the N.E.W.W. – the bulk of the remainder were objected to by a single Boston

10 Chapter 207, Section 15, of the Statutes of the Massachusetts Law. O'Faolain's analysis that follows is somewhat flawed: not only the vendor, but also the publisher and printer are specifically cited as liable for the material.
11 Charles William Eliot (1834–1926) was president of Harvard from 1869 to 1909. His forty-year term was the longest of any in the university's history. Harvard was founded in 1636. O'Faolain attended and graduated from Harvard as a Commonwealth scholar in the late 1920s.

clergyman. Another illustration of the importance of the individual factor: a bookseller, in doubt about a certain book, marked one major and one minor passage which seemed open to question, and, taking it to the Superintendent of the Police, pointed out the major passage, in which, however, the Superintendent saw nothing objectionable. Almost satisfied, the bookseller thought it better to mention the minor passage. In this two people, a man and a woman, are alone in a house at night, and, being awakened by a violent thunderstorm, come in night attire to their individual bedroom doors at the sound of a particularly terrifying crash. The gentleman said to the lady, "Hullo, dear, what's up?" whereupon the lady faints in his arms. At this the Superintendent was horrified, and explained to the somewhat puzzled bookseller that no gentleman should use the word "dear" to a lady dressed in her nightgown. This book was subsequently suppressed, but possibly for other reasons than this passage.

There is an appendage to the law as set out above, to wit, the surely objectionable decision of a Superior Court that a book, pamphlet, etc., tending to corrupt the morals of youth is one liable to "excite in the minds of those *susceptible to such influences* impure thoughts."[12] Such a definition, which could be construed to condemn "leg of the table" because for certain minds "leg" has but one indelicate connotation, and one only, leaves the bookseller almost wholly at the mercy of the prude. These are more than the anomalies of a poor piece of legislation: they are due to individual interpretations of what was supposed to be a perfectly static law – they represent the ever-changing core of society; they measure society, and they speak ill for Boston culture.

There is one other injustice in the working of this law which raises a fundamental question. It has been decided that a single "objectionable" passage condemns the whole book. This raises the whole question of the author's purpose in choosing to deal with situations which we may choose to call delicate, or subjects which we may choose to call morbid. In an attempt to amend the law, Mr. Ellery Sedgwick, of the *Atlantic Monthly*,[13] will probably introduce this Fall an Act which proposes the consideration of offensive words or passages, not in isolation, but in their context: it proposes, in other words, that an entire novel, for example, be considered *as a novel*. This, if we must have censorship, seems to be no more than the merest justice; it is exactly what any novelist would ask of his judges. But it does not seem likely that Mr. Sedgwick's amendment

12 This is from a decision of the Massachusetts Superior Court.
13 Ellery Sedgwick (1872–1960) was the editor of *The Atlantic Monthly*.

will pass the legislature. The *status quo* is dear to the hearts of its makers; it is simple and effective, and it has worked – to their minds – excellently, and it must be added that novels as novels are clearly not the business of such people as the N.E.W.W. Society. This is no more than natural; for them society has decided finally on what is ugly and impure – a bare knee, for example, is impure – and the efforts of well-meaning authors to find beauty even in the clay of humanity is contrary to the opinions of the *status quo* – the situation represents the strongest possible clash between the ideal of the individual and the immediate need of the masses. No doubt the main objection to Mr. Sedgwick's amendment from the booksellers' point of view is that it involves a lengthy and expensive legal struggle with appeals to the highest courts. Nevertheless, it stands for a principle which I think Irish publishers and authors should fight for in any Censoring Bill to be introduced into Ireland.[14]

The booksellers have also prepared an amending Act – one which is less concerned with the assertion of a principle for the censor's guidance than with the politics of the situation – they aim merely at achieving a more just arrangement than the present. This Act proposes that cases arising out of the existing law should be tried in equity instead of in a criminal court, which would have the desirable effect of taking the matter out of the hands of the district justices and putting it at once into the highest courts;[15] there, it is hoped, a more educated and liberal class of judge will pass on books brought before him, and there as well a criminal record will not follow a conviction. It would be the business of the booksellers to show at this court – public notice having been previously given to all concerned – why an injunction should not be placed on the importation of certain named books.

In all circumstances other than the present, it should be remarked, an undesirable publicity attaches to the whole business. Last year, when nine books were suppressed together in Boston, the affair became at once front-page news throughout the United States, and the New York publishers were immediately inundated with telegrams from all over the country

14 The Censorship of Publications Bill was introduced in 1928 and passed into law on 16 July 1929.
15 In England, Ireland, and the United States, equity is a system of law that exists alongside common and statute law and can supersede them. It renders a decision in accordance with the principle of natural justice and is appealed to when the law cannot otherwise provide an adequate remedy or the outcome would be deemed unfair.

ordering – frequently not even by name – "the nine books suppressed in Boston": the booksellers did not know the names of the volumes, but did know that they had become best-sellers overnight – which they had.[16] I was informed by the President of the Booksellers' Association that one New York publisher had on hand 2,800 copies of an edition of 3,000 of a first novel three months after publication, and was about to sell the lot as junk when the suppression of the book in Boston sold the entire stock in three days. I have heard it said, with authority, that publishers deliberately try to have their books suppressed in Boston so as to advance sales elsewhere. This result is deplored by all concerned – in Boston – for it is no satisfaction to a reformer to find that an evil which he has driven from his city breeds a hundredfold outside his walls. In an identical way it is certain that suppressed books in Ireland will be heard of in quarters in the North of Ireland and in Great Britain, which would never have heard of them otherwise, just as there is no doubt in my mind that if James Joyce's *Ulysses* were not contraband in America it would not be found in every second room in the Harvard undergraduate dormitories (mostly unread, I should add – just gutted).

I believe, and every writer must believe, that human nature cleanses itself like the sea, and that public opinion, when it is neither inflamed nor bullied nor cajoled, may well be trusted to look after itself. The occasion of sin is in the deep places of the human heart, and no law will purify those from the outside. There are people to whom a picture of a woman's breast is an obscene thing, and there are people for whom it is a thing of sacred beauty. There are people for which Rodin's *Kiss*,[17] let us say, is a mass of filth, and people for whom it is an elevation of the mind beyond this corporeal air we live in, but the filth and the beauty is in the heart only, and that cannot be dragooned.[18]

16 These books were largely unremarkable, but they did include *Elmer Gantry* (1927) by Sinclair Lewis (1885–1951).

17 *The Kiss* (1886) is often regarded as the masterpiece of French sculptor Auguste Rodin (1840–1917).

18 To dragoon is to coerce.

Celts and Irishmen[1]

The recent accentuation of the tempo of Irish politics is not due solely to the intransigence of a political leader. The music has quickened and become louder because latent emotions have come to the surface. It might be well to consider these.

Fundamentally, the clash is as ancient as history – Celt against Saxon,[2] now made more than ever violent by the self-consciousness of the modern "Celt." Outwardly it is a question of oath and annuities.[3] Actually a civilisation is – or is supposed to be – at stake. We may explain by a literary illustration, which is quite appropriate if we are speaking of civilisations and cultures.

First of all – is there a Celt alive? In his book on Synge, Professor Daniel Corkery made the first attempt to clarify the extreme, left-wing, ultra-nationalist Irishman's attitude to this question.[4] It is an attitude born of a patriotic idealisation of the position and function of modern Ireland, and it replies, in effect: Yes, the Celt lives, having miraculously survived

1 "Celts and Irishmen" appeared in *The New Statesman and Nation* (23 July 1932): 93–94.
2 The Celts were an Indo-European people who spread over much of Europe two millennia ago. The Saxons were a Germanic people who came to the British Isles in the fifth century CE. "Celt" and "Saxon" were sobriquets for "Irish" and "English."
3 Annuities in the context of Ireland at this time refer to the payments due to England for the transfer of land into Irish hands. See "Revamping Ireland," n. 1.
4 Daniel Corkery (1878–1964) was a novelist and nationalist literary critic. J.M. Synge (1871–1909) was the leading playwright of the Irish literary revival. O'Faolain refers here to Corkery's book *Synge and Anglo-Irish Literature* (1931). See also the essay "Daniel Corkery" in this volume.

his submergence of some two or three hundred years. According to this "submerged Celt theory," the Celt has been gagged by England for the past three hundred years – by the English and their allies the Anglo-Irish[5] – but he is now about to become again articulate, and when he does there will appear an unbroken line of tradition with the old pre-Elizabethan Celtic world. How leaky this theory is I will suggest presently, but in the meantime one must see how valuable it is to the nationalist politician. He stands before his people with the long line of Celtic heroes and writers fading into the dimness of antiquity behind him: he points backward to the days of Ireland's glory and then to the England that has crushed the language and traditions of those vanished days, and he says: We will be great again! We will have a culture and a civilisation all our own! We will weld them with our religion! But first of all we must smash every bond, great and small, that binds us to the tyrant, the pagan, the godless. The first portion of this imaginary conversation is admirable, and the second portion is intelligible, but that there is any connection between the two, at the present day, is not at all obvious. The whole thing may be nonsense, but it is at any rate an effective party cry and the mild suggestion of the Opposition that Ireland can do the first, and leave the second to wait, sounds very weak and watery beside so magnificent a cry as – Lazarus is come forth from the tomb.[6] And, as if to accentuate all this, the nationalist voter is shown Mr. Cosgrave in silk hat and morning coat at the marriage of the daughter of the Earl of Granard, while Mr. de Valera in humble soft hat and lounge suit bears the coffin of Mrs. Pearse – the mother of Patrick Pearse – to the grave.[7] So that if the voter does not quite follow the theory of the submerged Celt he has at least a vague idea that Mr. de Valera stands for a militant and enthusiastic and resurgent

5 Protestant Irish people, especially those of the aristocratic classes, were referred to as Anglo-Irish.

6 One of Jesus's miracles was to raise Lazarus from the dead.

7 O'Faolain makes class distinctions between William Cosgrave (1880–1965) and Eamon de Valera (1882–1975). Cosgrave was the first prime minister (taoiseach) of Ireland (1922–32), while de Valera held the same post thrice (1932–48, 1951–54, 1957–59), and was also president (1959–73). The Earl of Granard at the time was the 8th, Bernard Forbes (1874–1948), a leading Liberal politician. Patrick Pearse (1879–1916) was an Irish poet and educator who was executed for his part in leading the Easter Rising of 1916; his mother, Margaret Pearse (1854–1932), helped de Valera to found Fianna Fáil in 1926 when he broke away from Sinn Féin over his entry into the Dáil Éireann, the Irish Parliament.

nation, while Mr. Cosgrave is at best emulating a decadent Britain, and at
worst slavishly imitating it and bowing to its secretly conveyed desires. It
need hardly be said that Mr. Cosgrave would consider it an honour to
pay his last respects to the mother of Pearse, but his political opponents
are either much too astute to allow him to borrow their thunder, or much
too bitter to allow him to approach a grave that he is supposed to have
betrayed.

Actually, Mr. Cosgrave's government has done an enormous amount to
further the Gaelic revival in all its aspects, and the various departments
concerned were hard at work on practical schemes for the teaching of
Irish, the giving of financial support to the Gaelic-speaking areas, and the
financing of publications in Irish, while Mr. de Valera was trying to make
up his mind to enter the Dáil. But these practical demonstrations make no
appeal to Mr. de Valera's supporters, who are obviously so bitten by
Anglophobia that they can think of nothing clearly but their hate, and
whose vision of a great Irish nation, though it is essential to their enthusiasm, has never been expressed in any detailed, practical, human scheme.

The tragedy of all this, if one may say so without being irreverent, is
that there is no Lazarus in the tomb, and it is one of the greatest tragedies
in history, this not merely death but utter extinction of the Celt, an extinction for which England will never and should never be forgiven. Let us
return for a moment to the theory. What is the historian to do with the
last three hundred years while the Celt has been slumbering in the grave-
clothes? Surely O'Connell and Parnell were not submerged Celts?[8] And
as surely they were not Anglo-Irish allies of English rule? And those
others – allies or opponents of theirs – Mangan, Mitchel, Davis, Kickham,
Carleton[9] – where are we to place these? The propagandist has, it need
not be said, foreseen the objection and he has attempted to forestall it by
inventing a third class called "Colonial Irish." (So that, after all, Ireland,
despite its protestations to the contrary, *was* a British colony since 1600?)
In this colony, the theory goes on, there were three unblending races – the
Anglo-Irish (really English and living only, to be sure, in the big houses

8 Daniel O'Connell (1775–1847), known as the Liberator for his prominent role
in achieving Catholic Emancipation in 1829, and Charles Stewart Parnell (1846–
91), leader of the Irish Parliamentary Party, were the nineteenth century's great
Irish leaders.
9 James Clarence Mangan (1803–49), John Mitchel (1815–1875), Thomas Davis
(1814–1845), Charles Kickham (1826–1882), and William Carleton (1794–1869)
were influential Irish writers.

and the Viceregal Lodge);[10] the Colonials (Parnell and Davis and Pearse and Collins);[11] and the submerged Celt (unidentifiable after 1800, unless in places like Aran,[12] and before that represented by the Gaelic poetasters of the seventeenth and eighteenth centuries). Here the bottom falls out of the theory, for one would inevitably expect these tragically anonymous "submerged Celts" to blend gradually with the Colonial Irish – or as we would say the modern Irish, in which case there would be no submerged Celt left to-day. Which is obviously the pitiable truth. Take the case of Michael Collins. His father was an Irish speaker who knew several languages besides; he had been educated by a hedge-schoolmaster – a probable remnant of the eighteenth-century Gaelic world. Collins himself did not speak Irish. On the professor's own showing he is a Colonial.

But this is to anticipate a problem which Irishmen of all parties have yet to consider, and which was just coming into the open when Mr. de Valera and his enthusiasts seized on it and confused it by making the whole question of the Celtic revival ancillary to a party-cry of a "free" and "independent" Republic.

There can be no doubt that he has thereby given new momentum to an enthusiasm which was in grave danger of dying before the cold light of a reasonable survey; he has given his party a vigorous and popular appeal; but whether he can make any practical contribution to the development of a genuine Irish civilisation is doubtful. In other words, just as Ireland was beginning to find that, after all its centuries of fighting, life went on very much the same as before, he has given old dreams a new lease of life, and old dreamers and young dreamers naturally flock to him as men flocked to Moses from Pharaoh.[13]

The extreme, Irish nationalist, unhappily, has neither respect for nor interest in English culture. He has either heard of its superiority so often that he ends by hating and even fearing it, burying himself instead in

10 Built in 1751 in Phoenix Park, Dublin, the Viceregal Lodge was home to the viceroys who oversaw British law in Ireland until 1922. From 1922 to 1932, it was the residence of the Governor General of Ireland; since 1938 it has been the official residence of the president of Ireland.

11 Michael Collins (1890–1922) was an Irish politician and director of intelligence for the Irish Republican Army.

12 The Aran Islands are three limestone islands that lie off the west coast of Ireland, near Galway.

13 A sarcastic comment that links de Valera's leadership of the Irish people with Moses's leading of the Hebrews to freedom from Egyptian slavery.

thoughts of the real or mythical past of his own nation – or, if he has some interest in it, feels it difficult to find its outer manifestation in English life. He is not widely read, or cultivated, or leisured – the same is true, of course, of the average Britisher, but it scarcely matters so very much in his case since he has much less individuality and is willing to be led by his betters and when he pays a rare visit to England it is to be shocked by Brighton, or to lose himself in a Lyons' palace, or be wicked at the Holborn Empire, or watching the Regent Street night-parade.[14] And even if he scrapes a little deeper what will he find but a theatre that is either superficially smart or brainlessly naughty; an advance showing of cheap American films; a thriller-press; cities without a distinctive architecture, distinctive painting, or distinctive music? And when he returns home what does Great Britain send him but the same wretched Sunday press and the same wretched bedroom farces?

There is no part of the Fianna Fáil policy which is not inspired and invigorated by the enthusiastic vision of a resurgent Celtic nation. Its policy of an almost embarrassingly exaggerated protection of native industries, its historical approach to the question of annuities, its dread of compromising its position by discussion with British statesmen, all spring from the same intense patriotic emotion which, if it will only spill over into some practical human result and does not exhaust or satiate itself in hate and jingoistic display, is not to be derided. At any rate, it is something which Englishmen should attempt to understand. They should remember, too, that Ireland as little understands or sympathises with English points of view as they do with Irish, and no lasting peace can ever come between the two nations except by this mutual understanding, and sympathy, and respect.

14 Brighton is a popular seaside resort. One example of a palace owned by the Lyon family is Glamis, the childhood home of Elizabeth Bowes-Lyon (1900–2002), the wife of King George VI (1895–1952) and mother of Queen Elizabeth II (b. 1926). The Holborn Empire was a large West End theatre. Regent Street is a fashionable thoroughfare in the West End.

Literary Provincialism[1]

Provincial being one of those words which with the passage of time have acquired fresh connotations – in this case, quite unjustly, pejorative connotations – it is impossible to use it now without some attempt at a fresh definition.

First of all, it implies the metropolitan point of view; the provincial is judged and judges himself, if he ever does, not by his own standards but by those of the big city to which he looks for guidance and approval. It is not an independent point of view, but it is an inevitable one. The chief result in literature is that the provincial, because he is a Janus,[2] is in his most unhappy state incapable of making a true criticism of his own life or the life of anybody else; he is too self-conscious, and timid and restricted in almost all his mental activities.

Those who have had experience of this type of mind may be surprised at the words "timid" and "self-conscious," since nobody can be so aggressive and self-assured as, for example, the provincial critic, at whose hands every writer must at some time or other have suffered anathema. There is no contradiction however.

A man's aggressiveness in defending everything familiar – such as a local point of view or local standards – goes well with his timidity in judging anything new. But remove him from his familiars and one finds that he who is at first timid and self-conscious in the presence of all that is new and strange, becomes once again as aggressive and self-assured as

---

1 "Literary Provincialism" appeared in *The Commonweal* (21 December 1932): 214–15.
2 Janus is the two-faced Roman god of doorways and archways.

ever. Among metropolitans there are many provincials, and some provincials are incurable.

Yet there are many virtues in provincial life, if the provincial could only see them. There is a rawness and vitality and humanity which is missing in the more sophisticated urban centre. There is more fun if there is less humour. There is more colour if there is less drama, and what drama there is burns the brighter because of its rareness. I have known idealists in the towns and villages of Ireland who have spent, or are spending, their lives trying to persuade their fellow townsmen to be satisfied with and develop their own virtues independent of the cities. It is a vain task, for big centres are entitled to lead.

So much for what I mean by provincialism. It is in this atmosphere, strange and unsympathetic and uncritical in any good sense, that most Irish literature is written. Dr. Walter Starkie recently revealed to a meeting of the Irish Literary Society that much of the made-to-formula peasant drama presented to the Abbey readers is sent in by what appear to be Protestant Anglo-Irish landed gentlefolk;[3] in other words, the ladies and gentlemen of the big house have at last discovered rural Ireland via the Dublin theatre, which is an excellent example of the workings of the Janus mind.

It is obvious, therefore, that an original mind writing in this provincial atmosphere labours under great disabilities. The lack of valuable criticism is as devastating as a locust. There is a total lack of interest for the work of the young writer and he finds no outer stimulus whatever. *Cor ne edito*![4] There were times when Charlotte Brontë almost ate into her own heart daily; and she was fortunate and happy in her two sisters.[5] Hawthorne slept lazily for year after year in the heavy air of Salem.[6]

Worse than all these things the Irishman knows that he is writing for a mere handful of his own people, while his main public is at a distance from him and a stranger. He discovers for that main public an unfamiliar beauty, illuminates for it an unfamiliar scene, writes in a language which

3 Walter Starkie (1894–1976) was an author and specialist in Romance languages and history. The Abbey Theatre was founded in Dublin in 1904.

4 *Cor ne edito* translates from the Latin as "Eat not the heart."

5 Charlotte Brontë (1816–1855) and her sisters Emily (1818–1848) and Anne (1820–1849) were all accomplished English novelists.

6 Nathaniel Hawthorne (1804–1864), author of *The Scarlet Letter* (1850), was born and lived a great deal of his life in Salem, Massachusetts, where his family first settled in the seventeenth century.

it must find in many ways unusual, and as if to stress all the more this duality, this antimony, draws part of his inspiration from one literature, part from another – though the main part must naturally come from English literature of which he is bastard progeny without hope of posterity. His only consolation is that it is all very difficult and leaves no room for the third-rate artist. He will move at least in a good company.

The obverse of the picture shows the mass of Irish writers finding their standards in the whole of European literature and ignoring the merely temporary fashions because they do not know them and are not called on to supply them. There is, in brief, an urge to turn the parochial into the universal.

Under such circumstances it is natural that the Irish writer, ignored or misunderstood at home, should gravitate away from his own people – often in bitterness and disgust – even though he knows at the same time that all his interests and sympathies are forever anchored deeply and firmly in their lives. One recalls how terrified Charlotte Brontë was lest Haworth should discover who wrote of it so lovingly under the name of Currer Bell.[7] This revulsion-attraction complex has had a profound effect on Irish literature. It encouraged the Celtic mist – a release from the cruder realities of Irish life. It produced an excellent satirical comedy which the Irish public never took seriously, though when they occasionally thought it went too far, as in the case of Synge and O'Casey, they promptly bettered the actors and reviled the authors.[8] The prose-writers, who have been in the main realists, it would accept under no terms, and as a result the prose men are almost without exception in exile – to name a few, O'Flaherty, Moore, O'Leary, Boyd, O'Riordan, Strong, Miss O'Brien, Joyce.[9] Only those writers who have idealised Irish life, or whose orbit of interest is limited, or who treat of Irish life idyllically by a gentle

7 Charlotte Brontë published *Jane Eyre* (1847) under the pseudonym Currer Bell. Haworth is the town in West Yorkshire in which the Brontë family lived.
8 Sean O'Casey (1880–1964), né John Casey. Synge's *The Playboy of the Western World* and O'Casey's *The Plough and the Stars* provoked riots from upset nationalists in the Abbey Theatre when they were produced in 1907 and 1926, respectively.
9 Liam O'Flaherty (1896–1984), George Moore, Con O'Leary (1887–1958), Ernest Boyd (1887–1946), Conal O'Riordan (1874–1948), L.A.G. Strong (1896–1958), Kate O'Brien (1897–1974), and James Joyce.

process of tactful omission are really happy and at rest at home – e.g., de Blacam, Corkery, Hogan, Miss Smithson, Miss Somerville.[10]

It is therefore cruelly unjust and superficial to call these exiles "expatriates who are exploiting Ireland for gold" as they have been recently called in Ireland. I confess the phrase moves me to deep anger when I think of the young, half-ragged Yeats dashing back and forth between London and Sligo, of Colum now perpetually wandering between New York and Dublin, O'Flaherty never able to write without a visit to Ireland, of Frank Higgins or Lyle Donaghy literally half starving in Bloomsbury attics, of Sean O'Casey silent now in exile for three years, and all of us living on English hospitality because the Irish public, ungrateful as well as graceless, self-satisfied and aggressive in its priggishness, would rather kill off its writers than encourage and, if necessary, bear with them until they are certain in their craft and outlook.[11]

It does not really matter much where a writer lives. It is not the physical but the spiritual removal that is dangerous, for that is bound to produce odd and not always good results. It is weariness of the provincial rabble – I use Joyce's word – that has driven George Moore to write beautifully of mediaeval Europe when he had begun to write beautifully of Ireland; the loss is there merely national. But it is exile also, it seems to me, that has set Joyce thinking and writing esoterically, and that has caused O'Flaherty, at times, to write melodramatically. While it is that native provincialism gripping those who have remained at home which has produced the sentimentalism of the happy patriots.

O Liberty, I might well conclude, how many crimes have been committed in thy name!

10 Aodh de Blacam (1890–1951), Daniel Corkery, John Hogan (1897–1963), Annie M.P. Smithson (1873–1948), and Edith Somerville (1858–1949).
11 W.B. Yeats (1865–1939), Padraic Colum (1881–1972), Frank Higgins (1896–1941), who published under his initials F.R. Higgins, and John Lyle Donaghy (1902–1947).

The Modern Novel:
A Catholic Point of View[1]

The purpose of this essay is to suggest that some of the basic problems of the modern novelist arise from the history of the novel over the last sixty years or so, and are concerned with the disappearance from the novel of the ethic which until then informed it. These problems may perhaps be seen in a clearer light by considering them from the point of view of the Catholic novelist, for the Catholic novelist sometimes feels more sharply than the non-Catholic the disabilities which the disappearance of that ethic has brought about, even as he also feels that it may yet be his task to replace the vanished ethic of the older novel, either by a fuller ethic of his own or by a purification of the remnants of values which still inform the novel – one might almost say in spite of itself.

For the novel always has had, under whatever often disingenuous guise, some sense of moral and human values. So it has been from Fielding to Meredith.[2] Sometimes, as in the case of Jane Austen, one wonders if there is not a destructive scepticism playing upon commonly accepted values, but the main run of the English novel has definitely established and preserved what Saintsbury called a tradition of "moral and intellectual health, of truth and honour, freedom and courtesy."[3] It is patent in writers like

---

1 "The Modern Novel: A Catholic Point of View" appeared in *The Virginia Quarterly Review* (July 1935): 339–51.
2 English novelists Henry Fielding (1707–1754) and George Meredith (1828–1909).
3 English novelist Jane Austen (1775–1817); influential English literary historian George Saintsbury (1845–1933), who also held the Regius chair of rhetoric and English at the University of Edinburgh.

Thackeray and Dickens and George Eliot; it is implicit in others like the Brontës; it is basic in the lesser writers like Lytton and Marryat.[4]

Then, late in the day in England, but as early as the 'sixties or 'seventies in France, a break occurred. The still popular idea of the licentious Frenchman was gathered largely from the novels of the French Restoration – from Eugène Sue, Paul de Kock, Dumas père et fils, Flaubert, Balzac.[5] The dates are significant. Flaubert, for example, was sued for the alleged indecency of *Madame Bovary* in 1860, and that is the actual date of *Adam Bede*, a late date for Thackeray and Dickens, a middle date for Mrs. Gaskell.[6] Maupassant, Flaubert's literary son, contributed "Boule de Suif" to the *Soirées de Médan*, that manifesto of naturalism, to which Zola and Huysmans also contributed, in 1880 – at which date Tennyson was at his height.[7]

In that development of the novel, from realism to naturalism, which still rules the English novel, the old values were undermined. What produced this result need not concern us, though we may agree that nineteenth-century scientific research, the increasing complexity of the social atmosphere, and the rise of a sceptical democracy, had more to say to it than anything else. What we are more concerned with is the effect.

4 All of these are major British novelists of the nineteenth century: William Makepeace Thackeray (1811–1863), best-known for his novel *Vanity Fair* (1848); Charles Dickens; George Eliot (1819–1880), the *nom de plume* of Mary Ann Evans, author of *Adam Bede* (1859, not 1860 as O'Faolain suggests); Edward Bulwer-Lytton (1803–1873), titled as 1st Baron Lytton of Knebworth, was a politician, poet, and critic; and Frederick Marryat (1792–1848), also known as Captain Marryat, a member of the Royal Navy and writer of adventure tales and children's stories.
5 The French Restoration, also known as the Bourbon Restoration, refers to the period of 1814 to 1830 in France when the Bourbon monarchs were restored to the throne. Important French novelists Eugène Sue (1804–1857), pseudonym of Marie-Joseph Sue; Paul de Kock (1793–1871); father and son writers Alexandre Dumas père (1802–1870) et fils (1824–1895); Gustav Flaubert (1821–1880), author of *Madame Bovary* (1857); and Honoré de Balzac.
6 English novelist Elizabeth Gaskell (1810–1865).
7 Guy de Maupassant (1850–1893) was a major French short story writer; "Boule de Suif" (1880), which features a prostitute, is his best-known work and first appeared in *Les Soirées de Médan*, a collection of six stories written by leading naturalists, including, as O'Faolain notes, Émile Zola (1840–1902) and Joris-Karl Huysmans (1848–1907). Alfred, Lord Tennyson (1809–1892) is perhaps the most recognised poet of the Victorian era.

The effects are patent. Note, for example, the almost passive indifference to moral questions, linked with a greatly increased sensibility and compassion. The sentimental prostitute of Dostoevsky (to be compared with the little heroine – note that she is the heroine – of "Boule de Suif") has no prototype in the earlier novel.[8] Note, as arising from this "refinement" of sensibilities, the corresponding humanitarianism of men like Tolstoy.[9] And note, too, the inevitable swing towards irony, even bitterness and satire, in the humanitarian disappointed in humanity – as in Anatole France.[10] Note, finally, the sad fatalism of a man like Hardy, or the preoccupation with social tendencies of a man like Wells, the pessimist and the optimist of the new humanism.[11] And when you have noted these effects you cannot deny that the old ethic is gone. Saintsbury's description has no longer any pertinence to the novel. The phrase about a "tradition of moral and intellectual health, truth and honour, freedom and courtesy," has to be either scrapped or interpreted afresh.

The new notes are announced by Flaubert – "A man can breathe freely in a desert" – and echoed by Maupassant: "Tout le monde est bête."[12] They are: Let us bear with life since we cannot escape it, let us forgive our fellows who share with us the misfortune of life, let us pity ourselves.

In a sentence, the world is accepted with a bad grace and the universe and all creation is faced with an endless outpouring of questions. The old Christian attitude to life is, it is true, retained in part, but now without any genuine belief, and mainly because it is useful as the basis of a social code – not to be adhered to over strictly – and even more useful as an idiom of intercommunication. Love, charity, goodness, sacrifice – these are all terms too useful both to the commercial world and the writer to be discarded completely. But, in spite of these rag-ends of Christianity, one knows that at any moment a writer is capable of turning out a novel that is a gesture of pure unbelief, or of defiance, against the order of creation. Naked he will stand in the face of the lightning, and cry: "Very well, let me be another man to the dustbin!" (as Maupassant said when

8 Russian novelist Fyodor Dostoevsky (1821–1881); the reference is likely to Sonya Marmeladova, a prostitute in his novel *Crime and Punishment* (1866).
9 Russian novelist Leo Tolstoy (1828–1910).
10 French author and man of letters Anatole France (1844–1924).
11 Writer and socialist H.G. Wells (1866–1946).
12 The French phrase translates as "Everyone is stupid/silly."

he cut his own throat). And his fellows will probably murmur his requiem in the words of Hardy: The Gods have finished their sport.[13]

To the modern novelist life is evil and it is, apparently, his self-chosen task to prove it.

～

But the new development of the novel produced one more effect. It took the joy of life out of the novelist, *as novelist* (he could always be a cheery fellow as a man), and it isolated him from his fellowmen.

That is easily understandable. The first stimulus of rebellion in the new movement produced magnificent work. An artist is a man who takes himself seriously; and it helped the self-esteem of the artist of the 'eighties to feel that he was the pioneer – one might almost say of a new religion: the religion of honesty, disgust with sentimentality, hate of sham, the religion of pity and compassion and real Christianity, the religion of a new humanism. He might well feel that way when Tennyson was whitewashing the Industrial Revolution at the same time that men like Bakunin were wandering penniless over Europe.[14] Painting also, during the rise of the naturalistic novel, was in France breaking new ground. Artists were rebels.

But as usual life has caught up on art. And today the men who were in the 'eighties regarded as aggressive are accepted without query by everybody. The man writing in the naturalistic mode finds the critics hailing with joy the man who writes like Dickens as a vital, fresh, original creator. Naturalism is démodé.[15] And when one is writing in a way démodé one is writing by imitation, writing against the wind – there is no joy in it.

But there is more to be said than that. Men who write with something of the sense of the pioneer in them, reformers, even if it be no more than reformers of the novel, can accept *con amore* a bulk of life.[16] Dickens could write, for example, of the filth of London as if it were the most charming quaintness in the world. He almost made one love it. He certainly loved it himself. And he could well do so because he believed in the power of men, of Liberalism and Reform, to wipe that filth away. The men of the naturalistic movement had some of the same sense of elation. They

13 This is a paraphrase of a line in the concluding paragraph of Hardy's novel *Tess of the d'Urbervilles* (1891).
14 Russian author and chief propagator of anarchism Mikhail Aleksandrovich Bakunin (1814–1876).
15 *Démodé* is French for "unfashionable" or "outdated."
16 *Con amore*, an Italian phrase, means "with love."

did not specify their hopes. But they had some sense of power and some sense of belief in men. The modern novelist does not at all believe in men, or in Reform. Everything seems to have become chronically incurable. He sees all his hopes betrayed. He sits back from life and shrugs his shoulders at it. Or with one last despairing brutal effort of will he objectivises what he so hates. He is, none the less, isolated in the universe by his disbelief. He cannot, to any sufficient degree, accept the world he writes of.

What is the mentality of modern art? asks Eric Gill.[17] "Apart from the general enthusiasm for objectivity, and detestation of illusionism, and representation, and anecdotage, there is of course no one binding idea among modern artists ... But there is perhaps one tendency more noticeable than others [he is clearly thinking in terms of his own art] and that is the tendency to return to primitive and elemental ideas ... Any kind of elemental thing seems preferable to the dead and by now stinking frowziness of sham Gothic and sham Classic romanticism."[18] And even there, in that turn to elemental things, he sees the ghost of a genuine religious emotion at work, just as in the sham Victorianism he detests, he sees the ghost of a false religion producing in turn a false art.

In the novel, that taste for the elemental is often seen. One notices too, both in and out of the novel, a tendency to the biographical formula: one of the most obvious tendencies has been toward the chronicle novel, sometimes in many volumes. Apart from the novel there has never been before such a craze for biographies – at its height some years ago – and for the reminiscences of travellers, jockeys, salesmen, queens, dancers, statesmen, and what not. "The authentic story of!" That is the one thing which is certain to sell a book to-day. "The true story of Blank told for the first time!" Reality! The Goods! The inside Dope!

Well, it is one kind of search for truth. And for all their honesty, their brutal disdain for reticence, the realistic and the naturalistic novel do not seem to have satisfied that thirst.

The public is not alone in that feeling. The novelists themselves, I think, have begun to feel that naturalism and the modern lay-novel in general have exhausted themselves. There was a time when the spectacle of men like Balzac or Dostoevsky digging with renewed energy in the mud for the bottom of the well, excited themselves and excited the public, and

17 Eric Gill (1882–1940) was an English sculptor, visual artist, and writer.
18 From "The Right-Mindedness of Modern Art," *Order: An Occasional Catholic Review* 1, no. 4 (November 1929), 119.

created an atmosphere favourable to good work. Nowadays when we see a novelist digging in the mud ...

~

There being no hope of return, in modern society, to the old values, and society having in any case become infinitely more complex and in every way different, and the novel itself, above all, having learnt so much more in the absolute way of technique, I think we may say farewell to that old tradition of nineteenth-century England. Obviously there will never again be a *Vanity Fair*, since Vanity Fair itself is long since gone, and with it the rather ingenuous self-satisfaction of Mr. Thackeray. Gone, too, is the humour of Dickens – not to speak of his idea of the tragic – for the simple reason that the temper of our day finds quaintness unhygienic inside and in the way of the traffic outside, and as for the picturesque, our name for that is just Dirt.

But what offers to replace it? For a time it seemed as if Flaubert knew the answer to that. But it is nearly forty years since Hardy's last novel – Hardy, with such as Galsworthy and Bennett and Moore, caught the edge of the Flaubertian wind – and since then the novel has become poorer and poorer.[19] To-day it seems to offer no seed of growth.

We note two later arrivals – the Communist and the Catholic. They are neither of them capable of writing *of* as wide an audience or *for* so wide an audience as their predecessors, because they are limited by the common acceptance of their own beliefs. But they are something and they are worth considering.

To the Catholic novelist the world is a place that bears an aspect utterly different from anything so far seen in the novel. To find a counterpart to what the Catholic novelist is striving to create we must go to such work as Marlowe's *Faustus*, imaging it as treated in the naturalistic mode – for one cannot leap out of one's roots – and as treated by people of infinitely more refined sensibilities living in a much more mechanical and complicated age.[20]

The Catholic writer chooses to see man as midway between everything and nothing. He chooses to minimise the human drama, to belittle human glory, and to magnify the evil of life. He has the good fortune, on the

19 Novelists John Galsworthy (1867–1933), Arnold Bennett (1867–1931), and George Moore.
20 *The Tragical History of Dr. Faustus* (1604), by English playwright and poet Christopher Marlowe (1564–1593).

other hand, to see human actions as part of a cosmic drama, in which man can be both more noble and more terrifying for being, like Macbeth (only more so), like Tamburlaine, or Oedipus, the antagonist of the Gods.[21] This is his strong point. It restores at once to human action a significance it lost in the novel of the 'eighties, whose condemnation is that, in it, all human actions ultimately tended to have no significance at all because they tended to no significant end. It is also the strong point of the Communist, for to him, of course, life also takes on new significance in taking on new hope.

But in the Catholic novelists one knows, there is, so far, little or no improvement on unethical naturalism as we now know it. I find in all of them a painful self-consciousness, as if they could not forget they were Catholics, a timidity evident in their fear of the senses, a priggishness and a solemnity which has nothing to do with religion and for which there is no excuse, a lack of humour, and a tendency to underwrite about the emotions as if they feared to raise a storm they could not ride, and as by way of recompense for this slowness of the drama an overlyrical quality that verges on the sentimental and the neurotic.

These tendencies, though they may be well found and even for many edifying reasons highly laudable in the writer as a Catholic, are in the writer as a writer the signs of some basic weakness that is, apparently, fatal to his work. That weakness, I suggest, leads one direct to his chief problem.

In the first place, it points to an antinomy within him, a contradiction arising from the knowledge that in handling life he handles impurity. And that contradiction cannot be solved as he usually tries to solve it, by pretending that art can be a charwoman for religion, cleaning up life with her broom. I cannot hope, for example, to follow writers like Mauriac and Eric Gill in their tangled efforts to prove that culture and beauty are inspired by philosophy and religion.[22] It is, I think, going too far in the effort to give art a standing among the good works of the church to say that "it is primarily a religious movement that modern art exhibits" – merely on the basis that the artist is generally a hater of mammon, frivolity, hypocrisy, and flattery. In fact, Gide has well stated the position

---

21 Respectively, the protagonists of *Macbeth* (1606–07), by William Shakespeare, *Tamburlaine the Great* (1590), by Christopher Marlowe, and *Oedipus Rex*, by Sophocles (496–406 BCE).

22 François Mauriac (1885–1970), a noted Catholic writer and Nobel Laureate for Literature in 1952, authored *La Vie de Jean Racine* (1928) and *Dieu et Mammon* (1929). Jean Racine (1639–1699) was the major French dramatist of his day.

when he mocked at Mauriac as a man who could enjoy both God and Mammon, a man who in his *Vie de Racine* could rejoice that Racine had *fortunately* written his plays before he was converted.[23]

I pity the Catholic writer who suffers under this inquiet feeling that art is in some way or other a danger to religion. For such a feeling naturally deprives him of his equilibrium and self-confidence, and worst of all it deprives him of his necessary detachment. It produces all those peculiar effects which I have just listed. It induces the novelist to tone down the impurities of life, such as the sexual passion, to select from life what is an encouragement to his belief in a Divine Providence, to eliminate everything that seems to challenge it. And having pitied him I condemn him. He who would restore values, who would correct the error of the modern novel, himself falsifies utterly the wholeness of life.

No art can flourish, I said of the modern unethical novel, hating what it recreates. The Catholic novelist is falling into exactly the same foul morass in refusing to respect those impurities in life which are his material.

For, the whole human drama is surely the drama of the Seven Deadly Sins, and any novelist who attempts to avoid them is avoiding reality. That the Irish novelists have avoided them is certainly not true. Our critics usually charge us with having paid far too much attention to them. It is the greatest praise they could bestow on us, that we have the good sense to realise the glory of sin, its colour, its pleasure, its endless attraction, its repeated triumphs. Even as Tamburlaine respected its glory, and the Alchemist its colour, and Falstaff its endless pleasure.[24]

But we are almost alone in that, in this country or any other. On the stage what respect has been paid to evil during the last thirty years? It has been either buffooned or glossed over. In our Abbey Theatre we have tied a tin can to the devil's tail, painted his nose red, given him a Coombe brogue, and laughed at him. And that is not merely folly from the churchman's point of view, but it is a lie from the artist's point of view. So that I can truly say that while the Anglo-Irish stage has been, for the last thirty years, possibly the most edifying stage in Europe, it has been also, because it has fostered that lie, one of the most immoral and unreal stages in

23 French author André Gide (1869–1951) was awarded the Nobel Prize for literature in 1947.
24 The title character of *The Alchemist* (1610), by playwright Ben Jonson (1572–1637). Falstaff refers to Sir John Falstaff, a comic character who appears in Shakespeare's *Henry IV, Parts 1 and 2* (1596–98), and *The Merry Wives of Windsor* (c. 1597–1601).

Europe. In thirty years only three plays have riled our ostrich public, that public educated by an opportunist church to pretend that all sin comes from "across the water," and for the rest is better not spoken of in public – and those three plays were written by non-Catholics. I refer to *The Playboy, Countess Cathleen*, and *The Plough and the Stars*.[25] It gives me the greatest satisfaction to realise that in about three years as many novels have been banned in Ireland. It means that the Irish novelist has a proper respect for the devil.

How the novelist who is also a Catholic can put at ease his thus troubled heart is therefore his major problem. And it certainly will not solve that problem if the novelist is continually troubling himself about what may or may not give scandal. As Mr. Eric Gill observes, if a book does give scandal, then the princes of the earth may burn it, and no artist need be troubled at that since there are as good fish in the sea as ever came out of it.

I can well understand, I admire, indeed, the artist who is terrified by his own sensuality and by the sensuality of man. But that he should be made inarticulate by it I cannot understand. "La foi," says Pascal, "dit bien ce que les sens ne disent pas, mais non pas le contraire de ce qu'ils voient."[26] And after that comes the magnificent entry about the stars the eye sees and the stars it does not see. I quote it in full because it does help to suggest to the Catholic writer an answer to his *inquiétude*:[27]

How many telescopes have discovered for us stars hitherto unknown to philosophy! At one time they said, "But there are only one thousand and twenty-two as we well know." Very well. On the earth there are blades of grass invisible to the moon. And on these blades there is a little down. And on this downy beard are little animals. And after that, is there, then, nothing? O presumptuous soul! ... Here [he concludes] is a fine point to remember. That we may not say that there is

---

25 Like Synge's *The Playboy of the Western World* and O'Casey's *The Plough and the Stars*, W.B. Yeats's *The Countess Cathleen* (1892) caused considerable controversy when it was first performed in 1899.

26 Blaise Pascal (1623–1662) was a renowned French renaissance man especially noted for his religious philosophy. The phrase – which translates as "Faith tells that which the senses cannot, not the contrary of what they see" – is from *Pensées*, a collection of Pascal's writings that remained unfinished at the time of his death.

27 *Inquiétude* is French for worry, or anxiety. The block quote that follows is, as O'Faolain notes, from the next entry in Pascal's *Pensées*.

more than we can see: on that we must say just as the others say, who see no more. But – *there is no need to think as they think.*

~

Does not this point to another problem of the Catholic writer?

Here he is writing of the same things as every novelist writes of – the same hopes and desires, instincts, vices, ambitions that Balzac or Flaubert dealt with in their way. You do not need, says Pascal, to say you see anything that they did not see, but the effect of your picture – that is to say, what you think – will be different. But how will a novelist faithfully depicting what he sees convey his different values – convey that he feels differently from his unethical contemporary?

Or in other words, the Catholic novelist asks: Supposing I am prepared to embrace the fullness of life, evil as well as good, what is going to distinguish my picture of it from the usual modern novel?

Take a concrete example. What would a Catholic have made of "Boule de Suif"?

To begin with, he would, I suggest, have wished to make much more of it. And from that point of view it is true that to the Catholic every short story tends to be too short. That story of the little prostitute who is egged on by her righteous fellow-travellers to give herself to the Prussian officer is a great story. Supposing a Catholic writer with as much natural genius as Maupassant – which in all fairness we must – I think he would have made it even greater. For he would have enlarged considerably the implications.

The psychological novel is a mechanistic approach to human action. It is a biological view of man. It diminishes the power both of his will and his intellect, those forces striving towards good and towards beauty. Where we want, terribly, to know of the deepest conflict in the heart of that poor little Boule de Suif, Maupassant emphasises almost entirely the irony of her position in society, the mechanism by which society, in the persons of her fellow-travellers, profits by her even while despising her. Is conscience, then, nothing but pride and shame? we ask Maupassant. And we ask, too, whether Boule de Suif in relation to herself is not as important to a full and complete picture of life as Boule de Suif in relation to her fellowmen? It is the quality of good and evil to externalise themselves – *bonum est diffusio sui* – but what of the internal source which feeds them both?[28] In a word, I say that "Boule de Suif," magnificent as it is within

28 *Bonum est diffusio sui* is Latin for "goodness is self-diffusing."

its convention, is a partial picture of the life it pretends to crystallise into an incident.

What am I aiming at in asking this question about the manner in which the Catholic novelist differentiates his work from his fellows? I am tilting at the folly of the Catholic writer who adopts the technique of naturalism while contesting its general effect.

It has been the unfortunate effect of naturalism to externalise the life of the soul – and I here use the word soul in its common or literary sense. Originating as it did in a reaction from romanticism, its approach to human behaviour was almost wholly materialist and sceptical. So that when it said, This is how humanity really behaves, what it really meant was, This is *why* humanity really behaves. I shall not be so foolish as to say that it turned love, for example, into sensuality, but I do say that its tendency to turn all spiritual things into mechanisms is fully indicated by the cynicism, objectivism, and brutality of the novel as you have it at this day.

The general effect of naturalism has been to do exactly that thing I charge against the Catholic novelist – to oversimplify. It distinguishes the greater writers of that convention from the lesser – Hardy, let us say, from Galsworthy (there is twenty years of deterioration visible in Galsworthy) – that they took account of imponderables, of sudden aberrations from the accepted mechanism, of things like Fate, of conscience, of inexplicable fear and unrecorded instincts. All these and such-like things are necessary to the fullness of man. The psychology of the naturalists, on the contrary, meant the breaking down of character into unrelated parts. It was the psychology of men who would not have agreed with such a statement as that of Whitehead,[29] that God is the sum – the completion, that is to say – of the inconsistencies of the world. To them, to modern psychology, there are *not* more things in Heaven or on earth …

It is my point that a Catholic naturalistic novel is a contradiction in terms. And that since the problems of the Catholic are *sui generis*, so must his technique be free of earlier conceptions not merely of life in general, but of the geography of the individual human heart.[30]

~

My conclusion, then, is that the sole release from the tightness of the novel of the 'eighties is a transcendental conception of the *boules de suif* of life, expressed in terms of a most delicate balance between the

29 Alfred North Whitehead (1861–1947) was an English mathematician and philosopher.
30 *Sui generis* is Latin for "of its own kind" or "unique."

emotions and the judgment. We are united to people most closely by emotions felt in common, not by complexes, not by social effects suffered in common, not by intellectual agreement on the vapidities or pleasures of life. But whereas to the unethical novelist these emotions are self-suffi-cient and always explicable, to us they are often inexplicable because they come from secret and unexplored wells of being; and as for consid-ering them self-sufficient, they are to us, in Du Bos' magnificent phrase, the transparency of flesh.[31] Mark it down! *The transparency of flesh.*

Out of that concept of life, and an analogous treatment, has come great art before now, and out of it great art may come again. It will be, if it comes, something not seen before in the history of literature. It will indeed be the old drama of Faustus, the drama of sin, the drama old as Eve with the colours of the serpent twined about her eyes, the drama of naked Helen, but it will now be Cain and Salome and Solomon and Job, lit by the open gates of hellfire, lit by "Christ's blood streaming across the firmament" – and all seen by a generation for whom the geography of the heart contains few uncharted spaces, and who have much more to say and much more to feel about men and their world than was felt in the days when belief was a simple act, and the world solidly arranged.[32] It is a vision of life gambling with Eternity.

It is a concept of life that is difficult to retain. But it speaks to the chron-icler of our times in the comforting words of Alcestis, saying:

Vain hounds are baying round thee. But, O, forget them!
    Thou and I shall rule as kings
In this great House. We two at last will
    Order all things well.[33]

31 Charles Du Bos (1882–1939) was a major French critic of English and French literature. He wrote on a number of the authors that O'Faolain mentions in his essay.
32 The quoted line is from Marlowe's *Faustus.*
33 These are the final lines, spoken by Clytemnestra, not Alcestis, in *Agamemnon,* by Greek dramatist Aeschylus (525/4–456/5 BCE).

Revamping Ireland[1]

Turning the pages of my diary I find that a year ago just after the summer recess of our Dáil three elements defined our political course – a land bill of a revolutionary nature, conflict over General O'Duffy's Blueshirts,[2] and Mr. de Valera's promise to alter and reform, further, and in accordance with his republican ideals, the constitution of the Free State.

As I write the Dáil is still in session and in storm, but the course of things about which it argues remains fundamentally the same.

1 "Revamping Ireland" appeared in *The Commonweal* (30 August 1935): 417–18. It was preceded by the following editorial comments:

> The Irish situation is not merely of absorbing interest, particularly by reason of the social and economic experiments now in progress there, but it has now clarified sufficiently to make comment valuable. Mr. O'Faolain's paper, written on the spot, incorporates the views of one befriended with groups in all the parties. Another interpretation, by an American, will appear very soon. The interesting thing about Irish economics is their bearing on "emotional nationalism," says the present paper.

The economic situation that O'Faolain describes throughout this article was the result of the Anglo-Irish Trade War of the 1930s, in which the effects of the Depression were exacerbated. The Irish refused to continue to repay loans, annuities that were contracted to facilitate the transfer of lands to Irish tenant farmers under the Land Acts of 1891–1909. The British responded by placing tariffs on Irish products and the Irish retaliated by doing the same to British products.

2 Eoin O'Duffy (1890–1944) fought in the Anglo-Irish War and headed the Irish armed forces and police (1922–33). In 1933, he became head of the fascist Irish Blueshirts, who in 1936 fought alongside the Nationalist forces in the Spanish Civil War (1936–39).

That land bill speeded up the division of the large estates, or ranches, to relieve congestion. There were 170,000 farms in Ireland under £7 in valuation – too small, uneconomical. To relieve these, any farm over £2,000 in value has now to be developed or the owner must sell out. More tillage, less cattle – that is the government policy. And, to make up for the loss in our cattle trade, following our dispute with Britain over land annuities, resulting in tariffs on both sides ruinous to our cattle trade, the government policy extends to the development of industries which will, to put it graphically, eat our own cattle for us and consume the new produce of the land.

In other words, the land bill was merely part of a new economic policy which, in the meantime, has continued on its way with other enactments. The budget of this year annotates the position. The N.E.P. of rigid protection brought in a large harvest to the Minister for Finance in the shape of tariff income;[3] but insofar as the new factories of the Minister for Industry have been effective the tariff income has begun to disappear. That has been Snag Number One. The result has been a whole series of new levies on the consumer: still higher tariffs to protect and speed up the native industry (often non-existent at the moment), tariffs by way of revenue where there never will be a native industry (on rice, for example), and, most important of all, taxes on butter, flour, tea and tobacco. There is hardly a thing which is not spotted by the Minister's pen. One definite result is that cost of living has gone up here by, in my reckoning, 45 percent. I have compiled at random a list of a dozen articles bought by an Irish housewife, from canary seed to rolled ham-and-tongue, and compared the hole it made in her purse with the hole the same purchases would make, to-day, in the purse of a London housewife. The English housewife, I found, could do it cheaper by about $1.00 in every $2.50, i.e., for every two-fifty spent by the Irish housekeeper her English friend will save one.

On the other hand, if the tariff income has fallen because of the increase in home production, that should mean that unemployment here is dwindling. Unhappily we cannot be at all sure of that. These figures are elusive and one of the regrettable things is that the government refuses to issue a list of its new "factories." Besides, tariff income may have fallen simply because people do without things that are too dear to buy, even as, conversely, cost of living has not gone up solely because imported goods are

3 The N.E.P. is the National Economic Programme, which included the protracted and damaging tariff war against Britain.

dearer; the home product is generally more expensive than the imported article.

The government has, one must remember, forced the pace with its policy; for example, imported rubber footwear is taxed under the present budget because next October a factory will open in Cork for the manufacture of these goods which cannot, obviously, be on the market for next winter.

Recognising that hardship has resulted from this forcing of the pace, an important measure has been the special coal-cattle pact with Great Britain whereby a monopoly of the Irish market has been given to English mines, and a proportionate amount of our cattle is bought back by Great Britain. Again the consumer is hit, for while German coal was being imported the British mine owners dropped prices to compete, and we could buy their coal cheaply if we did not wish the far cheaper Silesian coal.[4] Mr. de Valera is quite honest in saying the farmers are not alone in the front line trenches during this economic war. Meanwhile it is a race with time. Those factories must go up as quickly as possible; they must become as efficient as possible; farm produce must be consumed by them; prices must fall. But Mr. Cosgrave is not dishonest either when he points out that to manufacture for forty millions and to manufacture for three means a difference of, for example, two shillings on every boot made in Ireland.

On the side of social services we have been generous. Unemployment relief is now given to men and women even where they have contributed nothing to any scheme. Free milk is available for the poor. A widows' and orphans' pensions bill is on the mat. Nobody denies the merit of such schemes. Nor, as long as we can afford to pay, do we grudge paying. Prophecy, as George Eliot said, being the most egregious form of error. I do not intend to say whether or not I think we can afford such schemes. I do say that if we can it is – paradoxically – because our standard of living is so low. There is little real wealth or luxury in this new Ireland; we are accustomed to the simple life. A more cultivated and luxurious civilisation would not stand for such schemes, such imposts, such burdens, in the name of a future possible better world.

The second element in last year's politics was O'Duffy. He may now be discounted. He has broken with his more constitutional allies in the Dáil and founded a national party aiming at a corporate state, but he lacks everything necessary for success: money, the help of clever men, a

---

4 Silesia was a German region at the time of O'Faolain's writing, but became a part of Poland in 1945.

parliamentary mouthpiece, even personal picturesqueness. His Wearing
of the Blue, which did the trick a year ago, is outlawed.

On the side of the fundamental position, the old struggle with English
domination, Mr. de Valera has not made any progress. The Oath to the
King was abolished in 1933, the governor general later reduced to a formula (nobody ever even thinks of him now), but after that nothing happened until just a week ago the English Privy Council in an important
case, Moore v. the Attorney General, decided that the Statute of
Westminster of 1931 has given the Free State Parliament power to disregard every limitation on its authority. Writing in the London *Spectator* of
June 21, Professor A. Berriedale Keith points out that this means, simply,
that "the Parliament of the Free State is recognized by the Privy Council
as absolutely sovereign."[5]

Here would appear to be the reality of absolute freedom achieved at
last by the Free State. It can abolish the governor general. It can forbid the
presence in Ireland of the Imperial forces who still have certain limited
rights in one or two corners of the Free State. But, as the professor also
points out, it is one thing to invalidate a treaty by legislation and another
to annul it. It can be made impotent. But its obligations remain until,
under international law, it is abrogated by mutual consent, or found inva-
lid by international law for good reason. We can have and can do
everything we wish to have and do; but England will always say that the
treaty obligations remain and that we are bound by it however much we
evade it. The charge of not recognising our word can always be thrown
at us. A nice tangle, which nothing but economic pressure is likely to
settle by some means or other.

Politics aside, the old everyday life carries on just as it always did,
though there is, as always, far too much preoccupation with politics and
little else is thought of or talked of. This becomes in the end an exasperation. It narrows down conversation and it tends to limit our interests.
One tries to deflect the conversation from Ireland but back it comes again
and again like the moth to the candle. Perhaps that is for the moment
inevitable where the economic stress is so powerful, but it is, none the
less, to be regretted. It breeds abstract minds and it threatens to end by
producing a metaphysical type of Irishman, all words and wind, endlessly
debating the theory of new policies. On the other hand, if it is true – as
some of us often think here – that our racial fault is an overdevelopment

---

5 Arthur Berriedale Keith (1879–1944) was a Scottish professor of both Sanskrit
and Constitutional History at the University of Edinburgh.

of sensibilities and an underdevelopment of intellect, will not the very stress of economics ultimately drag us down to the rock bottom of realities? Will we not be forced to reconsider our values of life and living? Will we not be astonished some day to find that after looking for a sunburst we produced a factory? And when we have overdeveloped life on the material side – it sounds such an odd development to fear in a Celt – we may, then, swing back to the opposite way of life. For the interesting thing about our new economics is that they are based, ultimately, on our emotional nationalism and have not been thought out fully in all their implications, as yet. They have for the time being led to "fumbling in the greasy till";[6] they must end by forcing us to remember what it was all for, and where it all started. Then we shall take leisure by the hand and realise that the spiritual and cultural side of life also requires attention.

As things are, however – and one must be realistic – that can hardly come until some truce is called in the political field; for however much one tries to persuade even the most intelligent people that cultivation can go ahead of political affairs instead of lagging in their wake, they will tell you, if they are at all bitten by the nationalistic bug, that "nothing can be done until the main thing is done." One sighs over such an attitude; one calls it an inhibition and a complex, but if one knows one's history one accepts it and does not call it obscurantism. It is in the blood of Irishmen, and whether it is good or bad, it has to be taken into account. That is why any review of Irish affairs is always, for the moment, almost wholly occupied with matters of political or constitutional interest, whose effect never touches on international affairs and the recounting of which must give to outsiders something of the feeling that we are being very insular, if not actually parochial, in this modern Ireland.

6 The line is from W.B. Yeats's poem "September 1913," a scathing critique of bourgeois Ireland.

Roger Casement[1]

In a letter to Cunninghame Graham, Joseph Conrad once spoke of landing at some African port of small dimensions and, as he strolled around
the outskirts of the town, seeing a man with two bulldogs and a walking
stick and a Loanda boy go off into the bush.[2] He was a finely-built man,
around forty, dark-bearded, deep and gentle of eye, with a beetling brow
like an Irish terrier – a handsome fellow, a bit of a conquistador. A few
months after, as he happened to be looking into the dusk of the bush at
the same spot, Conrad saw the same man, with his stick, his pack, his boy,
and his two bulldogs, walk out as calmly as if he had been for an afternoon stroll. "He could tell you things! Things I've tried to forget; things I
never did know." That was the British consul at S. Paola de Loanda, in
Portuguese West Africa, one Casement.

There are men like him in Conrad's books. They move in a cocoon of
indifference that one might mistake for the absentmindedness of a poet,
or a dilettante, or the incompetent grace of a country gentleman, if there
were not a slightly troubled or brooding look behind the heavy eyes.
Casement's only protection in the jungle, for instance, was that walking
stick and the two white and brindled bulldogs. Another man like that

---

1 "Roger Casement" appeared in *The American Mercury* (February 1936): 160–7.
It was prefaced with Casement's dates and places of birth and death: "*Born, Dublin,
Sept., 1864. Hanged, Pentonville Prison, London, Aug., 1916.*"
2 Robert Bontine Cunninghame Graham (1852–1936) was a Scottish politician,
author, and adventurer. Joseph Conrad (1857–1924), né Józef Teodor Konrad
Korzeniowski, author of *Heart of Darkness* (1899), is one of the most important
modern British writers. Loanda, also spelled Luanda, formerly São Paulo de Luanda,
is the capital city of Angola.

(and he also was executed for treason against the state except that in his case it was an Irish state and his loyalty was to an older Irish dream) was Erskine Childers.[3] He had been through the South African War with the Honourable Artillery Company, and later through the World War, and fought in the naval attack on Zeebrugge:[4] yet when he was with the Irish Republican guerillas on the hills in 1922, tough ragged-breeches who looked the part, he, too, had the air of the country gentleman out for a stroll – with his flat cap, his stiff linen collar, his long raincoat, and sometimes a walking stick. One never saw a weapon on him. There was another friend of his, also with the guerillas, who had been in the Tank Corps in France. Once when we were, under his leadership, about to start a surprise morning attack on the garrison of a little mountain village, he froze us by asking to be instructed in the use of an ordinary .45 Colt revolver, explaining that he knew nothing of such things. The attack deliberately fizzled out because our fellows, who were bristling with weapons, simply could not believe in that sort of man.

Yet such men are of a type common enough, although it takes wars and adventures to disclose them. Far from being the dilettantes for whom one might mistake them, they reject not merely all preoccupation with self but all worldly human values as well; instead of being dedicate to egotism they are dedicate to sacrifice. They have the air of old soldiers home on furlough, carrying themselves with the aloof but friendly air of men resting, looking at everything with the casual and slightly distinguished glance of men for whom all life is either an adventure or a sequence of periods between one adventure and another. Men of action, their minds move swiftly when they are in action: when they are not they become a little tormented and tangled, and yet not even then are they self-engaged, but concerned rather with a teasing out of the values inherent in the adventures to which they have given their support, which are imposed on

3 Robert Erskine Childers (1870–1922) was an Irish writer and nationalist combatant who was executed for his Republican actions during the Irish Civil War. The link made here between Casement and Childers is provocative: both former representatives and supporters of Empire, they were later executed by states for revolutionary Republican actions.

4 The second South African War, also called the Boer War, was fought between Britain and the Boers of South Africa, 1899–1902. The Honourable Artillery Company is the oldest regiment in the British Army, incorporated by Henry VIII in 1537. Zeebrugge is a major port in western Belgium; in April 1918, British naval ships attacked German forces there to deny the use of the harbour to German submarines.

them by more clever men, and which could never be brought to success except by their own particular brand of conquistador enthusiasm. There is something dedicate about them all, something of the martyr or the saint, as if they had indeed come out of a world of inveterate rebels against the despotism of fact. Note the deep-set eyes, or the gentle lips: note in Casement the lifted eyebrow, as if he were asking of the world that had suddenly impinged on his dreams – "Hello! Still carrying on just the same? How do you manage it?" I feel sure that Sir Galahad wore that lifted brow, and Francis, and Dominic.⁵ It is a brow that more worldly men should fear ...

The truth is that these men are rebels by nature, aberrants and solitaries. That is clear if you compare a man like Casement with a man, let us say, like Dwight Morrow.⁶ Here are two lives of dedication, immutably inconsonant, and not to be compared because the one worked only partially within the world's code and the other worked wholly within it, to support it even if, also, to amend it. Or put between them another type of man, either the man who prosecuted Casement at his trial for high treason, Sir F.E. Smith, K.C., M.P., later Lord Birkenhead, or his friend and companion in another kind of high treason, the late Lord Carson.⁷ Smith closed his speech for the prosecution with the words:

> The prisoner, blinded by a hatred to this country, as malignant in quality as it was sudden in origin, has played a desperate hazard: he has played it and lost it: today the forfeit is claimed.

In his last speech from the dock, the man who was about to be hanged replied to the man who had in his time led the Ulster rebels against the British Government:

5 Sir Galahad was known as the pure knight of Arthurian legend, the son of Sir Lancelot. Saint Francis of Assisi and Saint Dominic (1170–1221) founded, respectively, the Franciscan and Dominican orders of friars.
6 Dwight W. Morrow (1873–1931) was an effective negotiator and American statesman on the international stage.
7 Sir F.E. Smith (1872–1930) later helped to negotiate the Anglo-Irish Treaty in 1921. Edward Carson (1854–1935) was a lawyer who made his mark prosecuting Irish writer Oscar Wilde (1854–1900) for homosexuality in 1895 and later was known as "the uncrowned king of Ulster" for leading unionist resistance to Irish Home Rule. Carson was succeeded by Smith as Attorney General in 1915.

The difference between us was that my treason was based on a ruthless sincerity that forced me to attempt to carry out in action what I said in words, whereas their treason lay in verbal incitements ...

What would Dwight Morrow have said as between these men? He would probably have said that neither of them was as good a citizen as he ought to have been and that both had been foolish. But he would not be echoed by the majority of men, and in fact the cynical Birkenhead was right – they had both gambled and Casement had lost: that was all.

There is a sense in which all history is bunk, and these three or four careers annotate it. Had Casement died in 1914 he would be on the roll of England's splendid dead. T.E. Lawrence,[8] it is said, was willing, after the war, to come over to his native Ireland and fight with Michael Collins for Sinn Féin. Had he done so he would be now, quite possibly, on the roll of those who bowed their heads under Traitors' Gate.[9] Glory is a gamble and the definitions of history go to the winning side. History can never deal with men as men because it has to start from the premises laid down by victory and consolidated by power. Its values are the values of the *fait accompli*.[10] Occasionally, very occasionally, as with a Joan of Arc, a great power like the Church of Rome can redress a wrong;[11] or a vast revolution can rehabilitate, though even then only for some, the reputation of a prophet. But with little nations like Ireland and a great Empire like the British Commonwealth, there is small hope for gallant losers such as Roger Casement. His bones still lie in Pentonville under the quicklime, while men like Dwight Morrow or Lord Birkenhead can have justice done to them because their countries were victorious in a great war. Casement's little war was won too late to save him. So the judgments remain for all time, simply because – to paraphrase Macaulay's famous

8 T.E. Lawrence (1888–1935), also known as Lawrence of Arabia, is best known for his military exploits and his book *Seven Pillars of Wisdom* (1926).

9 Traitors' Gate was the entrance for prisoners to the Tower of London when it was used as a jail. It was also the name given by nationalists to the Royal Dublin Fusiliers' Arch on St Stephen's Green, which was dedicated to the 212 soldiers of the battalions who died in the Boer War.

10 *Fait accompli* is French for "accomplished fact," something that has already been done.

11 Saint Joan of Arc (1412–1431), or Jeanne d'Arc in her native French, was burned as a heretic and is revered today as a national heroine. She was canonised in 1920.

fantasy – the future African tourist, sketching the ruins of Manhattan, will not be bothered to remeasure them by new values.[12] Men should be measured as men, not as part of social trends. Lawrence knew that and so measured himself. Casement knew it and lived accordingly.

~

Yet, in and out of their cocoon of scorn, these aberrants do dally with worldly affairs. Though it was young Casement's ambition to be an explorer (and he was one for a time and toured America to tell it what an American expedition had discovered along the track of Stanley's march to the source of the Congo)[13] he later entered the British consular service. Then from the day he took the boat to Akassa on the Niger coast he came to know Africa as few men have ever known it. He was in the French Congo, in Nigeria, in Angola, in Mozambique, working for the British Government as trade commissioner or consul, so that when he found himself in 1903 at Kinshassa in the Belgian Congo he had lived north, south, east, and west of that seventh wonder of the world, the loop of river that cuts Africa like a reaping hook. Already the stories had begun to seep down to him out of the oily and slumbrous darkness of the Upper Congo's jungle-gloom, and when Lansdowne told him that the Foreign Office must have the truth about that private cozenage of old Leopold II, he knew what he must endure to get it, and he had some idea what it would be like when he got it.[14]

But he had only the very vaguest idea, and not even in a nightmare horror could he have imagined it before he went. He must have had many nightmare horrors after. Out of that vast insect-buzzing silence, that

12 This is likely a reference to Zachary Macaulay (1768–1838), an important English anti-slavery activist and governor of Sierra Leone.

13 Sir Henry Morton Stanley (1841–1904), né John Rowlands, was a British explorer known for rescuing David Livingstone (1813–1873) and for his navigation and development of the Congo region.

14 Henry Charles Keith Petty-Fitzmaurice (1845–1927), the 5th marquess of Lansdowne, was a British politician, governor general of Canada (1883–88) and viceroy of India (1888–94); during his time as foreign secretary (1900–06), Casement was in the Congo. Leopold II (1835–1909), King of Belgium, led the first European efforts to develop the Congo River basin with his agent, Stanley; Leopold is best known today for the exploitation, mutilation, and mass murder of native people and the large-scale environmental degradation caused by his efforts to extract the largest possible profit out of his African holdings. O'Faolain details some of this in the following paragraphs.

welter of hot rottenness underfoot, porous branches, fallen leaves, crawling life, and overhead submarine gloom; out of the long endlessness of parched grass ten feet high, an endlessness of what Englishmen would call "damn-all," he must come in two months with his story of how Wealth can make a beast of itself. Even before he went he knew how easily anything at all can happen in a place – if such a region could be called a place – so empty that one sees with a passionate delight a hill a hundred miles away, across the glittering, murmuring scrub. Anything that a white man wished to have or do in the heart of that oozy disintegration, he could have and could do and nothing would reply but the unbroken chirruping of the globules of obscenity that one sometimes squashed underfoot ...

Casement knew the shy native life, and had come to have a great liking for it. He struck off alone into the bush to question it, and he found whole villages gone, disappeared, since his last visit to the same region a few years before. There had been mud huts and savages then. Farther up at the junction of the Lulanga there had been cannibals and pygmies: and slaves had been driven in herds. But now, they were gone – and he felt lonely. He was one man against a whole system and he was on the side of the natives and the flight of these natives made him feel isolated. A new silence was added to the inexorable silence of Africa. The solitary was marooned.

Such loneliness is never kind, but it is terrifying when it is a man's direct enemy. For the thing that makes the gorge rise about the Congo brutalities is the impenetrable secrecy of the place where they occurred. The natives were safe once by reason of the darkness of Africa: it was now their foe. If they fled they knew that their taskmasters would follow them as implacably as the little cloudlets overhead, moving endlessly across the hot sky. The deeper they went into the glaucous dusk of the jungle the more did secrecy wrap their helplessness. In some clearing, because they had not brought in rubber forty times the value of what they were paid their black fellows would fall on them, worn out and tired as they were, and then ... women were shot ... a white man used to put six natives in a row, belly to back, and kill them with one bullet ... or they were tied up, even the chieftains, to a post in the settlement and flogged and made to swallow the defecations of the white man ... soldiers were told to unman their victims, and the human parts were brought back as the sign of the kill ... a youth was tied to a tree all night until the thongs of his wrists cut to the bone: in the morning soldiers battered off the hands with rifle butts ... Casement saw the hands ... he saw the stumps of arms. Day after day he wrote down the details, names, dates – saw missionaries who told him in heart-breaking voices of this frustration of all they taught. And he was

back at the coast under two months of the date he set out, with his mass
of documents. It is thanks to him and the energy of the British Government
that today Leopold-Kinshassa is ten times its size, that the natives have
come back, that if a white even strikes a native he may have to answer for
it to the commissioner. For his work Casement was made a Companion
of the Order of St. Michael and St. George.[15]

Eight years later he was Consul General at Rio de Janeiro, and was
inquiring into similar evils in the Putamayo rubber industry, 3000 miles
up the Amazon. He reported things that were not even printed in the Blue
Book subsequently issued;[16] for here he dealt with men who were not
merely brutal but perverted, men whose "civilization" suggested to them
ingenious forms of torture. A man named Jimenez took an old Indian
woman, strung her naked between two trees, and lit a fire of leaves under
her. The Barbados man who gave this evidence admitted that he saw the
great blisters rise on her thighs while she screamed with pain. They did
other things to women that one would not wish to recall. The voyage
went on for months. When it was over Casement's fight to effect real reformation continued for more than a year, for he and the British were
thwarted constantly by the sloth or indifference or graft of the Peruvians.
In the end it was largely through Taft and the British ambassador at
Washington that the report was published.[17] For his work, the last work
he did as a British servant, Casement was made a knight. There is a certain irony in the admission. He had always been a knight.

So far Casement had devoted himself to the magnificent task of uphold-
ing all that was best in the code of a great country. Now, forty-eight years
old, he retired from the consular service on a pension. ("I served the
British Government faithfully and loyally," he wrote in 1915 to Sir
Edward Grey, "as long as it was possible for me to do so.")[18] At his trial
the Crown Prosecutor was to speak of a hate for England "as malignant
as it was sudden." I do not believe he ever hated England, but I think he
never believed particularly in the code, and his disbelief in it was not

15 The Most Distinguished Order of Saint Michael and Saint George is a British
order of knighthood founded in 1818. The honour is conferred mainly on those
who have performed important duties in colonial or Commonwealth countries.
16 A blue book is an official report issued by Parliament or the Privy Council.
17 William Howard Taft (1857–1930) was president of the United States (1909–13).
18 Sir Edward Grey (1862–1933) was the British Foreign Secretary (1905–16).

sudden. As early as 1905, between the Congo and Brazil, he had been back in Ireland in the glens of Antrim, and like all these adventurers, brooding between their adventures, he had begun to brood on Ireland. He was a wanderer, however, and he was a Protestant Irishman, one of the minority; and he had left Ireland as a mere boy. It was in the worst period of Nationalist politics, the doldrums after Parnell's fall that he came, far from home, to his maturity. It took him a long time to work his way back, out of the tangle of his equivocal connection with the Empire, to a clear understanding of his own country's relationship to that Empire. But, even in 1906, after he had left Ireland for Santos, had the British secret service been more alert, it would have been shocked to peruse the letters of one of its apparently most devoted servants.[19]

For Casement had (he said so himself in his diary) in the nineteen months he spent so happily among the simple Ulster folk, and in conversation with the young men and women who were already laying the mine of the 1916 rebellion, sown in his heart the seed of all his subsequent actions. I have seen letter after letter, sent from South America to his devoted friend, Bulmer Hobson, one of the most active and persistent of the secret society of the Irish Republican Brotherhood,[20] in which he writes as an Irish Nationalist, pure and simple. He contributed to their revolutionary papers over a pseudonym; he even helped to write a pamphlet against recruiting; and, as always, his hand was ever in his pocket to help with hard cash.

Now, six years later, he was back again in Antrim, free of all avocations that might distract him from dedication to his own people. And he was back at a time when "King" Carson was already beating the big drum of Ulster and threatening the Liberal Government with civil war. But it was only a few years to the outbreak of the European war and Casement had long seen it coming; and if the fight for Home Rule had reached that stage when, as in a drawn-out boxing match, the antagonists were so weary that it seemed a matter of chance which would win, Casement had no belief in the Liberal Government, and less belief in John Redmond, the Irish leader, and he could understand Carson's deliberate defiance and the weight it would pull with the English Tories.[21] In Coleraine, in September,

19 Santos is a port city in southeastern Brazil.
20 Bulmer Hobson (1883–1969) was a leading member of the Irish Republican Brotherhood, a secret oath-bound nationalist organisation devoted to the creation of an Irish Republic.
21 John Redmond (1856–1918) became leader of the Irish Parliamentary Party after the downfall of Parnell in 1891.

1912, the autumn of his return to Ireland, he could have heard that saturnine, ruthless, and fearless man cry, as he fought for Ulster's right to remain within the Empire: "I do not care whether it is treason or not!" So that when, in a back room of a Dublin hotel less than a year later, a few Southern Irish founded the Irish National Volunteers, Casement felt it was the only proper reply, and at once gave his name as one of the trustees.[22]

After that things moved quickly. On the night of April 24, 1914, 35,000 rifles were landed for Carson's army at Larne from the Norwegian steamer *Fanny* out of Hamburg. On Sunday afternoon, July 26, Erskine Childers and his wife appeared off Dublin with a yacht containing 2500 rifles and 125,000 rounds of ammunition. Gun-running was the order of the day. Then at midnight on August 4, the whole Irish crisis was blown to bits by the outbreak of the World War. A month later, Casement, now in New York City plotting with the Irish revolutionaries, wrote in an *Open Letter to the Irish People* enough treason to hang any man. He had taken the last step. His journey to Berlin via Christiania, where he landed in October, 1914, was merely the implementing of what he said in that letter.[23] His last adventure was the effort to form in Germany, from among Irish prisoners of war, and bring to Ireland, a brigade of troops to be called the Irish Brigade. For that, precisely, they hanged him.

Casement was already worn out when he reached Berlin and, like Wolfe Tone with the French Directory in 1796, found it trying and wearying day in and day out to argue with the German General Staff, and the Foreign Office in the Wilhelmstrasse: for not merely were they troubled by doubts of their own, but even from left-wing Irish-American sources doubts were being instilled into them about Casement.[24] And he was not a young man, now, like Tone with his merry "'Tis but in vain for soldiers to complain"

22 The Irish Volunteers were founded in 1913 in response to the formation of the Ulster Volunteers; they were succeeded by the Irish Republican Army in 1919.
23 Oslo, the capital of Norway, was formerly known as Christiania (1624–1877) and Kristiana (1877–1925).
24 Theobald Wolfe Tone (1763–1798) was an Irish republican and a prominent leader of the 1798 Rebellion. He was tried and to be executed for treason, but he committed suicide before he could be hanged. In 1796, The French Directory – the Revolutionary government – granted Tone a fleet of ships to launch an attack on English forces in Ireland, but the expedition failed when a storm thwarted the invasion plans.

that runs all through that most vivid and amusing diary of his; or Lord Edward; or Emmet.[25] He was fifty-one, and he was a worn man.

The organising and the persuading and the plotting went on into the spring of 1916, and then, in March, the Irish revolutionaries informed the Germans that they had decided to rise on Easter Sunday, April 23. They asked for a shipload of arms, and officers. The General Staff, after the usual haggling, agreed to send 20,000 rifles, well over a million rounds of ammunition, some machine guns and ammunition; but no field guns, and no officers. The arms would be loaded on a steamer disguised as a Norwegian trader, under a layer of lumber. They refused to provide an escort, but finally decided to send Casement, his loyal friend, Captain Robert Monteith, and a Sergeant Beverley of the Brigade, a trained machine-gunner, in a submarine.[26] The plan was that the disguised trader, the *Aud*, was to be off the Kerry coast after ten o'clock at night, on either April 20, 21, 22, or 23. The Irish revolutionaries were to station a pilot boat off Innistusket Island from that hour to dawn on each of these nights. The pilot should bear two green lights that would flash at intervals, and so meet and guide the gunrunner into Fenit Harbour.

Casement, Monteith, and Beverley left Helgoland in the *U-19* on April 14, and for five days they battered their way around the north of Scotland and Ireland, and down the west coast towards Tralee Bay. Not once did they sight a British warship. Monteith was able to spend most of the day in oilskins on the conning tower. Casement was too ill and weak to climb up into the cold air through the tiny manholes. On April 20, after dark had fallen, they throbbed past the Shannon, and as they had sighted the gunrunner two miles to starboard a few hours earlier, they had good reason to feel that things were proceeding according to plan. It was a dark night. There were no stars. The sea moved in a slight swell. They crowded the conning tower and stared and stared for the two winking green lights of the pilot. They never came. Either Stack, the local commandant, or Dublin headquarters had made a fatal error.[27]

---

25 O'Faolain edited an abridged version of Tone's writings, *The Autobiography of Theobald Wolfe Tone* (1937). Lord Edward Fitzgerald (1763–1798) was a fellow leader of the 1798 Rebellion who died in prison of wounds sustained while resisting arrest. Robert Emmet (1778–1803) was hanged for treason, having led the abortive 1803 rising against English forces.

26 Captain Robert Monteith (1879–1956). Sergeant Beverley was the alias of Daniel Bailey (1887–1968).

27 Austin Stack (1879–1929) was commandant of the Kerry Brigade of the Irish Volunteers who was elected as a Member of Parliament (MP) to Westminster and a Teachta Dála (TD, the Irish equivalent of an MP) for the Dáil.

At last the commander of the U-boat would wait no longer. He turned and steamed swiftly into the bay. Casement was informed that they would all three be put ashore. They do not appear, any of them, to have questioned the wisdom of this, and in any case they were so ashamed and appalled at the disaster of the missing pilot and the abandoned *Aud* that they seem not to have been able, poor devils, to think at all. The submarine wallowed slowly inshore, a big gray fish of the night. They were put into a little cockleshell of a boat – it was produced later at the trial and looks rather like a big basin with a fat tube for gasoline around it, for an outboard motor could be attached – and then the submarine vanished into the night, and they began to rise and fall on the Atlantic waves.

They rowed. It seemed to take hours, although they could see the beach with its long line of foam and hear the dull sound of pounding breakers. The waves threatened them continually and once tossed them upside down into the sea; but they were wearing lifebelts, the boat did not sink, and with effort they righted it. They rowed again; they stuck on a sand bank; and in trying to push off, Monteith fell overboard once more. At last they felt the beach grate under them and they tumbled, soaked to the skin, utterly exhausted, waist-deep into the sea. Monteith's description of this landing, in his splendid book *Casement's Last Adventure*, is one of the most moving things I have ever read:[28]

> I found my companions stretched on the sand, weary and exhausted. I do not think that Casement was even conscious. He was lying away below high-water mark, the sea lapped his body from head to foot, his eyes were closed and in the dim moonlight his face resembled that of a sleeping child. I dragged him to his feet and chafed his hands and feet as best I could, while the water ran from his hair and clothing: then I made him move about to restore his circulation …
>
> When we had warmed up a little we wrung out our clothing and felt a little more comfortable. I said to Casement, with as much cheerfulness as I could muster, "Well, Sir Roger, we've had the little adventure and got through it alright." He patted me on the shoulder as was his way and answered smilingly, "Yes, Captain Monteith, we've had a little adventure, and are much nearer the end of the chapter" … Had I known what the end of the chapter was really

28 *Casement's Last Adventure* was first privately published in Chicago in 1932.

going to be, I would have let him sleep into eternity in the foaming water of Banna Strand, the water that had tried to be kind to one of Ireland's heroes.

They hid Casement – ill, stiff, discouraged – in an old fort while they pushed on into Tralee to give warning and get help. Unknown and suspected as they were, it took time; and before a car could reach the fort Casement had been arrested by police. Even in his misery he kept something of his urbane sense of humour, for he told the police he was an author. "What book did you write?" they asked. "A life of Saint Brendan," he said.[29] As he sat in the ancient fort, with his teeth chattering and his body feverish, he must have been ruminating on all the Irish voyagers he knew, for Brendan's *Voyage*, a ninth-century legend, is one of the most famous of the sagas of the old Celtic church. It was a voyage in which there were many visions of Heaven and Hell, and its aim was to reach the Happy Otherworld, or Land of Promise whose allure has so often inflamed the imagination of the Irish race.

The Rising broke out on Easter Monday. It was crushed in a week. By May 13 many men had been sentenced to death or to life imprisonment, and about 2500 had been deported. Among them was a young man named Michael Collins who, on his release, began to organise at once for the revolutionary years to follow. But by then Sir Roger Casement had been tried, found guilty, unknighted, and hanged.

There it is, then. Casement is dead, and Carson is dead, and Birkenhead is dead, and every Irishman thinks Casement a patriot, and nine out of ten Englishmen believe him a traitor, and legally and by all the forms that govern human relationships he was one. He was a traitor to British prestige, to the British code, to British history, to the long and truly admirable traditions of England – admirable *for* England, that is – a traitor to Elizabeth, and Peel, and Clive, and the Industrial Revolution, and Cobbett, and Tennyson, and Rudyard Kipling: in brief, to the *status quo*.[30] He was,

---

29 Saint Brendan (484/6–578) was an abbot and the hero of legendary voyages on the Atlantic Ocean. The tales appeared as early as the eighth century in Irish, and in the tenth century were translated into Latin as *Navigatio Brendani*.

30 Queen Elizabeth I (1533–1603). Sir Robert Peel (1788–1850) was twice British prime minister (1834–35 and 1841–46). Robert Clive (1725–1774) was the first British administrator of Bengal and helped to establish British power in India. The Industrial Revolution is acknowledged to have begun in England in the eighteenth century. William Cobbett (1763–1835) was a journalist and champion of

possibly, not a very clever man as cleverness goes, and of worldly wisdom he had little. (It might even be thought by some that because he belonged to a small nation he should have devoted his talents to a big nation: which is much like saying that there should be no small towns only big ones, no small farms only collective ones, no private ambitions only communal ones.) But we Irish revere him because, quite simply, he was that rare thing – an integrated man.

I do not believe his friends think of him entirely as that. They see him in some Dublin hotel and he is talking with the chambermaid or the boots like an old friend.[31] "Ah, yes," he smiles to a companion's questioning glance. "Paddy is a good fellow. His wife is getting on well now, and the baby is fine." For within ten minutes he seemed to know more about people he met casually, and who liked him on the spot, than others might find out in ten years. Or they recall that although he would always arrive with, maybe, half a year's salary, he would, before he left, be living on an overdraft – the whole thing given away.

But it is the penalty of fame that men become symbols, whether for good or ill. One passes no final judgment on Casement because one knows that all human beings read these symbols out of the past, according to their own ambitions, their own desires, their own hopes or their own fears as to what life ought or ought not to be.

As I write, they are laying Carson's body in reverence in the Westminster Abbey of Belfast. As I write, Roger Casement's bones lie under a prison wall, marked by a numbered brick. It is a strange world, one thinks – and having thought it, one realises that there is no more to say.

---

traditional rural English values. Rudyard Kipling (1865–1936) was an author who celebrated British imperialism in some of his works and was awarded the Nobel Prize for Literature in 1907.

31 "The boots" is the name for a servant in a hotel whose primary responsibility is to clean the boots of guests, but it can been applied to a male servant in general.

Dickens and Thackeray[1]

There never was and never will be a final judgement on any writer. All that is possible is a contemporary judgement, since there never was and never will be a critic who does not see the wood of the past through the wood of the present, and centuries are always either mutually antagonistic or naturally partial. With that apology for anything harsh that one may be inclined to say of Dickens, and with the confession that as a reader's novelist he is sufficiently a master to be beyond criticism, it must be said that, as a novelist's novelist, he is fallen on evil days – he is now at any rate a master without pupils. There is no question of our losing anything by this. It is simply a matter of times that do not match. Whether or not there will come a time when Dickens will influence other writers does not concern us. All we know or care to know is that he does not influence anybody now.

This is not merely because he was so personal in his triumph as to be inimitable, but because objectivity has given way to subjectivity, description to analysis, and acceptance to revolt, because we are in search of a new synthesis, a different wisdom, because the whole emphasis has shifted from common sense to individual sense; because since his day art has become a religion and every artist has as many airs and as much pride as an aristocrat. In his secret heart every modern writer would like to despise the Big Public, and a great part of the explanation of the fact that literature is none the less at a comparatively low standard is that Big Public approval today offers such prizes that few can be independent of

1 "Dickens and Thackeray" appeared in *The English Novelists: A Survey of the Novel by Twenty Contemporary Novelists*, ed. Derek Verschoyle (London: Chatto & Windus, 1936): 141–51.

it. Something of the same sort of thing happened to Dickens; and novelists will never condescend to learn from a best-seller.

This simply means that Dickens was not in the modern and rather priggish sense an "artist," for which we may be deeply grateful and proceed to rejoice in the results of his lack of "art." But it is not a highbrow attitude, nor is it as stupid as it might seem, since in essence it is nothing but a deep regard for integrity. It is a mixture of puritanism, intellectual snobbery, and resentment against a lack of exclusive devotion to the Muse. The only kind of writer who has any influence on other writers is either the lesser man who failed to exploit to the full a half-perceived idea, as in the case of Dujardin and Joyce,[2] or the aristocrat of letters who would have gone to the guillotine of oblivion for a book. Writers must have their martyrs and their heroes as well as everybody else. Dickens was neither. Of the two, Thackeray and Dickens, writers are the more likely to learn from Thackeray, who was both a snob of books, and one of those who half-perceived a liberty of which his successors perceived the full possibilities.

The main quality of the English novel is its grand balance of feeling and intelligence – Fielding, Defoe, Smollett, Thackeray, Trollope, Dickens.[3] Always there is feeling. A sense of life and its endless interest, a humanity, a restrained sympathy, even a breeziness near to vulgarity – the number of scenes in the English novel dealing with eating and drinking are extraordinary. It is eminently a social document, and wherever you find aberrants from the tradition you will find that they were solitaries in whom there is an excess either of feeling or intelligence: or in whom other untraditional, but not, of course, alien qualities preponderate over feeling and intelligence. The Brontës, for example, who had imaginations fostered in excess by their isolation – or rather Emily, and, apart from *Shirley*, Charlotte – are complete aberrants from the main English tradition. So is Hardy, and it is significant that in each of these three there is a touch of outlandish blood that is not quite yeoman. Jane Austen, too, in whom intelligence is all-powerful, has no imitators in the main stream of the English novel. The sentimentalists, Sterne and Richardson, are generally,

2 Édouard Dujardin (1861–1949) is best known for his novel *Les Lauriers son coupées* (1888), the first work to employ interior monologue and an inspiration to the stream-of-consciousness that James Joyce later developed.
3 Henry Fielding, Daniel Defoe (1660–1731), Tobias Smollett (1721–1771), and Anthony Trollope (1815–1882) are all important British novelists.

I think, regarded by English critics as outside the main stream, even as to me certainly Barrie is an infusion, not a growth.[4]

Feeling, restrained but warm, then, is the natural hall-mark of nineteenth-century fiction. The one thing, Emily Brontë apart, that it does not possess in excess or has never sought to exploit is emotion: that belongs to the Irish or the Russians. Rarely – Meredith and Jane Austen aside – has it exploited its restraining element and become analytical, tempering sensibilities with intelligence as finely as the French.

Now, to speak of Dickens as an aberrant would be absurd – he is too full of genuine feeling for that. But we have all observed that his feeling, or sentiment, goes over at the slightest excuse into sentimentality which is felt as a disproportion of feeling – embarrassing as an ornate but gimcrack gift. And we have observed, too, that the only thing that prevents him from sentimentalising all the time is his immense gusto, showing itself as a powerful sense of humour which is really a frolicking enjoyment of life, or as a powerful imagination which burns up every dross – both of them releasing him from that terrible social inhibition from which he suffered throughout his career, a complete lack of taste. In these two respects, gusto and imagination, he is the Dickens whom we all love, and what we love in him is his excess – the only thing in life or in letters that appeals to all writers, say what they will. In those two respects we see him approach the great aberrants of the English tradition, those outstanding ones who may not, so to speak, be as sound as the main procession but who are better than it – Emily Brontë, Sterne, Jane Austen, Meredith, undoubtedly Hardy, probably Lawrence, possibly Joyce – the novelist's novelists.[5]

But we do not actually class him with these, straightway and wholeheartedly, because he was not wholehearted himself, and we never know the moment he will betray us. He is often, frankly, disloyal to his Craft.

We know that he wrote for his public – his dear, darling Public – and that the reliable novelist writes for himself, even as we know that all great literature has a quality of being overheard, not announced. It is an exaggeration, but it is at bottom true. You read *Martin Chuzzlewit*, for instance, and you adore the man who created Pecksniff, and Mark Tapley, and Tom Pinch, and Sary Gamp and Chevy Slyme, and you wish you

---

4 Irishman Laurence Sterne (1713–1768), Englishman Samuel Richardson (1669–1761), and Scotsman J.M. Barrie (1860–1937).

5 D.H. Lawrence (1885–1930).

could do anything even a hundredth part as good.[6] And then you come to Eden and that truly shocking piece of flummery, the reform of Martin, and you begin to feel uncomfortable. You have held the good old gentleman's purse while he went around the corner: now he has gone around the corner with yours, and you are waiting for him to come back ... You need never feel like that about Thackeray; he may be a bore and a prig but he will never deliberately play you false.

~

Only writers who live their art, not play on it, affect other writers, or at any rate young writers for whom, as yet, ideals are more important than anything else. One feels that Dickens wanted to live his art, but would not. One feels that the real Dickens was the big-eyed solitary child who made his soul in the blacking-factory and saw the Golden Gates from the top of Bayham Street in Camden town where, across the docks and the dust in the fields, the cupola of Saint Paul's loomed out of the smoke.[7] One feels that the poetry of life held him, then, intact and complete, or when he was – his own words – "supremely happy" in the macabre gloom of Covent Garden or Seven Dials, with wild visions of prodigies of wickedness and want and beggary arising in his mind as he looked about him.[8] More than one critic has found the real Dickens in the adult version of that solitary child, and all his faeryland as a grotesque remaking of the bizarre ideas dilating behind those wondering eyes – a remembering of a magic that really never existed in fact and which gives us Pol Sweedlepipe for his uncle's decent barber in Dean Street, Soho, and Doctor Slammer for the old staff-doctor at Chatham, and Micawber for his father, and the odd bookseller in Copperfield for a quite normal bookseller in Hampstead Road, that gives us all the Blennams and Duftys and Duddles and Tuzzers and Meagles and Foggys and Boffins and Blodgetts (of his notebooks and his books) for perfectly unexciting people who would never have recognised themselves in his fantastications.[9] One feels that it is all

6 Dickens published *Martin Chuzzlewit* serially under the pseudonym "Boz" from 1843 to 1844 and in book form in 1844.

7 Camden is a northern borough of London that was densely populated and heavily industrialised in the nineteenth century. St. Paul's is an Anglican Cathedral whose tall dome has long dominated the London skyline.

8 The Seven Dials is a junction in Covent Garden, a major district located in the West End of London.

9 *David Copperfield*, which Dickens published serially from 1849 to 1850 and in book form in 1850, incorporates semi-autobiographical details from his childhood.

invented by him – that he is not, in a word, in the least a realist but an utter fantaisiste.

Yet, with such power has he impressed his poet's vision of his world on us that it is doubtful, now, if we shall ever be able to see his times clear of his remaking of them. So, after his pen had set to work the modern Christmas Card came in with the snow and the coaching-inn and the red robins – his faeryland, and it troubles us not at all that nine times out of ten there is only a dreary drizzle of rain at Christmas. He has made the poetry of the winter-fire and the creaking inn-sign so vivid and so inseparable a part of English life that today in the United States, wherever you meet people who have an affection for their roots, you get perfectly gratuitous ingle-nook fireplaces in centrally-heated apartment-houses, and there is hardly a village in America without its inn-sign and its Ye Olde Curiositie Shoppe. Who minds? Not the realists, certainly, since it has nothing to do with realism. It is enough that when he is writing in that vein Dickens is living his vision of life, living in his dream-world, locked against all the envy of time in the Quilp Castle of his bizarre and macabre imagination, the complete artist.[10]

Looking at him, so, we know that he could do anything while he followed that star. But there is no novelist but knows that a dream-world must be related in some way to life, and no critic but knows that more artists than have ever been heard of have gone out like a candle in that delicate process of attempting to make their dream-worlds persuasive. One look at Tennyson, say, trying in *The Princess* to tune his lyric pipe to the boom of contemporary ideas on education and the Rights of Woman, is enough to show us how the tragedy happens.[11] It is the most delicate part of the novelist's craft, and the pit that faces him is called The Commonplace.

Dickens was great when he followed his star with abandon, and his only – and quite astute and wise – compromise was to go back a little out of his times to days that were already becoming mellow by being past, the coaching days. But for the rest he took his world and moulded it like putty in the claws of his wildly romantic imagination. As long as he did that he is simply without peer. When he came down to fundamentals, however, like Tennyson in that dull, dull poem *In Memoriam*,[12] full of

10 References to Dicken's novel *The Old Curiosity Shop* (1840–41).

11 Tennyson's *The Princess* (1847) is anti-feminist. By contrast, *A Vindication of the Rights of Woman*, written by Mary Wollstonecraft (1759–1797) in 1792, calls for equality between the sexes.

12 Tennyson published *In Memoriam*, a popular, long, elegiac poem that mourns the death of his friend, the writer Arthur Henry Hallam (1811–1833), in 1850.

commonplace triteness – if you are shocked go to it again and see for yourself – Dickens hitched his star to the wagon of conventional thought and conventional morality, one of the shakiest wagons ever known. He became the novelist of bourgeois thought, and in the musty drawing-room with its plush overmantel and its lace curtains he lay side by side with the family Bible on the plush table-cover. He became the creature of his times – Hard Times.[13]

In the result even his qualities suffered. He who was a poet and a solitary by nature became prosy with mechanical universals, bespoke philosophies, and a painful cocksureness about imponderables. He who was fancy-bred could smell, even in his humour, of stuffed-heart. I possibly put myself out of court by saying that I cannot, on my heart, agree that *Pickwick* is anything but a slow, tedious book by a great humourist, even though it *has* incomparable interludes like Bardell *v.* Pickwick.[14] But, again, retest it with Mr. Winkle on the Ice, or the Shooting Expedition, and all that about the fat boy supplying fat food to a fat man, and say if, in honesty, you do not sigh for childhood memories broken by a re-perusal. Worst of all, he, who had seen Evil face to face, was content to call it Injustice and plead for reform with every air of smug content that the world would again in time, with the help of Dickens, become a jolly good place to live in. No, as if he were too dynamic to be daemonic, he had no Vision of Sin, and was satisfied that with his stuffed images out of a Chamber of Horrors, the claptrap, gentlemanly claptrap, of a man who knew the facts but would not face them, he had adequately presented his whores and fences and sharks and pimps. He, who could express his pity for humanity as no man ever did before him, would not as much as look at the light of hell in human beings or the impenetrable darkness of their souls. Read Quilp – a scarecrow for children. Finally, because he had not a trace of humility in him, he wrote as if he knew everything, and there is, as a result, no wisdom in him but the wisdom of Samuel Smiles.[15] He is, in short, the great comforter of the nineteenth century, and unhappily for him the nineteenth century is gone. The farther it goes the more will his

13 A reference to Dickens' novel *Hard Times* (1854).

14 Here O'Faolain discusses *The Pickwick Papers* (1837). Mrs. Bardell is Pickwicks' landlady; she sues him for breach of promise after a misunderstanding in which she believes that he has proposed marriage to her.

15 Scottish author and journalist Samuel Smiles (1812–1904), whose best-known work was the advice manual *Self-Help, with Illustrations of Character and Conduct* (1859).

reputation decline, and the higher will the reputation of Thackeray become, though – because Dickens *was* immense – it is unlikely if they will, even at that, ever meet.

Whereas Thackeray is not at all to the same extent sold to his times. The man who wrote a Novel without a Hero and almost made a heroine of Becky Sharp, is – whatever he may think – near enough to Maupassant who made a heroine out of Boule de Suif, to be company for Turgenev or Flaubert: possibly not very good company and they would have quizzed him a great deal, but let that pass.[16] He is no aberrant – he had not the forcefulness for it – he was too much of the commune, but he did do what Hardy did and Lawrence did: he slapped smug English morality in the face. True, he did it so gently they hardly noticed; indeed he hardly knew himself what he had done, for it was a little gentlemanly slap. But he did it just the same, and the proof of it is in the dedication to *Jane Eyre* and in the protests and the dirty stories of the shocked Victorians who read that book.

Even if one says that in so far as Dickens was a grand exponent of the nineteenth-century traditional novel all who are of that tradition must be indebted to him – it is not entirely true. He pushed down no fences in the traditional fort, expanded its limitations in no effective way; rather he took the fort by storm, planted his flag in it, and if anything left his successors little to conquer. He took the technique of the English novel, its loose narrative style, its interest in various life, in character seen by-and-large, and even its long interest in rogues and ragamuffins, adapted it to his material, and blew fantastic life into it out of his mouth. But he did it as a glassblower who blows out magic with traditional tools and who says when you ask him how he does it, "How do I do it? I just blows." He had no imitators because he was inimitable at his best, and at his second-best what was imitable in his work was equally available outside it. Journalists did seize on his style; in his *Portraits of the Sixties*, Justin McCarthy remembers hearing London editors complaining humorously about the Dickensian craze, so that if an editor asked some reporter to do a description of a big public ceremonial he was sure to get something like: "Seats everywhere. Seats outside the Abbey. Seats inside the Abbey. Seats in Palace Yard. Seats in Piccadilly. Seats in High Holborn ..." and so on

16 Becky Sharp is one of the protagonists of *Vanity Fair*. The Russian Ivan Turgenev (1818–1883) and the Frenchman Gustave Flaubert were also important nineteenth-century writers and precursors of Maupassant. All three influenced O'Faolain's writing.

for a half-column before there began anything like a plain and practical account in intelligible prose.[17] But otherwise ...

＜ﾞ

There is no greater critical folly than that of wishing a great writer was other than he was, and nobody need wish it for Dickens. That Mark Twain might have been better if he had not been inhibited by his times and his wife is true: it is also true that he might have been worse.[18] It suffices that he wrote *Huckleberry Finn*, and it suffices that Dickens wrote a dozen of them. Achievement is all. Dickens peopled the England of his day with the loveliest, most amusing, most touching, most fantastic hobgoblins and elves imaginable, giants and dwarfs, good fairies and bad. Among them he threw a few highly creditable but incredible Oberons and Rosalinds.[19] And his world shuddered and wept and laughed at the *reality* of them as a child might laugh or shudder with delight and joy at the lifelike figures in Madame Tussaud's.[20] Even Jeffrey, that crusted Whig reviewer, blubbered over "sweet Paul."[21]

I have said it is foolish to wish a writer was other than he was, but one may wish a public different, and if only the public of Dickens' day had the wit to take literature for literature's sake, which is to say for the sake of its charm and delight and awe, and not for edification's sake, how much better could he not have served them with fun and fear. But who are we to wish a public different? His public did him the grace of taking him seriously, even solemnly. While in our day the public, by making a giant of so many, insisting indeed on "giants only" as its motto, ends by taking nobody seriously. But even that wish about Dickens' public is stupid. They took Tennyson seriously enough, Heaven knows, and a nice mess they made of that delicate lyric poet – as Mr. Harold Nicolson gives us room to believe in his excellent biography.[22] And they took Mark Twain lightly enough,

17 *Portraits of the Sixties* (1903), by Justin McCarthy (1830–1912).
18 American author Mark Twain (1835–1910), né Samuel Clemens, author of *The Adventures of Tom Sawyer* (1876) and *Adventures of Huckleberry Finn* (1885).
19 Oberon and Rosalind are characters in Shakespeare's *A Midsummer Night's Dream* (1595–96) and *As You Like It* (1598–1600), respectively.
20 Madame Tussauds, a wax museum in London devoted to historical and topical figures, was founded by Marie Tussaud (1761–1850).
21 Lord Francis Jeffrey (1773–1850) was the editor of *The Edinburgh Review*.
22 Harold Nicolson (1886–1968) was the author of several works, including *Tennyson: Aspects of His Life, Character and Poetry* (1923).

too, and that prose lyrist went buffoon and thwarted his seriousness, as Mr. Van Wyck Brooks argues in another excellent biography.[23] It all ends in the balance between the heart of the writer and the opportunities of his times. If Dickens lived in our bitter day one wonders what would happen to his humour – and if he had lived in the eighteenth century, one wonders what would have happened to his romance – and one ends by believing that he made an excellent bargain with his own difficult age.

But it is not our age, and we have to make a bargain of our own in our way, that is not, and could not, be his way. We have broken with tradition both in literature and in life, and if we are to receive any inspiration it will not be from him. It will be from those who broke with tradition before and after him, those individual wanderers out of the orderly procession in which he, like a general, brings up the rear – those scouts and guerillas of the disorganised rebellion of our times.

23 The American critic Van Wyck Brooks (1886–1963), author of *The Ordeal of Mark Twain* (1920).

Daniel Corkery[1]

The chronology of Daniel Corkery's works is in itself an indication of the movement of his mind, and because he is representative of a tendency not uncommon in Ireland – among the general public – an indication of a great deal in modern Irish life and criticism.

His first works were plays, mainly one-act plays, produced often by himself in a little theatre in Cork city, called *The Dún*, or The Fort, a romantic title significant of the times. Here, working with enthusiasm, a small band of players and playwrights (and they were, wisely, keen on writing their own plays) produced plays by men like Corkery, T.C. Murray, Con O'Leary, Daniel Harrington, Terence MacSwiney, Patrick Higgins, and others.[2] They were plays typical of the Anglo-Irish revival in drama, forcefully conceived, tragic, even melodramatic, romantic – as with Corkery's own *King and Hermit*, or his unpublished and more ambitious *Israel's Incense*: all a little mannered and stylistic and literary. The play *Clan Falvey* came later, as did the three act play dealing with Labour strikes in Ireland, and

1 "Daniel Corkery" appeared in *The Dublin Magazine* 11, no. 2 (April–June 1936): 49–61. The essay was prefaced with a note indicating the year of his birth (1878) and the titles, genres, and dates of publications of his works at the time that O'Faolain was writing: *The Onus of Ownership* (unpublished); *Israel's Incense* (unpublished); *The Yellow Bittern* (play, 1920); *King and Hermit* (play, 1920); *Clan Falvey* (play, 1920); *The Labour Leader* (play, 1920); *The Threshold of Quiet* (novel, 1917); *A Munster Twilight* (stories, 1917); *The Hounds of Banba* (stories, 1920); *The Stormy Hills* (stories, 1929); *The Hidden Ireland* (criticism, 1924); *Synge and Anglo-Irish Literature* (criticism, 1931); *I Bhreasail* (verse, 1920).
2 T.C. Murray (1873–1959), Con O'Leary, and Terence MacSwiney (1879–1920). Daniel Harrington and Patrick Higgins do not appear to have left much of a trace as authors and theatre men.

evidently suggested by the whirling figure of Jim Larkin – *The Labour Leader*: first produced at the Abbey Theatre in 1920.[3]

Meanwhile the nationalist revival had begun to capture these young men's imaginations, and as if in a desire for a closer analysis of Irish life than the drama seemed to afford, Corkery turned to the writing of a novel and a volume of short stories. The stories, ineptly called after Yeats's *A Celtic Twilight* – *A Munster Twilight* appeared first: the novel was published the year after. These stories have little about them that is likely to suggest the delicacy and fantasy of Yeats's lovely verse: they are cast in a different key and came out of a more direct approach to life. Here and there, as in the opening story, "The Ploughing of Leaca Bán," the too-literary quality still asserts itself, but in the city stories, often, nearly always indeed, of the poor-folk in the slums of the city, the note is much more like that of a folk-tale. At the end of the book, grouped under the title of "The Cobbler's Den," we get stories that could with a little more shaping be called pure city-folklore.

This is an entirely original note in Anglo-Irish literature for though a novel like James Stephens' *Mary, Mary* may antedate *A Munster Twilight*, there is a self-conscious fantastical note of the more practised literary man in Stephens' little masterpiece of frolic, and the compact, intimate, "folksy" quality of life that is revealed, as typical of Cork city, in Corkery's stories could not, in fact, have been evoked in a metropolis.[4] Not that Corkery has not his own whimsical humour; it is the charm of his personality; but it is not whimsy because it is the laughter of a kindly delight in reality, and no doubt nothing would so please its author as to be told that in the grotesquerie of these little yarns there is a distinct echo of the mediaeval note in literature.

The novel, delicate, brooding, sensitive, tragic, not without a grotesque note – as in the character of Stevie Galvin – fulfilled absolutely the promise of the stories. It is, without question, a lovely novel, and for many even a perfect novel. Almost aggressively regionalist, it admits no view of life but the local, Irish view: a glimpse of other worlds serving only to support the sense of the inevitability of that view, and to sear the heart with a sense of the delimitation of life within a code, humbly accepted, loyally unquestioned, despairingly followed to tragedy in the one case, to renunciation in the other. It is a somewhat gloomy book, and the emphasis of the

3 James Larkin (1876–1947) was a leading labour and trades unionist in Ireland.
4 *Mary, Mary* (1912), by James Stephens (1880/2–1950). In the United Kingdom it was published under the title *The Charwoman's Daughter*.

motto that introduces it makes it almost unbearable to recall – Thoreau's
chance statement that "the mass of men lead lives of quiet desperation."[5]
Yet there is a balsam to soothe as one reads, a tenderness, almost too-
sweet, for the girl Lily Bresnan and her young brother Finbarr, both
secretly contemplating the renunciation of life in religion when, in despair,
the other brother Frank has abandoned an unequal struggle by suicide.
This feminine note in Corkery has to be noticed – it seems to vanish almost
completely in his later work: it could scarcely, indeed, survive a widening
of interest, an acknowledgment of the validity of other worlds.

> Bright grass, homely flowers – phlox, marigolds, gladioli – trembling
> poplar leaves, dancing shadows – Lily Bresnan's nook on the hillside
> was an Autumn lyric, mellow and glad, a sweet music that needed no
> heightening, no enriching, while that gentle girl, earnestly bent upon
> her task, lingered in the sun. She put the thread between her teeth and
> broke it. With a little clatter the scissors fell to the dappled ground.
> There it remained. A robin, quite suddenly, winged across her, and
> was lost in the sun-flushed foliage. Stitch, stitch, without hurry. The
> garment was held up and examined. She stooped and her fingers, but
> not her eyes, searched for the fallen scissors. Far away in the crowded
> valley a convent bell was ringing for evening Benediction. Then, again
> suddenly, the robin flung out a little phrase of melody. It ceased, but
> the far-off bell continued, very sweet, very faint. The scissors once
> again fell to the ground. There it remained.

There is no need to comment: the words convey the lyrical quality of
the mind that so pictured life – mellow; flushed foliage; lingered; dappled;
gentle; homely; sweet; very faint. If one had any criticism to make it
would be that life so gently imaged, and in a plot of such humble and
effortless evasion, could hardly offer many themes, little action, little
drama, and must end by reducing almost to inarticulateness so quietly
lyrical an observer. The characters of such a world, so will-less, so quies-
cent, so passionless, may – and here did to perfection – offer matter for a
lyric in prose: or might, if conceived with more masculinity, offer matter
for a Greek tragedy: but as for the novelist they out-Chekov Chekov who
wrote, also, many lovely lyrics, and with a wider experience of life, and

5 Henry David Thoreau (1817–1862) was an American essayist. The quote is from
his best-known work, *Walden* (1854).

an acceptance of a greater variety of valid worlds, many stories that were more than lyrics; but, he also, no series of novels.[6]

The influence of Corkery's novel was neither strong nor pervasive. It was, for one thing, what one may call a middle-aged novel: for another, and mainly, it was not followed by a second novel. But it was an event for some of us. One must remember that in 1917 the Irish novel had produced few examples: the game was still, in the main, with the poets and the dramatists. We had a dozen novels from Moore, but all, except *The Lake*, dealt with English life and in a hard French way: we had Joyce's *Dubliners*, but they were stories and were cruel and unpleasant and Flaubertian. *Mary, Mary* was a bit too metropolitan and too whimsical. What we wanted was a novel like this, come out of truly popular life, that would do for popular life what the Eliots and Hardys had already done for English popular life. When I say *we*, I suppose I mean youngsters like O'Connor and O'Flaherty and myself, who hoped one day to be novelists.[7] Unhappily the very perfection, and the controlled "middle-aged" quality of Corkery's novel, and above all, its limited scope, prevented its possible effect. Young men are rebellious – and it was the time of rebellions – and they are ambitious. In a phrase of O'Flaherty's, in a letter to me, we wanted to "bite off mountains with our teeth." There was not enough fire in this book to light any torch. We were far more excited, though horrified, by Joyce's *Portrait of the Artist* as *a Young Man*: we felt much nearer to *The Brothers Karamazov*, to *Torrents of Spring* even, to *The Death of Ivan Ilyich*, than to *The Threshold of Quiet*. After all, *The Kreutzer Sonata* was so wicked![8]

Corkery's later stories have not been, by any means, so good. We loved *The Hounds of Banba*, stories of the Irish revolution, as long as we were elated by being young revolutionaries ourselves: but the more we saw of revolution the less we liked Corkery's lyric, romantic, idea of revolution and revolutionaries. It is a personal kind of criticism, admittedly, and it is

6 Anton Chekhov (1860–1904), whose name O'Faolain consistently spells without the second "h," was a major Russian playwright and short story writer whose work was a significant influence on O'Faolain's writing.

7 Frank O'Connor (1903–1966) and Liam O'Flaherty were, like O'Faolain, former IRA members who had become leading writers of their generation.

8 *The Brothers Karamazov* (1879–80), by Fyodor Dostoevsky; *Torrents of Spring* (1872), by Ivan Turgenev; *The Death of Ivan Ilyich* (1886) and *The Kreutzer Sonata* (1891), by Leo Tolstoy. O'Faolain referred to the similarities between Russian and Irish fiction on several occasions over the course of his life.

not detached and it is, largely, the resentment of young men who had begun to compare romance with reality; and in the end it may well be astray. But it remains. The realistic novel and the realistic story were in the making. O'Casey was scratching out his first efforts: so, no doubt, were O'Flaherty, O'Donnell, O'Connor.[9] Against that convention Corkery could have easily smiled had he chosen to continue with his gentle and faultless lyricism, or with his homely, folksy, whimsical, grotesque humour of "The Cobbler's Den." These young men might know about the revolution, about blood, cowardice, fear, and horror, and courage. For wandering in and out of the hillside cabins, travelling by night, taking back-roads, sleeping in a different bed every night, they might even boast that they had come to know the country-folk as no would-be writers had ever chanced to know them before. But Corkery knew his lane-people, his city-types, far better. Alas, he chose to write after *The Threshold of Quiet* about the farmers and fisher-folk, in a mood and in a manner and with a preconceived approach that tended to falsify all he wrote, and for the understanding of which – and it is an approach that has found innumerable disciples, and has affected Irish emotions widely – we must turn to his two works of criticism.

In a few words – he began to idealise what he had observed from a distance, and worst of all, to idealise it according to a certain set of a priori ideas about life and literature which were wandering around Ireland at the time, waiting to be articulated by some able man. He has expressed these ideas in his *The Hidden Ireland*, and *Synge and Anglo-Irish Literature*. He has expressed them well, and they are thought-provoking books. But he has not since then written more than a few short stories on the level of his earlier work.

~

The book on Synge, coming later, contains the application to Anglo-Irish letters of the historical attitude outlined in *The Hidden Ireland*. The Introduction sums it all up, and is a marvellous piece of special pleading, though written in elusive English that is often vague and sometimes quite meaningless. In sum (according to this point of view) Anglo-Irish Literature, since 1900 in particular, is "astray" as an interpretation of Irish life, gives "no adequate expression" to the forces "that work their will in the consciousness of the Irish people," and – a typically suggestive

9 Peadar O'Donnell (1893–1986), another former IRA man, later took over as editor of *The Bell* upon O'Faolain's resignation in 1946.

but unprecise sentence – its practitioners did not "use such intellectual equipment as they possessed,"

sometimes admirable in itself, for the high purposes of art – the shaping out into chaste and enduring form of a genuine emotional content, personal to themselves but conscionable to the nation.

Writing for an English market ("keeps its eyes on the foreign merchants who are to purchase its wares") it has been "misled" from the start. In brief, Anglo-Irish literature is not an adequate interpretation of Irish life.

To illustrate this Corkery takes a hurling-match at Thurles, a crowd of thirty thousand country and town folk, and says:

It was while I looked around at that great crowd I first became acutely conscious that as a nation we were without self-expression in literary form. The life of this people I looked upon – there were all sorts of individuals present, from bishops to tramps off the road – was not being explored in a natural way by any except one or two writers of any standing … One could not see Yeats, Æ, Stephens, Dunsany, Moore, Robinson, standing out from that gathering as natural and indigenous interpreters of it. On the other hand there seems to be no difficulty in posing Galsworthy, Masefield, Bennett, Wells, against corresponding assemblies in England … Those English crowds are 100 per cent. English: and the writers who best express the individual souls that make them up are 100 per cent. English … The writers in a normal country are one with what they write of.[10]

To those who have accepted Anglo-Irish literature as literature this will sound painful. To those who approach it as the expression of a high-hearted Nationalism it will be (and was) a trumpet-call. With a little alteration it would equally well trumpet encouragement to all Nazis, Fascists, Communists, and every other type of exclusivist for whom the essential test of literature is a political, racial, or religious test. All a Nazi need do, to make that passage personally gratifying, is to put for "Yeats,

10 Yeats; Æ, the *nom de plume* of George William Russell (1867–1935); James Stephens; Lord Dunsany (1878–1957), né Edward John Moreton Drax Plunkett; George Moore; and Lennox Robinson (1886–1958) have all had difficult relationships with the definition of an Irish writer. John Galsworthy, John Masefield (1878–1967), Arnold Bennett, and H.G. Wells.

Æ, Stephens, etc." – Ludwig, Feuchtwanger, Toller, etc., with 100 per cent. Teuton in his mind and a meeting at the Munich Spielplatz instead of Thurles.[11]

One may pass over the disingenuousness of Corkery's choice of lyric writers from the Irish group (Yeats, Dunsany, Stephens, Æ) instead of O'Donnell, O'Connor, O'Casey, and such like as possible interpreters of the "mob"; and of Naturalistic writers from the English group, Bennett, Wells, Galsworthy. He is, after all, fighting here for a propagandist idea and may be forgiven a little sharp practice. But one does not so easily forgive his suggestion that "the writers who best express the individual souls of England" are Bennett, Wells, Galsworthy. Not because they may not but because one knows well that Corkery sincerely thinks these writers very small beer: one knows that his spiritual affinities are writers like Musset and Turgenev, the feminine lyrists;[12] that, if anything his own romantic image of life is far nearer to that of Yeats and Stephens, than to Bennett and Wells: that he is being disloyal to himself as an artist in trying to make his theory fit. And that is unforgiveable.

Of course, the fact is that *The Old Wives' Tale*, or *The Country House*, or *The New Machiavelli* do not interpret an English cup-final crowd at Wembley.[13] To ask art to do things like that is to socialise it, and that precisely is what Mr. Corkery's nationalism means – the nationalisation of culture.

That is the core of the weakness of this approach. It is not a critic's approach. It is a politician's, and clearly one cannot find any common ground for discussion under such conditions unless one agrees on the nationalistic premisses. That the emotional content of, let us say, *A Portrait of the Artist as a Young Man* is genuine, Corkery will not admit! He says Joyce is "astray!" He suggests of Stephens that his idyllic picture is "watery gruel." He has a good word, but not complete approval, for T.C. Murray and Padraic Colum, but for nobody else. That O'Casey is "conscionable" to the nation he does not admit, because O'Casey satirises Nationalism! But, one leaves the position in disgust – it is an impossible attitude which cannot allow a man to satirise what he honestly

11 German writers Emil Ludwig (1881–1948), Lion Feuchtwanger (1884–1958), and Ernst Toller (1893–1939); all three were Jewish and left-wing and thus antipathetic to the Nazis.

12 French Romantic author Alfred de Musset (1810–1857).

13 *The Old Wives' Tale* (1908), by Arnold Bennett; *The Country House* (1907), by John Galsworthy; and *The New Machiavelli* (1911) by H.G. Wells.

thinks deserving of satire. It is a position which leads Corkery into more than one baseness, more than one disloyalty. Typical is his scorn of Irish expatriates in America, when he says they do not even know the names of our Irish writers, and that those who do show an interest in Irish literature are of the type who "do not hasten home to do their bit when an insurrection is on," or "contribute to the funds of any political group," or contribute to "the funds of Irish cultural establishments." These are simply untrue statements.

~

One turns back to Corkery's later stories and to his *The Hidden Ireland* to see how these nationalistic premisses express themselves in theory and become effective in art. We may take a glance at the stories first, though their mould and technique is really not fully illuminated until we come to the other book which is a history, in effect, of 18th century Ireland from the point of view of the penalised underdog.

Anyone who might turn from the silvery, twilit, Musset-note of *The Threshold of Quiet* to the stories in *The Stormy Hills* might wonder if it were the same writer. Here all but one of the tales are in the country: all of these in the wilder, more outlying country, often Gaelic-speaking. Strange, rough words we now hear, in place of those other words we noted in the novel: words like splintery; lumpish; awkward; scraggy; harsh; gigantic; fierce; glaring; bearlike. In two stories we meet the phrase, "a blob of a hand." The hands are often "heavy." The eyes are "glaring eyes," or are "fiercely buried" in a person or object. Always the hero is very tall, big, broad, glum – almost, indeed, the type of the strong silent Englishman, a feminine idea of masculinity. "He stood there, a solid piece of humankind, huge, bigfaced, with small round eyes, shrewd-looking, not unhumorous." "The two women looked at himself, alert yet lumpish before them, noted his body's girth and depth, and felt that 'trunk' was indeed the right word to use of such bodies." "When he could not find words to fit his thought his left eye would close tight, and one big tooth, that he still retained in his upper gum, would dig itself into his lower lip, until the struggling words came to him. And they noticed that his two hands had clenched themselves, long before he needed them clenched, to illustrate how he had tackled the reclamation of the sluggish marshlands of Dunerling East ... Every now and then the timbers of the heavy chair groaned beneath the movement of his awkward carcase." "Murty, on the other hand, was a monumental junk of humanity, huge and staunch, lavish in flesh, resounding in laughter." "The end of the drawing away was, however, that four gigantic figures were left grouped about the coffin." "The wind was singing and whistling – *screeching* was the word used by themselves – in the long brown, wiry, bog grass." "He stepped in slowly and heavily ... " "Satisfied at last he lifted himself to his full height, six feet two inches, flung backwards his massively domed head, hoisted the instrument, and etc ... " "His dab of a mouth hung open: his unshaven lip trembled." And so on. This gigantism, as if in rebellion against the more moderated, more quiet, often lyrical quality of the Anglo-Irish literature he dislikes – forgetting that it is also the note of his own best work – can only be explained as an effort to come closer to the soil and the life of the soil. But that it is a convention just as much "astray" as the convention of the poetry he has put in the dock, and poetry has its own sweet liberties, is not likely to be denied by anybody who is familiar with the conventional Brutalist literature of the present day in America and England. Seeking after strength is a confession of weakness when the search produces a conventional idealisation that only impresses one with a sense of somebody blowing up a balloon.

The themes are not always informative, but some are. They now seek after powerful drama and wild action and a setting of storm and harsh landscape – a further convention of this romantic idea of strength. But, what is significant, they seek, too, the historical Irish peasant fated to resurgence. The story "Carrig-an-Afrinn" will illustrate. Old Hodnett had long held a farm of that name, so-called after the Mass Rock where in Penal Days the hunted priests said Mass in secret.[14] As he prospers, he sells it and buys Dunerling East, a rich pasture-land. But he leaves the old mountainy farm with misgivings: he has heard that angels hover over these old mass-rocks. He slaves to succeed in the new farm, and does succeed, but at the cost of the lives of his family. We see him at the end of his labours, still dreaming of that old mountainy farm – for he does not know the rock has been blasted by new road-makers to widen a road. In another tale, "The Wager," we get the Big House from the view-point of the serf-peasants whose historical dignity is stressed heavily:[15]

14 The Penal Days refer to the period of the sixteenth to the eighteenth centuries during which time the practice of Roman Catholicism was penalised through a series of legislative acts and law enforcement. A rock that served as an altar was known as a Mass rock.
15 A Big House is the equivalent to an English county house, the seat of an aristocratic family.

You will remember there is a great difference between the Brosnans who lie in Kilvreeda and those in Muckross Abbey. You might say 'tis only since yesterday, since they came down in the world, that the Brosnans are satisfied to lie in Kilvreeda. The Brosnans who lie in Kilvreeda were just poor common people like ourselves, but the ancient Brosnans, from time immemorial, they had been laid in the Abbey with the MacCarthys, the O'Sullivans, the O'Donoghues, the MacGillicuddys.

In "The Rivals" we get the rivalry between two folk story-tellers with the clan spirit well to the foreground.

One can see what the author has in mind. He will write stories that will be "conscionable to the nation" – if that means, as it appears to mean, acceptable to the self-proud race-memory. He will write regionalist stories whose values are the values of the locale in which they are set. Unsure of himself as an artist *sans phrase* he will be at least sure of himself as an Irishman.[16] Unhappily the self-consciousness of this approach, the deliberateness of it, has vitiated the spontaneity of the artist. The stories are mannered, the emotion is forced. The emotion may be "conscionable to the nation" – or may not, who knows that? – but it does not strike one as being in the least "genuine": it is pumped up.

In his book on Synge, Corkery spoke of writers who write for an alien audience; here he is writing for a native audience; in truth the genuine writer writes for no audience but himself. That is the rock on which the self-conscious Nationalist has broken. Art is a stern mistress. She brooks no rivals. It is possible, indeed, that in the course of a century, when we Irish have become a nation – as we are not yet a nation, the sediment of history not yet sunk to the bottom, the chemical elements not yet fully compounded – patriotic Irishmen may or may not read these stories with pride and other stories written to the same formula. So may Irish critics: but for the sake of Irish letters I hope not. Nor is it likely. We can still read novels like *Knocknagow* with a patriotic glow, but we are under no delusions – not even Mr. Corkery is under any illusion – as to their literary mediocrity (his own word).[17]

The progression, rather the decline, from tender and whimsical humour, and the gentle lyricism, of the earlier work is evident. It is a sad example of a fine talent thwarted by theorising. Not that some of these stories

16 *Sans phrase* is French for "without words," as in not needing to qualify.
17 *Knocknagow* (1879) is a novel by Charles Kickham.

have no merit. In this volume *The Stormy Hills* there is one story, "The Emptied Sack" that is as perfect and lovely as anything Turgenev ever wrote. There is lovely feeling in all of them, such as "The Lartys." The descriptions, when free of mannerisms, are often masterly; as when in a silent night, with drama moving to tragedy in the foreground,

> out on the reef a run of foam would catch the moon's rays for a moment, wriggle silver-bright, like an eel caught in the hand, and then go out, leaving the darkness vast and vacant.

~

All this deliberate pre-occupation with the historically-seen peasant arises from the conception of Irish history outlined in *The Hidden Ireland*. It is a biggish book and it would take a bigger book to dispel the illusion of veracity it creates: for its arrangement of facts, and of half-facts, and of pious beliefs, by a man with an inadequate knowledge of Irish history, is tendentious in the extreme. It is a book which needed to be written. But it should have been written by a historian; and as it stands – with no historian willing to engage his energies in challenging and disproving so many elaborate generalisations – it has had and will continue to have a profound effect on modern Irish (uncritical) thought. I give one or two statements from the book which will indicate the light-heartedness with which the author has handled whole periods of history:

> P. 153. Whatever of the Renaissance came to Ireland met a culture, so ancient, so widely-based, and well-articulated that it was received only on suffrance.

There is only one word for this: it may be inelegant, but it is the truth – and that word is, *Rubbish*.

> P. 42. The poet scarcely took even poetic licence with the facts, as is the manner of Irish poets. He invented nothing; he hardly even heightened the tint ...

Of this one may say that if one does not laugh outright at it one might weep at such a perfervid gullibility.

> P. 49. (*Speaking of the eighteenth century*) The language was a gateway to a complete and unique civilisation.

Possibly unique: but complete?

P. 152. The appeal of their (*the poets'*) work was primarily to an audience cultured in literature.

The comment is fifty pages farther back:

O'Bruadair, in 1692 ... goes on to say that knowledge is now so corrupt in Munster that nothing but vulgar poetry is understood.

P. 58. There was a common culture flowing up and down between hut and Big House in Irish Ireland.

(Of this I do believe that a few students ought to spend a few years in the examination of the problem.)
Speaking of a sophisticated Vision poetry:

P. 141. How used those peasants to take in such a song? One may safely reply, With perfect comprehension.

And one also may not.
These few excerpts, possibly too remote in interest for many readers, will suggest the kind of picture the romantic novelist has made, for himself, of the immediate ancestors of the historical (?) peasant of his own stories. They are the descendants of greatness, and of a cultivated greatness. There every Irish writer parts company with Mr. Corkery.
We do not see the Irish farmer in this lambent light of reflected greatness. We know his immediate history – we can follow it back to Parnell, to the Land League,[18] to O'Connell, his first popular leader (who, incidentally, threw Gaelic overboard). We can follow his rise back to the Hedge Schools,[19] where he was eager only to learn English and mathematics (to be able to keep accounts and measure his land), and Latin where the son of the house aimed to be a priest. We can follow the ideas that ultimately liberated him, back to Tone and the effect of the French Revolution. Behind that we cannot go. We look at him now, out in the

18 The Land League was an Irish agrarian organisation founded by Michael Davitt (1846–1906) in 1879 to push for reform of the colonial model of land ownership.
19 A hedge school was a popular local form of education in Ireland that was outside of the colonial system.

fields that are his own: and we look back to Tone – and back into the impenetrable night of the Penal Days – and he seems to us to be, thus regarded, a satisfactory unity. We hear him sing a song from Tom Moore and it takes us no farther back than all that.[20] We hear him applaud a song of Lady Dufferin's and it takes us back no farther than all that.[21] Only in the Gaelic fringe of Ireland do we hear notes that take us back behind the dark veil. But in that Gaelic fringe we see that life is, for all that, patterned exactly as it is in Meath or Limerick, only more colourfully, with more picturesque detail preserved out of the past, both near and remote. And where we have tried to puzzle out what really happened behind the darkness of the Penal Days we have – many of us – formed, in fact, the belief that the modern Ireland *is* a new and indigenous growth that began when the Irish folk, in disgust with this non-popular, aristocratic, effete, world (whose last dregs of culture lasted on into the nineteenth century for Mr. Corkery to slobber over as if it were the people's love instead of being the people's indifference), threw it all aside to build up, for themselves, and for the first time, a world of their own in the hovels to which that ancient curse, the Celtic state, had by its inefficiency reduced them.

To us the Irish fishermen and the Irish farmer and the Irish townsman is the result of about one hundred and fifty years struggle. And that, for history, is long enough for us. To us, Ireland is beginning, where to Corkery it is continuing. We have a sense of time, of background: we know the value of the Gaelic tongue to extend our vision of Irish life, to deepen it and enrich it: we know that an old cromlech in a field can dilate our imaginations with a sense of what was, what might have been, and *what is not*; but we cannot see the man ploughing against the sky in an aura of antiquity![22] Colum, the poet, may do so, asking if the plougher is thinking of Pan, or Wotan, or Dana.[23] The poet, so to speak, may do what he pleases. But as novelists, story-writers, dramatists, we know that the plougher is at most thinking of the Famine, which is a hundred years gone, and that his other thoughts that are too deep for him to express, weld him with such things (and Corkery rightly deals with such things) as the

20 Thomas Moore (1779–1852) was a Romantic nationalist Irish writer.
21 Lady Dufferin (1807–1867), née Helen Blackwood.
22 A cromlech, also referred to as a dolmen, is a prehistoric structure, with one stone resting on others to resemble a table.
23 Pan is a Greek deity of fertility; Wotan is one of the names of the Norse god Odin; Dana, or Danu, is the Celtic earth goddess.

Rebellion of 1798, the priest-hunters, the hedge-schools, the mass-rock – but definitely *not* with the now dead and forgotten Celtic world.[24]

So, outside of Corkery's short stories, and one or two plays, you will get nowhere else in the literature of Anglo-Ireland, for short call it Ireland, this grandiose note of the romantic peasant. Had he outlined his ideas twenty years sooner, in the period of the Celtic Twilight that he so despises, he would have had many more followers than he has now.[25] But realism, which has been for some time the cry in Irish fiction, has been against him. The Abbey Theatre, with its superficial satires, – which he dislikes, for the wrong reasons, as much as we all dislike them for the right, or artistic reasons – has formed the public mind. He does, I think, influence our political evangels considerably: all that is behind our system of education in the modern Ireland, much that enthuses and supports all our more fervent politics, has come out of his books and his lecturings. But as far as literature is concerned, because he has not spoken to it in the only language it understands, the language of literature and literary values, he has no influence except the influence he rightly exercised at the beginning with his pleasant book of tales *A Munster Twilight*, and his delicate novel that he has, so greatly to our loss, not wished to repeat.

For that limitation of such an influence we may be thankful to the loyal insistence of such as Yeats and Moore and Stephens on "the high purposes of art." They are content to live or die by Beauty's suffrage, the only suffrage that counts, knowing that all other writers are those who, grown weak in her service, put above her praise some popular cry, and become in the end, the impoverishment of the people they think to serve.

24 The Irish Famine occurred in the late 1840s and early 1950s with the failure of the potato crop due to a blight, a type of mould that infected the plants. Ireland's population fell from over eight million before the Famine to just over six million after it. More than a million died and still more emigrated.

25 The Celtic Twilight was the name of the Irish literary revival in the late nineteenth and early twentieth centuries.

The Dangers of Censorship[1]

Some renewal of interest in our extremely virulent Censorship of Publications has followed on the banning of three more Irish books – *The Green Lion*, by Francis Hackett, *The Singing-Men of Cashel*, by Austin Clarke, and *Bird Alone*, by myself.[2] Mr. Hackett contributes a trenchant article on the censoring of his own novel to the current number of *The Dublin Magazine*, and several letters to the press have protested against the banning of mine.[3]

What the public, the Minister for Justice, and possibly the five Censors whose word is law, and against which there can be no direct legal appeal (the chief source of disquietude among thinking people) do not seem to realise is this – that the main objections to the present method of working the Censorship of Publications Act do not primarily concern the wisdom or unwisdom, of banning certain, individual books. For while it is undoubtedly an indignity to be publicly proclaimed as a pornographer, we could bear with that, confident of our own integrity as artists, and indifferent, as artists, to a form of insult which is rapidly becoming quite

1 "The Dangers of Censorship" appeared in *Ireland To-Day* 1, no. 6 (November 1936): 57–63.
2 All of these novels were published in 1936.
3 Francis Hackett (1883–1962), "A Muzzle Made in Ireland," *Dublin Magazine* 11, no. 4 (1936): 8–17. The letters of protest began with O'Faolain's colleague and close friend Frank O'Connor, and continued for a week. See Frank O'Connor, "A Protest," *Irish Times*, 21 September 1936; Lynn Doyle (1873–1961), né Leslie Alexander Montgomery, "A Protest," *Irish Times*, 22 September 1936; Andrew E. Malone (1890–1939), "A Protest," *Irish Times*, 24 September 1936; F.P.F., "A Protest," *Irish Times*, 28 September 1936; Irene Haugh, "A Protest," *Irish Times*, 28 September 1936; and William M. Glynn, "A Protest," *Irish Times*, 28 September 1936.

meaningless by indiscriminate use, if we did not believe that the chief results of the Censorship are to debase the public conscience, to bring the law into disrepute, and to limit, not the growth of the author, but the growth of the nation.

We believe that any unnecessary interference with the public will is not merely a tyranny but a folly. It removes responsibility from the hands of the community before the community has had any adequate opportunity to exercise its own quiet methods of control. It thereby pre-empts the activity of a healthy public opinion, and prevents that public opinion from (so to speak) growing by exercise. It kills the national conscience by giving it no scope to take or leave, to praise or condemn, to exercise its will or exercise its wisdom. By depriving morality of its freedom it reduces it to a machine without virtue.

Undue legal interference goes even further with its folly than this, since, by denying to a free people so large an element of their freedom, it belittles human dignity and insults the essential nature of man. By removing from the community responsibility for its own behaviour it makes it the tool of others, and so reduces it to a condition of moral slavery under the pretence of "helping" it to "obey" the moral law. But obedience implies choice; and where there is no choice, as there is no obedience, there can be no conscience worth the name. The Censorship, in this way, recalls Milton's words – he, too, censored in his day by other Puritans:

"Assuredly," he makes his censors admit, "we bring not virtue into the world, we bring impurity much rather; that which purifies us is trial, and trial is by what is contrary. That virtue, therefore, which is but a youngling in the contemplation of evil, and knows not the utmost that vice promises to her followers, and rejects it, is but a blank virtue not a pure; her whiteness is but an excremental whiteness; which was the reason why our sage and serious poet Spenser, whom I dare be known to think a better teacher than Scotus or Aquinas, describing True Temperance ... brings him through the cave of Mammon, and the bower of earthly bliss, *that he might see and know and yet abstain.*"4

4 John Milton's *Areopagitica* (1644) was written to protest the government's licensing of publications, which was, in effect, a preliminary censorship to ensure orthodoxy. Blessed John Duns Scotus (c. 1266–1308), beatified in 1993, was a Franciscan philosopher and theologian; St. Thomas Aquinas (1224/25–1274) was a Dominican theologian.

Our Censorship, in a word, foolishly squeamish, tries to keep the national mind in a state of perpetual adolescence in the midst of all the influences that must, in spite of it, pour in from an adult world.

But it is even more disturbing to realise that the Censorship Act has brought the law itself into disrepute, since while lip-service is given to the major ordinances of the Act by everybody, only its minor ordinances – relative to flagrantly indecent and vulgar periodicals, of whose prohibition we all approve – are respected by those who advert to it. Not only is there no book which may not be read before the censors have had time to consider it (some books have been on sale for as much as two years before the censors became aware of their existence) but it is notorious, as it is natural, that no book is so much in private demand as the book which has been banned. In fact the Act is regarded with approval only by those who generally read next to nothing, or who are by nature extremely cautious in their reading, and for whom it was scarcely necessary to go to so much trouble to create it. The banning of some books, such as Sinclair Lewis's *Elmer Gantry*, has, furthermore, drawn outraged protests from the most orthodox Catholics. The banning of a book like Shaw's *A Black Girl in Search of God* has been shown by the Irish Academy of Letters to have been banned not for indecency but for irrelevant reasons not adumbrated at all by the Censorship Act.[5] Still, further, it is patent to everybody that the provisions of the Act are being evaded by the censors – such as the section which indicates to them that they are expected to consult the author or publisher in doubtful cases; and at all times to take into account the literary and other merits of every book before them. All this evokes much natural and entirely justifiable irritation whose chief effect is to provoke antipathies between the intelligent reading public and the puritanical Pussyfoots inside the Dáil and outside the Dáil who fail to see that they can enforce this particular law only at the cost of a weakening in public respect for the whole fabric of our public legislation. It is like to the Liquor Licensing Laws which are evaded without a qualm of conscience; or the Anti-Birth-Control ordinances which (as nobody but a foolish optimist, or a self-blinded hypocrite, would deny) are respected only by those who would normally never as much as advert to them.

These are considerations which we who suffer directly at the hands of the law consider of the utmost importance. The best that can be said of those in favour of the present working of the Censorship Act is that they

5 *The Adventures of the Black Girl in Her Search for God* (1932), by Irish writer and Nobel Prize laureate Bernard Shaw (1856–1950).

either consider these undoubted evils of less importance than the evils which, they maintain, would result from the alternative, i.e., the free circulation of books; or have never thought about the matter seriously at all. But observe, we do NOT ask for the free circulation of books. We ask merely that the circulation of books should be interfered with, only with the utmost circumspection; and nobody can pretend that a Censorship which has banned upwards of 500 books in about four years has acted with any sensible degree of circumspection. We do not (apart from the disgraceful absence of any machinery of appeal) object to the Censorship Act. We object to the censors who have exploited it with a stupidity amounting to malevolence.

As for the effect of all this on the growth of the nation, is it necessary to say much? A young nation cannot possibly develop if what is at one stage vulgarly accepted is to be perpetually regarded as axiomatic; if, that is to say, there is not to be at every point a reconsideration of traditional values. Perhaps an old nation may for a long period fold its wings – though one may doubt it. A young one, scarcely fledged, can do so only at the peril of becoming moribund. We are at the threshold of life. We should be full of eagerness and the lust for discovery. We are, instead, so far as the promulgation of ideas through literature is concerned, hedged, and walled, and fettered by five licensers more remarkable for their timidity than for their courage, their narrowness than their openness of mind. Well might we ask, with the *Areopagitica*, if five men are enough to estimate all the good sense and genius of the world, for these censors actually have taken not merely England, or Ireland, but the whole world for their province! Well may we ask if there is now a monopoly of knowledge which, like motor-tyres, has been granted by a tariff to these five men? Ask if the common people are not insulted by the suggestion that their famed morality cannot stand the impact of a flighty book by some English chit of a girl-journalist; or if the force of our clergy is so little, and all their labours so barren, that we, their flocks, are likely to be staggered by a whiff from Mr. John Dos Passos, a touch of anti-clericalism from Mr. Sinclair Lewis, a hearty laugh from Mr. Shaw?[6] We may well ask finally, why we are bred to be free souls, if we must now turn to the complacent idleness of the slave who feeds or starves at the flick of a bully's whip?

That individual books, therefore, should be banned is of little import to the authors thereof. As Mr. Eric Gill has said, there are, so far as that goes, as good fish in the sea as ever came out of it. The larger considerations are

6 John Dos Passos (1896–1970) was an American novelist.

important, however, and they are considerations which should appeal to
every type of mind which truly values the moral virility of Ireland, thinks
it well that the law should receive respect, and is jealous for the honour of
the nation.

There is one general conclusion of secondary interest to be drawn from
this. The combination of forces which is at present most active here in supporting such prohibitory ordinances as the Censorship Act is a combination of the Gaelic Revivalist who fears the influence of European, and
especially English, literature (for nationalistic reasons) and the Catholic
Actionist who fears the same influences (for pious reasons). Their motives
are of the best. Their methods are of the worst. Too lazy, both of them, to
inoculate the public with a lymph of education – which would have the
effect of causing the public to live and choose wisely – they are content to
act only by a method of absolute prohibition. The only ultimate effect of
this must be that they will both fall into utter disrepute, as the bully – especially the lazy and stupid bully – always must fall into disrepute. So, for
example, Mr. Peadar McGinley, the President of the Gaelic League, once
went so far as to say that he would prohibit the importation of all English
newspapers, and, yet, the Gaelic League, once so full of life and vigour, has
not within ten years been able to produce as much as a weekly paper in
our own tongue![7] On the other score, the clergy, active in denunciation of
late dances every autumn, when the application for Dance Hall licences
come before the courts, have not been able to offer a single, solitary, constructive suggestion as to how the people are to amuse themselves in the
countryside during the dull nights of winter. Rightly did a District Justice
recently chide the clergy, saying that they had broken up the cross-roads
dances, which never continued to late hours, and so were now faced by a
problem largely of their own making. This combination of forces, then,
which might be powerful for good in a constructive way, has, instead, by
its follies drawn upon both the Gaelic spirit and upon the Catholic spirit
the irritation of the people. The more compliant District Justices play into
their hands; the wiser ones are distracted and dismayed – like that court in
Waterford which angrily dismissed a case brought against an Amusements
Park manager who had installed a game of *push ha-penny*, or the Justice
in Kerry who listened in evident irritation to the curates who protested

7 Peadar McGinley (1856–1942), né Peadar Toner Mac Fhionnlaoich, wrote under
the names P.T. McGinley and Cú Uladh. The Gaelic League was founded in 1893
as a part of the national revival. It was, in its origins, a non-sectarian organisation
devoted to the preservation, maintenance, and promotion of the Irish language.

against a dance-hall on the score that it was so near to the presbytery that they could hear the dancers stamping and cheering!

This mentality is producing in Ireland an eleusinian, secret, subterrene life – a life of public silence, and private grumbling, public obedience, private revolt, a public morality to win place and please the powers, and a private morality of quite a different type.[8] Disintegration must be the inevitable result, a disintegration from below, making the crust, the ice, thinner and thinner, while all the while the surface appears pure, and white, and shining – an "excremental" or outward whiteness as Milton calls the blank virtue of mechanical acquiescence; only that it is worse than his "blank virtue" since we are learning the craft of *pretending* an acquiescence which we as constantly evade. When, or if, the ice cracks, the crust crumbles, it is not the intellectuals who are demanding greater circumspection in the use of prohibitory powers, but the Gaelic-Catholic combination who are never satisfied that these powers have been sufficiently exercised, who will be the first to wonder what has happened, and the last to realise that it is they themselves who are responsible for the ultimate, and to my mind (as things go) inevitable collapse into a moral pit.

So, a small handful of intellectuals (who earn their living elsewhere, though residing here, who, having been placed by outlawry beyond the temptation of place, or the fear of this hypocritical "public opinion," speak with the trebled influence of men who obviously can have no ulterior motive) are the sole bulwark between the national character and the disintegrating influences of the Censorial mind. But in so far as their influence is limited by the Censorship, the country hears them only by chance, and at random, and we are witnessing the extraordinary spectacle – though perhaps not so extraordinary in the Europe of to-day – of a country deliberately deprived of its own intellectuals by (in our case) a junta of misguided, however well-meaning, Gaelic Revivalists and Catholic Actionists. The position could be worse. The hope lies in the fact that both these forces rely largely on intellectual support themselves, and they have hitherto received that support from such as University professors, professional men, private students, journalists, and so forth. To these alone it is worth while appealing, and to these we must earnestly appeal, on the highest plane, either to affect by penetration the prejudices of their associates, or to dissociate themselves from their present methods

8 O'Faolain refers here to the Eleusinian Mysteries, the most famous of the secret rites in ancient Greece; they are directly related to Demeter's journey to the netherworld in search of her daughter Persephone, who had been abducted by Pluto.

by forming an independent Catholic – if necessary even a politically active – wedge; not a new Front, indeed, for they are not numerous enough, but a spear-head into the dullness of the mass that at present uses them to no sensible purpose, since what purposes these forces have in mind have, so far, produced only the most deplorable effects towards which nobody of any insight, or foresight, can have anything but that most devastating of all emotions, sympathy without respect.

Don Quixote O'Flaherty[1]

My friend Liam O'Flaherty is (to use one of his own favourite adjectives) such an *amazingly* serious person that I almost hesitate to knight him as the inn-keeper knighted his famous ancestor of La Mancha.[2] But a Don he must be made, for there is no modern writer who has so valiantly fought for his ideal Dulcinea, so often tackled the giants, so often been tossed in the blanket of his countrymen's scorn, so often been waylaid by the priest, and the barber, and the pious housekeeper, so often been thrown high by the windmills of his imagination. He has not, happily, yet joined the Company of White Knights, but he has, long since, won the affection of everybody who has read of his endless adventures.

I admit that while it is sometimes easy enough to define the enemies he attacks – those old Irish hobgoblins of Prudery, Hypocrisy, Deceit, Opportunism, Political Guile, Moral Cowardice, and so on – it is not at all easy to define the nature of the Dulcinea he defends. For he also spends so much of his time rushing headlong against a host of other well-known enemies outside Dublin and Connemara – in Russia, even, and he has a lurking weakness for Russia (in spite of *I Went to Russia*),[3] in London, in

1 "Don Quixote O'Flaherty" appeared in *The London Mercury and Bookman* 37 (April 1938): 170–5. It was later published under the same title in *The Bell* 2, no. 3 (June 1941): 28–36.
2 Most of what follows is, as the title suggests, an extended comparison between O'Flaherty and the eponymous hero of *Don Quixote* (1605), by Miguel de Cervantes (1547–1616).
3 O'Faolain discusses the following of O'Flaherty's works in this essay: *I Went to Russia* (1931); *The Informer* (1925); *The Black Soul* (1924); *Mr. Gilhooley* (1926); *The Puritan* (1932); *The Martyr* (1933); *The Assassin* (1928); *Thy Neighbour's*

Paris, in America – that one is left wondering whether the ideal beauty
that drives him on resides anywhere, even in an approximation, on this
mortal earth. He does not love the priest's niece, this Don Quixote de Los
Aran Islands: but has he not a very shrewd idea, also, that his Princess
Micomicona is nothing but that pimply young woman cunningly disguised? You may be, Don Liam, a rebel against the despotism of fact, but
you are no fool.

~

Wonder is his weapon – an undulled wonder at the things of life – and
folly is his enemy (in more senses than one). His own wonder sometimes
amazes him, and he transfers it constantly to his characters. I open *The
Informer* and on two pages I come upon:

> They were nodding their heads with that amazing prodigality of
> emotion ... Suddenly there was an amazing interruption ...
> Everybody, for some amazing reason or other, sniffed at the smell of
> fried sausages ... Gypo was unconscious of the amazement he had
> caused by his shout ... Mrs. McPhillip was not amazed ...

This round-eyedness is further dilated as we turn the pages.

> He had become seized by some violent emotion ... He was petrified
> ... For some reason or other he jumped to his feet ... Everybody was
> amazed ... Spurred by some sudden impulse ... He felt moved by an
> uncontrollable impulse ... There was an indescribable coldness ...

It is not the *amazings* and *terrifics*, though if O'Flaherty's typewriter
printed not letters but words these two words would be flattened bare by
now; it is the large vagueness of the *indescribable* that blows out the mind.
Always we feel that something vast has entered into the imagination of
the author, and we are impressed, and oppressed, by the weight of it.

How he can contain this emotion for any length of time we do not
know; and we have reason to believe that he does not. His books have the
impress of pressing time. Their violence, like the violence of his characters, suggests the scream of a safety-valve. In *The Black Soul*, one of his
earliest novels, he describes the madness of Red John, the island-man

---

Wife (1923); *Spring Sowing* (1924); *Famine* (1937); and *The Short Stories of Liam
O'Flaherty* (1937).

whose wife is seduced by The Stranger. Red John strips himself stark-naked and hides behind the door to attack his enemy, who, on coming out

saw Red John standing naked by the wall. He stood with wide-open mouth and staring eyes. His face got cold and then turned white. His nostrils distended. He stared into Red John's eyes and Red John stared into his ... Then Red John yelled and tore his jaws open to the utmost with his two hands, as if trying to vomit his fear in the intensity of the yell. He drew up his right leg to his buttock and struck against the wall with his sole. "Go away," he screamed, "go away; you are going to kill me ... "

It is typical, and it is almost symbolical, that yell with the jaws torn open by the two hands. It is primitive, epically wild, like the infant Achilles stuffing food into its mouth with its hands.[4] One feels that O'Flaherty writes in a kind of fury. Whether he does, or not, he whips us with his thyrsus until we are madly excited by communication with his emotion.[5]

Even the pattern of his novels suggests fury and speed in the writing, for in his favourite pattern he places one character at the centre, and the action whirls faster and faster around that centre with a centrifugal force that dazzles the eye. Gypo, in *The Informer*, Mr. *Gilhooley*, *The Puritan*, *The Martyr*, O'Connor in *The Black Soul*, and *The Assassin* are all pivotal characters in that way; and their brains, not unnaturally like ours who watch them, reel and stagger long before the end. There is no time for O'Flaherty to offer, or for us to demand, analysis of their behaviour. They act with an insane instinct, they shew their natures in external action – the quickest, as well as the least satisfactory, because least precise or positive, indication of what is going on inside. The priest in *The Black Soul*

blushed and fidgeted when talking. His face would darken suddenly and he would grip his side as if he had a stitch in it.

More definitely suggestive is the description of O'Daly's city-cultured daughter.

4 Achilles, a figure from Greek mythology, was said to be the greatest warrior of the Trojan War.
5 A thyrsus is a staff or spear.

Her eyes were just like her father's, blue, gleaming, fierce, cold eyes.
Her face was like her father's; the lips were thin and compressed. The
nose was straight and the nostrils were slightly distended. The rest of
her body was slight.

In the same way when his people labour under any emotion they have to
do something. The woman who dreams that she may yet have a child feels

the blood course madly up her neck swelling the veins as she shiv-
ered with passion. Often she rushed from the cabin of a Summer evening, her bodice open at the neck, her light shawl across her
shoulders, seeking love ...

It is nothing for these flesh-driven creatures to want to bite mountains, or
to want to swallow oceans; they gasp, choke, shiver, tremble, grip their
limbs, feel their muscles grow rigid, scream, sigh, weep. They never hide
or control their emotions; as if conceived dynamically, they must feel
daemonically. They must not cease from the dance until they drop, or are
sent hastily off the stage, like the priest who rows out into the Atlantic in
Thy Neighbour's Wife, or the Stranger who is hurried from the island in
The Black Soul, or the Martyr who is hurled blazing with petrol, with the
cross to which he is crucified, down into the lake hundreds of feet below
his Gethsemane.[6]

What commentary, what consideration, what remarks there are, by the
way, are not, naturally, impressive; they are too briefly and hurriedly
stated, and they are most often stated in faulty English. They are, indeed,
too often jejune and express childish prejudices, or judgments hardly
weighed before being thrown on the page. I gather these examples from
Thy Neighbour's Wife, O'Flaherty's first novel, because he shows his
weaknesses there more readily; later on he is more careful.

... just like women get the Order of the British Empire in England
during a war for upsetting hospitals or driving ambulances into
ditches.

6 Gethsemane is the name of the garden on Jerusalem's Mount of Olives, where
Jesus is said to have prayed before he was taken into custody to be crucified.

... the attitude of a bullock being herded to a slaughter-house that rushes hither and thither in an effort to escape.

... the mock-heroics that are labelled nationalism and the self-hypnotism that passes for religion.

... (the congregation) too busy with their own thoughts to pay any attention to the prayers.

He does not mind interpolating an "as O. Henry says,"[7] or "as H.G. Wells says," or "as Mr. de Valera would say." He does not mind breaking up his own well-created atmosphere with any kind of furious personal remark that comes into his head. But then, the immensity of his natural vigour, the undeniable fount of natural genius that has rightly put him at the head of the realistic school of his day, overwhelms our distaste and we are under his spell once more. He has more blemishes and more faults than any living writer of his rank, and he surmounts them all. He has only one serious enemy – the Second Reader.

I have spoken of O'Flaherty as being at the head of the realistic school of his day; it is realism with a difference, and strangely, he is far and away at his best when, in his short stories, he is not writing in that tradition at all.

The original realists, like Balzac, were men who merely used realism as a spring-board (I think that is Brunetière's word – *un tremplin*).[8] They dealt with types, as O'Flaherty does, and they aimed at effecting a generalisation, as he does; the aim of their work was moral, as his also is – they were, that is to say, to a large degree conscious reformers. But they embraced reality with a genuine affection, even for its most poignant things, so that one can feel Balzac revelling in what he overtly condemns, such as the struggle and revolt of Eugène de Rastignac, or the brutal independence of the ex-convict Vautrin.[9] There O'Flaherty, in common with all his school, parts company with the tradition that fed him. His work pulses with genuine hate. *Gilhooley, The Puritan, The Martyr* suffice to illustrate that. He

7 American writer O. Henry (1862–1910), né William Sydney Porter.
8 Ferdinand Brunetière (1849–1906), author of *Honoré de Balzac: 1799–1850* (1906).
9 Eugène de Rastignac and Vautrin are characters in Balzac's *Le Père Goriot* (1835).

is full of *saeva indignatio*[10] – he lacerates his heart – but where is the corresponding love? As I have said, we recognise the windmills of Don Quixote, but the Dulcinea we do not often see.

Nor is he that later acidulation of the realistic school – a Naturalist. For he could not, so vigorous a writer, so tireless a fighter, be called a pessimist; and he has not that "profound sympathy for humble toilers which is the very soul of English naturalism" – he kicks them soundly; nor has he anything of the exactitude of that school – which so loved facts, human documents, the exact anatomy of life, that they talked of fiction as if it were a kind of experimental science.

Essentially, I do believe, O'Flaherty is, like every known Irish writer, an inverted romantic. If he were a true realist he would look at life, and whatever faults he found with it, he would write of it with gusto. But there is in O'Flaherty less gusto than disgust. If he were a true romantic he would not see reality at all, he would see only his own dreams. But, as I have said, he is no fool, and when he has sought out, in his adventurous way, some fresh world, some hoped-for ideal, some smiling Dulcinea, he sees the old familiar pimply face of the priest's niece behind the powder and paint. Neither a realist, nor a romantic, then, nor yet a naturalistic writer, he sets out in the most self-conscious and deliberate way to attack with violence the things that hurt the inarticulated dream of his romantic soul. For he *has* a romantic soul; he has the inflated ego of the romantic, the dissatisfaction of the romantic, the grand imagination, the response to the magic of nature, the self-pity of the romantic, his masochistic rage, the unbalance. And these are the claws in which he takes reality and, like a gull with a shellfish, he lifts it up to an enormous height and lets it fall with a crash; while we are yet stunned by his gyring flight, and the reverberation of the impact, he then swoops to see if there is anything worth his respect in what he has already destroyed and, screaming, he flies away, unsatisfied.

In those lovely short stories, however, he is at rest. There he has found something that bears a resemblance to his ideal. Not in men, but in birds and animals; and often men are seen as cruel creatures who hunt and torment these dumb things. In *Spring Sowing* there is a perfect, a lovely, a tender story called "Three Lambs," and there, as in those other excellent stories, "The Hook," "The Cow's Death," "The Rockfish," one has the feeling that O'Flaherty has his ear to the earth, listening quietly.

The best of his short stories have now been opportunely collected into one volume, fifty-eight stories that are the pure distillation of natural

10 *Saeva indignatio* is Latin for "fierce indignation."

genius.[11] It is a bold saying, but I do believe that no book published this winter can come within a donkey's bray of it. Here, if anywhere, is Dulcinea – here, and in that more restless, more magnificent, almost Biblical last novel of his, *Famine*. It is the Irish "Exodus" in which there is no Moses to lead out the people of Israel, the starving Irish millions of the black forties to whom a moonstruck O'Connell was no help. It is characteristic of O'Flaherty that in *Famine* he lifts his theme out of the rut of despair by combining two of his best qualities – his power of describing natural phenomena, and his love for a big central figure to typify the things he hates or (as in this book) admires.

~

On O'Flaherty as on Joyce I shall always look as on men in search of a Holy Grail. It is, this grail, an ideal loveliness, and it is a loveliness that is different to all other forms of loveliness, as their natures, being the natures of Irishmen, are different to the natures of all other men. That juxtaposition in Joyce of the tawdry and the tender, as in O'Flaherty, though rarely in the same book – he is really less various than Joyce – of the gentle and the ferocious, is nothing but the mark of the disappointment these men feel at not finding anywhere in life enough ideal beauty to make a coat to cover themselves from the world's winds. More wise, more of an artist, a man of far more sensitiveness, a man of taste, Joyce knows what he is doing – knows that like Stephen Daedalus he carries through all the squalor of life the chalice of his heart's ineffable desire for beauty; he knows that however life may sully his dream, it can never destroy these grails that the Stephens of the world carry through the muddy streets.[12] O'Flaherty is not so sure. His grail slips from his grasp at every turn of the road. He has less faith, and little vision. He has more vigour, hardly any wisdom. He has great courage, no direction. He tilts too much at windmills. He falls more often. But since he is good-humoured enough about it all, we cannot but love him.

All modern Irish literature is a search after that Irish grail, and because there is so much that the mass of Irishmen interpose between themselves and its service, so much evasion, so much timidity, such an endless shoal of stinking red-herrings, so much brushwood of every conceivable kind, Irish men of letters only glimpse it in snatches. In England it could be

11 *O'Faolain's note: The Short Stories of Liam O'Flaherty.* Cape. 7s. 6d.
12 Stephen Dedalus, whose name O'Faolain repeatedly misspells, is the protagonist of James Joyce's *A Portrait of the Artist as a Young Man.*

called the English tradition, or the English norm of life. Here the tradition is not formed yet, the norm of life has not been established. "Let me get at it!" cries O'Flaherty, and he wastes his spirit in grappling with the obstacles, and his books are often a sour record of these fruitless fights.

I have no love for national literature as nationalists understand it. O'Flaherty's Irish nationalists would tear him limb from limb if they had their way, as their Welsh counterparts would with Caradoc Evans, and as some Scotsmen would with Eric Linklater, who is only occasionally pertinent to, and impertinent to, Scottish life.[13] It is purely a matter of life feeding literature, or life not feeding literature. In so far – to put it no stronger – as O'Flaherty is moved constantly by life near at hand to his emotions, he has always fought for a real thing, and a vital thing. And I think it matters not in the least that his Dulcinea is for ever, and will be for ever, masked and anonymous. She is the as yet uncreated beauty, and all the names – Little Dark Rose or Poor Old Woman – that others have given her do not in the least define her for him.[14] She is an ideal Ireland too lovely to describe except in terms of her shadows – those enemies of hers and his against whom he is for ever spurring his Rozinante.

13 Caradoc Evans (1878–1945) was critical of the Welsh in his unvarnished fiction, and Eric Linklater (1899–1974) was a noted satirist.
14 Little Dark Rose and Poor Old Woman are, like Cathleen ni Houlihan, pseudonyms for Ireland, which is often depicted as a downtrodden female and thus in need of knights like Don Liam O'Flaherty to be rescued.

Æ and W.B.[1]

When I look at the large book which constitutes Yeats's effort to explain the nature of life and thought, *A Vision*, I want to think back into a certain corner of the latter half of the nineteenth century.[2] That particular aspect of nineteenth-century life is represented for me by a few fragments that persisted into my time. I see a laneway somewhere behind the National Gallery in London where, in a dark and poky shop, painted a hideous blue, I bought my first books about what used to be called The Occult.[3] There is a familiar villa door – one of the hundreds such scattered all over London's suburbia – with a tarnished brass plate, rubbed into holes at the corners, faintly announcing séances for given nights in the week. Its only counterpart in Dublin is the stable door near the old Huguenot Cemetery by the Shelbourne Hotel where the Hermetic Society still meets.[4] Or I hear again a sibyl in Gordon Hall, Boston, answering the eager-timid questions of her audience about dead relatives, and I feel again the painful embarrassment of each palpitating questioner.[5] There is

1 "Æ and W.B." appeared in *The Virginia Quarterly Review* 15, no. 1 (Winter 1939): 41–57.
2 *A Vision: An Explanation of Life Founded upon the Writings of Giraldus and upon Certain Doctrines Attributed to Kusta ben Luka* (1925). Giraldus Cambrensis (c. 1146–c. 1223), was a Welsh archdeacon and historian, and Kusta ben Luka (820–912), also known as Qusta ibn Luqa, was a Byzantine Greek scientist.
3 The National Gallery, founded in 1824, is located in Trafalgar Square.
4 A Huguenot is a French Protestant. The Shelbourne Hotel is a luxurious establishment located on St. Stephen's Green. The Hermetic Society followed the occult religion of Hermetism.
5 Gordon Hall is a building belonging to Harvard University.

one evening spent listening to Annie Besant.[6] There is Yeats talking about a strange experience with a medium in Soho. These are all the personal scraps I have from that extraordinary period after 1850, when, as if in reaction from the despair of Darwinian materialism, there arose a fever of what I can only call pseudo-religiosity usually mingled with interest in the arcane. Buchmanism, in our day, is one such reaction from Marxist materialism and post-war pessimism, but there is no spookism worth talking about.[7]

And one reads up the period: reads that spiritualism arose, in America, some time around 1848; it still flourishes. That Madame Blavatsky was working towards Theosophy;[8] the Theosophical Society was founded in 1875; it had reached Dublin within ten years – Yeats gave the opening address to the Dublin Hermetic Society. The first paper dealt with spiritualism and the fourth dimension. Christian Science was founded by Mrs. Eddy in 1866; the First Church was established in Boston in 1879.[9] I think it fair to say that the defining motto was, "All Is Infinite Mind." There was at the same time a revival of interest in Swedenborg, Hinduism, Buddhism, the Hermetic Writings, Rosicrucianism, Egyptian religions, Jakob Boehme.[10] One may check up on that by looking at any good library catalogue under these headings, just as one may, in the future, check on the modern revival of interest in Kierkegaard.[11] There are, for instance, several English biographies of Swedenborg after 1854. The wide popularity of *The Light of Asia* would alone testify to the interest in Indian thought in the last quarter of the century if there were not, again, a striking increase in the number of books on Indian ideas from the same

6 Annie Besant (1847–1933) was a British social reformer and theosophist.

7 Buchmanism was a non-denominational revivalist movement begun by Frank N.D. Buchman (1878–1961).

8 Helena Petrovna Blavatsky (1831–1891) co-founded the Theosophical Society. Theosophy, many of whose adherents overlapped with the Hermetic Society, was an occult belief system founded in the nineteenth century.

9 Christian Science is a religion, known for its practice of spiritual healing, founded by Mary Baker Eddy (1821–1910).

10 Emanuel Swedenborg (1688–1772) was a Swedish scientist, philosopher, and mystic theologian. Rosicrucianism is an occult belief system that takes its name from the order's symbol, a rose on a cross. Jakob Boehme (1575–1624), or Böhme, was a philosophical mystic.

11 Søren Kierkegaard (1813–1855) was a Danish philosopher who influenced the development of existentialism.

period.[12] Not in the least pseudo, but indicative of the general interest in the unusual is the foundation of the Egyptian Exploration Fund in 1883. It happens to coincide with the first of the many exciting books since published by Flinders Petrie – a man as eagerly read by Æ as Sankara or Patanjali.[13] Scientific studies into the nature of the mind itself were further aërating the intellectual atmosphere. Hypnotism was taken out of the hands of experimenters and charlatans when it was favourably reported on by the British Medical Association in 1892. Charcot's studies in pathology were published between 1886 and 1890.[14] William James was simultaneously experimenting in psychology, in America.[15] The Freudian subconscious was about to be laid bare. Poetry, responding, possibly, to the general fermentation was, with such as Rimbaud, Mallarmé, Laforgue, subjective, symbolist, inhuman, non-realistic, twilit.[16]

The young intellectuals of the time had thus, if their natures had any such disposition – and we know that it was so with young Yeats and Æ – an entry into an excitingly Eleusinian subworld, half hocus-pocus, half sincere, now soporific, now stimulating, where thought could be levitated into the stratosphere like a dream. They generally entered that hangar of the mind via the poky shop in the back lane; and in its back room they ballooned out of it. For Yeats and Æ it could have been otherwise if they had grown up in London or Paris, in a certain cultivated milieu; for in such cities there are milieus where the intellect is rarefied without being fantastic, and one may sift the strangest ideas without having to mix with lunatics and cranks for the sake of heterodoxy. They need not have gone to Paris. Christiania, small as it was, would have done. But not Dublin. Dublin rotted on the stalk of the eighteenth century. In Dublin there was only orthodoxy or hysteria.

12 *The Light of Asia, or, The Great Renunciation* (1879), by Sir Edwin Arnold (1832–1904).

13 Sir Flinders Petrie (1853–1942) was a renowned British archeologist and Egyptologist. Adi Shankara (spelled Sankara by O'Faolain) (c. 700–750) was an Indian philosopher and theologian. Patanjali was a major author of Yogic thought in ancient India.

14 Jean-Martin Charcot (1825–1863) was a French doctor who co-founded modern neurology.

15 William James (1842–1910), the brother of American novelist Henry James (1843–1916), was a leading psychologist of his day.

16 French symbolist poets Arthur Rimbaud (1854–1891), Stéphane Mallarmé (1842–1898), and Jules Laforgue (1860–1887).

~

There are innumerable indications that both Yeats and Æ attracted to themselves some of these floating ideas. Their interest in Theosophy, for instance, is a matter of history; but Theosophy was such a hotchpotch, and so hopelessly non-intellectual and disorderly – especially at the start – that it led them both down many bypaths. Yeats playing about with Rosicrucianism, with alchemy, with magic, even with table rapping, doing such fanciful things as putting out all the lights but a little roman lamp in – was it? – Edward Martyn's castle and imagining himself taking part in some fantastic romance – all that kind of thing one knows about;[17] and, in so far as one bothers with it at all, one dismisses it as the natural caparison of young and febrile genius. What really is important is the subjection of the mind to what these things symbolised. George Moore, on the contrary, had his python and his incense, but did he subject his mind to La Bohème?[18]

This mental subjection is something more easily felt than defined. What synthesis Yeats managed to evolve out of his multifarious interests emerges, in so far as it ever emerges, in fits and starts, and was always subject to a kind of catalepsy.[19] I once spent months trying to list these interests for the fun of seeing what he got from each. It was my invariable experience that by the time I had plodded one-tenth of the way down any particular avenue, such as Indian philosophy, he was away down the second-next one, plucking up the golden apples as fast as he could run. He never, I saw, had studied anything deeply. His amazingly sensitive and receptive mind – were it trained he would have made an excellent scholar – were it, rather, capable of being trained – rapidly elicited the interesting thing, or the essential thing, and the rest was ruthlessly abandoned. He had and has no interest in knowledge, fact, or objective truth, for its own sake. All one can do, therefore, is to observe the essential fact that his subjection was an act of will, of need – he rejected the intellectual approach.

He wished for the lightning flash. He dreamed, accordingly, of a Sacred Book. He found many such. Now it was *Axël*. Now *Alastor*. Now *Manfred*,

17 Irish author Edward Martyn (1859–1923).
18 La Bohème refers to a bohemian life.
19 Catalepsy is a nervous disorder whereby the body becomes rigid, in a manner somewhat similar to rigor mortis.

Athanasius, or Ahasuerus.[20] Now the work of some Cambridge Platonist of the seventeenth century. When he found that Blake revered the revelatory imagination he bowed down and adored.[21] It is to be particularly noticed that all this is a private dream – revelation; the lonely thinker; it is separate; it is non-gregarious. So is his great idea of the unifying personality. Here he adored the man brought into unity by a mood – which is personality – as against static unity – which is character. That idea he may have taken – I believe he did so take it – from his father, the painter, and it has been one of his most important and formative ideas. His debt to his father has never been assessed; all his major ideas are better and more clearly expressed by John Yeats in *Evening Memories*.[22] For from him, too, he took another equally important idea – that the world had been broken into fragments shortly before the birth of Shakespeare, and therefore an artist who would try for Unity of Being (John Yeats gave him the term, Unity of Being) must find some traditional subject, in working over which the disintegrating separateness of the modern over-intellectualised artist would be countered, and the old breadth and stability and harmony return again. That subject Ireland gave him, and as it, too, had its magic, its folklore, its ancient memory, its mystery, and its passionate love of life, and its non-intellectual simplicity, he was able to alight there, safe for a time, out of the esoteric balloon.

It was an extraordinary voyage and it had an unexpected conclusion; and naturally we can more easily observe the end than record the fluxive currents that had, before he alighted, blown him this way and that. We know, however, that having thus published three or four books with an Irish flavour, he floated off again into the symbolism of the Rose poems. Of these he says in the autobiography that "there was something compelling me to attempt creation of an art as separate ... as some Herodiade of our theatre dancing seemingly alone in her narrow moving luminous

---

20 *Axël* (1890), by Auguste, comte de Villiers de l'Isle-Adam. *Alastor* (1816), by English poet Percy Bysshe Shelley (1792–1822). *Manfred* (1817), by English poet Lord Byron (1788–1824). Saint Athanasius (c. 293–373) was a theologian and Egyptian statesman. Ahasuerus is a name given to the Wandering Jew in a German pamphlet dating from 1602.
21 William Blake (1757–1827) was an English artist, poet, and visionary who was a major influence on Yeats.
22 The book in question, by John Butler Yeats (1839–1922), is actually titled *Early Memories; some chapters of autobiography* (1923).

circle."[23] So persistent was the attraction of the mysterious, the eclectic, the secret, the personal isolated communion.

But – and this is the interesting antipode and for him the vitalising influence, since he lives, one might say, deliberately by conflict – he was aware of a tidal movement in his nature, in and out of his private self. "It is perhaps because nature made me a gregarious man that I love proud and lonely things. When I was a child … I found one poem that delighted me beyond all others: a fragment from Aristophanes wherein the birds sang scorn upon mankind." Again: "In later years my mind gave itself to gregarious Shelley's dream of a young man studying philosophy in some lonely tower, or of his old man hidden from human sight in some shell-strewn cavern on the Mediterranean shore."

Later – far later, in the late 1920s – he discovered Hegel and was there confirmed in this idea of life as an antinomy.[24] For the formative period of his life he was simply groping about here and there, happy with any kind of imagery or crude expression of his innate feeling that the duality of a man's nature is the germinating element in him. It was an unhelpful period, I cannot help feeling, and I think how in the 'seventies, Ibsen, much better off in this respect, was reading Hegel, Schopenhauer, Hartmann; trying in *Emperor and Galilean* to resolve the conflict of the blind will of nature with the personal will of man; forcing his people to take part in a world struggle over ideas; inventing a Third Empire out of the conflict between opposing powers in life; posing Hegel against Comte; dissecting his own abilities and desires in terms of contemporary philosophy and religion.[25] No – Dublin was not helpful, nor even London. It was inevitable that Yeats should have had to serpentine towards his final position, and it is another tribute to the inviolability of genius, and his genius in particular, that he managed to sidestep so many provincial temptations – even to use them – and guard himself, and keep himself intact. The Marxist critic will never be able to do anything with Yeats.

∾

23 The line comes from Yeats's *Autobiographies* (1926); the quotes in the paragraph that follows are also taken from this source.
24 German philosopher Georg Wilhelm Friedrich Hegel (1770–1831).
25 German philosophers Eduard von Hartmann (1842–1906) and Arthur Schopenhauer (1788–1860). *Emperor and Galilean* (1873), by Norwegian playwright Henrik Ibsen (1828–1906). French philosopher and founder of sociology Auguste Comte (1798–1857).

Æ, meantime, was being much more obvious and direct about it all. He embraced Indian philosophy at the start, and as he kept close to it all his life it gave direction to all his reading and bottom to his thought. He did so because he was disposed to be much more simple of heart; and disposed, especially, to be intellectually persistent. He, also, believed in the lightning flash, but he chose a particular brand of lightning and "since then used no other." He was not arrogant, nor egotistical – the philosophy he embraced involved self-subjugation to the point of self-suppression – and he had a gift of accepting and rapidly adapting. He had not a father who put things endlessly to the question, fraying them away and away while insisting, in a typically Yeatsian manner, that no artist should have any opinions; a man sociable with his equals, antisocial with the masses; mischievous of mind, complex, saved from being a talker pure and simple by the fact that he had a tactile itch – was, that is to say, a painter. Æ was tolerant and unassuming, was so little sensuous that the imagery of his verse is as impalpable as a veil. He was mild and kind, was almost without sensuality, and could easily have been a priest. The main difference between him and his young friend was that he looked at life with the eyes of innocence and the other looked at life with the eyes of desire. The important element in him – the defining element – is his sweet toleration.

That tolerance was of the two main kinds that we meet in life. In the spirit of the first kind we say: "For an Atheist – or a Communist or a Fascist – he is a grand fellow"; and we view the world as a series of groups, and all activity emerges as compromise. In the spirit of the second kind of tolerance we say: "He is an Atheist, et cetera. *But* he is a grand fellow," and that means that we hold to our own ethic more firmly, and all activity emerges as indoctrination, apologues, propaganda, sorrowful friendship, and the tolerant man is either restless and self-driven, or he is shy and timid and withdrawn. Æ was now one, now the other. In his social work he was the propagandist. In his poetry he was both – integrated by what was virtually a form of religious verse. There is really no progression in that verse: it is the same note at the end and at the beginning; there is neither advance nor decline.

~

Obviously we have two dispositions that, though alike in a hundred ways, differ in some essential way; two men brought up in circumstances unusually similar, diverge at some crucial point.

Is it simply a conflicting conception of character and personality? Character which implies static morality, and morality which implies an order in nature, and an order in nature which, by implying co-operation, self-subjugation, rational control, brings us back to character once again? Personality, which (in the Yeatsian concept of what that term means) is fluid; which does not form the mechanical contrast to character of being amoral, or questioning an order in nature, but which *is* egocentric and therefore not so submissive to the order of nature? If anything it tends to mould the order of nature to its fancy; for it does not easily co-operate, or subjugate itself, as character does. Is this the distinction between Yeats and Æ? I think it is, mainly, this which distinguishes them. But I also see that Yeats has, in the conflicting duality of his nature, a concept of personality which is largely a reflection of his own bi-valvular nature, and is therefore at odds with itself.

I see this when I turn to *A Vision* to see what is the natural object of the natural ego, or Will, in his philosophy, and find that its "idea of good" is defined as something made for man, out of his dæmon's "memory of the moments of exaltation in his past lives," Here it is not necessary to discuss the question of reincarnation. The essential point is the phrase "moments of exaltation"; and its logical – I beg Yeats's pardon for the use of a hateful word – its logical implication is that all such moments unite only in the isolated ego, never in any permanent synthesis of themselves outside the ego, never in any order capable of being considered apart from the ego which gives them their sole value, and which therefore deprives them of all value for any other man's ego. What Kant calls the "reign of ends" is denied therein.[26] It means that exaltation is not only transitory – which we all admit – but fragile; which I, at any rate, and everybody who with me admits an order in nature must deny. In short, the object of the Yeatsian Will is not capable of being regarded objectively. It has no extra-personal continuity. It is an object like the Stoic's concept of virtue – pure form independent of realisation. It is most natural, then, that Æ should feel that a will which has no object is not a will, as without a target it is impossible to conceive of a gun.

~

A man with such a philosophy could never, it is evident, be anything but a disconnected man. There would be no evident continuity in his poetry, thought, feeling, colour, what not. But no such man could exist and Yeats is not such a phantasm. He is too firmly founded in life, too passionate,

26 German philosopher Immanuel Kant (1724–1804) developed the idea of a Kingdom of Ends in his *Groundwork of the Metaphysics of Morals* (1785).

gregarious, intensely sensitive, too arrogant to live in so dim a cavern. He has, indeed, as I have shown from his autobiography, liked to think of himself as a lonely sage in a lonely tower or a sea cavern, studying strange tomes; but he has outlived that. He thinks to find in a concept of personality, that does not bear examination, a symbol to unite his human gregariousness and his artistic loneliness. It is inadequate. It throws its weight on the loneliness far too heavily. It is a rôle, a self-dramatisation not powerful enough for the life in the actor himself. It is appalling in its self-consciousness, in its power to deceive and mislead him – as it has done time and again – as all ideas must that are incubated in isolation.

Above all, it is so unnecessary, so falsely romantic. Yeats is not, by nature, either so romantic or so lonely as his rôle might suggest. He is a public figure, if a rather vague one. And when I think of the modern men who seem not to have lived by static character but by personality, the names that come to me are the names of other gregarious men – Johnson, Landor, Donne, Dick Steele, Sterne, Horace Walpole, Goldsmith; and to these, none romantics, the one romantic, Shelley.[27] I think of men whose character was static, and think of lonely Arnold, Wordsworth, Gray, Tennyson, Rousseau, and possibly Browning – all romantics except Gray.[28] And surely it is to the former company rather than the latter that Yeats belongs. His poetry strikes me as having, at its best and most representative – the later, final poetry – the metaphysical quality of Donne, and the virile clarity of Landor. It has none of the particularisation of the romantic poetry of 1800–1850. How many concrete images could one collect from the whole corpus of it? It is wholly egocentric – man at the centre of the world looking out at the universe – which is the characteristic of eighteenth-century art. It has the true Aristotelian attitude towards nature – it is not subservient to it, it selects its beauties, it perfects its charms, it is never imitative of nature but it is nature wrought to a finer pitch; and these are Dryden's phrases.[29] It does what the old classical dogma about the twin arts of painting and poetry always asked poetry to do – "presents us with images

27 British authors Samuel Johnson, Walter Savage Landor (1775–1864), John Donne (1572–1631), and Horace Walpole (1717–1797); and Irish authors Richard Steele (1672–1729), Laurence Sterne, and Oliver Goldsmith (1730–1774).
28 British authors Matthew Arnold (1822–1888), William Wordsworth (1770–1850), Thomas Gray (1716–1771), Alfred, Lord Tennyson, and Robert Barrett Browning; and Swiss author Jean-Jacques Rousseau (1712–1778).
29 English author John Dryden (1631–1700); the quote that follows is taken from his essay "A Parallel of Poetry and Painting" (1695).

more perfect than the life in any individual and we have the pleasure to see all the scattered beauties of nature united in a happy chemistry without deformities or faults." Again, Dryden. If that is to be called Romanticism, it is at most the orderly "Romanticism" of the Pre-Raphaelites which was, in actuality, a turning back of the clock to the times behind the disorder of the soul in the eighteenth century. If the essential Yeats has any literary affinities it is with gregarious men of the eighteenth century.

In the eighteenth century men could live by personality because their world was ordered. In the nineteenth century men more commonly lived by character because their world was disordered. Every Romantic of the nineteenth century was either a moralist or a radical – like Rousseau, or the Radical Blake and the Radical Shelley. But because a man cannot but reflect his time the art of the eighteenth century is a formal and orderly art, and the art of the nineteenth century is explorative art. You cannot live by fluid personality in a fluxive world – you have to hold order within you as a bulwark against the chaos outside. It is the chaos which creates the internal order; the outer order which releases the internal flux. Yeats was born out of time. He should have been from the beginning in conflict with it.

In all Yeats's earlier verse that conflict was evaded. He found material to hand on which he expended a marvellous virtuosity, and gave us the shimmer of the tenuous but lovely poetry of his youth; all up to 1900. For another fifteen years he found a more practical object for his will in public affairs and private griefs. The volumes of 1919 (*The Wild Swans at Coole*) and 1921 (*Michael Robartes and the Dancer*) are turning points. He is facing up to the largest questions; thought is deepening as the conflict becomes intensified. By 1928 (*The Tower*), he is taut with fight. That volume and all after it to the two latest books (*The Herne's Egg*, 1937, and *New Poems*, 1938) are poetry from a mind which has consolidated, as a result of conflict, a non-intellectual, imaginative conception of order in life. The veracity of that conception is not in question. His concept was as adequate – which is all that was required of it – as the imaginative conception of order which Shelley formed on the basis of his pseudo-scientific reading, his radical disposition, his subjection to Godwin.[30] It is by these volumes since 1919 that Yeats will live. In them he was released – that is all one cares. They contain the man. His ideas no more concern us than the ideas of Shelley concern us. Did artists ever agree about anything?

30 English philosopher and radical political journalist William Godwin (1756–1836) was also Shelley's father-in-law.

I do not suppose, in the end, that it matters a penny what conflict engages a man's will and extracts his highest possible voltage out of him. But if one dared to grumble, at all, at chance, I should curse that early subjection of Yeats's mind to the Alastor complex, the Axël complex – the illusion of Faust that happiness and beauty and wisdom could be won in seclusion from life. Goethe could have told him the truth on that.[31] Shelley could not have told him, but Shelley's life would have – that angel whose reading and whose studies were like the reading and studies of some young radical out of Sheffield University or a Worker's College in Manchester.[32] I know what Yeats would say to that – that such things are fated. But are they? Is the brain a flea that can only jump, the will a louse that can only creep? The pride a wind not to be directed? Is art a slavery or is it not?

This poet of the eighteenth century, born by strange lot into that fantastically aërated, unsolid, feverish, dim, flibbertigibbety period at the end of the nineteenth century – which, because it seemed to be economically solid, only remembered in the dark patches of the night or in the honest minds of a few of its poets, or in the troubled mindlessness of its would-be seers, that it was emotionally a shifting bog – was, not unnaturally, disintegrated; as we are after the European War, and in this time of wars that break out like boils. And he, not unnaturally, hoped for some kind of revelation that would replace the blankness of life, as we, hopeless of revelation, have made our compromise with pointless subjectivity or crude realism. In his very latest book he still asks for the lightning flash:

Grant me an old man's frenzy.
Myself I must remake
Till I am Timon and Lear
Or that William Blake
Who beat upon the wall
Till truth obeyed his call;

A mind Michael Angelo knew
That can pierce the clouds
Or inspired by frenzy
Shake the dead in their shrouds,

31 German author Johann Wolfgang von Goethe (1749–1832).
32 The University of Sheffield was founded in 1905.

Forgotten else by mankind
An old man's eagle mind.[33]

An ironic folly, looked at in one way – for why should a man ask to write magnificently when he writes magnificently?

~

In a sense that nothing in a poet matters but his poetry, all this is folly unless it serves as a thread of Ariadne.[34] I take up the *Collected Poems*, 1934, and as I turn the pages slowly, recalling the flavour and scent of each flower of rhyme, I feel the silken thread slipping helpfully through my fingers. I have asked certain questions about his will, and his mind, and pride, and the answers are here. Here are poems that smell of the smoky lamp of the back shop, and the faded bookmarks left in little called-for books out of the British Museum, bog myrtle smell from Sligo and Gort.[35] From 'eighty-five – interested in Theosophy and attracted by the picturesque Ireland. Blake and Symbolism from 'ninety; for though he did not meet Verlaine until 'ninety-four, and Symons not, probably, until 'ninety-six, the general idea was abroad for years.[36] Here is *The Rose*, in 'ninety-three, and *The Wind among the Reeds*, in 'ninety-nine, with the last drops from the Symbolist flagon. Always, however, the Irish note sounds out like a dance to which this wine is but a drug. By 1903 we see the effect of the Theatre, of passionate fruity life from the heart of John Synge, controversy and fight, "the gutter" – "I am trying to put a less dream-burthened will into my work."[37] By 1906 he is driving out of the

33 "An Acre of Grass" (1938). The second line of the first stanza is often printed as "Myself must I remake."
34 In Greek mythology, Ariadne gave Theseus a thread so that he could find his way out of the Labyrinth.
35 The British Museum, located in the London district of Bloomsbury, was established by act of Parliament in 1753. Yeats was born in Sligo, and lived for a time near the village of Gort, County Galway.
36 French poet Paul Verlaine (1844–1896) and English poet Arthur Symons (1865–1945); Symons also wrote *The Symbolist Movement in Literature* (1899).
37 From the closing remarks to Yeats's collection of poetry *In the Seven Woods* (1903), which also included his play *On Baile's Strand*. Writing of the collection, Yeats's passage actually runs: "The first shape of it came to me in a dream, but it changed much in the making, foreshadowing, it may be, a change that may bring a less dream-burdened will into my verses." In O'Faolain's version, there is considerably more will and intent in Yeats's future direction as a poet ("trying") whereas the original is less certain ("may be," "may").

cocoon of mind, delighting in "the whole man, blood, intellect, and imagination running together."[38] But experience is costly and he is complaining in *The Green Helmet*, of 1910, about the poems he did not find time to write since his last previous volume – which was 1904. By 1916 he has written more than enough to establish him in his place, but he is far from the end of his long road, and it is a somewhat weary man who writes, in *The Wild Swans at Coole*, 1919:

I would be ignorant as the dawn
That has looked down
On that old queen measuring a town
With the pin of a brooch,
Or on the withered men that saw
From their pedantic Babylon
The careless planets in their courses,
The stars fade out where the moon comes,
And took their tablets and did sums;
I would be ignorant as the dawn
That merely stood, rocking the glittering coach
Above the cloudy shoulders of the horses;
I would be – for no knowledge is worth a straw –
Ignorant and wanton as the dawn.[39]

There, surely, still are webs of dream clinging to the will? The studious, self-conscious deliberation to appear unstudious – "the withered men," "pedantic Babylon," "took their tablets and did sums," "the pin of a brooch." And the old desire to escape, to be unchained like a hawk from the wrist. But take the whole volume of that year and there is a freshness of impulse and a purity of desire that, for not being what it had been, made the critics dislike the new note. What can one say of this, almost of the same time?

Never until this night have I been stirred.
The elaborate starlight throws a reflection
On the dark stream,
Till all the eddies gleam;
And thereupon there comes that scream

---

38 From "Personality and the Intellectual Essences." This appeared in *Discoveries*, which was published in 1907, not 1906.
39 "The Dawn."

From terrified, invisible beast or bird:
Image of poignant recollection ...[40]

Or, the same volume of 1921, *Michael Robartes*:

Turning and turning in the widening gyre
The falcon cannot hear the falconer;
Things fall apart; the centre cannot hold;
Mere anarchy is loosed upon the world,
The blood-dimmed tide is loosed, and everywhere
The ceremony of innocence is drowned;
The best lack all conviction, while the worst
Are full of passionate intensity.[41]

There is power, control, internal vision of order to match the outer chaos, a tragic vigour that is not rôle, or pose, but will, and brain, and pride pushing with all their might against the falling dykes of the world. There is genuine conflict in which the whole man, *not* "in harmony with himself" – self by itself is nothing – but in harmony with both his original or naked nucleus of being and with outer life, has produced a work of rare beauty that is the symbol or expression of self and world. And it has been so with Yeats from that 1921 volume, his turning point, to the present day.

For I know no other art but this; the art of a man who writes out of his naked nucleus of self, his original, primal cure of being, with and about those accretions of thought, habit, opinion, desire, that common or traditional life wraps about each one of us. These accretions are mostly alien, habits and sanctions that are merely habits and sanctions by chance of time and place and training; but a few are inherited wisdom; and all are bits of life as it is lived. We cannot go into a tower away from these things. They are our language with which we work on men's minds, symbols to hate or symbols to admire, the stuff of argument, the stuff of poetry and prose – cancer or coitus; Communism or Catholicism; that love is divine or that love is the Devil; that all fathers are fools, like Lear or old Goriot;[42] that Nature hears and sorrows for us; or that Nature is a stone. What is any literary movement but this opposition and alliance of naked self and

40 "An Image from a Past Life."
41 "The Second Coming."
42 Lear and old Goriot are characters in Shakespeare's *King Lear* (1608) and Honoré de Balzac's *Le Père Goriot*.

caparisoned self? A current life perfectly expressed by a man who has the clear-sightedness to see it as it is reflected in himself – Narcissus finding himself his own pool. Every artist becomes, thus, the critic of his times, which, though merged into him, may as easily evoke hate as love. As for who becomes the critic of the artist, that can only be another artist whose eyesight we may compare with his fellow's; so that Pope does not drop into his place until we have read Goldsmith, nor Goldsmith until we have read Defoe, nor Defoe until we read Sterne, nor Yeats until we read Æ.[43]

So, what is Balzac but the Monarchy of July loved and hated – loved with delight because it is life and Balzac, hated because it is not Balzac *tout nu*?[44] What is Ibsen but Norway hated because it is not Ibsen, would not with Ibsen fight beside Denmark, would not with Ibsen form a Scandinavian hegemony, would not be what Ibsen thought God made Ibsen – and loved because it is Ibsen's youth, wife, dreams, his mother who bore him naked into the world? What is Yeats but Ireland loved because it is life, and because it is what Yeats thinks he is – passionate, and proud, and gay, and noble; or hated because it is none of these things?

In all I have said about Yeats I have been thinking of him as a man who had factitious ideas about himself in his youth, in his maturity. He evaded life "early and often," as we all do, and what in those moments or years he wrote will not last because they are neither self nor life but merely mechanical pose, or mechanical opposition, or mechanical temper – the product of self-consciousness; in crude words, fake personality. But what in his years he wrote came out of his real and naked self, and came out of conflict between that self and his caparisoned self which is the image of what life in Ireland is like as far as concerns him as observer. All the Rose poems are factitious personality – splendid virtuosity, indeed, but what is that but to say "mere words"? Time alone, comparison with his fellows, will sift the real from the fake.

As for Æ, I loved him and we all loved him as a man. As for his poems, they are sweet and they are noble, but they are not Æ and they are not life. Yeats was right enough about Æ. He sought not himself but a way of life, and no man who does not find himself can find life. His best poems, like "We must pass like smoke or live within the spirit's fire,"[45] are the

---

43 English authors Alexander Pope (1688–1744) and Daniel Defoe.
44 The July Monarchy was the reign of France by Louis-Philippe from 1830 to 1848. The July Revolution installed the new regime. *Tout nu* is French for "stark naked."
45 The title of the poem in question is Æ's "Immortality" (1913).

perfect expression of traditional wisdom as he adapts it, hardly altering it. In the volume before me, *The Living Torch*, we have some of his best work, and it is almost exclusively day-by-day journalism, though journalism without peer.[46] There he is himself as the sage who sees all things, even the most commonplace, as part of the eternal procession. But his conception of order to which all things are related is a traditional conception, not, need it be said, the less admirable and satisfying for that reason, though the less interesting for being "found" rather than "self-won."

When one places Æ and W. B. in opposition to each other it is this that finally emerges – that the poetry of Yeats is the poetry of a personality; unsure, unequal, adventurous, most satisfying when it is most personal, dismaying when it is least personal – even tiresome then, of an egregious folly; while the poetry of Æ, like the poetry of Crashaw, or Herbert, or Vaughan, is the poetry of character, satisfying when felicitous, its enemy triteness and mechanical sentiment.[47] If I were to be wrecked with either on a desert island, or have the choice of either as a companion in death, I should not hesitate which to choose. For the desert island I should choose Æ – and read Yeats. For the end – Yeats. Because we live as we can, but we die as we must. I should get no companionship from Yeats; he is wrapped up in his own world, like Joyce – another gregarious man who writes like a hermit – and he is full of ideas but he has no intellect, having no continuity but his lyric mood. But, as against Æ's kindness, tolerance, journalism, sociability, and wisdom, he has what is more to the point of a crisis – pride, and passion. If God could only have mingled the two of them. Or if youth had not lured them with the bauble of the esoteric. But ... "all things can tempt us from this craft of verse"![48]

46 *The Living Torch* (1937).
47 British religious poet Richard Crashaw (1613–1649), and Welsh metaphysical poets George Herbert (1593–1633) and Henry Vaughan (1622–1695).
48 This is the first line of Yeats's "All Things Can Tempt Me" (1910); however, as the title suggests, the word "us" in O'Faolain's quote should be "me."

Essays: 1940–45

This is Your Magazine[1]

THE BELL has, in the usual sense of the word, no policy. We leave it to nature to give the magazine its own time-created character. A boy grows into personality. A man is worth calling a man only in so far as he defines his own character for himself – makes it up out of the gifts of his fathers, the memories of his childhood, the dreams of his boyhood, the ambitions of his youth, the passions of his years, the strength of his own four bones. This magazine will, likewise, grow into character and meaning. By the time you have read three issues you will be familiar with its character. By the time you have read twelve you will take its character for granted. That would not happen with every magazine, but this is not so much a magazine as a bit of Life itself, and we believe in Life, and leave Life to shape us after her own image and likeness.

That was why we chose the name of the THE BELL. Any other equally spare and hard and simple word would have done; any word with a minimum of associations. If you begin to think of alternatives you will see why we could not have used any of the old symbolic words. They are as dead as Brian Boru, Granuaile, the Shan Van Vocht, Banba, Roisin Dubh, Fodhla, Cathleen ni Houlihan, the swords of light and the risings of the moon.[2] These belong to the time when we growled in defeat and dreamed

---

1 "This is Your Magazine" appeared in *The Bell* 1, no. 1 (October 1940): 5–9.
2 All of these are nationalist symbols and figures: Brian Boru (941–1014) was high king of Ireland from 1002 to his death; Granuaile is the nickname of Grace O'Malley (c. 1530–c. 1603), Ireland's famous pirate queen; the Shan Van Vocht (Irish for "the Poor Old Woman"), Banba (a Celtic goddess), Roisin Dubh (Irish for "the Dark Rose"), Fodhla (Banba's sister), and Cathleen ni Houlihan are all pseudonyms for Ireland.

of the future. That future has arrived and, with its arrival, killed them. All our symbols have to be created afresh, and the only way to create a living symbol is to take a naked thing and clothe it with new life, new association, new meaning, with all the vigour of the life we live in the Here and Now. We refused to use the word Irish, or Ireland, in the title. We said, "It will plainly be that by being alive." Our only job was to encourage Life to speak. When she speaks, then THE BELL will itself become a symbol, and its "policy" will be self-evident.

All over Ireland – this is the expression of our Faith – there are men and women with things itching them like a grain stuck in a tooth. You who read this know intimately some corner of life that nobody else can know. You and Life have co-operated to make a precious thing which is your secret. You know a turn of the road, an old gateway somewhere, a well-field, a street-corner, a wood, a handful of quiet life, a triangle of sea and rock, something that means Ireland to you. It means the whole world. Men and women who have suffered or died in the name of Ireland, who have thereby died for Life as they know it, have died for some old gateway, some old thistled lag-field in which their hearts have been stuck since they were children.[3] These are the things that come at night to tear at an exile's heart. These are the true symbols. When Pearse faced death it was of such things he thought – the rabbits on the sloping field at Rosmuc, the field lit by the slanting sun, a speckled ladybird on a blade of grass.[4] That is Life. You possess a precious store of it. If you will share it with all of us you will make this bell peal out a living message.

THE BELL will ring a note this way and a note that way. The wind will move it and a faint sigh come from the top of the tower. Some passing traveller will finger the rope and send out his cry. Some man who knows how to ring a proper peal will make the clapper shout. People will hear these chance notes to the north and people will hear them to the south, and when they say, in field or pub, in big house or villa house, "There is the bell," they will echo the replication of its notes, and the air will carry the echo wider and wider. Each note a message, each echo an answer, each answer a further message – can you not imagine them a linking, widening

3 "Lag-field" is an odd compound that I have yet to come across in reference works. A lag is a rim of a barrel, so there is the possibility that the thistles in the field would be as high as a lag. Alternately, given the promixity of the "g" and the "y" on keyboards, it might be a typographical error for "lay-field." A lay (also spelled lea and ley) is a field that has remained untilled and thus has become a pasture, which would allow thistles to grow.

4 Pearse lived in Rosmuc, a village in Connemara, County Galway.

circle of notes, a very peal of bells, murmuring all over the land? It is said that four hammers can ring a peal of twenty-four changes; eight of forty-thousand changes; twelve can ring five hundred million changes. When, between us all, we have struck echoing notes so wide and so far, shall we not have awoken the innumerable variety of Life itself? Beside that would it not be foolish, impertinent to talk of "our" policy; unless by "our" we mean "yours" – the immeasurable Irishry of the world?

This magazine will be creative only in so far as Ireland is creative. Only the people can create an image of themselves. If, therefore, you have a fault to find with THE BELL blame us only in part. Blame us for not being alert to what is going on around us. But blame yourself, too. Here is the belfry, the bell-rope, and the bell. If it does not speak that is because you have not taken the bell-rope and swung out of it. Write about your gateway, your well-field, your street-corner, your girl, your boat-slip, pubs, books, pictures, dogs, horses, river, tractor, anything at all that has a hold on you.

There is, as I have said, one thing in which you must praise or blame us who are running THE BELL, and we need both praise and blame in order to know if we are on the right scent. It is our job to have a flair, a nose, a hound's smell for the real thing, for the thing that is alive and kicking, as against the thing that is merely pretending to be alive. We have to go out nosing for bits of individual veracity, hidden in the dust-heaps of convention, imitation, timidity, traditionalism, wishful thinking. In that search our only advantage is that of being professional writers, publicists and, after a mild and, we hope, civilised fashion, somewhat unconventional people ourselves. The professional writer's job, as for himself (as for others when he turns critic) is to be able to sense the synthetic thing a mile away.

You will notice that we do not ask, primarily, for perfection in the craftwork; we ask, first and before all, for the thing that lies lurking at the bottom of each man's well, and, if you look through this first number, you will see several things whose merit is not chiefly Art but Truth, but which for that are worth a hundred thousand things that are full of Art but, as for Truth, are as skinny as Famine. If, then, you are a professional writer we want your best and only your best; but if you are not, I want you particularly to read the invitation on page 92 from Frank O'Connor.[5] If you doubt whether you have the gift of the written word, and yet do want to set down something that is vital to yourself, there is a special section where you can try your hand.

5 Frank O'Connor, "The Belfry," *The Bell* 1, no. 1 (October 1940): 92–4. O'Connor was the poetry editor of *The Bell*; "The Belfry" was the title of the section devoted to new poetry.

This Ireland is young and earnest. She knows that somewhere, among the briars and the brambles, there stands the reality which the generations died to reach – not, you notice, the Ideal; our generation is too sober to talk much about Ideals, though we may think of it by any fine name there is, the Holy Grail, the Sacred Altar, the dream we have called by those hundred names now gone out of date. We are living experimentally. Day after day we are all groping for that reality, and many of our adventures must be a record of error and defeat. Some of our efforts must equally be steps nearer that practicable, possible fineness and decency. In recording them all, the defeats and the victories, the squalors and the enchantments, how can we have any "policy" other than to stir ourselves to a vivid awareness of what we are doing, what we are becoming, what we are? That is why we say that this is your magazine. Whether you know it or not, admit it or not, so long as what you read is true – you wrote it.

THE BELL is quite clear about certain practical things and will, from time to time, deal with them – the Language, Partition, Education, and so forth. In general THE BELL stands, in all such questions, for Life before any abstraction, in whatever magnificent words it may clothe itself. For we eschew abstractions, and will have nothing to do with generalisations that are not capable of proof by concrete experience. Generalisation (to make one) is like prophecy, the most egregious form of error, and abstractions are the luxury of people who enjoy befuddling themselves methodically. We prefer, likewise, the positive to the negative, the creative to the destructive. We ban only lunatics and sour-bellies. We are absolutely inclusive. We take our stand, for that, on the noble words of Alice Stopford Green in presenting the Senate with a casket to hold its Constitution:

> From the beginning, Ireland has been rich in her hospitality to men of goodwill coming within her borders. And at all times there have been incomers who have responded honourably to that generosity and have become faithful members of her people. She has had her rewards among the strangers who, under her wide skies, have felt the wonder of the land, and the quality of its people, and have entered into her commonwealth.[6]

Whoever you are, then, O reader, Gentile or Jew, Protestant or Catholic, priest or layman, Big House or Small House – THE BELL is yours.

---

6 Alice Stopford Green (1847–1929) was a nationalist Irish historian who was nominated to the Senate in 1922.

Jack B. Yeats[1]

The widest public will always prefer the Jack Yeats who drew for us donkeys, foreign sailor-men, jockeys, maggie-men, and all the strange characters and scenes of that grand book, *Life in the West of Ireland*.[2] His later more "queer" style in painting, they will admire, but never love in the same way as they loved the donkeys and the sailors. Yet, if you look through that early book you will surely perceive, in the light of his later work, a strange fancy playing over everything he has done, making it all in some way a little bizarre, even exotic. I am just now looking at a perfectly simple drawing in that book. It is called "The Music." It is the simplest drawing in the book. It shows the prow of a tramp-steamer and closer at hand the front portion of a rowing-boat creeping into the picture. There are three sailors in this boat, all smoking cigars, and the fellow in the prow is playing a melodeon.[3] The water is smooth. It is evidently evening. Do I persuade myself, or is it really so, that there is an elfish, wistful, pensive, melancholy air about these sailor-men, as if they knew themselves to have been lifted out of the common world of tarry ropes, shiny serge, engine oil, and Guinness, into a world of outlandish poetry?

1 "Jack B. Yeats" appeared in *The Bell* 1, no. 4 (January 1941): 33–6.
2 Jack Butler Yeats (1871–1957), the brother of W.B. Yeats, was a major Irish painter who also wrote plays, poems, and prose. He published *Life in the West of Ireland* in 1912. O'Faolain also mentions Yeats's *Sligo* (1930), *Apparitions* (1933), *Sailing Sailing Swiftly* (1933), *The Amaranthers* (1936), and *Ah, Well!* (1942). A maggie (from the Irish "gleas magaidh" or "object of ridicule") is a dummy at which sticks are thrown at a fair; hitting the maggie is said to bring good luck. A maggie-man is the person charged with collecting the sticks.
3 A melodeon is a type of accordion.

It probably is so, and not a self-persuasion. Irish realism never was realism in the accepted sense. Synge.[4]

It needs no genius, now, to see this outlandish note in the West. Columbus has discovered America. Most leave it at that. Yeats has gone on and on, developing the hint, drawing out finer and finer the light thread which connects the imagination with the original experience that excited it. However finely drawn out, the link is there. He is based on Life. There need be no hesitation to accept that. Jack Yeats, in his painting and his prose, may be what we please to call "difficult" (which is a way of saying that he is not obvious), but one thing is evident from the whole course of his work: he never bamboozles us. "Odd" – as we say: yes, and very wilful; but not tricky.

Really he is not so much "difficult" as "different." He is that because he is always himself. He resolutely follows his own nose. He never makes up books out of other books. His material and his methods are his own: his style and technique are his own – sometimes, possibly, a little too much so for complete clarity. But our reward is that we are admitted to the intimacy of an unalloyed personality which has retained all its primal freshness and individuality. He is, thus, among Irish writers singularly pure.

He is also one of our most independent writers. What he writes, he writes: take it or leave it. It carries no moral. It is a chunk of life played over by a vivid imagination. He did it because he liked to do it, and for no ulterior motive.

He is entirely free of the tyranny of the audience. Whereas most other writers always keep one eye on the audience. They are trying to add undertones of meaning to the thing they record – opinions, philosophies, conclusions, and to get those undertones across they must, necessarily, sacrifice something. They want to communicate widely, and to do that they will often use the most threadbare language, just because it will be understood. They do get results that he does not get. But it is an old artistic problem whether the sacrifice is worth while: whether the results of their methods are "better" than his results. Theirs is a more public art: like a statue among the seagulls: a little vulgar; less fine; aiming at a larger nobility; so often attaining less. W.B. Yeats said you should write poetry

---

4 There are a few possible explanations for this one-word sentence: it is an accidental inclusion of "Synge"; the rest of the sentence was cut off; or it suggests on its own that O'Faolain considered Synge typical of an Irish realist school that ran counter to a standard form of realism.

so that you could shout it across a street. What would Mallarmé have said to that? Public art versus the art of the few.

I have been re-reading his little book *Sligo*. The very name is wilful. A vagrant whom he met in a train said, "Call your book *Sligo*. It is a lucky name." So Yeats did. Why not? What is in a name? The book is full of glittering gifts, a bran-tub sifted by the fingers of memory – things lifted out, twinkled, tossed down. Nothing is exhausted. Some things hardly explained. For example: "I saw in a street in New York, a card writer, I mean a writer of visiting cards. He turned them out at ten cents a dozen in a lovely curling hand, and he sat at a little table by a doorstep and he wore a Buffalo Bill hat."[5] That is all. A scrap to delight and be left there. Or he remembers the time when tambourines were made of old lawyer's parchment and you could see scraps of writing on the skin. It all has very little to do with Sligo county. Accordingly, although I have read more satisfactory books, I have read few with such charm – even if the charm has a lot of idle bran clinging to it. But I never bothered much about the name. I should not have cared if he called the book XYZ.

A good deal of the fun of such wilful books as that – such books as his odd plays *Apparitions*, or his novel, *Sailing Sailing Swiftly*, or even *The Amaranthers* (which is more remote from common reality) – is the fun of spotting the man, his winning personality, and his actual, original life, behind the fancifulness. It is not difficult. It is overt in the novel – Ireland, Sligo, the boxing-booths of the East End, ballad-singers, Epsom Downs, Barnet fair, horse auctions, all the life of the 90's, old plays, yellow-backs, early loves among painters, too, such as Morland.[6] (Can he, possibly, be a realist *manqué*?)[7] These are the stuff that his dreams are made on. The stuff is not so overt in his latest, and I think, happiest novel, *Ah, Well!* (What a lovely name for a Memory Harbour of a book!)[8] Here we are deeper among his dreams. But I think that the flesh and blood is just as

---

5 Buffalo Bill (1846–1917), né William Cody, was famous for wearing what are more commonly termed cowboy hats.
6 Epsom Downs refers to the Epsom Derby, a horse race that takes place on Epsom Downs but has become as well known for the extravagant fashions of the race-goers. Barnet Fair is a horse fair that runs over a few days in September in the London borough of Barnet. A yellow-back is a cheap and often sensational or lurid novel. Influential English landscape and animal painter George Morland (1763–1804).
7 A realist *manqué* is a failed realist.
8 *Memory Harbour, 1900* is one of Jack Yeats's early paintings.

close, if hidden a little, behind the veil of fancy. *Ah, Well!* is to me like a ship sailing out free on the seas of the imagination – a ship in a folk-tale or a saga – and its name on its port and its stern are dim and almost rubbed out and indecipherable; but not quite.

To each man this town he describes in *Ah, Well* will be a different town. I could see it as Cork Harbour or I could see it as Sligo, and fancy that when morning welcomes the sailors home, the mists will be clinging to the surface of Sligo river, and the eddies of memory will be curling back on the flow of the tide up the Garravogue, and the cocks crowing among the shirts and shifts drying in the backyards will make the wanderers awaken to the smell of turf-smoke and bacon frying. But that fancy would not, perhaps, please Jack Yeats. Almost a vulgar "explanation!" Of *Ah, Well* we are printing one complete section – the description of the town and its inhabitants. We print it because we believe that our readers will delight in it for its power to be, at one and the same time, familiar, strange, simple, and lovely. It is lovely because its imagination is so free and so pure: because it is so homely and racy; because it is quite realistic though cast in fancy's mould: because, to borrow a phrase, it is "strong but sweet like the honey in the lion's carcase." It belongs in this magazine, just as surely as a translation of an old shanachie's folk-tale would belong, being made up, like that, of the life that we tread every day beneath our feet.[9]

Many readers will remember those little Irish textbooks called *Ceachta Beaga*, by Norma Borthwick.[10] Jack Yeats did the "pictures." They were enchanting. So is this word-picture of a town. With only this difference that fancy has grown up. Consideration, wisdom, experience have deepened and darkened it in the vat of the mature artist's imagination. The humour is a little mocking: even sardonic: the lighting is sometimes lurid and frightening. Otherwise, with him we can, in so far as grown people ever can, become children again; unabused; and disabused of the effects of more worldly-minded literature.

9 As this paragraph suggests, an excerpt of Yeats's *Ah, Well* followed O'Faolain's essay. See Jack Yeats, "Ah, Well," *The Bell* 1, no. 4 (January 1941): 37–43. A shanachie is a storyteller of Gaelic tales and legends.

10 Norma Borthwick (1862–1934) first published *Ceachta Beaga Gaedhilge* (*Irish Reading Lessons*) in 1902; as O'Faolain says, the book featured illustrations by Yeats.

Frederick Robert Higgins (1896–1941)[1]

It happens that in this issue we record the anniversary of the death of W.B. Yeats, on 28th January, 1939, and the death, on 7th January, 1941, of F.R. Higgins. The loss, as it must always be with any young poet, is incalculable: the juxtaposition of those two deaths annotates the nature of that loss whose scope nobody can measure. In his later years "Fred" Higgins was Yeats's closest friend; there was even sufficient physical resemblance to make somebody say, after meeting them walking side by side in O'Connell Street, "They are like father and son." They were bound by natural affinities. It is probable that Yeats found in his young friend a bridge across the generations: an assuagement of the feeling that "we were the last romantics"; found in him an Ireland more sweet than that pictured by Joyce and O'Casey and O'Flaherty, the critical generation. At any rate, Higgins does form that bridge between the obstinate anti-romanticism of our time and the lofty and fantastic imagination of pre-revolution poetry, with its pliable subjects, all ready to hand, caparisoned by mythology and traditional awe. ("We … chose for theme," Yeats wrote, "traditional sanctity and loveliness.")[2] For Higgins also loved the traditional subject, loved

---

1 "Frederick Robert Higgins (1896–1941)" appeared in *The Bell* 1, no. 5 (February 1941): 53–5. The title of this article as originally published erroneously gives 1897 as Higgins's birth year. O'Faolain published another article on Higgins to mark the first anniversary of his death: "F.R. Higgins," *The Bell* 3, no. 4 (January 1942): 251–3.
2 From Yeats's poem "Coole Park and Ballylee, 1931" (1932). The full two lines run: "We were the last romantics – chose for theme / Traditional sanctity and loveliness." The poem was a tribute, an elegy of sorts, written to Lady Gregory as she lay on her sickbed.

to see at all times behind the lore of the people, and folk-tunes and ways, and in the aerial, almost tenuous beauty of nature, the classically lyric face of life. Young Yeats might have written –

Over the limestone mountains
Where rain-blown roads run wild,
By limestone green in the moonlight,
I've seen through a ghostly wind
Strange princes down Glen Naefin
Like horse lords from Mayo
On geldings proudly riding
With bridles of shot gold ...[3]

The folk-tune is in –

By a field of the crab-trees my love and I were walking ...[4]

The traditional atmosphere and subject mingle in –

They've paid their last respects in sad tobacco
And silent is this wakehouse in its haze ...[5]

But in these poems there is something personal to himself which balances his debt to Yeats, since Yeats, I believe, was influenced by it in his own later work. That is a sturdy, genial, homely note, or even a gay, boisterous rapscallion note, muted in that lament for O'Conaire, singing out in the ballad he so loved to sing –

I'm old, very old, yet I don't need a wattle,
I'm old, very old, but I'm not a dry nettle;
I still need a fellow that's high in his mettle,
Glory O, glory O, so you'll serve mighty fine.[6]

One might call that the accordion-note from the far side of the bridge on whose hither end one hears sounding the delicate flageolet pastoral of

3 "Beloved of Nobles" (1940).
4 "The Three-Cornered Field" (1940).
5 "Padraic O'Conaire – Gaelic Storyteller" (1933).
6 "Glory O!" (1940).

I know a small lake that sails the palest shadows,
Trailing their frail keels along its waveless sand... .[7]

He was clearly moving rapidly towards the time when he would blend
the two sides of his nature. For if at times in his uneasy wrestling with his
problem he flopped into little short of tavern-room vulgarity he was constantly achieving the warmth and ease of –

If you draw secrets from the wind, O little birds – that neatly leap
From twig to twig – you've heard my cries, but these are secrets you
     must keep,
Until in far flights you should find her, dreaming of me at twilight
     time –
Then sing: though broken in my mind, I'll have her in unquiet sleep.[8]

Only his friends knew how much internal vibrancy and nervousness
there was to this genial, fat man, so full of good humour, always ready for
a joke, playing the jew's-harp at one of his own parties, or shaking his
belly at somebody's bawdy quip. They had the key to his special quality
of Irishness; a peculiarly native blend of *grossièreté* and sensitiveness, a
Keats disguised as a Falstaff.[9]

His death cannot fail to tell sorely against the development of a native
tradition in verse, for he was a most careful craftsman; his influence was
growing every day. As for his own contribution to that tradition, it was
remarkable, since it was a double achievement when he captured a native
vigour and pungency hitherto considered suitable only for novels and
plays and then held it in a net of the most iridescent verse written in
Ireland since *The Wanderings of Usheen*.[10] That must not suggest to us
that his death unfortunately breaks the Yeatsian continuity: on the contrary, he would have had to disrupt that tradition *had he lived* and done
it, thereby, a noble service. For unless a tradition is continually interrupted and redirected it dies. *Dans la littérature il faut toujours tuer son
père*;[11] one does it because, almost in Wilde's phrase, one loves deeply.

7 "Muineen Water" (1940).
8 "The Spine That Bears All Brightness" (1940).
9 *Grossièreté* is French for rude or rustic manners.
10 *The Wanderings of Oisin and Other Poems* (1889), by W.B. Yeats.
11 *Dans la littérature il faut toujours tuer son père* translates from the French as
"In literature, one must always kill one's father."

Literature moves like that – obliquely as the knight in chess cornering the king for a new game. From disciple Higgins would have become apostle, and perhaps begun a new canon. But a pawn has taken the knight, and the king has escaped again.

Ah, Wisha! The Irish Novel[1]

Forty years ago, verse in Ireland clustered about a nucleus; so did the drama. Anybody of Irish origin who could write gravitated like the atom towards this nucleus, and the result was a well defined little school of poetry. Today Irish verse and drama are at the ebb. A number of novels, equal in bulk to that verse and drama, have appeared ever since George Moore started that tradition going, but they have not coalesced into a school. To give but one example, a man like James Hanley, had he been a poet in the 1900s, would have become identified with Anglo- Irish literature.[2]

The reason for this dissipation is that there has never been any literary doctrine for Irish prose, as there was for Irish verse. Compare Yeats. He inherited, and used to effect, the gospel of the Symbolists and the Pre-Raphaelites.[3] He followed Pater, Mallarmé, Symons, *Axël*, Morris, Burne-Jones, Rossetti, and all that school.[4] He had no love for that range of social or psychological interests out of which Shaw made his plays and Joyce was about to make his novels, and of which, in his day, Bastien-Lepage and

1 "Ah, Wisha! The Irish Novel" appeared in *The Virginia Quarterly Review* 17, no. 2 (Spring 1941): 265–74. "Wisha" is derived from the Irish *mhuise*. It is a colloquial exclamation that indicates surprise or adds emphasis; as for the latter, it is roughly the equivalent of "indeed."
2 James Hanley (1901–1985) was a novelist.
3 The Symbolists and the Pre-Raphaelites were nineteenth-century groups that were against the strictures of realism and naturalism.
4 Walter Pater (1839–1894) was a major advocate of art for art's sake. *Axël*, by Auguste Villiers de l'Isle-Adam. William Morris (1834–1896), Edward Burne-Jones (1833–1898), and Dante Gabriel Rossetti (1828–1882) were all important artists of their day.

Carolus-Duran were the popular exponents in painting.[5] He developed a clean hatred for naturalism and science and the general mechanistic theory of life. Yeats sought a dream-world of symbol for all his earlier work; he sought remoteness; the heroic and generalised appealed to him; he made his soul on Blake and esoteric literature, not scorning even such shoddy stuff as spiritualism and all its trappings and rappings; he even worked inside a pseudo-personality, or poetic shell, cold to others, cosy and iridescent within. Later, when increasing gravity brought him down from this stratosphere, he was fortunate to find in Synge another exemplar whose poetic realism combined faëry and fact in an ideal fashion. One may doubt Yeats's spiritual "teachers," but that he had bodily teachers there is no doubt, and his biographer will have no difficulty in reconstructing his general doctrine from its always centripetal, if often inconsonant, parts. In a word, he had a line to follow – a line of many strands.

Irish prose has no such line. Had it started earlier it might have had. Had it been intellectual – had intelligence been an Irish quality, as it is not, the Irish mind being too undisciplined and imaginative – Æ might have set a habit in books like *The Candle of Vision*.[6] But Yeats's prose, which is almost impossible to read, and which is always breaking off just where the mind is about to grasp his muffled point, shows that the only effect of a suggestive or allusive prose style on the Irish mind is to cloud with further emotion a mind already lost in the dimness of its own conch. Nature, even in matters of the mind, has a care for its own self-preservation, and the Irish mind fled from danger. No young Irish prose writer, observing Yeats floundering through the Celtic mist, could do anything else but turn towards some more extrovert models. But where, bearing in mind that they were not and never could be extroverts or objective intellectuals, were they to find these models? Where could they get some exemplars midway between the intelligence and the imagination?

The prose writer, as novelist or biographer, uses the same material as all naturalistic and realistic novelists do: he uses what Flaubert and Balzac used. There is, in the National Gallery in Dublin, an excellent little portrait by Bastien-Lepage – it might be any old red-nosed, whiskered boulevardier. It might almost have been a sketch by Manet.[7] It probably made

5 Jules Bastien-Lepage (1848–1884) was a naturalist painter and Carolus-Duran (1837–1917), né Charles Auguste Émile Durand, was a portrait painter.
6 *The Candle of Vision* (1918).
7 The National Gallery of Ireland opened its doors on 30 January 1864. Édouard Manet (1832–1883) was major French Impressionist painter.

Yeats stand aghast. It is unashamed naturalistic reproduction. It delights me. For every novelist has to reproduce, if not as an end, at least as a method. Old men with red noses are our materials. The novelist cannot work with the symbolic language of the Rosy Cross, characterless characters like Michael Robartes or Ossian, shadowy scenery of the mind:[8] he uses direct and precise language, real people, muddy fields, streets with trams; the hiss of Emily Bovary's corset-laces is music to his ears. But while the Irish novelist, in common with every novelist, thus works in the Flaubertian studio, it is in his nature – which makes him both rich and poor – to hanker after that renounced symbolism and those regretted worlds of the mind. O'Flaherty will give you the old man with the red nose, but you can see him tearing himself to bits in the effort to burn up and melt down the poor old man in order that you may perceive behind him some Michael with a flaming sword and the gates of hell or heaven glinting in its fire.[9]

Evidently there are no established models in prose for this kind of thing. Moore attempted something vaguely like it in one novel, and in one only, *The Lake* – and it is the Moore novel most favoured by Irish writers.[10] For the rest, Moore was either the by-child of a crude naturalism, or else he escaped with Heloïse and Aphrodite.[11] Joyce did something glorious in *A Portrait of the Artist as a Young Man*, and if he had only been a little less subjective and preoccupied he might have given Irish prose a model as Gogol gave one to Russia with "The Cloak."[12] And we have a great admiration for James Stephens, especially for *The Charwoman's Daughter*.[13] But neither faces the problem squarely enough. They leave out too much for

---

8 Yeats was a member of the Rosicrucians. Michael Robartes and Ossian are two characters in Yeats's poetry.

9 A reference to St. Michael, the Archangel, who is often depicted as a warrior.

10 *The Lake* (1905).

11 Heloïse (c. 1098–1164) was the secret wife of theologian and philosopher Peter Abelard (1079–1142), to whom she bore a son. When her family discovered the liaison, they castrated Abelard, and the two lovers retired to a convent and a monastery, respectively. Aphrodite, the Greek goddess of love, is another romantic figure in whose story castration is a central element: she was born from the foam that formed when Uranus's genitals were cast into the sea by his son Cronus.

12 Nikolay Gogol (1809–1852) was author of "The Overcoat" (1842), a short story that is considered to have begun the nineteenth-century tradition of Russian realism.

13 *The Charwoman's Daughter* (1912) was Stephens' first novel; as indicated in an earlier note, it was also published under the title *Mary, Mary*.

the conscience of our times. And the later history of both writers is dismaying. A model which does not repeat itself is hardly a fructifying example.

When I think of the books that have, from time to time, excited a few of us, they are all anti-naturalistic books: Kafka's; all the Russians, but, alone satisfyingly and permanently, Chekov; one or two books by Catholic Frenchmen, such as Duhamel and Mauriac; a play like Obey's *Noah*; a Giraudoux or two.[14] Of English writers, Hardy stands on a pedestal. For myself, I was pleased by the sane fancy of the early Coppard and I have an almost uncritical admiration for Graham Greene.[15] As for the solid English writers, like Galsworthy, we acknowledge them and admire them, though with a detached lobe of the mind, reserved for people who are splendid in a world that is not our world. Jane Austen, for example, we regard with an adoration which must exceed that of any Englishman – she is somebody whose perfect perfection of its own kind we might as soon try to reach as reach the moon. But I think we would sacrifice every single one of these if we were left only with Chekov. From the beginning it is in the Russians that Irish writers have found their nearest counterparts, and of all the Russians most so in Chekov. That is, I feel, because he repeats, in the manner of a prose-writer, the Synge recipe of poetry and realism, mood and consideration, laughter and opinion, brutality (which we must always have) and tenderness (which is essential to us), and all sunk in a thick atmosphere. If Irish prose fiction ever does develop a distinctive quality, it will be as much by virtue of this influence of the Russians as Yeats developed his distinctive quality under the influence of the Symbolists and Pre-Raphaelites.

You cannot, however, develop a literary doctrine on a dislike (such as this dislike of naturalism), and anyway, literary doctrines are not cerebrated. Yeats gravitated towards the Pre-Raphaelites because he was the son of his father, and to the Symbolists because he was reared in Sligo – under the tomb of Queen Maeve. (It actually is not the tomb of Queen Maeve.)[16] Local conditions in Ireland, and the times, and a number of

14 Franz Kafka (1883–1924) was a Prague-born German-language writer. O'Faolain refers here to French writers Georges Duhamel (1884–1966), François Mauriac, and Jean Giraudoux (1882–1944); *Noah* (1930) was written by French playwright André Obey (1892–1975).
15 English writers A.E. Coppard (1878–1957) and Graham Greene (1904–1991).
16 The Queen of Connaught Maeve, or Medb, is said to be buried on Knocknarea, just west of Sligo.

other things counteract this aversion to the naturalistic method and theory. And, incidentally, re-impress Chekov.

·The material of local life is rebellious to art: but that makes small matter – novelists are always quarrelling with their models, and their models are always disliking them. The things Chekov said about his Russia, or that Flaubert thought about Rouen, are just what any Irish writer might say and think of Aran or Dublin. All or most writers have hated their country as much as they simultaneously loved it. The difficulty of the Irish novelist is one of an adjustment of sympathy: he cannot make up his mind as to what to love and what to hate. The norm eludes him. If a stranger could sit for an hour in any group of Irish people discussing either politics or religion he would soon observe this in a basic disagreement as to the premises. In sum, I think, this disagreement concerns a conflict between what one may roughly call faith and morals. All our writers are torn between the two.

We see our people living an easy-going life, happy enough, highly casual, often complacent – their complacency about this war has been shocking – and they are good-humoured, happy-go-lucky, warm-hearted to a fault, and charitable beyond judgment, vicious only in vendetta, and savage only in hate. All that, to a novelist, is excellent. Of morals as sin, they are made almost sickly conscious by the Church. But this is morals as obedience, orthodoxy, discipline. Of morals in action they have only a very vague conception. And this is emphasised by a self-preserving technique of evasion, as exasperating in practice as it is delightful in theory. All morality, outside the confessional, is covered by an umbrella of charity, striped by evasion, and wide as the sky.

What I have called faith covers a multitude of sins. In this respect the Irish motto of life might be described as "Ah, wisha!" So – "Ah, wisha, what harm if he did go off with a few pounds or so. He's a decent poor lad at bottom"; "Ah, wisha, even if he does take a sup too much now and again – we all have our weaknesses"; "Ah, wisha, why did they put the poor divil in jail? Sure, he didn't know what he was doing!" There is an excellent story by Frank O'Connor, in *Bones of Contention*, which gives a perfect illustration of this.[17] A local boy made good by embezzling the club funds. The priest, a moral man, condemned him at once. The parish came in wave after wave of deputation to plead for the "poor boy." But the moralist stood his ground, and the boy was duly charged, tried, and punished. The people thereafter turned against their priest. The charm of

17 *Bones of Contention and Other Stories* (1936).

this story lies in the complete, maddening, hopeless failure of the people
to see the moral point of view. This failure reaches its climax of absurdity
when they ask the priest "at least" to give "the poor boy" a character –
that is, they asked him to tell the judge that the boy was really "a decent
poor lad at bottom," and that "we all have our weaknesses," and "he
didn't know what he was doing," and so on and so on.

Now this charity-child of faith in our people is of itself a precious treasure, a human gift, a divine dispensation of laughter and pity; and every Irish
writer is torn between his admiration for it – a quality he shares, of course,
in common with his people – and his sane, human, rational idealism which
cannot stand seeing life and reason being driven mad by something half-
way between angelic soft-heartedness and lunatic soft-headedness. He
cannot see, in the wholly un-vulgar sense of the words, how any race can
ever get anywhere (not even into the all-charitable bosom of God the
Father) if it sublimates morality out of existence. If we protest to the
people for being so lax, they say, "Ah, wisha, we're doing our best and God
is good." If we protest to the priests for being too strict, they say, "God is
good, but we can't let the rein slacken." The end has been, astonishingly,
that the rigidity of the clergy, on the one hand, and the evasive humour and
charity of the people, on the other (for they resent all such discipline),
flings the writer not into the arms of the people but into a puritanism of
despair far beyond the asceticism of the priests. Every Irish writer is a
puritan at heart; the real priests are the writers, just as the only Catholics
are the Protestants; though if the writers were priests they would certainly,
in pity for the people, become libertines and let the people gaily go to hell.
No writer can love the priests, since it is the final prerogative of the priest
to forgive, after he has scolded; and, to put it crudely, the writer, and any
other sane man with him, is about fed up with all this forgiveness business.
So, the novelist, to his horror, finds himself (as George Moore did before
him) aligned with the Protestant tradition against his own folk. His
alternative is either that or laugh himself sick.

There we come back to naturalism and Chekov. The situation is very
like the situation of Chekov. No figure is so common in Russian literature
as the benevolent but strict landowner whose serfs are incorrigible.
Change landowner for priest and serf for farmer and you have the same
antagonism. There the peasant came to the noble, and asked for corn, or
roubles, or wood, or manure; and the master gave it, with plenty of orders
and lots of advice, and the serf took it with loud thanks and firm resolutions, and then he went off, and gambled away the roubles, or the corn,
or drank them, or lost them, or in some other way dodged the problem

– and, in due course, came back for more and for forgiveness. Like Chekov the Irish novelist has to pass judgment on all this folly.

For people who say that Chekov never passed judgment simply do not know their Chekov. All they can know of him is one sentence which has passed into a cliché. He was a violent reformer. "I hate violence and false-hood in all their aspects. My Holy of Holies is the human body, health, mind, talent, inspiration, love, and the most absolute freedom – freedom from violence and falsehood in whatever form they may be manifested."[18] This was not said by a man who did not pass judgment. In *The Cherry Orchard*, "How beautiful life will be in three or four hundred years" was not said by a complacent man: the price of such optimism as to the future is depression as to the present.[19] The man who went to examine conditions in the penal settlement of Sakhalin, and raged at people (e.g., Suvorin) for saying that Sakhalin was of no interest to anyone – he was not a man to fail to pass judgment.[20] But in fact, the sub-audible judgment of his irony is in every story, and it is strident in some: "The Grasshopper," "The Duel," "The Wife," "The Chorus Girl"; I could quote endless examples. "You once told me," he wrote to Pleshcheyev, angrily, "that my stories lack the protesting element, that there are no sympathies and antipathies in them. In this story ("A Tedious Story") do I not from beginning to end protest against falsehood? No? Well, then, I cannot bite, or I am a flea."[21] One has only to read his letters, for his praise of Germany, his rage against Russian smugness, his gospel of "normality," to know that he too had to find for himself a literary doctrine to cover this identical problem – which in some shape or form faces all writers – of the adjustment of a novelist's ideas to the ideas of his people. Or, let us not call it a literary doctrine any longer, but a doctrine of life, since for such writers as Chekov there is no wall between living and writing.

Balzac once said that he wished, in the *Comédie Humaine*, to make society wear upon its brow the reasons of its being; it is his way of saying

18 Chekhov wrote this in a letter to the Russia poet Aleksey Pleshcheyev (1825–1893) on 4 October 1888. Pleshcheyev was an important editor for Chekhov.
19 *The Cherry Orchard* (1904) was Chekhov's final play.
20 Sakhalin Island, located in Eastern Russia, was for a long time a notorious penal colony; Chekhov visited it and later published his findings in *The Island of Sakhalin* (1893–94). A.S. Suvorin (1834–1912) was a wealthy newspaper owner and publisher of Chekhov's work.
21 Letter from Chekhov to Pleshcheyev, 11 October 1888. The story in question was "The Name-day Party."

that he wished to write a criticism of life.[22] Every novelist wishes to do this, and for that reason he must be more concerned with morals, i.e., with men's actions, than with faith, i.e., with men's declarations. It is natural. Faith and all declarations are universal, and in the end, even the most materialistic declarations are mystical, since they answer a mystery with an assertion incapable of proof. Morality is individual and human, and the test of these generalisations. If both are felt there is a conflict. If either is not felt there is no conflict; then there is comedy, or the Aristophanic ringmaster making the dogs look silly even while they are being clever.[23] That is why Shaw is a success. He observed that his society wore upon its brow neither the furrows of worry nor the suavity of its reason. He did the only thing possible. There is no room, in that society, for anything else but laughter – or autobiographies of self-nudation.

The Irish novelist, in a society that may be crazy but is conscious, is thus driven back to objectivity, reproduction, almost to photography. He must depict the fact, or his comment, his Chekovian judgment, will be unjust. For all comment on life is on life as it is felt, seen, heard, smelled by those who live it. Only when he meets that evasion of which I spoke earlier is he defeated. He is there in the same position as his English brother: up the gum-tree, laughing like hell. Intensely as he may dislike naturalism, he has to use it. I suddenly remember, here, Yeats's rooms, with all those drawings by Blake and Rossetti, so lovely, so mysterious, so ethereal, so remote; and I think of this crude world of common life, and I envy from the bottom of my heart that exquisite world of the senses in which the imagination of the poet fed and contemplated itself hourly. For, as Chekov says, once a man sees the rope he must pull it, and no fastidiousness must prevent him from mucking his hands.

Yet this dislike of naturalism must mean something, since it is wholly instinctive, a cry or whisper from the heart for some kind of food it desires but cannot define. Perhaps that is precisely what this dislike of ours for naturalism and all its offshoots does mean: that the solution of all conflict is indefinable; we are against all those positivist solutions which began with Zola and still go on repeating their formulas in proletarian novels and brutalist novels, and all those novels about the dried egg on the heroine's spoon, and the fly crawling up the Hamlet-hero's windowpane. The

22 *La Comédie humaine* is the collective name for much of Balzac's oeuvre, comprising dozens of novels and novellas.
23 Aristophanes (c. 450–c. 388 BCE) was the foremost Greek writer of comedic plays.

conflict must appear to us indefinable because the antagonists are invisible, imponderable, and insatiable. It is a pertinent question whether such a concept lends itself at all to the novel form, whether the Irish mind can control its own lusts. Yet, the greatest Irish novel, *Ulysses*, has just that virtue of exciting the mind by its record of a young man's search for something inexpressible by the very naturalistic tools it employs, so that in the end all the characters are dilated into symbols, and the climax is a gesture of no meaning and of every meaning, when, in a nightmare, Stephen Daedalus raises his ash-plant and smashes a chandelier to bits.

That must be why we love Hardy and Chekov. We like Hardy because he was, as Duhamel once said in conversation, *un misérable*. Were his characters more sophisticated they too would have wanted to go to Moscow. Eustacia Vye might have been one of the three sisters.[24] Jude suffers from Russian longings.[25] Hardy is on the Celtic fringe. Keats knew what he wanted; you might meet him in any village pub. Moore, who was a first-class critic, said well that he was a boy with his nose pressed to the sweetshop window. We love his passion but his certainty chills us. But Chekov was more civilised than Hardy, and being uncivilised, we want to be civilised. He was a doctor, Hardy was an architect, and we like the human calling. And being a doctor he knew, with Novalis, that when a man's body is sick it is his soul that is sick, and vice versa.[26] We see that his people are not so much frustrated as they are romantically averse to satisfaction. There is nothing to stop the sisters from going to Moscow except the fact that they do not sufficiently will it, and they do not will it because they really do not want it. They want the moon. They are happily miserable. We, too, want the moon, and we, too, are content with our insatiable desires. Like Hardy and like Chekov we live in conflicts to which there is no solution, as there is no explanation to the mystery of life whose coloured balls we so love to juggle in a similar melancholy delight.

24 O'Faolain suggests here that Eustacia Vye, the flawed heroine of Hardy's *The Return of the Native* (1878), could be one of the eponymous characters in Chekhov's play *Three Sisters* (1901). All of these women yearn to escape their staid provincial lives.
25 Jude Crowley is the titular protagonist of Hardy's last novel, *Jude the Obscure* (1895); Jude constantly strives for a better life, but is defeated by the rigid norms and values of Victorian society.
26 Novalis (1772–1801), né Friedrich Leopold, was a German poet who later influenced the Romantics.

Standards and Taste[1]

Have we got 'em? Well ... Has anybody? The memory roves from London to New York: and one wonders. I do think that, strange as it may appear to some people, we have more of them than we even realise ourselves. But they are quite undeveloped and unapplied.

I am sure most people would agree, at any rate, that a people like ours are as yet comparatively unspoiled, living as we do a natural existence as farmers, or as townspeople still close to the farm – most townsmen are only a generation or, at most, two, removed from the land. And most people would agree that there are natural decencies attached to that sort of life, dictated, one might almost say, by the necessities and hardship of that life. For instance, hospitality, co-operation, generosity, or human charity cannot easily die where to-morrow it may be any man's turn to need them from his neighbours. (There are, to be sure, the corresponding faults of these qualities, acting possibly as a check on their too easy exploitation, such as hardness, suspicion, timidity, excessive individualism; but we are not now talking about that side of the matter.) And most people would even go farther and agree that from these natural virtues there do come some elementary ideas of what is in taste both in life and literature. To follow the "office rule" of trying to be concrete about generalisations, I can give one small example from the field of journalism. It is a tradition in Dublin newspapers not to exploit personal scandals, however juicy as news. You can call that anything you like – Hush-Hush, Cowardice, Prudery, Decency. I am not concerned with the morality of it, for the moment. I am merely pointing to the fact that there is there an elementary example of an elementary idea of what is and is not done.

1 "Standards and Taste" appeared in *The Bell* 2, no. 3 (June 1941): 5–11.

Whether the thing is good or bad it is an instinctive approach to standards of behaviour in Journalism.

Now, from the first number, the attitude of this magazine has been that this country is at the beginning of its creative history, and at the end of its revolutionary history. These are mere words. By a twist of thought you could change them about and say that since the days of Hugh O'Neill we have been trying to create certain conditions in which the people could get down to that Job of Work which is the epilogue of all wars, and that that Job of Work is the real beginning of our revolutionary history.[2] But the idea should be clear enough. The period of political and military struggle is over, or virtually over (we devoutly hope!); and the period of creation has arrived. And one contributor has shrewdly pointed out one example of the fact that this is not realised sufficiently – that we teach history in the schools as if 1916 and the years after were the end of the story, instead of the end of one phase and the beginning of another, in some ways far more important.

That being the attitude of this magazine it follows that, as regards Taste and Standards, we must recognise that they are still entirely undeveloped out of their elementary instinctive condition. We are groping. We make endless mistakes; and, worse still, endless evasions – for standards are not comfortable things to live with, and it is dismayingly easy to jog along with a sort of rough and ready rule-of-thumb, or with no rule at all except what you can "get away with." In this issue there is, for example, a slashing attack on the Abbey Theatre for getting away with something that it should not have tried to get away with; the distressing thing being that it did get away with it thanks to an apparently complete lack of standards on the part of that theatre's public.[3] Again I am not concerned with

2 Hugh O'Neill (1540/50–1616), 2nd Earl of Tyrone, was the subject of O'Faolain's *The Great O'Neill* (1942). Sources vary as to O'Neill's year of birth.
3 Frank O'Connor, "Public Opinion: The Stone Dolls," *The Bell* 2.3 (June 1941): 61–7. This was O'Connor's scathing review of *The Money Doesn't Matter* (1941), by Louis Lynch D'Alton (1900–1951). The play was a crowd pleaser that ran at the Abbey for a record-breaking nine weeks. O'Connor was not alone in his disappointment with what he saw to be the play's rather empty comedy: *The Bell* published another negative review alongside his, "Public Opinion: The Abbey Theatre," *The Bell* 2.3 (June 1941): 67–8, by author and politician Denis Ireland (1894–1974). Most reviewers, however, saw D'Alton's move into comedy from tragedy as successful. O'Connor was reacting, in part, to what he considered to be an unflattering caricature of Lennox Robinson. D'Alton wote a lively and highly critical response to O'Connor: "Public Opinion," *The Bell* 2, no. 4 (July 1941): 72–6.

whether the writer or the theatre is in the wrong – as a matter of fact I personally believe that the Abbey Theatre has behaved badly: what I am pointing out is that there are apparently no standards at all for certain things and that we (the public) are either not keenly concerned or are moving in a fog partly composed of ignorance and inexperience, and partly of *laissez-faire*.

It is going to take a long time before we develop our instincts in these matters. But they are not going to develop the way grass grows. We have to keep wide awake, keep aware, be jealous for our sense of honour, and jealous, too, for our rights. There is no use in putting a tooth in this matter. There will have to be divergence of opinion, and those opinions must be defended actively. Take the Literary Censorship, for example. That was an effort to codify certain alleged native instincts about literature, and what has been the result? Time has proved that these alleged instincts are *not* native. I listed in the April issue, and here list again the almost complete roll-call of Irish writers banned by the Censorship Board, or by the unofficial censors who follow in its wake. These writers are Frank O'Connor, Liam O'Flaherty, Kate O'Brien, Norah Hoult, Austin Clarke, Francis Stuart, F.R. Higgins, Brinsley MacNamara, James Joyce, W.B. Yeats, George Moore, Sean O'Casey, Paul Vincent Carroll, Elizabeth Connor, Synge, Con O'Leary, Rearden Connor, Louis Lynch D'Alton, and others (including, I suppose I should add, myself).[4] All that means is that it is the instinct of these writers against that of five censors, none of whom has ever written a piece of fiction, a play, or a poem. For the third time, I am not concerned with which is right and which is wrong but with the fact that our taste and standards are in the most debatable state of flux.

Just as we go to press I have come on an interesting example of this divergence of opinion. It is valuable because we can document it. This is the banning by the Censorship Board of Kate O'Brien's novel *The Land of Spices*.[5] Here are three quotations which give the gist of the reviews of this novel in our national dailies. "This character may indeed complete a

4 Norah Hoult (1898–1984); Austin Clarke (1896–1974); Francis Stuart (1902–2000); Brinsley MacNamara (1890–1963); Paul Vincent Carroll (1900–1968); Una Troy (1910 or 1913–1993), who published under the name Elizabeth Connor; Rearden Conner (1905–1991), né Patrick Rearden Connor.
5 The scandal that exploded in the press and the Senate was caused by the banning of O'Brien's *The Land of Spices* (1941); *The Tailor and Ansty* (1942), by Eric Cross (1905–1980), excerpts of which first appeared in *The Bell* from February to April 1941; and *Laws of Life* (1935), by Halliday Sutherland (1882–1960).

trilogy of saintly types in the Roman Catholic Church, depicted in modern Fiction." (*Irish Times*, 8/3/41.) "It is a picture of rare fidelity and charm, with the portrait of the Reverend Mother, splendidly life-like in every line. But there is one single sentence in the book so repulsive that the book should not be left where it would fall into the hands of very young people." (*Irish Independent*, 11/3/41.) "It is a pity that the author should with a single offensive point mar for sensitive readers an otherwise magnificent character-study of a gallant soul, a truly valiant woman." (*Irish Press*, 18/3/41.) The official notice declares this book to be banned in Eire because it is "in its general tendency indecent." Clearly that is a lie. What is more important at the moment is that the newspapers, circulating all over Ireland, two of them definitely and cautiously Catholic, warmly praise this book (while demurring at "one single sentence," and "a single offensive point"), and speak of it as "splendidly life-like," and a "magnificent character-study of a gallant soul." The five gentlemen of the Board of Censors disagree violently; obviously so violently that they ban the book absolutely. Patently, nothing could be more controversial than the question here raised. In other words Standards and Taste are not established at all here, yet, and one man's opinion is just as good as another's, and the Censors, certainly, cannot be taken as authorities.

Like everything else here, as we have been saying over and over in THE BELL, we have in this to build up from the bottom. What France or England has done cannot help us very much. Imitation is fatal. There are, indeed, certain guiding first principles, universally accepted. To state them is useless. It is only by repeated experiment that we establish the convention which relates these universal principles to native practice. For in this, practice is everything, and theory deceives itself. There are foreign models, too. They are no use to us. Take architecture. You see a perfect-looking building in California or Vienna or Copenhagen. You cannot just lift it up and lob it down in a field in Limerick and make it look as if it belonged. It would not only look ridiculous there, but actually ugly – devoid of association, sentiment, propriety, of that sense of having evolved gradually which made the very same identical building so perfectly adapted to its original site, in its native country. We cannot jump the centuries: we have to travel them; just as a young man can learn everything out of books and yet be a ninny for lack of experience.

The same is true of, say, poetry. Our poets, having for generations been moved by the natural pieties, humanity, the affections, the gods of time and place, cannot from reading Mr. Eliot or Mr. Spender, suddenly start to write that kind of poetry out of their rational appreciation of it, however integral and natural it may be to the original writer.[6] The Arts grow out of living devotion and unrest, nourished and tested alike by long and intimate and intense experience. All the reading and reasoning in the world, without that, must end in work that is derivative and imitative, and without life. That is why to imitate is to be like the tortoise who hung on to the tail of the hare: he got somewhere; he achieved nothing; he remains a joke for the children of the earth.

Meanwhile, we continue to print here all that seems to come up out of that living devotion and unrest, that long and intimate experience of which I have spoken and some criticism, and some analysis, and a little controversy. We try to let life speak for itself, record its own experiences, its own experiments, its own nature, that by long practice and possibly certain repetitions, some kind of pattern may, conceivably, emerge. We try to encourage people to speak of the things they like, rather than the things they dislike – that a kind of natural selectivity may reveal some kind of natural desire for, as Frank O'Connor says, a "desirable vision of life."

The final critic and judge will, as always, be Time. Time has, for example, selected from a mass of Russian literature a few that drank from the source of Life, and rejected the many who had not Life in them. We can form from Chekov, and Tolstoy, and Dostoevsky, and Gorki, and Turgenev, and Aksakov, and Gogol a vague image of the Russian soul, of its ideas as to what is decent and what is rotten, what is desirable and hateful, what is in taste and what is not in taste.[7] We, also, must await Time's final decision, but, in the end, let us never forget that Time is but the conflict of effort and of opinion about it come to some kind of conclusion. Time will not tell if we do not make it tell. As I say, standards do not grow like grass. The intensity of our minds is the measure of the growth of our lives. And it cannot but be that by searching life for the material of literature, and by searching our literature for the pattern of our lives – much as Taine did with English literature – we shall extract the instinct of our race for certain affectible things that it is natural for us all to like and prize. That is, for the good and creative, by examining Sean O'Casey and Synge, and Yeats, and O'Flaherty, and Corkery, and O'Donnell, and Higgins, and others such whose achievements are indisputable, we may with wisdom discover in them a common line of thought or emotion – the repeated

6 T.S. Eliot (1888–1965) and Stephen Spender (1909–1995) were major poets of the twentieth century.
7 Maksim Gorki (1868–1936), also spelled Gorky, né Aleksey Maksimovich Peshkov, and Sergey Timofeyevich Aksakov (1791–1859).

image of the soul's yearning. As for the barren and destructive, Heaven knows we can never be charged here with being too lightly critical of that. And wherever further such examples continue to occur (as with this recent unpleasant incident at the Abbey), there will always be the one or two not only to hasten but to forestall the contempt of Time for those who choose the cynical or idle attitude to Taste and Standards that they are commodities which one may purchase but need never bother to sell.

Help us in this. Whenever you see something fine that any of our people are doing anywhere tell us about it. Whenever you see anybody creating something cheap and ugly, and a large number of people being deluded by him, tell them and tell us about it. Only in that way can we build up real standards worthy of our dreams about a great, modern Ireland.

Ulster[1]

This issue is an Ulster issue: apart from one or two of the regular features everything has been contributed from the North. It was a natural instinct to want to publish, in this Ireland, a little of the work of writers living in that Ireland, and it has made some pleasant contacts; but it has also caused us a certain amount of heart-searching and heart-burning since it is never easy to indulge a particular desire without inviting a general problem. This problem is not primarily the problem of Partition.[2] On the contrary the ghost that it has inevitably raised is the whole question of the future of small cultural entities in a world where Borders fall every day. That problem has been finely stated in this issue in Hubert Butler's article "The Barriers," and there is no need to outline it again, although we may try to apply it more specifically.[3] Applied, it calls not for the destruction of a political Border so much as of a mental Barrier, that both North and South may be saved from the evil results of an unnatural rivalry.

1 "Ulster" appeared in The Bell 2, no. 4 (July 1941): 4–11.
2 The island of Ireland was partitioned under the Government of Ireland Act, 1920, thereby creating two political entities: the six northeast counties that make up present-day Northern Ireland, and the twenty-six others that make up the present-day Republic of Ireland. Although Ulster has nine counties, three of which are in the Republic, it is a term often used to refer to Northern Ireland. The contentious issue at stake for some people is whether the island should remain partitioned with part of it under the authority of Westminster.
3 Hubert Butler (1900–1991), an Anglo-Irishman who was born and died in the same years as O'Faolain, shared many of O'Faolain's perspectives and attributes as an essayist. The article referred to here is "The Barriers," The Bell 2, no. 4 (July 1941): 40–5.

For here we have, apparently as remote from the world as Crete, a small island, divided in two, one portion comically minute;[4] and of this island, the southern portion has been for a long time intent on self-sufficiency, while the little corner clipped off the north has been linked politically to a vast empire and, through it, to every distant corner of the world; and that outward-looking eye, and this introversion and exclusiveness not only help to distinguish, and therefore to divide the two parts of the island, but, as time goes on, they must increase the gap beyond bridging by creating two completely dissonant modes of life. That would be sad, but one might say, at least, that each could go its own fruitful way. Unfortunately, however much there is to be said for those two modes of life – for that international way to the open sea of world-ideas, or for this national way of cultivating our own garden – it cannot be said that either is being at all as fruitful as that undivided Ireland of, say, forty years ago. The emphasis on inward and outward is possibly to blame, this passionate, and therefore almost always stupid, rivalry of hyper-nationalism and hyper-internationalism that has resulted from Partition.

Take the example of literature alone. Forty years ago a magazine such as this would have been in a happier position in many ways. It would have had a larger population of writers to draw upon. Yeats, Æ, Eglinton, Stephens, Colum, Moore, Boyd, Joyce, Robinson, Higgins, Murray, Shan Bullock, Susan Mitchell, Seumas O'Kelly, Conal O'Riordan, Lady Gregory, Douglas Hyde, Stephen MacKenna, O'Grady, Synge, Fred Ryan, Thomas Keohler, Alice Milligan, Daniel Corkery, St. John Ervine, Seumas O'Sullivan, Rolleston, Moira O'Neill, Stephen Gwynn ...[5] The list could go to the size of a bibliography of our old friend the Irish Literary Renaissance: it would include great talkers and scholars and good company like T.W. Lyster, James Montgomery, J.F. Taylor, Gogarty, Cassy Markievicz; men about to win immortality in mortality like Pearse or Thomas MacDonagh,

4 Crete is an island off the mainland of Greece.

5 John Eglinton (1868–1961), né William Kirkpatrick Magee; Shan Bullock (1865–1935), né John William Bullock; Susan Mitchell (1866–1926); Seumas O'Kelly (c. 1875–1918); Lady Augusta Gregory (1852–1932); Douglas Hyde (1860–1949); Stephen MacKenna (1872–1934); Standish O'Grady (1846–1928); Fred Ryan (1876–1913); Thomas Keohler (1873–1942); Alice Milligan (1866–1953); St. John Ervine (1883–1971); Seumas O'Sullivan (1879–1958), who was also known as Seamus, né James Sullivan Starkey; T.W. Rolleston (1857–1920); Moira O'Neill (c. 1865–1955), pseudonym of (Agnes) Nesta Skrine, née Agnes Higginson; Stephen Gwynn (1864–1950).

or Joseph Plunkett or Arthur Griffith; men able in the field of critical journalism like A.E. Malone or James Winder Good;[6] and a host of people
difficult to classify who kept the air vibrant with their patronage, curiosity,
optimism and width of interest. Some of these have died: some have arrived
at the Collected Edition stage; or at the stage when they have retired from
the activity of youth; some are in Exile; only a very, very few like Gogarty
are as active now as they were then. Perhaps Gogarty alone possesses at
the age of sixty-three this gift of perennial youth. It was a period of amazing vitality. It was also a period when not one of these writers would deny
that he was indebted to the literatures of the world. They were national.
They were not nationalistic. The difference is in the arrival of the Ism.

What is the position of Irish literature to-day? What has the second
and third generation been doing in this field? It answers the question to
say that the average age of the thirty-five members of the Irish Academy
of Letters is between fifty-six and fifty-seven. In other words a representative collection of active Irish writers to-day is dismayingly near the average age of sixty. We have been cultivating our garden assiduously, without
interference, for twenty years, spending great sums of money on education, subsidising schools, and theatres, and Gaelic writers, and the results
are that we have hardly any young writers at all.

In a magazine most obstinately devoted to the cultivation of our own
garden it may appear strange that we should suddenly question the wisdom of that exclusive occupation – I might even say pre-occupation –
which we ourselves appear to illustrate in the most extreme degree. I will
answer that in a moment. Just now I want to emphasise how the question
naturally arises in connection with Ulster, and how well it annotates our
chagrin at the loss of the North.

It arises in this way. We have observed that the works we get from the
North and the South are informatively and strikingly different. They
point to the fact that the two parts of the island are – outside politics,
though no doubt because of them – sheering away from one another. The
two sets of manuscripts have qualities and faults apparently now peculiar

6 T.W. Lyster (1855–1922) was a librarian at the National Library; James
Montgomery (1870–1943) was the first Irish film censor; Oliver St. John Gogarty
(1878–1957) was an Irish doctor and writer; Constance Markievicz (1868–1927),
née Gore-Booth, Thomas MacDonagh (1878–1916), and Joseph Plunkett (1887–
1916) were nationalist revolutionaries; Arthur Griffith (1871–1922) was a journalist,
the founder of Sinn Féin, and the president of Ireland in 1922; John Francis Taylor
(1853–1902), Malone, and James Winder Good (1877–1930) were journalists.

to north and south. (This will not shew itself so clearly in what appears in print: the printed thing always shines with its own self-justifying merits; one would see it much more readily in the rejected manuscripts where the exaggerated distortion of the facts is like a magic-lantern projection of some minute microcosm on a slide.)

From the South come a great number of manuscripts that tell, chiefly, of this extreme self-preoccupation which is, in any case, obvious everywhere. Our people are, it would seem, self-absorbed to an amazing degree – so self-absorbed as to cut out, in a way that one would hardly have thought possible in this modern world of constant inter-communication, all detachment, critical sense, a sense of proportion, a sensible objectivity, even a sense of humour. I think it is most significant, for example, that two things which are rare – so rare that they sometimes do not appear at all in THE BELL – are poetry and humour: two poles of detachment. The decline of poetry is almost complete in Southern Ireland – an extraordinary thing in a country which was once prolific in poets. (In that list of the writers of forty years ago almost every one wrote poetry.) On the other hand there is, in what is now being written here, a greater homeliness, a greater intimacy, a new solidity, as of people who do live a natural if not very sophisticated life; and we may feel that the public approval of this magazine is in large part due to the fact that it is honest about that. It does what it can do. It faithfully reflects. If we have any longing it is that we might reflect a more varied world; but that is not in our hands since we have to take the world as we find it.

From the North there come, as a rule, manuscripts of another focus. They are generally not such good photography: they are not preoccupied with depicting a traditional mode of life: they are interested in sidelights, *curiosa*, and ideas. At worst this type of work is chromium and metallic; and at best knowing and acute within a fixed range. Belfast seems to dominate everything here and it is Belfast which seems to owe more to London or Manchester than to the Glens or the Sperrin mountains.[7] One fears, in short, that the roots are cut. On the other hand, one feels that these people of the North are much more detached, and extroverted, have a nice sense of humour, do more thinking, and live a more varied life. I asked one of Ulster's shrewdest observers why so much work from the North has this colouring and he replied, sensibly: "They write like that because that is the background against which they live – which does not

7 The Glens of Antrim and the Sperrin Mountains are major geological features and regions of Northern Ireland.

amount to saying that they are not Irish but merely that they are twentieth-century industrialised Irish, and, if you will pardon my language, the
South has bloody well got to get that into its head. Shan Bullock and
Upper Lough Erne is Ulster, but another kind of Ulster just as the
Gaeltacht is one thing and Dublin is another.[8] That seems to me to be a
very important issue for Irish unity." And surely it is. I think I have been
honest in describing this contrast and the feelings it evokes.

Here, then, in this small island, are two very different modes of life in
a process of consolidation. The results in each case leave something out.
When we look back at that great period of forty years ago we see what
the ideal might be and what has been lost – an extraordinary catholicity
of interest, a fine intellectual curiosity, a bond with the civilisation of the
wide world, a sympathy and understanding with all human sorrows and
tragedies which gave a universal quality to the best work of the time –
one thinks of the width of interest of men like Æ and Stephen MacKenna
– now not at all evident. And, on the other hand, that period of forty
years ago was surely as Irish, as indigenous, as anything ever achieved in
any country by a like group of men and women?[9]

What, then, can enlarge our nationalism? What shall humanise their
metropolitanism? Surely a greater amount of intercommunication would
at least *help*? For it seems to me that each part of our country, South and
North alike, is in grave danger of losing an enormous amount by being
kept in a state of mechanical isolation from one another. Like a sulky
child who retires more and more into itself when refused what it wants,
the fantastic irony and tragedy of the thing is that we in the South are
shutting the door tighter and tighter not only on Ulster but on the world
by our extreme self-preoccupation, and they in the North are bolting and
barring the door by cutting away every possible contact of contamina-
tion with our common heritage of history.

Down here, especially since the war, life is so isolated now that it is no
longer being pollinated by germinating ideas wind-borne from anywhere.
As I write this I see, on the contrary, yet another example (one sees them
every day) of the characteristic hyper-nationalism of the South which
resents and fears outside ideas – a thing the northern mind not only

8 The Gaeltacht is the collective name of the regions, mainly in the west of Ireland,
in which the Gaelic language and culture are predominant.
9 The question mark is O'Faolain's. It is difficult to know whether it is an error
that resulted from a change in phrasing, or a rhetorical device intended to make
the reader question the statement.

cannot understand but positively dislikes. "To-day," says the Most Rev. Dr. Lyons, Bishop of Kilmore, "there are obstacles to the revival of the language that were non-existent then, chief of these being the radio and the cinema, with the ever-persistent danger that the young people may absorb ideas inimical to native culture."[10] We may understand that in the South: we may in sympathy read into it qualifications which are hardly implicit. But that is precisely the kind of statement which is calculated to alienate the North: even as, and I say this as (like his Lordship) an old Gaelic Leaguer myself, it is illustrative of an attitude which, in the words of Hubert Butler's article, is likely to smother all culture behind the very barriers intended to preserve it. As I correct these proofs another example comes in. Professor Corkery, of University College, Cork, says that painters, not writers, are our only really patriotic artists because they alone have cut themselves off from England. It is the language of 1912. Change England to Southern Ireland and it is the language of Sir Edward Carson. It is patriotism gone mad.

Up there, on the other hand, a ruthless industrialism, and an equally devastating hyper-internationalism, are at the same time preventing life from being cultivated with humanity. *There* it is not that there are no barriers – there is no sieve – everything comes flooding in on a people cut off from their roots and will as effectively smother them as our introversion will indubitably smother us if it continues.

We cannot avoid a political opinion on all this. Anyway, no man to-day can say that he does not meddle with politics when politics are meddling all over the world with the humblest peasant. For when we speak of being kept in mechanical isolation we only say what is a political fact. The political, social, and cultural division of this country, and the institutions that arise out of it, and the attitudes it breeds – I might almost say foments – amount to a mechanism. This Ireland is not an organism. It is the result of a theory imposed without consideration for the nature of things, an artifice with only the most superficial roots in life, in history. Our condition to-day, and this applies to both South and North, is largely the inevitable result of a few bright ideas on the part of that civil servant mentality which loves to regulate the lives of millions of people by the typical "quite simple solution." One cannot be simple about political institutions, or about history, or about the interpretation of it, and our feeling is that the interpretation of history in this Ireland is hideously and destructively over-simple. So that when, on the other side of the attack, the Catholic

10 Patrick Lyons (1875–1949) was appointed Bishop of Kilmore in 1937.

Tablet blames us here, in a recent issue, for not assessing the historical heritage of the North, all we can say is that what every intelligent man cries out for, both North and South, is that, in fact, both Ulster and Eire should be given back their common history, in all its complexity, unconstricted by notions forced on us by the zealots.[11]

One wishes, therefore, that this Ulster issue could be merely a little part of a constant interchange of ideas between our people – between the common people on both sides; not for political or commercial reasons but for those purely human reasons which are so much more likely to create a real and fruitful affiliation. The continuance of such a natural relationship might end by a proper understanding of both our difficulties, and the working-out by intelligent, non-political people South and North of some more elaborated and therefore more natural scheme than the present ingenuous mechanism which we call Partition. For until some such intelligent scheme is put forward in a concrete form by disinterested opinion, representative of both the North and the South, all our talk is helplessly in the *vague*.

Lastly – there is nothing in all this which conflicts with the pattern of THE BELL. We have held to one or two ideas firmly from the beginning: we set out from the beginning to be absolutely inclusive, to take in everybody who wished to write for us, without exception of religion or class; we set out to keep to what we do know about, which is only sensible; to acknowledge that we are at the beginning of our creative history and therefore to stick, as far as possible, to our own way of doing things; and, if we have no way, to try to create a way suitable to our national character. I do say, and I think it is true, that foreign models are of little use to us since in this practice is everything, and theory is subject to all sorts of local and individual conditions. But there is nothing to prevent us from taking germinating ideas from wherever we can get them and making our own of them. And one insistent idea of that order is that our fellow-Irishman in the North may not have precisely the same picture that we may have in the South about what constitutes "a native culture." And I sincerely trust that nobody will suggest that because a man is an Ulster Presbyterian, let us say, or even a Belfast Orangeman, he is not therefore a "fellow-Irishman" with as much right as any Southern Catholic to speak on such matters. One wonders how many people do face that fact. One wonders whether many people are not being dishonest, or self-deluded about

11 *The Tablet* is a London-based weekly Catholic review that began publication in 1840.

Partition because, in their hearts, they have no intention of facing that fact. One wonders how much would we sacrifice down here to face that fact? Censorship? The full blast of the Gaelic Revival? The "patriotic" attitude to culture typified by a Professor Corkery? Perhaps, in short, the barriers are not on the Border alone, but also deep within our own minds?

Our Nasty Novelists[1]

The other day I read a little sketch by T.C. Murray, the playwright. (What an honourable title that is, by the way: "playwright" – with its air of the honest craftsman. If a novelist could only be called a "novelwright" I feel that it would help to dissipate some of the vulgar feeling that he is midway between an alchemist and a hypnotist instead of a *makar*, or storymaker, as the old Norse sensibly called his predecessors.) This little sketch of Murray's was called "Conversation on the Bridge."[2] It was a conversation about books; about books by Irish writers; and the Adversary said the usual nice things about Anglo-Irish novelists. "In that world," he said, "our Bluebottle writers ignore everything that is good, or decent, or lovely in the life of our people to batten on the sordid elements that are no more typical of the race than a dead rat in my garden is typical of the garden's everyday life."[3] And then the Adversary went on to say how harmful to the morale of a small nation (though it is not clear what smallness has to do with it) such books can be; and that their merits, as of style and imagination, are merely lures, and that any recommendation they may get in England is due to the Englishman's eagerness to praise anything that flatters his own sense of superiority and denigrates Ireland. And so on.

I do not know whether this was an imaginary conversation between Thomas Murray and his doppelganger, Thomas Doubting, or a true record, but it is a familiar argument which will no doubt go on cropping up

---

1 "Our Nasty Novelists" appeared in *The Bell* 2, no. 5 (August 1941): 5–12.
2 I have been unable to track down another mention of this story elsewhere let alone a copy of it.
3 A bluebottle is a type of fly that subsists on carrion and excrement.

as long as books are written.[4] It is as old as the hills. It is no more confined to Ireland than any literary problem is. But a painful violence characterises it here, and it is argued here with the additional zeal of nationalism to exulcerate the more common zeal of social conventionality or moral devotion.

Thus, in this conversation, the word "typical" inevitably crops up. "These books are no more typical of our race ... " One never hears that argument when the realistic novel is discussed in France, or England, or America – except, possibly, from the Daughters of the American Revolution or the Britain First fanatics.[5] To these people also, literature, painting, music, everything indeed from Mothers' Day to Primrose Day, from West Point to Dr. Barnardo's Homes is assessed solely on its propaganda value.[6] Though they are not intelligent even at that assessment since it never dawns on them that the works of Erskine Caldwell, say (he wrote that grim play *Tobacco Road*)[7] could possibly increase European admiration for America; just as it never dawns on our zealots that Synge, and Yeats, and James Joyce, and O'Casey, and O'Flaherty, have done something to eradicate from American opinion the idea that Irishmen make good cops, excellent ward-bosses, and moderate gangsters, and nothing much besides.

Not that the propagandist idea does not work as powerfully in other brackets. We have just come through a lengthy period during which a great

4 Saint Thomas, one of Christ's apostles, became known as "Doubting Thomas" when he refused to believe that Christ had been resurrected until he had physical proof.

5 Daughters of the American Revolution is a patriotic organisation founded in 1890 that bases its membership on bloodlines. Britain First was a far-right political movement with direct ties to Oswald Mosley (1896–1980) and the British Union of Fascists.

6 Primrose Day is celebrated in Britain to mark the death of Benjamin Disraeli on 19 April. Disraeli (1804–1881) was a popular novelist and prime minister of Britain in 1868 and again from 1874 to 1880; the day is so named because Queen Victoria, who considered Disraeli her favourite prime minister, sent a wreath of primroses, reportedly his favourite flower, to his funeral. The day is still observed by many in Britain who wear primroses to mark the occasion. West Point, in New York State, is a name for the United States Military Academy, where officers are trained. Dr. Thomas John Barnardo (1845–1905), an Irish-born medical missionary, founded homes for destitute children, the first of which began operating in 1870.

7 *Tobacco Road* (1932), by the American author Erskine Caldwell (1903–1987). It was adapted into a successful Broadway play in 1933.

many critics seemed to approve of a book in proportion as it exposed social squalor. Thus it was the combined chorus of the squeals of hogs in Chicago and soft-hearted reviewers in New York that put one of America's worst novelists on the map – Mr. Upton Sinclair, with *The Jungle*, a novel about the "horrors" of the meat-packing industry.[8] England has come right out of that phase since the war began, and with the exasperating capacity of the human mind for going to extremes has swung back to a bullnosed patriotism which – and this in an extraordinary gamut of periodicals, ranging from *The Times* to *Horizon*[9] – has begun and continues to growl that this Joyce fellow was not up to much, and Proust was not very much better, and (so it would seem) what they really want is *Three Daughters of the British Empire* and more classics like *An Airman's Letter to His Mother*.[10] One might be inclined to excuse either brand of intellectual servility in times of war – whether it comes from the Right or the Left (and the Left felt itself at war from 1920 to 1940) – were it not that the trouble about saying so is that the gentleman whom Mr. Murray met on the bridge at midnight would thereupon reply, "But *I'm* always at war!"

What is wrong with this Type idea, this All-Art-must-be-Representative-of-the-Race idea, is that it is just *not* a critical implement. It does not work. There is no such person as a typical Englishman, or a typical Irishman. The infinite variety of human nature rejects such an intellectual abstraction for what it is, and literature illustrates the depths of its folly. Thus, Hamlet can hardly be a typical Englishman (or Dane) except to those who believe that all Englishmen (or Danes) believe in ghosts, behave outrageously to women, kill their uncles and their uncle's employees, and spend their spare time mooning about in graveyards. (It is not surprising, however, that Mr. Murray's doppelganger should have no compunction about telling us exactly what "the typical Englishman" considers to be "the typical Irishman.") I would offer the gentleman a test. I am pretty sure that he would exclude such writers as Kickham and Corkery from

---

8 Upton Sinclair (1878–1968) was an important American naturalist writer. His popular novel *The Jungle* (1906) so ruthlessly depicted the conditions of Chicago slaughterhouses that the American government passed legislation to reform the meat-packing industry.

9 *Horizon* was an influential British periodical that ran from 1939 to 1950.

10 *Three Daughters of the British Empire* has not been traced, but it is likely similar in tone to *An Airman's Letter to His Mother* (1940), a patriotic pamphlet first published in *The Times* and later made into a documentary-style propagandistic short film (1941).

his general detestation of realistic novelists. Yet a more *miserere* of a novel than *Sally Cavanagh* it would be hard to find; and *The Threshold of Quiet* runs it close with a drunken father, a suicidal brother, a melancholic sister, and a couple of gabsters who end up in a Strindbergian gloom sheltering from the rain in a shebeen somewhere outside Kinsale.[11] It is nevertheless one of the finest novels ever written in Ireland. But that it is, or should ever be, typical of life here may the Lord forfend. On the "typical-of-the-race" argument one could proffer to every Jew some grounds for the banning of the Old Testament. On the "typical" argument I should not care to have to defend any Irish character from Queen Maeve to Parnell. To ask that a work of art be "typical" of anything is patriotism gone balmy.

What these people who dislike Realism in our literature do not sufficiently consider is that Realism is purely a matter of convention, and that its opposite – which I take to be Romanticism – is largely, if not wholly, a twist of the convention. An amusing book, published this spring, *Hardy of Wessex*, by Carl J. Weber, illustrates the way the conventional graph wobbles.[12] It shows how cynically Hardy had to alter whole incidents of *Tess of the d'Urbervilles*, to please Victorian primness, after two periodicals had refused it on the ground of its improper explicitness. A third editor agreed to publish *Tess* but even he drew the line at the scene where Angel Clare carried the four milkmaids, one after another, in his arms across the pool. Hardy thereupon kindly substituted a wheelbarrow. (Possibly the gentleman on the bridge with Mr. Murray will here laugh at the hypocritical English.) Every reader of that novel will also remember the manner in which the murder of Alec Stoke is disclosed: the scarlet bloodstain slowly forming on the ceiling beneath the room where he was killed. A "Gentleman with Daughters" wrote in at once to say that this was "Indecent." Now – are these objectors psychopathic cases? Not in the least: they merely reflect the convention of their day – or more usually the day before their yesterday. The outcry against both *Tess* and *Jude the Obscure* was terrific. Yet, so far had the convention altered that when

---

11 *Miserere* is a Latin term, taken from the phrase *Miserere mei Deus*, or "Have mercy on me, O God," in Psalm 51, one of the Penitential Psalms. *Sally Cavanagh* (1869) is a novel by Charles Kickham. *The Threshold of Quiet* is a novel by Daniel Corkery. August Strindberg (1849–1912) was an avant-garde Swedish dramatist. A shebeen is an unlicensed public house.

12 *Hardy of Wessex* (1940).

Hardy died he was buried with pomp in Westminster Abbey.[13] We have had examples of these changes in our own time here. O'Casey is one example. The last book of verse by F.R. Higgins was withdrawn by his Irish publisher for reasons never disclosed: yet on his death Radio Eireann nobly paid him several high tributes and his funeral was attended by Cabinet Ministers.[14]

I have been upbraided here, in the correspondence section, by my friend Frank O'Connor for saying that the censorship (of whose unofficial side all this silly conventionality is a part) is "understandable."[15] With a little more attention to history it would be patent to everybody that this sort of thing is a permanent part of literature, and that the proper response to our censors – as to Mr. Murray's apoplectic bridgehead companion – is not to say that they are monsters but to say that they are naturals. In twenty years time the Dáil will be scratching its head to know how it can rescind the ban which now covers almost every known Irish writer, without exposing the patriots of 1929 for the silly idiots they were – and are. Hardy had the right angle. When the film people gave *Tess* a happy ending he just shrugged. He had made a masterpiece and the masterpiece was indestructible. When the conventions of the rather tiresome Ireland of to-day grow up people will make jokes about it all: like the famous one about the original Comstockian censor who charged a woman with having been so indecent as to give birth to a naked baby.[16] The Censor, like the Law, is always an ass.

Anyway, *our* realists are actually three-parts romantics: even as most of the great romantics were three-parts realists. The stuff of some of the greatest and loveliest romantic literature in the world is not composed of what Mr. Murray calls "all that is good, or decent, or lovely" in life. It has very differently been fashioned out of the most unprepossessing sort of material – Death, Jealousy, Despair, Melancholy,

13 Many believe that the backlash against his last two novels, *Tess of the d'Urbervilles* and *Jude the Obscure*, caused Hardy to stop publishing prose and to commit himself to poetry. His cremated remains were interred in Westminster Abbey's Poet's Corner, though his heart was buried in Stinsford with his first wife.
14 Radio Éireann was founded in 1925.
15 Frank O'Connor, "Public Opinion," *The Bell* 2, no. 3 (June 1941): 61–7.
16 Anthony Comstock (1844–1915) was a moral and social crusader who founded the New York Society for the Suppression of Vice.

Ay, in the very Temple of Delight
Veil'd Melancholy has her sovran shrine.[17]

Horror, Disease, Sin, Corruption, and Shame. One has but to mention Goethe; Villon (the "Ballad of the Hanged," or "Les Regrets de la Belle Hëaulmière"); Baudelaire; Verlaine; the anonymous author of the *Caillech Beire*; Shakespeare,

Ay, but to die, and go we know not where
To lie in cold obstruction and to rot ...

Wordsworth (on the old ragged fellow collecting leeches, or on Lucy); James Clarence Mangan; Poe ("The City in the Sea," or "The Raven"); Whitman; the unknown author of the saga of Deirdre, which is not a pretty story; or of Diarmuid and Gráinne, which is a far from "decent" story; "The Night Before Larry was Stretched"; "The Ancient Mariner"; Robert Burns; Shelley ... The examples are endless.[18]

Conversely it is open to the Romantics to retort that the Realists take things of an apparent pulchritude and make them look forbidding – or worse. It is more than arguable. But in that case there can be no question of our Realists not choosing *nice* subjects. I do not think the argument would get us very far, but it might, at least, get us far enough to make us realise that there is just a little more complexity in the whole subject than may be dismissed in a two minutes conversation on a bridge. In fact like the ancients' arguments about Classic and Romantic there is no end to it.

17 "Ode on Melancholy" (1820), by John Keats.
18 Johann Wolfgang von Goethe is considered by many people to be the greatest German writer; François Villon (1431–1463) was a major French poet; Charles Baudelaire (1821–1867) wrote *Les Fleurs du mal* (1857); Paul Verlaine; *Cailleach Beira* (spelled *Beire* by O'Faolain) is a Scottish legend. The lines quoted are spoken by Claudio in act III, scene i of Shakespeare's *Measure for Measure* (1603–04). William Wordsworth; Edgar Allan Poe (1809–1849); American poet Walt Whitman (1819–1892); Deirdre, Diarmuid, and Gráinne are figures in Irish legends; "The Night Before Larry was Stretched" is an Irish execution ballad from the early nineteenth century; "The Rime of the Ancient Mariner" (1798) is a poem by Samuel Taylor Coleridge (1772–1834); Scottish poet Robert Burns (1759–1796); Percy Bysshe Shelley. Many of these people are writers who led bohemian lifestyles. Several of the works would have been considered risqué or immoral had they been penned by a contemporary writer.

It is about as fruitful as a debate on Document Number Two,[19] or "What did the Bishops say in 1922?" It should be left to the novelists to work out as best they can, and I am sure nobody is going to be corrupted by their experiments. Of all the people in Ireland who even have heard of James Joyce, how many have even read a line of him? I remember my long debate with a commercial traveller about *Ulysses* which ended when I found that he thought the author was George Bernard Joyce.

It is not the subject that matters. It is not the treatment. It is the intensity of feeling that a man brings to bear on life, and that intensity will be affected, naturally, by his intellectual integrity. He must not kid himself, that is, work up a synthetic emotion, argue himself into some attitude which is neither really inherent in the subject nor essential to his own unabused nature. But whether he writes about dead rats or live squirrels does not matter a damn, so long as, if he has to write about dead rats, he can make us feel for the rat. And one of the loveliest poems in English was, as we know, so written about a dead mouse.[20]

Implicit in the objection to realism in literature is, of course, the idea that art is inevitably mixed up in some way with morality. That there have been great artists who were also moral teachers nobody would deny, but that artists must *inevitably* concern themselves with morality is patent nonsense. Is the famous picture of Mona Lisa in the least concerned with morals? And had the painter chosen to paint a Madonna instead, would that make any closer connection with morals? I raise my eyes from this page to a little reproduction of Van Gogh's wonderful painting of an old kitchen chair, and I fail to observe therein any connection with the Ten Commandments, and I think of several fine poems about the moon, such as Shelley's

> And like a dying lady, lean and pale,
> Who totters forth, wrapt in a gauzy veil,
> Out of her chamber, led by the insane
> And feeble wanderings of her fading brain,

19 Eamon de Valera proposed Document Number Two to the Dáil as a challenge to the wording of the Anglo-Irish Treaty; it would have made Ireland more independent and would have refused the contentious oath of allegiance to the King that was demanded of Irish politicians.

20 The poem mentioned is likely "To a Mouse On Turning Her up in Her Nest with the Plough, November, 1785," by Robert Burns (1759–1796), especially given O'Faolain's reference to Burns earlier in the essay. The poem is written in Scots dialect.

The Moon arose upon the murky Earth
A white and shapeless mass ...[21]

What has that got to do with "all that is good, or decent, or lovely" in life? It has been seen, felt, and said, and that is all. Mr. Murray's friend on the bridge may acidly remark, "Pagan!" and he would be partly right: although Shelley was really a Deist. And it is just barely possible, let us say, that the eighteenth Psalm by the poet, David, with its exultant oriental comparison of the Lord and the sun to the bridegroom and his bride, may be a finer poem. Even if it were, Shelley's poem remains – a magnificent lyric: composed, characteristically, of the moon, a skinny woman who has gone off her rocker, a motoring veil, and Death; all welded into an imperishable moment and an immortal image.

I can never understand this latter-day fastidiousness of ours towards common and familiar subjects. Our life is close to the earth. Our ancient literature is far from fastidious. Our conversation is racy and homely. Our manners are not at all fastidious – as an occasional visit to the Dáil may show. In the Gaeltacht we are familiar with a speech and an imagination of the most burly and Rabelaisian kind.[22] If we are to conclude that this modern censoriousness is the result of the invasion into a cheap, urbanised middle-class of the "refainement" which flourishes in the purlieus of Putney then there exists at least one solid reason for the revival of Gaelic.[23] But, alas, even our Gaels are all going villa-ish, hastening as fast as they can to Rathmines and Killiney.[24] They have tucked away the founder of the Gaelic League in the Viceregal Lodge among the Victorian bric-a-brac.[25] One of our best Gaelic writers dresses like the President of Woolworth's.[26] And about the only natural Gael I know is Mr. P.S.

21 From the poem "And like a Dying Lady, Lean and Pale," although Mary Wollstonecraft Shelley (1797–1851), the poet's widow, titled it "Waning Moon" when she published it in 1824. Vincent Van Gogh (1853–1890) was an impressionist painter. The painting is likely *Vincent's Chair with his Pipe* (1888).
22 Rabelaisian refers to that which is representative of the French author François Rabelais (c. 1490–1553), whose stories are marked by earthy humour or bawdiness.
23 Putney is a district in south London.
24 Rathmines and Killiney are fashionable towns that have since become suburbs to the south of Dublin; O'Faolain lived in the latter for much of his adult life.
25 In addition to founding the Gaelic League, Douglas Hyde was the first president of Ireland (1938–45).
26 The F.W. Woolworth Company, a major American retailer, operated from 1878 to 1997.

O'Hegarty, any reference to whose costume would be as dangerous as the famous reference to Tom Casement's hat.[27] While the Dáil, still shoving Irish down our children's throats without once consulting the opinion of their parents, is still at the stage of "I'm-sorry-I-can't-talk-the-Irish-but-me-son-is-learning-it."

Ah, dear! Twenty golden years ago how simple they made it all seem for us, and what a sad mess they have made of "native culture" ever since ... By comparison the only real sanity in this island, as far as culture is concerned, is in the novels of our Realists whose only frailty has been that they have not sufficiently excoriated such ridiculous objects as the ancient mariner who halted Mr. Murray on O'Connell Bridge.[28]

27 P.S. O'Hegarty (1879–1955) was an influential Irish nationalist, historian, and author. In February 1933, Tom Casement (1862/3–1939), Roger Casement's brother, launched a libel suit against the London-based *Daily Express* when it published an article on 22 October 1932 describing his hat as "battered and weatherbeaten," claiming that it suggested that he was "dissolute, debauched, and incapable of managing his affairs."
28 O'Connell Bridge, named for Daniel O'Connell, is the major bridge over the River Liffey in central Dublin.

The Gaelic League[1]

I have just been reading two pamphlets issued by the Gaelic League, and they are so depressing that I find myself pondering all over again on the way politics have ruined so many fine things in Ireland – ruined them as some mad, vinous drug ruins a man's brain. Here is, or was, one of the finest institutions we ever had – fine, potentially, and in its inspiration – and now, when we need it as much as we ever needed it, we find it at its lowest ebb. There are, no doubt, many concomitant explanations, but I am convinced that the main one is this, that, in Ireland, political nationalism has for too many generations absolved us from the need for intelligent, constructive thought. The result has been that we have forgotten (if we ever knew) that ultimately every problem is not a problem of nationality but of civilisation. Let us look at the history of the Gaelic League and see briefly what its story has been.

The Gaelic League was founded in 1893, a year short of half-a-century ago, by a small group of people which included the man who is now President of Ireland, Dr. Douglas Hyde. At first, since its chief aim was to encourage the speaking of the Irish language, and a live interest in its literature, it seemed natural to its founders that it should be non-sectarian and non-political; thus, the President of the League for several years was Dr. Hyde himself, a Protestant, with little practical interest in current politics. It was not by any means the first organisation with these objects as will be known to all readers of Mr. Desmond Ryan's history of the language-revival, *The Sword of Light*.[2] But in those early years it did far better than the others because it came at a better time, had abler men behind

1 "The Gaelic League" appeared in *The Bell* 4, no. 2 (May 1942): 77–86.
2 *The Sword of Light* (1939), by Desmond Ryan (1893–1964).

it, profited by the accumulated interest roused by these preliminary efforts, and was more popular in its appeal. Then, as the century crept on, Ireland saw the rise of the new revolutionary movement fostered by the re-organised Irish Republican Brotherhood, a wholly political body with a wholly revolutionary ancestry. The Brotherhood took an early interest in the League, helped to rear it in the spirit of political nationalism, far differ-ent to the purely cultural or pedagogic atmosphere of its predecessors, and in the upshot the League was steered towards political aims. The first overt result was the resignation of Dr. Hyde in 1915, and the second, less overt, was that after 1915 the League associated itself more or less actively with the general political revolutionary movement. For example, it was in the League organ that Dr. Eoin MacNeill first proposed the founding of a Volunteer Army, and it was its secretary, The O'Rahilly who, under the guidance of Bulmer Hobson, the most active I.R.B. man of the period, invited a representative group (carefully larded, of course, with I.R.B. members) to meet and found the Volunteers, the progenitors of the I.R.A.

Here it is well to note that the Gaelic League has always been some-what evasive about its relation to politics. This was partly due to the well-known fact that everything touched by the I.R.B. inevitably became un-candid by association with the methods of secret conspiracy. But this evasiveness arose too, because, when all is said and done, there really is nothing sectarian or political about the idea of reviving a language or a literature, so that whereas many members remained members for polit-ical reasons, which they preferred to keep more or less quiet, others who had no interest in politics would have left the League if it had declared overtly that its objects and methods were not to be so much cultural as political. At any rate, as everybody who has worked in the League knows, the political colouring was there. Indeed there arose in it a kind of mental, unexpressed schism between the men of action and the men with purely intellectual interests. There was even among the younger an air of slightly patronising superiority on the part of the fighters which certainly did not assist the thinkers. The essential fact is that on the cultural and intellec-tual side the League was weakened, indeed bled white. It stands to rea-son. When men like MacNeill and The O'Rahilly, to mention only those two, and to omit mention of their scores of lieutenants down through the organisation, began to devote themselves to political and military affairs they had very much less time and interest for the main business of their society. One example, out of many, of a studious man deflected in this way is Terence MacSwiney. The arguments used at the time seemed impregnable. "Autonomy first, and everything else will follow."

So this semi-political League continued to exist, until such time as the revolutionary period ended and a native government was established in 1922, with every political party clamatory in its loyalty to the Language Revival. Then one would certainly expect either of two things to happen: (a) the League would either disband itself, as other organisations of the period did; or (b) the League would announce candidly that it now had no political objects and that its aims were entirely linguistic and cultural. It did neither. It dived deeper than ever into political lobbying. That is probably sufficiently inherent in human nature to be called natural – men hate to give up any activity to which they have devoted years of their lives – but that this "activity" has not in recent years been very fruitful one may see in the pamphlet referred to: the opening pages admit it in these words: "During the last twenty years … the Gaelic League has not been there, or there only in name." Meaning that its political activities have been a complete failure. In spite of that, as we shall see, the League has not learned its lesson.

Now, in what did the original appeal of the Language Revival, and of the Gaelic League lie? For it once had a considerable power of inspiration. Its appeal was that the League never regarded Language merely as Speech – merely, that is, as a mechanical means of communication. How could it? Almost any other modern language was, in that, superior to Gaelic, and still is, owing to the historical fact that Gaelic was relegated for two centuries to the veriest poor in out-of-the-way places, and in complete desuetude everywhere else. As a practical language in this country English is at present unarguably the better language for all purposes. Everybody speaks English fluently; its commercial utility is apparent; it possesses an interesting modern literature, dating from the seventeenth century; it opens avenues to the literature of every country in the world; and it has so long been the practical language of our national resurgence that all our political ideas, every single token of patriotic nationalism that concerns us, with only one exception, has been expressed in English. The one exception consists of the two-words "Sinn Féin." These priceless historical associations are, indeed, the only retort to the basic plea of the language-revivalist that Gaelic is *not* merely a speech-form but is a vessel of great spiritual content.

Nevertheless, the language-revivalist is in an unassailable position. For although modern Ireland, by which we mean Ireland from 1750 onward, has expressed herself in English, there is behind 1750 a long, long story. For those centuries Gaelic, both the language and the literature, is like a well in whose dark silence one sees an image of that shadowy other-self which is our ancestral memory. And unless we can communicate, even if it be only in stumbling, half-understood whispers, with those drops that are part of the whole stream that fed us, we are, to put it no higher than the coldly intellectual plane, the less wise as to our own natures, so variously and often so incongruously formed by the flux of history. But there is, in this knowledge, as one can never explain to those who have not had the experience, in these sudden glimpses of the *vestigia veteris flammae*,[3] something far more than a merely intellectual illumination. There is something, to explain which one would have to speak of pieties and philosophies that only one so remote from it all as Pater has ever properly expressed; there is the whole traditional "religion of usage," of habit, of custom; the merits of those humble "household gods" whose veneration conveys a sense of personal distinction that separates every "ancient house" from newly-made people; whose indefinite history and almost total lack of interpretation provoke also those speculations which are the beginning of all personal understanding. Those who have not had this – if one may so call it – "romantic" experience of association with the immemorial past cannot imagine how illuminating it is to discover that, by virtue of it, even the most plebeian memories, the most vulgar tales, the most humble customs, suddenly become in the literal sense venerable, indeed sanctified, by becoming an intimate part of one's own inheritance, one's own story, one's own nature.

That entire and so slowly formed psychosis which, in Arnold's word, we sometimes call the "genius" of our race opens itself fully only to those who can touch, through Gaelic, the folk-world of our people's imagination, their ancient ways, the charm of their literature, their wilful modes of life, even their tabus and fetishes and pious simplicities, all preserved uninterrupted for too many centuries to be worn out of us by even two centuries of Europeanisation.[4] In a word, Gaelic is essential if we wish to inform ourselves about ourselves. It is a need and a gift which our Anglo-Irish friends must sometimes envy us, as we sometimes envy them their gifts and memories of another kind, less ancient, not less gracious, more

---

3 O'Faolain appears to have reversed the phrase *veteris vestigia flammae*, which is Latin for "the embers of a former flame." It was famously uttered by Dido, the Queen of Carthage, in book IV, line 23, of Virgil's *Aeneid*, when her capacity to love is rekindled by a new lover. Virgil (70–19 BCE) was a renowned Roman poet.
4 Matthew Arnold discusses the Irish in *On the Study of Celtic Literature* (1867). Some of O'Faolain's claims in his essays that the Irish lack intelligence but have an abundance of creativity can be traced to this source.

informed by that intelligent experience which ours lacks. All of which, of course, assumes that we are talking the language not of politics or insular nationalism, but of civilisation, which we here apprehend by becoming, through Gaelic, a richer part of it.

Now is this, or indeed has it been for many years, the strength of the Gaelic League? I am afraid not. These things are of the mind, and are only won by the exercise of the mind, by tedious study, by patience and humility, by consideration, by taking thought. These are the things that have attracted to Ireland, over and over again, poets and savants who were prepared to delve for this gold. When the Gaelic League turned to politics it turned from these things to a policy of quick-returns, of opportunism which could never win them. The only thing that opportunism could win was an opportunity, i.e., to achieve them more easily. And it did win it in 1922. But, by then, the Gaelic League had vulgarised itself and betrayed itself, and it has gone on doing so ever since 1922. The result is that, now when the politicians are in power, the League is without power. It has thrown away its weapons, and it can only whimper and beg and complain – as the pamphlet to which I have referred does from beginning to end – being starved mentally, being without constructive intelligence, having turned so early from it. The sad part of the story is that the politicians are quite ready to fulfil their part of the bargain if only there were some cultivated society there to tell them what to do.

The fatal error of the Gaelic League has been, in short, that it has neglected its business; and Douglas Hyde has lived to be proven right. During the last twenty-seven years it should have been engaged in study, deciding what must be done when the critical moment came, been creating a body of civilised intellect, been as I have already said – and nobody can use the phrase too often – "taking thought." Take the example of Education – a specific interest of the League. When the critical moment came, when Gaelic Leaguers found themselves in power, when the Government was ready to take advice from any expert body available, there was no plan. And we all know the result. But, then, not one solitary, useful, constructive plan emerged from the League in all that quarter of a century which was half its life.

And now, we turn to this most recent pamphlet issued by the League to see how much thinking has been going on in the immediate present; to see how many constructive ideas the League has been pondering; the fruit of its bitter experience; and what do we find? Alas, we find only the old, useless, rambling rhetoric, the old veiled threats of every League platform since 1915. We find, moreover, that the League proposes to intensify its interest in politics, speaking of its "anxiety about politics" as if it had not ruined its mental stamina on that drug twenty-five years ago. Its enemy, we find now, is not England, but the native "bureaucracy," "the State," the Ministers of State, the Civil Service, and even the Church comes in for its whack. It is going to work on these, i.e., "instruct" them; lobby with them; if necessary bully them. Anglo-Irish writers, too, are trounced on page after page, with sneers at O'Casey and Yeats by name, and others by innuendo. This attack on Irish literature in English is particularly deplorable. Thus, it says that sixty or seventy years ago this literature was mere "comic relief," made by the Ascendancy for the "amusement of others." That is blindly malicious; it ignores Kickham, Gerald Griffin, Carleton, the Banims, Lefanu, Edgeworth, Robert Dwyer Joyce, Thomas Davis, Mangan, Mitchel, and so on.[5] This hatred of the Gaelic League for Irish literature in English is not nice to contemplate, and by putting two good things against one another it is simply creating an utterly pointless dissension. Is it really even good propaganda to say that the "people feel that Anglo-Irish literature to-day is colonial, and leave it for the most part to the English and *the denationalised Irish to read*?"[6]

But there it is. The League is apparently quite content with that by way of constructive thought – ready to abolish utterly all books other than those written (or to be written) in Gaelic, and to abolish English utterly as the general, practical language of the island, feeling that the special Nationalism within its keeping cannot otherwise exist here. Then, if we ask what is this special kind of Nationalism, it proposes, in the most perky tone, to instruct us freely:

It would seem that the very first plank in the rebuilt platform of the League must be the interpretation of nationality to the people at large; but more especially to politicians and Anglo-Irish writers, they

---

5 Gerald Griffin (1803–1840); John Banim (1798–1842) and Michael Banim (1796–1874); Sheridan Le Fanu (1814–1873); Maria Edgeworth (1767–1849); and Robert Dwyer Joyce (1830–1883).
6 *O'Faoláin's note:* These attacks are continuous and unscrupulous. In *An Glór*, April 11th, there is an attack on the Book Fair. "The majority of these books are published in London and it is the same publishers who finance the Fair. It is clear that whatever influence there is at present behind our culture is coming from London." The Fair, of course, is financed in Ireland. In a current *Rosary* Daniel Corkery contemptuously dismisses Nationalist verse in English. [*Editor's note: The Irish Rosary* was a monthly Catholic periodical founded by the Dominicans in 1897.]

do so mix things up. And if on occasions it will also find itself saying a word or two to such publicists and professors and others who would settle for us what Nationality really is, it will do so in sheer human kindliness and not for the purpose of shutting them up ...

The Gaelic League, in its despair, seems to wish to go even farther still into the realm of politics than this: for if a vague suspicion begins to dawn on the reader of that nicely gloved threat he will find corroboration for his fears in the League's new-found contempt for the Scottish and Welsh language-movements, and in its admiration for more drastic tactics, expressed hardly without a glove in these sentences:

From such movements we cannot learn how to do what we want to do. *From certain Continental movements we have much to learn. As a fact the temper of our movement, and the energy and daring of it, have more in common with them than with those nearer home.*

In the other pamphlet to which I referred, one on Film-making in Ireland (issued by a branch of the League),[7] we come on exactly the most kind sort of rodomontade. Here are some examples. "We cannot permit film-making to remain in the hands of the Jews, the eternal enemies of Christianity, for Ireland's sake at any rate." "Let us make Ireland the master of Europe in the twentieth century!" "Eire's vocation in the twentieth century is to renew the love of Christianity throughout the world." "Griffith spoke of a wall of paper built about Ireland by England. It is nothing to the wall of celluloid. This Branch will level both of them, by force if necessary – with dynamite, if necessary!" "We must also (sic) look ahead to the time when Europe, or what is left of Europe, may once more look to Ireland for leadership."[8] "But is there such a thing as Europe? It seems all very remote now, except in terms of newspaper reports and air-raids."

This is surely a long, long way from Douglas Hyde's ideals for the original League, from the patient absorption of all that Gaelic has to offer. This is not mental stuff at all but, as the Germans say, up-from-the-stomach,

---

7 *O'Faolain's note:* In justice I must add that this pamphlet contains a few quietly sane suggestions from such wiser heads as Liam Gogan, the Revd. R.S. Devane and Ernest Blythe. [*Editor's note:* Liam Gogan (1891–1979), R.S. Devane (1876–1951), and Ernest Blythe (1889–1975).]
8 The parenthetical remark is O'Faolain's.

dark-blood-stream stuff. It is a kind of emotional hæmorrhage bearing no
relation whatever to that true intellectual and spiritual illumination which
comes, and comes only, from earnest speculation on the past. Listening to it
the young men of the League will want not to sit down and devote themselves to thought, but to do exciting things, noisy things, perfectly in accord
with it, and utterly futile; like the branch of the Gaelic League which we saw
marching through the streets of Dublin a few weeks ago exclaiming for
more and cheaper land for the cottiers in Meath; as if these cottiers will only
speak Gaelic by the con-acre, or as if they were not utterly pampered already
by a terrorised Civil Service.[9]

And yet the Gaelic League has many valuable things of its own on
which to work – Gaelic music, folk-songs, traditional folk-lore, literature,
the language itself, the technique of teaching it, problems of education
connected with it, dances, sport. The revived annual Oireachtas has done
good work with some of these.[10] Why not be content to do a little more
constructive work on those lines? One could name a dozen societies busily
occupied with interests that do not offer a tenth of the problems those
things offer. Why not, for instance, publish a magazine in Gaelic? But why
continue? The whole thing is absurd. The organ of the Gaelic League itself
published a complaint a few weeks ago that the players employed by the
Gaelic Dramatic Society do not always talk Gaelic off the stage; and yet,
that same paper, in the same issue, was so humourless as to say – "It is we,
and we alone, who practise the true spirit of Nationalism!"

There *is* room for a creative, constructive Gaelic League – for any intel-
ligently informed body which will be modest, and patient, and realise
that its own immense problems can only be solved by – once again – taking thought. But the other kind of thing is merely so much loud noise,
so much sentimental sludge, and if any reader would wish to see a good
example of this he may turn to that fortnightly penny paper of the
Language Revival, *An Glór*, under the date of March 28th, and read the
front page article on Migration – full of the old sentimental rhetoric, but
too lazy to make one single constructive proposal of any kind – beyond
calling on the Clan of Gaels to answer the voice of Eire in her misery with

9 In the Irish land system, conacre is the renting of a plot of land that has already
been ploughed and prepared for seeding.
10 Oireachtas is now more widely known as the name of the Irish parliament, but
it is also the name given to an annual festival organised by the Gaelic League. It is
an Irish term, meaning "assembly" or "gathering."

the "fiercely national spirit, the truly national spirit" – etc. and da capo.[11] This while civil servants are doing their best to work out some scheme; while men like Peadar O'Donnell have been working and studying for years, in every country in Europe, to understand the problem of migratory labour here.[12]

The moral is general. Twenty-five years of politics have infected a generation with monomania. The loss is as great as a European War to the intelligentsia of one of the combatants. All we may do is to direct the younger generations towards the fields left barren by their fathers. If we do not, the Old Man of the Sea will simply ride this country in another quarter-century to its intellectual grave.[13]

11 Éire is the official name of Ireland in the Irish language. Da capo is a musical term that directs the musician to repeat from the beginning.

12 *O'Faolain's note:* As an example of the political acumen of the Gaelic League when it *does* make a concrete suggestion, see *An Glór* for April 11th, front-page banner-heading, UNEMPLOYMENT – proposing that unemployment is caused by allowing women to work for salaries, quoting Leo XIII and asking for a Christian Code to defend the hearth. [*Editor's note:* Leo XIII (1810–1903) was elected Pope in 1878.]

13 At the end of "The Mart of Ideas" (the next essay) an editorial note reads: "*The Gaelic League:* Professor Daniel Corkery has sent us a fourteen-page reply to the May editorial on the above subject. We have refused to print this reply because it introduces personalities into what should be an objective discussion, and because the writer expressly refuses to make any excisions whatever. Readers will, no doubt, have an opportunity of reading the professor's reply elsewhere."

The Mart of Ideas[1]

It is one of the most dangerous illusions of your man of action that he can starve the public mind and keep its conscience alive. He will hope to rely on the public to boycott a Black Market in goods while he himself runs a Black Market in ideas. For that is how the illusion works in any country where only the few, usually economically independent, are given free access to ideas and where intellectual indifference is encouraged as a virtue in the masses. One clear sign that this intellectual indifferentism to ideas is being encouraged is the contempt of the public for anything which is not a popular political issue, and it was illustrated here a little while ago when somebody declared that the average man in this country does not care a rap about the Literary Censorship. If he was correct he should have wrung his hands with sorrow. Instead he was, apparently, quite pleased.

This attitude to ideas is based, ultimately, on the theory that the public can be divided into those who do not think, those who do not care, and those who act. At the top are the intelligentsia. These, since they *do* think are dangerous people, and therefore they are commonly mocked. "Our pseudo-intellectuals"; "the intelligentsia, God-help-us"; "the literary cliques"; "our scribbling journalists." How well one knows the contemptuous phrases, all intended to suggest that they do not, in fact, think at all – are, in brief, charlatans. At the bottom are the masses who can be kept quiet with bread and circuses. In between are the men of action who do the real work of the country. Now, nobody will deny that in most countries the mass of the people are, in normal times, indifferent to almost every plea that does not concern their own comfort. But it is astonishing

1 "The Mart of Ideas" appeared in *The Bell* 4, no. 3 (June 1942): 153–7.

that anybody should think this indifference a matter of no importance. Indeed, time and again, even your man of action comes up against it, as when in an hour of crisis, forgetting how long he has played upon that indifference, even counted on it in the tactics of his benevolent despotism, he will suddenly begin to assault his public with the most honourable and intelligent arguments. And nobody is more pained than he is if his pleadings fall on deaf ears. Look out of any office-window. Those crowds who pass and re-pass – it is of those that any man may say that not one in a thousand cares tuppence about such things as the Literary Censorship. But if there are also thousands who do not care tuppence about the Black Market, the Gaelic Language, A.R.P., the Licensing Laws – except in so far as it is fun to break them – is it not simply because they never do consider?[2] And how can you possibly expect any man to think about the Black Market when for thirteen years you have been employing a Literary Censorship to keep him from thinking about anything at all?

There is no connection between the two? Ah, but there is. There is this danger of encouraging people "not to care." For it is not a question of whether what they do not care about is, or is not, in itself, of vital importance. Three weeks ago, for example, Eugene O'Neill's *Mourning Becomes Electra* was staged in one of our provincial cities.[3] In two churches condemnatory sermons were preached about the play, presumably because it dealt with an incest theme. I am quite certain that these good provincial audiences have no more than a very mild academic interest in incest, and that the greater part of them hardly knew, or even still know, what it is. Ignorance of the subject would therefore be small loss to them. But, what an attitude, to want to cherish their ignorance! What it amounts to is "Don't think about anything that does not concern you." Combined with the implication that there is very little which does concern us. And although it is, indeed, very pleasant and easy to have such an obedient and innocent populace, surely if their obedience and innocence is automatic, i.e., based on indifference and not on an intelligent appreciation of what is involved, it will inevitably crack when they do come face to face with some difficult task which *does* concern them. And then it becomes futile, because it is too late, for your man of action to argue and plead on reasonable grounds, since he has for years been deliberately nourishing

2 A.R.P. refers to the Air Raid Precautions, a series of measures to protect people and property in the event of air attacks. The Air Raid Precautions Act was passed into law on 26 July 1939, just over a month before Britain declared war on Germany.
3 *Mourning Becomes Electra* (1931), by Eugene O'Neill (1888–1953).

what is tantamount to a contradiction in terms – a brainless morale, a moronic mass to which he can make no intelligent appeal whatever.

If the reader hesitates to believe that this kind of populace is being created I would ask him how long it is since he has himself heard, or heard of, a frank, *public* discussion of any three of the following subjects – Birth Control, Freemasonry, The Knights of Columbanus, Unmarried Mothers, Illegitimacy, Divorce, Homo-sexuality, Rhythm, Lunacy, Libel, Euthanasia, Prostitution, Venereal Disease, or even Usury – to take only a few subjects which do concern us closely.[4] Surely it is the fact that we are not having enough public discussion of all sorts of things that breeds the "not caring" attitude? Surely it is this indifferentism that made it possible for a pamphlet issued recently by one of the best-known organisations in the country, the Gaelic League, to say – with the amiable idiocy of a mental sleep-walker – "But is there such a thing as Europe? It seems all very remote now except in terms of newspaper reports and air-raids?"

Thirty years ago nobody would have denied the importance of a live intelligentsia here. Then those same people who now deride it made use of it day in and day out to disseminate all those doctrines which have resulted in a free Eire. That intelligentsia exists still; small; naturally uneven as it always is; composed of every man and woman who keeps his brains burnished and is neither so snobbish, nor so cautious, as to hide his light under a bushel; every paper and every periodical in the country is a member of it – though what each sells is of course a very difficult matter, and the investor has to be supremely cautious lest he should suddenly wake up to find that he has been dealing for years with a Bucket Shop.[5] For in this mart there is no Committee to elect members, and every man who opens his mouth in public is a legitimate broker.

And that, of course, indicates the whole point and purpose of the Literary Censorship as it is worked. It does not propose to defend fair-trading in ideas. It does not aim at making ideas more easily marketable. It does not aim at establishing a smooth machinery for their interchange

---

4 The Knights of Saint Columbanus was founded in Belfast in 1915. In mid-century Ireland, it was a very powerful Catholic fraternal lay organisation; a number of high-ranking Irish politicans were members. Rhythm refers to the natural method of birth control that demands periods of abstinence in line (or in rhythm) with the woman's fertility cycle.

5 A bucket shop is a brokerage house that "buckets" – or secretly sets aside – a customer's order instead of executing it in the hope of obtaining the stock or commodity at a lower price.

but rather, a smooth machinery to prevent their interchange. And, of course, it could, even under the present Act, and would if the public demanded it, do these positive things. It could, for example, assist publishers by allowing them to present manuscripts for pre-publication inspection. It could, and is, in chosen cases, actually supposed to open up negotiation with authors and publishers. It never does. It could take into account the aims and intentions of writers, and again is supposed to do so, but does not. It may revise its decisions – but never once, in the case of a book, has it done this. All of which omissions have turned it into a wholly negative and destructive piece of machinery; and all of which it has done and failed to do because people "do not care."

We beg anybody who may be glad at this "not caring" to revise his ideas. After all, if a man is not interested in the Literary Censorship, why should he be interested in any public issue at all?

It is not too sweeping to say that ideas, as we will agree if we have anything of sane idealism in us, are the substance of life. They do not come from the bottom upwards. They come from quiet corners of life which make no fuss, and seep slowly downward to inform the whole of society. To give a tiny example, when Ann says to Angel "I have a complex about such-and-such," it does not occur to either of them that they are, for the moment, dominated by the minds of two or three old professors in Western Europe.[6] It is against all such, against every man who takes life seriously, who takes thought seriously, who takes art and culture seriously, that the Literary Censorship is directed by those who would establish in place of thought a rigid orthodoxy that no man must even discuss, let alone question or deny. For any man to say, to be pleased, that nobody cares about that is, in the absolutely literal sense, to take leave of his senses. It is to prepare the way for the handing over of all power to the caucus and the mob.

6 It is assumed that Ann and Angel are stock names.

That Typical Irishman[1]

A friendly correspondent asks, "Why do you object so strongly to talk about the 'typical Irishman,' or 'the traditional Irishman'? If you allege that there is no such person would you explain why this is so? I never have noticed any objection to talking about 'the typical Englishman' or the 'typical Frenchman.' Why should we be so different?"

I think it might be interesting to try to put the viewpoint of THE BELL on these questions.

As it so happens I had just been finishing Charles Seignobos' *History of the French People*, the day before I got this letter, and at the end of that book I had come, quite properly as it seemed to me, on a definition of the typical French nature: a brilliantly clear and unsentimental definition.[2] It is very much to the point of our correspondent's enquiry to ask why is it that one does not feel any such objection there as one would have felt had the definition come at the end of a *History of the Irish People*. I think that reason is patent. Seignobos summed up at the end of a long, complex, formative story of the life and growth and consolidation of a free people, and only after he had carefully indicated the many varieties (Gascon, Fleming, Norman, etc.) that exist inside the general bracket of their ultimate synthesis. Centuries of free development had gone into that welding. To the story of no people is one ever able to put the word *Finis*, but in so far as something clear and rounded has emerged from the

---

1 "That Typical Irishman" appeared in *The Bell* 5, no. 2 (November 1942): 77–82.
2 *History of the French People*, by Charles Seignobos (1854–1942), was originally published under the title *Histoire sincère de la nation française: essai d'une histoire de l'évolution du people française* (1933). It was a major influence on O'Faolain's *The Irish* (1947).

complex history of that most complex people, one can roughly say that the modern Frenchman has the finality of an achievement. That seems to me to be fair enough. But, surely, with us the case is utterly different? We have been free only for, by comparison with France, a breath's length. We do indeed possess some ancient traditions, but we do not possess, are not possessed by, one clear Tradition. That synthesis is not yet, and it will not be for many centuries to come.

We have insisted on that repeatedly, saying that we are now at the real beginning of our adult history. And we have put it before ourselves consistently that we shall never even begin to build until we do realise the challenge of our comparative nakedness. For, indeed, all we have achieved so far is to have clarified a certain continuity of desire – to have preserved some few precious strands from the past – to have established our insistence of desire for our own way of life – and to have won an opportunity to get down, at last, to the manufacture of our own house out of these few sticks and stones that the centuries have not wholly destroyed. One has only to look about to see that we have built very little, so far, to which we can point and say, "*There* is the sort of thing we have always wanted to do."

Now the people who want to put the "typical Irishman" across on us are denying all that. They are trying to make us imagine that what has barely begun is finished. They are describing the baby before it is born. They are buying History before it is written. They are trying to block or thwart the natural development of our people. They are trying to squeeze us, as the feet of Chinese women used to be squeezed, into an ideological shoe. And some have not the slightest objection to mutilating us in the process; not even to destroying without pity the little we do possess from antiquity.

Thus, there is here a small but very vocal number of people who – with a complete disregard for the mixed nature of our blood – call themselves Gaels; people, sometimes, of such good old Gaelic stock as the Cunninghams and the Blackhams.[3] These people would like to throw aside the Anglo-Irish strain in Irish life. Even normally intelligent men, like Professor Daniel Corkery, or Professor Michael Tierney, will lend themselves to this; as the former did in a book which dismissed Yeats and tied itself up in knots to try to preserve Synge, and as the latter did, recently, in *Studies*, when he posited that the only typical Irishmen are the peasant and the

---

3 Cunningham and Blackham are names that are, respectively, Scottish and English in origin.

priest.[4] To such lengths will this curious Procrusteanism go that even what we have of true Gaelicism is itself liable to mutilation.[5] Thus, readers of this magazine may remember reading here with pleasure extracts from a recent book called *The Tailor and Ansty* – the authentic record of the fireside conversation of an old tailor in West Cork, a well-known Gaelic speaker and folklorist. (As I have sat many a happy night by his hearth I can vouch for the genuineness of that racy talk.) The book has just been put on the censored list as "in its general tendency indecent." One may say, sardonically, that this conception of decency is indeed building from the bottom up. It is, at least, new! And the pure traditionalist might well tell us that we are "asking for it" in our pleas for "beginnings." But this is not building. It is merely destroying and mutilating the little that we have, wiping out the old foundations on which we must build our new house.

Professor Tierney would condemn this treatment of his "typical peasant." But does he realise that this sort of thing is inherent in the effort to force on us a Master Type of one kind or another? Does Professor Corkery realise it? Does Aodh de Blacam? Do the starry-eyed young fanatics of Craobh na hAiseirghe realise it?[6] Does the Gaelic League as a whole realise that in attempting to impose a narrow differentiation upon us ("It is we alone who possess the true spirit of Nationality.") they are in fact digging their own graves – since, obviously, it is open to any powerful group to invent some new differentiation which may as sensibly exclude them? Such differentiation is always double-edged. To go out of Ireland for an illustration it has been observed that there is a certain amount of anti-Semitism among American Catholics. Nothing could be more unwise, since there are just as many people in America who could work up an anti-Catholic feeling as there are Catholics to work up an anti-Jew

4 Michael Tierney (1894–1975), a TD, a senator, and professor of Greek at University College Dublin, was a regular contributor to *Studies*, an Irish journal that has been published by the Jesuits since 1912.

5 In Greek mythology, the robber Procrustes compels his victims to lie on his iron bed. If they are too short, he stretches them, and if they are too long, he cuts off their legs. His name has become synonymous with those who impose an unnatural uniformity.

6 Craobh na hAiseirghe (Branch of the Resurrection) was a pro-Axis, fascist organisation that sought such measures as the prohibition of English and moving the Irish capital from Dublin to Tara. Its political wing, Ailtirí na hAiseirghe (The Masons of the Resurrection), won strong first-preference votes in the 1944 Dáil elections.

feeling. To return, there is here a growing feeling of fed-upness with the Gael. (I know one man, a former Gaelic Leaguer of great enthusiasm, who now always spells the words – Gaelic £eague.) So that it may yet happen that it is we Anglo-Irish writers who will have to save the Gaelic tradition, to which we owe so much, from the follies of its more narrow-minded professional exponents.

A good deal of this narrow differentiation comes, no doubt, from the fact that our knowledge of our own history is still incomplete, and that a great part of Irish history as it is written is such a refraction of the facts that our books of history are not so much lenses – through which we see more clearly that which happened – as prisms through which we see coloured distortions of what happened. Thus, anybody with a cold knowledge of our story need but evoke half a dozen of our great names to realise what widely differing "types" we have thrown up from time to time. What Master Type, for example, could possibly contain in one all the varied elements of seven or eight such men, to take them at random, as Archbishop Croke, J.K.L., Thomas Davis, Dan O'Connell, Edward Martyn, Michael Collins, Jo Biggar, Parnell, O'Conaire, and Yeats?[7] One may indeed find aims held in common. But what a contrast of personalities, of techniques, of morality, of human nature. If Davis is a "typical Irishman," then O'Connell, his opposite in every conceivable human way, most certainly cannot be a "typical Irishman." Dr. Croke and Jo Biggar? Martyn and Collins? Parnell and Bishop Doyle? But we have not yet studied our great personalities enough. They remain, all too often, not as men but as myths.

Some day somebody must study the rise here of this extraordinary warping of Tradition which might well make one cry out – Oh, Tradition, how many crimes are committed in thy name! There must be many conjoint explanations, but one, I think, is that the ideas of a former time are being applied to this time without the necessary adjustment. We have about us too many elderly men and women whose minds are still steeped in the psychosis of the Besieged City. They were the Irishmen with their backs to the wall. They cannot adjust themselves to the open air of political liberty. They go on thinking of the Anglo-Irish as if Landlordism still

---

7 Thomas Croke (c. 1823–1902) was appointed Archbishop of Cashel in 1875; J.K.L., the acronym for James, Bishop of Kildare and Leighlin, né James Warren Doyle (1786–1834), was appointed in 1819; nationalist politician Joseph Biggar (1828–1890); nationalist leader Charles Stewart Parnell; and writer Pádraic Ó Conaire (1882–1928).

existed. They go on hating England as if this were still the nineteenth century. There are men and women who still go red in the face about Proselytising Protestantism as if the boot were not now on the other foot. These people are unable to begin to build a free Ireland because their minds stopped dead thirty years ago in an Ireland that was not free.

The essential thing that we have to keep on dinning into our heads is that History is not a verb in the past tense. It is now, and it is in the future. History is a vast landscape constantly unfolding. To view the past one withdraws, as a photographer might, to a great distance, and in a small view-finder one compresses a mighty scene. The great features stand up clearly. Time has washed away the minor ones. But the more closely one approaches the scene the more confusing it becomes. A hill here seems large and important until the camera panning onward meets a bigger hill. Yet, as it were around the corner, there may be a yet larger feature which will alter the whole composition and upset all previous judgments. And that constant unfolding goes on until, as seems to happen, periods become framed off, and every subsequent event clusters about some new nucleus. That is what happened to us. The events of our generation have framed off a period, which we might call the Period of Preparation. The appeal to the exclusive judgment of that period on the events of this period is obviously close, but it is not, and could not by any reasonable view of our story, be the only appeal.

And that is what makes living so difficult here to-day. Where the Past is no sure test of the Present and a great part of life has to be lived pragmatically and experimentally, even the most absurd and outrageous ideas can find a momentary support. But the difficulty is also that other difficulty of being so close up against things that nobody can possibly distinguish major event from minor, or even tell what is fructive from what (though it may now seem strong) is, if we only knew it, doomed to die. Much is, in such a time, unpredictable and all that is clear may be easily summed up. It is clear that any man who says he knows what is traditional – in the sense of what will become traditional – is being very foolish. It is clear that much that we are doing is experimental and will not persist. Our statesmen have had the courage to admit as much – more than once; have gone back courageously on their tracks and confessed error. It is clear that if we cease to be experimental, if we cease even to make mistakes, we are ceasing to learn and therefore ceasing to progress: so that one of the best criticisms I have ever heard of our first two governments is that they have not enough gallant failures to show in proof of their enterprise. It is, above all, clear that in such a time free intellectual discussion is of first importance, and any effort, in the name of any ideology, to check it is a disservice to us all.

There is, for all those reasons, no typical Irishman yet. Just as there is, as yet, no clear Irish tradition. And you cannot improvise a Tradition. To try to do it is, as Æ said, to be like the child who dibbles flowers in the sand to make a garden. The danger is not merely to pre-define. The danger, at this stage, is to define at all. Most of the things to which we object, such as the Literary Censorship, arise from that. They are the efforts of small groups to impose their narrow-minded definitions on the rest of us.

The Senate and Censorship[1]

Anybody interested in Irish literature might easily be depressed by a casual perusal of the Official Report of the Senate debates on the Censorship in November and December. He might even feel that for the greater part of its length the debate showed the intelligence of the Senate to be on a pretty low level. On a more considered reading both these impressions vanish.

In the first place, most of the time of the Senate was taken up by Professor Magennis, who, as Chairman of the Censorship Board, had to defend himself and his colleagues.[2] He was permitted to wander a great deal. He spent a great deal of time on ingenious legalistic arguments to justify the extraordinarily elastic meaning he would personally like to give to the term "indecency." But he mainly occupied his time in the attempt to cover up with verbiage the banning of Dr. Halliday Sutherland's *The Laws of Life* which received the imprimatur of the Westminster Diocesan Council six years ago.[3] Had he here said frankly: "We made a mistake. We did not realise that the book now bears a *Permissu Superiorum*"[4] – and have done with it, he could have reduced his speech to, at most, one hour instead of five and the debate would have been far

---

1 "The Senate and Censorship" appeared in *The Bell* 5, no. 4 (January 1943): 247–52.

2 William Magennis (1867–1946) was chair of metaphysics at University College Dublin as well as a former TD and a sitting senator (Independent).

3 *Laws of Life* argues against artificial means of contraception; instead, it promotes the rhythm method. Sutherland was a noted physician and a convert to the Catholic faith.

4 *Permissu superiorum* is Latin for "permission from the Superiors," meaning that the book had been approved by the Church Hierarchy.

less depressing. For it is always depressing to see a man whorling about in the mazes of his own mind in the effort to stave off the humiliating admission that he has done a wrong thing. One sympathises with him. It is, nonetheless, an embarrassing public spectacle.

Secondly, only about one-third of a Senate of sixty spoke to the motion.[5] Of these, Sir John Keane (who moved the motion that the Board has lost the confidence of the public), Senators Johnston, Tierney, Rowlette, Douglas, and Michael Hayes made the most intelligent and liberal speeches.[6] Indeed, one felt that if the Censorship Board were composed of five such men we should have little cause for complaint. Speaking for myself, I appreciated even more than any of these the humane and broad-minded speech of The McGillycuddy of the Reeks, with almost all of which I agreed.[7] Mr. Desmond FitzGerald also spoke as a cultivated man, though, as always, he tended to lose his humanity in the folds of his philosophy just as Professor Magennis loses his candour in the mazes of his metaphysics.[8] That left eleven speakers. If it has to be admitted that most of these were deplorable I hasten to say that this was not because of their views but simply because they were not fitted by nature or education to intervene on such a subject at all. To what depths of – perhaps the kindest word is "incomprehension" their inexperience led them it is impossible to describe.

Thirdly, the majority of the senators wisely refrained from speaking at all; businessmen, professional men, and farmers. I do not know what they would have said – possibly nothing that would have pleased me; but I hazard a guess that they felt that this sort of question is as technically alien to them as farming-problems are to somebody like myself. If the reader studies not just this one debate, but several – the discussion on the

5 On 18 November 1942, Sir John Keane (1873–1956) (Labour Party) moved: "That, in the opinion of Seanad Eireann, the Censorship of Publications Board appointed by the Minister for Justice under the Censorship of Publications Act, 1929, has ceased to retain public confidence, and that steps should be taken by the Minister to reconstitute the board." The discussion continued on 2, 3, and 9 December. After much debate, two voted in favour, thirty-four against. Those in favour were Keane and Joseph Johnston (1890–1972) (Fianna Fáil).
6 Robert James Rowlette (1873–1944) (Independent), James Green Douglas (1887–1954) (Independent), and Michael Hayes (1889–1976) (Fine Gael).
7 The McGillycuddy of the Reeks (1882–1950) (Independent), né Ross Kinlough McGillycuddy.
8 Desmond FitzGerald (1888–1947) (Cumann na nGaedhael).

Trade Union Bill or the School Attendance Bill, for example – he will find
that these senators discuss practical matters in a perfectly efficient and
generally liberal-minded way. Of course, those present voted against Sir
John Keane. That was to be expected. We are not, for a long time to come,
going to see public men voting otherwise on a subject about which they
do not feel deeply, and which only touches a minority: some know perfectly well that it would not, for obvious reasons, be good politics: some
honestly disapproved the form of the motion.

It may be said that all this being so there should be no discussion in the
Senate on such a subject. Far from it. In this mortal world we have to work
with what we can work with. The sum of the debate was satisfying. People
are now agreed, on all hands, that the Censorship Board does make mistakes. It is a small admission to have extracted out of three days' debate
and thirteen years' sporadic criticism. But it is made and has gone widespread. A more important thing has been placed indelibly on record. That
was the Minister's breath-taking "I am the Law" attitude that whether or
not a book was legally banned he would over-ride or ignore the Act of
Parliament and ban it on other (unspecified) grounds.[9] This is what we
have been trying for years to get the public to see and the Government to
confess – that the Law is being abused, and that many books are quite
improperly proscribed under cloak of it. Magennis took a quite different
position: he tried hard to defend the banning of *The Laws of Life* on legalistic grounds because he saw that this exposure was in the offing. He tried
to make the word "indecent" a mere technicality capable of interpretation
almost at will, an endlessly expanding portmanteau-word.[10]

I do not think that either he or the Minister would ever have come to
that were it not for the case of *The Laws of Life*. It is quite clear that they

9 O'Faolain's note: "*Professor Johnston:* What does the law of the State say about
the safe period with regard to birth-control? *The Minister:* I am not prepared to go
into the Law of the State, but I repeat that I take full responsibility for the banning
of this book. Whether the Board was technically and legally correct, whether the
book in its general tendency was indecent and obscene, may be open to question,
but on the ground that it was calculated to do untold harm I was perfectly satisfied
it should be banned." (Official Report.)

10 O'Faolain's note: "The book (*The Laws of Life*) was not condemned as indecent
… It was banned for indecency within the meaning of the Act – a very important
difference … As I was saying, if we disapprove of the sale and distribution of a
book the mode in which we convey that disapproval to the Minister, and asking
the Minister to prohibit the sale and distribution of that book is to report: 'In its
general tendency indecent.' A technicality!" (Official Report.)

would not have banned it had they known it bore an *imprimatur*. Once that grave blunder was exposed they preferred to stick to it, and try to brazen it out, rather than withdraw the ban. And the only reason the Minister would not is the human one that he wished to protect himself and his Board from the admission that they do make these serious blunders.

The next step will be to force the Board and the Minister to correct some of these blunders. Once that is done the autocratic power of the Board will be smashed. At present the Minister fears to thwart the Board because if he does so the Board may resign, and, on the express admission of the present Minister's predecessor, it is most difficult to get anybody to undertake the task. That, incidentally, is one of the great arguments for paying the Board a proper remuneration. The work is unpleasant, time-absorbing, and socially speaking the title of Censor is rather blown upon.

But it is behind the face of these debates, as everybody familiar with parliamentary technique knows, that the real work goes on. Ministers and officials wash only their clean linen in public. As well as the Board there is the Bed: to every party its curtain-lecture. Attend any debate and you find the spokesman rejecting nine-tenths of the proposals and criticisms put forward. In his office there is the post-mortem. Senators and T.D.'s know this well and, indeed, if it were not so there would be no use in parliamentary discussions at all. No Minister likes public criticism: you never know where it ends. The Censorship Board will watch its step more carefully in future. The Minister will choose his next Censors more cautiously. That is why it behoves the recently-formed Council of Action on Censorship, representative of about ten different organisations, to keep on pressing this matter home. The Chairman of the Board is over seventy, two other members are not in good health, and resignations must soon be expected. Everybody is now quite clear that the abolition of Censorship is not in question but the fanaticism of the members of the present Board and their predecessors. The Act as it stands has flaws, but if it is worked in the spirit and not in the narrow-minded letter of the law, the check of public opinion will save us from such repeated humiliations as it has, up to the present, imposed on individuals and on the nation.

Once more, it is well worth any reader's while to study the Senate debate on the School Attendance Bill, which took place on the very same day. This Bill has had a stormy passage in the Dáil on the head of Article 4 which – if passed will give the Minister power to force all children to attend National Schools. It would even give him the power to prevent parents from sending their children to be educated outside the State, in England or the Continent. The principle at stake here is, obviously, of immense importance, and the assault on that principle is a cynical comment on the views held elsewhere, most strongly (against Communal Restaurants for the Poor, for example) that the State must never interfere with parental authority. It is significant that Senator O'Buachalla, who was so illiberal on Censorship, was strong for taking from parents the right to send their children out of Eire;[11] and (not as if he was merely assailing the rich) he was equally keen on wiping out the whole fraternity of gypsies, tinkers, and travelling-folk in general in a typical totalitarian lust for absolute State control over the individual. It is equally significant that the opponents of this State-ism were far from silent. They included Senators Desmond FitzGerald and Michael Tierney, and even the humanity of Mrs. Concannon was outraged so far that she taunted Senator O'Buachalla with wanting to corral vagrants into reservations.[12]

One statement by Professor Tierney, indeed, might have been made as trenchantly on the Censorship debate. It was this: "If you have not liberty for the exceptional people, for the people who will not conform to your dead-level pattern and fit into your machine, then you have not got liberty at all. When you talk about the State being free, and of the citizen being free in this country after so many years of slavery, you are simply using a lot of meaningless words which you, by your own action, would deprive of the meaning that so many centuries of struggle have sought to give them. There is a grave danger in all this kind of legislation, by this introduction of uniformity, that we are taking a step in the direction that Europe has already taken with such disastrous consequences … I feel that the whole tendency is to set up the Machine first, and then to get that Machine geared up more and more until it tries to bring every single person in the community within its workings. Ultimately, of course, what happens is that that sort of machine breaks down, and that its effect is negatived by the very attempt to do that. I am almost tempted to say, not that I am afraid, but that I hope this machinery of compulsion will not do the work which the Minister expects it to do."

In short, the old fundamental principles are being fought out not on one issue but on several. There are weak brethren, and selfish brethren, and, worst, short-sighted brethren. Thus I suspect that the Teachers are supporting the Minister wholeheartedly on this Bill – it is not yet passed – because the principle of compulsion will jack up the averages of attendances on which their jobs depend, rather than because they have Education

11 Liam Ó Buachalla (1899–1970) (Fianna Fáil).
12 Helena Concannon (1878–1952) (Fianna Fáil).

at heart. (Senator O'Connell, Secretary of the Irish National Teachers' Organisation, was one of those who attacked the right of parents to send their children to private schools.)[13] These men may pay far more dearly in the long-run for their blindness than they will ever gain in cash.

That is what makes the stand of writers against an autocratic Censorship of national, and not of minor, importance: they defend a principle for principle's sake. It will take time before, from the tangles of all our legislation, it is the fundamental principles which emerge, and not the opportunisitic advantages of a moment. When that time comes it will, once again, be the writers who will extract the fundamental thing from the mass of superficial arguments that now, like Professor Magennis's verbiage, try to conceal it. They will be able to do it because they have always kept the fundamental rights of the individual Irishman in the forefront of their minds and have persistently fought for it in the face of every obloquy.

13 Thomas O'Connell (1882–1969) (Labour Party).

Gaelic – The Truth[1]

First of all let us see what this bright dream that we call Gaelic and the Gaelic tradition was before our witless generation manhandled it.

We treasure Gaelic for one outstanding reason – that, beside the religious motif, it is the one solitary remnant of *living* tradition that links us back to the centuries behind our breaking. In it are embedded, or from it have come, the few customs, no matter how humble, that we have preserved from the native life-way; the few broken shards of the traditional life-mode of our people. It is our victory to have preserved any of them, and our defeat to have preserved so little.

In speech, Gaelic seems to contain our natural poetry as a race. On a windy day over Clew Bay an old man behind Westport says to me: "There is a blossom on the sea to-day," and my heart jumps with delight at this dignity of speech which I like to think is natural, racial, embedded. Gaelic is our history. Off Wexford I see an island and ask its name, and am told "Beggery Island." I ask the meaning of this odd name, but nobody knows, and I sense a chasm, a loss, a breaking in time. Then somebody is found who says: – "The true name of that island is Becc Eriu – or Beag Eire – meaning Little Ireland. A saint went there one time and he called it that name to remind him, in his hermitage, of the big Ireland he had left for ever." Once again, we feel the presence of a coherent wholeness in time and memory. And there is not a place-name in the whole of Ireland that does not, in this manner, thus contain some piece of history as a jewel contains a concentration of light. In Gaelic is the reality of a folk-life which is almost wholly disappeared from the world. The maid comes back from her holiday and tells me that her aunt has borne her ninth

1 "Gaelic – The Truth" appeared in *The Bell* 5, no. 5 (February 1943): 335–40.

child, and at each child-bearing she lies up for nine days, and that on the ninth day her grand-aunt goes out into the field and picks nine thorns and comes in and burns them in the fire, and she says, "It is all over then. She gets up and her pains are forgotten." It is a trifle, but multiplied a million-fold it gives us a flitting glimpse of a vast general loss. For wherever (which is almost everywhere) the English language has replaced Gaelic a mass of these traditional life-ways is gone for ever.

Our regret for this general dilution is not merely an aesthetic regret: though it is that, too. Our regret is for the impoverishment of each man's mind and life. The significance of this has been well put by a man who realised it fully. In the words of Æ: "A nation is cultivated only so far as the average man, not the exceptional person, is cultivated and has know-ledge of the thought, imagination, and intellectual history of his nation. Where there is a general culture its effects are seen in the houses, the pic-tures, the homes and gardens, the arts of life. Almost insensibly beauty enters the household and what is meant by civilisation is apparent."[2] He implied, of course, "a distinctive civilisation." One has only to compare the simple, perhaps one might even say crude, yet always gracious and almost indigenous ways of a country cottage in Connemara with the ways of a suburban bungalow in any town to see, immediately, what has been lost. For while one must agree that there is no reason why life in the sub-urban bungalow should not be equally a civilised life the *distinctiveness* is undoubtedly diminished, where it is not wholly gone. There is much to pride in, a great deal to pride in, but there is, surely, less to pride in than if that were not gone.[3]

Now, in the hey-day of the idealism of the Gaelic Revival every contact with that distinctive thing was an increase of joy and pride to us. We went to the Gaeltacht, and at once we felt an enlargement of mind and soul. We over-idealised it, but that was natural. We learned Gaelic. We delighted in the folk-lore of Gaelic, the hero-tales, the folk-ways, its popular songs. We brought them back to the towns and cities, and they became part of our racial mind. They gave us a little more of that precious sense of dis-tinctiveness, and pride in proportion. Our daily lives were on another plane, and we could not live, think, feel, or work like western fishermen or country wives: it was not to be expected and if anybody suggested that

2 From *The Living Torch*, page 381–2. O'Faolain has altered some of the punctuation in the passage.
3 This an archaic use of "pride" as a verb, which nowadays tends to adopt the form "to take pride in."

we should we would have stared at him. Still we honoured the Gaeltacht as a well of racial memory and drank from it repeatedly.

And now ... ? The Gaeltacht, the language, the Revival, everything associated with what was once so honoured and so nourishing, is now a bitter taste in the mouth, sometimes positively nauseating. These once precious things are associated in the mind of the average man with jobs, with money, with dishonest speeches from public men (who, we know, have no intention of ever learning the language themselves), with politics, with mean and petty racketeering. I do not think that even the most ardent revivalist would deny this regrettable picture.

If this be so why is it so? And how may this tragedy be undone?

For a particular answer we cannot go far wrong in trusting the man-in-the-street on things which concern him intimately; and, after we have made every allowance for his exaggerations and prejudices, we must realise that he, after all, is the one man concerned in the revival of the language. His phrase is universal. *"Ramming it down our throats."* We have choked the Irish cat with Gaelic butter. There is no arguing about so patent a fact.

Is it, then, just a question of easing off? Far more – infinitely more than that. For it is greatly to be feared that the so-called revivalists – vivisectionists would be more like it – have done irreparable harm to the Language. The very sight and mention of Gaelic is now what the sight of butter would be to the half-choked cat.

To see what is required let us ask what a phrase like "ramming it down our throats" means on the intellectual plane. It means that we have taken an inspiration and thwarted it. How often have we not met, to take an analogy from another experience, young men reared so strictly, in some pious but arid household, that their whole manhood is a reaction of utter disbelief? For them, too, an inspiration has been thwarted. It has been deprived of its life, its esprit, its poetry, its beauty, by being reduced to the dry rattle of the prayer-wheel, and the priggish tones of self-righteousness, to empty formalisms and severe strictures and fanatical compulsions; at best to the saccharine of a sentimentality which the first touch of real life proves to be a sham. The same thing has happened in the pious Gaelic household. Gaelic, like this *faux-religion*, has been for twenty years in the hands of idealistic, fanatical, self-righteous, and domineering men, who have vulgarised it almost beyond redemption, and from whom nothing now can be hoped. If anything could be hoped from them one would hold silent still longer, or speak kindly of them. Their murder hangs about their necks. They found a living inspiration, a thing full of poetry, warm with popular affection, revered by popular respect, and they have left us with this pitiable wry-necked guy for whose condition they blame everybody but themselves.

There is another implication in that phrase about "ramming" Gaelic. It is that the social welfare of the people is sacrificed, at times, to Gaelic. Thus, when the public hears (as it has done) of a doctor with first-class qualifications being set aside for a doctor with far inferior qualifications but with a knowledge of Gaelic, it is dissatisfied. In Education the public is dissatisfied with the penalisation of children for the sake of Gaelic, though perfectly willing that an extra reasonable effort should be made for the sake of Gaelic. It is particularly exasperated when these penalisations are enforced by men who have themselves either long left the Gaeltacht or have no intention of at any time submitting themselves or their children to the disadvantages of the Gaeltacht standard of living, and its lack of opportunities. We are not making original statements here – we are merely relaying in print in a particular way what is crackling on all sides in the air.

Let us also be constructive in a particular way.

Briefly what is necessary, we suggest, is this: The essential preliminary is to call in another doctor. The Gaelic League, with what last shred of decency is left to it, should disband promptly, in silence, and without recrimination. Much of the error attending the Revival is not its fault, but it is the representative body and must bear the brunt alike for its own faults and those of others who have hearkened to it. It is now a totally discredited organisation. Simultaneously, we should be clear that the new aim is to restore this inspirational quality of Gaelic as we have spoken of it. Two primal things then face us. First: the restoration of the voluntary technique. Secondly: that we be honest and realistic, and admit that our object is not unilingualism, but that we should speak, according to our moods and needs, both Gaelic and English.

On that dual clarification, and only on that clarification, a voluntary scheme may be developed; on which the vast expenditure wasted hitherto in thumb-screwing the schools had been far better spent during the last twenty-odd years. Local teaching, local entertainments of every kind, plays, dances, socials, cards, billiards, gymnasiums, talks, concerts, and periodicals, through, or partially through Gaelic – but offered on a purely voluntary basis to the public – would, if that red blood of inspiration but once began to creep back into the anaemic body of the language, bring back honour to dishonour, warm the hearts of a chilled populace, and set alight again a fire that only the will and wish of the populace can kindle.

There will be work in plenty here for those at present wandering in the fog of the Gaelic League, and they can here do that work which the whole atmosphere surrounding Gaelic now makes impossible; for they will have to sell Gaelic and sell themselves to the people on merit; and there will be an end to this devastating bullying and cockiness which has swollen beyond bearing the arrogance of men with no other gift but the accidental possession of a linguistic gift, and with little or nothing else to recommend them.

As for the schools, that, too, is simple, as all these problems are if only we would hear the voices of those to whom experience has given knowledge. "Irish should be made the language of instruction in districts where it is the home language, and English the second language taught as a school subject. I would not, at any stage, use English as a medium of instruction in such districts. Where English is the home language it must of necessity be the first language in the schools, but I would have a compulsory second language, satisfied that this second language in five-sixths of the schools would be Irish ... But in all details of their programmes the schools should have autonomy."⁴ So, the voluntary note, trustful of the spirit of our people, not bullying and abusing them, not mocking and sneering at them, but firing their hearts and imaginations – and all technical matters in the hands of the people whose job these matters affect, the teachers themselves.

All of which one may sum up by saying that the truth about Gaelic is that the people are still with all their hearts behind the revival of Gaelic, but that they have long ceased to have anything but distrust for the conspiracy of intellectual bankruptcy which has come to be known as the Gaelic Revival.

Whether there is any public man with the drive and vision to restore to Gaelic its power of inspiration is, in itself, a test of that latent power. Perhaps that power is indeed gone, drained away by twenty years of malnutrition. It remains to be seen. But if it is so then it is also terrifyingly true that we freed our country too late to save it. And stronger words than those no man could use to express his belief that an Irishman without a knowledge of the language is politically free but intellectually and spiritually disinherited.

4 *O'Faolain's note:* The quotation is from *The Murder Machine* [1916], by Patrick Pearse.

Ireland and the Modern World[1]

The two words which have probably had the greatest influence on Irish lives during the last forty years are Sinn Féin. And so well they might for, in their day, they were inspiring words. They meant then a creative gospel; they asked Ireland to think originally, not to be imitative, to be self-proud and self-dependent. That was what we took then from their literal meaning – Ourselves Alone. But something seems to have happened to their inspiration which we had not foreseen in the days of their glowing youth. Imperceptibly those two words have been squinted into meaning Ourselves All Alone. Self-reliance has taken on the astonishing implication of estrangement from the world. We have become, that is to say, alienated from Europe to such an extent that we sometimes seem less to belong to it than barely to adhere to it – as if by no more than a mere accident of physical propinquity. Indeed our more ardent nationalists appear, at times, to regard our present geographical relation to Western Europe as one of the less explicable errors of taste of the Almighty, who might better have chosen to put us near any other country except Britain, or, better still, have preserved His chosen-people from the temptations of the world by putting us well out in the middle of the Atlantic. I am sure that there are lots of people here who, if they woke up some morning to find that we had slipped our moorings and were rocking gently somewhere in the region of Trinidad, would feel that Ireland had at last achieved her true destiny as the Fortunate Island.

The world is wicked: we are good. The world will contaminate us: we must keep out of the world. The whole mental outlook of our

1 "Ireland and the Modern World" appeared in *The Bell* 5, no. 6 (March 1943): 423–8.

neo-puritans and neo-nationalists is of that order, and all their efforts are correspondingly directed towards protecting us by insulation and isolation. The peculiar statements of some of our Senators quoted last month in our *Mise Eire* section were along these lines.[2] It is a sad declension from the gospel of self-reliance if any of our people really do place so little reliance on themselves as to want to retire to a funk-hole from the traffic of ideas.

There is nothing whatever in our healthiest traditions to anticipate this tendency. Whenever we failed to be internationally-minded we became weak, and our defences fell. Our worst period (barring the 18th century) was from about 1350 to 1550 when we sank into a stupefied insularity, lost touch with world movements, and were therefore unable to orientate ourselves to them when they burst unexpectedly upon us in the great 16th century Tudor thrust for *lebensraum*.[3] Our only bulwark then was O'Neill, an utter internationalist, who realised the circumstances and could therefore meet them.[4] We did not flourish again, after 1690, until Tone and Dan O'Connell who had drunk deep of Europe; and all our revolutionary tradition thenceforward has been similarly nourished abroad and applied at home.

Not but that the tendency is understandable. Every ambitious youth has felt the urge to complete independence: but before he realises it what he is experiencing is the limitations on human independence. Economic pressure, stubborn resistance, greater pressure, greater resistance culminate not so much in an acknowledgment that in this world we are all bound together as in an angry and hurt withdrawal into a greater and still greater seclusion. Self-reliance and isolation thus lure us down the long railroad in whose distant perspective, like a Charlie Chaplin exit, we see ourselves still erect, without a Thank You to anybody.[5]

Unfortunately it does not happen quite that way with nations. To be sure, we all know the self-made man: but the phrase invariably means the half-made man, and the sons who see what he has missed, and are not so proud of Father as Father is of himself, and there are phrases that

2 *Mise Eire* translates from the Irish as "I am Ireland," which is also the name of a famous poem by Patrick Pearse, written in 1912. This section of *The Bell* was a selection of quotes, generally taken from notable public figures.

3 *Lebensraum* is German for "living space"; the concept is usually employed by countries who seek to justify their territorial expansion.

4 Hugh O'Neill.

5 Film director, actor, and writer Charlie Chaplin (1889–1977).

slightingly measure the halfness of his achievement. It is not that the man lacks tradition, family, or pride of stock – on the contrary these men have fine qualities of that order, and their sturdy self-pride commands respect on all sides. There is no lack of Self Reliance in these men. What they have missed is that priceless intercourse with various humanity, and all that it produces, without which any man is less than wholly civilised.

If any country could arrive at some such crude achievement under her own steam – it is, of course, impossible in any full sense in this viable world to-day – the generations would make wide comparisons and quickly become dissatisfied. I have never met a young man or young woman from countries like Hungary or Finland, countries much more bottled-up than we are, who did not hate having to go back. They had tasted the fruit of a wider life. Lilliput had immediately become inadequate.[6] So with our young men and women. Bottle them up, make life wholly local, simple, circumscribed, traditional, unvarious. They bust. Economic reasons do not fully explain why in the last two years one in every forty, in the Twenty-Six Counties, left this country: a total of 78,222 young people. Before the War they were crowding just as fast out of the fields into the towns.

But the whole history of the world, as we all know, is, in fact, one long persistent interchange. It is the natural process of human development. France, in the 16th century, was influenced powerfully by the Italian Renaissance, and by the German Reformation. In the 17th century she was influenced by the Catholic revival from Rome. In the eighteenth century she was influenced by the English revolution of 1648 and the history of the American colonies. It was from England that Voltaire and Montesquieu derived the formulas of religious toleration and political liberty that they propagated at home.[7] Indeed, many of the very words which political revolution later acclimatised in France reveal their origin – *libre-penseur*, *comité*, *religion de la nature*, *juge de paix*. Even in dress and social manners she was equally prehensile, taking the *redingote* from London, *tabac* from America, *sucre* from the Orient, down to the tall-hat

6 Lilliput was the island of inhabitants whose small stature was a metaphor for their small-mindedness in Book One of *Gulliver's Travels* (1726), by Jonathan Swift (1667–1745). In many of his writings, O'Faolain refers both to Ireland and to his native city of Cork as Lilliput to emphasise their parochial and petty provinciality.
7 Voltaire, the pseudonym of François-Maire Arouet (1694–1778), and Charles-Louis de Secondat, baron de La Brède et de Montesquieu (1689–1755), were the leading historians and philosophers of the French Enlightenment.

and umbrella of Louis Napoleon, the *boxe*, *cycle*, and *football* of the present-day artisan of Paris.[8] And if, before all this, the traditional folk-ways of France have disappeared ...

It was not until our own day that States began to resent and check this natural process of human development. How this Stateism arose has been a fruitful subject for speculative historians. Æ used to say that this rise of the State as the watchful father was largely due to Hegelianism. Hegelian philosophy spread the idea that history was, loosely speaking, not so much a free process as the projection of the Divine Will in human terms. (Which is almost as determinist an idea as the Marxist theory that history is the inevitable projection of economic forces.) Once God and the Nation were put on an equal footing it was obviously only a matter of time before the Absolute State was born – the State masquerading as God Almighty. It was said that when Hegel saw Napoleon in the streets of Jena, he declared: "I have seen the World Spirit go riding out."[9] What he was duped into admiring was a complex of extreme nationalism, despotic absolutism, and ruthless imperialism. He was admiring the defeat of the French Revolution – which had undertaken the complete overthrow of these things in 1789 – even as England partially overthrew them in the Revolution of 1642. But these tendencies are in human nature. We see them, in little, in the character and behaviour of individuals. We will see them for all time in peoples. Even in our own little island we get that complex in our extremists who first want to boss everybody at home and then order Ireland to ride out as the torch-bearer of the post-war world.

Let us not be misled by cant-phrases. An Internationalism that tries to stifle national egos is inhuman. We have never tolerated it. It is Imperialism. Neither should we tolerate a Nationalism which would go to extremes – exploit the worker or assail the Jews or outlaw the Protestants or gag the writers or penalise any class whatsoever. That sort of thing is usually a phoney nationalism pushed forward by private cadres for their own ends. The test of a true national spirit is whether it is inclusive. If it is propped up on the bodies of one class for the benefit of another it is an exploitation. And there is certainly something very groggy about it if it

8 Charles-Louis-Napoleon Bonaparte, or Napoleon III (1808–1873), was the president of the Second Republic of France from 1850 to 1852 and the Emperor of France from 1852 to 1870.

9 Jena, a city in Germany, is home to Friedrich-Schiller University, where the philosopher Georg Wilhelm Friedrich Hegel taught. Hegel was reacting to Napoleon I, Napoleon Bonaparte (1769–1821).

has to ask for laws (like our present Education Bill) to "shield" it from contact with the rest of the world.

Are we so afraid of the world that we let our rights go one by one in order that our Ministers may protect us? From self-reliance have we descended to mere pupillage – a cowering, timid pack of children afraid of the dark bogey-men? It is a curious development, but I imagine that the innate individualism of the Irishman will resist it savagely as soon as he realises what is happening. His religion, in any case, is too catholic to approve of it – or it should be, which is a rather different matter. Besides, we have too many of our own folk scattered all over the world ever to become knotted into a little island fragment, a piece of casual flotsam, as disconnected as the Eskimos, as odd and peculiar as a hermit's rock-refuge. And that influence must work on us even though too often

Their place of birth alone is mute
To sounds that echo farther west
Than your sire's Islands of the Blest.[10]

So, in this little magazine, which has persistently devoted itself to the cultivation of our own garden, we here take a peep and a smell at some other gardens. They will not, we hope, give us hay-fever, or Spring fever. They will not, we sincerely trust, evoke any evil desires. It is only a little peep, and we have had to prick holes where we could in a very large and very tall fence. But, even so, those other people, we will observe, seem to be quite human?[11] True, those back-street folk in Paris seem to have read far more than Mr. Boland or Professor Magennis might think good for them: but what is our contrary achievement, or is Dominick Street really so much brighter and happier than the Rue de la Huchette?[12] I could imagine that Mr. Jimmy Montgomery, our late Film Censor, who has just been suggesting that Ireland should, after "the present Dark Age" has passed, "spread a new light on a wounded world," might in his more benign moments rejoice in Mr. Osbert Sitwell's recreations of a London

10 This excerpt is from "The Isles of Greece," a poem within *Don Juan* (1819–24), by the English Romantic poet Lord Byron.
11 The question mark here is likely a rhetorical device: a statement is made and the audience is asked to reflect on it.
12 Patrick Boland (Fianna Fáil). Dominick Street is located in Dún Laoghaire; Rue de la Huchette is a street in the Latin Quarter of Paris that is renowned for its nightlife.

contemporaneous with the unsullied childhood of Mr. Joyce and the blessed innocence of little Buck Mulligan.[13] The art of Mr. P.G. Wodehouse has long been so popular in our seminaries, and recently so unpopular elsewhere, that nobody is likely to suggest that Mr. John Hayward's serious exegesis on the Master is a cunning form of British propaganda.[14] Really, when all is said and done, the only trouble about this International Number of THE BELL is that, in the main, it merely forecasts what any Irish magazine might well produce after the war when normal intercourse can again return.

13 Osbert Sitwell (1892–1969); an unpublished excerpt from Sitwell's auto-biography followed O'Faolain's editorial in this issue of The Bell. Buck Mulligan, a character in James Joyce's Ulysses, is a rather unfavourable fictional portrayal of Oliver St. John Gogarty.

14 P.G. Wodehouse (1881–1975) was an English comic writer. John Hayward (1905–1965) was the author of P.G. Wodehouse (1942).

On State Control[1]

On all sides we can feel one question tormenting every thinking mind of to-day – the problem of balancing State Control and Individual Liberty. On this only one thing is certain; there is no simple answer to the problem. It is also certain that it is risky to attempt to give a simple or generalised answer to it since the danger is that in generalising too freely you give birth to a shibboleth. Within the last few weeks I happen to have met two or three such which are worth while examining.

The first deals with man's natural desire for greater achievements and greater efficiency. It tends to end up as a whole-hog demand for complete State Control. We are not fitted in this magazine to speak of other fields than the arts and learning. There, I think it is fair to say that the student and the artist generally takes up a very distinct and firm attitude. He fears State Control, not on any general principle, but because he knows that all his achievements are painstaking, slow, imperceptible, and not to be judged by any other critic than Time – the only critic who is never deceived.

There is nothing undemocratic about this. On the contrary it is based on a real awareness of democracy's position in relation to the arts and to learning to-day. We know that the age of social privilege is gone. We know that the happy chances of birth will never again put a heritage of power into the hands of specially fortunate men. Great homes, great collections, the power of patronage, vast personal influence due to wealth or birth – it is all either gone or going. I am neither rejoicing in this nor deploring it. The fact is that the general level of culture will henceforth rise or fall almost imperceptibly and the whole movement of civilisation

---

1 "On State Control" appeared in *The Bell* 6, no. 1 (April 1943): 1–6.

in these matters will be as unobtrusive as Nature. An Ardilaun could once give a Stephen's Green to Dublin.[2] Who could do it to-day?

Æ said this well, and prophetically, when he said that a nation can now become cultivated "only in so far as the average man, not the exceptional person, is cultivated and has knowledge of the thought, imagination, and intellectual history of his nation. Where there is a general culture its effects are seen in the houses, the pictures, the home and garden, and the arts of life: a better taste is manifest. *Almost insensibly* beauty enters the household and what is meant by a civilisation at last becomes apparent."[3] Or to apply the democratic Boswell to this later age: "Life consists not of a series of illustrious actions or elegant enjoyments. The true state of every nation is the state of common life ... They whose aggregate constitutes the people are found in the streets, the villages, the shops and farms, and from them, collectively considered, must the measure of a general prosperity be taken. As they approach delicacy a nation is refined. As their conveniences are multiplied a nation, at least a commercial nation, must be denominated wealthy."[4]

The flowering of a narrow society here is over. There is hardly an inch left here, from end to end of the island, of the sophisticated life of the upper classes. We shall do the achieving, now, one by one, little by little. So that, for the one man or woman who makes a neat garden, keeps a serene and gracious home, practices good manners, builds a solid piece of furniture, weaves a fine piece of material, paints a good picture, cooks a good meal, or clears an old field, I would give all the prating but unproductive propagandists that surround us.

The artist and the student, working quietly, thus claims the privilege of his own special liberty. Even Communism recognises this to a large degree. No real student or artist could agree with the recent assault (led by the Gaelic League) on the Universities, which, also, have always been given an enormous amount of autonomy in a wise recognition that there are some things outside national planning, some things which the State cannot handle, which, indeed, its function is to protect from

2 Arthur Guinness (1840–1915), also known as Lord Ardilaun, made the financial gift necessary for St. Stephen's Green to become a public park in 1880.
3 From Æ's *The Living Torch*, 381–2, quoted in the earlier essay "Gaelic – The Truth." O'Faolain again slightly alters the passage, including adding the italicised emphasis.
4 James Boswell (1740–1795). The quote comes from his biography, *The Life of Samuel Johnson, LL.D.* (1791).

interference.⁵ Yet, there are those who deny that they approve of State Control, but work for another control far more dangerous. They do so in the name of a second shibboleth – National Culture. And here note how these shibboleths confuse men's minds.

The President of the Gaelic League, for example, in leading an agitation against the autonomy of the University protected himself by saying that he did not want State Control of the University. (He was, in effect, leading a demand for mob-control of the University.) Meanwhile his colleague Senator Liam O'Buachalla has been demanding State Control over the Primary Schools, even to the point of giving the Minister for Education power to prevent parents from sending their children to schools or Convents in England or Switzerland. Where do these two men agree? They agree in being ready to use a little "pressure" all round for the sake of this mythical "National Culture."

The truth, as our eyes can show us, is, that nowhere to-day, neither here nor elsewhere, and never again, can there be a National Culture as those people understand it. And what they mean by the words is sufficiently clearly indicated by the official organ of the Gaelic League (in its issue of February 27th, 1943) which quotes Professor Eoin MacNeill as follows: "In Ireland there is no possible foundation for a national culture except the national language. It can easily be shown that an attempt to base Irish culture on the English language can only result in provincialising Irish life." (It is to be noted that, in point of fact, we here plead for bi-lingualism.)

Had one not known the date of that statement (it is 1909) one might have guessed it. It was a false *prophecy*. Take literature. It was made before the bulk of Yeats's poetry appeared. And is Yeats a provincialising poet? It was made before Joyce's *Ulysses* was published, and one can hardly call that book provincial? One may call it many other unkind things but not that. Is O'Casey a provincialising influence? Are the short

---

5 *O'Faolain's note:* For the interest of overseas readers: this controversy arose over the decision of the Governing Body of University College, Dublin, to appoint as Professor of Education Mr. W.J. Williams, M.A., whose knowledge of Gaelic was held by the Gaelic Revivalists to be inadequate. The Gaelic League and others held protest meetings. There was a street riot in which the students manhandled this opposition.

The Government, in effect, did not support the University: for when the Senate, by an overwhelming majority, ratified the decision of the Governing Body, the Chancellor Mr. de Valera, in the Chair (so our information goes), led the Opposition in his own Senate and University.

stories of Frank O'Connor? Is Corkery's *Threshold of Quiet?* Are the
songs of Fred Higgins?

What, then, has happened to the professor's prophecy? It has gone out
of date. It was made at a time when all Irishmen feared English influence
with a dreadful, natural, and, for the time, proper fear. To-day the influence of England is far less than the influence of America – and of Europe.
One has but to think of films, books, political ideas. We have, meanwhile,
done what every country has done – we have learned from *all* countries.
We have come out of parochialism, side-stepped the danger of one particular and exclusive influence, and become an international people,
much as we were in the seventeenth century.

If you doubt this take up a half-dozen modern novels. There is not any
real scrap of difference between the novels of France, Russia, America,
Ireland, Italy, or England – apart from differences of subject-matter.
Silone's *Fontamara* could have been written by Peadar O'Donnell on an
Irish valley.[6] Peadar O'Donnell's *Adrigoole* could have been written by
Erskine Caldwell – on a Georgian valley.[7] The same is true of Science. The
world has moved on a great deal since 1909. I am afraid these good
people are still away back there. Once again it must be evident that if the
State were to attempt to interfere with the natural development of the
arts and learning there is no reason to believe that it would be any wiser
than these enthusiasts.

For all that it would be an utter folly to maintain that we should have
no State Control at all. And a third shibboleth is arising to say so. After all
it was the State which established the National University itself. The State
it is which gave us our fortnightly Symphony Concerts, so that it can even
sustain and assist the Arts. We have, in fact, long accepted the principle,
and a current *Tablet*, in trying to argue that "negative" state-interference
– i.e., police action – is all right, but that "positive" state-action is another
story, is indulging in that sort of tricky argument which always infuriates
one from the Catholic Right. This State has complete control over the Post
Office, Broadcasting, – which might be better if it had not – the Army,
national electric and water power, mining, the Police, a growing amount
of control over industry and agriculture, and, during the Economic War, it
did virtually what it liked with one branch of agriculture – cattle-raising.

In general, surely, State Control is to be welcomed when it transfers the
responsibility for all public troubles – say Hunger, Poverty, or Disease

6 *Fontamara* (1930), by Italian author Ignazio Silone (1900–1978).
7 *Adrigoole* (1929).

– to the shoulders of Government, i.e., to us, the public, through our representatives. We can then fight out these questions freely, as public political questions. Otherwise what happens, as we all know, is that these public questions are clutched away into private corners by interested parties, so that the public cannot get at them. Hunger and Poverty, for example, are too often shoved away into a private corner plausibly called Charity, and the public court, called Justice, where social evils should be tried and condemned, is thereby shut against the hungry and the poor.

The appearance of the Beveridge Report has stirred up a great deal of opposition from the Right against the idea of State Control.[8] The shibboleth employed to damn both is "The Servile State." In the last few days I have met it several times. The Rev. E.J. Coyne warns us of this danger.[9] The Rev. Dr. Lucey of Maynooth is not happy about it.[10] The Catholic weekly, *The Standard*, has begun to tremble at the danger of Stateism.[11] The Catholic *Tablet* has been throwing cold water on the Report for weeks.

We may look forward to an increasing movement of this fertile opposition to the whole idea of giving our own Government power to control our own problems. It is a tricky situation, and I freely admit that I could easily see myself being lured to line up – in an alleged defence of things like "individual rights" and "national culture" – on the side of reaction and conservatism. All I know, by way of guide, is that all my reading of our history teaches me that whenever we were without a powerful central control the game was lost. And all I feel by way of deterrent is the knowledge that reaction and conservatism can only achieve powerful central control over the heads – over the minds and bodies of the populace. There my instinct finally urges me to trust in the spirit of my own people. That spirit, with the freedom of art, learning, religion and the press, will be our guarantee against abuse.

8 The Beveridge Report, known officially as *Social Insurance and Allied Services* (1942), was written by the economist William Henry Beveridge (1879–1963). It is considered to have laid the foundation for Britain's post-war welfare state.

9 Edward Joseph Coyne (1896–1958) later founded the Catholic Workers College in 1951, which is now known as the National College of Ireland.

10 Cornelius Lucey (1902–1982) was at the time the chair of philosophy and political theory at St. Patrick's College, Maynooth; he was later (1952–1980) the Archbishop of Cork and Ross.

11 *The Standard* (1928–78) was a conservative Catholic weekly newspaper with very close ties to the Hierarchy.

Books and a Live People[1]

I suppose it is to say the obvious to point out that whatever a country loses by large imports of books and other prints, it is not Literature: not even if one follows the effects of this dependence out to its last ramifications. For, as far as our reading is concerned, what does it matter where we get the books so long we get them? Even if it is true that the influence of Irish dependence on British publishing – like that of Scotland – takes most native writers away to London; that does not necessarily matter to Literature. It hardly matters, either, to the writer, who is generally – like the scientist and the scholar – indifferent as to where he lives, so long as he is let alone and can earn a living. Moreover, thanks to British and American curiosity about the writers of other lands those countries get therefrom a number of books about themselves that they would not otherwise get – as we in Ireland do.

Ireland's dependence on Britain for her books does not even hurt our national pride: or if it does it cannot hurt it very much since we do nothing about it. For let us never be heard saying that Ireland "produces" writers, or "produces" a literature. Far from "producing" a literature what Ireland does is to eject it by the front-door, creep around to the back-door and take a bit of it in again (marked *Published in Great Britain*); have a quick look at it in the back-room, approve of some, spit on the rest, and then run around to the front-door again shouting: "Look what *we've* done!"

What, then, is involved in this vast importation of books that we should be concerned about it?

1 "Books and a Live People" appeared in *The Bell* 6, no. 2 (May 1943): 91–8.

The richness or poverty of life is involved. Those imported books are mainly not about ourselves, and when we close them, and look about us we cannot help having a rather empty feeling. When we close these travelled books we must feel that in other lands, made interesting by their writers, there is colour, excitement, ideas crackling like rockets, great men rising, great events continually happening, but here – a contrasting emptiness, darkness, and silence. It has been said that if there were no God man would have had to invent Him. If we had no books every man would have to write his own. That is what makes books. The shanachie by the fire, and Shaw in his study, are moved by the same vital urge. Mere dumb, uninterested, existence is the prerogative of the brute.

Our dependence on Britain and America for our reading is undeniable. If I may be pardoned for taking the example nearest to hand – my own – I have written four Irish biographies: Countess Markievicz, Eamon de Valera, Daniel O'Connell, and the Great Earl of Tyrone.[2] I could get no American publisher to take two of those four biographies; and I am a fairly well-known writer in America. Britain would not have published any of these biographies if I were not an established writer. No Irish publisher would finance any of these books. That means that the Irish public could not have read them. And yet – I need hardly say that I speak only of the subjects of such books, not of their merits – it is such books, hundreds and hundreds of them, that Ireland needs. In the same way if you liked Joseph Hone's Life of Yeats you must thank his London publisher who invited him to do it, and financed him while doing it.[3] If you liked, say, that fine book The Irish Countryman, by Dr. Conrad Arensberg, you must thank the late President-Emeritus of Harvard, Lawrence Lowell, who invited Dr. Arensberg to prepare it.[4] It is the same with the late Edmund Curtis's History of Ireland; all but one of the novels of Peadar O'Donnell (he financed himself for the first); O'Connor's Life of Michael

2 At this point in his career, O'Faolain had actually written five biographies, two of them on de Valera. He notably distanced himself from the rather hagiographic first one, The Life Story of Eamon de Valera (1933), and wrote the second, more critical De Valera (1939) to reflect his changing vision. The miscount in the essay appears to be an attempt, conscious or not, to expunge the first from the record; or it could be more generously interpreted as O'Faolain considering the later de Valera biography as a revision or a second edition of the first.

3 W.B. Yeats, 1865–1939 (1942), by Joseph M. Hone (1882–1959).

4 The Irish Countryman (1937), by Conrad Arensberg (1910–1997). A. Lawrence Lowell (1856–1943) was president of Harvard from 1909 to 1933.

Collins, *The Big Fellow*; the poems of Austin Clarke, of Fred Higgins, of Roibéard O'Faracháin, and so on.[5] The only well-known writers I know who have been produced by an Irish publisher are Francis MacManus and Daniel Corkery.[6] Writers in Gaelic are alone paid for by ourselves, i.e., by Government subsidy.

That makes one ask – If MacManus and Corkery, why not others? *Ní hannsa*, as the old Irish glossaries say – Not hard. Any Irish publisher will print a book if you take it to him under your arm, and if it is a hundred per cent. safe. These two provisos are rigid. Elsewhere if I want to devote my life to the art of literature I go to a publisher, with some stories, or an unfinished manuscript. His reader looks over my work. He says "Not promising" – or "Promising." The publisher asks me about my hopes and fears for art, and if he is a man of enterprise – i.e., if he really is a publisher – he says: "I will give you enough to live on for the next two, three, or four years. In return you will give me the next two or three books you write. If they sell enough to cover my advances you will, of course, get whatever they earn over and above that. If they lose me money, that is my funeral." No Irish publisher has ever done this.

Why not? First of all – and this is at once both heartening and a little dismaying – it is not a question of sales, or population, or of a poor Irish public. That was more true twenty years ago than now. I happened to begin life as a commercial traveller for an Irish publisher, and I know that it was most difficult to sell fiction in the country in 1921. To-day things have altered in a most encouraging fashion. An Irish novel, in Ireland alone, can now sell as much as, or more than a corresponding novel in England. One popular Irish author is alleged to sell up to 15,000 copies of each book, in Ireland. A recent first novel by a young Irishman, I am informed, sold, without difficulty, over 2,000 copies – which, for a first novel, is very good. I have other examples, equally pleasant to record. But, as I say, these books must be what is called "safe" books. There must be no come-back from the convents or the clergy. For example, an Irish publisher handled the Irish edition of the poems of the late F.R. Higgins. They were reviewed adversely, more or less on Catholic grounds. That publisher does not now handle the Irish edition of the poems of the late F.R. Higgins. I am not blaming our publishers in the least for crying ca'canny.[7]

---

5 *A History of Ireland* (1936), by Edmund Curtis (1881–1943); *The Big Fellow* (1937), by Frank O'Connor; and Roibéard Ó Faracháin (1909–1984).
6 Francis MacManus (1909–1965).
7 Ca'canny is a cry for caution.

Some of them are not only publishers of secular books but of religious books, and most of them rely for the greater part of their trade on educational books, supplied largely to religious. These are facts which any publisher will frankly admit. I have seen books which became near-best-sellers in Britain and America turned down by Irish publishing houses for this reason. They had to let the money go out of their hands. (Those books, I may add, were subsequently acclaimed here and had a wide circulation here.) It is obvious that Irish publishing is thus very circumscribed.

If one asks why all Irish writers do not write "safe" books it is only necessary to point out that in every country in the world there are two main brackets of readers – the sophisticated and the unsophisticated. (We all belong to both: you and I will leave the Library with, say, a serious biography and a detective story: unsophisticated readers will sometimes, though less often, do just the same.) In the main, the bulk of serious writers nowadays write for the sophisticated public. In Ireland, however, all things are ordained for the simple. Thus, to revert to our tiresome old friend, the Literary Censorship, the summing-up sentence of the Jesuit Quarterly *Studies* on "Art, Morality, and Censorship," December, 1942, is: "Our censors have the common people of Ireland on their side, and it is in the interests of the common people of Ireland that they exercise the unpleasant and unrequited functions of Censorship." You cannot have a literature on that basis. Neither can you have a genuine publishing business. And if you have not got a genuine publishing business then you can only have what we have – such books as we are fortunate to be able to import. They feed our interest about the wide world – for which our bitter thanks to the English Conquest of Ireland,[8] and to its elimination of the Gaelic language, whose total revival would, of course, shut out everything – except the "safe" books that Gaels would permit us to read in translation. For the rest, we get a few books by Irish writers about Ireland. Many of these are banned. The rest are blessed spurs to our interest in the lives we lead. If these should become still fewer we shall be as the little birds on the trees – or the cows in the field – so that when on the Day of Judgment Peter at the Golden Gate hears a faint and distant mooing coming up from the West he will say: "Here come the Holy Irish!"

That is why only one or two Irish writers are published inside Ireland. Ask a publisher if you doubt it.

A common excuse for our failure to establish a publishing business, and to produce our own books is that we have a small population. This is

8 The English Conquest of Ireland began in the late 1160s.

nonsense. Denmark, with a similar population, in one year published 2,004 periodicals, 293 news-sheets, 3,295 books, 69,195 pamphlets. Compare the English figures for books alone. Although the English-Danish population figures far exceed the ratio of five to one, England in one year – take a flourishing year, 1933 – barely published five times the number of Danish books. I wonder does the Irish issue, in any one year, of all publications put together, amount to the number of Danish news-sheets alone. There are in Finland more than two hundred newspapers. Generally speaking, every larger village in Finland has its own newspapers: not every one is a daily paper but most of them appear at least four times a week. Every year Finland publishes several hundred native books, and about the same amount of translations. In Sweden the total number of books of every kind, from Poetry to Military Literature, published annually, in the years 1932, 1936, 1937, and 1938, were between 2,000 and 3,000. See the schedule below.[9] How many books did Ireland publish last year?

9 *O'Faolain's note:* Here are some detailed figures of the production of books in Sweden during recent years, kindly supplied by the Swedish Consulate:

	1932	1936	1937	1938
Bibliography	15	22	26	20
Encyclopaedias, &c.	55	65	66	61
Religion	249	323	290	347
Philosophy	28	35	42	36
Education and text books	98	84	89	92
Languages and Philology	112	149	130	118
History of Literature	29	23	22	24
Fiction and Poetry	638	793	794	859
Art, Music and Theatre	77	62	76	88
Archaeology	21	18	20	18
History	91	122	113	118
Biography and Genealogy	120	143	111	108
Anthropology and Ethnology	13	14	10	10
Geography and Travel	140	176	181	157
Sociology, Law and Statistics	220	242	212	137
Technics	59	52	65	62
Economics and Commerce	188	178	190	152
Athletics and Sport	42	42	35	38
Military Literature	14	26	19	38
Mathematics	31	48	52	39
Science	172	183	204	221
Medicine	93	86	87	91
Totals	2,505	2,886	2,834	2,834

Why are we alone so backward? We are backward because no native government has given a moment's thought to our national culture since the first Cosgrave Government gave the Abbey Theatre a small subsidy of £1,000 per annum – which some members of the Dáil still wrangle over every year. Denmark, Sweden, and Finland know that they are comparatively small countries sandwiched in between large and powerful countries, and know that they cannot adopt our so casual policy of letting Nature take its course. In Sweden, for instance, writers receive such encouragement as scholarships, rarely more than about £100 a year, or even less; sometimes up to £250 a year for outstanding authors. Assistance and subsidies are further distributed by an Authors' Association known as *Samfundet De Nio,* and by the publishing firm of Bonnier. There is a fine and highly-developed system of free libraries. Publishers of scientific works are assisted by subsidies to cover printing costs, and so on. In Czecho-Slovakia authors are pitchforked into Civil Service sinecures. I once asked a Czech Minister whether this did not spancel authors.[10] He smiled – he was in Dublin at the time – and said: "Religion? Political views? Oh, no! A man may be a Moravian, a Catholic, a Socialist – it does not matter. You know, this is the first country I have ever been in where I have heard people say: 'He is a Protestant, but he is quite a decent fellow.' Or: 'Of course he is a Catholic, but he is *quite* intelligent.'" I once asked at the Finnish Legation in London how it is that so small a population publishes so many books? Nobody could give any answer except that it was to be presumed that the Finns like literature and are very keen readers. (Obviously, they have never heard of the "safe" book limitation.) But it is of practical interest that Finland has, in comparison to her population, the largest number of public libraries in the world.

One could be bitter about all this, but I think we have enough of bitterness, and that it would be much more profitable if we could all forgive and forget and start all over again – and *do* something. Literature will not, I repeat, suffer if we do nothing. Our writers will not expire. They will export. As they leave us they shift their interests, of course, partially or wholly away from Ireland, and write of the greater world outside – as have done Shaw, Shane Leslie, Elizabeth Bowen, L.A.G. Strong, George Moore, Denis Johnston, Dunsany, Colum, Helen Waddell, and many

10 A spancel is a rope used to restrain or hobble livestock to prevent them from moving.

more;[11] and what of local interest we get from them become as the occasional gifts that Scotland gets from her expatriate authors. And you cannot expect a people to be very much alive on a feast once or twice a year and starvation for the rest of the time?

I know quite well all that is involved in the problem of State support for art, books, publishing – just as well as if I were sitting at this moment at a Cabinet meeting in Government Buildings. Somebody is gallant and far-seeing enough to move, let us say, that State pensions for authors, painters, musicians, or actors, be established. A shrewd look comes over those faces. "Yes, it would be nice to do that. But who will get the first pension? It would, after all, be tantamount to State approval of that man's works." The real check is caution and prudence, and a calculating eye on Elections. The spoken argument is all about Morality and Duty, and Responsibility ... How disgusting men can become after a few years of politics! How moral cowardice eats into their very souls! Yet, I could believe that some big man like Mick Collins, or some human man like Wolfe Tone, or some genuine idealist like Pearse – who defended Synge against the sharks – would say: "Are we a Government or are we not? It is for Ireland we legislate, not for a caucus! To hell with this puny-pandy sort of argument. Yeats was honoured all over the world as an Irishman. For God's sake let us have the courage of our convictions. These are our own people. Others think them worth while. Let us do so, too."

Until some such man arises again, we shall not have a live literature, a live country, or live thought. We shall have neither honour on this Irish earth, nor beauty, nor belief nor, what is more important than all, the courage of our own brains.

---

11 Shane Leslie (1885–1971); Elizabeth Bowen (1899–1973); Denis Johnston (1901–1984); and Helen Waddell (1889–1965).

The Strange Case of Sean O'Casey[1]

I came away from *Red Roses For Me* at the Olympia last March cursing London, Dublin, the Abbey Theatre, Willy Yeats, The Protestant Boys' Brigade, the Civil War, the Gaelic League, the Smuthounds, Lady Londonderry, C.B. Cochran, and everybody and everything else (including Sean O'Casey) who drove or lured O'Casey out of Dublin, and for nearly twenty years now have been inhibiting or thwarting him – and apparently still do it.[2] In my mind were Baudelaire's lines –

Qu'as tu fait, o toi que voilà
Pleurant sans cesse.

1 "The Strange Case of Sean O'Casey" appeared in *The Bell* 6, no. 2 (May 1943): 112–18.
2 In this essay, O'Faolain mentions the following of O'Casey's works: *Red Roses for Me* (1942), *The Star Turns Red* (1940), *The Silver Tassie* (1927), *Within the Gates* (1934), and *Juno and the Paycock* (1924). The Olympia is a theatre in central Dublin. Robert Baden-Powell (1857–1941) was an early administrator of the Boys' Brigade, which was founded by William Alexander Smith (1854–1914) in 1883; the organisation's emphasis on militarised Christian manliness influenced Baden-Powell's creation of the Boy Scouts in 1908. Lady Londonderry (1878–1959), née Edith Helen Chaplin. Charles Blake Cochran (1872–1951) was a British theatre impressario. Although he neglects to mention it, O'Faolain wrote a negative review of *The Silver Tassie* that O'Casey took great offence to and that further deepened his antagonism toward Ireland. See Sean O'Faolain, "The Silver Tassie Staged," *The Irish Statesman* (19 October 1929): 134–5.

Dis, qu'as tu fait, toi que voilà
De ta jeunesse?[3]

I was saying: "There's more heart in this absurdly faulty play than in anything that has been put on the Dublin boards since *Juno*. There is more genius in *Red Roses*, more poetry, more humanity, more hope, more belief. In short, there is more *lift*." And it is donkeys' years since we have had a play with a lift in it. For all that can you, if you have been to the play, see yourself going to *Red Roses* a second time? I do not think so. And one reason, at least, is plain enough: the poetry is more in the heart of O'Casey than in the words of the play.

You can see the man smouldering with it. You see his flicker of fire break up gallantly now and again through the smother. And what on earth this smother is, nobody can tell – least of all, of that I am quite sure, Sean O'Casey himself. Just as I am sure that if he were sitting in the stalls of the Olympia watching his play, he would not see what you and I see – who have only the words and those flickers and our belief in the man to guide us. He would see things behind the words which are not in the words, or the scenes, or the appearances of the people. He would see in every moment his unexpressed, inhibited vision which we barely glimpse. What is checking him?

O'Casey's exile is probably the key to the problem – if we could but understand it. When a man goes into exile one expects that everything that drove him out will be limelit in his later work. We expect that his revolt will show us things in him that, for one reason and another, he had hitherto either suppressed or at least toned down. His denial of us should define him.

With O'Casey the definition has been very indirect. One can see plainly enough, for instance, that much of his later work is of the sort that Dublin would not want to produce – so that it has been left to the courage of Shelah Richards and Michael Walsh to take a big gamble with this play, as they did with Paul V. Carroll's *The Strings are False*.[4] In the same way,

---

3 From the poem "Le ciel est par-dessus le toit" (1880) by Paul Verlaine, not Baudelaire. The title translates as "The sky is above the roof" and the lines as "Oh what have you done, you who comes here, / Constantly crying, / Say, what have you done, you who comes here, / with your youth?"
4 Shelah Richards (1903–1985), a noted actress, and Michael Walsh (n.d.), né Nigel Hazeltine. Paul Vincent Carroll's *The Strings Are False* (1942), later published as *The Strings, My Lord, Are False* in 1944.

The Star Turns Red was blocked here by the pious papers which pre-reviewed it as Communist and anti-clerical: and, as we know, even one such pre-review in Ireland can kill a play. (And, as was to be expected, the Catholic *Standard* duly tore the guts out of *Red Roses*.)

One may guess also that not merely would he foresee that Dublin would not want to produce these later plays, which he must have been incubating when he left us, but that he would know that it would be difficult even to write them in the atmosphere of Dublin. It would be, no doubt, an unconscious foresight, an artist's instinct – sometimes faulty, sometimes sure. And, certainly, *The Silver Tassie, Within the Gates, The Star Turns Red*, are not the kind of plays that normally occur to Irishmen living in this Ireland. It no more occurs to them to write such plays than it would have occurred to Shaw, had he remained in Dublin, to write *Mrs Warren's Profession*, or *The Doctor's Dilemma*, or *Heartbreak House*.[5] Even the problem of *Widowers' Houses* – the slum problem – would have seemed to him a local and lesser problem in this mainly ruralised society, bred of a farming country. And Shaw, like the later O'Casey, was interested in the whole international world-problem of a reorganised society. He has plainly given us this reason for leaving Dublin in a well-known passage. "A certain flippant, futile derision and belittlement which confuses the noble and serious with the base and ludicrous seems to me peculiar to Dublin. When I left Dublin I left (a few private friendships apart) no society that did not disgust me ... " Then he speaks of Socialism and how other countries were working out new ideas on those lines. In short: "My business in life could not have been transacted out of an experience confined to Ireland. I had to go to London just as my father had to go to the Corn Exchange."[6]

Now, that, as Shaw is careful to elaborate, was written of a time before the 1916 Revival; before the Anglo-Irish Literary Revival; before the Gaelic League's hey-day: it was written of a period as dull and idle-hearted as we have ever had – that soggy, whinging, conscienceless, barren period before Jim Larkin and Jim Connolly, Pearse and the I.R.B.,

5 Shaw, a major precursor for O'Casey's politicised drama, was the author of *Mrs Warren's Profession* (1893), *The Doctor's Dilemma* (1906), *Heartbreak House* (1919), and *Widowers' Houses* (1892).
6 From Shaw's Preface to his novel *Immaturity*. The novel was written in 1879, but not published until 1930; the Preface was written in preparation for the publication of the novel.

started to wake us up.[7] The comparison thrusts itself on one. O'Casey left Ireland in an equally *detraqué* period: that disordered, backward period after the Civil War.

His mind, clearly, had expanded tremendously after the 1916 Rising, and during the period of the subsequent Revolution. New ideas, far larger than Nationalism, were growing in him. By 1925 what had he come to? He had come to find himself at the height of his powers, with his mind open to the world, in an atmosphere clogged with local personalities, half-baked, babyish ideas, all belonging to the 19th century, racial and religious bitterness, disillusion, despair, with the job-grabbers clawing for their chances, and the pious smuthounds smelling out their victims. It was the inevitable aftermath of courage and glory, no worse here than, let us say, America after the Civil War – when exactly the same forces came creeping out from the smoke of battle. It may have occurred to O'Casey that his genius must get out or choke. There would be nothing new in that. The list is long: Stephens, Joyce, Moore, Ervine, Boyd, Eglinton, Leslie, Helen Waddell, Elizabeth Bowen, Shaw, Francis Stuart, Liam O'Flaherty, Gogarty, Colum, Stephen Gwynn, Kate O'Brien, and many more of his kin who have chosen exile.

This is a thing one cannot probe. They do it. It is evidence. We drive them out. They are lured out. Nobody can blame them. The atmosphere is, undoubtedly, hellish. They would not do it if they did not think it wise to do it. One can only measure the wisdom by the fruits, and exile has been fruitful – that is also evidence – for more than a few. But it has not, in the main, been fruitful for O'Casey. It is, of course, more than possible that it would have been even worse for those few had they remained in Ireland.

Mind you, it is not the material that goes bad on us. For the point about the material is that the worse it is the better it is. It was not the beauty of Dublin but the filth of Dublin that nourished O'Casey. He had flourished on its poverty. His passion flamed in its damp and chill. (And in the Third Act of *Red Roses For Me*, see again how the old fire is fed on that misery; and I say this although it is in every way a bad act, and poor theatre, and I know that what I am watching is that smothered, passionate fire trying to get up and out through its inhibiting smudge.) He had got a lift, in some mysterious way, out of the dull exasperation of his native city. His

---

7 James Connolly (1868–1916), like Patrick Pearse, was one of the leaders of the insurrection in 1916 and was executed for his part in it. Like Larkin – and unlike Pearse – he was committed to left-wing politics and was a major organiser of the labour movement in Ireland.

gall-sac had fattened on its fungus. *His* weed had never rotted itself in ease on Lethe's wharf: it had bloomed, wondrously.[8] He had even had no need to go into physical exile to be lonely; for, as a poet, he had always been marooned here, brooding alone on a dropsy of evil and dirt and slummery that meant more to him than the Rose of All the World had ever meant to Yeats. Gauguin, who went into exile among the yellow Polynesians in Tahiti, never got more excitation than O'Casey got out of the yellow tuberculars of North Dublin.[9] Whatever disillusion came over us this did not cease. The more we rotted the more incense there was to our foetor.[10] Mollser is always with us.[11] The only betrayal Dublin could have been guilty of was not to become more ugly but to become more beautiful, less exciting in her cruelty, less brutal, more humane, a moral city. And I hardly think anybody would announce that miracle.

We all know the immediate occasion of his withdrawal – the row with the Abbey over *The Silver Tassie*. Personally I can see in that not a reason but an excuse.

The world knew that the Abbey had turned it down and the affront was great, though I imagine that it was less the rejection that angered him – for O'Casey should have been big enough to shrug off a mere disagreement of opinion – than the manner of the rejection, especially the unsympathetic dogmatism of Yeats. "Your statements," he said, angrily, to Yeats, "are to me glib, glib ghosts. It seems to me that they have been made, and will continue to be spoken for ever and ever by professors in schools for the culture and propagation of the drama. (I was nearly saying the Gospel.) I have held these infants in my arms a thousand times and they are all the same – fat, lifeless, wrinkled things that give one a pain in the belly looking at them." But what chiefly got O'Casey's goat, perhaps, was Yeats's equally dogmatic suggestion that he was only pretending to be interested in the Great War – the subject of the *Tassie*. "Impudently ignorant" was his word for that, and with all my dislike of bad manners in controversy, I must say that our sympathy there goes out to O'Casey. For the essence of the whole thing was that the war had made

8 In Greek myth, Lethe is the name of a river in the nether world; drinking from the River Lethe causes total amnesia.

9 French post-impressionist painter Paul Gauguin (1848–1903) settled and died in Tahiti.

10 A foetor, or fetor, is a stench or putrid smell.

11 Mollser is a young girl who dies from tuberculosis in O'Casey's *The Plough and the Stars*.

O'Casey passionately concerned about the fate of humanity; that his imagination, indeed, was, for the moment, less interested in scenes and characters for their own sakes (if he had ever been interested in them in that exclusive way) than in scenes and characters for the sake of their widest, social, human implications.

The Abbey had enjoyed Juno. The Abbey had rocked itself sore with laughter over the Paycock. O'Casey, for the time, no longer gave a curse about Juno as Juno, or the Paycock as the Paycock. Something bigger was bursting in his heart and he wanted desperately to let it out, and to get a way of letting it out. He had, indeed, thrown those characters at Dublin with as much fury as delight, as Swift threw Gulliver. We underestimated this *saeva indignatio* of O'Casey, and when he followed his Lilliputians with his Houyhnhnms we, or the Abbey, said NO! But we need not be too hard on ourselves. London took the *Tassie* only because it had become a *cause célèbre*, and the later plays found just as cold a reception there as here.

That was one justification for exile. But again – what was the *reason*? When a man is unhappy he seizes the nearest object for attack. A man will quarrel with his wife over his slippers when he is secretly upset in his heart over the slums. "This coffee is cold," I can see myself shouting to-morrow morning, when what I am really thinking is: "This letter is written by a ruffian who should be shot." It cannot have been just a row over a play. A man does not remain in exile for a thing like that.

No, I cannot see that the reason was the row over the play. And it was not that Dublin let him down. Even if the Abbey behaved badly the Abbey was not Dublin – and I wish O'Casey could have seen how his Dublin audiences, appropriately packed into the popular old Olympia, took his play last March, with a warm-hearted welcome and an instinctive sense that he was on their side even if they could not wholly understand him. Besides, Dublin is not as parochial now as it was in 1925. The pressure of world-forces is beating a way into us, and the middle-class revolution – which is what came out of 1922–1924 – is not able to keep world-ideas out, not even with every obscurantist weapon they possess, Censorship, Pietism, anti-Trades Unionism, doles and bribes of every sort to drug the poor. It might have been all right, therefore, for a George Moore to get out, because he wanted sophistication, or a Shaw, because he wanted Socialism. And any writer who needs sophistication and does not work on the common stuff of the life of the people will always be wise to leave us. But not an O'Casey. Why, then, did he leave Dublin?

I hesitate to come to the only other alternative I can imagine: one stated in the phrase of a recent American critic of those post-last-war American novelists who went into exile to Paris: "loss of nerve." They lived in America but they couldn't take it; they left the dullness of Minnesota for the romance of Montparnasse.[12] Gertrude Stein called them "the lost generation."[13] Of them all only Hemingway got away with it.[14] We who remain in Ireland, and sometimes grow bitter and warped and silent – are we, also, a "lost generation"? And those of us who *unwisely* go, flying from bitterness and the thwarting bend-back of frustrated hopes and ideals, are they, also, of the "lost generation"? You grow up in a small town or city like Cork or Dublin, dully exasperating, narrow, circumscribed, sometimes indescribably unhappy, but your body and soul are shaped by it for good or ill. Can you jump off your own shadow? I have no regard for the sight of Belfast, but it was out of Belfast and County Down that St. John Ervine got his best book and his best play – *Mrs. Martin's Man*, and *John Ferguson*.[15] He left it, and what did we get? We have to find some synthesis, some technique, some way of sublimating what we work on, as did those Americans whom 1929 anchored in America – Caldwell, Faulkner, Saroyan, Cain, Halper, or Steinbeck.[16] Old Father Chekov has warned us: "If the rope is put into your hand you must pull it" – dirty, tarry, smelly, muddy and all as it is, you must pull it.

Red Roses for Me is a fascinating play to watch from this point of view. We see him going back, here, to the old dirty rope and trying to pull it. But one halts there, perturbed, uncertain, fishing for some way of explaining what it is that fogs us as we watch the struggle. For some fog does come between us and his people as we listen: some fog came between him and his people as he wrote. My only way of saying it is that these people are "literary" people: they lack the simplicity of life: sharpness, edge, dramatic dimension. They are not given to us: they are like dolls whom their owner loves to dress up and play with. Instead of shoving them out boldly from him he is all the time cuddling them and petting them in the nursery of his imagination. Are they his youth which he cannot let go?

12 Montparnasse, a district in south, or left bank, Paris, was renowned for its artistic community in the early twentieth century. Leaving Minnesota is likely a reference to F. Scott Fitzgerald (1896–1940), who was born in St. Paul and spent some of the 1920s in exile in France.

13 Gertrude Stein (1874–1946).

14 Ernest Hemingway (1899–1961).

15 *Mrs. Martin's Man* (1914) and *John Ferguson* (1915).

16 American authors William Saroyan (1908–1981), James M. Cain (1892–1977), Albert Halper (1904–1984), and John Steinbeck (1902–1968).

Qu'as tu fait, o toi que voilà
    Pleurant sans cesse.
Dis, qu'as tu fait, toi que voilà
    De ta jeunesse?

The very stage directions are literary, unreal, often quite impracticable in terms of the stage, which insists on clearcut and unprettified character, and an atmosphere created *only* by the players' speeches. Here he is describing the Breydon's tenement:

Under this window, on a roughly made bench, stand three biscuit-tins. In the first grows a geranium, in the second, musk, and in the third, a fuschia. The disks of the geranium are large and glowing; the tubular blooms of the golden musk, broad, gay, and rich; and the purple bells of the fuschia, surrounded by their long, white, waxy sepals, seem to be as big as arum lilies. These crimson, gold, and purple flowers give a regal tint to the poor room.

What good is that to you or me in our seat in the theatre? That is not play-writing. It is a man fondling his material subjectively inside himself, as the literary novelist so often does – and safely can: as a dramatist *never* can. Here is another example, Sheila, the girl who loves Ayamonn, the hero of the play:

She has large sympathetic brown eyes, that dim, now and again, with a cloud of timidity. Her mouth is rather large, but sweetly made; her hair is brown and long, though now it is gathered up into a thick coil that rests on the nape of her neck.

Can't you hear the producer saying: "Now, Miss X! That cloud of timidity in the eyes? Dim, please!" And what if Miss X happens to be a blonde? The Olympia actress, for no earthly reason, actually did wear a false bun behind her head, as if it matters a damn whether or not "a thick coil rests on the nape of her neck."

In Act Three, "*Ayamonn's head is set in a streak of sunlight, looking like the severed head of Dunn-Bo speaking out of the darkness.*" (Does he mean Dunboyne, by any chance?)[17] Later: "*the houses on the far side of*

17 O'Casey's reference is to the singer Dunn Bó, who was killed in the Battle of Allen in 722 and whose severed head was said to sing in praise of the slain Fergal

the river now bow to the visible world, decked in mauve and burnished bronze." Not theatre. None of it. And yet, that Act, for all its gawkiness, does give us a throb and a lift, proving that genius cannot blind or choke itself once it touches, even touches, the hem of reality.

The speech of the characters hold them, also, away from us. On them, again, the eyeballs have turned inward: some opium covers them with a haze; they speak as in a dream, until you want madly to take a grip of the dramatist and shake him and say, "Wake up. Stop communing with yourself. Give us our people! Give us back our people!"

Obviously O'Casey is under the impression that this rhapsodical speech heightens his characters. It blurs them – like a bad microphone. It is a dramatist crooning to his own breast. Listen to it:

> I am drifting away from you, Mother, a dim shape now, in a gold canoe, dipping over a far horizon ... Time's grey finger puts a warning speck on the crimson rose of youth ... Let the timid tiptoe through the way where the paler blossoms grow ... Sheila, we've gone a long way in a gold canoe, over many waters, bright and surly, sometimes sending bitter spray asplash on our faces, forcing forward to the green glade of united work and united rest beyond the farther waves ...

It is a medley of Ella Wheeler Wilcox, Swinburne, Sam Goldwyn, and the Salvation Army.[18] In one speech of Sheila's the thing is like the frenzy of a Primitive Methodist – a vertigo of 21 adjectives in 14 lines, not to speak of murmuring adverbs and pendent participles, so that the poor actress had to pour it out like a bath emptying and nobody could follow a word.[19] All that comes to is – that we hear words that are not poetry, while we are thirsting for the true poetry, which is deep in the heart of Sean O'Casey, to come out, as it should come and used to come, simply and purely, in the natures of Dublin men and women moving and speaking in their ordinary clothes.

And yet – say what one likes – it does come out in this play, in fits and starts; and how it survives the smother, or how it comes at all, God only

---

mac Máele Dúin, the defeated High King of Ireland. O'Faolain could be referring to any of the Lords Dunboyne in his query.

18 American poet Ella Wheeler Wilcox (1850–1919) and film mogul Samuel Goldwyn (1879–1974). The Salvation Army, a charitable religious organisation, was founded in England 1865 by William Booth (1829–1912).

19 O'Faolain provides the parenthetical citation of page 78 for Sheila's speech.

knows. It is the mystery of genius that nothing can utterly destroy. I think
that it comes, above all, because O'Casey believes in life and believes in
men. He is not one of those on whom Conrad called Woe. "Woe to the
man whose heart has not learned while young to hope, to love, to put its
trust in life."[20] And because of that we can forgive everything. We came
away from *Red Roses For Me* with a gulp in the throat, and a smile for
this "black and bitther city" (as his apple-woman calls it) over which he
has cast his glow, and, as for how it ever came, as the First Man of his play
says, all I know is that "Something funny musta happened, for, 'clare to
God, I never noticed her shinin' that way before."

As for the Olympia performance it was the producer's play.[21]

20 This is a passage from Joseph Conrad's novel *Victory* (1915) (part 4, chapter 14).
21 At this time, "producer" referred to the position of "director"; O'Faolain likely
means that the show was defined more by the director's vision than the actors's
performances.

The Stuffed Shirts[1]

A few weeks ago in Dublin, at a Convention of the Gaelic Athletic Association – a body which has done a great deal of fine work in reviving through sport the spirit of manhood among our people – it was proposed that the Minister for Defence be at once removed from office.[2] If any Irishman outside Ireland (for within Ireland we have become pretty alert to the meaning of these motions) should read that sentence he will probably conclude that the Minister for Defence has been grossly remiss in his work: possibly that he has not built up our Air Force, or that our Tank Corps are under strength. The actual complaint was that some members of the Army play golf, or hockey, or soccer – which are not "national games." With a world-war raging at our shores, boiling up from the Papuans to the Aleutians, from Iceland down to Madagascar, I think that this is, of all recent Celtic lunacies, the most lunatic that I have ever met.

But, about the same week, a whole batch of zanies seemed to have performed a mass-escape from Grangegorman Asylum![3] A second idealist

1 "The Stuffed Shirts" appeared in *The Bell* 6, no. 3 (June 1943): 181–92.
2 Oscar Traynor (1886–1963) was the minister for defence from 1939 to 1948 and from 1951 to 1954. While Gaelic Athletic Association (GAA) sports had been intimately linked with recruitment and training, Traynor was a noted soccer fan who wished to open up the armed forces to other sports. See the *Anglo-Celt*, 1 May 1943. The chairman of the GAA, the Very Rev. J.J. Meagher, still expressed his anxiety over what he deemed a preference for foreign games in the Army the next year in the *Irish Press*, 7 February 1944.
3 Grangegorman, which derives its name from the north Dublin suburb in which it is located, was Ireland's oldest mental asylum and psychiatric hospital. It opened in 1815 under the name Richmond Lunatic Asylum and was later called St. Brendan's Hospital. St. Brendan's closed and was replaced by a new facility, Phoenix Care Centre, in 2013.

proposed at the Dublin Corporation that the Press be henceforth prevented (note how constructive they all are) from reporting the details of
unpleasant crimes: this, in Holy Ireland where such things do not happen;
in a country where the Press is almost sepulchral in its reticence; where
courts are commonly cleared at the slightest provocation; where Press
reports are frequently killed by editors out of sheer human sympathy; and
where it is a firm Press tradition that newspapers just will not exploit any
human embarrassment, or any purely personal misfortune outside crime.
The next straws-in-the-hair were the Censors: they banned the last two
volumes of Marcel Proust's *A la Recherche du Temps Perdu*:[4] this, in a
country where, I suppose, about .02% of the population ever heard of
Proust, and where the rest (in the old joke) think Sodom has something to
do with Begorrah. A fourth gentleman, down in Limerick – he might be
called the anti-Marx brother – of the name of O'Mahony was meanwhile
raising Cain crucified because the Readers' Union of London had refused
to send him any more books – for the very good reason, that he had, on his
own admission, refused to send out to R.U. members in Limerick their last
choice, a book by H.G. Wells.[5] Mr. O'Mahony was maintaining, in fact,
that it was his duty, and right, to censor the Readers' Union choice for
these members. There were other blokes dodging about in the shrubbery,
quacking at us through their fingers, but it is enough; and a good bag at
that. It is enough to make one sit down and seriously try to find out what
on earth has happened to our native Irish mixture of realism and humour.

The only thing to do is to look back and see just where the crack began.
Goodness knows if I am right – and when fissures appear they probably
break all over the place – but I have come to the conclusion that where
the crack began was about 1913; and that it was wide open in 1922: and
that what came crawling out of it was an appalling and quite alien,
stuffed-shirt, middle-class mentality.

The year 1913, it may be remembered, was the year of the great Dublin
Tramway Strike, when Mr. William Martin Murphy, a "strong man" of
the old régime, locked-out his workers, organised his fellow-employers,
set to starve the poor of the city, and unwittingly created a fermentation

4 The seven volumes of *À la recherche du temps perdu*, a semi-autobiographical
novel by Marcel Proust (1871–1922), were published from 1913 to 1927.
5 The Marx brothers, known for their chaotic humour, were a successful American
comedy team composed of Chico, né Leonard (1887–1961), Harpo, né Adolpho
(1888–1964), Groucho, né Julius (1890–1977), Gummo, né Milton (1892–1977),
and Zeppo, né Herbert (1901–1979).

of ideas that long outlasted the strike.[6] It was the year, too, of the founding of the Irish Citizen Army. It was, in addition, the year of Carson's defiance of the British Government and his enrolment of the Ulster Volunteers; which gave birth in turn to the Irish Volunteers in the South; who were, in turn, to raise the Rebellion of 1916. In 1913 Revolution was on its way.

So far, good. But what lay behind those dramatic incidents is more important – the old, multiple, traditional life to be sought and found in every cabin in the country. This is the social history of our times which has been almost wholly subserved to their political history. That human background may be summed up in three commonplace observations.

The first observation of all social historians is that the more powerful elements in every country use the weaker elements to exploit Nature for them. Here the more powerful men were not ourselves, whom a too devoted love of ancient custom had debilitated and made unadaptable; they were the various Tudor and pre-Tudor conquistadors who broke us on the wheel of our own conservatism, and whose descendants exploited us for centuries afterwards in a manner as ruthless as it was natural.[7] We shared the fate, that is, of all races who had grown old in the joints, and, in a too-remote Gaelic isolation, ignored the threats of approaching World Change.

The second commonplace of social history is that there can be only one satisfactory outcome to Conquest – the assimilation of races into a new, hybrid society. And native Ireland was, to a great extent, thus assimilated. We adopted the English language (perforce); English law (perforce – we still rule ourselves by means of it); and most modern European customs and ideas were passed on to us by Britain. Indeed, the sum of our local story is that long before 1900 we had become part and parcel of the general world-process – with a distinct English pigmentation.

On the other hand the original and subsequent colonists had taken on an Irish colouring – Butlers, Fitzgeralds, Lacys, MacMurroughs, de Burgos, de

---

6 William Martin Murphy (1844–1919), a journalist, press baron, member of Parliament, and chairman of the Dublin United Tramways Company, co-ordinated owners to combat the rise of trade unionism in the Dublin Lockout of 1913. Murphy used his press to rail against the unions, and the police were brutal in their use of force against the workers. The Lockout lasted from August 1913 to January 1914.
7 The modern conquest of Ireland began under Henry VIII (1491–1547) and was completed under his daughter Elizabeth I.

Angulos (who became Burkes and Costellos respectively), Boyles, Floods, Grattans, Magennises, Wilmots, Hydes, Cunninghams, Redmonds, Parnells, Skeffingtons, and so on – all men of Norman, Tudor, or Cromwellian Conquistador descent. This mutual absorption, however, must be fairly swift, generous, and mutually advantageous if it is to succeed; and it was too slow in Ireland and never generous enough to be a complete success.

Now we come to the third and most important commonplace of social history. As the powerful parasite begins to enjoy the fruits of victory he inevitably shares them with those whom he exploits. Fumbling and foolish Handy Andy making ludicrous mistakes with his squire's letters, and his soda-water, and his silver forks is all the time learning far more than merely waiting at table: so is Tom, Dick, and 'Arry, Sans Culotte, Simon Bolivar, Hyder Ali, Lajos Kossuth, or Dan O'Connell.[8] Besides it is the grace of civilisation that men become ashamed of crude exploitation and sincerely wish to help and share with the weaker – at first, no doubt, out of pity and human charity, but, gradually, on terms of human responsibility, duty and liberal emotion. The whole history of Grattan's Parliament here is this history of this growth of fellowship between colonists and natives.[9] The history of the whole colonial empire of Britain shows just the same process, and sometimes reveals (as in India) the same fatal evils of adjournment and procrastination. So your weaker element steadily gains in strength, and your stronger as steadily grows less powerful. The last stage of the process is generally a sharp economic struggle. All liberal emotion begins to vanish. Old ties snap. Ancient memories revive. The basic fight remains the same but is now expressed in national or political terms. That is what happened here from O'Connell to Davitt – 1800 to 1900 and after.

8 *Handy Andy* (1842), a novel by Samuel Lover (1797–1868), is considered a source for the stage Irishman. Tom, Dick, and 'Arry (or Harry), is an unspecified reference to characters that might represent anyone. Sans Culottes, or sans-culottes, were the more militant supporters of the French Revolution, so named because they were without (sans) knee breeches (culottes), wearing instead the long trousers or pants of the lower classes. Simón Bolívar (1783–1830) was a South American revolutionary who fought to achieve independence from Spanish rule. Hyder Ali (1722–1782) was a ruler in India who fought successive battles against the British army. Lajos Kossuth (1802–1894) led Hungary's fight for independence from Austria.

9 The Irish parliament that was founded in 1782 and disbanded in 1800 under the terms of the Act of Union is often referred to as Grattan's parliament, in reference to Henry Grattan (1746–1820), the leader of the independence movement.

The social history of modern Ireland, when we thus clear it of the murky smoke and flame of patriotic emotion, had been, up to 1913, the history of a gradual undoing of the economic exploitation of the peasant which followed the original military conquest. All through the nineteenth century, in Land Act after Land Act, and in various other reforms, the people were slowly lifting their backs and lifting their heads. By 1898 the farmer had already won real political power on the establishment of the County Councils, under the new Local Government Act. By 1905 he was getting solid possession of his land. All the time, his sons were going steadily into business, clerical posts, crafts, trades, and the professions, so that a native town-class had become consolidated by the first decade of this century. By 1914, except for Home Rule, and the economic hang-over of Time, the country-folk had retrieved an astonishing amount of ground. In fact, many of the remaining larger evils such as Emigration, then attributed to misgovernment, have proved insoluble even under native rule.

When one thus considers the whole record up to 1913 it is only natural that our people should have wanted, mainly, this material basis of Freedom, and that the title of Freedom should wait on the solid meaning of it. The people had wanted, first and foremost, fair play, solid leases, education – the elements of existence. In their circumstances no politicians who tried to lead them without a social policy could have succeeded: and none who tried, like Butt,[10] did succeed. Even O'Connell failed after Emancipation, and it was not until Davitt founded the Land League that the people rose again. Once the Land Acts had been won, John Redmond was the weaker for it: as every politician is always the weaker for a lack of material grievances – so much so that his success in perceiving them is threatened by his success in removing them; and he as often goes down in defeat less because he has been a failure than because he has been a success.

The final social picture around our time is given objectively and dispassionately in Elizabeth Bowen's *Bowen's Court*, which covers the whole story of a typical Big House, as in the south we call the home of the big landowners, from the Cromwellian Plantations on.[11] Anybody who has read that book must have seen that towards the end the Big House had ceased to be a fortress: it had become something between a besieged city – besieged by growing economic pressure – and an anachronistic remnant

10 Isaac Butt (1813–1879) was a barrister and Irish nationalist politician.
11 *Bowen's Court* (1942).

of such dearly-bought grace and incomplete comfort that it had already become "quaint" to English visitors (or even funny: e.g., Somerville and Ross)[12] while all about it there was growing up a sturdy peasant society, whose grace and comfort was a hundred times, a thousand times, more incomplete, but whose outlook for the future was rosily promising. All this is, of course, part of the now neglected story of the magnificent labours of the Irish Parliamentary Party, and of the generations who supported it by all those methods of political agitation, not short of violence, initiated by Dan O'Connell – who was indubitably the greatest political agitator who ever lived.

That is the material ground of 1913 and after. And since it is often remarked that the meaning and value of ideas depend not only on themselves but on the nature of the soil on which they fall, this retrospect is essential in order to remember what kind of soil took in the ideas of Sinn Féin.

But here we meet the most important thing of all. The last great political movement before Sinn Féin was the Land League – i.e., a rural movement. Sinn Féin was a town movement, started by a townsman (Arthur Griffith), and plugged by townsmen almost without exception. There was, probably for that reason, far more sheer idealism about the original Sinn Féin movement than any other previous political movement; except only that other townsman's movement, The Young Irelanders.[13] That very fact gave it its strength. It rose above all material appeals. It was, like the Young Irelanders, inventing a sentiment, an ethic, almost a philosophy of life out of the material struggle.

But let us not deceive ourselves. If the country people were roused by that appeal, as to this day they can still be roused by some old magician of that remaining little clan, such as Mr. de Valera, it was not because they were not interested in the material advantages of freedom but because, thanks to the Irish Party and the Land Leaguers, they had – as I have shown – a firm grip on most of the possible material advantages already. They had turned the corner of the bare struggle for existence, and could at last take risks out of crystal-pure and unselfish patriotism. As we know, they took them nobly.

---

12 E.Œ. Somerville and Martin Ross, the *noms de plume* of Edith Somerville and Violet Martin (1862–1915), were cousins who co-authored a number of novels.
13 Young Ireland was a nationalist movement of the 1840s; it was broken when a revolt was suppressed in 1848.

For the townspeople, however, there was far more yet to be gained and as the movement increased in power the idealism took on a more material shape. Those generations in the towns and cities had developed an incipient social sense. In some, such as the socialist James Connolly, that sense was strong and clear. He was always trying to interpret abstract terms like "Freedom" in human forms. In most this was little more than an instinct. I think Griffith had little of it. Instinctively Sinn Féin hated the sight of Dublin Castle society; of snob-Catholics, whom they called Cawstle Cawtholics;[14] a good deal of the attraction of the Gaelic language and Gaelic games was that they belonged to the life of the common people and brought us closer to the rude cradle of our history: we all had an instinctive mistrust of what one may call clubby people.

That is why I go back to 1913 and all that. Politics became, after 1913, as urbanised as they ever can become in a country where 51 per cent. of the people are engaged in agriculture and where 63 per cent. live outside towns and cities. The people who ultimately profited by the success of Sinn Féin, as the farmers had profited by the Land League, were mainly townspeople. Then the farmers' sons took a sudden step up. They became, from 1922 on, our new industrialists, businessmen, Civil Servants, professionals. (In recent years many of the urban and village poor have also profited by our improved social services.) That was where the break came.

Had these new men had any real sense of history they would have wanted to weld the new Ireland into a coherent society. They did not. They cut their roots, as so often happens with their like. The final stage of the Revolution around 1922 became – and is to this day – a middle-class *putsch*. It was not a society that came out of the maelstrom. It was a class. You had only to look about you in the streets – at the crowds of motorcars, at the over-dressed women, or in their homes at the cheap mass-produced furniture, to see that they had lost their own world and were lost in the new.

Now, with all that in mind, if we look at the face of Ireland, at this date, many things become clear. The foremost is illustrated by the fact that about two-thirds of our representatives in the Dáil are townsmen. In the Senate likewise, name after name is that of a cityman or a townsman – with only a very dubious one-fourth from the country. There is, obviously, no question

---

14 "Cawstle Cawtholics" is a derisive term for those Irishmen who paid allegiance to the ruling British forces, whose headquarters were in Dublin Castle. They were so named to imitate the phrase "Castle Catholics" as spoken with a posh English accent.

as to who is running this country, or in whose major interest it is being run: so that Mr. de Valera may think that he is representing his twenty-five acre farmer of North Cork, but in practice nothing he wishes to do can be done unless his solid urban backing agrees. In any case the economic policy of the present government has been an industrialist's policy.

But behind politicians are those organisations which pretend to represent, and often affect public opinion. It was in this critical period after 1922 that bodies like the Gaelic League, and the Gaelic Athletic Association, even semi-religious bodies like the Catholic Truth Society, or purely cultural bodies like the Irish Academy of Letters, could have done a great deal to direct us.[15] Alas, most of them were just as lost as the politicians. I have shown in other articles how the Gaelic League, for example, sold itself to politics, became vulgarised, forgot its true cultural function, with the result, obvious now to all, that the Gaelic language became synonymous in the popular mind with racketeering and inefficiency. Worst of all, the Labour movement hastened to cash-in on self-government, and threw ideas and idealism overboard: so thoroughly that when I, myself, interviewed the present leader of that Party in January, 1934, he refused to admit that his Party was "Socialist." (And, incidentally, because I recorded the fact the *Daily Herald* refused to print it.) In the Election of 1923 Farmers were 10 per cent. of the Dáil; in 1932 they were under 3 per cent.; and in 1938 there were none at all. Semi-masonic (Catholic) bodies rose overnight; and pietistic bodies flourished as never before. Everything was so swallowed up by the middle-class *putsch* that by the time Mr. de Valera – who had so far resisted it – came into power it swallowed him and his "republicans" up, too.

Look at the most idealist, if wrong-headed, young organisation we have to-day, Ailtiri na hAiseirghe (The Masons of the Resurrection): one has only to glance at its unmistakable policy to see its origin, and to guess – which is the fact – that the main interest in it comes from the Civil Service, industrialists, and, surprisingly, but it is so, one or two of the landed gentry.[16]

---

15 The Catholic Truth Society of Ireland was founded in 1899 to provide religious publications for the Irish people. It continues to do so under the name of Veritas publishing.

16 *O'Faolain's note:* Its first proposal is to abolish the farmers' sole local representation – the County Councils. There will be no democratic government. There will be, instead, one Leader, one National Organisation, and a Council, meeting once a year. The Leader will personally elect 15 per cent. of the members of this Council,

One need probe no further. It is plain that our generation has lost all sense of its origins. The healthy, generous, humane sweep of feeling that we associate with the traditions of our countryside no longer runs through society or political life. The very history being pumped into our children in the schools and the image of life being offered to them is all alien alike to our nature and to fact. It is a complete fairy-tale – I have examined scores of these books and speak by the book – based on a fanciful Celtophilism of which you will find no living example if you get on your bicycle and wander through the countryside in search of its exponents. The main notion of it is that we have since the dawn of our history been united here in our efforts to eject all foreign ways, peoples, manners, and customs – which is, of course, arrant nonsense: on this fancy there has been piled up a gospel of the sanctity of the West and the evil of the East, the generative power and utter purity of all native custom and tradition, as handed down by an army of, mainly legendary, saints and heroes; a thirst for not only what little remains of this custom and tradition but for the revival of what of it is actually dead or obsolescent; a drive towards authoritarianism to enforce these ideas and a censorship of cold-blooded economic pressure (which we all feel, and which businessmen carefully watch) to down everybody who opposes them. This farrago is called Nationalism.

There is here a very interesting continental analogy which deserves an article to itself. In the first half of the nineteenth century there grew up in Russia a group of Nationalists called Slavophils. They adored the native soil, declared that Russia was killing her native strength by imitation of Germany, as Germany had done with France before Frederick the Great, and before Lessing, Schelling, and Herder raised the cry of national culture.[17] These Slavophils were opposed by the Westerners who wanted

the one Organisation will elect 35 per cent., and Trade Associations will elect the other half: and anyway this Council will have *no* power other than to elect the next Leader for seven years. Parish Councils and Provincial Councils will be allowed – all, obviously, controlled members of the one permitted Organisation. And so on. Obviously the sort of thing which would appeal profoundly to the heart of a man like Michael Davitt! [*Editor's note:* Ailtirí na hAiséirghe was an Irish nationalist fascist political party founded in 1942.]
17 Frederick the Great, the more colloquial name for Frederick II (1712–1786), king of Prussia, was best-known for his military campaigns that enlarged Prussia's territories and made it into a world power. Gotthold Ephraim Lessing (1729–1781), Friedrich Wilhelm Joseph von Schelling (1775–1854), and Johann Gottfried von Herder (1744–1803) were German writers and philosophers.

Russia to learn from Europe, to progress, to be modern. There was a very similar clash in modern China. Now, both these ideas were generative, if only by virtue of their conflict, but the point is that those Slavophils evoked sympathy mainly from just the same class of people as our rabid Nationalists – the middle-class stuffed-shirts, Civil Servants, landed gentry, professionals. For like our Nationalists they wanted not Change but the momentary *status quo*. They liked to think of the peasant safe in his cabin, the worker safe at his bench, the lord safe in his manor, and the Czar safe in his palace. And some, I agree, may well say, Why not? They had just the same colossal evangelism, the same Messianic delusion as our Celtophils – one of whom declared recently and rather vulgarly: "Ireland must be the shop-window of Christianity for the world." The Russian historian Klyuchevsky said it better when he called Russia "this dirty village cradle in which restlessly tosses and helplessly cries the future of the world."[18] And like ours they had the same alluring watchwords of Tradition, Piety, Custom, Obedience, Authority.

Our Celtophils – many of them misguided idealists, for whom one can have a great respect and a great regard, mind you – think themselves revolutionaries and democrats. They think, in everything they do, to apply the words of Father Gannon, s.j., on the Censorship, that they are working "in the interests of the common people."[19] I see in them only reaction, conservatism, sentimentality, and intellectual cowardice. I feel that if you took every element of them, from the Gaelic League to the Catholic Truth Society, the Censorship Board to the Aiseirghe, The Knights of Columbanus to the Legion of Mary, and rubbed them all into a ball they would stick into an indecipherable lump like plasticine – and you could pull the bits apart, and make little homunculi of them again, and not one of them would notice any difference.[20] They are all different names for the same thing – a lump of mush softened out by the manipulations of that uprooted middle-class which has cashed-in on 1913–1922, all of whom, instinctively no doubt rather than in callous deliberation, see in this kind of thing a bulwark against those final changes that they naturally fear and would do anything to prevent.

18 Vasily Osipovich Klyuchevsky (1841–1911) was a major Russian historian. The quote likely comes from his four-volume work *A History of Russia* (1904–10).
19 This is from the concluding sentence of Father Patrick J. Gannon's article "Art, Morality and Censorship," *Studies: An Irish Quarterly Review* 31, no. 124 (December 1942): 409–19.
20 The Legion of Mary is a lay Catholic organisation founded in Dublin in 1921.

So, the Gaelic Athletic Association has its own good work to do in fostering sport: the Gaelic League has its own good work to do in the revival of the Gaelic language: the bookseller of Limerick has his own good work to do in selling intelligent books: the Dublin councillor need not look for unpleasant stories in the Press, he will find them in the slums of his own Ward. They have all (unknown to themselves) in one way or another been lured to play politics – the politics of buttressing the fake-society which is being thrust on us by the successors of Mr. William Martin Murphy and his colleagues – rather than help to form the kind of society that liberal men would shape for the people who rose in 1913 and were thwarted in 1922. And if, here, the G.A.A. should ask, "What have Gaelic games, or golf, or even soccer to do with any sort of social policy?" – we answer: "Nothing. That is the point. It is just a smoke-screen of Bunk." For these things are all one vast smoke-screen sent up to hide the corruption of this bastard thing that we have unforeseeingly created out of martyrdom and blood.

How differently we had once dreamed it all! We had not merely seen the English flag and the English army go, and the Royal Irish Constabulary, and the sepoys of Dublin Castle.[21] That was but the clearance. We had not merely seen even those first steps of the new thing – land for the land-less, homes for the poor, factories rising, rivers harnessed, a fair share of our own people in business, an end to emigration and unemployment. That was but the framework. We had looked forward to seeing all classes united, all religions equal, all races welded, all ideas welcome, that hammering and clanging of a young nation at work which Milton so finely describes in his famous "Speech for the Liberty of Unlicensed Printing."[22] We visioned fresh and eager life sloughing its old skin. Those things I poked fun at in the beginning of this article are not young and eager. They are very old, and very silly, and very cowardly. I do not believe that they are in the least characteristic of our people, or of the kind of world our people will ultimately make.

But wishful thinking will not make it, and as to how it will come nobody knows. It will probably come very slowly – unless, by chance, some other Man of the People, like O'Connell, should rise to lead us, or some

21 The Royal Irish Constabulary (1814–1922) was the name of the police force in Ireland; O'Faolain's father was a member of the R.I.C. in Cork. A sepoy is a native of India employed as a British soldier.
22 The subtitle of Milton's *Areopagitica* is *A Speech of Mr. John Milton for the Liberty of Unlicenc'd Printing, to the Parliament of England.*

circumstance re-enliven the old spirit. All intelligent men can do is to cast scorn on the fake thing wherever it shows itself, and try to save, in every small way, the unspoiled living People. It was all summed up for me a few years ago in a picture of the old President of Finland in his home – a simple, graceful, modest, original, Finnish house: and then I consider why we should not find a more fitting setting for our own old Gaelic Leaguer President than the aspidistras and tawdry bamboos of the former Viceregal Lodge.[23]

That is what our middle-classes have done for us. That is what we must, with patience, work to undo.

23 It is unknown which picture of which Finnish president O'Faolain refers to here, as four presidents had already served terms since the country achieved its independence from Russia in 1917. The official residences of the president of Finland are the grandiose Presidential Palace in Helsinki and Kultaranta, the summer residence, located on the island of Luonnonmaa. O'Faolain compares the more natural, national setting of the residence of the president of Finland with the seemingly artificial, colonial one of the president of Ireland, Douglas Hyde.

Shadow and Substance[1]

Now and again, when the bats are more numerous than usual in the Irish belfry, and in this past election-month they have been whirring about us in their myriads, I look up from the newspaper over one of the most pleasant landscapes in Ireland. Trees in groves are so numerous about this southern valley of Dublin that they merge from a little height into a forest, and any trick of the light will arrange them into a series of petty horizons stepping off to that bold, continuous line which in North Dublin and the County Meath stretches like a long affectionate arm about the bay of our capital. In the soft trenches of those woods there are big and little houses, cool as mushrooms; a clock-tower in the foreground; a gazebo pricking an inky rim of trees; and below it the obelisk at Stillorgan is glinting like a little spire. From the delicate blue smoke which reclines over the Liffey there uprise cupolas, domes, chimneys, spires, gasometers, masts and funnels. It might be any great port of the world. It might be a distant prospect of Edinburgh, or London from Jack Straw's Castle.[2] Keats or Stevenson would not have found it unfamiliar.[3] It is all urbane, and civilised, and soothing. Each little villa, with its red roof below me, will have its busy housewife – dusting in mob-cap, or taking in the joint from the butcher's boy, or welcoming sonny back from kindergarten. In the nearer fields the cattle lie up to their throats in the buttercups. From

1 "Shadow and Substance" appeared in *The Bell* 6, no. 4 (July 1943): 273–9.
2 Jack Straw's Castle refers to the wagon from which Jack Straw, a leader of England's Peasant's Revolt of 1381, purportedly addressed his fellow rebels. In Hampstead Heath, a pub reputed to have the highest in elevation of any such establishment in London was erected bearing this name.
3 Robert Louis Stevenson (1850–1894) is a renowned Scottish author.

a yet nearer garden there comes the amiable clack of a hoe. A busy puff of steam reveals a train chugging down to Bray. A distant bell murmurs the Angelus. It might be the portrait of a contented land: a solid land; with everybody going stolidly about his own business.

And, then, I look down again at the paper, where the bats are squeaking and whirring as madly as ever; and the firm landscape begins to vanish, and everything seems to shimmer and shake. It is not at all like the view from Hampstead; it could not be Edinburgh. I have a notion (Is it as daft as the most batty notion of the bats?) that, down there, in that wide, wooded valley, and that gently veiled city, everybody is going about everybody else's business, and that nobody knows what his own business is, or has enough business to occupy his own mind, and that it is full of people gnawed by a restless, unsated, questioning, unconsidered, bothered – and, possibly, idealistic – anxiety for they know not what; that, indeed, it might all blow up at any moment in fire and rainbows, in the name of God, or of Ireland, or of Goodness, or of the Republic, or of Social Credit, or of Purity, or in the name of Hell or Heaven alone know what. For, to read our papers and periodicals, and to listen to our endless arguments and disputations, we seem to think and talk of nothing that is not as passionately speculative as the controversies of the Hindu gymnosophists.[4]

If only, one thinks then, we could become as intense about the best way to cook a steak! But, says Gil Blas, *comme ces Irlandais aiment se disputer*: and that was in scholastic Salamanca![5] And I remember, in a profound sympathy, that when my friend Liam O'Flaherty wrote to *The Irish Statesman* about the eagerness of the young cubs and bears of Ireland, with the foam still on their jaws, Æ wearily replied that it would be such a relief to us all if they would only wipe off the foam, and lie down, and go to sleep for a change.

We all know that there *is* this restlessness and disputation and what in German means interference-one-with-another. The forms it takes are many. We are told by some that we ought to speak only in Gaelic – though nobody wants to do so, and in fact nobody does. We are told by others that we must not dance after midnight, though everybody (who dances at all) wants to and, where they can, do. We are told by others that we must not play soccer, hockey, rugby, golf, tennis – though why these interdictions are not extended to ping-pong, kif-kif, basket-ball, dominoes, draughts, billiards,

---

4 Hindu gymnosophists were ascetic Hindu philosophers of the ancient world.
5 *Gil Blas* is a four-volume picaresque novel (1715–35) written by Alain-René Lesage (1668–1747). The French phrase translates as "My, how these Irish like to quarrel."

and kiss-in-the-ring, nobody has yet said, and possibly nobody can.[6] We are told that we must not read to the end of Marcel Proust, though it is doubtful if more than six human beings in Ireland ever have done it, or would ever want to; and those few who want to naturally do so. Some people want a more severe censorship of films. Some want less. Or, again, it was proposed recently at the Dublin Corporation that no reports of crimes should appear in the Press, while, simultaneously, one of the most dramatic cases of *crim. con.* that we have had here for a generation was totally suppressed in all our local papers, but was appearing in full in Northern and English news-sheets, freely imported in the usual way. And so on, from day to day.

No! Definitely not a view over London: nor Edinburgh: though there is a faint suggestion of the non-conformist purlieus of Aberdeen on a damp Sunday afternoon. My pleasant landscape cannot possibly be said to enfold a stable or contented community. In fact, the real question is whether it enfolds a community at all, or whether it is not populated by a swarm of internecine sects rather in the tradition of the less hearty of the early schismatics – say, Donatus, or any such masochists with a leaning towards martyrdom – for others.[7]

One of the many wise things said by that very sensible man Shaw is that an addiction to goodness is as bad as an addiction to badness. The slogan of One Good Deed per day made him as ill as if he had heard One Good Drunk per day – not only for the implicit smug acceptance by all such good-doing people of a state of affairs so bad that there should be endless facilities for good deeds by all – but because this self-sanctification easily becomes the vice which induced Savonarola to upset all Florence, and induces many pious folk here to think that because *one* man *can* live for an hour on top of Mont Blanc *all* men *must* live there for ever.[8] Which is really what our idealists want us all to do.

---

6 Kif-kif is an uncertain reference; in French, it is an expression meaning "all is even" or "all the same." Draughts is another name for the board game checkers. Kiss-in-the-ring has many variants, but one is essentially selected or caught by the person who is "it" and given a kiss.

7 The Donatists, named after their leader Donatus, separated from the Roman Catholic Church in 312 over the election of the Bishop of Carthage. Their goal was a life of penance followed by martyrdom.

8 Girolamo Savonarola (1452–1498), a Christian preacher and reformer who battled corrupt clergy and tyrannical rulers, led the creation of a democratic republic in Florence.

One respects idealists; but only as long as they recognise that in being exceptionally good people they are the worst possible example for the commonalty. Great causes have been initiated by idealists. But no tolerable community, which means no community, no tolerable society, which means no society, was ever established on idealism. When an idealist tries to make a community live by his rule he should at once be put into prison; so that when Mr. de Valera once suggested that, in order to be independent of British-imported tea, we should all drink milk or weak beer for breakfast, he was perilously near being fit for Mountjoy.[9] In fact, there are a lot of people in Mountjoy not because they are so wicked that we had to put them away, but because they are so good that it would be dangerous for us to let them out.

Where did this starry-eyed idealism begin?

Here if you say anything you are held to be attacking somebody. There is a useful French word which, as one of our best historians, the late Edmund Curtis, used to say, describes something never really understood here: that is *constater*, to make a declaration, as a witness does, irrespective of judgment, of praise, or blame. When I say that this uncontrolled idealism whose envelope now has folded itself about Irish life began with the Young Irelanders I am constating an idea which does not belittle anybody. The romantic, visionary nationalism of those young men was like some powerfully stimulating drug: it hyper-invigorated us spiritually. It gave our poor cottier forefathers – men engaged in a bloody, pitiless, unpretty, relentless struggle to regain what they had lost – the poetic personifications, and the idiom of a dream that illuminated their drab lives and lifted their struggle on to an imaginative plane. But to do this Young Ireland had to ignore the practical aspect of life and politics, and they never could create a homely image of tolerable or attainable life. We have inherited that spiritual balance so thoroughly that, to this day, we are devoid of any humanist concept of life.

It is probably from their day that we get the common iconography of patriotism, the Celtic cross, the wolf-hound, the round-tower, the pike, the Maid of Erin, the shamrock. It was no great harm *then* if this tradition was entirely faked-up since our poor people had to have some symbolism or they would have starved spiritually; nor any harm, *then*, that the sun was always promising to burst, and the chains to fall, and the dark beauty to come across the sea with wine from the royal pope, and the little old crone prophesying that there will be vast armies on the

9 Mountjoy is a Dublin prison that began operating in 1850.

Curragh of Kildare.[10] Yet, it was all utterly remote from actuality. One dud meeting – O'Connell's fiasco at Clontarf – explodes it.[11] It was the sort of thing, with Mitchel's and Maher's foolish talk of revolution that inevitably resulted in a side-car and two policemen at Ballingarry;[12] a couple of unpleasant knives in the Phœnix Park, and poor Joe Brady crying in bewilderment in his cell the night before his execution for "poor old Ireland."[13] Had it ended with 1916 and after it would have ended, and been justified, magnificently. Unfortunately it ended – if it *has* ended – in the bewilderment and confusion of our day.

Nobody would dream of deriding it. It played its useful and even its noble part. But the fact remains that before it became practical militarily Collins and his fellows had to deromanticise it brutally, and the fact remains that politically it was *never* deromanticised. We paid dearly for that hyper-idealism and unrealism, in the unpreparedness of 1922, by a bloody Civil War. We are, to this day, still tugging at the balloon, trying, in Yeats's phrase, to bring it into its narrow shed. We shall probably not succeed fully until every man associated with 1916 and 1922 has passed away and men, now unknown, will have taken over control, and in concerning themselves solely with the humane and the practical will resume contact with that other more merciful political tradition which this romantic tradition has always interrupted. That is the tradition of O'Connell, of Davitt, of Parnell, and, I think, of Michael Collins.

10 The Curragh of Kildare is a twenty-two square kilometre plain that has been a military training area since 1646.

11 Clontarf, a north-side Dublin community, was the site of the beginning of Daniel O'Connell's downfall in 1843. He refused to hold one of his rallies, or monster meetings, as they were called, at Clontarf when the authorities threatened to intervene, fearing that there would be bloodshed. He was arrested, fined, and imprisoned, and died not long afterwards, eventually succeeded by the more radical politics of the Young Ireland movement.

12 The Maher referred to here is likely Thomas Francis Meagher (1823–1867), who was sent to Van Dieman's Land for treason in the Young Ireland Rebellion of 1848, and was later a Union officer in the American Civil War (1861–65). During the Rebellion, Ballingarry, in County Tipperary, was the site of a shoot-out between rebels and police.

13 Joe Brady (c. 1857–1883) was a member of the Invincibles, an Irish nationalist secret society. He was executed for his role in the 6 May 1882 stabbing deaths, known as the Phoenix Park Murders, of Lord Frederick Cavendish (1836–1882), the British chief secretary of Ireland, and Thomas H. Burke (1829–1882), the undersecretary.

That more humane tradition has had no poetic literature to give it colour: mere scraps here and there – a street-singer's ballad or two for Dan
O'Connell, who was nothing if not humane: or a few Land League songs.
There is much more prose literature to its name though little of it is first-
class, and most of it, in the nature of the case, is not happy reading. The
English novelist Anthony Trollope wrote one or two books that bring us
towards that common life, such as *The Land Leaguers*: there are the neglected lesser books of Lever, such as *Saint Patrick's Eve*; Kickham's
Knocknagow; the tales of Carleton; Liam O'Flaherty's *Famine*; Peadar
O'Donnell's novels; a few histories like Davitt's; a poor life of Davitt;
Asenath Nicholson; O'Neill Daunt – and so on.[14] Yet, even without a
literature, that tradition of the endurance of the simple folk who were our
fathers goes deeper into us than the romantic and dashing, but also more
exclusive and less representative, tradition of Mitchel and Smith
O'Brien,[15] of Emmet, Lord Edward, James Stephens and the Fenians,
Pearse and Plunkett, which has had all the publicity and which has created a kind of "sword and cloak" concept of life and history and politics:
an idea of history which has no social sense whatever behind it.

If we were steeped in that realistic nationalism, rather than in this
romantic nationalism, if we listened to the breathing of our dead people
and less to the bellowing of our live politicians, we would, I feel, think of
Ireland and her problems more quietly, more constructively, and more
happily. For if we could call up our parents and grandparents, to-day,
what do we suppose they would wish us to show them? Surely, they
would ask to go to the old homesteads and see how the hovels have
grown into homes; examine the barns and the byres; the boreens and the

14 *Saint Patrick's Eve* (1845), by Charles James Lever (1806–1872). Peadar
O'Donnell had authored a number of novels by this time, including *Storm* (1925),
Islanders (1928), *Adrigoole* (1929), *The Knife* (1930), and *On the Edge of the
Stream* (1934). O'Faolain possibly refers to Michael Davitt's *The Fall of Feudalism
in Ireland: or The Story of the Land League Revolution* (1904). The poor life of
Davitt might be the biography *Michael Davitt: Revolutionary, Agitator, and Labour
Leader* (1908), by Francis Sheehy-Skeffington (1878–1916). Asenath Nicholson
(1792–1855) was an American missionary to Ireland who detailed the lives of
the Irish poor in the 1840s in her book *Ireland's Welcome to the Stranger* (1847);
O'Faolain cites her work in his biography of Daniel O'Connell, *The King of the
Beggars* (1938). W.J. O'Neill Daunt (1807–1894) was an Irish nationalist politician
and author of several political works, including *Ireland and her Agitators* (1845).
15 William Smith O'Brien (1803–1864) was an Irish nationalist politician.

haggards;[16] the stock and those fields on which they slaved; handle the implements; note the lives of the children; admire their health, their strength, their ambitions, their opportunities and their achievements. If those generations did, indeed, "die for Ireland," – which is a phrase I detest – was it not that this living community might rise on their struggles? Or perhaps I am being a mere materialist? Perhaps they might be interested in Marcel Proust? And they might ask eagerly about hockey? And they might agree with Mr. de Valera's famous dictum that it would be better to live as they lived, in dirt and misery, talking Gaelic in hovels, than to be what we are and what they chose to make us? Perhaps our forefathers, yours and mine, would eagerly and delightedly applaud that fanatical pseudo-religiosity which no longer compresses people to go about their religion as quietly as possible, but to go about it as loudly as possible? Or, perhaps, they who danced so freely by the roadside, and walked home under the stars, or threw their doors wide when the travelling fiddler passed their way, would no doubt fully understand that they must now have a licence from a policeman, or fight for permission from court to court, to have a dance on their own hearths? Or would they ask, as so many of us ask, what the blazes we have come to?

Our more humane leaders, from Collins to O'Connell, established the nearest thing we have to a broad, humanist tradition in politics. Our idealists interrupted it with something almost sectarian: so that, however lofty in the abstract, their course has been to dehumanise and disrupt. This is an indisputable fact which people like the G.A.A. and the Gaelic League have to face. We believe that there is a strength in our people that no misfortunes can destroy: but it can be retarded; and it will be, until we realise that the summary of History and the test of Politics is, in the last resort, the physical content of the People.

That elementary lesson every other country in Europe learned a hundred years ago. It is the substance beside which almost all our so-called Nationalism is the shadow.

16 A boreen is a country lane; a haggard is a yard or enclosure in which crops are stacked.

The Plain People of Ireland[1]

One hears this phrase used so often and so loosely that it may be well to ask who are those so-called Plain People of Ireland?

Surely, what we chiefly do when we speak of the People is to make an historical reference to certain more or less defined loyalties, and to those who fought for them whether under Collins, Redmond, Parnell, Davitt, O'Connell, or Wolfe Tone. It is a term, that is, which frankly excludes and frankly sets a boundary. It marks as the origin of modern Ireland that eighteenth century which, for its misery, we call the Bad Century, but for its amazing resurrection we might equally well call the Great Century. Everything, virtually, behind O'Connell and 1700 we thereby instinctively leave to the student of abortive civilisations: everything after it which is not in line with the democratic resurrection under Tone and O'Connell we thereby implicitly exclude, even where we admire and revere it – such as the generous and gallant gestures of Lord Edward Fitzgerald or William Smith O'Brien. Those words, The People, have an aggressively democratic ring.

It is likely that research will shew that the words "The People" do not occur before Wolfe Tone. Before the year 1700 there are, indeed, passing references – but they are, so far as I know, no more than when Fynes Morison speaks of the Irish as "a people," of such and such bestial habits, as if he were Captain Cuellar referring to them as "savages," or Campion to the "mere Irish."[2] Even later when the common folk first arrive in history

---

1 "The Plain People of Ireland" appeared in *The Bell* 7, no. 1 (October 1943): 1–7.
2 Fynes Morison (1566–1630), also spelled Moryson, was the author of *An Itinerary* (1617), which recounted his travels through Europe, including Ireland. Captain Francisco de Cuellar wrote an account of his adventures in Connaught and Ulster in 1588 when his ship, which was a part of the Spanish Armada, was shipwrecked off the coast. Saint Edmund Campion (1540–1581).

en masse they appear to be thought of not as a commonalty but as a sect. As when the early Tone speaks of them as The Catholics, or the Roman Catholics. But when the United Irishmen begin to change from a semi-humanitarian constitutional body into a revolutionary organisation under the influence of events in France the new terminology becomes established. Already in 1791, resolutions passed at an October meeting at Belfast demand "a complete and radical reform of the representation of the people in Parliament": and Tone himself clearly records the French influence there:

In a little time the French Revolution became the test of every man's political creed, and the nation was fairly divided into two great parties, the Aristocrats and the Democrats (epithets borrowed from France), who have ever since been measuring each other's strength, and carrying on a kind of smothered war, which in the course of events, it is highly probable, may soon call into energy and action.[3]

Later (April 27th, 1798) after he has spoken of the United Irishmen as the "Chiefs of the People" he makes the clear connection between the Spirit of the People and the Spirit of Revolution:

They (the Government) have begun by seizing almost the whole of the Chiefs of the People, and now they are about to draw the sword in order to anticipate the possibility of assistance, and to reduce them to that state, that, if assistance should at length arrive, they may be unable to profit by it. In this last design, however, I am sure they will find themselves mistaken; the spirit is, I think, too universally spread to be checked now, and the vengeance of the People, whenever the occasion presents itself, will only be the more terrible and sanguinary. What miserable slaves are the gentry of Ireland! The very sound of independence seems to have terrified them out of all sense, spirit, or honesty. If they had one drop of Irish blood in their veins, one grain of true courage or genuine patriotism in their hearts, they should have been the first to support this great object. The People would have supported them; the English Government would never have dared to attempt the measures they have since triumphantly pursued, and continue to pursue; our Revolution would have been accomplished without a shock, or perhaps one drop of blood spilled; which now can succeed, if it does succeed, only by all the calamities of a most furious and sanguinary contest.

3 This and the next quote are from *The Life of Theobald Wolfe Tone* (1826).

Those democratic ideas impregnate all subsequent Irish politics. Thus
O'Connell, replying to Sir Henry W. Jervis, of County Wexford, in 1843
(Correspondence: edited by Fitzpatrick: Vol I, p. 397) says:

> You ask who are to be understood as "THE PEOPLE; the source of
> all legitimate power?"
>   I reply. All those not possessed of prerogative or privileged capaci-
> ties. *Not* the King in his corporate capacity – *not* the peers, in their
> privileged state – but all those who are neither Kings nor peers. In
> short, the Commons, for whose benefit the King *ought* to reign; and
> for whose benefit alone the privileges of the peers *ought* to exist.

As a matter of fact this letter is a very interesting document in the history of the rise of an Irish democratic spirit. It is in O'Connell's best vein.
For Jervis had rashly talked of the "dregs" of the people, and O'Connell
was not the man to fail to ask who these "dregs" were:

> Not the rich and the titled, I warrant, but the laborious and poor?
> Now, as to the poor and labouring classes I will not allow you to
> claim any superiority over them. You thought fit to bestow on me
> your tediousness for a long half-hour, during which you conde-
> scended to exhibit to me your views on various local and general
> topics, and I can confidently assert that I have frequently received in
> five minutes, from one of the poor and labouring classes, more infor-
> mation, and more sound views of public policy, than I did from you
> in your entire half-hour. Again, Sir, you presume to assail the spirit of
> democratic liberty – the only rational spirit of freedom – by calling a
> Democracy "the worst, the most brutal, and senseless of tyrannies."

To which O'Connell replies by a brilliant sweep of reference to Venice,
to America, to England herself whose superiority owes so much to "that
greater portion of the spirit of Democracy which mingled with her
institutions."
    These are the first instinctive associations of the words "The People" for
modern Irishmen. There are other less vibrant associations which gathered around it elsewhere on the rise of Socialism in the nineteenth century,
and which men like Michael Davitt and James Connolly found no difficulty in harmonising with the nationalist-democratic tradition – Davitt in
his daring ideas for the nationalisation of the land (whereon he fell foul of
Parnell, and of the Vatican) and Connolly in his re-interpretation of Irish

history. In any case, the link with the republicanism of the French Revolution naturally opens these wide paths to all who choose to travel on them.

Now, if we cast our eyes about us to-day, is this what is meant by all those who like to speak of the "plain people of Ireland"? If it is, it is intelligible, traditional and honourable. But if it is not in this political sense that we hear the words used, in what other sense can they be used?

Why, one asks, are the people suddenly become "plain"? Is this a previously unheard-of Irish love for the homely, the ordinary, the unaffected? Is there a desire abroad that we should be artless and simple-hearted, as guileless as children, as candid as the dawn? Or has somebody formed an Arcadian vision of Pat and Sheila carrying Mayblossoms and dancing jigs (with a licence from the District Justice) at the cross-roads?[4] I am tempted to open my Roget's Thesaurus to see against what other sort of people these plain people are being put into opposition: what strangely variegated people there are who must be thrust aside to make way for the plain ones. I find, according to Roget, that the antithesis of the plain Irish are "the cunning, crafty, and artful," the "subtle, feline, and vulpine," the "strategic, diplomatic, and politic," the "slim, sly, and stealthy," the "ornamented, the beautified, the tesselated, and the festooned." When, I wonder, did we last see a festooned Irishman?

Alternatively whom can these good folk mean by the plain? I think quickly of some of the most unaffected and homely men and women I know. I recall an old tailor and his wife sitting by the turf-fire in a labourer's cottage in the Cork mountains – old Mr. Buckley, and his wife Ansty.[5] But these will not do. These are apparently too plain, since the record of their fireside chat has been banned "as in its general tendency indecent." If I turn for guidance to those who will neither have festooned people nor mountainy people, to see just what possible sort of people they do mean all I can find to guide me is the revelation of one Senator O'Donovan, in the Senate last December, when he said that whatever sort of people we are "we are better than other people, and our standards are better than

---

4 This is a sarcastic reference to de Valera's oft-quoted St. Patrick's Day radio address in 1943 in which he spoke of his ideal rural, athletic, morally upright Irish society.

5 Tim Buckley (1863–1945), the tailor of Gougane Barra, County Cork, and his wife Anastasia (1872–1947), also known as Ansty. O'Faolain wrote of the Tailor's death in his short story "The Silence of the Valley" (1947). They were the title characters of Eric Cross's *The Tailor and Ansty*.

those of other people."[6] Or I may find a hint in the speech of another Senator, one Kehoe, who has discovered at least one sort of people whom he can praise – "those people at the ports, custom officers, who sometimes usurp, even in their spare time, the functions of censorship."[7] Beside which may be the statement of Father Devane that the Censorship officials exercise their unpleasant functions in the interests of "the common people" of Ireland.

Does a glimmer of light begin to break through the fog? Does it begin to appear that whatever associations those noble words, The People of Ireland, may have for these new patriots, they are no longer the old, historical, political, democratic associations? Does it appear that, as if they had no interest in these things – as if they felt, rather, an instinctive recoil from them – these men would shift the whole meaning away from the virility of politics and history by proposing a quite imaginary People who never had any existence in either? In short have we begun to create a myth, like the famous eighteenth-century poetic myth of the Noble Savage, which it is worth remembering was also promulgated by equally sentimental townsmen, and equally imprudent missionaries? "Lo, the poor Indian," chanted Alexander Pope, in his phoney grotto at Twickenham.[8] "Lo! The Plain People," chants the citified modern in his phoney villa at Ballsbridge ...

Lo, the plain people, whose untutored minds
See God in clouds, or hear him in the winds;
Their souls proud science never taught to stray
Far as the solar walk, or milky way;
Yet simple nature to their hopes has given,
Behind the cloud-topped hill another heaven;
Some safer world in depths of woods embraced,
Some happier island in the watery waste:
There slaves once more their native land behold,
No fiends torment, no Saxon thirst for gold. ...

6 Timothy Joseph O'Donovan (1881–1951) (Fine Gael).
7 Patrick Kehoe (n.d.) (Fianna Fáil) was the founder and editor of the conservative journal *Catholic Bulletin*.
8 The quote is from Alexander Pope's poem *An Essay on Man* (1733–34), Epistle I, Line 99. What follows in the longer quote is O'Faolain's slight rewriting of lines 99–108.

I think one's resistance to any such fake is the counterpart of one's admiration for our people as they really are.

We are all involved in the conspiracy to foster this modern illusion. It is part of the Celtophilism manufactured by Civil Servants in that Murder Machine known as the Department of Education, with their fairy-tale textbooks on history and their quite unrealistic school-readers. The spurious picture drools out week after week from the Radio, where nobody is allowed to discuss anything frankly. And this Arcadian fairy-tale has been further protected year after year by the banning of every book that denies it, so that, to-day, almost every known Irish author is safely on the list of the damned. Worst and most pitiful of all even the countrymen themselves, when they come into the cities, find it profitable to leech on it, arrogate to themselves a superiority on the basis of it that their own behaviour mocks, lay down the law for all and sundry, and end by destroying the very thing we most need – an affection for our common stock. A great part of our present exhaustion with the Gaelic Revival centres around that pitiful vulgarisation of men who, on their own soil, are our tutors and our friends.

There is, of course, everywhere – in England, in America, in Spain, in Ireland – what we casually and naturally speak of as the general or common people. It may be thought that the distinction is small, between people without the capital letter and with it: between plain people in Ireland, or in a pub, or in a railway carriage, and The People. Or it may be thought that it is pedantic to boggle at a preposition, and insist that there is, again, a vast difference between people in Ireland and the people *of* Ireland. But that is how the mind slips and deceives itself. Let us beware. There is an effort being made here to "take the harm" out of political history by pretending that it does not exist or function. There are plenty sentimental, or self-seeking men here who would like to forget the political People – the men and women of Tone, of O'Connell, of Davitt, and Parnell, and Collins, and to put up instead of them an incoherent, helpless mass with no political integration and no political pedigree. Man is essentially a political animal. He can only live in political societies. If we do not persist in seeing our people politically we shall fall back into that chaos of our history which O'Neill failed to hammer into a shape, but to which Tone, and O'Connell, and Davitt, and Parnell, and Collins gave a form when they made The People a definition. It would be a betrayal and a calamity to dissolve that bond which the generations have so painfully welded.

We are all plain people. The question is, how many of us are with *The People*? And if we are not with them – where *are* we?

The State and its Writers[1]

Somewhere about a year ago E.M. Forster wrote one of his all-too-rare, ironically intelligent articles, under a similar title to the above.[2] He foresaw a time when the State would become the chief patron of the arts, and imagined the effect of this distant impersonality on art and the artists. He amused himself with the notion of an "old-time," individualist painter being commissioned by some Government department to decorate the inside of a fire-station, and his disgust on being told that it would not do at all to paint it in blue and red stripes! No – he must paint it according, no doubt, to Form XB 125 – "Fire Stations: redecoration." The joke is far-fetched, but it drives home the point that under the present system – or the remnants of what we call "the present system" – individual taste is still the chief influence. With the decline of privilege the influence of individual taste declines.

Hitherto the patrons of art have been wealthy men or men in control of wealth. A Bishop would order his tomb at Saint Praxed's.[3] A Pope could supervise the building of a cathedral. A peer or a rich business-man would commission an architect, give some famous painter a free hand on the murals, buy individual pictures for the walls, and the curtains and upholstery and fittings would all come from individual designers, and

1 "The State and its Writers" appeared in *The Bell* 7, no. 2 (November 1943): 93–9.
2 E.M. Forster (1879–1970), "The Duty of Society to the Artist," *Listener*, 30 April 1942.
3 This is a reference to Robert Browning's "The Bishop Orders His Tomb at Saint Praxed's Church" (1845), a poem about a dying bishop who asks his illegitimate sons to give him an expensive funeral. The Basilica of Saint Praxedes is in Rome.

into his shelves would go the books of individual writers. Even where the patron is a big Corporation – such as the British Broadcasting Corporation – the taste of one or two men will still dominate the Board and the repute of the chosen artists dominate them. Even when, to-day, something so chilly as a Government department controls the outlay there is still (*a*) a tendency to go in for Competitions, (*b*) to employ skilled judges from outside, and (*c*) which is most important of all, the artist is not expected to conform to some stated idea or ideology. Within normal limits he may be as individual as he thinks fit. E.M. Forster sees in the gradual elimination of this private wealth a greater and greater influence falling into the hands of the impersonal bodies, and inside these bodies the passing away of men with a tradition of culture and a love of individual work.

Now, what is our position? Here, almost everything that we have of beauty in the open air about us is the fruit of privilege and the taste that it developed – our buildings, our streets, our statues, the whole of the incomparable, if somewhat decayed, beauty of the city of Dublin, of many corners of other Irish cities. One thinks of the Crescent in Limerick, the North Mall in Cork, that lovely hilly street of Derry, some Protestant churches like Christ Church, many striking and perhaps not much looked-at buildings like the Ulster Bank in College Green, or Powerscourt's town-house in a back street of Dublin, not to mention the great public buildings which give us casual delight every day or the many rural seats that please the traveller's eye, such as Rockingham or Charleville. This is our Anglo-Irish heritage. Almost everything that the unprivileged have done in the same period – one could not expect it to be otherwise – is bad and ugly. One will look twice at one Catholic church in a hundred and avert the eye from the other ninety-nine. In modern times, when privilege has almost gone, we have improved a little: but how little one may measure if one recalls what a rash of mean little statues sprang up all over the country after 1922: only one or two tolerable or fine, like the lofty cross in Midleton designed by Seamus Murphy.[4] Only one of our twenty postage stamps (see the illustrated article in THE BELL of June, 1942) can be said to be a really good stamp: that is Atkinson's design for the R.D.S. Centenary.[5] The reader may turn back to our issue of April, 1942, to see eight pages of photographs illustrative of the best modern Irish architecture, and he will

4 Cork sculptor Seamus Murphy (1907–1975).
5 W.D. Robertson, "The Postage Stamps of Ireland," *The Bell* 4, no. 3 (June 1942): 180–7. The stamp he refers to was designed by George Atkinson to commemorate the bicentenary, or two hundredth anniversary, of the Royal Dublin Society.

form his own opinion as to our progress there. But he would do well to do so because three very attractive things noted there are Butler's church at Newport, Hicks' church in Cathal Brugha Street, Dublin, and a little technical school at Castledermot, County Kildare, by Buckley and O'Gorman.[6] As a matter of fact I happened to race by that school in the bus a few weeks ago, not expecting it, and I was struck with astonishment at its beauty, and started a train of thought which has resulted in this article. For if a country technical school and two churches, one Catholic, away in the West, the other Protestant, bordering a slum, can all be so satisfactory, it does seem to mean that privilege is not always necessary for taste and beauty.

At a Brains Trust session last year it was agreed that two of the most striking things in modern English architecture are of public origin – the public pavilion at Bexhill-on-Sea, and the Saint James' Underground. Again one of the best pieces of public artistic work produced in modern Ireland are our coins. And one need hardly add that the fact that they are designed by an Englishman is as irrelevant to the present point as that an Irishman, Foley, designed the statue for the Albert Memorial in Hyde Park, that Frenchmen have designed public memorials in many American cities, that the fingers of Italians have moulded beauty in great houses all over the world, or that the Dane Thorvaldsen surpassed them in their own work in some famous *tondos* of the Villa Albani in Rome.[7] One outstanding example of work done here under impersonal contract is the magnificent aerodrome at Collinstown which has been awarded the Triennial Gold Medal of the Royal Society of the Institute of the Architects of Ireland. The State, then, can do these things well – when it bothers enough.

6 St. Patrick's Catholic Church in Newport, County Mayo, was designed by Rudolph M. Butler (1872–1943), the chair of architecture at University College Dublin, and built in 1914. St. Thomas, Church of Ireland, in Cathal Brugha Street, Dublin, was designed by Frederick G. Hicks (1870–1965) and built in 1931. Castledermot Vocational School, County Kildare, was designed by Eoghan Dominic G. Buckley (1907–1995) and John Joseph O'Gorman (1908–1994), both of whom studied under Butler, and built in 1936. The article that O'Faolain refers to is "Eight Pages of Photographs in Illustration of Modern Irish Architecture," *The Bell* 4, no. 1 (April 1942): 29–36; it includes photographs of these three buildings and several other excellent examples of modernist architecture in Ireland.

7 Irish coins were designed in 1926 by Percy Metcalfe (1895–1970). The Albert Memorial was designed by George Gilbert Scott (1811–1878) and built in 1872, while the statue, which was sculpted by John Henry Foley (1818–1874), was installed in 1876. Danish sculptor Bertel Thorvaldsen (1768/70–1844).

But taste is not enough – something else is also necessary as we see when we come to literature. There we have very few examples of intelligent State patronage anywhere. We have here a small subsidy given to the Abbey Theatre: it is a pleasant gesture but the example is inadequate for obvious reasons. In the United States alone, so far as I know, has a Government devised schemes for writers, such as a recent series of books on the life and ways of each one of the states. The trouble is that writers deal in words, and words convey ideas, and only a really imaginative and courageous Government will encourage ideas. It is noteworthy that since the Russian revolution very little literature of merit has followed on the great masters of the nineteenth century, and I think that it is agreed generally that all the later work of the last of them, Maxim Gorki, is very poor stuff indeed. Even popular literature weakens under State watchfulness. An anthology from *Crocodile*, the Russian *Dublin Opinion*,[8] has just been issued: the spirit is magnificent, but the level of intelligence is as feeble as a school-magazine.

Music, architecture, painting – these have some chance: literature has little. Though one remembers the committee here which refused to accept a gift of the Rouault "Christus," and one may record that while Radio Eireann seems interested in music it is continually clamping down the lid on its writers.[9] Yet even musicians do not always go free. When Shostakovich gave the first performance of his (commissioned) opera about the Collective Farms, it is said that Premier Stalin burst out: "It isn't Collectives! It's Chaos!" And the poor musician went into disgrace until out of the siege of Moscow he was free to create what "chaos" he pleased. Musicians tell me that his Moscow Symphony is a very impressive work.[10]

Yet, the fact is that writers in Ireland have become, and are likely to remain, perhaps for generations, the responsibility of the State. And that for a very illuminating reason, which reveals the great problem of modern Ireland. Let us be quite clear about this. I speak of writers *en masse*. For you must have the mass to have a literature – you must have critics, journalists, poets, pressmen, novelists, biographers, columnists,

8 *Krokodil* (1922–1992), like *Dublin Opinion* (1922–1968), was a satirical magazine. The focus of its criticism was Western imperialism and capitalism as well as Soviet dissidents.

9 French artist Georges Rouault (1871–1958).

10 Russian leader Joseph Stalin (1879–1953) was said to be furious with the composer Dmitry Shostakovich (1906–1975) after attending a performance of Shostakovich's *Lady Macbeth of the Mtsensk District* (1930–32) in 1936.

Essays: 1940–45

publicists, every class from the men who write the songs that the funny
men sing at the pantomime to the chaps who write hardly anything at all,
but whose conversation is often worth more in the way of excitation or
incitement than the written words of a lot of writers: you must have all
these, as well as the rare genius. For a writer, like a tree, cannot grow
alone. Any artist will tell you that.

In the old days we writers were part of a large community – the writers
of the world, for we had the interest of that world, and we were interested
in the wide world, and this livingness of thought kept us together here. In
becoming independent, it is undeniable that the community has shrunk,
and fallen apart. We have, in many ways, exchanged big questions for
little local questions. The ideas agitating the world find less and less
expression – chiefly, let us be frank, because it is dangerous for writers or
anybody else to express them. There is a lid down on all that. The questions that now agitate us are all anterior or intellectual interests. They are
fences to be got over, such as the Censorship and all this discussion about
Gaelic. Such fences have long since been got over in every other country,
and the world is bored with our childish lolloping over them, and our own
writers are also bored with it, and exasperated, and exhausted, because
the whole thing is really just like the lolloping of kids at a riding-school.
The writers cannot breathe in that air, and what has resulted is a neurosis
of frustration. A set-up has been allowed to develop which stamps across
the forehead of the Ireland of to-day the words "Frustration Complex."

The truth which we have to face, sooner or later, is that the culture,
which Mr. de Valera sometimes pretends will not persist without the
Gaelic Language, does not, in fact, as yet exist at all. The idea of it exists:
nothing more. There is a political frame: there is the canvas of a racial
identity: there are the palette and colours of our historical memories and
urges, and the remnants of a native culture. But there is no picture.

The people cannot reform their ranks unless they have the courage to
admit the reason. A clamp was put down on all intellectual activity here
almost from the first day that the Free State was set up. In the verbatim
reports of the Dáil proceedings from 1919 to 1921 it will be found that
on the very first day that the Dáil met in the Mansion House a deputation
was thundering at its doors, composed partly of laymen, partly of clerics.[11] Michael Collins tried to scotch them and moved that they go to the
proper Minister, the Dáil not being a public meeting. But the voteens in
the Dáil already began to crumple up before the invisible threat, Collins

11 The Dáil's first meeting took place in the Mansion House on 21 January 1919.

was outvoted and they were admitted.[12] For columns of print they spoke – This at the height of a country's agony! – of "evil literature" and "evil plays." That intrusion into the Parliament of the People by a small private group, with no Church sanction, is a symbol of what has been going on here for over twenty years. Drops will wear away a stone. When the State, the Government, cringed and submitted like that at the outset of its career the only result possible could be that the whole moral fibre would be finally eaten away.

Let no man reply to us by talk about the writers' loyalty to the State. I pass over the implicit idea of the God State, and merely refer any such man to a book like Maritain's *The Rights of Man*, or to his fascinating book *Three Reformers*, in the course of which he nobly asserts the independence of the person.[13] It is enough that, taken all in all, our writers ever since the days of O'Connell and the Young Irelanders have been behind every liberal and national movement in the country. They backed O'Connell; they backed Parnell; they backed Griffith; they backed Jim Larkin and the workers in 1913 – no man more courageously, selflessly and nobly than Æ; they backed the whole national struggle from 1916 onward. Irish writers have over and over given full proof of their national, social, and literary integrity. No! It is not the loyalty of the writer to the State which is in question. It is the writer who must to-day cry *J'accuse*.[14]

If we want the reality of nationhood we must have the courage of it. We must speak the truth. We must have the intellectual energy to look for it. We need that inner dynamism that small groups have so often generated in the past and communicated to a whole People. For you cannot make a nation out of a Civil Service office, with blue papers, and niggling green-tape – all the rope a Civil Servant is given or can give. A coherent live society is an organic thing that grows of its own power, and all it asks is to be allowed to grow. The writers of this country are, in that sense, the responsibility of the State, because the State – seeing this Frustration

---

12 Voteen is a derogatory term; it refers to one who is ostentatiously religious.

13 *The Rights of Man and Natural Law* first appeared as *Les Droits de l'homme et la loi naturelle* in 1942 and *Three Reformers* was published as *Trois réformateurs: Luther, Descartes, Rousseau, avec six portraits* in 1925. They were written by French philosopher Jacques Maritain (1882–1973).

14 When the Jewish officer Alfred Dreyfus (1859–1935) was convicted of treason, Émile Zola published a letter on 13 January 1898 in the newspaper *L'Aurore*. In the letter – often referred to as "*J'accuse*," French for "I accuse," its opening words – Zola rightfully charged that the authorities concealed the truth of Dreyfus's innocence.

Complex on all sides – can alone now give the People the example of courage, vision, and imagination that will free us all from the repressive forces that threaten to destroy us like a paralysis.

I do not speak of the present. The present is a bad period, and may be marked off as a dead loss. Our leaders are old and tired, and it is their successors who will have to face the problem, i.e., that a small community cannot be left to itself in these things. A writer like the Nobel Prize winner, Grazia Deledda,[15] wrote about the simple life of her Sardinian peasants, as O'Flaherty or O'Donnell do of ours. But she wrote not for them, but for Rome. Peasants do not support literature. Daudet wrote about the simple Midi.[16] He was inevitably part of the literary community of all France, and won his fame in Paris and in the wide world. Can Dublin become a Rome, a Paris, a London, a gateway to Europe? For I speak not of money but of the open arms or the shut mouth, the eager welcome and open mind, or the repression and the infantilism. The picture is tragic, but we must paint what we see. Yeats, Moore, Joyce, Shan Bullock, MacKenna, Gregory, Æ, Higgins have all gone. No young men are appearing. If our leaders of opinion do not act quickly Irish literature will virtually cease to exist within ten years.

15 Italian writer Grazia Deledda (1871–1936) was awarded the Nobel Prize for Literature in 1926.
16 Alphonse Daudet (1840–1897); the Midi is a region in the south of France.

The University Question[1]

An important and interesting incident occurred in February. The Lenten Regulations of His Grace the Most Reverend Dr. McQuaid, Archbishop of Dublin, announced the closing of Trinity College to all Catholics resident within the Dublin Diocese – if not, ultimately, to all Irish Catholics.[2]

Hitherto the Hierarchy has, in practice, left it to parents and guardians whether or not they will send their children to T.C.D., merely insisting at intervals that no priest can advise a parent to do so. The February regulations apply only, of course, to the Dublin Diocese, and are not equal to an absolute interdiction; but their intention is obvious, and in their wider influence and repercussions they are poles apart from that spirit of conciliation which marked earlier efforts to establish a unified National University in Ireland.[3]

The general effect of the Regulations may be illustrated by the opening statement which propounds the general teaching of the Church on Education. "Therefore," says His Grace, "the Church forbids parents and guardians to send a child to any non-Catholic school, whether primary, or

1 "The University Question" appeared in *The Bell* 8, no. 1 (April 1944): 1–12.

2 John Charles McQuaid (1895–1973) was appointed archbishop of Dublin in November 1940. The statements were part of McQuaid's Lenten Regulations, which were issued on 7 February 1944. Trinity College Dublin, often shortened to T.C.D., is officially known as the University of Dublin. A non-Catholic institution, it was founded by Queen Elizabeth I in 1592.

3 The National University of Ireland was established in 1908. It is composed of three constituent colleges: University College Dublin, University College Cork, and University College Galway. The latter two were first founded in 1845 and known as Queen's College, along with Queen's College Belfast.

secondary, or continuation, or university. Deliberately to disobey this law is a mortal sin, and they who persist in disobedience are unworthy to receive the sacraments." That is, whether a parent deliberately sends a child to a Kindergarten or to Dublin University, neither being denominationally Catholic, he automatically puts himself outside the benefits of the Catholic Church. The National University is excluded from this general proscription as being just "sufficiently safe," thanks to certain measures taken by the Church "to protect Faith and Morals" inside that University. A great deal depends here, in theory, on the technical connotation of the word "deliberately," and a minority of the laity may possibly ask for instructions as to the application of the law to their personal circumstances: but the majority are likely to regard the interdict as unqualified.[4] Again, the reference to the grave penalties incurred by the priest who "in any way assists in sending a Catholic to be educated in a non-Catholic educational establishment" will be interpreted not as to the letter – e.g., of "assists" and "in sending" – but rather as to its spirit. In any case, as far as Trinity College is specifically concerned the laity is now reminded that it is reserved to the Archbishop himself to grant or withhold permission to enter T.C.D.; and the laity is further warned that this permission will only be granted "for grave and valid reasons and with the addition of definite measures," as yet undefined, for the protection of the student. Everything taken into account, nobody can be under any illusion as to the uncompromising aim of the order.

4 *O'Faolain's note:* The word, deliberately, one presumes, means "by one's own decision." That is to say, the interdict is general (in Ireland); it is a mortal sin to break it, where it is enforced locally; it is not a mortal sin if one asks and is granted permission. There is nothing odd about that. The State does the same every day of the week. Thus, there is a general prohibition on the export of some commodities; it is a crime to break this prohibition; it is not a crime if one asks and receives permission. It is a fact that the State is constantly "inventing" crimes. Why should the Church not also "invent" sins, e.g., of disobedience?

As to whether *the Church* "forbids parents and guardians, etc." in the sense of the Universal Church, is something beyond our scope. The above statement which says so possibly only means that "the Church," through its representatives, the Irish Hierarchy, has done so *for Ireland?*

It should be added that there is nothing new in this prohibition on attending non-Catholic Colleges in Ireland. It is laid down in the Maynooth Statutes: even the words "sufficiently safe" are there applied to the National University. But these Statutes had become obsolescent in so far as it had ceased to be the practice to apply for permission. Nor is it necessary even now outside Dublin. The Regulations, that is to say, have revived locally something long obsolete elsewhere.

Let it be said, at once, that we are not proposing that any Catholic should attempt to evade obedience. For a Roman Catholic nothing can deprive the Church of its prerogative as a divinely constituted guardian of the Faith: he must recognise his Faith as a defined Faith and his church as a living authority. That is his choice while he remains a Catholic, and if he does not cling to that position firmly he is, at bottom, less a Catholic than a Protestant. He must acknowledge that there is no least pore of human life, no minutest cranny of his behaviour from birth to death, which his Church may not control. Whether he agrees or disagrees he must obey – provided only that the law at any time propounded to him is, in fact, the law of the Church. He may then not only question the law but refuse to obey it; though the results, in such a case, cannot be other than unhappy and chaotic. We all have, for example, a vivid memory of the state of affairs which arose in the Diocese of Cork during the Revolution when the Ordinary there laid an interdict on the Irish Republican Army which most, if not all, of the laity refused to recognise as binding.

Such matters are, however, outside the layman's scope. He will be interested, rather, in social and political implications and reverberations. To understand these, and to dispel some misconceptions, he would do well to go back a little to the history of the whole Irish University dispute. Many of our Protestant fellow-countrymen, for instance – we but record the observed fact, which might, in any event, have been anticipated – have been exacerbated by what they regard as an insulting form of "sectarianism." It might help to calm the atmosphere to remember that all universities were originally "denominational," with daily prayers, religious services, and so forth. Oxford, Cambridge, Trinity College, had all been, at first, houses of religion. Less than a hundred years ago, it was still a tradition that Fellows of Oxford and Cambridge should remain celibate. It was the scientific spirit of the 19th century which really finished clerical control in the universities and established secular education, with specialists in charge of every department. In addition, as we all know, Irish Catholics were excluded from University education from the Reformation to about 1793, when Trinity College opened its gates to them: though no real effort was made to cater for them until the establishment of the Queen's Colleges at Cork, Galway, and Belfast.[5]

5 *O'Faolain's note:* The first two of these are now constituent colleges of the National University of Ireland, and may, if they wish to recognise their origins as Queen's Colleges, celebrate the centenary of their incorporation next year. They were not opened for the actual reception of students until 1849.

It was with these Queen's Colleges that the University dispute began. Some of the Catholic hierarchy, such as Dr. McQuaid's predecessor, Archbishop Murray, wished to try to make these Colleges work.[6] They asked for certain amendments, e.g., dual chairs in History, Logic, Metaphysics, Moral Philosophy, and curiously (to our modern ears) Geology and Anatomy. These being refused, Cardinal Cullen tried, in 1854, the famous experiment which we popularly call Newman's University.[7] Before it collapsed, something like a quarter of a million of Catholic money was swallowed up in this tragic fiasco.[8] Nothing of it now remains but Newman's exquisite little chapel in Stephen's Green. From that onward, effort after effort, in Commission after Commission, was made to provide a form of University education which would satisfy both Irish Catholics and British public opinion.

Why did these efforts fail? It was not that British statesmen did not wish Irish Catholics to have University education: far from it. It was not that the Catholic bishops were unwilling to compromise: far from it. The contentious questions were of the order of episcopal control over organisation, clerical censorship over professors, strict denominationalism, and the unwillingness of Trinity College to co-operate. On these questions non-Catholics were adamant and Catholics were not agreed: again, far from it. Outstanding Catholics like Wilfrid Ward – I quote his daughter's biography – "felt that it would constitute not merely a bar to efficiency but actually a danger to faith if it seemed that the Church could not allow the sciences to develop on their own lines without constant interference. The Galileo case had remained for centuries a scourge for the Catholic apologist because the theologians had been too ready to fear that a scientific discovery might endanger revelation."[9]

6 Daniel Murray (1768–1852) was appointed archbishop of Dublin in 1823.
7 Paul Cullen (1803–1878) was appointed archbishop of Armagh in 1850 and of Dublin in 1852, and was elevated to cardinal in 1866. John Henry Newman (1801–1890), a Catholic priest who was appointed the first rector of the failed Catholic University of Ireland, published his thoughts on the project in The Idea of a University (1852); O'Faolain later wrote a book about him titled Newman's Way: The Odyssey of John Henry Newman (1952).
8 The currency used at the time was the pound.
9 Wilfrid Ward (1856–1916) wrote a biography of his own, The Life of John Henry, Cardinal Newman: based on his private journals and correspondence (1912). The biography O'Faolain mentions is The Wilfrid Wards and the Transition, published in two volumes (1934–37), by Masie Ward (1889–1975). Galileo Galilei (1564–1642) was an Italian scientist who was persecuted by the Church for advocating the heliocentric system.

But it is still more important to remember that politics also entered into the matter. I again quote Maisie Ward:

Newman's book (*Idea of a University*) remains as a monument and a witness to the possibilities of Catholic education. My father held that its ideals were being largely carried out at Louvain University, yet he saw, too, the dangers and difficulties in the light of what Newman had suffered. One of the lectures in the *Idea*, although printed, could not even be delivered in Dublin because it awakened the alarms of Cardinal Cullen. "The Irish bishops," wrote Newman, "treat the laity like little boys." Cardinal Cullen objected to Newman's bringing professors from England and Scotland. He objected equally to the appointment of Irishmen of pronounced political views – "Young Irelanders" as they were called in those days. Newman had cared nothing for a man's politics or nationality. All he had wanted was the best possible professor in every subject. He had desired to get the sympathy of the laity, but the fact that he had come there under the aegis of Cardinal Cullen made this impossible. Cardinal Cullen, he came to hold, and some of the Irish bishops with him, did not want an educated laity.[10]

This cautious interest of the clergy in the possible effects of education on political thought must never be lost sight of.

Not until the century was well dead, in 1908, was the problem solved by the establishment of the present National University of Ireland. It was and is, in theory, undenominational: as, in practice, Trinity College has also become. Very few Protestants attend the National University. The proportion of Catholics to Protestants in Trinity College is now about one-third to two-third.

Time and experience have thus allayed many fears and prejudices on both sides, and justified many hopes and beliefs. But our Protestant fellow-countrymen should remember, too, that it is not the fault of Catholics if the two Universities have not come even closer together. Catholic bishops like Bishop O'Dwyer of Limerick, and Archbishop Walsh of Dublin, favoured the idea of a truly National University which would put a Catholic College side by side with Trinity College inside Dublin University.[11] Yet, when a

10 The Catholic University of Leuven, or Louvain in French, was founded in 1425 in the Belgian city bearing that name.
11 Edward Thomas O'Dwyer (1842–1917) was appointed archbishop of Limerick in 1886; William Joseph Walsh (1841–1921) was appointed archbishop of Dublin in 1885.

Catholic college, open to Protestants, was first mooted, Provost Bernard spoke of the idea with horror, saying that it would constitute a terrible danger to the faith of young Protestants.[12] Had such a University been established – and would for Ireland's sake that it had! – nobody would then have seen anything "insulting" in the efforts of the authorities of either Church to forbid or dissuade their flocks from attending the college of another persuasion. It might help to soothe hurt feelings if the present Regulations were regarded in the light of these events.

Nevertheless it would be unrealistic not to perceive that behind those oppositions, then, the social and political struggle for power and influence affected what was on the surface a purely religious question. And that very passage of time which has since produced wholly amicable relations between the universities, and produced equally good relations between Catholics and Protestants outside them, must in itself make the revival of these old antagonisms correspondingly painful now. The question therefore which must trouble our fellow-countrymen is not "Why?" but "Why *now*? Why, in 1944? When the two universities have existed side by side so fraternally for over thirty years? When students have long interchanged hospitality, and professors interchanged knowledge? When the course of politics has gone so far to obliterate distinctions and differences of all kinds?" For the thing the history of these disputes teaches us is that religion, held by ordinary human beings in ordinary human circumstances, however divine in its origins, is human in its course. Though, surely, if *any* ideal does not follow the contours of human nature it must evaporate, and both ideal and humanity be the loser?

One therefore welcomes in the warmest possible manner the alternative suggested in the leading article of *The Irish Times* of March 11th: "Is there no way to overcome this unhappy schism? A solution, obviously, would benefit both sides. We suggest that it would be worth while for both to make substantial concessions, in order to secure these benefits – to think not in terms of sectional interests but of the nation as a whole." If there are three hundred Catholic students in T.C.D. could they not be given a chapel, a chaplain, a club? Of wider matters I give below the example of the English Universities.

One cannot, in short – Who should know this better, to our cost, than Irishmen? – touch Religion without touching Politics and affecting Society. We cannot, to give a homely example, tell our children not to mix with our neighbours' children on religious grounds, and at the same time

12 John Henry Bernard (1860–1927) was appointed provost of T.C.D. in 1919.

expect our neighbours to believe that we have no personal objection to them. Irish Protestants would have to be angels, not human beings, not to feel a sub-implication that there is something sinister about their creed, and their society. And all this, of course, in its enlarged form is of vital importance to us in connection with Partition and the whole political future of Ireland.

But suppose this point is granted. Suppose it be said that the shape of a *Catholic* society, of a *Catholic* order, is paramount and that no political consideration, no social consideration, no human consideration of any kind or description can take precedence over it? Very well. Let us accept this as a great ideal, and without casting the mind over those vast reaches of history east and west during which similar ideals caused untold human misery without achieving the desired result, let us glance merely at what happened in England about eighty years ago, in this very same matter of the University dispute, when a similar ban was laid on the Universities of Oxford and Cambridge.

That interdict of 1864 was carried through mainly by the influence of Cardinal Manning in opposition to Newman whom, one regrets to say, he so persistently opposed and uncharitably suspected – of the vice of being a Liberal.[13] His impression, surely mistaken, was that no Catholic really was interested in University education for its own sake: his own words were that what arose was merely the snobbish desire of certain Catholic parents to "get their sons into society and have a latch-key to Grosvenor square" – as we could say to Merrion Square.[14] He therefore tried, instead, as Cardinal Cullen had earlier done in Dublin, to establish a denominational Catholic University in Kensington. What happened? As with the Dublin scheme, it collapsed pathetically, with an enormous financial loss, while Catholics continued to attend the banned Universities in increasing numbers. Not until Manning died was the question ever fully reconsidered. Then Cardinal Vaughan, his successor, had to petition the Holy See to remove the ban, and in 1896 Catholics freely attended these and all other universities.[15] The analogy with Ireland is not complete, since we

---

13 Henry Edward Manning (1808–1892) was appointed archbishop of Westminster in 1875.
14 Grosvenor Square is a park and expensive area in Mayfair, London; Merrion Square is its Dublin equivalent.
15 Herbert Alfred Henry Vaughan (1832–1903) was appointed archbishop of Westminster in 1892.

already have a University at least tolerated by the Church; but the comparison is informative.

Not the least interesting feature here suggested by the name of Newman is the fact that he defended the strong democratic spirit of the laity in this whole university question, not only in England but in Ireland; for in defence of the rights of the laity he resolutely opposed the efforts of some of the bishops, of a less liberal mind than his, to get "the most absolute power over University organisation in every detail." He went so far as to say of the kind of university which the anti-Fenian Cardinal Cullen desired for Ireland that, if such views prevailed,

it will simply be priest-ridden. I mean, men who do not know literature and science will have the direction of the teaching. I cannot conceive the professors taking part in this. They will be simply scrubs.[16]

Or again:

On both sides of the Channel the deep difficulty is the jealousy and fear which is entertained in high quarters of the laity. Dr. Cullen seems to think that Young Irelandism is the natural product of the lay mind everywhere, if let to grow freely. And I wish I could believe that he is singular in his view. Nothing great or living can be done except when men are self-governed and independent. This is quite consistent with a full maintenance of ecclesiastical supremacy.

Of the whole incident Abbot Butler, the biographer of Ullathorne, who, like Newman, disliked Manning's extremism, was to write:

After thirty years' experience of Catholics at Oxford and Cambridge we look back with wonder at the violences and fears and hesitations of sixty years ago, and the theorisings of Manning on the inevitable consequences that have not happened, and that there is no reason for supposing would have happened any more then than now.[17]

16 These passages are quoted from Ward's biography of Newman.
17 Cuthbert Butler (1858–1934); the biography O'Faolain mentions is *The Life and Times of Bishop Ullathorne, 1806–1889* (1926). William Bernard Ullathorne (1806–1889) was appointed bishop of Birmingham in 1850.

In our own time Denis Gwynn, the historian of Catholic Emancipation, writes of the results of the more liberal and far-seeing policy of Newman:

At both the old universities Catholics have formed flourishing Catholic Student Societies, and Catholics have attained high positions on the staffs of the Colleges. At Oxford, especially, the Catholic position has been strengthening and developing with most remarkable progress in recent years. In all the new universities of the great cities also Catholic students are now enrolled in large numbers and have begun to exercise a considerable influence everywhere.[18]

That is what I mean by saying that if ideals do not follow the contours of human nature they evaporate: though in this case, and perhaps it happens often, the people most directly concerned found in nature another way of keeping their ideals about them. But the idealist – here Cardinal Manning – did not recognise this truth; and the extreme idealist never does. Mr. de Valera's "milk for breakfast instead of tea" is a comical case in point. You may bring your horse to the milk but he won't drink it: and you may bring your people to any ideal but the rest lies with them. No doubt a great many more wonderful things would have been accomplished, if it were otherwise: and, indeed, this cuts both ways, for a great deal of human misery would also have been avoided. For what is at work is the fact that humanity is merely all too human. People do not make fine intellectual distinctions; impersonalise what affects them personally; take long and wise historical views on every question; and so on. A poor, ragged poet may do it, a martyr, a hero, but a whole people only in brief moments of ecstasy. And I confess that I find it very odd, and a little amusing, that these things should have to be said in this of all periodicals, which is sometimes taunted for being Leftist. Because these are thoughts that lead us away from all radical action, and towards the humane conservatism of wise men like Thomas More, and John Henry Newman, and Edmund Burke, and Bishop Ullathorne, and Wilfrid Ward, and many such.[19] Thus, it was More who, having in Utopia granted to every man

18 Denis Gwynn (1893–1973) was the author of *The Struggle for Catholic Emancipation (1750–1829)* (1928).
19 Thomas More (1478–1535) published *Utopia* in 1516. Essentially executed for remaining true to his Catholic faith and refusing to recognise Henry VIII's marriage to Anne Boleyn, he was canonised in 1935. Irish politician and political thinker Edmund Burke (1729–1797).

"free liberty to believe what he would," gave up his own life for the mere right to believe, in silence, what he did believe. If Protestantism in Ireland, South and North, must be regarded as an "evil," it was Burke who said that "it is no inconsiderable part of wisdom to know how much of an evil ought to be tolerated."[20] As it was Ward who said to Bishop O'Dwyer, on this very matter of the universities and of episcopal censorship, that "to rule wisely is not the same thing as to meddle much."

To the historian of our times all these matters are of a great fascination. Every new incident must strike him as part of the birth-pains of a new order, or the death-pangs of an old order. What is being born here? What is dying? It is far from easy to say. Nearly seventy years ago Mahaffy wrote in the *Nineteenth Century* that "in the course of the next fifty years it seems inevitable that well-nigh the whole country will pass under Romanist influences."[21] That is one thought. But another one is suggested strongly in the reply given by Bishop O'Dwyer to the question, put to him at one of those Commissions: "Do you believe that a Catholic University will strengthen Roman Catholicism in Ireland?" He replied, sagely and cautiously:

> It would educate Catholics in Ireland very largely, and of course a religious denomination composed of a body of educated men is stronger than a religious denomination composed of a body of ignorant men. In that sense it would strengthen Roman Catholicism.
>
> As far as religion is concerned I really don't know how a University would work out. If you ask me now whether I think that that University in a certain number of years would become a centre of thought, strengthening the Catholic faith in Ireland, I cannot tell you. It is a leap in the dark.

One can understand, in the light of that answer, the desire for what Newman called "the most absolute power over University organisation in every detail."

Is it possible, then, to believe that the middle and upper classes are slipping? Or that some modern equivalent to "Young Irelandism" really *is* the natural product of the lay mind everywhere? In other words, are our Universities, unknown to us all, breeding a new liberal Nationalism? That would not be out of keeping with the natural course of a middle-class

20 From Burke's *Thoughts on the Cause of the Present Discontents* (1770).
21 John Pentland Mahaffy (1839–1919), professor of Ancient History at T.C.D.

society whose sons have a disconcerting way of striking off at a tangent from their origins. In passing on, this warning one may respectfully offer to all concerned: it is not among the poor or the rich that anti-clericalism traditionally begins. It is among the middle-classes who associate all superior power together, as in the France of the Revolution or in modern Spain. In Ireland, where the aristocracy had always been felt as foreign, or at best suspect, the middle-classes have hitherto traditionally been with the Church. Yet they *have* been capable of revolt, as when, in 1799, the Catholic gentry under Fingall, together with the bishops, supported the royal Veto on the appointment of bishops.[22] O'Connell at once led the poor and the merchants against both, disowned both, defeated both, threw out the Veto, and originated the famous phrase about taking our religion from Rome but taking our politics from Ireland.

Perhaps it is all a matter of what our middle-classes want. If they want Power they will sacrifice anything for it, short of honour, as all ruling classes do everywhere – even life itself, as when they accept the inevitability of war, and in war proudly take the van. If they want Security, they will sacrifice everything to it, including honour, as the ruled classes do everywhere – excepting only life, as when in war they let themselves be led, but no more. In this Ireland the question to be decided is whether we have *any* lay leaders or rulers: Of what kind? With what aim? With what image of life? And from which university – in so far as they come from universities at all – will they come? The National University was once the fortress of "self-government and independence": does that Spirit still breathe there, or is she already beginning to take flight, abandoned by her ancient friends, to light among her ancient foes, there hoping for a second Spring? Whichever institution chooses, in the end, to house these principles may well hold the future of Ireland in its hands.

But is it necessary that such clashes should be invited, and cannot a wise statesmanship patiently evolve a solution which can surely, as the *Times* has said, be worked out if we "think not in terms of sectarian interests but of the nation as a whole." That, after all, was Bishop O'Dwyer's attitude when asked if the reason why he sought a Catholic University was simply to strengthen his own Church. "No! It is not, by any means," he replied. "We are Bishops, but we are Irishmen also, and we want to serve our country."

22 Arthur James Plunkett (1759–1836) was the 8th earl of Fingall.

Toryism in Trinity[1]

Ever since the first issue of this journal these pages have been written in a lofty, impersonal style like, but one hopes a little less frigid than, an encyclical. This time I feel drawn to the more modest egoism of the first person because I am dealing with a pamphlet to which I feel the only fair and reasonable sort of reply is to permit the author to watch its more or less instantaneous effect on an average Irishman of, I hope, normal intelligence and tolerance. This pamphlet is called "A Recognised Church": the Church being the Church of Ireland, recognised formally by the Constitution.[2] Its author is Professor W.B. Stanford, of Dublin University. Its burthen is a grievance: a popular subject in Ireland since we are adepts at grievances, but a dangerous one since any Catholic knows more about grievances, ancient and modern, than all the Anglicans of Ireland and Great Britain put together. Briefly, the Professor sees that his Church is a minority Church with a dwindled influence; that it is not vital (which one regrets to hear, since it is a Christian Church); that, in a rather opposite sense to the usual one, it is getting more than its fair crack of the whip; that Protestants are shabbily treated in one way or another, in public appointments, or the social life of the country; that they are being proselytised by the Catholics; that they are, in short, allowing themselves to be pushed away into a corner and left severely to themselves – a fate, incidentally, which many Catholics might sometimes envy. Farther on in this

1 "Toryism in Trinity" appeared in *The Bell* 8, no. 3 (June 1944): 185–97.
2 "A Recognised Church: The Church of Ireland in Éire" (1944), by William Bedell Stanford (1910–1984), who held the position of Regius Professor of Greek at Trinity College from 1940 to 1980. The Church of Ireland is the Anglican Church within both Ireland and Northern Ireland.

journal the reader will find an extract from the pamphlet, with comments by seven of the Professor's co-religionists. For the moment I would merely point out that if Eire is in danger of being divided by pamphleteering of this sort into two warring sects the Church of Ireland seems to be divided against itself. Thus I have before me a statement made in July, 1924, by Primate Day, that almost legendary figure in the modern Church of Ireland: "To say, that Protestants are in any way ignored, despised, or ill-treated is entirely contrary to the facts."[3] That was the old Free State. Fourteen years after, in May, 1938, I find *The Irish Times* approving an address by Dr. Harvey, Bishop of Cashel, by saying: "In the new Eire Protestants hold positions of high honour in every branch of public life. The first President is a son of a Church of Ireland clergyman. There are four Protestant judges in the High Court; and there is not a town or village in the country in which Protestant citizens do not exert an influence that is out of all proportion to their numbers."[4] It might seem as if the nineteen-twentieths have merely to sit back and leave the one-twentieth to carve itself up into two-fortieths.

Unattractive as any such divisions or disputes would be, they would be preferable to what has already happened: the inevitable joyous entry of Catholic controversialists into the arena. And this is my first reason for deploring this pamphlet, deploring it even with annoyance: because until I read these things I never think of myself, in relation to Ireland, as a Catholic at all, and I strongly resent being compelled to think of myself as a Catholic, or of seeing other people compelled to think of themselves as Protestants, when we should all feel quite content to think of ourselves as Irishmen. Thus we can all sympathise with the Protestant minority if we think of it as an Irish minority, since all such minorities call for our special interest, but once Protestants begin to assail Catholics or vice versa I am no longer whole and entire, I am to my disgust driven to take sides – which is an image of what sectarian argument does to the whole country. Professor Stanford may not understand this, I do not profess to understand it myself, but it is what happens. One ends up by cursing both their

3 Godfrey Day (1874–1938) was Primate of All Ireland and archbishop of Armagh in the Church of Ireland for only two months before his death.
4 Thomas Arnold Harvey (1878–1966) was bishop of Cashel and Waterford in the Church of Ireland from 1935 to 1958.

houses.[5] I have no doubt at all that Protestants have minor grievances: who has not? It is hurtful that Dublin University should be put under a Catholic ban, for example, not because the Catholic authorities have not every right to do it but because there was no need to do it, since (as the President of University College, Cork says in a recent issue of the Catholic *Standard*) "Protestantism does not appear to us Catholics to be a serious danger at all."[6] Or it is a grievance if some local clergyman should use his power to persuade his congregation not to deal with some Protestant shopkeeper, as has happened. But when such things occur I am angered not as a Catholic, but as an Irishman, and if one had to speak publicly of such things one would apologise for speaking as a Catholic – again not because one was ashamed of some Catholic's discrimination but for the same reason that Dan O'Connell apologised for speaking as a Catholic the first time he came before the Irish public, i.e., because what his people wanted was not the Catholic thing, or the Protestant thing, or any other kind of thing but the normal, healthy Irish thing. It was on that occasion that he said, putting the great grievance of his time into its proper place:

> Let every man who feels with me proclaim that if the alternative were offered him of the Union or the re-enactment of the Penal Code in all its horrors we would prefer without hesitation the latter as the more sufferable evil ... I know that Catholics still remember they have a country and that they would never accept any advantages as a sect that would destroy them as a people.[7]

I have every belief that on consideration Irishmen of every persuasion would normally agree, including the Professor: what he is nevertheless doing, in practice, is to foster something which is not normal, and which we normally and properly forget, to wit our religious differences, and once you do that and make a list of grievances or disabilities you stick a sectarian label on the Irish thing to the general loss.

~

5 In Act III, scene i, of Shakespeare's *Romeo and Juliet* (1594–96), Mercutio, when he is mortally stabbed in a battle between the two feuding families, says: "A plague o' both your houses!"
6 Alfred O'Rahilly (1884–1969) was president of University College Cork from 1943 to 1954; he was ordained a priest upon his retirement.
7 O'Connell made the speech at the Royal Exchange, Dublin, on 13 January 1800.

I cannot help feeling, next, that even from the minority point of view sectarian controversy is unwise. It is all too easy, for instance, to prove by means of Census figures that *The Irish Times* is correct in saying that Irish Protestants do "exert an influence that is out of all proportion to their numbers"; and Catholic controversialists have straightway done it all over again, and of course with every justification. The result is that instead of inducing sympathy with Protestants for their disabilities – and there are obvious disabilities in being a Protestant in Ireland, as there are in being a Catholic in England, or America, or Russia, or Tibet – the effect of such controversy is to induce an assault on Protestantism for any privileges it may have out of proportion to its numbers. And if this went on long enough, and sank low enough, as low let us say as unscrupulous men and bigoted men, the result would be a madness of party and religious dissension until our people found themselves caught up in the stupor of one of the most ancient of human insanities, and both Catholicism and Protestantism would then suffer. Whereas I am sure that the attitude of all sane Irishmen to privilege is that if any body of men do possess great wealth and influence, if, for example, the majority of the Dublin Stock Exchange, or of the governors of the Bank of Ireland are Protestants, or Mohammedans, or Moravians, or anything else except morons, then nobody will envy them so long as they are also good citizens. It is more important to me at any rate – since I am offering myself to Professor Stanford as an average reader of his pamphlet – that men of influence should be read in Lecky than in Luther, or in O'Connell than in Calvin, because I can then think naturally of them as my fellows: whereas everybody will strongly resent being distracted from that gift of common ground by some Protestant dragging in the Book of Common Prayer, or some Catholic making protestations about Crux Ansata.[8]

8 W.E.H. Lecky (1838–1903) was an Irish historian and political theorist. German theologian Martin Luther (1483–1546) was the catalyst of the Protestant Reformation. John Calvin (1509–1564) was a French theologian and Protestant Reformer. *Crux ansata*, "cross with handle," is the Latin term for an Egyptian ankh, a hieroglyph signifying "life" in the shape of a cross topped by a loop; this form of the Cross is traditional in the Coptic Orthodox Church. However, "Crux Ansata" here likely refers to the H.G. Wells book of that title, published the year earlier in 1943, although O'Faolain does not italicise it (as he sometimes neglected to do for book titles); its subtitle is "An Indictment of the Catholic Church."

But whenever one comes on this sort of thing I think that one is almost always most offended by somebody's lack of a real sense of history. And that the Professor has no real sense of the past is evident from his opening historical summary; packed as it is with the most tactless references, e.g., to the grand evangelical work of the Achill mission, and with almost magnificent understatements.[9] To give one example, would anybody casually reading the following paragraph guess that it genteelly passes over one of the most horrible periods of religious persecution, or since we are being euphemistic should I say "religious discrimination," in the history of Europe?

Besides this, there was clearly, after the 16th century a strong party in the governing classes who had no wish to see all Irishmen enjoy the material, to say nothing of the spiritual, privileges belonging to the "official faith." These foresaw a dissipation of their wealth and power if no religious caste differences remained in Ireland. With subtle and persevering opposition they impeded any extension of the fruits of the Reformation as they saw them. Only an Irish-speaking John Wesley, two centuries before his destined time, could have overcome their cold policy of exclusiveness.[10]

If my friend, Gulliver, at the end of this magazine, should care to start one of his competitions for "Famous Understatements" I offer him as a jewel of the first water that last elegant euphemism – "a cold policy of exclusiveness" – for a jungle of the vilest passions that ever disgraced a creed, an abattoir of blood and torture whose effects are still rooted in the marrow of our memory.[11] After that one is not surprised to realise that the Professor seems utterly unaware that behind all this there lies that old historical conflict, Church versus State. How else but from an historical obtuseness could anybody who had even once glanced at the face of Europe, even at the face of France alone, not know that he was handling dynamite in talking about Protestantism's "loss of influence in making Government appointments," or its need for "strong political and economic supports"?

9 The Achill Mission was a colony of proselytising Protestants founded in 1831 on Achill Island, County Mayo.
10 John Wesley (1703–1791) was an English clergyman who founded the Methodist movement.
11 Gulliver, named after Swift's famous hero, was the *nom de plume* of Michael Farrell (1899–1962).

Would not even such evocative words as Gallican, the Veto, Ultramontane, Napoleon, Gambetta warn him that what he is doing is inviting a new rivalry of churchmen for political contacts?[12] I am sure he would draw back in dismay from the charge. Would he draw back also if it were put to him, as it is often put to all of us, that "this is a Catholic country" – not meaning, as all would agree, that it has formed over the centuries that quality of life which we equally expect to have developed in France, Spain, or Italy from the great influence of the Catholic Church on those countries in their formative periods, but adumbrating the principle that every country must be designated, shaped, and governed by the dictates of a majority Church, and that all in it must accept the political consequences of that dominant power. That has, in fact, been put directly to Professor Stanford in *The Leader* of April 22nd: "Protestants cannot understand that this is a Catholic country" – and put to him indirectly in the Catholic journal *The Standard* by the President of University College, Cork, when he speaks of "the fact of (Protestants) being faced by a majority which believes in democracy."[13] Would not Professor Stanford reject such a principle as utterly undemocratic? For if this country is, in that sense, a Catholic country, then another country is a Protestant country, another a Confucian country, another a Buddhist country. In that case the miseries of Spain are to be charged to the Catholic Church and the follies of Italy laid at the doors of Rome, and because England has a majority of about 70 per cent. Anglicans, the 5 per cent. Catholics (one-twentieth, like the Irish Protestants) have to submit absolutely to all majority decisions. (They have only recently been contesting the principle hotly in the new British Education Bill.)[14] What would be the effect of such a conception of Democracy on the Catholics of the Six Counties? But while I am sure

12 Gallicanism was a movement in France to restrict papal power. The Veto was a proposal in the early nineteenth century that the British government should have veto power over the appointments of bishops in return for the restoration of the Catholic Hierarchy. Someone who is Ultramontane, contrary to one who is a Gallican, believes in strong papal authority. Léon Gambetta (1838–1882) was a French republican politician.

13 *The Leader* (1900–1971) was founded by Irish nationalist D.P. Moran (1869–1936).

14 The British Education Bill eventually became law in 1944. It was popularly known as the Butler Act, after R.A. Butler (1902–1982), the president of the Board of Education. The legislation importantly raised the mandatory minimum school-leaving age to 15 and made all schooling free.

that the Professor would deny that it is democratic for any modern country to be subject to the economic and political influence of a majority church, just as Irish Catholics for a hundred years rejected the economic and political influence of a minority church, here he is, as calm as you please, demanding "influence in making Government appointments," and asking for greater "economic and political supports" for Protestantism. If that is not adumbrating a rivalry between churchmen for political power, then words mean nothing. Far better for Protestants to take the firm attitude that when they meet some proof of "religious discrimination" they meet a proof that discrimination has nothing at all to do with Religion – for how could such unChristian behaviour have anything to do with Religion? – and declare themselves satisfied that the existence of bodies like the Knights of Columbanus, the Orange Lodges, or the Masonic Order proves likewise that there is no organised interest in Protestantism but a well-organised interest in profits.[15] Just as when Catholics protest against the Literary Censorship they should never be so irreligious, or so anti-clerical, as to suggest that it is a religious or a clerical Censorship but maintain firmly that it has nothing at all to do with priests or with religion, least of all with Catholicism. Then everybody can deal with this so-called Catholic defence of modesty and this so-called Catholic defence of democracy, as Irishmen irrespective of creed and class. I feel that this is the core of the thing, and that it is this which makes it worth while dealing with the Professor's pamphlet at length, not so much to defend or warn Protestants and Catholics as to defend and warn Irishmen against being involved in these disputes as anything else but Irishmen. But when a distinguished member of the Church of Ireland only speaks to his co-religionists as Irishmen at the very end of his address I feel that he does not see that this *is* the core of the thing. What he does say, finally, is finely said:

> Above all considerations of loss and gain I put my conviction that if you are a true Irishman you love Ireland before all countries and if you do not love Ireland before all countries you are not in your heart an Irishman.

Or, again, in his last paragraph when he sees the necessity for Protestants having "roots deep in the soil and history of Ireland." But he does not see

15 The Orange Order, which is composed of individual Lodges across the globe, is a Protestant fraternity founded in 1795. The Free and Accepted Masons, a secret fraternal society, was founded in 1717.

that not only should that have been said first, as O'Connell said it, but that it should be the ground and framework of the whole. For he goes on to say, "Not that I believe that a Church depends on its political attitude for survival"; in which I believe that he is absolutely wrong as far as his own Church is concerned, and indeed as far as all Churches are concerned in the modern world. Where the Catholic Church is weak or strong to-day it is weak or strong – as it is the one in Spain and both in France – as it remains, for one reason or another, separated from the common lives of the people or comes close to them. Here, the names of Parnell, Smith O'Brien, Butt, Thomas Davis, Lord Edward, Tone, Emmet, Yeats, O'Casey, Hyde and many more such – all Protestants – prove that where a man's political attitude was sound his religion has never been anybody's concern.[16] I am not sure that *as a religion* Irish Protestantism was ever as strong as it should have been, but I am quite certain that it will not be even as strong again until it is not merely above suspicion politically, but until it is strong politically, and that what keeps it weak is that it is sulking in a vestry. There is no reason why it should, for it has many things to offer in the creation of a rich Irish mode of life.

This brings me to my last reaction on reading this pamphlet, which is that in some unfortunate manner the writer of it has given me an impression of Protestantism at its most protesting and least creative. Thus, I cannot tell why, I read with a slight shiver of distaste – and let this be another personal confession for the Professor's englightenment or entertainment – such sentences as these:

> To be a *good*, and not just a *law-abiding* citizen, one must do much more than this. One must keep the spirit of the law, as well as its letter, and, further, each of us should be vigilant to detect the faults of the existing laws or projected laws, and eager where necessary to work for their amendment …
>
> Having our principles, we must protest when they are publicly infringed, whether the infringement is against ourselves personally or against any citizen …

16 Charles Stewart Parnell, William Smith O'Brien, Isaac Butt, Thomas Davis, Lord Edward Fitzgerald, Wolfe Tone, Robert Emmet, W.B. Yeats, Sean O'Casey, and Douglas Hyde.

If necessary we should be ready to gather in large meetings, to walk in processions of protest, if our rights are gravely imperilled.

Especially two constant allegations must be resolutely met: "Your faith is false. Your political and social situation is hopeless." The first can be met if the full force of Anglican apologetics is exerted in pulpits, schools, and in publications. (To which I and nobody else, of course, can object. It is the adjective in the next sentence which chills me.)[17] The second can be met by internal co-operation and comradeship.

Why on earth so exclusively internal? As to why all that seems like a voice from another island, rather puritanical and even inhuman, I cannot easily say. Perhaps, however, since I am, as it were, sacrificing myself experimentally to him I might tell him two recent personal experiences which have, to be frank, bothered me a lot. They are experiences which a great many people must have had these last four years: both trifling. Here is the first. I ordered four tons of cut logs from a wood-cutter. He delivered what, to be brief, turned out on reweighing to be 35 cwt. 8 lb., so that he had blatantly defrauded me of about £7.[18] The point of my story is that I did not prosecute him, and that with two exceptions everybody whom I told of the fraud admitted that he would not have prosecuted the man either. They would have "frightened" him, abused him, got the money back from him – all of which I did: but they would have, in end, let "the poor devil" go. The two exceptions were a Protestant clergyman and a Catholic priest. I am a little ashamed of myself for my part in this affair: yet, I would do the same again: and I am quite ready to agree that the moral is that the only people in all this incident who showed the promise of an Irish ruling class were the parson and the priest. The other incident is even more familiar – to millions. I fell into a discussion in London, some weeks ago, with a distinguished English churchman on the subject of the effect of the war on English society. I had been saying that English society never seems to me so warm and coherent as Irish society, and that I would have expected that the terrible experiences of the war, especially of the air-raids – "so many dangers and discomforts shared in common" – would have gone far to wipe out class feeling. He corrected me gently. "You are not quite correct. Dangers, perhaps, but not discomforts. You see, the English middle and upper classes have always known

---

17 The parenthetical comment is O'Faolain's.
18 Cwt. is an abbreviation for "Centum weight" or "hundredweight"; it is a British measurement of 112 pounds ("lbs").

that war is part of the price of power. They have always sacrificed their eldest sons in war. They sacrifice themselves. They will encounter even more danger than the poor. When those raids of 1941 were at their worst the poor were not ashamed to crowd miserably in the deep underground shelters, but the middle and upper-classes insisted on going on with their dinners, or at best retired to the merely comparative safety of the base-ment of the Dorchester.[19] Security is what poor people want. Power is what the middle and upper classes want." Then he went on, fascinatingly, to prove from history that no country which has not been ready to bleed in war has produced a strong ruling class – Italy for instance, whose spirit was broken by the unaccustomed sacrifices of Adowa and Abyssinia.[20] By chance, I went on that evening to dine with an imperious woman, in a big restaurant where there happened to be a wide, glass canopy over our heads. A raid began, and the guns rumbled, and the shrapnel pinged on the streets, and between guns and bombs the whole house shook, and the waiters moved the other diners away from underneath the canopy for fear of falling shrapnel. But my imperious friend just simply would not stir, and I had to pretend not to want to. I suppose that if I told her that she represented Power, as she did – and that I preferred Security – she would have raised her eyebrows. A curious thing happened then. I noticed that one other diner had refused to stir, and I recognised her as a well-known courtesan. I saw in those two obstinacies two symbols, of Power with Responsibility and Power without Responsibility – the prerogative of the Imperialist and the prerogative of the Gangster. Thinking back on them later, while my mind was worried by wood-cutters and ruling-classes, I felt quite sure that both of these women would have ruthlessly prosecuted my rascally "poor devil" who is trying to make a living by fraud. I thought that Shaw would have made a very nice group of the lot of us: the parson and the priest, the courtesan and the imperialist, the wood-cutter and the writer – and I imagine that he would point out to people like me that every one of those four would not only put the wood-cutter in jail but would prosecute me, too, if I dared to oppose their power. To which I would have nothing to reply except that I wouldn't be there: I would be in the Underground. Does it begin to occur to Professor

19 The Dorchester is a luxury London hotel that opened in 1931 and was fashionable with artists.
20 The Italians lost the Battle of Adowa in March 1896 in their failed attempt to secure Abyssinia, the former name of modern-day Ethiopia, as a part of their colonial expansion into Africa.

Bedell Stanford why I do not much like his "good" and "law-abiding"
citizen, any more, indeed, than I like our industrialist gangsters – because
behind all these virtuous or unvirtuous exteriors there is simply the same
lust for Power.

∼

But, to be sure, the great and final question is, "Power to do what?" Power
to create what kind of society, according to what desirable image of life?
That is the only thing I really want to hear from the Protestants, and from
the Catholics, and from everybody else who wants power. I do not give a
rap what Professor Stanford thinks about the Unity of the Churches. I
want to know what he thinks about the Unity of Ireland. When he talks
to me about the life of Julian the Apostate I want to ask him about the life
of Julia Murphy.[21] Just as when the Legion of Mary talks about the evil of
smut what I want to talk about is the evil of slums. Or when *The Standard*
talks about a living Democracy in Catholic Ireland I want to recommend
it to read Belloc on the death of Democracy in Protestant England.[22] For
Democracy, as Gilbert Chesterton said, does not fail; it dies.[23] It died there
when Plutocracy took its place. Does *The Standard* ever wonder whether
anything might not be usurping its place here? Democracy ceases to be a
reality when, for various reasons, there is nothing but a kind of public
front – shirt-front, stuffed, period 1930 – and a private silence; or it may
be a Front Bench packed and a Back Bench gagged. Nor has anything less
than this been happening to us all in Ireland in the last ten years or so. The
Parties have ceased to represent the people since they have ceased to represent anything in particular, certainly anything that differentiates them
particularly from one another, until in practice we have become virtually
disfranchised. We go innocently to the polls but our votes cannot make a
scrap of difference to our lives as long as what really counts is not our
wishes – we have no way of expressing them – but the, of course, benevolent wishes of the influences behind the scenes. That is why Chesterton
said that it was not the Kaiser or the Czar who precipitated the last war
but people like that mild religious man Mr. Cadbury, with their spare

21 Julian the Apostate (331/2–363), né Flavius Claudius Julianus, was the Roman
Emperor from 361 to 363. It is assumed that Julia Murphy is simply a common
name, meaning anyone.
22 Hilaire Belloc (1870–1953) was a French-born English author, notable for
his essays.
23 English author Gilbert Keith Chesterton (1874–1936).

millions and their inhuman, that is to say non-human because unreal, ideals of universal benevolence and goodwill, which prevented every English government before 1914 (and he might have added), every government before 1938 from arming to the teeth.[24] Frankly the "good-and-law-abiding-citizen" ideal gives me a belly-ache. Talk like that reminds me of the man who spoke so genteelly at a dinner, in the presence of Augustine Birrell, about Dr. Johnson's style; whereupon, in true Johnsonian anger, Birrell told him that if he wanted to understand this great man's English he should look up the passage in which he calls somebody or other a son of a bitch.[25] As for walking in processions are there not enough Gaelic Leaguers and Legionnaires to do that, all very good and law-abiding citizens so long as they are inside the general racket? If Protestants merely want to muscle in on that general scheme of things nobody can have the slightest interest in them. But, actually, nobody can know what the Protestants do stand for, and they have been so long silent on every question that even though Professor Stanford has made many mistakes, and above all the major mistake of talking not as an Irishman but as one-twentieth of an Irishman, I feel glad that he has at least shewn that Protestants are not all stone-dumb. From his recognised Church would he not, in simple words, go on now to a recognisable Government and tell us what, if any, are the political and social views of the Church of Ireland?

In conclusion I must make a small confession. I do not think that this rather negative pamphlet would have produced any effect on me at all – it is the replies to it which have affected me rather than the thing itself – if I had not gone on from it to a very positive pamphlet, this time by a Fellow of Pembroke College, Oxford, called "How Britain is Governed."[26] Because, suddenly, as when a negative and a positive current meet, the two together set up this rather random course of thought which I have followed publicly for the Professor's entertainment and at least my own illumination. I might sum up those thoughts by saying that I had a wicked

---

24 George Cadbury (1839–1922) was, along with his brother Richard (1835–1899), the owner of Cadbury chocolate; he was also an important social reformer and philanthropist.
25 Augustine Birrell (1850–1933) was a British politician and man of letters who served as British chief secretary for Ireland from 1907 to 1916.
26 This is likely a reference to *How Britain Is Governed* (1939), by R.H.S. Crossman (1907–1974), who was a fellow of New College.

desire to reverse the titles of the two essays. I would have liked to call the English pamphlet "A Recognised Government," as a reminder to us all of those days when it was patriotic to refuse to recognise any government whatsoever, and in a growing conviction that we are fast reverting to that same position. And I would have liked to call the Irish pamphlet "How Ireland is Churched," because Cathleen Ni Houlihan apparently was after giving birth to the Free State, and has ever since been locked up in the sacristy lest she should do anything worse. In other words, would it really be very much better, if Cathleen Ni Houlihan were now to be locked up occasionally in the vestry of Christ Church or the crypts of Saint Michan's?[27]

Does the Regius Professor of Greek see my point? Or is it so vulgar as to be Greek to him?

---

27 Christ Church Cathedral was founded c. 1030. Saint Michan's was consecrated in 1096. Both Protestant, they are located in Dublin.

One World[1]

It must have been noticed that during the elections of May very little mention was made of the relations of Eire and the Commonwealth of Nations, and no serious mention at all was made of Partition. That silence was informative, since elections are fought over things on which the electorate feels strongly. The impression a stranger might have gathered from that May election, indeed, was that the people either did not feel strongly about anything in particular, or were considered by the candidates – who ought to know – not to be feeling strongly about anything in particular. The candidates were probably right. Taken all in all Ireland to-day has few problems that she can worry about. So much so that far from being concerned about the personnel of government a great many people obviously feel that we should probably get on very well, for the time being, if we had no government at all.[2] Thus, Mr. de Valera has not spent so much of his public time, for the last two years, on the Gaelic language for any other reason than the simple one that he either knows how helpless he is in other directions or is using it as a smoke-screen, and he is a very self-blinded man if he does not see that the public sees that. This does not mean, however, that the problems are not there – in ambush so to speak, ready to spring: it merely means that Partition and our relations with the Commonwealth are not things that we can do much about in 1944. Nevertheless, if we have had any real and sincere intention of facing either of them in the future – if we have any attitude about them to present to the world when the world is more ready to listen – our statesmen should be now preparing the public

---

1 "One World" appeared in *The Bell* 8, no. 4 (July 1944): 277–86.
2 *O'Faolain's note:* E.g. In some districts the percentage of the electorate which voted at the May elections was as low as 55 per cent.

mind against that time. That they are, on the contrary, keeping mum on these matters can only be explained in various ways: (*a*) that politicians have a pragmatic, empirical, opportunistic preference for crossing bridges when they come to them; (*b*) that our leaders guess that the state of Europe in general and of the Commonwealth of Nations in particular may be very different after the war, and indeed it is true that the term "Commonwealth of Nations" does appear to be facing a dissolving or expanding period; (*c*) it may be that our politicians have, in fact, long studied these problems, and have either concluded that their possible solutions are not tactically attractive to expound, or even that they are insoluble; (*d*) there is lastly the not at all unlikely and quite human explanation that politicians, unlike journalists, do not like to make their mistakes in public, and would rather leave it to people like us to worry out these questions in the intervals of peace.

～

Three large volumes to hand give an opportunity for a large perspective on one of these questions – the unity of Ireland. These volumes are the Canadian *Report of the Royal Commission on Dominion-Provincial Relations*, popularly known as the Rowell-Sirois Report, dated 1940.[3] These heavy volumes tell us, with masses of documentation, largely financial, how the disparate units of North America came together and have prospered as a federation. Like us they had their minorities problem, racial and religious, their international economic problems, their imperial political problems, their financial and fiscal problems, their domestic cultural problems. In a hundred ways the analogy diverges: but the fundamentals of racial, social, religious, economic and political fissuration are all there. And what one feels after following the long and tangled story of this vast region up to and after the British North America Act of 1867, which united the various colonies as a self-governing Dominion, is that nobody here has yet made us realise what a vastly difficult question we face in our, by comparison, microscopic problem of Partition.[4] Certainly, the study of that

3 The report was named for the two presidents of the commission that wrote it: Newton Rowell (1867–1941) and, when he resigned from the position in 1938, his replacement Joseph Sirois (1881–1941).
4 Enacted on July 1 of that year, the British North America Act, 1867, divided the Province of Canada into Canada West and Canada East (present-day Ontario and Quebec) and joined them with New Brunswick and Nova Scotia to form the Dominion of Canada.

analogous story of Canada would at least prepare our minds to accept a few hard truths about Partition. Of these the first is that even if the problem is ever solved on paper, by some legal concordat, it will never be solved in the sense of laying completely [to rest] all regional frictions. Secondly, in so far as regional antagonisms ever can be laid they can only be brought to rest by a trembling balance of tensions only nominally at rest – in that sense talk of "ending" Partition is obviously simple-minded. Thirdly, no "solution" is likely to be anything but progressive, i.e., spread over generations; and, perhaps most vitally important of all to appreciate, one decides that these are problems that no amount of speeches or propaganda can even remotely touch. And that, possibly, may best account for the present silence of our statesmen. Pressure for union, that is to say, is almost certain to grow, if it comes at all, not out of sentiment but out of circumstances. Here these circumstances do not exist. Without them talk is futile, and publications like *Orange Terror* are merely whistling to keep our courage up until circumstances now wholly favourable to Partition begin to alter radically.[5] In fact as long as we are obliged to talk of "the problem of Partition" and not of "the problem of Union" we are admitting the real position.

Let us glance at the circumstances leading up to Canadian Union. Firstly, of course, we have to remind ourselves that the Dominion now called Canada was originally a French settlement around the St. Lawrence region, that great waterway which, assisted by canals and the Great Lakes, opens up a whole continent by an unequalled system of inland navigation. This French core held for a century and a half after the founding of Quebec, a name that will remind every schoolboy (though only those of an earlier generation, perhaps) of the famous scaling of the Heights – it is sometimes called the Gibraltar of Canada – by General Wolfe: shortly after which event Canada was ceded to Britain.[6] Other independent provinces are to be added to make up the sum of original British possessions: such as Nova Scotia – once won by Jesuits and English from the French, subsequently passing to and from French hands at various times, with settlers of British, German, Indian origin, some Catholic, some Presbyterian, some Baptist.

---

5 *Orange Terror: The Partition of Ireland* was published under the pseudonym Ultach in 1943.
6 James Wolfe (1727–1759) commanded the British army's attack on Quebec City. He died on the outskirts of the city at the Battle of the Plains of Abraham on 13 September, the victory of which led to the British gaining permanent control of the colony. Many French Canadian schoolboys would not remember this event with such fondness.

Or add Newfoundland – whose settlers were Portuguese, French, Biscayans, even Gaelic-speaking Irish, a region well known to that rambling poet Donnchadh Ruadh MacConmara, whom many will at least know as the hero of Francis MacManus's Harmsworth Prize Novel *Men Withering*.[7] These alone will indicate the mixed nature of the population which Canada has accepted and by tolerance and patience at last welded – so different to our simplifiers who think to level everything down to some such draper's footrule formula as "This is a Gaelic, Catholic country." Or one could further complicate by adding that Ontario and New Brunswick were purely British-loyalist in origin – they were founded after the American Revolution by loyalist emigrants from across the border. Now, the first thing we note is that as these pockets developed they developed away from one another. And this division of interest and occupation is apparently natural in young countries. Groups do *not* naturally tend to coalesce: their self-interests steer them on their own roads. The only thing that gave them any cohesion was the British flag: or, more crudely, the imperial commercial system which sheltered and nourished the colonies by the mercantile privileges supplied by British navigation laws and trade preferences. To quote the Royal Commission Report: "This was their world and they would be compelled to find an entirely new scheme of existence if it disappeared." As we know it did disappear:

Great Britain, for the time being disillusioned with empire, reversed her military and commercial policies ... By adopting free trade at home, she swept away the privileges on which the provinces relied. With the grant of responsible government, imperial control over colonial fiscal policy was relinquished. The imperial authorities insisted that responsible government carried with it the responsibility for defence and the colonies were notified that the garrisons would be withdrawn. The threatened recall of the legions marked the end of the sheltered world the colonies had known.

Which is a note of regret that will sound strange on many southern Irish ears. And might possibly strike a warning note on some few northern ones? But there comes after that, when the colonies begin to get into every

7 Nova Scotia was not an independent province: it was part of Confederation; Newfoundland and Labrador, at the time of O'Faolain's writing, was a dominion, becoming part of Canada only in 1949. Donnchadh Ruadh MacConmara (1715–1810) was a real-life Gaelic poet as well as the protagonist of three of MacManus's books, among them *Men Withering* (1939).

sort of financial trouble in a fiercely expanding and aggressive age and continent, another interesting note. "If their southern neighbour had shown herself pacific and eager to trade on advantageous terms they (the provinces) might have permitted themselves to be drawn quietly and separately into her orbit." Faced, instead, by threats and rivalry the North-American isolates began to see the natural advantages of huddling tightly together. In short, in what we now call Canada the merger began to come not out of a mutual sentimental attraction, as in marriage, but out of stern pressure from without, as in business. French-speaking Canada, in fact, then and since, had every cultural reason to distrust the union. And, lest anybody should imagine that nothing but economic forces govern these matters – or lest, in making analogies with our own case we should minimise the formative power of cultural or religious feeling, i.e., the culture and religion of the North and the South *equally* – that internal tension worked most powerfully, wherever cultural heritages were involved, to retard union; and when union was legally completed they constantly kept it restless. The rights and loves of French-speaking Catholic Canadians have always been a hard lump to mould into the unified Dominion. Just as the rights and loves of English-speaking Protestant Ulstermen will always stand out here. As a matter of sardonic interest, those French-Catholic-minority rights in Canada have always been protected, in essence, by England. When the Statute of Westminster opened up to Canada the same possibilities that it opened up to the (then) Irish Free State – and which Mr. de Valera exploited to the limit – French-Catholics were the last people likely to think of cutting Canada off from the British Commonwealth: not, necessarily, from love of Britain, but from fear of the rest of the Dominion. One could wish that all our simplifiers could grasp that point.[8]

∾

To follow the detailed and technical history of Canada's subsequent adaptation to the new circumstances would be a study not immediately relevant to our interests. But one or two main trends grip the attention. We, with our nostalgic clinging to patriarchal images of life, will find that early period known as the Golden Age in the maritimes fascinatingly self-sufficient and self-enclosed. At one stage, for example, fishing, lumbering, ship-building – a trilogy of wood-wind-water – often bulked under the

8 The Statute of Westminster (1931) granted equal status to the United Kingdom and its dominions: Australia, Canada, Ireland, New Zealand, Newfoundland, and South Africa. This ensured that the sovereign right of each of the dominions was recognised and they were thereafter responsible for their own internal and external affairs.

white sails of an Atlantic schooner the enterprise of a single family or trading-group. To quote A.R.M. Lower's *The North American Assault on the Canadian Forest*:

> The lumber of these assorted cargoes came from small local mills. Many of these mills would be owned and managed by men who had farms in the neighbourhood and whose interest also extended to the sea and ships. The Bluenose farmer, proclaimed the handiest man in the world, was commonly credited with raising the potatoes for his cargo, felling and sawing the lumber for it, building his own schooner in his spare moments and finally sailing her down to the Islands where he turned merchant and disposed of her wares.[9]

But we must also note that, as with our Golden Age, the system was too simple to face the complications of modern commercial specialisation and fine-drawn competition. For one thing machinery was hooting its ominous defiance across the prairie – steamships and railways were introducing long-term factors that cast clouds over the lush prosperity of the 1850s. A non-industrialised Canada – I had almost written a non-industrialised Eire – was facing problems that it could barely understand. The world was crowding in, slowly making those altered circumstances in which all apparently fundamental ideas began to melt away into new shapes – which, of course, in turn would begin to imagine themselves just as eternal and unalterable. Yet, even when infant manufacturing began to arise in Canada the gospel of self-sufficiency held its place, so that the patriarchal-minded might even still find there attractive models and analogies – the small local factory, the comparatively simple needs, almost on a par with Mr. de Valera's "milk-for-breakfast" dream and the Pietist's "Weren't-our-grandfathers-better-off-on-butther-and-spuds?"[10] Again quoting:

> The increase in cash income and the high prices for many products during the American Civil War were coaxing farmers away from self-sufficiency into specialisation. This movement, however, was just beginning and the farm household in Upper Canada was still

9 *The North American Assault on the Canadian Forest* (1938), by Arthur R.M. Lower (1889–1988). Bluenose is a nickname for a Nova Scotian.
10 Pietists exaggerate their religious devotion and stress feeling over intellectual engagement in their practice.

a basically self-sufficient unit ... The farm of the period was a minia-
ture factory or combination of factories. Much of the work of the
large industrial army of to-day, concentrated in highly specialised
factories in the cities and towns, was in that early period performed
in a multitude of rural households.[11]

Alas this stage was soon exploited to its limit. If the Canadians wanted to
expand agriculture any farther they would have to find buoyant foreign
markets for their exports. As for the manufacturers, industrial expansion
depended likewise on expanding markets. Now and again local booms
came – as with the gold boom. In general public debt mounted. In some
provinces the budget could not be balanced. Gradually the separate units,
"travelling their separate and well-nigh independent economic paths,"
reached the cross-roads at the same time. Finding that the external world
threatened them all alike they hoped to find new strength in political
union. They decided – as the two parts of Ireland might some day decide,
if the circumstances force it into their heads – that federal union was *a
plan*. It was a plan whereby through mutual concession, cultural and
local loyalties could be preserved and reconciled with the political
strength and solidarity of the whole, whereby the minorities in abandoning their rooted objections to a superior political authority would
reap the benefits of a single control in matters of general interest. The
British North America Act was the result. If anyone wishes to see an
example of legislation reconciling far more diverse interests than ours he
should study that Act, which, in sum, visualised the Union as a great
holding company designed to unify the efforts of the partners and realise
their opportunities to the full.

∾

But the student of confederation should not stop there. It induces a considerable amount of political realism in dealing with such matters to
observe how intense was that continuing and persistent clash of racial and
religious differences. In those years, they could blaze up at any moment
and threaten the precarious bond of Canadian union. For example, students of Fenianism, or even readers of Sir William Butler's *Autobiography*,
must vividly remember the insurrection of the Franco-Indian-Irish Louis

---

11 The American Civil War lasted from 1861 to 1865. It was fought over the right
of the eleven southern states to secede from the Union and their desire to maintain
slavery. Upper Canada was in present-day southern Ontario.

Riel who championed the cause of the Metis or half-breeds in 1884, captured Fort Garry, set up a provisional government, awaited a Fenian raid
across the border, and was finally taken and executed.[12] Quebec's deepest
feelings were outraged by Riel's death and a wave of resentment against
the Federal government swept the province. It is but one example to prove
that deeply-rooted traditions never really die, and that, once again, there is
no such thing as ending these partitions in any sense that implies an end to
inter-provincial frictions. These frictions have always shaken the substance
of Canadian union – differences on tariff questions, provincial dissatisfac-
tions with general federal projects, disputes on the incidence of taxation,
and here we even have this Royal Commission, still at work while the War
was in progress, still struggling seventy years after confederation to reconsider the economic and financial basis of the union and the distribution of
legislative powers between the central and provincial parliaments.

It becomes patent that while we, here, spend much of our time on short-
term propaganda about alleged present religious discrimination we spend
far too little in long-term analyses of the economic basis of possible future
Union; and it is on that plane and at that distance that our minds should
be constructively working. It cannot be entirely unanalogous that the
main preoccupation of other federal governments, such as the Australian
and Canadian, has always been economic development. Even our different attitudes to the War have this concrete aspect and will leave different
marks north and south of the Border. Thus the consciousness of Britain
has been so profoundly impressed by the total efficiency of wartime government in conscripting every last ounce of manpower and labour – a
conscription so ruthless that it must be experienced to be believed – and
the British public has come to expect almost with passion that an equal
efficiency will be shown in organising for social welfare in Peace. The
North, too, will have these expectations for Peace and will doubtless try
to put them into practice in proportion as it is now partaking in the haz-
ards of War. That, incidentally, happened in Canada too where the last

12 William Francis Butler (1838–1910) was a British Lieutenant-General who
recounted his life and times in *Sir William Butler: An Autobiography* (1911). Louis
Riel (1844–1885) was executed for treason after the unsuccessful rebellion that he
led against the Canadian government; the conflict came only after he had failed in
his efforts to have Métis land claims in the west recognised through more peaceful
means. The Métis are an indigenous people who have both native and European
ancestors; the French word *métis* refers to something that is hybrid or of mixed race.

War considerably hastened the acceptance of the philosophy of the social-service-state. Postwar reconstruction likewise will much more definitely involve the North in the British postwar boom or postwar depression – whichever may occur – than it will involve us. In all these actual conditions the factor that will chiefly affect the minds of people in the North in relation to Southern Ireland will be the economic factor. What will we then have to offer them in a united Ireland? What economy to give them the greatest commercial dynamism? Would the federal schemes we could outline, with their co-operation, be dynamic and expanding, or would they be conservative and emasculate? Would the shape of society that we plan to create suit them? The whole point, in short, is that when we talk, as we sometimes do, of the North "coming in" we must realise that the South would also be "coming in" – to a wholly different and planned entity in which neither the present ideas of Mr. de Valera nor the present ideas of Sir Basil Brooke could have any validity.[13] For while both these statesmen now probably consider themselves very modern and progressive, if there ever is a Federal Union of Ireland it will come in such a complicated time that they may both by then have come to be regarded, in perspective, as some lovable old patriarchs of the Canadian Golden Age would now be regarded by a modern Mackenzie King.[14] Let somebody be honest about this. Union and Partition to-day are lifeless questions. They will remain lifeless, to be referred to only now and again with a mawkish please-God, or a cliché about "an aim to be kept steadily in mind," until we create so dynamic an Ireland that they will jab into urgent and screaming life. If we do not – they will slowly sink into a sort of tubercular decline, hoarsely spitting old blood in dark corners like other once-living, once-urgent phrases such as National and Individual Liberty for all Irishmen, the Gaelic Renaissance, or the Irish Republic. They are questions that, to live, must be given the broad view which does not try to pretend that they are purely local, domestic, or national questions, which realises and which admits that they are linked up inextricably, like the tangled problem of Canada, with the whole international question of the economic and political future of Europe and the World.

That, certainly, is how the North looks at those questions. Why should not we? It is One World. And we *are* part of it?

13 Basil Brooke (1888–1973) was the leader of the Ulster Unionist Party and prime minister of Northern Ireland from 1943 to 1963.
14 William Lyon Mackenzie King (1874–1950) was Canada's longest-serving prime minister (1921–26, 1926–30, 1935–48).

The Pleasures and Pains of Ireland[1]

A friend of mine holds that Ireland is a paradise for the *homme moyen sensuel* – that untranslatable compound of sense, sensibility, and mere sensation, a purgatory for the artist, and a hell for the intellectual.[2] That, at least, gives us an understandable classification and one may welcome it since in order to describe one must first distinguish. Sometimes he adds a fourth class, but these one may postpone, if not pass by, since they pass us by: they are the "sports," using the word in the gardener's sense – "odd plants that deviate strikingly from the general type or species." Such have been, in the literary world, Yeats, Joyce, Moore, Shaw; one has heard of Irish pressmen abroad; the list of businessmen, soldiers, politicians and other local boys who have made good elsewhere is endless. For these odd-men-out (very much *out*) Ireland is a place or state of punishment where some souls suffer for a time before they push on somewhere else. One hesitates to say any more about them, because a larger description would have to mention that these "sports" or aberrants are not generally approved by the majority whom they aberr; and that grim word "approve" would introduce a process outside our fiscal audit of Loss and Gain. It would introduce the admonitory reformers. It would introduce that popular modern Irish game of tying oneself up in theological knots for the fun of trying to untie oneself again. Let us be content to consider our three types.

∼

1 "The Pleasures and Pains of Ireland" appeared in *The Bell* 8, no. 5 (August 1944): 369–79.
2 *Homme moyen sensuel* translates as the "average sensual man."

What and where is this Ireland of the *homme moyen sensuel*? Surely we all know it and him, indeed are at some time and to some degree it and him – that average, substantial, unmetaphysical man who is both Fielding's lusty Tom Jones and Sterne's innocent My Uncle Toby whom Hazlitt thought the finest compliment ever paid to human nature.³ He is you and me when we are neither morose nor melancholy, neither arguing nor being philosophical, Shakespeare's "good easy man," any land's Happy Man.⁴ A thrown twig at any racecourse will hit him. He is at Mask in May, in a wag at Dunleary, tingling at the heels of the hounds, watching his pointer stiffen like a ramrod, voluble at the Bloodstock sales, putting down his half-crown at the dogs, slipping a couple of ferrets into a leather bag on a Sunday morning, queueing for the pictures, watching Mr. de Valera talking to thousands in O'Connell Street or Mr. O'Cuinneagáin talking to himself, sucking a perpendicular bottle at a Point-to-Point, or prone in a punt behind a duck-gun, or playing poker in a train on a rain-coat⁵ … For all such Ireland is the Golden Land. He loves – indeed he has manufactured its lazy tempo, its friendly air, its good-heartedness, its warm charity, even its humanising touch of graft. But is there any need to describe *him*? The whole world knows the Ireland of the amiable Irishman, the argumentative Irishman, the hotheaded Irishman, the roguish Irishman, the kindly Irishman. It knows it and him, so well, and is so predisposed to find them where they aren't as well as where they are, that there is none of us who does not sometimes try to contrive the effect from a sheer desire to please. That Happy Man and that Happy Ireland are authentic.

3 The eponymous hero of Henry Fielding's novel *A History of Tom Jones, a Foundling* (1749); My Uncle Toby is a character in Laurence Sterne's *The Life and Opinions of Tristram Shandy, Gentleman* (1759–67); William Hazlitt (1778–1830) made this observation in *Lectures on the English Comic Writers* (1819).
4 In Shakespeare's *Henry VIII*, Act III, scene ii, lines 350–8, the ambitious Cardinal Wolsey (1475–1530), whose downfall has begun, attempts to draw sympathy by describing himself as a "good easy man," or an average man.
5 Lough Mask, in County Mayo, is a well-known fishing lake and is reportedly best fly-fished in late May and early June. A wag is a small boat; they are quite popular in Dún Laoghaire. A bloodstock sale is an auction for horses. Putting down a half-crown at the dogs refers to placing a bet on a dog race, a crown representing a value of two shillings and sixpence. Ferrets, like dogs, have long been used for hunting other animals; they ferret the prey out of their dens and burrows. O'Faolain possibly refers to Gearóid O'Cuinneagáin (1910–1991), who founded the nationalist fascist Ailtirí na hAiséirghe. A point-to-point is a horse race.

~

Just as I was wondering, at this point, if the outstanding quality of the
Happy Irishman is not Personality I was suddenly reminded that in his
autobiographical book *Orientations* Sir Ronald Storrs – speaking of that
Irish "sport" Lawrence of Arabia – deplored the increase of personages
and the decline of personalities in modern England;[6] and I cannot help
thinking that, on the other hand, one of the exuberant faults of our
Happy Irishman's exuberant qualities is the incontinence of his personality. I mean that he is probably much better at exuberant living than at
estimable creation. To every country its own virtues and its own faults.
After all Storrs also admires sobriety of thought and act, and reckons it
as one of England's great virtues: one can hardly have it both ways. Or
can one? And do they? If we admire exuberant personality must we also
abjure soberly thinking and soberly doing? But I would never blame our
Happy Irishman for any lack in that direction. We cannot expect to have
an array of "personages," with titles and orders and medals and their
quota of space in *Who's Who* until we get to a much later stage of our
career as a nation. To make a personage you have to possess an established tradition of living, a convention to define him, a formal society to
support him, and that is what we have not and cannot have, until this
unfinished revolutionary period is over. No doubt there are a great many
stuffed-shirts here who would love to be "personages." The first Free
State government was not well in office before there was a proposal to
establish some sort of Order or Award – The Order of the Sons of Saint
Patrick or some such register – a pleasant addition, no doubt, to any
shirt-front.[7] No, our traditions are only potent as mystical diffusions in
the air, emotionally powerful, accursedly so, but not yet point-out-able in
many of those solid things into which other peoples have woven *their*
national mystique – such as laws, food, music, painting, sport, dress,
architecture. Indeed this must be granted to the Happy Man that he is the
possessor of the two only really perfect *things* we yet posses, each of them
alive with the aura of the hills and fields – horses and whiskey. We have
the beginning of a few more things that can match any in the world – the

6 *Orientations* (1937), by Sir Ronald Storrs (1881–1955). T.E. Lawrence, also
known as Lawrence of Arabia and T.E. Shaw.
7 *O'Faolain's note:* Not that one objects to Orders or Medals; not that one objects
to anything in particular so long as the spirit is sound. The French Republic, that
historic inspiration of modern Irish republicanism, adored panoply. Why not?

basis of a literature, a sound tradition in medicine, rich dairy-products, several manufactures, fast dogs, good manners; but it is nevertheless true that the Happy Man is more lively than civilised, and has a long way to go yet on his own plane to perfect his art of living. For instance, this holiday month, one thinks, how tolerantly he endures the most inadequate hotels who is so exacting a connoisseur of good company, good sport, and a good time. The point of all that being that while the Happy Man and his Ireland are enviable, and admirable, they are not inexhaustible.

~

And then what happens? Why, then, you want something more and something other. You want a bit more of those elaborations of life that canalise personality into recognisable shapes, forms, and conventions which it becomes the delight of the artist to describe, paint, analyse. George Moore, that odd mixture of artist, cad, gentleman, liar, buffoon, critic and connoisseur, said a sharp but apt thing when he arrived in Dublin – in search of the Irish Literary Renaissance – and found no Edward Martyn, and indeed nobody at all, to welcome him. "He never thinks of the gracious thing to do, not because he is unkind but because he is a little uncouth." That is true of all of us. We just don't bother to remember: but we will be exuberantly "all over you" in the morning – when we do remember. ("How are you at all? Sure, I needn't ask! Delighted to see you! Did you have a nice crossing?") And, unfortunately, there is an almost traditional patriotism about this careless informality. I remember with embarrassment that when I was at College some twenty-five years ago we associated all the formal people with Shoneenism and West Britonism,[8] and even made a cult of shagginess. You remember Turgenev's Bazarov?[9] Something like him crops up in all revolutionary periods, and lasts on and on – and on. One thinks of those receptions at Dublin Castle. One remembers the jeers Republicans used to throw at the Governor-General's levees in those far-off days before, as my friend Peadar O'Donnell once said, the Republic became a lamp-post for the Hounds of Banba.[10] There is no Governor-General now; there is not

8 "Shoneen" and "West Briton" are derogatory terms that refer to Irish people who adhere to English values.
9 Yevgeny Bazarov, an arrogant, nihilist physician, is the protagonist of Turgenev's *Fathers and Sons* (1862).
10 This is likely a sly reference to Daniel Corkery – one of his books is titled *The Hounds of Banba* – and those who shared his political outlook.

much panoply; even the Blue Hussars are gone.[11] Was nothing else lost? And, once again, this is probably not just Ireland alone: it is part of the whole world's modern levelling-up. The other night somebody who had studied in Heidelberg and Königsberg remembered the vanished ceremony of the gay Sunday morning students' processions, with their caps and banners, their exclusive "korps," their various sports-clubs, the traditional groupings with their parties and plots, their flirtations and formalities, all swept away by the intense pressure of Social Democracy. Yet, if you have once known that world you bring some of its traditions with you into a less formal age. We have never known it. Our Anglo-Irish compatriots did: but they will apparently only share their skill with the rest of us on their own terms. The Americans and Australians and South Africans and Canadians never knew it.

The result is that their artists and ours have some mightily unmalleable material to work on.

~

Everything is grist to the artist's mill: or should be. But it seems that when Ireland was more of a folk-world than it is to-day it was a richer inspiration for the artist. Yeats knew what he and his cadre of writers were doing: they were writing by the sunset of the folk-Ireland:

John Synge, I and Augusta Gregory, thought
All that we did, all that we said or sang
Must come from contact with the soil, from that
Contact everything Antaeus-like grew strong.
We three alone in modern times had brought
Everything down to that sole test again,
Dream of the noble and the beggar-man.[12]

But he could not endure the 1930 stage, and small blame to him since we cannot endure the stuffed-shirts ourselves.

11 The Blue Hussars, also known as The Mounted Escort for their role in accompanying the president and visiting dignitaries, were founded in 1931 and disbanded shortly before World War II. They were reformed in 1945 but were permanently disbanded in 1949.
12 From Yeats's poem "The Municipal Gallery Revisited" (1938).

Hurrah for revolution and the cannon-shot!
A beggar upon horseback lashes a beggar on foot.
Hurrah for revolution and cannon come again!
The beggars have changed places, but the lash goes on.[13]

But since Synge's hey-day the folksy Ireland has almost gone. It has all been to Reading and Birmingham and Dagenham, there to imbibe culture from the *Sunday Dispatch* and eat such rare viands as spam and *ersatz* Ale.[14] There are fewer and fewer villages left that have not gazed on the beauty of Jinx Falkenburg and Greer Garson.[15] *White Cargo* has gone into remote hamlets.[16] It is vain for some innocent P.P. up in Monaghan to have denounced Anew MacMaster's *Othello*.[17] And what is all that to the artist but the stuff of more and yet more exhausted Abbey farces? The artist cannot certainly feel that a romantic "contact with the soil" is now sufficient. Contact with the people, yes – but a very different people to Yeats'. His brain begins to work. He is driven to examine his conscience. He asks questions.

And what does that mean? Why, it means that you want something more and something other. You want the world of the mind, the world that is not merely local but universal, the world of the intellect. To describe that Ireland seriously is too much to ask. The would-be Irish intellectual about to let loose an idea for the benefit of the stuffed-shirts, reminds me of a ring-master about to fire a man from a cannon at a circus. He must first say: "Now, ladies and gentlemen, before I fire off this idea, I want every-body to be perfectly assured that there is absolutely *No Danger*. I assure

13 From Yeats's "The Great Day" (1938). The first line should read "Hurrah for revolution and more cannon shot!"
14 Reading, Birmingham, and Dagenham are English cities. The *Sunday Dispatch* was at one time the biggest-selling Sunday newspaper in Britain.
15 Famous for their beauty, actress and athlete Eugenia Lincoln "Jinx" Falkenburg (1919–2003) and actress Greer Garson (1904–1996) were known in their day as "pin-up" girls for the many posters bearing their likenesses that were pinned up on walls.
16 *White Cargo* (1942) is a film starring Hedy Lamarr (1913/14–2000).
17 A P P. is a Parish Priest. Irish actor Anew MacMaster (1891–1962) was an actor-manager who actively toured provincial Ireland with Shakespeare's plays, such as *Othello* (1603–4).

you, ladies and gentlemen – I can call you my friends, I hope? – in fact I
will call you *A Cháirde!*[18] – I assure you, I say, that I am the last man in
Ireland who would wish to endanger the most tender little head amongst
you. What I am about to do is merely to make a very small and entirely
safe ... I cannot call it 'explosion,' I can only say a slight 'percussion.' This
idea will now fly into the air some four hundred feet ... What? You think
I go too far? Well, let us say, two hundred feet? No! One hundred feet
then? Very well, since you have (of course) much more wisdom and much
more knowledge of the world than I have, shall we say fifty feet? I entirely
agree. Prudence! Prudence above all things! So be it. Twenty feet ... And
there is more, *a cháirde.* There will be a net beneath this idea, so that it
should not endanger you by bouncing on the earth – the Holy Earth of
Ireland! See, I remove my hat as I mention it. And, in fact, on final and
careful consideration just before I entered this Ring I decided to give you
this last assurance. I decided that, after all, it would be best that we should
fire not a real live idea, but a dummy!" Whereupon the drums roll, and
the match is applied, and everybody applauds, and the stuffed-shirts go
home saying: "You see! We let them fire cannons just like every other
country in the world!"

Or, perhaps, a better image is that the intellectual flies his kite with
weights attached – so many prettily-coloured reservations, qualifications,
applications, equivocations, evasions, annotations, all dangling brightly
at the tail, all dragging the poor idea

down,

and down,

and down,

until it is about as like a kite as a kipper. You think this is just a bitter
joke? Ask any politician. He will probably assure you, bravely, that he
speaks exactly as he thinks. If he does all one can say is: "Oh, grand-
mother, what big thoughts you've got!"

At this point, if the reader has been following these rambling ideas with
a proper degree of attentive scepticism he should say: "Hold hard! You
have suggested earlier that the Happy Irishman might be more creative if
he were more sober? How can you now consistently complain if he
refuses to be pyrotechnic when he is handling ideas?" But I do not complain. I merely describe; *je constate* (to adapt the old verses) that

18 *A cháirde* is an Irish greeting, meaning "Dear friends."

It's the intellectual Irishman's fate
To stumble and stutter in state
    On the semi-illiterates' chariot
Or be called an effeminate
If not a degenerate
    Pilate or Judas Iscariot
Without any alternative
Offensive affirmative
    Than to badger the mob and to worry it
With – "When will you start thinking
Instead of thinking you're thinking
    When Dev takes his heart out to harry it";
Which is like chasing, I fear,
Our most equivocal steer
    With a highly illusory lariat.

Besides, there are serious reasons for this. The fact is we have to keep our ideas close to the ground because our people live close to the earth. We either have to put our brains humbly to the service of our own people, who gave us suck, from whom we rose, to whom we are tied by so many memories, or leave Ireland and put them to the service of the world.[19] Ireland is thus never likely to produce men like Shaw or Wells (to say that we produced Shaw would be sheer hypocrisy) – men, that is to say, whose ideas are thrown out gaily like balloons into the bright air of the intelligence. Writers like Wells and Shaw are flamethrowers. They live in a world so large, so free, so loose, so wide, that not merely is there room for all sorts of men and ideas in it, but it is, also, so solid a world, and so given as by its very weight to settling heavily down on itself that the best gift any intellectual can give it is the gift of shocking it. Such men are in the best sense Anarchists, always shaking their people out of a state of ossified, and indeed stony-hearted Smug Morality. You remember, for instance, Shaw in *The Sanity of Art* – a little pamphlet that every Irishman should have by his bedside:

The continual danger to liberty created by law arises, not from the encroachments of Governments, which are always regarded with suspicion, but from the immense utility and consequent popularity

19 *O'Faolain's note:* Not that there is any patriotic reason why the Irish intellectual *ought* to stay at home. Intellectuals, like scientists, are citizens of the world.

of the law – and the terrifying danger and obvious inconvenience of anarchy. So that even pirates appoint and obey a captain. Law soon acquires such a good character that people will believe no evil of it; and at this point it becomes possible for priests and rulers to commit the most pernicious crimes in the names of law and order. Creeds and laws come to be regarded as applications to human conduct of eternal and immutable principles of good and evil; and breakers of the laws are abhorred as sacrilegious scoundrels to whom nothing is sacred. (Which, he goes on to shew, is, of course, a very serious error.)[20]

And just because these men keep on shaking up the human mind the human mind dislikes them, and I have no doubt that even we, in our mild and modest way, with our much-ballasted little kites, and our dummy cannons, are often regarded by some of our readers as tiresome and nagging folk who won't let the Irish people sleep in peace. But when you have not got – as we have not – ossified law or stony convention to shake up, and when what our intellectuals are doing is trying to keep law and convention, rather, from shaking down before it has done its day's work, it is natural that all ideas here tend to be localised or applied. There is, thus, small room for universal ideas in Ireland. They are all tied, like our kite, to a whole lot of local things like the Gaelic Myth, and other myths like the Noble Peasant, and a host of susceptibilities born of History, which have a confining effect on all Irish thought. And indeed, that, really, is why we get so weary of our Tame Thomists whose ideas have no application at all to our immediate problems: try them, for example, on Family Allowances, or Slums, or Old Age Pensions, or V.D., or Censorship, or an Oath of Allegiance, or Trinity College, and they at once start to wrap themselves up in a cocoon of knots like some poor bothered Charlie Chaplin.

∽

But it is Summer and let's take a rest from thinking; and for a while let Ireland be all *gemütlichkeit,* good-humour, and easygoingness, good-nature and *plamaus,* kindliness and feather-bed cosiness, the veritable Golden Land.[21] Time enough, a life-time, for the job of jacking-down those too-near horizons so that there shall be room enough for us all, a wide spacious Ireland planned on that prime need of our times, so much

20 *The Sanity of Art: An Exposure of the Current Nonsense about Artists Being Degenerate* (1908). The parenthetical digression is O'Faolain's.
21 *Gemütlichkeit* is German for "cosiness," while *plamaus* – or *plámás* – is Irish for "flattery."

threatened on all sides – respect for persons however much we disagree with them: indeed, that art in which our nearest neighbours are so long skilled, the art of civilised compromise.

~

And, there, just when I had risen to look over the dark gleaming humidity of the woods that creep towards the haze of Dublin – "No older nor more weary nor less patient of subjection than in the days of the thingmote?"[22] – a friend, looking over what I have read, says: "Or there is Italy?" and we go poking in Daniel Binchy's book for this sentence that sums up the skill of Latin civilisation. "One of the great characteristics of the Latin mind is its ability to combine theoretical intransigeance with practical tolerance."[23] After which Binchy directs attention to the example of the civilised relations between Leo XIII and his great opponent Francesco Crispi – rebel, revolutionary, republican, rationalist, Mazzinian, Garibaldian, premier, one of the founders of Italian unity, the man who virtually drove the Italian government to occupy papal Rome;[24] yet the man, too, who could receive from Leo a private message of admiration for his fine quality as a fighter.

Well … Who knows? Perhaps, down there in that once seventh city in Christendom, some day, a leader of a government may dine with a leader of an opposition, a Catholic Archbishop sup with a Protestant Provost,[25] even a banned novelist with the censor who banned him. It is, one thinks, looking out again at that dim fabric of the capital and at the low, far horizons of three counties, such a lovely country to look at, its Happy Men are such good companions, it has so much natural warmth and natural wisdom: a very little more and a very little less – shorter memories, longer rope for everybody, less peasant caution; more courage, more efficiency, more tolerance, and She would be – shall we say She will be – the land we all dreamed of thirty golden years ago.

22 From Joyce's *A Portrait of the Artist as a Young Man*. A thingmote is a Viking site of assembly where rules of law are made; such a place existed in Dublin, which was founded by Vikings.
23 *Church and State in Fascist Italy* (1941), by Daniel Binchy (1899–1989).
24 Francesco Crispi (1819–1901), Giuseppe Mazzini (1805–1872), and Giuseppe Garibaldi (1807–1882) were republicans who fought for the unification of Italy; Crispi eventually became premier of the united country from 1887 to 1891 and again from 1893 to 1896.
25 A reference to T.C.D. Provost John Henry Bernard and Archbishop John Charles McQuaid.

The Gaelic Cult[1]

To the historian few spectacles are so fascinating as mass-delusions. For, as we all know, and nowadays more than ever, it is quite possible to delude whole peoples into believing that they are living or dying for causes that are not the really effective causes, and which are in effect forms of the imagination. One of the commonest and simplest exercises of the imagination, for example, is the attempt to unify those scattered incidents and accidents, those various and often conflicting human urges and ambitions which we call a country's story, into a neatly bounded stream of purely local event, flowing from start to finish to one single sea – as if they were not all, rather, streams of the many tributaries of the great river which is the story of the world. Thus there is no such thing, in this sense, as the History of Ireland. You might as well say there could be such a thing as the History of Yeats, or the History of the Liffey. You could, it is true, as Croce distinguishes, tell the Chronicle of Ireland or the Chronicle of Yeats – born, worked, married, wrote, died.[2] But once you tackle the essential thing, i.e., the problems of Ireland or of Yeats, then the whole world and all time float in. Yet people do commonly think and feel about Ireland as if they were thinking of a personal demi-goddess, and one may agree that it is a noble fancy, and even an inspiring fancy, to speak of "her" as a beautiful queen, or as a poor little woman. It is nevertheless a fancy and not a fact, and it is well to keep that in mind because the great danger of this sort of thing is that while it often inspires noble deeds it can also end up in a complete mystification of the mind and a stultification of the heart and of all human feeling, and make men act very stupidly. For one certain

1 "The Gaelic Cult" appeared in *The Bell* 9, no. 3 (December 1944): 185–96.
2 Benedetto Croce (1866–1952) was an important Italian philosopher and historian who published most of his writings in *La Critica*, the journal he founded in 1903.

effect of these efforts to unify and localise and simplify is to produce what is called Nationalist, and, if you choose, also Imperialist histories, which are inevitably and invariably a pack of lies, because they inevitably and invariably produce wildly passionate exhalations that obfuscate and madden like a drug – cults and myths and mystiques in the adoration of which all rational thought and all pity for human life is forgotten. We have seen many examples in contemporary Europe – indeed there is scarcely a country in Europe that has not, at some period of its history, succumbed in this way: Spain, France, England, Austria, Germany, Italy, and let us add Ireland. It must be one of the greatest attractions of America that she is still too young to have developed a historical cult.

In our own small way we have, in recent times, created one such very wonderful delusion. It is variously called the Gaelic Tradition, or the Gaelic Nation, or simply The Gael. It is a mystique, and like all mystiques it has a basis in fact, or rather an impossible bundling together of disparate facts. In sum the mystique has tried to discover in the old Gaelic world a model, or master-type – rather like the National Socialist mythology of the Pure Aryan[3] – to which we must all conform. Now, this imagination of an Avatar, or incarnation of race or nationality at its purest, almost in its divine perfection, is a natural poetic flight, and all peoples indulge in it in moments of ecstasy: but they do not really believe in it, and they do not keep it up, and they certainly are not so foolish as to try to *live* according to it. On the contrary, they usually have a second and more homely image of themselves for the purposes of day-to-day existence. Thus "Britannia" sits nobly on the coins of Britain: but it is "John Bull" who pockets her.[4] Even America, like France, has her goddess of Liberty but it was an inspector of food named Sam Wilson who created for her the practical image of Uncle Sam.[5] What one might call the iconography

3 The National Socialists, better known as the Nazis, were members of the German totalitarian movement led by Adolf Hitler (1889–1945). The Aryans were a people who originated in Asia but, beginning in the mid-nineteenth century, gradually became associated with the notion of a white race and its superiority over other peoples.

4 The figure of Britannia, the female incarnation of Britain, has existed since the first century CE; John Bull, the male incarnation of Britain, was invented by John Arbuthnot (1667–1735) in *The History of John Bull* (1712).

5 O'Faolain refers here to Lady Liberty in the United States and Marianne in France; they are based on Libertas, the Roman goddess who is the female personification of liberty, and have their analogues in Britannia and Cathleen ni Houlihan. The figure of Uncle Sam rose to prominence during the War of 1812; he is said to have been based on the Troy, New York businessman Samuel Wilson.

of Irish symbolism is various, chiefly women, mainly unrepublican queens, but we have yet to find a really homely effigy – having long discarded the one which the 18th century foisted on us, Paddy with the pig.[6] But, whatever he may turn out to be when we begin to see ourselves sanely enough to define him, a Gaelic avatar will certainly never appear in homely caricature: for the very solid reason that he has not even yet appeared in apotheosis. The attempt to conceive the master-type as "Gaelic" could not succeed since it is, as we will see, based on a fundamental delusion.

This history of the Gaelic mystique is fascinating. It is really dual, partly cultural and partly political. For that reason it will be simplest to speak of it in the bivalvular term – "The Gaelic Nation." The story of its gradual arrival is likewise dual, partly a matter of politics and partly of literature, and it is comparatively recent. For if we cast our minds back over any distance – say over a couple of centuries – we do not find any of our political leaders or observers aware of it at all. I do not think that you will even as much as find the word "Gael" in Swift, Molyneux, Grattan, Wolfe Tone, Lord Edward, Robert Emmet, Dan O'Connell (except when he said that he had no use for the Gaelic language), nor is it in John Mitchel, Michael Doheny, Fintan Lalor, Michael Davitt, Parnell, John Redmond, or, though this may surprise some, even in our *pater patriae*, the founder of Sinn Féin, Arthur Griffith.[7] He, like all those others before him, is content to speak of "Ireland" and "Irishmen." Some of them, of course, speak in favour of the Irish language – but that has nothing to do with the political cult, or the imaginary master-type of the "Gael." Thus, Davitt, for example, presented Parnell in 1882 with a political programme whose ninth point advocated "the cultivation of national literature and the encouragement of the Irish language"; and we can well believe, too, that all our political leaders were naturally inspired by a knowledge of the past.

There was only one man who, it might be argued – though I think, after reading his essays, not very convincingly – did make some small effort to make some sort of actual link between contemporary politics and the old

---

6 The negative stereotype of Paddy with the pig was meant to characterise the Irish as a backward people who lived closely with their livestock.

7 William Molyneux (1656–1698) was MP for Dublin and author of *The Case of Ireland's Being Bound by Acts of Parliament in England, Stated* (1698). Michael Doheny (1805–1862) was an Irish historian. James Fintan Lalor (1807–1849) was a political essayist. *Pater patriae* is Latin for "father of the fatherland" or "father of the country."

Gaelic world. That was Thomas Davis.[8] Even his essay on the language would have to be carefully edited by any modern enthusiast hopeful of using it to-day. And it might be noted, in passing, that several of his colleagues on his paper *The Nation* opposed his revivalist ideas – even the antiquary, John O'Donovan – being eager, instead, for a modern cosmopolitan culture.[9] In any case, on all political matters, Davis was overshadowed by the colossus from Kerry whose defined policy, and whose clear contribution to the development of native political thought – agree or disagree with it now as one chooses – was to say, in sum, to his ragged army, "Start afresh. Modernise." As we know, they did, throwing overboard every scrap of the past that had not already, like The Wild Geese, abandoned the sinking ship.[10] Davis and we might bewail the harsh necessity, but he had no political alternative to O'Connell's modernisations. So far, then, the Gaelic Nation as a political theory has no pedigree.

Some may here say: "But what about what Professor Corkery called 'The Hidden Ireland'? Maybe the inarticulate people held to it in secret?" They did not. The "inarticulate" people found a voice in O'Connell (1775–1847). If anybody wants a line on the political theory of the last of the Gaelic poets, from the ruin of the old Gaelic society to his day, I venture to suggest that he might read the Preface to my biography of O'Connell, *King of the Beggars*.[11] In sum, all the poor devils could think of was the return of the Stuarts, and, presumably, some kind of Anglo-Irish monarchy to patronise poetry.

Neither had the militant separatists any alternative to O'Connell's ideas, though they had, of course, to his methods. That was natural: the rebels of '48 and '67 were insurrectionists, not revolutionaries.[12] All

---

8 *O'Faolain's note:* Possibly one might base the argument for Davis as a pro-Gael on his essay "Udalism and Feudalism." By Udalism he meant a form of titular peasant proprietorship with an over-riding State Control. We have something very like it now and I do not see anything particularly Gaelic about it. His ideas there, of course, all went out of date with the Land Acts. [*Editor's note:* "Udalism and Feudalism" was published in 1841.]

9 *The Nation* was a nationalist newspaper that became associated with the Young Ireland movement. John O'Donovan (1806–1861).

10 The Wild Geese refers to the Irish Jacobite forces that fled the country to France after their loss in the Williamite War, as agreed to under the terms of the Treaty of Limerick on 3 October 1691.

11 *King of the Beggars* (1938).

12 1848 was the year of the Young Ireland rising; 1867 was the year of the Fenian rising.

they knew was that they craved something that would satisfy racial pride. (Nationalism and racialism were in the air of Europe, it was part of the Romantic movement, winging westward on the words of Herder, Lessing, young Wordsworth, Shelley, Mazzini, Garibaldi, Hugo, Lamartine.) But what that *something* was the '48 and '67 men could not define, and all that emerges from them is the craving to be "different," to "separate." They had no more idea of what they meant by that – in terms of life, of human beings, of social order – than the kids who used to chant at school in my young days "A Nation Once Again."[13]

But the Romantic movement was now about to satisfy the craving that it had thus helped to create. That same romantic urge that had in England produced Percy's *Reliques of Ancient English Poetry* in 1765, had produced Charlotte Brooke's *Reliques of Irish Poetry* in 1789, as it had Walker's *Memoirs of the Irish Bards* in 1786: two literary landmarks.[14] There followed many little societies interested in antiquities and the Gaelic language; local archæological societies; more and more publications; scholars native and foreign; until by about 1900, there began to emerge – almost wholly in English, it may be said – a vivid awareness of the existence of an Ireland that had been completely forgotten. That was Gaelic Ireland. What was even more wonderful and exciting, there were still places where men and women told ancient folktales by the fireside, believed in the *sidhe*, held in their rude hands the thin thread of Ariadne back to the forgotten labyrinth.[15] All one needed to get back to that wonder-world was to be able to speak Irish. One could even touch that world without it. Yeats, Lady Gregory, Synge, Colum, all the poets of the Anglo-Irish Revival drank eagerly at the fountain, and handed the winy goblets back to such of the populace as had the wit and heart to gather around them. No young man reading these lines – not even young Gaelic enthusiasts of to-day – can realise what that discovery of the "ancient mother" meant. Its outward signs were Anglo-Irish Literature and the founding of the Gaelic League in 1893. But let us keep our eyes on the point – there is still no mention of the "Gaelic Nation" as a political ideal.

13 "A Nation Once Again" (1844) is a patriotic song by Thomas Davis.
14 Thomas Percy (1729–1811); Charlotte Brooke (c. 1740–1793); *Historical Memoirs of the Irish Bards*, by Joseph C. Walker (1761–1810).
15 The *sidhe* (pronounced like the English pronoun "she") are fairy folk in Irish lore.

So far, then, we see the three elements: constitutional politics, in pretty low water after the fall of Parnell, the Separatists now burrowing underground, and this new Gaelic inspiration. Arthur Griffith established Sinn Féin in 1905–1906. (I repeat that there is, so far as I have been able to see, no mention in all his writings of the "Gael.") The first modern politician after Parnell whom I have found seizing on Gaelic Ireland *as a prototype*, or model, to be reincarnated in a politically free Ireland is, of all people, the Socialist Jim Connolly in his *Labour in Irish History* (1910). Whether it is with him or with somebody else that the grand delusion begins he had it badly. He was apparently under the impression that the antique social order enshrined for those whom he called "our Gaelic forefathers" certain nobly desirable democratic rights and institutions, and that the modern, debased commercialised Irish stood between the people and these admirable traditions. Alas for the glory of Tara's Hall, nothing could have been farther from the truth. He could have saved himself and thousands of others much disappointment and more folly had he done no more than look at the Gaelic preface to the great collection of Gaelic Laws known as the "Senchus Mor," which lists all the awful things that existed before these laws were codified – plagues and disorders of every kind, and, as the crowning worst, such general anarchy that "even the churl's son dared to consider himself the equal of the son of a king."

Whoever began it, there it is, in one example, already at work: and if some student of our universities should make the whole question a subject of research he would find other examples. I seem to remember that Mr. Sean Milroy (Heaven forgive him) wrote a book, also in praise of the Brehon Laws.[16] Constance Markievicz gave lectures about the subject – an extraordinary medley of Marx, Republicanism, and Gaeldom. The general idea of the "Gaelic Nation" is implicit in the very title of Mr. P.S. O'Hegarty's interesting book *The Indestructible Nation* which, note, was originally given as a series of lectures to the London Gaelic League "in (I quote the author's own words) the first and best decade of Sinn Féin, in 1911–1913."[17]

There one can see the idea of a Revival shake hands with the idea of a Revolution. As we know, the Gaelic League was shattered by that handshake. The first President and founder, Dr. Douglas Hyde, now President

16 Scan Milroy (1877–1946) was a TD and Senator for Cumman na nGaedheal. The Brehon laws were the written legal code in ancient Ireland; they date from the seventh and eighth centuries. A brehon was the Irish equivalent of a judge.

17 *The Indestructible Nation* (1918).

of Ireland, resigned from it in 1915 when the militant separatists inside
the League – they had deliberately gone into it in order to control it politically – insisted on making Independence one of its avowed objects.
From that day onward politics infected Gaelic; and the idea of the "Gael"
and the "Gaelic Nation" infected politics. It is all summed up in a well-
known phrase of Pearse – "Not merely free but Gaelic as well, not merely
Gaelic but free as well."

I am afraid that we have become so accustomed to the jargon of this
mystique that some, reading that phrase again, will dumbly react to it in a
reflex now almost mechanically conditioned by twenty years of propaganda. They may say, "A Gaelic Nation? Well – why not? It sounds all
right." It sounds all right. But let us shake off the drug and ask: What did
Connolly and Pearse mean? They refer to a period when the people of
Ireland possessed and lived by an indigenous culture of their very own –
laws, dress, language, social order, and so on: and they refer, simultaneously,
to later periods when various Irishmen, finding themselves misgoverned by
the British people, propounded the solution of the absolute and unqualified
separation of Ireland from Britain as a modern Republic. Two entirely different ideas are there thrown together – one cannot say "mixed" together
because they are immiscible. For the antique Gaels never heard of and
would have fought to the death against the idea of a Republic and all it
connotes, and the men who first initiated the idea of Republicanism – Tone
onward – knew nothing about the antique Gaels and would, whether
Davis, Lalor or Jim Connolly, have been appalled by the reality of those
days and conditions. If anything other than common-sense were needed to
prove that the men of 1916 were, like the men of '48 and '67, not social
revolutionaries but romantic insurrectionists, this idea of an Ancient-
Modern-Republican-Gaelic-Nation should suffice. It is obvious that
nobody could base anything like a social revolution on the lines of this
fairy-tale fantasy.

Actually long before 1916 a very real revolution in Ireland had been
brought about by the pressure of the Irish Parliamentary Party, or really
by Davitt – a true and genuine social reform of the largest kind – when
they won the land for the people: so that the most serious social grava-
men had already been removed before the political change-over occurred.
That marks off Davitt as a man apart in Irish history: one of our very few
real revolutionaries, perhaps our only one. It shows us, too, how revolu-
tions occur, on the pressure of actual not imaginary circumstances. The
only other big thing waiting to be done after that was perceived clearly
by another realistic man, Griffith – the need for autonomy in order to

make possible an industrial revolution. So that what is needed, and perhaps alone needed to-day is not so much a further revolution as a revolutionary *approach* to both land and industry to set the dynamo going full-blast.

We can see, now, why the insurrectionists seized on the Gaelic Nation ideal, absurd and impossible as it was: their hearts were full, but their minds were vacant: into the vacuum there swept the first exciting idea to hand. Far be it from me to assail the memory of brave and noble-hearted men whose courage and idealism we will for ever honour. But we must not imagine that they had all the virtues; and the virtue of political thought they had not. Yet, to this day, their dual theory dominates the minds of our legislators, or of most of them – I find it hard to think that men like Mr. Sean Lemass, for instance, are thus affected – so that all you have to say to them is "Not merely free but Gaelic as well, not merely Gaelic but free as well," and their mouths will begin to water like Pavlov's dogs.[18]

It is an amazing hypnosis. But still more amazing is the manner in which it affects the minds it dominates. For it produces nothing positive. On the contrary its effect is wholly negative and inhibitory; as with some mumbo-jumbo that is feared for its destructive powers and given mere lip-service to keep it quiet. Anything that has been done has been done without reference to it or without any assistance from it – whether it be the Shannon Scheme, or improved rural housing, or the growing of wheat, or migratory schemes to lessen unemployment, or the efficiency of the Army, or the development of Air Transport, or Tourism, etc.[19] Thus all that the more perfervid Gaelic addicts have ever contributed to any of these things is a nark.[20] Why should the Army play rugby! Tourism will ruin the West! Keep the Gaelic migrants inside a kind of Red Indian reservation – as was proposed last month by the Gaelic League at its Annual Conference. This

18 Sean Lemass (1899–1971) was a long-time Fianna Fáil TD; he was taoiseach of Ireland from 1959 to 1966. Ivan Petrovich Pavlov (1849–1936) was a Russian physiologist known for developing the concept of the conditioned reflex; it arose from his experiment to train a dog to associate the ringing of the bell with the arrival of food, resulting in salivation even when the bell rang and no food arrived.
19 The Ardnacrusha hydroelectric power plant, located in County Clare, was originally known as the Shannon Scheme; construction on it began in 1925 and it was completed in 1929.
20 In Ireland, a nark refers to a stitch, in the sense of a small rag of clothing; O'Faolain thereby implies that these Gaelic addicts have not contributed anything of value.

is natural because the mystique is the opponent of all modernisations and improvisations – being by nature, in its constant reference to the middle-ages – terrified of the modern world, afraid of modern life, inbred in thought, and, so, utterly narrow in outlook. All its ideas of life are mediæval. Take even industry which might be thought safe from it. Can we seriously hope to develop a dynamic industrial future with a system of education which is based on an uncritical adoration for Finn MacCool (or Thomas Davis) and which has no interest in encouraging, let alone in producing, young technicians?[21] Look even at the school-readers *in English*. For all the reference they make to the world of science or industry they might have been prepared for Ancient Britons. And does the mystique not affect politics – its politics are shiveringly isolationist; and is not our industrial future close bound to politics, seeing that we can have no large commercial future unless we look to the wide world as our market? In culture the mystique is equally fearful and inbred. That should be evident in our literary censorship alone which strives to keep out anything that savours of a bold facing-up to modern problems – banning even books by reputable Catholics abroad, books and pamphlets sanctioned by the most reputable members of all churches. How utterly different all that is to the magnificent courage of O'Connell, who said to our people, "There is another world outside. Follow me. I will lead you into it."

But we are not yet finished with the wonders of this hypnosis. We know, as I have said, the many good things our legislators have done without thanks to it. That means that when they do anything effective they are, for that time, free of the Cult and do not really, in their clearer brains, then dream any longer of harking back to the mediæval myth. Yet, not one single man of them will admit it. They still imagine that they are carrying out the Gaelic gospel. They are thus in the delightfully befuddled condition, and this is the most wonderful wonder of all, of being under the delusion that they are under a delusion.

Is this just a joke? Simple examples of the result offer themselves frequently. Thus, last month, as I write, the Gaelic half of the delusion was under the delusion that it was holding an Oireachtas or annual all-Ireland Festival of Gaelic Culture. Apart from a couple of ceilidhes in the Dublin Mansion House, and a boxing tournament, there was little sign of a Cultural Festival at all.[22] Yet, even such hard-bitten businessmen as Mr.

21 Finn MacCool – or Fionn MacCumhaill – is a hero of Irish myth.
22 A céilidhe, or céilidh, is an Irish session of traditional music, dancing, and storytelling.

Louis Elliman of the Gaiety Theatre, who is a Jew, and his genial English-born manager, Mr. Hamlyn Benson, were apparently hypnotised into believing in the pleasant fancy.[23] They must have been slightly puzzled when, in due course, the curtain for the Gaelic play *Deamar agus a Bhean* rose on a theatre apparently quite empty.[24] The Dublin *Evening Mail* reported that it was not, in fact, quite empty;[25] the Minister for Education with a party of eight held the dress-circle;[26] and there were also six critics in a bunch; the Gallery was empty; on searching the highways and by-ways of the Parterre and the rest of the house 14 other devotees were discovered in the darkness. There was also, during the week, an Exhibition of Paintings, reported by the *Irish Times* as being mainly reminiscent of South Kensington. Though how a painter, or a boxer that, for the rest of the year, has been just a painter or a boxer can suddenly become a Gaelic painter or boxer is difficult to understand.

An even more puzzling example of the stultifying effect of being under a double delusion is the political fact. The whole argument of those hypnotised by the ideal of the "Gaelic Nation" is that we are being infected by the English language, by English and American books, by English and American music, by English radio, by English manners and customs. If that be so, it surely seems more than illogical if these people should deliberately decide to go on enjoying all the advantages of polit-ical association with the country which is so constantly proclaimed as the source and origin of all these allegedly offensive things.

The reason for that is clear, too. For what has happened is that the separatist half of the thing has been quietly dropped, or exchanged for a variety of subterfuges whose final effect has been to muddle us com-pletely as to our true relations with Britain and the world. It was dropped, of course, because to be a genuine separatist you have to possess that revolutionary approach which I have mentioned. And whatever else we have got, we have not got that. The whole thing is thus a dead mouse that our leaders go on playing with – possibly because they do not yet realise that the unhappy mouse died about two hundred and fifty years before

---

23 Louis Elliman (1903–1965); Hamlyn Benson (n.d.). The Gaiety Theatre, located in central Dublin, was opened in 1871.

24 *Deamar agus a Bhean* (1941) was written by Séamus de Bhilmot (1902–1977); his surname sometimes appears anglicised as Wilmot.

25 The *Dublin Evening Mail* (1823–1962) was renamed the *Evening Mail* in 1928.

26 Thomas Derrig (1897–1956) (Fianna Fáil) was minister for education from 1932 to 1939 and 1940 to 1948.

they discovered it. But the whole thing is very foolish, and rather painful. Though there is something touching about it too. It is all part of the natural tendency of an inexperienced people – without insult and indeed in a certain oblique pride we might call ourselves a primitive people – to go on myth-making long after the age of myths. It would appear in fact that there is a lot of Hans Andersen still left in men like Mr. de Valera.[26]

Let us not confuse this political mystique or cult with the specific matter of the Language itself. That is a quite different matter. That is a simple and clear matter. Let us, by all means, learn and read and, when we choose, speak our language. It has its value, it has its pieties. You can, it is true, be free men and not speak a native language: but that is obvious – as the example of America and thousands upon thousands of good Irishmen to-day can shew. You can speak your native tongue and not even desire to be politically free: as Wales can shew. Yet, if we do not possess our own native language, and what it contains, we are spiritually and intellectually the poorer. On the other hand, a language is in itself only a noise. It has no mysterious therapeutic value. As many unpleasant people speak Gaelic as English. But the unfounded notion behind the present Gaelic cult is that you can "think" Gaelic: as if, did I choose to write this article in Gaelic, I would think it out to a different conclusion! No – unless a language is a door to a rich store of thought, political thought, social thought, philosophical thought, scientific thought, it can only be a doorway to those indefinable things – often foolish, but always warm, human and precious – that we call our memories. Gaelic will do that for us, but only that, since of all those other kinds of thought the Gaelic world has nothing to offer us. Let us then drop the cult. The course will be simple after that.

Irish should be made the language of instruction in districts where it is the home language, and English the second language taught as a school subject. I would not, at any stage, use English as a medium in such districts. Where English is the home language it must of necessity be the first language in the schools. But I would have a compulsory second language (*voluntarily selected*) satisfied that in five-sixths of the schools it would be Irish. But in all details of their programme the schools should have autonomy.

That seems a reasonable proposal. Would it satisfy the devotees of the Cult? Would it satisfy Mr. de Valera? I hope so, because with the exception

26 Hans Christian Andersen (1805–1875) was a Danish writer best known for his fairy tales.

of the two italicised words – inserted solely by way of explanation of his meaning – it is a quotation from Patrick Pearse, and his solution. If it were adopted we would be free of the mental miasma that has resulted from the Cult, free to think out our problems with unconfused minds as a modern people in a modern world.

Eamon de Valera[1]

I began these notes as a short review of Mr. M.J. MacManus's recent book on Mr. de Valera. They have expanded so much and contain so many personal opinions that I feel it unfair to press them into any other compartment but my own. So, here they are as a personal reaction which may or may not be shared by other Irishmen who, like myself, once held Mr. de Valera in an admiration "this side idolatry" and, even yet, consider him gifted with immense, if dammed or thwarted, potentialities.[2]

The first thought that came to me as I closed this rather bland record of Mr. de Valera's career was that the Taoiseach is a bad subject for biography. He is a man of pleasant personality, though in private rather than in public, for he has small art of public living, speaks badly, goes about little, does not patronise the arts or sport. But he is not an interesting personality as Disraeli's personality was interesting, or Palmerston's or O'Connell's: there is no quiver of light and shade, no surprise, hardly a paradox.[3] That is not his fault; it may be his virtue – in another sense, indeed, if he were a little less blatantly packed with virtue he might be a

1 "Eamon de Valera" appeared in *The Bell* 10, no. 1 (April 1945): 1–18. The essay's title had a note appended to it stating that *Eamon de Valera*, by M.J. MacManus (1891–1951), was published by the Talbot Press and was on sale for 7s. 6d. The book came out in 1944.
2 In *Timber: or, Discoveries* (1640), Ben Jonson (1572–1637) says of Shakespeare: "I loved the man, and do honor his memory, on this side idolatry, as much as any."
3 Benjamin Disraeli. Henry John Temple (1784–1865), 3rd Viscount Palmerston, was prime minister of Britain from 1855 to 1858 and from 1859 to 1865.

more attractive subject – but it is definitely the misfortune of his biographers. Indeed I can only think of two kinds of books about Mr. de
Valera that might grip one to the end, and both would really be prolonged
essays – a murderous attack or a comic satire. Not that either would be
just; both are possible. I have heard old opponents do the former with
merciless brilliance on the lines of The Great Splitter – the man who split
Sinn Féin, split the I.R.A., split Cumann na mBan, split Clan na Gael,
double-split Sinn Féin, double-split the I.R.A., split the whole country,
and spends the rest of his time splitting words.[4] Of the satirical style there
are such examples as Oliver Gogarty's opinion that he has been the greatest national fiasco since Jem Roche;[5] but, apart from such lavish gusts of
laughter, there are many segments of Mr. de Valera's career that should
only be recorded with a Lytton Stracheyish irony, such as his wonderful
American tour, that complete comedy of misunderstandings between de
Valera the young revolutionist who miscalled himself a republican, and
John Devoy the old republican who miscalled himself a revolutionist.[6] Or
there is the hilarious absurdity of the shadowy Second Dáil in which
(while Mr. Cosgrave in the real Dáil was making the laws as President of
the Free State) Mr. de Valera was pretending to be the President of the
Irish Republic but was in fact presiding at solemn scholastic arguments as
to whether the Republic did, in fact, really exist. There are all these prolonged hesitations about taking the Oath and entering the (actual) Dáil,
the expulsions from the Party of men like Mr. Dan Breen who took it, the
actual final swearing and entry into the Dáil and then these – Oh! so earnest! – arguments to prove that nobody ever took an Oath at all.[7] There are
many other occasions on which Mr. de Valera has indulged his passion for
being cruelly wronged. But Mr. MacManus, one must agree, is under a
disadvantage here. One would not expect the Literary Editor of *The Daily*

4 Cumann na mBan, which translates as "the Society of Women," was an all-female
auxiliary corps formed in 1914 to fight alongside the Irish Volunteer Force. Fine Gael
was founded in 1933 to accommodate the amalgamation of Cumann na nGaedheal
with two smaller parties: the Farmer's Party and the National Guard.
5 Jem Roche (1878–1934), an Irish boxer, lost against Tommy Burns (1881–1955),
né Noah Brusso, the Canadian-born world heavyweight title holder, in a first-round
knockout in Dublin on 17 March 1908.
6 Lytton Strachey (1880–1932) was an English biographer and critic. John Devoy
(1842–1928) was a prominent Fenian.
7 Dan Breen (1894–1969) won back his seat in the 1932 election as a reinstated
member of Fianna Fáil.

Express to be ironical about Lord Beaverbrook as long as the most important event in Lord Beaverbrook's life has yet, happily, to occur.[8]

~

But if a biographer cannot be ironical there are other slightly promising alternatives. The biographer of Mr. de Valera might, for instance, act as official apologist. And is it really feasible to avoid entirely the position of apologist (if one will not adopt the position of critic) when dealing with a life not wholly innocent of inconsistency? Facing every biographer of Mr. de Valera there is, to give the outstanding example, that crucial date on which he at last did enter the Free State Dáil, and the question, "Why did he not do it in 1922 since he did it several years later?" Mr. MacManus slides around this question as if the whole character and reputation of his subject were not involved in the answer to it – or rather in the method of answering it. The plain answer is, of course, as plain as one of Mr. de Valera's 1916 pike-staffs.[9] All of us Republicans who followed his lead in 1922 refused to accept majority rule: that is to say we tried to do what E.L.A.S. recently tried to do in Greece and we were licked.[10] Not until then, or rather not until several years after – for Mr. de Valera is a man who takes a long time to make up his mind, or he certainly was in those days – did he decide to reverse the famous epigram of Clausewitz about war being the continuation of politics by other means.[11]

~

I personally still think that he was on every ground, moral and political, entitled to refuse to accept the majority decision under the circumstances because the Treaty was a decision by force – whether he was politically right is another matter – and when he failed to defeat the majority he was

8 Maxwell Aitken (1879–1964), 1st Baron Beaverbrook, was a Canadian-born British politician; he bought the *Daily Express* in 1916. Since 1931, MacManus had been the literary editor of the *Irish Press*; the newspaper was founded by de Valera in 1931 and ceased operations in 1995.

9 A pike is a weapon consisting of a long wooden staff and a pointed metal head.

10 E.L.A.S. – Ethnikós Laïkós Apeleftherotikós Strátos, in English the National Popular Liberation Army – was the military wing of the Greek communist resistance formed in 1942 to fight against the occupying Germans and Italians. When resistance groups united to form the Greek government in 1944 after the departure of the Germans, E.L.A.S. refused to decommission, resulting in combat from December until February 1945, at which time E.L.A.S. surrendered.

11 Carl von Clausewitz (1780–1831) was a Prussian general and military strategist.

certainly right to accept the inevitable. But what nobody with an ounce of honesty, not to mention humour, can stomach is the prolonged pretence by means of ingenious argufying that he never did what everybody knows he did, or that "it is different now." He may keep up the pretence if he wants to, but the biographer must either defend or condemn, because if he does not he is simply not doing his job of bringing the character of the man out from behind the camouflage of words. In fact that pretence is far too illuminating to be ignored. It means that Mr. de Valera is not really a man with any sense of history, and has neither a cultivated nor a sophisticated mind; if he had he would realise that from the beginning of time determined minorities have forced their reforms and decisions on unwilling majorities. At the present moment a determined minority of fanatical Gaelic enthusiasts have for years forced on the whole people, who have, of course, never been consulted on the matter, an educational scheme (better called "a schame") of compulsory Irish, led by Mr. de Valera himself who, with characteristic inconsistency and a characteristic desire to have his own way (by constitutional means) – whether anybody likes it or not – is convinced, and has even said, that he is merely implementing the will of the majority. As to how he knows the majority's will on this subject his heart tells him that.

The whole of the Civil War period must force every normally percipient observer to agree that when Mr. de Valera's devotees present him as an utterly honest man they are quite right if they mean honest according to his lights, but that those searchlights which he turns on his heart have some very well-timed blackouts.

Actually one could make too much of this notorious goodness and infallibility of Mr. de Valera, those annoying virtues of his which, to his sorrow, his opponents are occasionally so ungenerous as to question. I believe myself that he is a good man; and he has, since his great days when he used to be a revolutionist, done very few wrong things, though chiefly because since then he has done very few practical things of any kind whatsoever. To be good and to be infallible is a common element in the egomania of all leaders. It is dangerous only when it is not offset by political shrewdness and political caution and a good deal of common humanity, and Mr. de Valera is now an unusually cautious and humane statesman. In his idealistic days when he was ready to take great risks, and not afraid to ask other men and the whole country to take great risks, he had less of these qualities: idealists cannot afford to be humane. But, as the Americans say,

he learned the hard way and the de Valera of 1945 is a very different man
to the de Valera of 1915–1925; much more canny and much less imaginative. One does not therefore mind, one would even be tolerant of his goodness and infallibility if he did not make such a fuss about it at a time when
his present masterly policy of inaction places so little strain on either quality. If we quarrel with him it is not because he is in fact wrong as often, or
as rarely, as his critics but because he has decided to be always right on the
good old Civil Service motto – "When in doubt do nothin'."

It is not information to list a man's qualities: one must measure the quality of his qualities. Mr. MacManus by not bothering to do this is so foolish as to compare Mr. de Valera to Abraham Lincoln, presumably because
each came from the equivalent of a log-cabin and reached the equivalent
of a White House, each could amuse himself solving problems in Euclid,
each had to do with a Civil War, each is tall, each has two eyes and two
legs and two hands, and unless something is done to make it possible for
artists to live in Ireland it may yet be possible to say that each was assassinated by a mad actor.[12] The comparison, of course, is too sentimental
to stand a moment's examination. Lincoln's virtues were formidable virtues. Think of his attitude in the American Civil War – clear, hard, logical,
unwavering. Compare his power of decision then with Mr. de Valera's
ambiguous hesitations in our Civil War when the Republican section of
the Army of Independence simply took the whole matter out of his indeci-
sive hands. Lincoln's mind was a hard logical mind, and that is something
very different to the mathematical quality of Mr. de Valera's mind –
which, for instance, loves to work on words and formulas. Can one
imagine that if Lincoln lost the Civil War he would have been so formu-
listic as to go on for years playing make-believe at governing? Would he
try to blind his mind to the fact of a partitioned continent by inventing a
name for one part which had associations with the whole – such as
Columbia: which corresponds to Mr. de Valera's childishly hopeful use of
the word *Eire* as if, on the principles of M. Coué, you can make a thing
so by saying it often enough.[13] "Every day and in every way these twenty-
six counties become more and more."

12 Abraham Lincoln (1809–1865) was president of the United States from 1861
until he was assassinated in 1865 by the actor John Wilkes Booth (1838–1865).
13 Émile Coué (1857–1926) was a French pharmacist and psychotherapist who
developed the method of autosuggestion with the mantra: "Every day, and in every
way, I am becoming better and better."

~

The truth about Abraham Lincoln is that he was tough and formidable. (I think the adjective "formidable" is Cecil Chesterton's.)[14] Mr. de Valera is sinuously persistent, and his enemies would use a harder word. The persistence is undeniable; the sinuosity tends to lose the persistence in a maze. For example, if we are to take the Lincolnian parallel seriously can the question of North and South be maintained within it? On this question of secession Mr. de Valera was magnificent when, as Frank Pakenham showed, he planned and directed the strategy of the Anglo-Irish discussions so as to make them break, if they had to break, on that vital question of the dismemberment of Ireland.[15] Unfortunately, Mr. Lloyd George (as he then was) also saw the point and manœuvred Arthur Griffith into such an untenable position that we did not and could not break on it.[16] But once the Treaty debates began Mr. de Valera paid comparatively little attention to this question. He did not see that if Anglo-Irish discussion could not break on Partition it was the one cause on which inter-Irish discussion might then have come together. Lincoln was firm and clear on secession. He fought the South on that question – on slavery he was willing to compromise and did compromise. He joined the country, in the end, by his uncompromising Americanism, not by humanitarian principles. All the finicky constitutional pother in those awful Dáil debates about Document Number Two, the King, the Oath, and the so-called Republic was pure scholastic blether compared with that dismemberment.

Even now nobody knows – and Mr. MacManus does not cover the question – whether Mr. de Valera realises how literally vital the question of North and South is, i.e., that the loss of the North is depriving Ireland of half its vitality. For the case for Irish Unity is not merely legal, or merely rational, or merely constitutional. It is purely and simply a natural human necessity. Our Irishism is only half-Irish without the Northern strain, just as the North is only an artificial half-alive thing without the blood of Ireland running through its veins. The late Alexis Carrel put a chicken's

14 Cecil Chesterton (1879–1918) was an English journalist, the author of *A History of the United States* (1919), and the brother of writer G.K. Chesterton.
15 Frank Pakenham (1905–2001), who was later made Earl of Longford, was the author of *Peace by Ordeal: An Account, from first-hand sources, of the Negotiation and Signature of the Anglo-Irish Treaty 1921* (1935). Coincidentally, given O'Faolain's discussion, Pakenham later wrote biographies of both Eamon de Valera (1970) and Abraham Lincoln (1974).
16 David Lloyd George (1863–1945) was prime minister of Britain from 1916 to 1922.

heart in a machine invented by Colonel Lindbergh and it has been beating there for years.[17] That is the North to-day. It is open to the North to observe that our miracle of a chicken without a heart is even more wonderful and less inspiring. Partition now inspires Mr. de Valera only to the use of meaningless clichés. On the North he has become our great stand-patter.

∿

In any case, Lincoln dealt with great universals and set a precedent to the world in his clear and direct way of handling them. Mr. de Valera may be just as honourable a character in his own way but he just is not that sort of human being at all, and to compare him with Lincoln is to prove that one has either no sense of proportion, or no knowledge of history, or no knowledge of Mr. de Valera. One has only to think of our present relations with Great Britain in which there is neither clarity nor direction to see that the comparison is inept. On that, as well as on our present general static position, the best one could say for Mr. de Valera would be that his policy may be to give Ireland twenty years of undisturbed peace in order to stabilise and reconstruct. Against which one can only confess that the speed of reconstruction and the things which seem to engage his own interest – the revival of Gaelic, and the Higher Mathematics – are utterly depressing. He may be making the great mistake of thinking that any really dynamic reconstruction is possible without dynamic politics. And as I said editorially last month Irish politics to-day are not politics: our two main parties are indistinguishable not because their political ideas are alike but because neither has any political idea at all.[18] Socialism, Communism, Imperialism, Distributivism, Fabianism, Toryism, Liberalism, these are political ideas.[19] The "Fenians of Destiny" and the "Race of Gaels" are just silly Romantic titles that confess a complete intellectual vacancy as far as the realities of political ideas are concerned.[20]

---

17 Alexis Carrel (1873–1944) won the Nobel Prize for Physiology or Medicine for his work on suturing blood vessels. Charles A. Lindbergh (1902–1974) piloted the first non-stop transatlantic flight in 1927. The men co-authored *The Culture of Organs* (1938).
18 "One World," *The Bell* 9, no. 6 (March 1945): 461–71.
19 Distributism, as distributivism is more commonly known, is a political system in which property is distributed to the largest number of people; the Chesterton brothers were two of the theory's main proponents. The Fabian Society was founded in London in 1884 to propagate social democratic reforms in Britain.
20 The "Fenians of Destiny" and the "Race of Gaels" refer to Fianna Fáil and Fine Gael, respectively.

~

If a biographer will not discuss his hero's personality, or analyse his character, or act as his apologist, there are two other things left for him to do.
The first – which is more or less what Mr. MacManus has done – is to rely
on the interest of the event, neither re-assessing each crisis, nor measuring
his hero's quality in the face of it. This is not a very interesting or illuminating procedure intellectually but it can make a fine dramatic tale. The
man, enlarged by the event, will become the noble embodiment of the
Great Adventure if he has the dignity and stature to carry it off well.
Some men do this with themselves deliberately, as Patrick Pearse did in
1916. He rose to that height of great drama in which all personal character falls away, the dross of human nature burns into pure flame, and a sort
of poetic impersonality emerges. It is a rare thing and beloved by the
poets themselves for whom the gesture is in itself sufficiently eloquent; as
when Yeats became excited by a story he heard of how the O'Rahilly,
dying in the Insurrection, leaned upward from the pavement of Moore
Street to write his own R.I.P. in his own blood on a door.[21] There have
been many times in Mr. de Valera's life when he has finely performed this
role of the national hero, and the first part of this, as of every biography
of the man, thrives on this nobility which Ireland can always lend to its
children. So, when people say that he is a great man I would myself prefer
them to say that he is a great Irishman, a distinction with an immense
difference which annotates the common observation about his lack of art
in public living. For in this one thing, though in no other, he has a great
public gift. As a person I do not think his qualities could possibly be
called great, but he has always had the height of the great pedestal on
which he stands and the dignity to fit the position. Some, thinking that
his original pedestal is inscribed not "Eamon de Valera" but "The Irish
Republic" – as if he were standing for a sculptor not as an individual but
as a personification – will say that he has lost in stature since he stepped
down to a lesser pedestal whose title nobody has yet been able clearly to
decipher. He himself, as I have remarked, has tried to give it the honour
of a most honourable name, Eire. But somehow there is an ambiguity

21 Yeats memorialised Michael Joseph O'Rahilly (1875–1916), a founding
member of the Irish Volunteers, in "The O'Rahilly" (1938): "Sing of the O'Rahilly, /
Do not deny his right; / Sing a 'the' before his name; / Allow that he, despite /
All those learned historians, / Established it for good; / He wrote out that word
himself, / He christened himself with blood ... / They that found him found upon /
The door above his head / 'Here died the O'Rahilly. / R.I.P.' writ in blood."

about this, almost an evasion, certainly a character of controversy that makes the spectator more than uneasy about what the figure on top really represents. If in some generation yet to come the hope of the title is ever fulfilled, then the future biographers of Eamon de Valera, far from finding his story dwindle into an anti-climax, far from seeing – as we now more and more tend to see – his procrastinations of 1922 and his long pause since 1932 as aimless and weak, his Constitution a mere scrap of paper in so far as it is constantly being blown aside by the harsh winds of reality, and his ambiguities in relation to Great Britain irritating if not dishonourable, may see in all those demurrings and hesitations that we now take for indecision and irresolution the prescience and patience of a prophet.[22] That it may be so. That we may all eat our words with the worms. That in this, at any rate, he may be proved right even if it is too late for us to admit it. But it is a very long shot, and if one may say so in this context, into the dark and the dust. Nobody can now say whether Mr. de Valera has written the word EIRE on his coffin or his cenotaph.

To return to the present book this method of keeping to the story of the Great Adventure is vitiated by the fact that these hopes are in the future: in other words, once the Insurrection and the "Troubles" and the Treaty are disposed of the rest is not sufficiently exciting, either in a national or universal sense, to enlarge the man. Party-politics make poor drama.

The one other way of handling a biography, apart from analysis, apology, or what one may call epic description, is to consider the social significance of a man as a type. To the world and to us Mr. de Valera is at the moment the representative Irishman. In the natural foreign presumption he is a mirror. Native opinion will expect its leader to be a lighthouse, that is a guide, an example, almost a fashion. For although all periods are coerced into certain conditions by the evolution of political or economic necessity, public men and women do inside these compulsions create the metaphors of life. It is not merely that if King Edward VII wears a grey bowler the rest of the country may safely wear grey bowlers; or that because Queen Victoria delivered one of her children under an anæsthetic the more ignorant doctors had to stop quoting the Bible about bringing forth children in pain; or that when a Government bestowed a title on an osteopath the whole of the medical profession could thenceforth defy the stick-in-the-muds of the

22 O'Faolain refers here to the 1937 Constitution.

General Medical Council;[23] or that because Mr. de Valera occasionally attends a rugby-match the army is free to play any game it likes and the fanatics are powerless. In the largest ways public men serve as models for the whole nation. They can disseminate a general philosophy of living, popularise certain attitudes of mind, set standards and create values, apart altogether from what they can do for the lesser graces of living. (It has been, in passing, a great loss to the nation that our President's health has almost entirely prevented him from doing any of this: and one devoutly, and tremblingly, hopes that our next President will do it with intelligence and grace.) Mr. de Valera's biographer has not made any real effort to relate the man in this way to his times. He does quote him about a full human life for all, but it has to be admitted that Mr. de Valera's truly frugal notions as to what constitutes an ideal full human life are so lugubrious that they may have been too much even for Mr. MacManus who, one knows, is a writer with civilised ideas. The "milk or light beer for breakfast," the "frugal sufficiency for all," the Gaelic-nostalgia complex, not to mention how very tentative our present government has been about urban slums, Social Security, [and] Educational Reform, are not things to encourage the consideration of Mr. de Valera's desirable (?) images of life.[24]

This is probably the thing which more than anything else has gradually lost him the admiration if not the support of most forward-thinking persons. The trouble here, no doubt, goes back again to his lack of sophistication and a tendency to think along the simplest traditional lines. Having been reared in a labourer's cottage he has apparently made up his mind (quite illogically) that he represents the small farmer. This is just as silly as if a writer, because his father was a policeman, or he was reared in a lodging-house, should decide that he must take his ideas from the police-constables of the world or write novelettes for land-ladies. I can imagine no more stultifying and stunting standard of living or back-reference than the Irish small farmer. Whether asleep or to all appearances awake the small farmer follows an occupation which Shaw once rightly called "politically stupid and barely half-civilised," and if anybody, however much he

23 The General Medical Council, which controls admission to the profession of medicine, was established in Britain by the Medical Act of 1858. Osteopaths operated on the margins of the medical profession in Britain until the passage of the Osteopaths Act of 1993 established the General Osteopathic Council.
24 The parenthetical question mark is O'Faolain's.

may like the human qualities of the peasant, should take his political star-
dards from them he is committing intellectual hari-kiri.[25] On this somebody should try to tell Mr. de Valera that in taking the measure of every
statement two preliminary questions are essential. Is it a fact? If it is a fact,
so what? Ireland is mainly a farming country. True. Does it therefore follow that we must all accept the intellectual, political, and conservative
inanition of this most primitive of all human professions? There is abroad
here a notion that because a thing is simple it must therefore be a good
and holy thing, and should be preserved intact. Apart from a passing reference to the sanitation and cooking of the average Irish small farm I can
only say of this modern Irish urban sentimentality about the Land – especially about the Land if it is in the Gaeltacht, and especially if its admirers
are in no danger of being sent there to live – what somebody once said
about Chesterton's sentimental slushery about Merrie England, namely
that it is a form of "cockney idolatry." Russia is far more of a farming or
peasant country than Ireland, and if Lenin or Stalin had therefore decided
that they must "represent" the small farmer or take their notions from
him and his ways, I hate to think where Russia would be to-day – if anywhere.[26] The result of Mr. de Valera's unsophisticated and uncritical nos-
talgia for that land of North Cork and South Limerick is that when he
tries to form his ideal image of life he sees something so dismal that beside
it the Trappist rule of Mount Melleray is a Babylonian orgy.[27]

As a matter of history this is a very old story in the development of modern
politics. Several countries illustrate the tendency to "go back" to the land
for inspiration. Some of the nineteenth-century Russian revolutionaries
developed this same curious romantic complex of finding all the virtues

25 The quote comes from Shaw's book review of *The Evolution of Revolution*
(1920), by Henry Mayers Hyndman (1842–1921), "The Old Revolutionist and
the New Revolution," *Nation* 28 (19 February 1921): 703–5. Hyndman was an
influential British Marxist agitator and thinker and leader of the Social Democratic
Federation. The term hari-kiri, generally spelled either hara-kiri or hari-kari, is the
method of suicide by disembowelment practised by the Japanese samurai when
they are disgraced or sentenced to death.
26 Vladimir Ilich Ulyanov (1870–1924), better known as Lenin, led the Bolshevik
Revolution in 1917 and was the first head of the Soviet state.
27 Mount Melleray is an Abbey located in the mountains of County Waterford,
run by Cistercian, or Trappist, monks; they are known as Trappists because their
order was founded in La Trappe, France, in 1662. Babylon, a city from antiquity
located in present-day Iraq, was renowned for its splendour.

among the "people" in this narrow and restricted sense of the "peasant." Others gave it the slant of going down to the lower depths in the cities. Even in England one could find examples of it. William Morris is, perhaps, one example in his efforts to form the workers into new Socialist Societies instead of developing and studying the kinds of organisation they had gradually been creating for themselves, as the Webbs did.[28] I came across an interesting example the other day (students of social history will forgive me for saying I had never before heard of him) in a reference to a book called *The Record of an Adventurous Life* by Henry Mayers Hyndman in a review of the book by G.B.S. (See *Pen Portraits and Reviews*, 1931).[29] One very telling sentence there summed up the danger of this romantic fallacy that men of intelligence, like H.M. Hyndman or William Morris, or Mr. de Valera, can learn *from* the people, though they may work for them and believe in them. The sentence is – "He took up the democratic burden (as he regarded it) of working with men and women not of his generation, not of his class, not of his speed of mind and educational equipment." When people like the Webbs refused to do this Hyndman regarded them as snobs, and the result was indeed an "adventurous life," an heroic and generous life, but a fearful waste of energy and talent and much mental obfuscation. But men like Hyndman did want to lift these people up. When Mr. de Valera hitches his star to a Croom milk-wagon he takes the L.C.M. of Irish life as his band-wagon, and wants us all to crowd into it contentedly.[30] The difficulty of persuading him or his followers that they are making a terrible mistake in this is that it is all so plausible: "We are a farming country." "Our people are a simple people." That old romantic idea that simplicity is a virtue, might surely have been shaken by the sight of what happened to antique China and antique Turkey before Chiang Kai Chek, the Communists, and Kemal Ataturk.[31] Unfortunately a corollary

28 Sidney and Beatrice Webb (1859–1947 and 1858–1943, respectively) were leading English socialists and important early members of and pampleteers for the Fabian Society.

29 *The Record of an Adventurous Life* (1911). The review was "Hyndman," *Nation* 10 (21 October 1911): 135–6.

30 Croom is a village in County Limerick. L.C.M. is an acronym for the least common multiple. O'Faolain uses the image of a Croom milk-wagon to symbolise de Valera's rural ethos.

31 Chiang Kai Chek (1887–1975), also spelled Chiang Kai-shek, was head of the Nationalist government in China from 1928 to 1949; he did much to unify and modernise the country during his time in power. Kemal Atatürk (1881–1938), né Mustafa Kemal, was the first president of the Republic of Turkey; his massive reforms included Europeanising Turkish society.

of the adoration of the simple life seems to be – "We don't want the world
to swamp us" – meaning, "We prefer to stick in our own mud," or, "All this
but Heaven too!"

~

And yet when one has said all that, Mr. de Valera remains, and sits apparently firmly in the saddle. Is he the true realist and are his critics just beating the wind? If to be a shrewd politician is to be a realist he is one. If to
ask for more than one can reasonably expect to get is to be beating the
wind then we are beating the wind. But are we asking for more than he
might reasonably give us? There are two angles on that – his and ours.
His angle is the angle of the politician who says, "I cannot give you more
than the people will stand for." Ours is, "Do you know the words the
American wits put into Governor Dewey's mouth in 1944? 'I am the
leader. There are the people. I must follow them.'"[32] In defence of Mr. de
Valera (as politician) it must be said that it is true that the source of his
strength at the polls is the source of his weakness as a leader. He has won
the support, that is to say, (if I may use one of his own phrases) of a
"mixum-gatherum" that he can only hold together on their own terms.[33]
Examine the matter for a moment. His policy to-day is alarmingly the
same as that of the Opposition, who are the lineal descendants – mainly
the identical personnel (what is left of them) – of the first Free State
Government. The question therefore becomes – how did he manage to
snaffle their supporters throughout the country? And, what is as important, how does he manage to retain this support? Think who these essential voters were. Some of them had, originally, backed Arthur Griffith
because they were sick of war, some because they knew a good thing
when they saw it, some (perhaps the majority) because they had never –
and were in this quite honest – wanted more than what one may call
industrial autonomy, and had made sacrifices and risked their lives for
this solid thing; some backed Griffith because they disliked him less than
de Valera; and some without much interest in Ireland's aspirations chose,
as they considered, the better or safer man. The present younger generation knows little about Griffith, I suspect, but if they could be bothered to

---

32 Thomas E. Dewey (1902–1971) was a three-term governor of New York,
from 1943 to 1955. He lost the presidential elections in 1944 and 1948 as the
Republican candidate.
33 A mixum-gatherum is a hodge-podge of people from varied backgrounds
and beliefs.

go back to his pamphlets and papers they would find his programme very mild politically; he was satisfied for far the greater part of his life, and so far as I can see to the end, with his idea of the Constitution of 1782, "the King, Lords, and Commons of Ireland" within the golden circle of the crown; and he wanted a national Ireland in the sense that it would be self-sufficient economically and racy of the soil. He was in no sense a republican, and, if anything, he was reactionary towards Labour. The people who in 1922 threw their weight of influence behind him, and their money into the party-chest, were therefore an extraordinary amalgam of hard-headed idealists (if such a term is possible), members of the Irish Republican Brotherhood, businessmen, all the former Unionists, self-seeking gombeen-men, the two Churches almost to a man and certainly to a bishop, most of the former Irish Party following, and, I venture, only a scattering of the more intense nationalists who sadly yielded against conviction to *force majeure*.[34] Of this odd grouping a deciding balance-of-power bulk fell slowly away from Mr. Cosgrave. They had, presumably, as many reasons as their components. But they surely did not swing over to Mr. de Valera for his Republican past, or on nationalist grounds, or because he would settle the Anglo-Irish question once for all? For if these were their reasons they could hardly, on his record since 1932, continue to support him, since his policy now, so far as anybody can see, is in no radical way different from that of General Mulcahy – with the one exception that the General is more clearcut and honest about those relations with Great Britain that Mr. de Valera will neither boldly break nor frankly foster.[35] One thing, however, must be said in justice to Fianna Fáil and Mr. de Valera: if the Opposition is now level with them on every count they have taught the Opposition a good deal and in social reforms they were far ahead of the Opposition when they took office. The attitude of Mr. Cosgrave's government towards the unemployed was shockingly cynical – he did not even register them; in Land Division he was slow; he was beaten to a frazzle in Rural Housing by Fianna Fáil. But nobody could yet dare to say (the abnormal circumstances of the War apart) that Mr. de Valera's agrarian policy is yet proven, and whatever about the

34 A gombeen man is a shopkeeper or a usurer in Ireland; this pejorative term is also used to refer to the bourgeoisie more generally. *Force majeure*, from the French, refers to an overwhelming force or power.
35 Richard James Mulcahy (1886–1971) was the chief of staff of the IRA during the Anglo-Irish War, a Fine Gael leader (1944–1959), and a TD for most of the forty years after Irish independence.

theory of his industrialist policy the outstanding effect of his manner of handling it was an enormous rise in prices.[36] What is certain about that change-over is that the Economic Depression of 1929 hit Mr. Cosgrave hard, and that Mr. de Valera's guarantees of tariff-barriers to the new industrialists won him support in every town and city, and kept on winning him more and more support as people began to respond to the propaganda of his most efficient party-machine about factories, here, there, and everywhere – a picture never adequately realised, whether because his government got cold feet as they saw the first snags appear, or whether because the idea was not driven forward hard enough, or whether the theory was leaky, or whether it was complicated by his unfortunate handling of Anglo-Irish relations nobody now seems able to tell. As for the poor and the unemployed we all know what has happened to the latter; the poor he has kept afloat by every kind of State charity; he has no constructive policy for either. Whatever be the full picture therefore, to imagine that he is, to-day, the great leader of an enthusiastic Irish Nationalism would be to chase a *chimaera bombinans*.[37] On the contrary, odd as it may seem to an outsider, he is held in power by the conservative middle-part of the community; and that basic fact accounts for his handy-cum-dandy leg-in-both-camps attitude to almost every question. In fact, since he must realise his ambiguous position quite well it is much to his credit that he goes even as far as he does with what he has salvaged from his early idealisms, such as the Gaelic Revival in which that middle-part has no real interest. The war has been, politically speaking, a godsend to him. It has transmogrified Ireland's Stormy Petrel into her Guardian Angel, and as the one rides and foretells the storm and the other protects us from it the change has not been too obvious.[38] Really all that was needed was a sartorial change of a kind to cause him the least inconvenience – a mere change of wings. But, badinage aside, it will be seen that his idea of what it is unreasonable to ask of him, and our idea what it is reasonable to ask of him, are not two different things: they are two different angles. He now considers, has to consider, everything from the restricted angle of the politician. We ask him for leadership.

36 The idiomatic phrase "whatever about the theory" should be read as "whatever one might think about the theory."

37 A *chimaera bombinans*, or a chimera, is a Greek mythological monster that has a fire-breathing lion's head, a goat's body, and a serpent's tail.

38 A stormy petrel is a small seabird, but it is also a person whose presence foretells trouble.

~

What is going to happen in this impasse? What the Marxists call the "historic moment" may decide that, some arrangement of circumstances that will shatter the frozen pool. But this is vital – since 1935, or 1936, a whole generation of twenty-one-year-olds, who have no experience of any other Ireland, indeed any other world, any other life but this one, have been voting. They have been moulded by our present system of education, whose effects are certainly not to inculcate a sense of proportion *vis-à-vis* the world abroad, or even to give young people any sane idea of the world or of history. Nobody can prophesy about their tendencies on the basis of the past, as one might about their elders. If the Church and Mr. de Valera (who have now long become reconciled apparently on the basis of the Simple Life, Isolationism, not being too keen to get the Orangemen in, Puritanism, the Gaelic Revival so long as it does not interfere with religious teaching, and so on) can hold all these young people to the de Valera notions of what a "good" Irishman is, then the picture of to-day is the picture for ever, and there may be no "historic moment" to shatter the ice that binds the Children of Lir.[39] But can Youth be gagged? Will the thousands who have gone abroad return as unaware of life as they were when they went away? Will their humble toil mock at our gombeen-men's ambition? That is the thing we all wait to know.

~

To conclude, nothing here said about Mr. de Valera is said in any spirit of party-politics. Probably as many readers of THE BELL vote for Mr. de Valera from conviction, or because there is nobody better to vote for, as do not vote for him. But we cannot be expected to be as enthusiastic as Mr. M.J. MacManus is about Mr. de Valera, because there is at least one kind of politics about which we can be explicit – we are not conservative middle-part men. And so, we are constantly aware that thousands of our people have to be sent abroad to work, that thousands of them are probably lost to us for ever, that our slum problem is hardly being touched, that if the poor were not kept alive by doles of every kind many of them

39 An Orangeman is a member of the Orange Order, an Irish Protestant political society founded in 1795 and named after William of Orange, King William III of England, Scotland, and Ireland (1650–1702). The children of the sea god Lir loved their father immensely; jealous of those bonds of love, their step-mother turned them into swans. Eileen O'Faolain (1900–1988), Sean's wife, published a version of the story of Lir's children in her book *Irish Sagas and Folktales* (1954).

would simply starve to death, that it is only in the thirteenth year of office that the present Government introduces legislation to deal with tuberculosis, that our educational system is antediluvian, that we are in many respects a despotism disguised as a democracy, that the dismemberment of our country has been allowed to become a frozen problem, that our relations with Great Britain are as ambiguously unsatisfactory as ever they were. We know that Mr. de Valera has deserved well of his fellow-countrymen. But just for that reason nobody knows better than he that a country is a hard taskmaster. To finish on the mildest note possible I would merely suggest to his biographer that in future editions he might at least give some slight hint of the *real* state of affairs by quoting from a well-known American, if not so well-known as Abraham Lincoln – the late President Eliot of Harvard: "Things seem to be going fairly well here now that a spirit of pessimism prevails in all departments."

It is, after all, the duty of a biographer to wink at least once in the direction of his audience.

Romance and Realism[1]

"Romantic Ireland's dead and gone, it's with O'Leary in the grave." So wrote Yeats in "September 1913" thinking of his old friend, John O'Leary, that picturesque and dignified link between the Irish Republican Brotherhood of the 19th Century and Sinn Féin of the 20th.[2] When he wrote the line Yeats felt the matter-of-fact hardness of the 20th century closing in on an Ireland which to him was a folk-world full of colour and mystery, ancient memories and ancient ways. As to politics, which to him meant only heroism, Paudeen with his greasy till, adding "the halfpence to the pence and prayer to shivering prayer," seemed to have obliterated every unselfish ideal.

Within three years the Rebellion came to prove that the old fires had merely been smoored, and in September 1916 Yeats, as the voice of Ireland, acclaimed it:

> Now and in time to be,
> Wherever green is worn,
> Are changed, changed utterly:
> A terrible beauty is born.[3]

He lived to see the fires either smoored again or wholly smothered by the dust and destruction of Civil War, in which he took the side not of

1 "Romance and Realism" appeared in *The Bell* 10, no. 5 (August 1945): 373–82.
2 John O'Leary (1830–1907).
3 To smoor is to smother. Yeats's famous poem "Easter 1916" was written in September of that year.

Romantic Ireland but of a hardheaded and calculating Ireland whose future he could not foresee. He became one of our first senators, and has left on record his own growing uneasiness among the bankers and the businessmen. He found himself very soon in a minority on such questions as Censorship and Divorce, discovered that he was an old Liberal and that the new Conservatives were in a majority, and gradually he began to hate the Ireland they were making.

His later development is fascinating. We get a good insight into his mind in his last pamphlets, such as *On the Boiler*, and in his letters to Dorothy Wellesley; those from about the Summer of 1936 onward especially.[4] We see him flare up whenever his rage or his old passions seized him, as when he defended Roger Casement's memory or when he finally became so disgusted with all post-1922 politics as to write that splendid poem "The Statues" in which he calls Ireland back to the world of symbol and imagination. It was there that he wrote:

When Pearse summoned Cuchulain to his side
What stalked through the Post Office?

Meaning that we Irish,

born into that ancient sect
But thrown upon this filthy modern tide
And by its formless, spawning fury wrecked,[5]

must climb again into "our proper dark" of passion and the imagination as the boys and girls of Greece may have climbed by night to kiss some statue of Phidias that gave shape to their dreams.[6]

He there returned to his own youth. For he always delighted in violent or heroic gesture that lifted men out of the rut of character into the fiery element he called personality, and never had much patience for the muck and ruck and pedestrian toil of everyday political endeavour. In that he showed himself a natural poetic type – though, also, a rather dangerous and not unfamiliar type of this era of ours which in growing weary of the slow machinery of democracy has been tempted to turn now to this now

4 *On the Boiler* (1938). Yeats's letters to the poet Dorothy Wellesley (1889–1956) are collected in *Letters on Poetry: From W.B. Yeats to Dorothy Wellesley* (1940).
5 From "The Statues" (1939).
6 Phidias (c. 490–430 BCE) was an important Athenian sculptor.

to that violent and spectacular avatar. It was one of Yeats' minor follies
to have written some fine marching songs for General O'Duffy.[7]
  Not that he ever sold himself to any narrow party-line – he was too
human and intelligent and civilised behind the poetic flare. His end,
rather, was that of the despairing Liberal surrounded by fountains of
ideas which when analysed proved to be no more than the glitterings of
brackish water. In his last years he flails both Left and Right with equal
fury. He writes a cursing ballad on Cromwell whom he called the multiple Lenin of his day – the great leveller. He writes of O'Duffy's Blue Shirt
movement – "A movement called The Christian Front is gathering all the
bigots together."[8] Or – "A woman to whom I had sent the Casement
poem writes approving of what she supposes to be my hatred of England.
It has shocked me … I have written to my correspondent. 'How can I hate
England owing what I do to Shakespeare, Blake and Morris. England is
the only country I cannot hate.'"[9] When *The Daily Worker* attacked his
friend's poem he raged:

One reason that these propagandists hate us is that we have ease and
power … You say we must love, yes but love is not pity. It does not
desire to change its object. It is a form of the eternal contemplation
of what is. When I take a woman in my arms I do not want to
change her. If I saw her in rags I would get her better clothes that
I might resume my contemplation. But these Communists put their
heads in the rags and smother.[10]

His attitude to Ireland is that in his Casement ballads he is not fighting
for any country.[11]

I am fighting in those ballads for what I have been fighting all my
life, it is our Irish fight though it has nothing to do with this or that

7 "Three Marching Songs" (1935).
8 Letter from Yeats to Wellesley, 9 December 1939, in *Letters on Poetry*, 121.
9 Letter from Yeats to Wellesley, 10 December 1936, in *Letters on Poetry*, 122.
O'Faolain omits a word from the opening phrase that indicates the woman's
country. Yeats specifies that she is an "Irishwoman" and not simply a "woman."
10 Letter from Yeats to Wellesley, 23 December 1936, in *Letters on Poetry*, 126.
The *Daily Worker* was a communist British newspaper founded in 1930; since
1966 it has been published under the name the *Morning Star*.
11 "Roger Casement" and "The Ghost of Roger Casement" (1938).

country. Bernard Shaw fights with the same object. When somebody
talks of justice, who knows that justice is accompanied by secret
forgery; when an archbishop wants a man to go to the communion
table, when that man says he is not spiritually fit, then we Irish
remember our age-old quarrel against gold-braid and ermine and
that our ancestor Swift has gone where fierce indignation can lacer-
ate his heart no more, and we go stark, staring mad ... I am an old
man now and month by month my capacity and energy must slip
away so what is the use of saying that in both England and Ireland
I want to stiffen the backbone of the high hearted and high minded
and the sweet hearted and sweet minded so that they may no longer
shrink and hedge when they face rag-merchants like ――― . It is not
our business to reply to this or that but to set up our love and indignation against their pity and hate.[12]

He sums up this politics in three verses, totalling eleven lines of which
the first four say it all:

Hurrah for revolution! Let the cannon shoot,
The beggar upon horseback lashes the beggar upon foot.
Hurrah for revolution! Cannon once again.
The beggars have changed places but the lash goes on.[13]

Or when he says that in England the educated classes are politics-mad
but that the mass of the people have free-minds; whereas in Ireland the
educated classes have free-minds and the masses are politics-mad. But
what politics! Nobody here seems to care, for instance, which side wins
in Spain or anywhere else, and even as to Irish politics (he presumably
means what we mean by the word, i.e., ideas not personalities) "there is
complete indifference."
    All this – I agree that I have selected, but I can only say that I have not
been trying to prove anything – makes a fairly clear picture of an aristocratic intellectual poet, revolted by the end of the last phase – perhaps the
dying kick – of Romantic Ireland, cursing all parties, still a nationalist in
the only sense which can have any meaning for an Irish writer, i.e., one

12 Letter from Yeats to Wellesley, 10 December 1936, in *Letters on Poetry*, 126–7.
Some phrasing is not exactly transcribed, but O'Faolain also excludes the second
last line, following the deleted word: "Indeed before all I want to strengthen myself."
13 "The Great Day." See note 13 of the essay "The Pleasures and Pains of Ireland."

who thinks world and describes Irish, saved from Fascism by his natural humanity and liberality of mind, fearing if not actually despising the masses, full of that undefined arrogance which rounds off all in his famous testimony to Irish writers who, he says, must sing whatever is well-made, scorn the shapeless sort now growing up, sing the peasantry, country gentlemen, the holiness of monks, porter-drinkers' randy laughter, and all our lords and ladies who were beaten into the clay for seven centuries; concluding:

> Cast your mind on other days.
> That we in coming days may be
> Still the indomitable Irishry.[14]

The romantic picture is clear; it is not simple – which is right and proper, since only *simpliste* minds and doctrinaire minds such as Party Men possess think that life or thought can be railroaded. But on one point he is both simple and clear. Romantic Ireland *had* died – for him.

As I wandered, delightedly, through his brother's Exhibition in June and July at the National College of Art – forty or fifty years of wonderful painting – I could not help thinking, excitedly, "Dear God, was W.B. wrong after all? Can it be that this is Romantic Ireland, all of a piece, *still* living?"[15] And for days I went around, bothered and excited, wondering if it really has died or, if it is, yet again, only smoored over? Two things sustained a persistent doubt – that no other painter, writer, or poet but this one only still sees and presents it; and the curious fact that the farther on in time one goes from the 90s and the 1900s – from those early, direct paintings of tinkers and porter-drinkers and horsecopers and gypsies and peasants and sailors, the farther back one has to stand from these pictures, until at the very latest paintings of all one must stand anything up to twenty yards away, and then drop the curtains of the lashes to focus – even at that as in a glass darkly – what has evidently of late been seen by the painter only in a form of visionary longsightedness, as of a man on a mountain-top seeing – or is it remembering? – beauty at the world's rim.[16]

---

14 *O'Faolain's note:* I take it that "cast" here means to cast, as the sculptor does, i.e., model, not cast back or think. [*Editor's note:* The lines are from "Under Ben Bulben" (1939).]
15 The National College of Art and Design, as it has been called since 1971, has existed in one form or another since 1746.
16 A tinker is an itinerant craftsman; a horsecoper is a horse dealer.

But, then, one may say, all romance is a *princesse lointaine*?[17] The far-off hills are greenest. Did W.B. ever look at life close-up? Should one ever? In twilight, in memory, in age, and in exile, Ireland is at her loveliest and most indubitable. I can still think, for example, in a mood of the most nostalgic longing, how lovely my native Cork could be on one of those unsummery summer mornings of childhood, which are all the summer we ever seem to get in this tender, grey island; when the light is sifted and diffused by unbroken flocks of clouds whose shadows are so delicately moulded that one has to gaze at them for a long time before one can observe their stealthy creeping; when every little roof is so placid in this sunless clarity that we feel hardly more awake than what we see, for those grey walls do not then show a spot of colour, and only in the memory does one know that even the hills are green – to the eye they are confused and purple as if by an injection of dark blood under the line – and all so calm and restful that one lonely cockcrow will not disturb the hooded dawn. But I know how kind our memory is, and that one does not live on monochrome and scenery, and that Cork and all such small towns have in them a life that is far from romance and prettiness.

If Jack Yeats has made this ophthalmic adjustment, and if W.B. never really was so foolish as to look things between the eyes (until the Revolution grimaced at him) have the realistic novelists of our time been wise in their insistence on ruthless close-ups? Or can one ever push back life so far that it looks pretty if it is not? There is a point beyond which one cannot retreat, a point described as having one's back to the wall. There is a point at which old values and interpretations have to be discarded, a point at which you simply throw away all your lenses and adjusting gadgets and realise that the animal has been transmogrified. In simple words it may be that no romantic world now exists – not merely in Ireland but anywhere on the face of the globe.

True – the old elements are all still there. There are still tinkers and horsecopers and sailors and porter-drinkers: but we all know that life is largely a matter of what a dramatist might call a balance of characters, and that when a new balance of the characters takes place it is no longer the old play.

I think back, for example, to the days when our generation first discovered this Romantic Ireland in the Western Gaeltacht. I think of the Festival or Pattern which is still held every Autumn in that little coom or closed valley of which Callanan wrote the wonderful poem beginning:

17 A *princesse lointaine* is an unobtainable woman of one's desires.

There is a green island in lone Gougane Barra
Where Allua of songs rushes forth as an arrow
In deep-valleyed Desmond – a thousand wild fountains
Come down to that lake from their home in the mountains.[18]

I recall the faintly blue autumn air, tinged with melancholy, studded along the roads at dusk by tinkers' fires; the smell of turfsmoke and of myrtle; the clear tinkle of the mountain streams; the linch-pin that rattles in a cart making for that hidden lake which becomes at sunset a bowl of lead in a mountain-glen; the bleating of lost sheep, like kittens in a lonely house; the long white winding roads; the huddle of porter-drinkers by the lighted inn at the lake's edge; the white cottages huddled under the scarps of the mountains; the white streaks of floodwater falling down the cliffs almost perpendicularly, silent by day, heard by night ... It was a dramatic background to the life of our West Cork cottiers who were all that Yeats would have wished the "folk" to be. It was like the wild, lovely, traditional Russian festival that Chekov describes so beautifully in his story "Easter Eve."[19]

By the time these lines appear I will have been down there to those mountains and back again. But it will not be the same. And will it ever be the same again? Certainly not, for our time. The balance of characters has altered too much.

To think of only one – our old friend Tailor Buckley – he is now under the green sods of that little graveyard by the lake. He was never a romantic figure, not to me or to anybody. My own first contact with him was unfriendly; the local people said he was a "Stater" (meaning that he thought us Republicans a lot of fools or playboys). I do not know whether what they said of him was true or not; my guess is that his ironical and realistic mind – a much more realistic mind than any of us had – could no more have refrained from sharp comment on our cock-eyed "civil war" than a Shaw could. One saw, too, as well as the next man that he was a bit of a show-box; as if, Heaven help us, every Irishman isn't. There was nothing romantic or Celtic about his cottage; a bare, bald, unattractive labourer's cottage. Above all he was a satirist and satire and romance are not bedfellows. So we were under no illusions about him.

But the old man was *alive*, he was real, he was vital, he was traditional, and as Frank O'Connor said of him in a recent tribute he was above all

18 From the opening stanza of the poem "Gougane Barra" (1825–26), by J.J. Callanan (1795–1829).
19 "On Easter Eve" (1886).

else a gentleman – one of Yeats' natural lords who had been beaten over
the centuries into our Irish clay; and his talk was the best of that sort of
talk you might have heard any night in any Gaelic glen – that natural, gay,
human blether which is a form of folk-art, that rollicks along with a
healthy earthy bawdiness such as must be familiar to everybody in Ireland
who has ever sat by a labourer's cottage fire.[20]

Well ... we know what happened to him. Our respectable citizens from
Foxrock and Ballsbridge, who were never intended to be characters in
that play – least of all leading characters; they have been the butts of
Gaelic humour from time immemorial – given the power and given the
blessing of our new Gaelic Revivalists, took the transcript of this old
man's fireside gabble, the gabble of the Gaelic hearth since the days of
Bricriu or Conan Maol and with their refined fingers wrote across it – "in
its general tendency indecent."[21] Later, the priests made the old man
take up his own copy of his own fireside talk and throw it behind the fire.

When that happened those other intrusive characters of the modern
Irish comedy, the "Gaels," never said one word in his defence. But other
equally intrusive characters said many words. It will suffice to recall only
one of these connoisseurs to the rostrum, a Senator named Kehoe, who
assured us that he had been reading various works for the last thirty
years, "discriminately and indiscriminately," and that he had never read
a finer collection of what he was pleased to call "smut" than this Tailor's
fireside chatter. "And," added the erudite gentleman, "I have read all the
authors from Rabelais down." It was the same Kehoe who cried contra
mundum: "Authors of repute! From what point of view? From the point
of view of world standards – which, mark you, are not the standards of
Ireland."[22] He suffices because had romantic Yeats been then alive he
might have had this man as a fellow-senator.

No! Romantic Ireland was a royal play and the clowns have taken it over
and destroyed it. To be sure they, too, were always there, for Senator Kehoe

20 Blether is noisy, unfocused talk.
21 Foxrock and Ballsbridge are fashionable neighbourhoods in south Dublin.
Bricriu is a trickster figure and Conan Maol is a great warrior in Irish myth. The
phrase "in its general tendency indecent" is used to justify bannings under the
Censorship of Publications Act. O'Faolain refers here to the banning of The Tailor
and Ansty and its aftermath, in particular the treatment of the Tailor at the hands
of the Censorship of Publications Board and, later, by a few priests, who forced
him to burn his copy of the book in his own hearth.
22 The phrase contra mundum means, literally, against the world; it is used to
describe someone or something that defies or opposes everyone.

and his likes are no worse than the idiot who asked thirty-five years ago, "Have you seen this awful play of Lady Gregory's *The Cowboy of the Western World?*" or the woman who said of a famous line in the same play "the word omitted but understood was one she would blush to use even when she was alone."[23] Nor is there any reason why we could not hear to-day what *The National Hibernian* wrote then – we hear far worse: "Brothers and Sisters everywhere, place a little history of Ireland in the hands of each little boy and girl of the ancient race and all the Lady Gregories of the world will not be able to destroy an atom of our splendid heritage."[24]

What has happened is equally obvious, simple and horrible. Romantic Ireland has given way to Sentimental Ireland. Yeats adored the talk of Biddy Early but he would never have been such an ass as to make a hero-ine of her, any more than you or I would be such an ass as to make a hero of Tailor Buckley.[25] To him Biddy Early was but a part of a vast and elaborate complex of ideas – the depersonalising power of the folk imagination, hatred of realism, love of personality, "the red rose-bor-dered hem," Unity of Culture, Unity of Being, woven with a score of other ideas into an aesthetic theory whose only test is the excellence of what he got out of it.[26] Our intrusive characters have certainly not made a hero of Tailor Buckley: on the contrary, they have denied that he ever existed – saying, for instance, that such talk as his never goes on in our western cottages; what they have done is to sentimentalise him into a coloured postcard, which is, of course, the form of evasion practised by every nation when the national will becomes so weak that it wants to avoid every human complication and evade every human challenge. It is a thou-sand miles removed from Yeats' lifelong search for that image or symbol by which nations, races and men are brought to face the greatest obstacle that can be contemplated without despair – an obstacle that in rousing the will to the fullest intensity unifies them at a blow.

When the will of Ireland becomes intense again Romantic Ireland will return. When the will of the world, now barely hanging on by its finger-nails, becomes intense again romance will warm life all over the globe. For romance is not made of pretty things. As a movement, it began in France out of dissatisfaction and despair; it was heralded in England by a poet who wanted to speak the language of simple men and describe the

---

23 This line is purported to have been said by the Abbey's charwoman.
24 *The National Hibernian* is the monthly magazine of the Ancient Order of Hibernians, an Irish fraternal organisation founded in New York City in 1836.
25 Biddy Early (c. 1798–1874) was a traditional Irish healer.
26 The quote is from "To Ireland in the Coming Times" (1893).

most common and actual things; romance comes out of blood and toil and tears and sweat,

> A mound of refuse or the sweepings of a street,
> Old kettles, old bottles, and a broken can,
> Old iron, old bones, old rags, that raving slut
> Who keeps the till ...[27]

Yeats created his lovely play *The Countess Cathleen* out of his puzzlement at a woman whose soul was being destroyed by fanaticism and hate. Baudelaire's flowers were made of evil. Villon's songs were made of rags. Chocolate-box colleens are made for money. The Sentimental Ireland is made of pound notes. The essence of both is pretence and escapism: Cathleen ni Houlihan as a pin-up girl; though the Gaelic poet, Geoffrey Keating, had a better name for her.[28] If we wish Romantic Ireland to come again, it will only come not by closing our eyes but by opening them, indeed only by following the advice of Yeats' epitaph, cut on the limestone flag over his empty grave under Ben Bulben:

> Cast a cold eye
> On life, on death.
> Horseman, pass by![29]

The hard and realist literature of our time is performing its own rôle. It keeps us looking both life and death coldly in the face until, some day, the Jacob's ladder of our vision will rise again out of this Irish clay and lift us to where we were in the days when we were not afraid to shudder at our dreams.[30]

---

27 From Yeats's "The Circus Animals' Desertion" (1939).

28 Geoffrey Keating (c. 1580–c. 1644), né Seathrún Céitinn, was an Irish priest, poet, and historian.

29 This is the final stanza of "Under Ben Bulben"; it became the epitaph on Yeats's gravestone. Yeats died in France. At the time that this essay was written, he was still buried there, but in 1948 his body was disinterred and taken back to his native Sligo, where it was laid to rest in Drumcliffe, the town that lies beneath Ben Bulben Mountain.

30 In the biblical tale, Jacob dreams that he sees a ladder lined with angels that ascends from the earth to Heaven, from which God reassures him of his future.

One World: An Irish Council[1]

Ten years ago in Britain a number of public-spirited citizens inaugurated a very characteristic British institution known as The British Council.[2] Its general aim was the diffusion of knowledge about British life and British achievements, mainly in the sciences and the arts. It was a typically elastic and typically independent body, so that even when it became evident that it was too valuable an institution not to be fostered by public money – after it extended its activities to the Empire its expenditure came under the head of the Colonial Office estimates – it still retained its autonomy, remains a wholly self-governing body, and its only definite link with the British Foreign Office to-day is in the appointment of its chairman.[3]

Its activities have been most extensive. It publishes its own pamphlets; over two million copies of *British Life and Thought* and *Britain Advances* have been circulated in twelve languages during the war. It issues its own monthly publications, *Britain To-day*, *Monthly Science News* and the *British Medical Bulletin*.[4] It sends out documentary films. It has established libraries of music in scores of countries. It has organised exhibitions of paintings, drawings, sculpture. It has arranged visits to other lands of

1 "One World: An Irish Council" appeared in *The Bell* 11, no. 1 (October 1945): 557–64.

2 The British Council was founded in 1934; it is still active in over 100 countries.

3 The Colonial Office was created in 1801. It was originally directed under the auspices of the Home Office and the Board of Trade, but by the mid-nineteenth century it became its own governing body.

4 *British Life and Thought* (1940); *Britain Advances* (1943–46); *Britain To-day* (1939–54); *Monthly Science News* (1941–47); *British Medical Bulletin* (founded in 1943 and still publishing four issues per annum).

theatrical companies like the Vic-Wells theatre and ballet.[5] It has established British Institutes in many countries – there are thirty-four such at present in Europe and in the near and middle East. It has arranged reciprocal exhibitions from other countries in Britain. It has, during the war, met the problem of "mutual understanding" by opening a score of houses, offices and centres to welcome members of temporarily exiled European, Commonwealth, and American forces. One of the most interesting of these bodies, for example, is the so-called Lawyers' *Foyer* in Lincoln's Inn which has about 500 overseas members.[6] Hundreds of students from abroad have been given scholarships and grants to study in Britain – students from Turkey, students from the East, students from Africa, students from all over the world.

There are, in short, few ways of diffusing interest and knowledge about British ways that the British Council has not adopted and few countries where it is not represented: it has taken over the Carnegie Library in Trinidad and from that base developed a sort of county-library scheme for all the islands of the neighbouring group, set up a Children's Library in Jamaica, is planning a central library for the whole of British West Africa, has five institutes in Cyprus, one with over two thousand members, a concert room in Lagos, English classes for Arab women in Aden, and so forth, almost *ad infinitum* and *in extremis orbis terrarum*.[7] In short this Council covers the whole cultural field – books, pictures, the drama, study, photography, music, films, sculpture, folklore, the sciences. Obviously a most valuable, practical and patriotic body.

I am not here proposing that we should avail ourselves more of this admirable institution, though there is no earthly reason why we should not do so if we wish to. And, indeed, to harp on the old string, as long as

5 The Vic-Wells Ballet was established in 1926 as the Academy of Choreographic Art but changed its name in 1931 to reflect the two theatres in which it began: the Old Vic and Sadler's Wells. The school, having received a Royal Charter in 1956, is now known as the Royal Ballet School.

6 Lincoln's Inn is one of the four institutions that admit people to practise law in Britain, the other three being the Inner Temple, the Middle Temple, and Gray's Inn; all are located in London.

7 Scottish-American industrialist and philanthropist Andrew Carnegie (1835–1919) created over 2,500 free public libraries around the world. Lagos is the chief port and, until 1975, was the capital city of Nigeria. Aden is a city in Yemen. The Latin phrases *ad infinitum* and *in extremis orbis terrarum* mean, respectively, "to infinity" or "endlessly forever," and "to the furthest reaches of the globe."

we remain a member of the British Commonwealth of Nations we are foolish not to take the overt as well as covert advantages of our position, and it would be more honest and honourable to do the one since we make no bones about doing the other. Some of us do. We have, here, never hesitated to avail ourselves of every such kind of institution, whatever the country of its origin. About two years ago when the editor was in London and saw the wonderful Yugo-Slav Exhibition of paintings, sculpture, and folk-art, he made every effort to have it sent to Dublin and would have succeeded if our Government had not been too timid to co-operate. Some years ago, again, the Dublin Gate Theatre Productions were able to arrange visits to Greece, Roumania, Yugo-Slavia, Bulgaria, through the medium of the British Council – which was very useful publicity for the Irish Theatre. I am not certain whether some films have not been shewn here through the medium of the same body. The main point of this article, however, is that we possess no such organisation of our own and that without it the diffusion of knowledge about Ireland, its institutions, ways of life and culture, is left to the comparatively rare and wholly accidental activities of a few individuals: while, on the other hand, the diffusion of knowledge here about the achievements of other countries – excepting Britain and America – is even more occasional, inadequate and accidental. All we have abroad are a few legations, poorly financed, understaffed, and overburdened with administrative work of a consular and industrial nature. The handicaps under which Ireland labours as a consequence are too obvious to need elaboration.

What lies behind our failure to do this kind of essential work? To answer this one has to do what one has to do with almost every Irish problem – draw back from the immediate question and watch it fall into position in the whole scheme and history of modern Ireland. Two things converge upon it. The first is our comparatively recent isolationism, accentuated if not caused by the romantic chauvinism of the insurrectionary movement of our time. And here, before going any farther, we should make an important distinction. Romantic nationalism here, of the 19th and early 20th century, was a great and invigorating force, for resistance, for unity. As such we must never belittle it. But that stage is now over and done with it. It corresponds to the great revolutionary period in France, say 1789 to 1802 or so: followed by a period of hard work and re-organisation – and ruined, as History shews, because Napoleon preferred romantic glory to political and social achievement. The original Chauvin was, in fact, one of Napoleon's veterans – a sergeant of the line, proud bearer of more than twenty wounds, who on his deathbed commanded that his shroud be dyed in the revolutionary colours, red, white and blue, and that the ropes for lowering his coffin be woven from strands similarly coloured – whose blind hero-worship and jingoism have given a word to two languages.[8]

One symbol of our chauvinism, which has been almost wholly narrowing and limiting if not negative, if not indeed positively destructive, is not the Gaelic Revival in itself (the ideal there is natural and invigorating) but the manner in which it has been handled and the narrow interpretation which has been given to it. In brief this interpretation has been unmodern and unEuropean. It was not always so. Last month we celebrated the centenary of Thomas Davis and the Young Ireland movement which might be said to begin the revival of popular interest in Gaelic. Davis was no antiquary and he was no isolationist: on the contrary, his most famous Address, that to his fellow-students in Dublin University in 1840, roundly condemned a too-concentrated study of the past (of any country) and pleaded simultaneously for a modern outlook of the widest scope. Note his words, first the modern emphasis and secondly the European:

Men cannot master all knowledge. If you believe this, conclude with me that a knowledge of his own nature and duties, of the circumstances, growth and prospects of that society in which he dwells, and of the pursuits and tastes of those around him, accompanied, too, by the running comment of experience, is what every man should first learn. If he does learn this he has learned enough for life and goodness; and if he finds this not enough, he is prepared in the only feasible way to profit by studying the works and thoughts of ancient Italy, or Greece, or modern France, or modern Italy, or Germany. If the student take more interest in the history and feel more admiration for the literature, or even derive more profit from the contemplation of those moderns than of these ancients, let us not condemn his taste or doubt his wisdom ... And still more strongly should we oppose the cultivation of any, or all of these to the neglect of English and, perhaps I should add, Irish literature.[9]

8 Nicolas Chauvin; his dates are not verifiable, and there is some conjecture that he did not even exist, but a number of sources claim that he was born in 1780.
9 From *An Address Read Before the History Society, Dublin, on the 26th of June, 1840* (Dublin: Webb and Chapman, 1840), 18–19.

From a man who so passionately and frequently drew us back to the inspiration of our own past this sanity of balance is an impressive contrast with the Little Irelandism of our day which seems to interpret nationality mainly as a bulwark against the challenges of the contemporary world, a desire to live for ever in the past.

From that mentality it is difficult to expect any enthusiasm for the idea of an Irish Council disinterestedly interested in bringing in to us the world outside. It is only right, however, especially for the benefit of any non-Irish readers who may come on these pages, to say that this isolationist attitude is, though tragic, historically understandable. Because our main contact with the wide world has for long been through Britain, whose influence has naturally been tremendously powerful and proportionately feared. The three essential elements of Irish life which every visitor must never fail to note are that we are an English-speaking country; of different race to every other member of the British Commonwealth; and are preponderately Catholic; with the inevitable result that in all our relations with other English-speaking countries there are special factors of tension. That we do not cope with these tensions is, admittedly, our own fault.

The second reason why we have been so shamefully backward both in spreading our own culture abroad and in bringing the culture of other lands to Ireland lies in the social tensions of Irish life and history. Of defined groups in Ireland the most cultivated (leaving the churches out of the question) is, for historical reasons too obvious to need recapitulation, what used to be called the Anglo-Irish. After these the next most cultivated group is the writers. Now the most outstanding illustration of our failure to cope with the problem of forming a unified society out of the many elements which, as in every country in the world, diversely compose it (or should compose it) is the extraordinary fact that these two groups, the Anglo-Irish and the writers, are virtually treated as outlaws. Is there, for example, a single Protestant dispensary doctor in Eire? A county librarian? A county commissioner?

That, too, was not always so. Return to Davis and the Young Irelanders, the men, almost wholly from that same University, some Catholics, some Protestants, who may be said both to have begun popular Irish literature in English and to have had as a main ideal the unification of Irish life, irrespective of class and creed. To-day Catholics in the Dublin diocese are forbidden under pain of mortal sin deliberately to send their sons and daughters to that University of which Davis himself, speaking of the idea of nationality fostered by his group, one "indifferent to sect and independent of party," said: "That notion has been made in the historical

societies of Dublin and belongs to Trinity College Protestants and a few
Roman Catholics of Trinity College, Dublin."[10]

We do not set out these facts for any other reason than that which we
have always declared to be an essential preliminary to the posing of every
problem, i.e., that one must first look all the difficulties in the face. If one
is proposing an autonomous, non-political Irish Council for the diffusion
of knowledge of Ireland in foreign countries, and knowledge of foreign
countries in Ireland, one has not merely to say that it is a necessity, and
that its creation would be an admirable achievement, but that it would
also be a difficult and delicate thing to do; and one must see exactly why.
These distrusts and these narrownesses of outlook must be put aside;
above all, these official timidities must be exorcised by an act of faith not,
for a change, in that metaphysical entity called "Ireland," but by an act of
faith in Irishmen. It so happens that the committees engaged during this
summer in preparing for the Davis Centenary have given an illustration
of the full capacity of Irishmen of every creed, class, and idea, to work
together effectively: for the first time in my own experience of modern
Irish life I found no doctrinaire ideas at work, no political prejudices at
work, no weedings-out and selectings. Every modern writer, for instance,
without exception, was represented in the Contemporary Literature stall
at the Book Fair (or if not was overlooked inadvertently). Conceivably
these cultural committees could be an actual nucleus for an Irish Council.
Lastly, there should be, at first at any rate, no Government interference,
and no Government patronage: it has, by and large, in the opinion of
many people, worked badly in the Abbey Theatre. But if Government

10 *O'Faolain's note:* Coming forward from this, his attitude towards denominational education may be seen in one of his more controversial articles in *The Nation:*
The objections to separate education are immense; the reasons for it are reasons
for separate life, for mutual animosity, for penal laws, for religious wars. 'Tis
said that communication between students of different creeds will taint their
faith and endanger their souls. Those who say so should prohibit the students
from associating *out* of the colleges even more than *in* them ... Let those who
insist on unqualified separate education follow out their principles – let them
prohibit Catholic and Protestant boys from playing, or talking, or walking
together – let them mark out every frank or indiscreet man for a similar
prohibition – let them establish a theological police – let them rail off each sect
... into a separate quarter; or rather, to save preliminaries, let each of them
proclaim war in the name of his creed on the men of all other creeds, and fight
till death, triumph, or disgust shall leave him leisure to revise his principles.
[*Editor's note:* from "Academical Education," *The Nation* 17 May 1845.]

assistance should eventually prove desirable it should have some generous vision behind it, for this is not a question of a few thousand pounds a year but of something in the region of a quarter of a million pounds a year – if the thing were to be effective at all.

In any – or no – event, it is proper that the whole question should be posed and the need realised. During the war it was pathetic to observe our defencelessness on this front: never so pathetic, for instance, as when this writer found himself being approached by Government officials (unofficially, of course) to write "something" in the American press – pathetic and comical seeing that another Ministry had been meanwhile presenting practically the whole forum of Irish writers to the world as little better than common pornographers. Well, that is an old and rather boring story now, and a bad reputation at home has never prevented Irish writers and artists from building that country's reputation abroad: what is to the point is that they, and a great many other Irishmen, scholars, scientists, industrialists, could do a hundred times more to keep that world-reputation high, to our enormous benefit morally and economically, if organised for the purpose of diffusing a better and fuller knowledge about Ireland and her achievements to the world.

All Things Considered – 1[1]

Having pontificated for over five years in these front pages I propose (see the announcement below) to retire after this issue to the body of the magazine in order to give the experts a chance to speak freely and myself a chance to think more freely.[2] What I propose to do, in these occasional pages, is what every schoolmaster might well like to do after being widowed from his work – stop being didactic (which is an art of particulars) and consider *generally*, and away from the scene of his former

---

1 "All Things Considered – 1" appeared in *The Bell* 11, no. 2 (November 1945): 649–57. The essay was accompanied by the following editorial note:

During the War and under the Censorship we innovated the series "One World" as our modest contribution against Isolationism and Little Irelandism. As long as the War and the Censorship lasted, imposing both a unity and a circumscription on all comment, the task was just barely possible for the editor, though nobody realised better how inadequate, indeterminate, over-generalised and merely allusive these articles have, perforce, had to be. With the Censorship gone and in the complexity and swift developments of the post-war period the editor will, from December, hand on the task from month to month, to specialised students.

We hope to present the sort of inclusive and authoritative world-survey we would always have wished to give our readers and which, at the moment, no other Irish periodical is attempting to supply. In order to retain some degree of impersonality these articles will be signed only by initials. These initials will be recognised by many: but we assure all our readers that these articles will be written, as far as possible within the obvious limitations of the times, only by writers with first hand knowledge and personal experience of their subjects.

2 Although he withdrew from the front page after this issue, O'Faolain continued to write essays for the journal; the final one he wrote as the editor of *The Bell* was five months later: "Signing Off," *The Bell* 12, no. 1 (April 1946): 1–7.

labours. To be sure, it won't work. I can already see Cathleen ni Houlihan pushing her bitter red nose into the den, the unburyable corpse. However, if she will not die she may fade away and on one thing, at least, I can be certain – these occasional pages have nothing to do and shall have nothing to do with Irish politics. These are intelligent discussions conducted with myself. No politicians admitted unless accompanied by an adult.

It is raining. (You see – Ireland will keep on weepily intruding.) Very well, I will accept the rain. ("Mr. Carlyle," said the earnest lady,[3] "I have decided to accept the universe." "Madam," said Mr. Carlyle, "you'd better.") Shaw also accepted the rain. He once proposed that a public subscription should be collected to send Chesterton to Ireland for a year in order that he might find Reality in the rain. He was himself in Ireland at the time, contemplating the magic of our weird climate – this constant interweaving of mist and shower that comes and goes, so gently that everything solid shimmers and wavers, disappears and reappears, until the sun bursts out again and through a million invisible particles of sunshot moisture Reality is refracted in a dancing, blazing, babbling ballet of silver and blue. One cannot see that Gilbert Chesterton would, in practice, have been likely to learn any more about Reality amid all these quiverings and reincarnations. Do we ourselves? True, you would not find a Kerry farmer proposing Distributivism even under the lovely lunacy of a Parknasilla rainbow.[4] But even Kerry farmers are not free of our national subjection to the supernatural and the eschatological, the fantastic and bizarre, the emotional and violent. However, we are all saved from the more extreme effects of this shimmering moisture by a divine dispensation which takes care to follow up this beautiful rain with more beautiful rain, and yet more beautiful rain, and had G.K.C. lived amongst us he might well have learned that, as occasionally happens, Shaw was dreaming, and that the place to find Reality is not in the water but in the whiskey. Truth lies at the bottom of the glass. An excellent thing to hold up to nature.

The effects of climate on Irish economy could be measured accurately. I am sure that The Statistical and Social Enquiry Society of Ireland could,

3 Likely Margaret Fuller (1810–1850), American writer and educator.
4 Shaw often vacationed at the famous spa resort at Parknasilla, County Kerry.

with the aid of a comptometer and a few records from the Meteorological Services, measure the value of every drop of rain in a year's fall.[5] For heavy soils, soft winters, generous moisture are the basis of our husbandry and cattle-trade, a generally secure dependence of potatoes, a fair electricity supply, excellent horses, ample supplies of sugar, the thickness of our pigs' hides and the thinness of our own. Even those who have maintained for years that our preference for cows rather than tillage is an economic calamity cannot deny that what has been authoritatively described (at the above Society) as "our great advantages in the production of grass" must affect any decisions as to alternative systems. What can never be measured is the profound social and spiritual effect of this combination of climate and country-side in patterning our minds.

For there *is* a visible and sensible pattern of Irish life, rooted (where most things are rooted) in the earth. There are certain, stable, recognisable traditional values which did for generations past, and will for generations to come, refer back ultimately to this life of the fields – life felt, suffered, enjoyed, endured in a constant manner. Here we have something which can be observed anthropologically. It has been by Arensberg in *The Irish Countryman*. It can be described objectively. It has been by Estyn Evans in *The Irish Heritage*.[6] Here we have a formative influence that has woven itself into the genius of our people and created rhythms of habit, some good, some appallingly bad, as easy as breathing, into which even strangers slip without effort and from which we never escape without effort. We all understand these metaphors of life, we respect them – even when we dislike them; they are the language of our daily behaviour.

They are that indefinable quality of every country which can only be understood without explanation. "Si nous nous expliquons," said M. de Talleyrand, "nous cesserons de nous comprendre."[7]

~

5 The Statistical and Social Inquiry Society of Ireland was founded in 1847; it analyses the Irish economy and society and organises debates to instigate reform. A comptometer is a calculator. The Irish Meteorological Service was established in 1936 in order to provide accurate weather information for aviation.
6 *Irish Heritage: The Landscape, the People and their Work* (1942), by Emyr Estyn Evans (1905–1989).
7 Charles-Maurice de Talleyrand (1754–1838), prince de Bénévent, was a notable French politician. The French phrase translates as "If we explain ourselves, we will cease to understand ourselves."

You cannot scan this Irish line without, I believe, referring constantly to its basic rhythm of delicacy of feeling – that extraordinary sensibility to human feeling for which we Irish are at once notorious and famous, loved and despised, our well-known desire to please. All our human contacts and social relationships return to this emollient delicacy, so good for art, so weak for work; which must, in turn, be related to the harshness of rural existence. Hardness as the father of softness. We shall never know what we owe to the wet sack on the shoulders, the dunging cow, the steam from the frieze pants before the fire.[8] You will find it all, hardness and softness, in that wonderful poem by Patrick Kavanagh, *The Great Hunger*.[9] You may see it in the way we handle Religion, as if it were made of glass, Love as if it were a tigress, Education as if it were a percussion-bomb. It all proposes not a proud and arrogant spirit but a sad and slightly battered spirit. It is as if we cherished – perhaps we do – the monkish theory, so widespread in the Middle Ages, that life was made hard in order that man should, in finding no sovereign content on earth, the sooner drag himself to the feet of God. "Thy laws, O my God, Thy laws from the master's strap to the martyr's trials." That was Saint Augustine whose Confessions made Juan-Byron envy his transgressions.[10] But then it is likely that all peasant countries, whether inured to bear hardship by Nature or induced to accept it by Religion, have something of this exhaustion of pride, mutual forbearance, eagerness not to hurt or offend: plus, of course, the natural corollary of sudden passions, skilled cruelties, and excessive repentances. Somebody, for example, has well described the character of the Welsh as composed of sanctimoniousness and venom.

This may all seem much too much about Ireland: but I really am thinking about a general thing – that all "natural" qualities, being the outer and human echo of a protean and earthy heart-beat, are, however admirable in their potentialities, in effect merely our instincts and our passions and our emotions, never our ideas and therefore never under secure control. Instincts and passions are egocentric, erratic, indiscriminate, wasteful. That peasant kindness, for instance, is always indiscriminate, often

8 Frieze is a coarse woollen cloth.
9 *The Great Hunger* (1942).
10 Saint Augustine (354–430) wrote *Confessions* c. 400. Juan-Byron refers to the Romantic poet Lord Byron, author of *Don Juan*, who is famous for his rebellious lifestyle.

frightening and frequently disgusting. The slaverings at Irish funerals are a hideous invasion of human privacy. As that famous character of the Irish Bar, Jack Fitzgerald, used to say, "we Irish are congenital mourners."[11] Nobody can carry pity farther than the peasant – even to the pitch of lunacy and to the pitch of sadism. You doubt it? Remember the pity we waste on the common drunk. Think of the pity with which we choke all rebellion, all "difference": "Ah, sure, the poor fellow, he has no sense." Do we not all know how the people of little towns refuse to believe that any leprosies can exist inside their citadel – all human despairs belong to elsewhere, never to Ballymoruv.[12] And this is not merely because the sufferers and rebels of these small holes hide inside truly gigantic coils of concealment but because, too, rebellion or aberration or suffering is least noticed and last understood by those who take all suffering submission as the normal mortal lot. Does Main Street ever see anything horrible, if it sees the thing at all, in, let us say, that smothered bud of boyish and girlish restlessness which stirs and aches in Sleepy Hollow but never has the strength to climb from its breathlessness;[13] flutters into a petal of weak gaiety, withers into some casual marriage, not so much falls as wilts into a contemptible resignation.

I was discussing Irish poetry the other day with a young American soldier. He had been reading *Poems from Ireland* and he said, "What surprises me is how direct and immediate they all are, none of them are scholarly or intellectual as so much of English and American verse is."[14] Naturally, when the emotions are so easy to hand they are rarely or ever worked over, never rationalised. And yet how easy, too, it would be to rationalise some of these natural peasant gifts, of our's and others'. This same kindness, for example,

---

11 Likely the Irish politician and lawyer James Fitzgerald (1742–1835).

12 Ballymoruv is likely just a name to represent any small town in Ireland. However, it is possible that O'Faolain means to evoke Ballymore, County Westmeath, which is near the Hill of Uisneach, or Ushnagh, the centre of mythological Ireland and home to many important ancient archeological sites.

13 Sleepy Hollow is the small-town setting of "The Legend of Sleepy Hollow" (1819–20), the short story by Washington Irving (1783–1859) that introduced into popular culture the characters of Ichabod Crane and the Headless Horseman.

14 *Poems from Ireland* (1944) is an anthology published by the *Irish Times*, including an introduction by Donagh MacDonagh (1912–1968) and a preface by the newspaper editor R.M. Smyllie (1893–1954).

has been intellectualised over and over for us by Maritain in his well-known distinction between the "individual" and the "personal." Or even better by Garrigou-Lagrange in *Le Sens Commun*, which is Maritain's main source here.[15] The individual, he points out, is a mathematical concept common to man and beast and thing, to microbe and atom; it is incomplete and isolate, it makes us mere fragments of matter – individual cows, individual men, individual stones. A person, on the other hand, is a complete individual substance, intellectual in nature, master of his actions, *sui juris*, autonomous, free.[16] The word person implies some sort of moral impulse and acceptable social order. Whereas "We shall see individualism culminate quite naturally in the monarchic tyranny of a Hobbes, the democratic tyranny of a Rousseau, or the tyanny of the God-State of Hegel and his disciples."[17]

There is, of course, no use in talking about respect for persons to Marxist Communists, just as there is little use in talking about it to our own pious and much-regimenting Irish Catholics. On the contrary respect for the personal is what Arthur Koestler makes his Marxists call "the metaphysical brothel."[18] Is it not Ivanov in *Darkness at Noon* who presents Gandhi and Tolstoy as criminals?[19] The personal is nothing compared with the communal, whether to Fascists, National Socialists, Communists, or the sort of half-savage Nationalist Catholic who has begun to pullulate here. After all is not the whole theory of our Censorship, as outlined by people like Professor Magennis or Father Gannon, S.J., the totalitarian idea that the writer must be sacrificed to the common good? It is exactly the argument which Gletkin applied to Busharov in that Koestler book

15 *Le Sens Commun: La philosophie de l'être et les formules dogmatiques* (1909), by Réginald Garrigou-Lagrange (1877–1964); Jacques Maritain.
16 *Sui juris* is Latin for "of one's own right," referring to one who is now legally liable for one's self and no longer under the rule of a parent or other guardian.
17 The references here are most likely to *Leviathan* (1651), by Thomas Hobbes (1588–1679); *Discourse on the Origin of Inequality* (1755) and *The Social Contract* (1762), by Jean-Jacques Rousseau; and *Elements of the Philosophy of Right* (1821), by Georg Wilhelm Friedrich Hegel.
18 Arthur Koestler (1905–1983) was a British writer best known for his novel *Darkness at Noon* (1940), which is set in the Stalinist purges of the 1930s. O'Faolain also discusses Koestler's *The Yogi and the Commissar and Other Essays* (1945).
19 Mohandas Karamchand Gandhi (1869–1948), also known as Mahatma Gandhi, was a prominent leader of the Indian nationalist movement and a proponent of nonviolent protest.

– "Be a scapegoat for the sake of the masses. Admit yourself a traitor and a criminal. You aren't really, and we all recognise your honesty in the inner circle. History will disclose this in due course and rehabilitate you. But as we haven't time to teach our poor proletarians and peasants to make distinctions we must have somebody like you to take their sins on his shoulders. Once we've discredited some scapegoat they will feel better, and continue to believe in us. You must be a big man and take it." There is not a damn bit of difference between that Marxist rationale and the rationale behind our Jesuit's statement that the Censorship must work "in the interests of the common people." There is a pseudo-poetic idea behind them both – a myth, a faith, a flag, an ideal, and a murder. If only they could here get some writer to get up and make a Russian confession – "I have sinned, I am a criminal, I deserve to be liquidated" – everything would be quite in order.

~

In an age so regimented and authoritarian as this when every people is girding against state-control and yet cannot evade the cruel necessity for it *distinctions* are the one essential to save Man from the New (invisible) Machine. The new world-cry must be – "We defend the liberty of the individual by respect for the person." Otherwise the Machine will run true to the ancient Frankenstein myth and kill what it set out to preserve.[20] It did it in Germany. It is killing it in Russia. It is killing it in Spain. It is killing it in Ireland. Even the British are terrified of it. The Holy Joes (of Holy Russia or Holy Ireland) point across their own borders, but they never look inside.[21] Thus the Catholic *Standard* recently ran a gleeful editorial on the attacks Arthur Koestler made on Russia in *The Yogi and the Commissar*, as if the whole point about Koestler's objections to the Russian Left is not that it is Left but that it is gone Right. Your Tory Nationalist and your debased Socialist sleep in the same bed,

---

20 Frankenstein is not an ancient myth as such. Mary Wollstonecraft Shelley created the figure in *Frankenstein; or, the Modern Prometheus* (1818). The novel's protagonist is a young scientist named Victor Frankenstein who creates an unnamed monster, which in the popular imagination has taken on the name of his creator. The monster chases Frankenstein around the world, tormenting him in his quest to have him make a mate for him; their long battle results in the death of Frankenstein, which the monster laments. In the end, deprived of human company and his creator, the monster drifts away on an ice flow to commit suicide.
21 A holy Joe is a prudish, narrow-minded person.

go down side by side on their knees before the ikon of the Machine. Who was the last Irishman charged with adoration of the Machine? It was our Catholic Minister for Education when he illegally (as the Courts proved) tried to force a Bill preventing parents from sending children to school outside of the Irish "State": and the man who charged him was a Catholic, Professor Michael Tierney, in these words:

> If you have not liberty for the exceptional people, for the people who will not conform to your dead-level pattern and fit into your machine, then you have not got liberty at all. When you talk about the State being free, and of the citizen being free in this country after so many years of slavery, you are simply using a lot of meaningless words which you, by your own action, would deprive of the meaning that so many centuries of struggle have sought to give them. There is a grave danger in all this kind of legislation, by this introduction of uniformity, that we are taking a step in the direction that Europe has already taken with such disastrous consequences … I feel that the whole tendency is to set up the Machine first, and then to get that Machine geared up more and more until it tries to bring every single person in the community within its workings. Ultimately, of course, what happens is that that sort of machine breaks down, and that its effect is negatived by the very attempt to do that. I am almost tempted to say, not that I am afraid, but that I hope this machinery of compulsion will not do the work which the Minister expects it to do.[22]

After all if the *unco guid* Catholic journalists here are all of a sudden so fond of personal liberty why did they not protest when their fellow-Catholic journalist Count Michael de la Bédoyère had a perfectly pure and decent novel – which they *knew* was perfectly pure and decent – banned here as "indecent"?[23] Awfully kind and decent chaps these Catholic journalists – but, dear God, this amoral Irish "kindness" and undirected "goodness" would make anybody sick.

～

22 The debate occurred 3 December 1942 over the School Attendance Bill. Thomas Derrig was minister for education at the time.
23 The *unco guid* are those who are morally strict. English writer Michael de la Bédoyère (1900–1973).

Yet, praises be that we *have* these natural qualities, even if all these natural racial and rural instincts *are* unguided, unintellectual and erratic. It is as well, and more than well, to have so much natural tolerance and decency and generosity as you will find in any normal Irishman. It makes Ireland one of the easiest and most friendly countries to live in – so long as you are not an intellectual or don't want to be different to the mass. And, in the end, who would wish this natural instinct for living to be intellectualised if it were not that nothing is so easy as to debase, nothing so easy for selfish and unscrupulous men to harness to their own ends. About two years ago I wrote an article called "The Stuffed Shirts" in which I shewed how it has already been happening through the gradual urbanisation and vulgarisation of these untrained peasant qualities at the hands of an unscrupulous middle-class. One great consolation we have, however, one great encouragement. If we now have to give our raw emotions a rest and sit down and think out a rationale of living – if, in a word, we have to become civilised, in that at least we are now about level with the whole of this tortured world, which in this year of the Lord is setting out, wearied but with determination to do exactly the same thing.

All Things Considered – 2[1]

Recently, in Dublin, a man has died to whom, since he was one of the greatest modern Irishmen, it is pressing and proper to pay tribute. One does it the more readily because, as it happens, his life-work touches on an urgent problem – i.e., our power of assimilation. Eoin MacNeill (1867–1945) was one of the best of our Gaelic scholars. He was also either more or less than that – he was the best conceivable type of what we have come to know as "Gael." He believed – if one might so translate that – in the perpetuity or continuity of the old Gaelic tradition in Irish life and the Irish nature; though with this large difference between himself and most "Gaels" of his day, that he was too much of a humanist not to admire and desire, also, the invigoration of the great stream of European and world-civilisation. Where his special emphasis of attitude as "Gael" came in was in his tenderness to the least criticism of that old Gaelic world which did not accept its own criteria and standards, which did not assume it to be a wholly valid and unique type of civilisation. That is to say – if it had its faults, they were *its own* faults. So that if somebody had said, thinking in terms of other civilisations, that it was "primitive" he would have denied it furiously and said that it was, rather, "peculiar." To historians like Orpen, for example, speaking of the "tribal anarchy" of the old Gaelic system he would react violently, perhaps too much so; just as he was unduly suspicious of those legal historians who have counted it valuable material because it has preserved in fossilised condition certain early Indo-European elements now long superseded.[2] If you wanted to

---

1 "All Things Considered – 2" appeared in *The Bell* 11, no. 3 (December 1945): 761–9.
2 Goddard Henry Orpen (1852–1932) was a historian of Norman Ireland.

provoke him to high battle – though he always retained an extraordinary urbanity in controversy – you need only say something like: "But the Ashanti tribes had also developed 'peculiar' laws and systems of their own."[3] He would not merely reply, most reasonably, that the Ashantis had not written down and codified and commented elaborately on their laws and systems, and had not created a complex and special caste for the development and preservation of their systems, so that there was no comparison between their elementary oral tradition and the massive records of old Irish law, but he would have held the whole *comparative* approach to be dangerous. The Gaelic system was *sui generis*, suited to the Gaelic mind, intact, doubtless imperfect, but certainly unique.

This standpoint may, at first glance, seem reasonable; but, surely, on consideration it can be thought reasonable to judge native things by native needs and standards only if these native standards and needs are themselves inclusive. As I have put it here more than once, the only sure test of nationality is civilisation, i.e., one can only test a thing by asking what does this thing contribute to the whole body of world-civilisation. To this the orthodox "Gael" replies, speciously, that all civilisation is an amalgam of national gifts, and that everything national is therefore important to civilisation. It does not, of course, follow. Some national characteristics are far from appearing precious to those who perforce receive them from others. Was Cecil Rhodes a national gift to the South African Dutch?[4] There have been ungrateful Americans who would have wished that we Irish had preferred to emigrate to some other country. But, of course, the real point is that even a very real native achievement is often outstripped by other and foreign achievements. I have little doubt that when Matthew Arnold's Tyrian trader, fleeing from the merry Grecian coasters, came to the "shy traffickers, dark Iberians," and undid his corded bales upon the beach they opened their eyes not only in delight at what he revealed but in annoyance at not having thought of these

---

3   The Ashanti – or Asante – are a rural tribal people of Ghana.
4   Cecil Rhodes (1853–1902) helped develop South Africa through the diamond mining company De Beers, which he co-founded in 1888, and was the prime minister of the Cape Colony (1890–96). He is also known today for having created the Rhodes scholarships, which are paid for out of the fund of his estate to allow foreign nationals to study at the University of Oxford.

wonderful things themselves.⁵ And one may be equally certain that when
these same shy traffickers undid their bales on the beaches of Wexford or
Lambay the Celts must have said, in effect, "What slowcoaches we have
been. Look! They put handles into the axeheads. We have been putting
axeheads into the handles these two thousand years!" What a wonder the
first iron sword to men of stone and bronze, what wonder the first Arabic
numerals in Rome, what wonder the first page of writing, what wonder
to hear for the first time that the Son of God had come down into this
world and had talked to people like an ordinary man. And if one had said
all this to MacNeill, when he spoke of the ancient Gaelic world as unique
– implying that it was self-contained? – he was much too much of a
scholar and a humanist not to have agreed at once that this was, of course,
all quite true; and we know, for example, from his *Phases of Irish History*
how critical he could be on that old Gaelic world for its incapacity for
assimilation and adaptation.⁶ But I think that he would also have said
that this common property of mankind must in each case be welded into
a local culture, which must be a finished vessel ready to receive it and
welcome it; and that, for us this local culture must be a first thing to create, develop, study, define, and defend.

One might pause there – at the word defend – to ask if he was, then, in any
degree a "bit of a propagandist." The most just and accurate answer I
could give to that would be to say that he was a pragmatical scholar. It
does not seem that he had much interest in pure knowledge, *die reine
Wissenschaft*, knowledge for its own sweet irrelevant sake.⁷ He applied
himself. He would, I imagine, have appreciated Chesterton's shrewd idea
that to be free a man must be aware of limitations: i.e., a man knows
where he is in a field, he is lost in a boundless expanse. Yet, it must be
agreed that his was a rôle not without risks to complete objectivity. For is
it really possible to define a local culture in its own terms without being
partial to those terms? Only a very stern scholarship, such as, for example,
Alice Stopford Green did not command (not to mention a host of even
less-equipped and more blatantly "patriotic" historians) can resist the
natural temptation to "make the best of things." MacNeill's scholarship

5 This scene is from the last two stanzas of Arnold's poem "The Scholar Gypsy"
(1853).
6 *Phases of Irish History* (1919).
7 *Die reine Wissenschaft* is German for "the pure science."

was sound but it was not stern. He had, moreover, the dangerous gift of being able to intuit conclusions on slight material; a gift by which other students have also profited – Kelvin for instance – and lived to be substantiated by later and more thorough investigators.[8] But they are not *always* substantiated and many a scholar has had to bay furiously at some of his less happy "inspirations." One could collect several examples: his statement, for instance, that ancient Irish law was national, not local, was a large claim since it would have been an achievement which did not occur in places where there was much more organisation than in ancient Ireland. (His basis, apparently, was that the jurists alone could keep guard over the unity of the law and he could find no evidence of local variations in the laws: a point suggested, obviously, not by evidence but the lack of it.) And since one uses the word "stern," it is to be said, too, that he was never as devoted a toiler as say, Thurneysen, and the corpus of his work is by comparison probably not one-tenth in size.[9] But there again, the refusal to devote himself to pure knowledge came in: he could not think of research *qua* research as adding to knowledge, and therefore all his work has not that same utter trustworthiness of the great line of German *gelehrte*.[10] Thus I have heard it said that he seldom copied out a manuscript. His mind and gifts were of a different kind – more the gifts, possibly, of sheer genius; a mind of bold and audacious sweep, sometimes too audacious; not the mind of a "digger" – he was inclined to shirk the drudgery of "digging"; a mind that should have been born a hundred and fifty years hence when the donkey-work will have been done, when he might have gone about with pocket-volumes of the texts, and when he might then have made – securely instead of riskily – those brilliant syntheses and conclusions that no man was better fitted to hurl through the clustering perplexities of the Celtic chaos. As to this special fitness, the very quality of his mind seems to have been attuned to the ages he dealt with. I believe it was Alice Stopford Green who said, "Eoin MacNeill has an old mind." With that old mind he had little trouble in thinking "then-mindedly."

～

8 William Thomson (1824–1907), Baron Kelvin, was an influential Irish-born Scottish engineer, mathematician, and physicist.

9 Rudolf Thurneysen (1857–1940) was a Swiss-born German linguist and Celtic scholar.

10 *Qua* is Latin for "as being." The German *gelehrte* means "scholar."

There remains the obstinacy or pertinacity (as one chooses) of his *modern* Gael-ery. A contemporary has called him our "scholar-patriot," forgetting that if the term were applied to a poet or a painter it would almost be an insult. A patriot-painter? A poet-patriot? It conjures up something as unlikely (both ways) as a "scholar-gypsy." Carlyle's scholar-hero is a compliment: or Browning's heroic Grammarian.[11] It is true that within this ascetic and ungrateful and almost utterly lonely vault of scholarship, a vocation rather than a profession (one thinks of the devoted, one might almost say martyr's life of that father of Celtic scholarship, Zeuss),[12] MacNeill did properly overthrow men who in being themselves for the moment less than scholars were not merely incorrect but had smirched the fair name of his Dulcinea del Toboso: and he was, thereby, for that moment happy in the double rôle. But that secondary rôle was an accident. What they are thinking about when they call him a Scholar-Patriot is another thing altogether: they are thinking that he helped to found the Irish Volunteers, went to jail, took his part in the first government of a freed Eire, and there, and as such, was a "Gael." This will puzzle us if we do not dismiss, first of all, those vulgar modern connotations that have made the word hateful.

Even then? Grant the ancient world's validity: grant that you cannot graft without having something on which to graft: but, having gone so far with MacNeill, one must then ask where is the continuity? Where is that parent stem to-day? If MacNeill would not have it that it was ever a "primitive" world, the humanist in him, the learned man also knew that if that world lacked little for the childhood of the race it now offers almost nothing concrete to the race in adult manhood: for it had a wonderful romance – all that, yes – but it had no philosophy, no science, no metaphysics, virtually no sculpture, an undeveloped architecture, no theology, no drama, no criticism, no painting, hardly a dish, not a wine. As George Moore bewailed – it has the steak, yes, but not the sauce; as John Eglinton said, it had not even enough religious vigour to make a heresy. What does all that mean? It means that the Gaelic vessel did not receive the new

11 Carlyle's scholar-hero appears in his work *On Heroes, Hero-Worship, and the Heroic in History* (1841). Browning's heroic Grammarian is found in his poem "A Grammarian's Funeral" (1855).

12 Johann Kaspar Zeuss (1806–1856) was the founder of Celtic philology and author of *Grammatica Celtica* (1853).

wines. The Gael did not assimilate. Wherefore Toynbee calls it the "abortive" Celtic civilisation.[13] MacNeill would have admitted it all, but he would also have pounded the table (metaphorically, for he was too gentle a man ever to lose his quiet poise) and insisted that the hard core remains. And, again, we may agree that we *are* indelibly and racially "different." Where he would also, however, have pounded the table would be with any nincompoop of a modern "Gael" who would have tried to maintain that a modern man could make the hundredth part of his soul on that Gaelic tradition *alone*.

∽

For MacNeill, as I have mentioned, not only chided the Gaels he loved for their failure to adapt themselves to Change, but was himself a man of boundless interests.[14] He had an amazing fund of knowledge, was at home with all sorts and conditions of people: so much so, indeed, that he might have been a more hard-working scholar if he had been a less varied and divided man. And it worked both ways: as witness that famous sally of one of his colleagues when he sat on the Boundary Commission and should, for once, have laid his scholarship aside and stuck to politics.[15] "Ah, well! MacNeill may have lost the North – but he has found the birth-place of Saint Patrick."[16] He was a man who could talk to you about greenfly like an entomologist. He invented half a dozen new games of Patience.[17] His reading knew no nationalist bounds. He, in a word, had not followed the bad example of the ancients he so loved. He *had* assimilated. Perhaps it was from the worldly communion, as well as from the natural sweetness of his nature, that he was so extraordinarily urbane. As another colleague has said, "One would expect Thurneysen to be urbane – a learned man living in an urbane, learned world. But MacNeill

13 English historian Arnold Toynbee (1889–1975) analysed the fortunes of civilisations in his twelve-volume *A Study of History* (1934–61).
14 *O'Faolain's note*: See *Phases*, page 355: "Glorying in the long vista of their past, they did not look before them. They were conservative, inadaptable, unproviding."
15 The Boundary Commission met from 1924 to 1925 to establish the frontier between the Irish Free State and Northern Ireland, but its report was not issued when its details were leaked and caused considerable scandal owing to suggested land transfers on both sides. The result was the maintenance of the status quo of the Anglo-Irish Treaty. MacNeill, who at the time was the minister for education, was the Irish government's representative on the five-member commission.
16 Although he is Ireland's patron saint, St. Patrick was born in Britain.
17 Patience, also called solitaire, is a card game.

– a politician in a politics-ridden country. That was the miracle." Whereby, he was probably one of the few Irishmen, if not the only Irishman of a period of internecine hates, who has died without an enemy.

So, we draw our memories away from the graveside of this great Irish scholar, not only grateful for the work he has left us but for the clarification his life implies. He draws our minds insistently to the truth that all culture is both individual and one. The Celts were themselves: they were also receptacles. They shared – and should have shared more – in that vast store of culture which is the result of endless graftings and pollenisations, over thousands upon thousands of years, from that mysterious parent Indo-European stock which the philologists have revealed to us from its words and its broken sherds of words, once the bright vocables of a civilisation that, some say, lay and has been lost somewhere west of the Hindu-Kush – those last verbal echoes of buried towns and time-erased gardens and forgotten cosmogonies, ghosts of the land that is to-day Soviet Uzbek and Turkmen.[18] That Aryan Adam had only two great sons – who became in turn source-countries for the civilisation of modern Europe, the Greeks whose art it was to think, and the Romans whose art it was to apply.[19] For although prophets went into the desert in their thousands – all prophets seem to have gone first into the desert to find wisdom – only One came out to lay His mark on Europe, and Greece and Rome were the channels for His message. Philosophy and criticism and science and government likewise all have come to us through these creative and recreative giants, and those who could not create for themselves had to borrow these gifts from them; the Celts, the Slavs, the Teutons were all their borrowers. The Celts certainly had to borrow: they were, as we can see, a race with no capacity for generalisation themselves. The study of Celtic law, alone, proves that: where time and again the jurists will ask a general question, and inevitably collapse at once into a particular answer. It was no shame to borrow: it was the lands that had the brains to borrow most and adapt most that in their turn became again

18 Sherd is another form of the word "shard." The Hindu Kush is a mountain range in central Asia. Soviet Uzbek and Turkmen are known today as Uzbekistan and Turkmenistan, respectively.
19 Adam had more than two sons. Seth was born to replace Abel, who had been killed by Cain. Cain's and Seth's descendants formed, respectively, the Cainites and Sethites, the two human stems.

most creative and recreative – Spain, France, Britain, Germany. The old wine in the new bottles made them magic bottles. Was our receptacle too small, too narrow-necked? Sometimes MacNeill obviously thought so, while insisting that it was his rôle to insist, and rightly, that it was, nevertheless, the only vessel we had. It was his curse and ours that this generation has taken the second point without taking the first. For the modern "Gael" loves not the magic bottle but the bottle-neck, so that the work of men like MacNeill, misunderstood by our ignorant chauvinists, has begun to breed evil instead of good. In token of which I remember how, it was a few months before he died, one of his own colleagues found one day by a casual question in a University class that no student knew the love-story of Deirdre and none had read the wonderful magic Celtic love-tale of Tristan and Iseult.[20] Whereupon I went to my own child's school-texts and there found much about Saint Patrick and Saint Brigid but no word of Deirdre and the three sons of Usnagh – the bottle closed and corked and thrown into the Holy Sea;[21] some day, perhaps thousands of years hence, to be washed up on another shore of Time to puzzle whoever those new creators may be – Russians? Americans? Chinese? Some dazzling cities on the shore of Africa? – with the scent and smell of a culture that if it had been more adventurous might-have-been. Can such things happen? Do races really die? Could Ireland vanish? The world is dotted with the trails of aborted cultures, the detritus of peoples who have left only a wrack behind – the empty chocolate-cartons, torn letters, and obscene hair-combings of the lodgers of the globe.[22]

20 Deirdre elopes and flees to Scotland with Noísi, one of the three sons of Usnagh, in a tragic Irish myth; her story was dramatised in plays by W.B. Yeats and J.M. Synge. Tristan and Iseult are lovers in a Celtic medieval romance; versions of the tale abound, from Le Mort Darthur (c. 1470), by Sir Thomas Malory (n.d.), to Tristan und Isolde (1857–59), by Richard Wagner (1813–1883).
21 The child that O'Faolain mentions is likely his daughter, the writer Julia O'Faolain (b. 1932); he also had a son, Stephen (b. 1938). St. Brigid (451–525) is one of Ireland's patron saints.
22 A wrack is a wrecked ship; wrack can also refer to rubbish.

Essays: 1946–76

Shaw's Prefaces[1]

I must have been not much more than thirteen when I saw my first Shaw play, it was *John Bull's Other Island*.[2] For I know I saw my first Irish play – it was Lennox Robinson's excellent drama *Patriots* – about the same time, in January, 1913.[3] These two plays blew through the theatre like the fresh winds of April. I had been seeing, and was to go on seeing, plays and musical comedies that had no reality in them: *Eliza Comes to Stay, Mrs. Wiggs of the Cabbage Patch, Bella Donna, Two Little Vagabonds, An Englishman's Home, My Umbrella, The Whip, Gypsy Love, The Marriage Market, A Girl in the Taxi. Hindle Wakes* or *Rutherford and Son* were sheer realism compared to these.[4]

This has been said many times before. Shaw came to a weary theatre and woke it up. Young people of our day cannot know *how* weary it was.

---

1 "Shaw's Prefaces" appeared in *The Bell* 12, no. 5 (August 1946): 425–32.
2 *John Bull's Other Island* (1904). O'Faolain also mentions *Candida* (1897), *Man and Superman* (1903), and *You Never Can Tell* (1898).
3 *Patriots* (1912).
4 *Eliza Comes to Stay* (1913), by Henry Vernon Esmond (1869–1922), né Henry Esmond Jack; *Mrs. Wiggs of the Cabbage Patch* (1911), by Alice Caldwell Hegan Rice (1870–1942); *Bella Donna* (1911), by James Bernard Fagan (1873–1933); *Two Little Vagabonds* (1896), by George R. Sims (1847–1922) and Arthur Shirley (1853–1925); *An Englishman's Home* (1909), by "A Patriot," pseudonym of Guy Du Maurier (1865–1915); *My Umbrella* is untraceable; *The Whip* (1909), by Cecil Raleigh, né Cecil Rowlands (1856–1914), and Henry Hamilton (1853–1918); *Gypsy Love* (1911), by Franz Lehár (1870–1948); *The Marriage Market* (1913), by Miksa Bródy (1875–1924) and Ferenc Martos (1875–1938); *The Girl in the Taxi* (1911), by Jean Gilbert (1879–1942); *Hindle Wakes* (1912), by Stanley Houghton (1881–1913); and *Rutherford and Son* (1912), by Githa Sowerby (1876–1970).

If we think the Abbey Theatre is dead to-day – and it is, because it is not keeping abreast of life – the whole theatre then (outside Ibsen) was a mausoleum. The greatest tribute I can pay to Shaw is that, to-day, *Candida* or *The Doctor's Dilemma* still has a hundred times more vitality than almost any other comedy written since the Restoration.[5]

His Prefaces do, in book-form, what his plays do on the stage. They shock. Just as Robinson's *Patriots* shocked me upright with delight in the real thirty-three years ago. I had been seeing other "Irish" plays. A trouper named Chalmers Mackay used to pack the Cork Opera House with the old green-and-scarlet melodramas – like *Arrah-na-Pogue*.[6] Robinson and the Abbey plays made these dummy conventions look silly. In the same way Shaw's Prefaces take conventional ideas and send them to the canvas for ten. If we do not see the country dramatic societies now doing buncombe Irish plays like *The Colleen Bawn* year after year, as they once did, the thanks must go to the original minds in the Abbey Theatre of thirty or more years ago.[7] Likewise, if the social conscience of the world has become proof against buncombe morality (on such things as slums, for example) a good part of the credit must go to Shaw.

Until he came along it was not considered good manners to attack conventional morality in the theatre. Compare, for instance, a play like Wilde's *An Ideal Husband*.[8] Dismiss the absurd mechanism – the plot and counter-plot, the wheels within wheels, the impossible situations. The really shocking point is that it is shocking not because it is unconventionally moral but because it is conventionally immoral. Thus Wilde's title may be ironical – the "ideal husband" (a cabinet minister) may be exposed as a fraud: but surely the ideal wife is presented as a heroine? And was there ever – though Wilde obviously does not realise it – a more detestable, hateful, priggish, corrupt and dishonest woman? For, in the end, after all her high-falutin' talk, both she and her husband, with her connivance, go on profiting by that dishonourable action on which he based his entire fortune and his fake reputation. We are told, with regard to the villainess, Mrs. Cheverely, "once a thief always a thief." The rule is

5 The Restoration refers to the re-establishment of the Monarchy in England in 1660.

6 *Arrah-na-Pogue* (1865) and *The Colleen Bawn* (1860) are melodramas by Dion Boucicault (1820–1890).

7 Buncombe refers to something that is uttered or performed merely to cater to and please the audience.

8 *An Ideal Husband* (1895). Shaw and Wilde referred to themselves as the Hibernian school of drama.

permitted to fall into polite abeyance when it comes to cabinet-ministers. After Shaw, nobody could write a play like that and get away with its half-truths and whole-lies. True, Shaw might well have gone to another extreme – he is always willing to say a thing in so extreme a form that one wants to contradict it, content if he has at least woken us up to the argument. He would probably have exposed the wife, lacerated the husband, and pointed out that the villainess was the only person who was honest in her dishonesty, and he might even have pinned a medal on her for exposing middle-class and upper-class pseudo-morality.

It is the same with the Prefaces. Even one sentence, I pick an example at random, from the Preface to *Man and Superman*, can be an immediate stimulant to contradiction or consideration. *Those who administer to poverty and disease are accomplices in the two worst of all crimes.* One must debate the "worst," immediately: but one must also pause at the startling word "accomplices." Is poverty, then, not a blessing (as we here in our defeatist, pietistic resignation sometimes even still dare to think it); or not even a misfortune; but a crime – of omission – committed by the poor and connived at (merely) by the rich? To throw part, at least, of the responsibility back on the dumb, pauper oxen – like throwing the responsibility for Ireland's "wrongs" back on the dumb, Irish oxen – is blessedly invigorating. This is to get behind morals (*mores*, as conduct, habit, so often dead habit) to a genuine decency beyond and outside custom, seeing through custom, seeing through so-called "morality" itself. This has been Shaw's ceaseless preoccupation and gift.

To get behind fine "principles" was what, for example, he did in *Widowers' Houses*, wherein a young man full of the highest "principles" discovers that he has all his life been drawing an income from slum property. And in the Prefaces he will explain, gently, what the general and genuine moral of that play is, simply by asking you and me (who braggingly agree with his play) to show him our box of matches, or the label on our coat, and to consider whether we have ever bothered to consider under what kind of conditions the people who made the coat or packed the matches work – and live. What a blessed thing it would be if to-day, in the Abbey Theatre, somebody wrote a play like that to ask our nation-builders under what conditions they permit to live those young city gamins whom they stuff with inflated ideas and ideals, not quite so happily reflected in the homes from which they come – or, often, in the very schools in which they are taught.

Critics of Shaw say that he puts up ninepins to knock them down again. The thing about him, rather, is how fair he is. For instance, he believes in progress. He is fully aware of the dangers that follow on the crazy lust for progress. Read him on public inoculation. He balances the common desire for public health with the duty of individual responsibility for private health. He will not let us get away from our consciences by saying that it is the doctors who have imposed this or that nostrum upon us. On the contrary, he is scornful of us, the public, who are always running to the doctors for charms against disease which we are too lazy to prevent by taking proper precautions beforehand. And, in passing, can there be any people more given than we Irish are to paying large fees to specialists – usually too late?

But, I suppose, to the romantic-minded, such things as slums, and disease, will always seem base subjects for literature, and they will be dismissed as didacticism or propaganda. The romantic subjects – the theme of an *Asmodée*, a *Three Sisters*, a *Deirdre of the Sorrows* – are, indeed, nobler and lovelier; they are not the only subjects.[9] Perhaps, however, what those who dislike the Shavian mind really dislike is not the subject but the treatment – they dislike his refusal, or inability, to transmute. If an artist wishes to paint a pub it must be transmuted into the *Bar at the Folies Bergères*, the prostitute into a Verlaine poem.[10] That, I agree, Shaw cannot do. Shaw is not a poet.

But it is unfair to expect poetry of him. Shaw is a special kind of man who had to invent a special kind of writing. He is a Puritan and a Reformer. Had he not also been a wit – rare combination – he might have been content to write poems like "London."[11] As it was he wanted to write comedy with the one hand and preach sermons with the other. His comedy became a cerebral fantasy, in effect a morality-play, a fairy story in short, in which his repressed romanticism found its revenge by forcing him to create forms of life whose figures of wisdom and unwisdom are complete fantastications. Shaw is a writer of fantasies full of common-sense. The dissidence is obvious. He has never resolved it.

This dissidence quite stumps the French, for example, who have more regard for living too well than for living wisely, and certainly do not appreciate intrusions of common-sense into the art of living. A recent

9 *Asmodée* (1937), by François Mauriac. *Three Sisters* (1901), by Anton Chekhov. *Deirdre of the Sorrows*, by J.M. Synge, was unfinished at the time of the playwright's death in 1909 and was first performed in 1910.
10 *A Bar at the Folies-Bergère* (1882) is a painting by Édouard Manet. Verlaine wrote a few poems on the subject of prostitutes.
11 "London," a poem from William Blake's *Songs of Experience* (1794). Shaw used an excerpt from this poem as the epigraph to *Mrs Warren's Profession*.

production of *Candida* in Paris left the critics saying something like this: "Eve here rejects Adam. The parson's wife rejects the poet. And for what? For a parson and for wisdom! Is this love among the English?" It is not, of course. Nor among the Hottentots. Poets like Marchbanks never existed, nor parson's wives like Mrs. Morell. He has rejected the fatality of love, the movement of passion towards its end, the theme of all romance, to confound love, passion and romance in gusts of laughter. It is funny. It is plausible given the puppets whom he has made to feel as he thinks. But it is not life.

And, yet, I said at the start that he blew fresh gales of reality through the theatre? So he did. The reality is in (*a*) his problems, and (*b*) his way of working them out: but not (*c*) in his people. There the bridge is down. They are vehicles: puppets if you prefer. He sometimes complains that the British public has been stupid in not taking him seriously in his plays. How could they? They do not recognise Life in his plays – though they do recognise this Reality which I have defined. They perceive him as a romantic puritan with an Eden of his own. The bridge from the problem to the person they do not see. And being a people of much more common-sense than he will admit, they just laugh and go home. But the last people who should quarrel with him, for that, are the people who say he does not sublimate – if anything he sublimates, though it be cerebrally, far too much. I, for one, being also a romantic and a puritan (most native Irish-men are romantics and puritans, whence their internal dissidences) am content. I am as willing to enjoy Marchbanks as Millamant – for different reasons.[12] But when I come to make the bridge to reality which he has not made I turn to the Prefaces because he there leaves it to me and to each man to make the bridge in our own way not impugned by fantasy. In short we go to his plays for the duel's flashes: to the Prefaces for the more solid fighting.

There are other reasons why these Prefaces may, yet, have a larger audi-ence than the Shavian theatre. They glimpse an emotional side that he has wilfully clamped down in his plays. The autobiographical Prefaces expose, sometimes movingly, that weakness in him for hiding his own weakness. The Punchinello Shaw has so often been useful to the emo-tional Shaw that it has ended by deceiving G.B. Shaw.[13] He will attack

12 Millamant is the heroine of *The Way of the World* (1700), a play by William Congreve (1670–1729).
13 Punchinello, a fairly mean-spirited marionette also known as Punch, often plays against authority.

romanticism night in and night out: he can slump into the most shocking sentimentality by refusing leeway to his own romanticism. (*You Never Can Tell*.) This duality in him comes to rest in the Prefaces – and would that he took the opportunity more often. For here he can afford to be serious, and here he might dare to be emotional. We all remember, for instance, the famous passage about Ireland and Dublin:

"In 1876 I had enough of Dublin," he writes. "James Joyce, in his *Ulysses*, has described with a fidelity so ruthless that the book is hardly bearable, the life that Dublin offers to its young men, or, if you prefer to put it the other way, the life that its young men offer to Dublin. A certain flippant futile derision and belittlement, that confuses the noble and serious with the base and ludicrous seems to me peculiar to Dublin. When I left Dublin I left (a few private friendships apart) no society that did not disgust me."

He then describes the vitality and enthusiasm of the early Fabians and the interest people took elsewhere in live, social questions.

"So," he goes on, "my sentimental regard for Ireland does not include the capital. I am not enamoured of failure, of poverty, of obscurity, and of the ostracism and contempt which these imply, and these were all that Dublin offered to the enormity of my unconscious ambition. My business in life could not have been transacted out of an experience confined to Ireland. I had to go to London just as my father had to go to the Corn Exchange. London was the literary centre for the English language, and for such artistic culture as the realm of the English language (in which I proposed to be King) could afford. There was no Gaelic League in those days, nor any sense that Ireland had in herself the seed of culture. For London as London, for England as England I cared nothing. If my subject had been science or music I should have made for Berlin or Leipsic.[14] It was not until I went back to Ireland as a tourist that I perceived that the charm of my country was quite independent of the accident of my having been born there, and that it could fascinate a Spaniard or an Englishman more powerfully than an Irishman, in whose feelings for it there must have been a strange anguish because it is the country where he has been unhappy ... "

"The country where he has been unhappy." "A strange anguish." A personality begins to emerge here which the plays conceal. In all that

14 Leipzig, as it is better known, located in eastern central Germany and just to the south of Berlin, has long been a seat of culture and learning. The University of Leipzig was particularly renowned in the eighteenth and nineteenth centuries.

essay, behind the sheer brain-power, the satire, the wit, it is touching to feel the swagger soften into feeling – and quickly run away from itself. The explanation is all over the Preface to *Immaturity* and in *John Bull's Other Island*, too well-known to need quotation – the hatred and terror of romance, of Irish gush, of our suicidal emotionalism and unrealism.

The essays have to be read in bulk, in, say, the one-volume edition of 1,000 pages, tight double-columns, to appreciate their accumulative, overwhelming force. There have been far better critics in English – Hazlitt, or Coleridge, even (when he is in the vein) George Moore; essayists of far greater delicacy (the word is out of place in speaking of Shaw) – three essays by Lamb are worth all these columns as far as pure literature goes. But, in his own particular field, there is nobody so stimulating. Indeed, the fact is, there is nobody in any language of the same order: nobody who can at one and the same time shock so stimulatingly, so amusingly, and with so much originality of mind. And only Sam Johnson had the same *instantaneous* power of soaring over any question and falling on it like a hawk, with speed and thrust, and nobody, not even Johnson, has had the same felicity of word. His only frailty is that he likes too much to astonish. And this witty and oblique common-sense of the Celt will never impress so much as the straight-forward common-sense of the Saxon. Or, perhaps, never impress any Saxon, who always suspects brilliance in a writer, even while he enjoys it.

Rebel by Vocation[1]

This essay was written to commemorate the death of one Citizen Smith, alias Mr. Hutton, alias Adjutant-General T.W. Tone, a gay young Dublin Protestant, fond of wine, women, song (and quotations), educated (or otherwise) at Trinity College, who tried the profession of law, gave it up or failed at it; grew disgusted at the state of his country, tried to rouse the Dublin and Belfast tradesmen and intellectuals (God bless the mark!), partly succeeded, partly failed; went off in a huff (and for the sake of his health, politically speaking), to farm in Philadelphia; failed at that, came back to France one blustery February morning with the cool proposal that the Directory ought to man a fleet (or two) to free Ireland (whatever that may mean); persuaded Carnot and Buonaparte to try it;[2] tried it himself (both invasions complete failures); was arrested in all the glory of his regimentals, condemned to be hanged (and to have his young head hacked off afterwards and stuck on a pike to grin at Dame Street); and in the Provost's prison, Dublin, cut his throat with his pen-knife (he almost failed at that) and died, November 19th, 1798.[3] There are monuments all over Ireland to numbskulls and blatherskites and brave men. T.W.

1 "Rebel by Vocation" appeared in *The Bell* 13, no. 2 (November 1946): 97–114.
2 Lazare Carnot (1753–1823) was a French general and statesman; Buonaparte refers to Napoleon I.
3 Dame Street is major thoroughfare in central Dublin. Provost's Prison was a part of the the Dublin Barracks. Provost's Prison has long been demolished, but the Dublin Barracks were renamed Collins Barracks, in memory of Michael Collins shortly after his assassination in 1922, and in the 1990s were transformed into the part of the National Museum of Ireland that is responsible for the preservation of the decorative arts and history.

Tone lies away down in the County Kildare in an ancient graveyard under an old rusty cage, as if the young lion were still not quite dead and might jump out any moment at some of those speechifying politicians who – to their credit (as to his) – come year after year to remember him in person: the only Irish patriot who is thus personally and individually never forgotten.

> In Bodenstown Churchyard there is a green grave
> And freely around it let winter winds rave;
> Far better they suit him, the ruin and gloom
> Till Ireland, a nation, can build him a tomb.[4]

The nation (whatever or whomsoever that may signify) has not yet had the courage to give him his statue. Money was collected in 1898 and it still lies in the Bank. A plaque was set in the ground at the corner of Stephen's Green to mark the site of his memorial – but the Board of Works took it up (after dark). (He thus even failed to get a statue!) He puts the politicians in a sad stew. They love him (secretly), commemorate him (openly) but, alas, he was a *Protestant*! He was a *suicide*! He made one or two disrespectful references to convents, bishops (who, at the time, thoroughly deserved a great many disrespectful remarks) and Catholic services. And every now and again the pious, the inexpressibly pious, the indescribably Catholic papers revive that sort of canting deprecation of poor Tone with which, in his time, all such men as he were sniffed at by their likes. Lastly, he knew nothing about the Gaelic Revival! So, we honour Davis (as we should) and praise God that Tone's grave is away down the country (where he can be honoured quietly). The bi-centenary of his death will come round in 1948.[5] What about that money in the bank?

After the Boyne and Limerick, 1690, the old aristocratic Gaelic world went underground. "The Irish language descended into the ranks of the peasantry, who themselves, as a result of frequent confiscations, were soon a blend of names of the oldest order and the blood of the common people." The aristocratic tradition continued to be represented as late as

4 The final stanza of "Tone's Grave" (1843), also known as "Bodenstown Churchyard," by Thomas Davis.
5 Tone died in 1798. The bi-centenary of his death was in 1998; 1948 was the sesquicentenary of his death.

the mid-19th century only by the Gaelic poets – whom, as they became more and more debased, one must call versifiers and songsters – with no rich patrons now, except such few of the new order as sympathised with them, or tolerated them, or took a purely cultural or antiquarian interest in them. The poems of a man like Darthi O'Bruadair, a typical remnant of the 17th century, show pathetically how nonplussed and helpless they became in this chaos of their antique world, for as he wanders through the country, apparently with little aim, he will halt at any house that will open a door to him and warmly praise its people for that kindness, no matter what their origin, as if he believes or persuades himself to believe, that it is not in pity or generosity that they shelter him but to honour the noble tradition of his caste and the wonder of his craft; and yet at the same time he, like the contemporary satirist of Clan Thomas, bitterly abuses the rebelly natives who after The Flight of the Wild Geese took to the hills as guerillas, calling them the "proud and rapacious children of serfs."[6]

On this unhappy picture any Irishman may hastily turn the page. The house fell. Its owners abandoned it. Their followers sheltered in its out-houses, lodges, cabins and sheds. That is all. And for a hundred years more, after 1691, that is all, except that the new masters employed these poor and crushed them with an indescribable brutality under The Penal Laws, of which it is enough to say that in 1759 a judge declared from the bench that the law did not presume a single Papist to breathe in Ireland, that Chesterfield considered them treated worse than negro slaves, and that Swift found them quite unmanned, as harmless as women and children.[7] History might there have taken up its pen and written Finis to a race. It would seem that there was no more to be conquered.

We flick back the page, are about to throw away the book, and are astonished at what we see. For, though a nation could not grow out of the glory and strength and variety of the old rich Celtic world, with its kings and subkings and lieges and clients, its brehons and its bards, priests and friars and schools of learning, its horsemen and kernes and gallowglasses, all so arrogant, so potentially creative, so free, so wild, so untameable;[8]

6 Darthi O'Bruadair, or Dáibhí Ó Bruadair (1625–1698). Clan Thomas refers to Pairlement Chloinne Tomáis, which translates from the Irish as "The Parliament of Clan Thomas"; a satire of the drinking habits of the anglophilic class – those referred to as Clan Thomas – it was written in the mid-seventeenth century by Aodh Buidhe Mac Cruitín (c. 1680–1755).
7 Philip Dormer Stanhope (1694–1773), 4th Earl of Chesterfield, was Lord Lieutenant of Ireland from 1745 to 1746.
8 Kernes and gallowglasses were ranks of soldiers that served Gaelic chieftains.

though all that was politically barren – out of rags and tatters, from tumble-down huts and cabins, from one of the most debased peasantries of which there is record in history, from Paddy with his pig, humbly and humorously plodding from birth to death, almost illiterate, next-door to a beast, incredibly, almost miraculously, we see a thought emerge, a mind begin to bud, a nation grow.

~

In 1791, in Ulster, that house built upon a house, among the Presbyterian Dissenters, there was founded a secret society known as the United Irishmen aiming at a "brotherhood of affection and a communion of rights and a union of power among Irishmen of every religious persuasion."[9] The source of this generative idea was France. It is striking that, in the end, it is not in culture but in politics, not in Gaelic Ireland but in Anglo-Ireland, not among Catholics but Nonconformists, that the fog suddenly lifts on a bit of clearcut logic. But no word must be said that would suggest for a moment a cold or abstract mind. The chief figure of the United Irishmen was a man of charming personality, merry wit, and civilised ideas about life in general. He had had noble precursors and contemporaries – Swift may stand for the one and Grattan for the other – but, to steal the words of a famous pass-word about another amiable Irishman, "Wolfe Tone is the name and Wolfe Tone is the man." This young Protestant Dubliner, educated at Trinity College, that alien nursery of native causes, was to unite the logic of the Northern Scot to the passions of the Southern Irish, to scatter the timidities of the peasants and the vacillations of the tradesmen with his vision of the new revolutionary age. In Tone's hands the French Revolution became a trumpet, unheard indeed by the dust of antiquity, and one can only laugh to think what the bardic caste would have said of him; heard by only a small number of the millions of slaves about him; but heard by enough men to have handed down to our day a gay and passionate republican spirit that is never likely to die wholly in Ireland.

The cleavage with the past is immense. A century before and the fumes of a thousand years are still lingering about us. Wolfe Tone flings open the doors of the modern world like a thunder-clap. Nothing less dramatic can describe a change so great as to see Jacobin ideas spreading, at whatever highly simplified remove from their original form, among a Gaelic-speaking peasantry.

9 A Dissenter, also called a Nonconformist or Free Churchman, is a Protestant who does not conform to the doctrine of the Church of England, or Anglicanism.

~

This combination of what one must call a controlled Anglo-Irish intelligence and a passionate sense of injustice among the native Irish – in so far as there was by 1790 any blood unmixed enough to be called "native Irish" – is the formula of modern Irish nationalism. The common people burned with a sense of their undeniable wrongs: the new middle-classes, of whatever religion, found their country – or the country of their adoption – being misruled by an utterly corrupt, inefficient and pandering Parliament in the selfish interests of Britain. But the peasantry had no ideas; the middle-classes had no force. The peasantry did, indeed, form into secret, local and violent societies (The Whiteboys and Shanavests and so forth)[10] to revenge themselves on local tryants; and for the enlargement or sublimation of their hates and hopes could still listen to the wandering Gaelic poets weaving Vision Poems, or *Aislingi*, in which the ancient world was once again restored by the Stuarts returning in triumph from France or Spain. But neither these impossible dreams nor those sporadic outbursts could be of much help except as a heady drink may keep up a poor devil's spirits until his real chance arrives. Neither could the timid methods of the Catholic Whiggish middle-classes achieve much by loyal addresses since they were content to accept the current social order provided they could remove the restrictions under which their own class suffered: they were otherwise indifferent to the real canker of their country, i.e., the hideous economic slavery in which the masses of the people existed as mere cottiers without rights, without security, without a vote, without hope. It was from the top alone, from the free-minded intellectuals, such as Tone, and from the more humane aristocrats of the new Anglo-Irish order that fighting leadership could come. Since, in the end, the aristocracy was subject to the corruption of its own vested interests, which not even the devotion of Grattan and his "Patriot Party" could hold at bay, that leadership of the people devolved in the end on the intellectuals.[11] They became the interpreters of the new

10 The Whiteboys were formed in 1761. The Shanavests were a later formation of the same movement that splintered into several lesser known factions.

11 *O'Faolain's note:* It was not, in fact, until Tone and his comrades expelled the tame Catholic aristocrats from their committees that they won, by the Relief Act of 1793, the removal of the major disabilities under which Catholics had suffered since Limerick and the Boyne, e.g., they could carry a gun, go to Dublin University (Protestant – the only University), vote as forty-shillings freeholders in the counties, hold minor offices, act as grand jurors, take commissions in the army.

America and the new France. Thanks to their propaganda the vacuum left in the Irish mind by the fall of the Norman and Gaelic aristocracy was filled by the most explosive ideas of modern democratic Europe.

Things have so much changed since that century, there are now so many other quarters from which leadership might at any moment emerge for a national agitation – the Church, the writers, the Labour movement, our political parties, the Press – that we must emphasise this isolation of Tone and his companions in the Ireland of the 1790s. I have mentioned five modern alternatives; obviously the last four did not then exist. We must see, too, why the Catholic Church was to all intents and purposes wholly supine at this period.

It was not until the first decade of the following century that any signs of spirit appear among the Catholic clergy, and then a man like the famous "J.K.L.," James Warren Doyle, Bishop of Kildare and Leighlin, forms an astonishing contrast not only to his predecessors but even to his contemporaries. This is not surprising. We remember that for generations the official – and legal – title for a Catholic was "Papist"; that the Catholic Church was never referred to as such but as "the Roman Catholic communion in Ireland," as if it were a peculiar local sect; that priests generally dressed in brown so as not to attract attention; are always (as in Tone's diaries) spoken of as "Mister" So-and-so; that an Archbishop of Dublin, in forwarding a curate's letter to Dublin Castle for perusal, could add, "You note he calls me 'Lord,' but I do not claim the title, and I can't prevent him from using it"; that, as Tom Moore noted in his Diary, whereas Archbishop Troy, the Catholic, died worth tenpence the Protestant Archbishop of Armagh left £130,000, having throughout his life enjoyed an income of £20,000 a year, largely made up of the pence of peasants (Catholics) unwillingly subscribed as tithes.[12] It sums up the dispiritedness of the Catholic Church that when Dr. Doyle became Bishop – Tone then seventeen years dead – he found that nobody had dared hold a confirmation service in his diocese for twenty years, his chapels were thatched cabins, the vestments were worn and torn, the chalices were old or even leaked.

12 Thomas Troy (1739–1823) was appointed Archbishop of Dublin in 1786. William Stuart (1755–1822) was appointed the Archbishop of Armagh in 1800; Lord John George de la Poer Beresford (1773–1862) held that office at the time of Troy's death.

Essays: 1946–76

"J.K.L." did, in his day, give magnificent encouragement to his people. On the other hand he was a rigid constitutionalist: his great opponents were the secret societies that the rebelly spirit of the century before had set flourishing among the tough men of the collieries, and he fought them to his dying day – often literally with the sweat pouring off him, haranguing them in their basalt thousands under the open sky.[13] This horror of physical revolt, of all revolutionary defiance for established law and order, goes so deep into the spirit of the Church of the time that it is worth probing a little farther into the causes of it, and its prolonged effects.

As we know, Maynooth was founded, long before Catholic Emancipation, even before the '98 Rebellion, out of British Government funds.[14] We need not enquire whether the Government hoped to purchase the loyalty of the Church; for though it certainly got it, that was because of chance circumstances that it could not have foreseen. In 1795, the year of Maynooth's foundation, there were a great many French refugee professors and teachers to whom any haven, the most frugal pension, would have been welcome. This suited Maynooth perfectly, for it was not a rich foundation, and, as one may imagine, Ireland (just emerging from the Penal Code) was in no position to supply it with sufficient native scholars. It gave posts to several of these distinguished men, such as Delahogue and Anglade for moral and dogmatic theology, thereby importing a French school of thought whose teachings so carefully, indeed fanatically, cultivated the spirit of Gallicanism among the Irish clergy that the Irish church soon became Gallican to the core, and remained so for nearly half a century.[15] That is: in politics, through their hatred of the Revolutionary spirit, in their devotion to the old monarchical absolutism, they filled the mind of most Irish priests, all through O'Connell's great fight against Britain, with the traditional Gallican belief that all things, even many of the privileges of the church, must lie in servile subjection to the throne; and, in morals, they encouraged a repulsive rigour in the management of consciences which rendered the following of Christ's teachings anything but

13 Basalt is an extremely hard igneous rock that often resembles tightly fitted columns; the Giant's Causeway in Northern Ireland is one such example of basalt formation.
14 St. Patrick's College in Maynooth, County Kildare, was established in 1795 and is the largest Roman Catholic seminary in the British Isles. It became a college of the National University of Ireland in 1910 and began to accept lay students in 1966.
15 Louis de La Hogue (1740–1827) and F. Anglade (n.d.), author of *Institutiones philosophicae* (1816).

a *jugum suave*.[16] They proscribed many of the classic theologians of the church, such as Suarez or Molina, both Jesuits, the first of whom had written against the Oath of Allegiance to the crown, the second of whom had humanely tried to reconcile free will and predestination.[17] Liguori, even after his beatification, was not safe from the censure of those bitter French exclusivists at Maynooth – one actually told his students that the saint was *perdite laxus*.[18] They were so far from all accommodativeness, benignity, mildness, so far from trying to make the Law easier for the people, that one of the prevailing class-books at Maynooth, that of Bailly, had to be put on the Index in 1852.[19] "An alien theology possessing for us neither national nor other interest thus balefully affected the youth and manhood of the Irish church, narrowing their views, misdirecting their professional studies and if not entirely estranging their feelings of allegiance at least sensibly weakening them towards the true object of Catholic loyalty."

When this mentality was finally exorcised from Maynooth I do not know; it cannot have outlasted the 1850s but it had by then been carried through the length and breadth of Ireland by priests educated under the old régime, and when a sharp controversy (from which I take the last quotation) developed in 1879 over a sudden lifting of the veil by Dr. Henry Neville, Rector of the Catholic University, ex-professor of Maynooth, one of the reasons why his would-be refuter, Dr. Walsh, later Archbishop Walsh (died, 1921), was angry with him was that so many priests who had passed through the College in the epoch under question were still working among the people. One feels that a tradition like that eddies on. Even in our day readers of Canon Sheehan's *The Blindness of Doctor Gray* will recognise a familiar priest of the old school, the stern moralist for whom "The Law" was a second god.[20] One meets its eddies constantly in the

16 *Jugum suave* is Latin for "a sweet yoke."
17 Francisco Suárez (1548–1617) and Luis de Molina (1535–1600) were major Spanish Jesuit scholars whose systems of thought are considered significant enough to have warranted being designated Suárezianism and Molinism.
18 Like Suárez and Molina, the Italian Saint Alfonso Maria de' Liguori (1696–1787) was a theologian; he also founded the Redemptorists. *Perdite laxus* is Latin for "recklessly lax."
19 The book in question is *Theologia dogmatica et moralis ad usum seminariorum* (1789), by French theologian Louis Bailly (1730–1808); it was published at Maynooth under the title *Theologia moralis ad usum seminariorum* in 1828. His book was banned because he claimed in it that marriage was valid without being a sacrament.
20 *The Blindness of Dr. Gray* (1909), by Patrick Augustine Sheehan (1852–1913), a priest known as Canon Sheehan.

political and clerical history of the 19th century, as in "J.K.L.'s" disagreements with Delahogue and Anglade (see Fitzpatrick's *Life*, page 83, page 156), MacHale's with O'Finan (O'Reilly's *Life*, I. 345), or again in Doyle's brush with the Jesuits at Clongowes (op. cit. 142) whom he tried to *stop* from hearing confessions because he thought them too lenient![21] And, of course, as we know, both Doyle and MacHale were anti-French because of their youthful experiences, the latter in Ireland, the former in Portugal when Napoleon invaded it in 1807: (he stood sentry at Coimbra during those exciting months, and went to Lisbon to act as interpreter for the English under that other famous Irishman, Wellesley).[22] But if one grasps this key one understands a lot of things much better, especially why it was that O'Connell had to fight not merely the British but his own bishops, the English and Irish Catholic aristocrats, and even defy Rome herself in the famous Veto question, i.e., the "right" of the Crown to hand-pick Ireland's Bishops, as Grattan weakly offered – that being the occasion of O'Connell's famous pronunciamentos that if the Catholics of Ireland must accept the order of Pius VII to accept royal nomination of their own bishops he would, in future, rather take his politics from Constantinople than from Rome, and that such bishops would, in fact, be the means of uncatholicising the land.[23] One understands best of all what a task poor Tone had, away back in the 1790s, to rouse the Catholic laity and priesthood.

21 *The Life, Times, and Correspondence of the Right Rev. Dr. Doyle, Bishop of Kildare and Leighlin* (1861), by William J. FitzPatrick (1830–1895); *John MacHale, Archbishop of Tuam: His Life, Times and Correspondence* (1890), by Bernard O'Reilly (1823–1907). John MacHale (1791–1881) was appointed Archbishop of Tuam in 1834; upon his promotion, Francis Joseph O'Finan (1771–1847) replaced him as Bishop of Killala. Clongowes Wood College, located in Clane, County Kildare, is a boarding school that was founded by the Jesuits in 1814.

22 The reference here is to Arthur Wellesley (1769–1852), the 1st Duke of Wellington, who had been ordered to Portugal to help the country, which was attempting to fight off Napoleon.

23 *O'Faolain's note:* It sums up the period, 1805 to 1845, to say that O'Connellism in the presbytery was fighting, and defeating, Gallicanism in the seminary. Long before O'Connell there were, of course, noble exceptions among the priesthood: one has only to recall the priests who died with the gun in their hands in '98, or who were hanged or shot after the Rising ended. [*Editor's note:* Luigi Barnaba Gregorio Chiaramonti (1742–1823) became Pope Pius VII in 1800.]

There were, then, no other fighting leaders but Tone and The United Irishmen.[24] They were trying to build up a new mentality, a new mind, against every opposition. Of that new mind Tone, first and before all others, is the personification. That was his main contribution, to give to his people the dynamism of his own nature, the example of his own life. Overtly he and the United Irishmen were to achieve, directly or indirectly, very little: the bloody Rising of '98, a failure; two abortive efforts to invade Ireland from France; a brief rising in the West. But he was to sow ideas broadcast. He was to present common men with their first personal hero of the new democratic age. He was to leave behind him a diary in which his merry, insuppressible, eager, all too human nature, so sceptical, so serious, so gay, so indiscreet, so utterly removed from all posing or false dignity, is a happy definition not merely of the man but of his ideals. It and he are the only sensible definition that exists of what Irishmen mean to-day when they talk of being Republicans. He was to become the beau ideal of Irish rebels, the great prototype on which all later would-be revolutionaries instinctively modelled themselves.

This rebel mentality has become so rooted in Ireland and has so coloured all our other characteristics, and so profoundly affected our social behaviour, our symbolism, our literature, even our conventions, that we should strive hard to understand it. Irishmen themselves possibly understand it least of all since with them it is not so much a question of understanding as of the dissection of something too familiar even to propose self-questions.

The rebel seems to fall into two types or stages. The one rebels against an immediate injustice – peasant risings follow, peasant societies of revenge, workers' associations. He sees no farther. The other sees beyond the immediate thing to the larger implications: he is the man who uses words like Emancipation, Liberty, Freedom. The one is clear as to his object; the other is never clear. He cannot be because his desirable image of life is not something which forms in a vacuum but something whose instruments are flesh and blood. He is subject to the limitations of his followers and times. This intellectual type of rebel is always the national leader, as against the local leader, and it is his dilemma that, in the ultimate, he is leading people to a Promised Land which *they*, not he, must define and create. He is riding a raft on a swirling river, and like all leaders

24 The Society of United Irishmen was founded in 1791 by Tone to fight for Roman Catholic emancipation and parliamentary reform.

of masses of men it may well be his constant problem whether he is riding the torrent or the torrent is driving him.

The Rebel probably never cared. He was devoted to failure. He was a professional or vocational failure. Not that he did not dream of and hope for success. But he always knew the odds were against him and if he was a Wolfe Tone, laughed cheerfully at his possible, indeed probable fate. (Tone joked over the usual fate of his kind – to be hanged and disembowelled. "A fig for the disembowelling if they hang me first.") There was only one thing at which the rebel wished to be a success and that was at rebelling. Death did not mean failure so long as the Spirit of Revolt lived. The rebel did not even mind obliteration and anonymity, and thousands upon thousands of Irish rebels have never been recorded and their sacrifice will never be known.

Nor are Irish rebels peculiar in this. One of the most eloquent tributes ever paid to anonymous sacrifice occurs in that remarkable, and too little known English novel, *The Revolution in Tanner's Lane*, by Mark Rutherford.[25] I think it worth giving here in full:

> To work hard for those who will thank us, to head a majority against oppressors is a brave thing; but far more honour is due to (those) who strove for thirty years from the outbreak of the French Revolution onwards not merely to tend the chains of the prisoners, but had to achieve the far more difficult task of convincing them that they would be happier if they were free. These heroes are forgotten or nearly so. Who remembers the poor creatures who met in the early mornings on the Lancashire moors or were shot by the yeomanry? They sleep in graves over which stands no tombstone, or probably their bodies have been carted away to make room for a railway which has been driven through their last resting-place. They saw the truth before those whom the world delights to honour as its political redeemers; but they have perished utterly from our recollection and will never be mentioned in history. Will there ever be a great Day of Assize when a just judgement shall be pronounced;[26] when all the impostors who have been crowned for what they did not deserve will be stripped, and the Divine word will be heard calling upon the faithful to inherit the

25 *The Revolution in Tanner's Lane* (1887), by Mark Rutherford (1831–1913), né William Hale White.
26 An assize is a sitting of a court; a Day of Assize refers to a Day of Judgment.

Kingdom, – who, when 'I was an hungered gave me meat, when I was thirsty gave me drink; when I was a stranger took me in; when I was naked visited me; when I was in prison came unto me'? Never! It was a dream of an enthusiastic Galilean youth, and let us not desire that it may ever come true. Let us rather gladly consent to be crushed into indistinguishable dust, with no hope of record: rejoicing only if some infinitesimal portion of the good work may be achieved by our obliteration, and content to be remembered only in that anthem which in the future it will be ordained shall be sung in our religious services in honour of all holy apostles and martyrs who have left no name.

Even of those who are recorded, honoured and well known what *is* known clearly? The one thing about them which is always clear is their personalities. Thus, what Tone would have done had he been first President of an Irish Republic nobody knows because he has not told us. But from the nature of the man we can see the kind of life that would have pleased him, and the things (for example) in this modern Ireland that he would not have tolerated, such as the least sign of sectarianism, puritanism, middle-class vulgarity, canting pietism, narrow orthodoxies whether of Church or State. One feels that his laughter and his humanity would have blown all these away, would have defined political liberty not merely in terms of comfort but of gaiety and tolerance and a great pity and a free mind and a free heart and a full life. And if few rebels have been so gay as Tone, except perhaps in our own time Mick Collins, wherever the Rebel appears he will always reveal the same composition – even the most solemn and subjective of them, such as Pearse – or else he is a faux-rebel or a lapsed-rebel, that most common and pathetic type in the history of all peoples.

The thing could not have been otherwise. Rebelly Tone was doomed to leave so little behind him, to be unclear in his ideas, to be fuddled even, to be a failure, because he chose to lock-knit himself with the common people, with the poorest and most ignorant of his countrymen whose whole lives, day after day, were themselves the very epitome of befuddlement and failure. He was not their tutor: he was their torch, their friend, their lover. He went down into the huts and cabins and took the people to his heart. He was not telling them about their future – they had no future. He was telling them about their present – about themselves. He was their second priest. It was Rebels like him whom in turn the poor have always loved with an unbreakable loyalty, made ballads about them, hung their likenesses in cheap pictures about their walls, revered as their symbols – Tone, Emmet, Lord Edward, Napper Tandy, O'Connell, Mitchel, Parnell, and all the Rebels of Sixteen and after.[27]

~

This is not to detract from those other Irishmen who, in their humanity, kindness and sensibility, contributed throughout the 19th century to the spirit of liberalism, but who pledged their minds to success in the sense that as gradualists they were satisfied to win reform little by little, and to clearsightedness in the sense that they would not look beyond those immediate and possible goals. These were our pure constitutionalists like that devoted and patriotic first leader of the Irish Party, Isaac Butt, and its last leader John Redmond, and there were earlier men, like John Keogh, and hundreds of others earlier and later still, and doubtless there always will be, whose natural sense of decencies ranges them, though at a remove of prudence or qualified disapproval, on the side of (if not beside) the rebelly-minded.[28]

A good example of these men was O'Connell's lieutenant O'Neill Daunt whose autobiography, well-named *A Life Spent for Ireland*, loyally veils but does not conceal his distaste for O'Connell's techniques.[29] But just as it is quite evident that O'Neill Daunt could never have accomplished what O'Connell accomplished by his rumbustuous, indeed often, if not always, slightly vulgar, flamboyant, defiance, his – call it if one wills tricky or even dishonest methods of inflaming the people to the very edge of open revolt and as in the Tithe War well beyond it, in short by his use of the rebel-mind in thought and action, so never once, I dare say, did any constitutionalist win one of those gradual reforms without the rebel as the real force behind him.[30]

27 James Napper Tandy (c. 1737–1803) was an Irish politician and revolutionary.
28 John Keogh (1740–1817) is considered a pioneering leader in the emancipation of Catholics.
29 *A Life Spent for Ireland* (1896), by W.J. O'Neill Daunt.
30 The Tithe War in Ireland occurred in the early 1830s. Catholic farmers rebelled against the laws that forced them to pay tithes, a form of taxes, to the Church of Ireland (which is Anglican). It was more of a movement than a war, with some violent outbursts over the years. The outcome was that the government charged the landlord the tithe, and the landlord then passed this cost on in the form of a tax to his tenant farmers.

This is illustrated over and over during the hundred years after Tone. It is that century in a nutshell. Tone died in 1798. O'Connell was at work from 1807. The next rebel movement, The Young Irelanders, began in 1842 and broke into armed revolt on his death. Ten years later Fenianism began under Stephens and O'Donovan Rossa, and there were attempted outbreaks in '65 and '67.[31] That "life and death question" of Ireland in the 19th century – Land trouble, which had scattered violence all over the country ever since O'Connell's day with its inevitable aftermaths of evictions and emigrations – was boiling ever since 1852, and was to be the centre of the Parnellite campaign. Interwoven with all this was the constitutional effort. Isaac Butt, to lead the Irish Party from 1870 on, defended the Fenians in '65. Parnell was converted to Nationalism by the execution of the three Irish Fenians who attempted the famous prison release in Manchester in 1867. The first of a series of Land Acts that were, ultimately, to change the whole character of the peasantry, namely Gladstone's Act of 1870, came out of violence and murder in Tipperary. The Land Bill of 1881, which at last fixed the tenant's rent and prevented landlords from practising any longer that brutal and ambition-destroying trick of increasing the rent whenever a tenant by his own industry improved his holding, came out of one of the most violent periods of Davitt's Land League agitation. And so on.

If there is in all this a distinction between the "common people" and others who are not "the people" I can only say *Circumspice*.[32] That is the way the story has gone. I say it in no spirit of democratic enthusiasm for the "common people" who are, to the artist and the intellectual, so often a bore and an aggravation, whose lives and minds are most creative and interesting when they themselves are most poor and least emancipated, as when Yeats "discovered" them, still a traditional peasantry.

Can we make no recompense to the Rebel for what he sacrificed? What was it that he sacrificed? His life, or the better part of his life? Far worse, far more exhausting, harder far to bear, he sacrificed the better part of his mind. Men like Tone, Mitchel, Doheny, all of them, had smothered talents.[33] They were presumably men with as much human ambition as anybody else, and more sensibility than most. It was a drudge to them to "go

---

31 Jeremiah O'Donovan Rossa (1831–1915).
32 *Circumspice* is Latin for "look around."
33 Michael Doheny.

down into the cabins of the people." How bored Tone was by these talks and meals with dithering, half-educated, Catholic tradesmen and farmers; and he was the last man to whine or complain. "Cowardly enough." "A dirty personal jealousy." "Our mob, very shabby fellows." "Shabby." "A blockhead, without parts or principles." "The parish priest, a sad vulgar booby." "Egan of Galway is flinching." "Sick." "Victuals bad, wine poisonous, bed execrable." "Sad, sad." "Dinner with the Catholics, dull as ten thousand devils. Dismal, dreary." "Damn them, ignorant bigots." (This about two Catholic bishops.) "Gog (this is John Keogh, the most pious of Catholics and most devoted, though timid) tells me he begins to see the Catholic bishops are all scoundrels." "Cowardly! Cowardly!" (This about men who are trying to dodge taking the chair at a meeting.) And so it goes on. But how even that far tougher metal, the great and burly Dan O'Connell, used to curse those "common people" as when he called them "animals," and "crawling slaves!"

All these men deprived themselves, and us, of as much as they gave us: they choked the critical side of their minds, they were good rebels in proportion as they were bad revolutionaries, so that their passion for change and their vision of change never pierced to organic change, halted dead at the purely modal and circumstantial. It had to be that way since they devoted their lives and all their beings to passion rather than to thought, or in Arnold's words describing the French Revolution "had their source in a great movement of feeling, not in a great movement of mind." Not that Arnold's ideas in the first of his *Essays in Criticism* have any political validity, and certainly no validity as between Ireland and England since (as he recognises freely, certainly by implication throughout) you might as well try to change an Englishman's political views about his Empire by reasoning with him as hope to stop the charge of an elephant with an epigram.[34] And, furthermore, as Arnold also agrees, though so subtly as to gloss over the inherent contradiction, the Revolution "undoubtedly found its motive-power in the intelligence of men ... The French Revolution derives from the force, truth and universality of the ideas which it took for its law, and from the passion with which it could inspire these ideas, a unique and still living power; it is – it will probably long remain – the greatest, the most animating event in history. And as no sincere passion for the things of the mind, even though it turn out in many respects an unfortunate passion, is ever quite thrown away and quite barren of good,

34 The first essay of Matthew Arnold's *Essays in Criticism* (1865) is "The Function of Criticism at the Present Time."

France has reaped from hers one fruit – the natural and legitimate fruit, though not precisely the grand fruit she expected; she is the country in Europe where *the people* is most alive." Yet, it is for all that still true of our Irish rebels that it was upon the emotional content of the Revolution that they seized and not on its intellectual content, with the result that the whole of Irish patriotic literature ever since has either concerned itself with matters of sentiment rather than thought; or with interim solutions of immediate problems that time has since dealt with otherwise.

There is, surely, only one real and obvious recompense that we can make to the Rebel for what he gave up, and that is the same recompense that Englishmen have made to the revolutionaries of Tanner's Lane. We can go back and attach to their names the original sense and force of their inspiration. The later course of the French Revolution, from its origin through all its vicissitudes and redefinings down to our own day, has been so little studied; all its implications, social, cultural, political, so little realised that our oldest statesman can to-day be so childish, so insulting to the passions of the past and to the intelligence of the present as to fob away the "greatest, most animating event in history" by lifting his wide eyes, as of innocent wonder at our questions, from a *dictionary*! (As if, thereupon, we might model our lives upon, let us say, the life of Venice of which his beloved Machiavelli said that "of all forms of servitude that under a Republic is the worst.")[35]

Ever since 1922 there has been a sly campaign, conducted by all the same shabby-genteel forces that he himself disliked so much, – revived under new forms, new names – to draw us away from Tone's presumably "dangerous" concept of Republicanism that he, like so many other rebels, had not the time to elaborate. He introduced Ireland to the word. If that word means anything to Ireland it means what it meant to him. It means the flash and thunder of other words that lit his mind and lit the mind of dying Ireland, and for which, at least once, poor ragged Irish peasants fought and died – France, La République, le serment de la liberté, the beginnings of a great and generous experiment in human happiness fluttering and falling, like seed from the sower, under the Republican tricolour, into the poor soil of Mayo.[36] We could do worse than go back to those beginnings.

35 Niccolò Machiavelli (1469–1527) says this in *The Prince* (1513).
36 Le serment de Liberté-Égalité, translated as the Oath of Freedom and Equality, was created on 14 August 1792 to swear allegiance to the Republic.

On Translating from the Irish[1]

Have we not done enough and more than enough of it? Why do we translate from the Irish: or from any other language? What does "translation" mean? Is it possible? To what extent is it possible? Is it a poetical exercise, or is it an excavating of old beauty?

I confess I begin to grow impatient with any translating from Irish other than translations from the Old Irish. Most of us can read Irish poetry in the original, and enjoy it in its original form, as far back as, say, 1600 at the latest, and perhaps to an earlier date with comfort. I am grateful for translations from Middle and Old Irish as I am grateful for translations from Latin and Greek, or for translations from Mallarmé, or Lautreamont, or Rimbaud – as, in the old schoolboy sense of the word, "keys" to the actual poems themselves, which I am too lazy to work over with gloss and grammar and dictionary.[2] But this does not apply to poetry in modern Irish, and when I am given a translation of that modern poetry I am being invited, it seems to me, either to take the translation instead of the original, or to enjoy the skill or virtuosity of the translator rather than the poem as a poem. Who would prefer to read translations from modern French instead of the original? I wonder if this habit of translating is not a habit chiefly; a hang-over of the nineteen-hundreds? Is it not an echo of the years when Mangan, or Ferguson, or Yeats *had to* get at Gaelic Ireland through English?

One has to be rather cold and objective about this and all such problems to-day when both prose and poetry are working their way out of the

---

1 "On Translating from the Irish" appeared in *Poetry Ireland* (January 1949): 14–17.
2 French author comte de Lautréamont, the pseudonym of Isidore Lucien Ducasse (1846–1870).

conditioned-reflexes and conditioned emotions of the first and second stages of the Irish literary movement. Of what help is it to talk to a modern Irish novelist about the charm of Charles Kickham? I can imagine nothing more stultifying to a young Irish poet than a devotion to Aubrey de Vere, or Sir Samuel Ferguson.[3] They have an antiquarian interest for us; a sentimental interest; occasionally a poetic interest, but does it go beyond that? They were the first stage. And is it likely to be much more helpful to have a devoted interest in Æ, or Ledwidge, or Synge, or Colum, or Seumas O'Sullivan?[4] (I deliberately omit Yeats – one must always omit the great, who are above and beyond the battle by reason of their greatness.) These were the second stage, and it is no more an abstraction from their merit to say that anybody who wrote now as they wrote would be using clichés than it is to say that, in our time, and for our time, Keats is fast becoming unreadable. The fashion of translating from Irish belongs to that second stage. It was part of the elementary exploration of a Gaelic world that was, then, still living, and that, then, because of politics, had a lively value as an excitation and inspiration. That Gaelic note, that Gaelic thought, that emotion, is to-day a cliché. It is worse when a modern employs it: it is sentimentality. Anybody thinking about life in terms of a Gaelic-speaking peasantry, in this year of Satan, 1949, is sleep-walking.

Why is it that when I read a volume of modern English poetry, say *The Song of the Cold*, I feel that, whether it is or is not poetry of the first order, it is poetry of my time?[5] But when I read poems of young, or middle-aged, Irishmen who are still devoted to the Gaelic cult it is all as remote as William Morris.

I may as well confess that I think that the technical influences of Gaelic are of a piece with this general soporific effect of the content. Higgins and Clarke seem to me to have exhausted the usefulness of the old assonantal modes.[6] Indeed, I feel that Clarke has taken the technique to the fair. It is impossible even for a trained ear, reading English, to hold an assonance beyond three lines; and, as for multiple assonances, their obvious effects are, firstly, to induce a highly artificial language – in the search for assonating vowels; and, secondly, to slow up the speed of the lines, and verses, to a dead march. Note that I have said "reading *English*." By this I mean that assonance, like the use of classical metres, is alien to the language. It

3 Irish writers Aubrey de Vere (1788–1846) and Sir Samuel Ferguson (1810–1886).
4 Irish poet Francis Ledwidge (1887–1917).
5 *The Song of the Cold* (1945), by Edith Sitwell (1887–1964).
6 F.R. Higgins and Austin Clarke.

lies there as uncomfortably as the elegiac pentameter. It just does not belong. To force Gaelic technique into poetry in English is a sign of an extravagant absorption that is all of a piece with the general "hanging-on-to-the-past" illustrated by translating from the 18th and 19th century instead of creating in the 20th. It is a brain-spun thing to persist in beyond the point where a pleasant technical innovation is received as a pleasant technical innovation – and no more. I take it that it is as such, for example, that Frank O'Connor translated recently "Pangur Bán" with extraordin- ary faithfulness to the Old Irish style.[7]

I do not, of course, suggest that poets should not translate from Irish. They always will. They will in doing so give us poems so near to original poems that they will wrest from the original creator half his due. The game of translating has given us some poems we would be the poorer without; and a whole volume of delight in O'Connor's *The Fountain of Magic*. But let us be clearheaded about this. That volume was issued in 1939. In the Preface O'Connor said it represented the work of ten years. In fact it represents the work of nearer twenty years. He began translating Irish poems in his 'teens and was publishing them in *The Statesman* cer- tainly as early as 1925. This work belongs to those years when we were all passionately learning Irish in the Gaelic League under the nationalistic influence of the post-1916 fervour. When he switched to prose he had outgrown that period and exhausted that inspiration, as we all soon did, being occupied now with finding our own roots, and seeing no future for literature as a grafting on the 19th century or a sentimental echo of a dying world. If O'Connor had decided to be a poet and not a prose-writer would he have gone on translating? *The Fountain of Magic* is a delightful *Ave atque Vale*.[8] All translations from the Irish now can be no more than either the occasional technical amusement of a poet, or a flower cast gratefully on a grave.

If this seems the wrong note to sound in a Number devoted to transla- tions from the Irish it is not meant in any ungracious spirit. The poets, I am sure, know very well what they are up to in translating from the past. The public may not be so clear. Perhaps I do not state the poet's position sensitively enough. The Editor may intend to do so. If I induce him to do so, this will be not an ungracious or ungrateful note but a critical and constructive note – and of that we need a great deal in Ireland to-day.

7 "Pangur Bán" is a popular Irish poem about a scholar and his cat; it is presumed to have been written by a monk in the ninth century.
8 *Ave atque vale* is Latin for "hail and farewell."

The Dilemma of Irish Letters[1]

In 1932 W.B. Yeats and Shaw founded a society which has since become moribund: the Irish Academy of Letters. It has become moribund for the usual reasons, age and lack of fresh blood. Some of its members are very long-lived. Half a dozen such as Shaw, Stephen Gwynn, T.C. Murray or Seumas O'Sullivan could, between them, nearly knock up five centuries. The average age of members is between sixty and sixty-five. The deliquescence of this Academy has been rapid; it had hardly been well founded before it began to founder. Ten years ago the total list could, at least by courtesy, have been called active. Since then several members have definitely died. Active is hardly the word to describe the majority. A striking thing about the list of thirty-five members, when last it was thirty-five – the maximum – is that almost half then lived in exile. It need hardly be said that the Academy, having been founded by two writers, has no money. In latter years vacancies have not been filled. I seem almost to be describing a Big House in Cork or Kerry with no glass in the windows, no money in the bank, no smoke from the chimneys and not much whisky in the decanter.

It may be said that it is unfair to present this picture of modern Irish letters since all Academies are much of a muchness, composed that is of ancient monuments. It is not true of this Academy. Some writers were elected to it when still in their thirties – Frank O'Connor, Francis Stuart, myself, Peadar O'Donnell, Elizabeth Bowen. We are now all in our middle years, and are still moderately prolific. Yet, as far as public acclaim is concerned – not that this is ever solid evidence – I do not think that any

1 "The Dilemma of Irish Letters" appeared in *The Month* 2, no. 6 (December 1949): 366–79.

of these less ancient members, except perhaps Miss Bowen, has arrived at the stage of consolidated achievement. None, certainly, is in the unassailable position of such founder-members as Yeats, Æ, James Stephens or Shaw. And while one does not expect a literature to be composed of writers of the first order one does expect it to include a few large figures. To-day we have nobody in Ireland of the stature of Joyce, Moore, Synge or Yeats. (I say "in Ireland" so as to exclude Shaw and leave the way open for a question which I want to consider in considering this general decline – the Irish literary diaspora which the Academy's list so well illustrates.) We have in Ireland, to put it in another way, no *chef d'école* among our elders, and no rivalry for the position among our middle-aged juniors. In any case, even outside the Academy's list, it is difficult to see any budding grove to alter the impression that the two outstanding marks of Irish literature to-day are exile and lack of originality.

Irish writing was last like a bay-tree some thirty or thirty-five years ago, which, if the members of the Irish Academy range between sixty years and ninety years, is about what one might expect. The year 1915 is a safe middle date; the year after *Dubliners* appeared; the year just before the Rising which, ultimately, was to alter everything and, unpredictably, create the circumstances in which Irish writing would begin to wilt: that is by over-simplifying the social picture. For a while it might have seemed quite otherwise. The poets had helped to inspire the Rising; three of its leaders were poets; for ten or more years after it the excitement of the revolutionary period was reflected in writing – the obvious example is the work of Sean O'Casey. Then, imperceptibly at first, literature began to feel the water getting colder and colder – the obvious illustration is the Censorship Act of 1929 under which practically every Irish writer of note has, some once, some several times, been banned by his own government. When Æ died, and George Moore, and Yeats, and Lady Gregory and Joyce, a period came to an end. Irish writers continue to achieve distinction; Irish literature still carries an honourable prestige; but nobody would care to maintain that it has as much prestige as it had around 1915.

∽

In casting about for the fundamental reason for this falling-off I suggest that we may find the clue in the tendency towards exile. I always like to quote in connection with the Celtic diaspora the entry in the Anglo-Saxon Chronicle which runs: "Three Irishmen came to King Alfred in a boat without any oars, from Ireland, whence they had stolen away because they desired, for the love of God, to be in a state of pilgrimage – they recked not where."² Such exile is splendidly irrational. It is the imagination in search of itself, or of its own insatiable satisfaction. The beginning is wonder and so is the end. This spring I was in Capri.³ Midway between Anacapri and Axel Munthe's castle there is a crumbling ruin to which a friend in Rome had directed me because he had seen there, in a niche, a few withered flowers and been told that it once had been a chapel dedicated to a saint called Cataldo.⁴ This Cataldo came from Lismore in County Waterford, one Cathaldus or Cathal. In Norman Douglas's *Siren Land* you will remember his story of how the Caprilians, being threatened by a Saracen invasion from the sea, decided that their patron Saint Cataldo was not much good for sea-matters; whereas, across on the mainland, at Massa Lubrense, at the end of the Sorrento peninsula, near where Virgil is supposed to have died, were the bones of an excellent seagoing saint called Costanza, who had, tradition said, sailed up from the Bosphorus and who is pictured with a lantern on his breast.⁵ So, one day, the Caprilians, full of terror, and of the wrath and courage thereof, gathered up the remains of poor Cataldo of Ireland and rowed off to Massa where they fought a bloody fight, won it, put the bones of the Irishman in the church and seized the bones of Costanza, who has ever since remained the patron saint of Capri. But how persistent the atavistic memory is when the imagination has once fed it! There in the crumbling wall, inhabited now only by the darting lizards, lay again the tribute of withered flowers to an Irish wanderer.

If we do not remember these early wanderers, driven by the passions of the heart, we may take too shallow a view of Irish emigration. The same necessity that drove Cataldo to Capri drove Shaw to Saint Pancras.⁶ It was not always belly-hunger alone that drove Irishmen out of Ireland. They have always gone, by the tens of thousands, for sheer devilment – or for sheer sanctity. Shaw would have died if he had not gone to Saint

---

2 Alfred (849–899) is also known as Alfred the Great and King of Wessex.

3 Capri is an island in Italy, near the Bay of Naples.

4 Axel Martin Fredrik Munthe (1857–1949) was a Swedish physician who achieved wide popularity with *The Story of San Michele* (1929), which recounted his experiences in Paris, Rome, and Capri. Saint Cataldo lived in the seventh century.

5 *Siren Land* (1911), by Norman Douglas (1868–1952), who wrote of and died on Capri. In the Middle Ages, Muslims were called Saracens. Massa Lubrense and the Sorrento peninsula are located in the south of the Gulf of Naples.

6 Shaw lived for some time in the London borough of St. Pancras, for which he was a vestryman and councillor from 1897–1903.

Pancras in the same sense that Saint Pancras would have died if he had
not been able to go to Rome to be beheaded for Christ. This is not an Irish
bull. It is a useful Irishism, this "dying" to do something. I use it in the
sense of the old woman in Cork, praying devoutly to a black Dominican
saint, a statue as oxydised as the hands of Santa Clara in Assisi, who said
the other day, "Sure he's dying to be canonised."[7]

"I went to London," Shaw has said, "as my father went to the Stock
Exchange": because it was necessary for his business.[8] So Goldsmith went
into exile, and Wilde, and Joyce, and so it seemed to many other Irish writers a necessity to leave their own country. But this sense of necessity is an
accusation. It puts in an extreme form the accusation that in Ireland the
writer feels some inadequacy, and he goes from it, drawing its blood; his
price, its loss: the alternative apparently being that if he stays his country
may draw his blood; its price, his loss.

Is there in Ireland a real inadequacy? If we shift the scene and the time to
America in the fifties we come upon what I think is a fair analogy. It is
stated explicitly in Henry James's *Nathaniel Hawthorne*.[9] And that James
is not fully percipient, and may be even considered more than a little crass
about what that America had, and had not to offer does not take from the
value of his statement. On the contrary it makes it a still more valuable
statement since this is an American exile who utters very much the same
sort of complaint about America that an Irish exile might about Ireland.
We are not concerned here with what is so, but with what seems so to the
restless heart, and with the conclusions that the restless draw from this
seeming-so. For example, when James looks, at the very start of his story,
for the moral of Hawthorne's achievement – one of "three or four beautiful talents" that are the sum of the "modest transatlantic nosegay" – he
says that "the flower of art blooms only where the soil is deep, that it
takes a great deal of history to produce a little literature, and that it needs
a complex social machinery to set a writer in motion." When he says this,
our interest is not alone to consider whether he is right or wrong but to

7 Saint Claire of Assisi (1194–1253).
8 He misquotes here from the Preface to Shaw's *Immaturity*, which he correctly
cites in his earlier essays "The Strange Case of Sean O'Casey" and "Shaw's Prefaces":
Shaw's father worked in the Corn Exchange, not the Stock Exchange.
9 *Hawthorne* (1879).

observe that this is the sort of feeling that any writer anywhere, including Ireland, might have towards his environment.

It is true that James is more articulate than Hawthorne could have been: and in his excellent essay on Hawthorne (in the collection called *The Sense of Glory*) Mr. Herbert Read is, I feel, right in suggesting that Henry James is also speaking out of his own terror for what he himself fled from; and we make allowances accordingly.[10] But James is not exaggerating grossly when he speaks, with a shudder, of History as leaving in the United States "so thin and impalpable a deposit that we very soon touch the hard substratum of nature, and Nature herself in the Western world has the peculiarity of seeming rather crude and immature"; nor when he speaks of "the large juvenility stamped on the face of things"; nor when he thinks of "the social dreariness of a small New England community," or outlines the considerable practical difficulties of authorship there, and the social discomfort of being an author, or a would-be author, in a society still so provincial-minded that a man could hardly be counted a regular fellow unless he was also a regular businessman.

He cannot be exaggerating since what he says is still true of large expanses of the United States. (Fifty years later Willa Cather's *The Professor's House* reflected a similar background in the Middle West.)[11] Indeed a modern Irish writer will read much that he says in a very intimate understanding.

If the American tone at large was intensely provincial that of New England was not greatly helped by having the best of it. The state of things was extremely natural and there could be now no greater mistake than to speak of it with a redundancy of irony. American life had begun to constitute itself from the foundations; it had begun to *be* simply; it was at an immeasurable distance from having begun to enjoy ... Hawthorne must have vaguely entertained some such design upon destiny; but he must have felt that his success would have to depend wholly on his own ingenuity. I say he must have proposed to himself to enjoy, simply because he proposed to be an artist, and because this enters inevitably into the artist's scheme ... He proposes to give pleasure, and to give it he must first get it. Where he gets it will depend upon circumstances, and circumstances were not encouraging to Hawthorne. He was poor, he was solitary, and he undertook

---

10 *The Sense of Glory: Essays in Criticism* (1929), by Herbert Read (1893–1968).
11 *The Professor's House* (1925), by American author Willa Cather (1873–1947).

to devote himself to literature in a community in which the interest in literature was as yet of the smallest.

We understand that very well in this Ireland.

I repeat that it matters nothing for our purpose if this is James speaking with special feeling because he is thinking of himself in terms of Hawthorne; it merely means that he is the better fitted to sympathize with Hawthorne. We know that Hawthorne *was* poor, and *was* solitary (he spoke of his "cursed habit of solitariness"); and that he did slave at menial and unrewarding hack-work; and that he struggled with these melancholy circumstances unaided; and that the struggle boiled down to "How to be an Artist although an American." It is right to remember at once that Hawthorne triumphed, and that James fully acknowledges that when he did triumph the American public generously hailed him. But even this very hailing seems to irritate James. With the greater generosity of his greater understanding, perhaps with some suppressed anger for this easy acclaim, this throwing a rope to a man who has struggled to land unassisted, he insists on the discomforts endured and the risks involved in that solitary struggle:

The best things come, as a general thing, from the talents that are members of a group; every man works better when he has companions working in the same line, and yielding the stimulus of suggestion, comparison, emulation. Great things have, of course, been done by solitary workers; but they have usually been done with double the pains they would have cost if they had been produced under more genial circumstances. The solitary worker loses the profit of example and discussion; he is apt to make awkward experiments; he is in the nature of the case more or less of an empiric. The empiric may, as I say, be treated by the world as an expert; but the drawbacks and discomforts of empiricism remain to him and are in fact increased by the suspicion mingled with his gratitude of a want in the public taste of a sense of the proportion of things ...

As an Irish writer of to-day reads the story of Hawthorne's uncomfortable struggles, as recorded by another American writer who found his own way of evading these discomforts and dangers, the analogy, though not exact, strikes him forcibly in its larger elements. He understands the meaning of "social dreariness"; "juvenility"; the life that has "begun to constitute itself from the foundations; begun to *be* simply"; the difficulty of "enjoying" as an artist the ungenial circumstances; the lack of companionship as an artist; the "provincialism"; the frightening meaning and challenge of "empiricism" with all its humiliating implications of botched jobs, leaps in the dark and pigs in a poke. An Irish writer of to-day very well understands why any colleague should feel that the only way to avoid all this dreariness and waste of time is by exile, not for his comfort but for his safety. It is another question whether this feeling and this solution is fallacious. Goldsmith, Wilde, Joyce, Shaw and Moore worked well in exile. Synge, Yeats and O'Casey worked best at home. One cannot draw the noose tight. All we must conclude is that there are and always have been circumstances in Irish life that perturb and that drive some to flight; just as they perturbed Hawthorne (he is not entirely silent about his discomforts) and drove James into exile.

James summed up those circumstances in New England under the word provincialism; his description is well known. At first glance it is devastating. One may read it with modern Ireland in mind, comparing happily, or uncomfortably.

> Everything … indicates a simple, democratic, thinly-composed society … No State in the European sense of the word, and indeed barely a specific national name. No sovereign, no court, no personal loyalty, no aristocracy, no church, no clergy, no army, no diplomatic service, no country gentlemen, no palaces, nor castles, nor manors, nor old country houses, nor thatched cottages nor ivied ruins; no cathedrals, nor abbeys, nor little Norman churches; no great universities nor public schools – no Oxford, nor Eton, nor Harrow; no literature, no novels, no museums, no pictures, no political society, no sporting class – no Epsom, nor Ascot … The natural remark in the almost lurid light of such an indictment would be that if these things are left out everything is left out.[12]

And he asks – "What remains?" (To this William Dean Howells explosively replied, "Why, simply the whole of life.")[13]

12 The University of Oxford has no clear date of foundation, but it has been the site of teaching since the late eleventh century. Eton College and Harrow School, both English independent schools, were founded in 1440 and 1571, respectively. Epsom and Ascot are English racecourses with historic ties to the upper classes.
13 William Dean Howells (1837–1920) was a close friend of Henry James, and also a novelist and critic in his own right.

I can well imagine what would be the emotions of any fervently patriotic Irishman, not a writer, at the suggestion that there could possibly be
any sensible comparison between America in the 1850s and Ireland in the
1950s. He would reply (if he bothered to reply), and reply quite reasonably, that James has been answered fully by the effects of time. He would
say that the answer has been supplied by the appearance of Hemingway,
Dreiser, Lewis, Saroyan, O'Neill, Cather, and a score besides.[14] He would
say that Hawthorne himself answered it by his own achievement. And yet,
though that is all true, it is not for a writer, or any artist, the whole truth
about the frustrations, challenges, difficulties, problems and discourage-
ments of, to use James's phrase, "a thinly-composed society." Indeed to
flourish such names as Sinclair Lewis or Theodore Dreiser or Ernest
Hemingway is to give one answer to this question of James. Literature,
that is, could not develop in America other than side by side with the
development of society. When society "thickened" letters could grow
thicker. Not before. At the earlier period too much had been missing, as
James's list insisted, for literature to flourish.

"What remains?" James had asked, and Howells had answered crossly,
"Why, the whole of life!" It is not true. The ground has been shifted
between question and answer. From a ground of civilised or sophisticated
life we have been taken to a ground of "natural" (in the Romantics' sense)
or elemental life. We see this very clearly in Ireland to-day where the stratified, and fairly complex, social life which a writer of 1915, say, could have
known in Dublin has given way to a far more simple and uncomplex, a
much "thinner" social life. The life now known, or knowable, to any modern Irish writer is either the traditional, entirely simple life of the farm
(simple, intellectually speaking); or the groping, ambiguous, rather artless
urban life of these same farmers' sons and daughters who have, this last
twenty-five years, been taking over the towns and cities from the Anglo-
Irish. They have done it, so to speak, by rule of thumb, empirically, with
little skill. Their conventions are embryonic; their social patterns are indis-
tinct. True, the "whole of life" remains. But at what level of intelligence
and sensibility? True, we do possess many of the things James missed in
Hawthorne's America; but they are largely inherited by us, not made by us.
They are not marks or measurements of *us*. Their quondam significance,
of that order, is lost in a general jelly-like mass of friendly egalitarianism
which is as comfortable as it is indeterminate and where hammered-out
convictions and ideas are so few or so elementary as to suggest a quite
unperplexed and uninquisitive communal mind.

14 Theodore Dreiser (1871–1945).

~

These sentences, whose connotations will be clear enough to anybody who has lived in Ireland of recent years, may be too general for the stranger. He would do best, I think, to seize upon the word "egalitarianism." He must remember that since the foundation of the Irish Free State in 1922 a large social upheaval has been occurring, and that the sort of values which a visitor to Ireland previous to that date would have found dominating us have been largely replaced by quite another set of values. For example, in theory we struggled, up to 1922, for Liberty; in practice, as we now see, Liberty was a very secondary goal. Liberty is an English ideal; it is expressed in terms of personal rights, often hard won, usually embodied in class and convention. The English gentleman (even still) knows his place, and the taxi-man (even still) knows his place. It is an ideal which is not so highly considered outside of Britain; or, even when it is jealously cherished as in France, it is not so firmly protected by form and usage and class and convention. In republican countries, like France, America or Ireland (or must I add "Southern" to Ireland?) this idea of Liberty is constantly struggling with the idea of Equality, and so far as I can observe from the course of events in modern Ireland, if there were a toss-up between the two ideas Equality would always be much more likely to win. We are a friendly, sociable, light-hearted and easy-going people, and we do not, so far at any rate, take kindly to the notion that we must protect our liberties, that is our rights, from our neighbours, or that our neighbours should protect their rights from us. I have only to mention poaching to a fisherman to give him a vivid, and perhaps painful, picture of one result. I have only to mention the free-and-easy atmosphere of an Irish race-course to any man to evoke a vivid and happy picture of another result.

From the point of view of the *homme moyen sensuel* this may, or may not, according to his taste or upbringing, sound delightful. In many ways it *is* delightful.[15] (I find it so.) But from the point of view of the novelist it is a total disaster. The novel is a social document; it is what Trollope wrote and Balzac wrote; it does not deal with amorphous crowds but with closely organised and stratified society; it deals with the play of personality on personality; with accepted or debated values and conventions; with the clashes between the aberrants and the tradition; unless, as with Scott or Stevenson, the novel roves into adventure or fancy, forms which may be thought of as compensations, or as evasions from its more usual

---

15 For more on the *homme moyen sensual*, see O'Faolain's earlier essay "The Pleasures and Pains of Ireland."

role.[16] Well, there is only one firmly outlined social institution, if I may be allowed to call it that, in modern Ireland: the Catholic Church. Aberration from its codes (the reader must take my word for this) is virtually unknown in Ireland to-day otherwise than in the secrecy of the heart. If rebels exist they are most cautiously silent. A Mauriac novel is unthinkable here, where lust is furtive and passion as simple as among animals.[17] We sin, but with no intense feelings about it, other than fear. Our sins are tawdry, our virtues childlike, our revolts desultory and brief, our submissions formal and frequent. In this Ireland a policeman's lot is a supremely happy one. God smiles, the priest beams, and the novelist groans. In short Irish life to-day is not really so far removed from the simple America of the fifties as superficial appearances might at first suggest. The other day I took a film-tycoon into the Gresham Hotel in Dublin.[18] It was his first visit to Dublin. "Now this," he said, looking around, "corresponds, I suppose, to Claridges?"[19] I looked around, in astonishment, at the good folk up from the country. "No," I sighed. "It corresponds to the Garden of Eden. Except that they are all dressed." And I thought to myself that they certainly have not eaten of the apple of knowledge.

One sees the effects on letters? The limitations? The fewness of available subjects for plays or novels? Rural life fed the first years of the Abbey Theatre with rich food for farce and melodrama; its dramatists quickly and joyously exploited the obvious – mixed marriages, land-hunger, peasant greed, religious fervour, political passion, small-town intrigue, family feuds. We have had them all in various shapes and guises, over and over, and to tell the plain truth plainly we are rather bored with them. Elizabeth Bowen, George Moore, Somerville and Ross, Lennox Robinson, Daniel Corkery, James Joyce all got one novel each out of the social picture in Ireland, and no more. Lord Dunsany has always wisely written fantastical novels about Ireland, never realistic. Austin Clarke has written wholly about medieval Ireland. All of James Stephens is fantasy. As one glances over the lists one becomes more and more aware of the limits set by "the thinly-composed society," as far as concerns prose. And while poetry can feed on air it is not an eagerly poetic period in Ireland now; it is a period in which the stage is set for prose and prose is starving for something to write about. No! William Dean Howells is not right. The "whole of life"

16 Walter Scott (1771–1832) was a popular Scottish historical novelist.
17 François Mauriac.
18 The Gresham is, to this day, one of Dublin's poshest hotels.
19 Claridges is a luxury hotel in London.

does *not* remain when social conventions and social institutions are simple, few, or in flux. In such an unshaped society there are many subjects for little pieces, that is for the short-story writer; the novelist or the dramatist loses himself in the general amorphism, unthinkingness, brainlessness, egalitarianism and general unsophistication. Speak of simplicity, or of Arcadia, if you will. All one can write about Arcadia is a treatise or a musical comedy.

~

"The play of personality upon personality." It is all there. How on earth can anybody play this game if the characters themselves are not interesting personalities? And when I cast about me in modern Ireland for the possible personalities of a Henry James novel I see at once what is missing in Ireland to-day. For such a play one needs three elements in every character, or main character: self-awareness, sensitive conscience, refinement. (One does not, of course, require these elements to a degree amounting to complete self-possession; on the contrary a character is more interesting when he contains these elements to a degree short of self-possession.) In modern Irish life these eloquently are, alas, either completely missing or embryonic. We constantly evade conscience, often by that awful self-destructive Irish gift of jocosity, cynicism's great ally, often by simply refusing to develop an instinct which, it must be admitted, is an uncomfortable sort of daemon to nourish in one's bosom. Self-awareness, therefore, is inevitably slight. Refinement we can boast of, and I would not insist on it apart from the other two, without which, however strong it is in nature, it must be of small intellectual interest. The writer of novels and plays is thus constantly thrown back on the semi-articulate, or inarticulate peasant, on his surges of passionate feelings, which are often of a terrific, primitive force but which are so unrelated to intelligence that we soon tire of them. Indeed we begin to think of their victims as sheep butting and groping in a furze-bush where chance has entangled them and from which they can only extract themselves with crude violence. It all boils down to Hawthorne's "thin" society, stuff for the anthropologist rather than the man of letters.

~

I think it is obvious that realism as a technique for dealing with such material soon arrives at a dead-end. The realist, content to describe, without comment, the local life he knows intimately, will get one powerful book out of its surges and thrustings and gropings. After that he will either have to repeat himself endlessly, or stop. Man is, after all, a thinking animal, and *a writer must want to think* – think through and with his people. If *they* will not think, how can he use them? (Such a consideration would not trouble the Americans; e.g., men like Erskine Caldwell, who go on writing their "So What" novels *ad infinitum*.) If a writer cannot rise above or transmute this unpromising material (as Thomas Hardy did), or get out of its clutches in some way (as Stevenson did) he soon gets bogged in its not-so-rich soil.

In Ireland the two dissolvents of this earthy material have always been, hitherto, humour and poetry. The humour, thank heaven, is always with us; sometimes low; sometimes not so low; always welcome. The poetry has ebbed; poetry in the sense in which we warm, because of it, to *The Charterhouse of Parma*, or to *Il Santo*, or James Stephens' *The Charwoman's Daughter*, or *Dead Souls*, or *Tess*, or *The Torrents of Spring*, or Aymé's *Uranus*, or any novel that lifts us out of the toils of naturalism; poetry which is partly wit, partly romanticism, partly fancy, partly a sort of intoxicated, sharpened, gay intelligence – Stendhal and Gogol – poetry which breaks the mould.[20] It is an element which cannot be brought back into literature by an act of will. All we can do, in this period of pause, is to experiment with it, to be empirics, to incite writers coming after us, by our very failure, to see and to say how much better it could be done.

∾

On one thing I must insist: this is not just an Irish dilemma. It is the dilemma of all regionalist or provincial writers. That excellent essay by Herbert Read to which I have referred indicates how some of them solved it: he mentions the Brontës, Hardy, Sterne, even Wordsworth. He might have made much play with the most remarkable example of all, Jane Austen. And indeed, when we look carefully into the other names, it is she, more than any of them, who faced the problem squarely. (She offers, for the reasons I have given, but little encouragement to Irish writers, beyond the passionate wish that Miss Elizabeth Bowen, who could still do it, might yet apply Jane Austen's technique to what is left of the more complex forms of life in provincial Ireland; that life of the Big House which, as her one Irish novel *The Last September* shows, she knows so well.)[21]

20 *The Charterhouse of Parma* (1839), by Stendhal (1783–1842), the *nom de plume* of Marie-Henri Beyle; *Il Santo* (1906), by Italian author Antonio Fogazzaro (1842–1911); *Dead Souls* (1842), by Nikolay Gogol; *Uranus* (1948), by Marcel Aymé (1902–1967).
21 *The Last September* (1929).

The question "How to be an Artist although an American" easily becomes "How to be an Artist although living in Stoke-on-Trent"; with Bennett doing his best work about the Five Towns and then coming up to the metropolis, and, with the exception of *Riceyman Steps* falling off sadly.[22] The Swiss must know this problem intimately. All the French provincials must know it. George Sand knew it, and occasionally solved it.[23] Balzac knew it, and met it by not bothering his head too much about realism; for *The Country Doctor* is not authentic – the whole background life was made up out of his head.[24] Flaubert, as we know, did not solve it: he got the usual one book out of the provinces, and that was not a solution but a *tour de force*. The Italian novel and theatre has never flourished, largely, in my feeling, because of this same lack of self-awareness, conscience and refinement in the Italian nature.

There is nothing like being gloomy when one is being gloomy. It may well be that the novel as a literary form is in a pickle everywhere to-day. It may be that whereas the provinces have not arrived at the conditions suitable for fiction, like babies who are too revolting to be photographed, the centres have outlived those conditions, like cheese that has become too ripe to be eaten. On the one hand values are not established and codified; on the other hand they have become disestablished and disintegrated. One adultery sufficed for a Hardy novel. A hundred would not make a modern novel. Men like Graham Greene get thereby driven back to fundamentals, such as God and Hell and Sin, and the public sits up at the sight of those novel words. Or does it? Or does it not, rather, sit up at the thriller-stuff; mentally translating Scobie's or Pinkie's religious conflicts into the terminology of the psychiatrist – "abnormal" and so forth.[25] And anyway Graham Greene and Mauriac, as novelists, *are* abnormal. One could not wish for many more Mauriacs?[26] One Graham Greene is magnificent; two would be a comedy; three would be the Marx Bros. If we have to say that the only hope for writing is the constant violent injection of one part God and two parts Satan it would really be better to lay the typewriter away in some sort of Shangri La until this

22 *Riceyman Steps* (1923), by Arnold Bennett.

23 French novelist George Sand (1804–1876), pseudonym of Amantine-Lucille-Aurore Dudevant, née Dupin.

24 *The Country Doctor* (1833).

25 Pinkie Brown is a gang leader in *Brighton Rock* (1938); Henry Scobie is a police commissioner in West Africa in *The Heart of the Matter* (1948).

26 O'Faolain again ends a statement with a question mark, apparently to provoke thought.

dancing mass of atoms we call modern society settles down sufficiently to be observed again calmly by that imaginative recorder and truthful liar, the writer of fiction.[27] By that time Ireland, catching up as usual, will probably be in the throes of the Reformation or the Black Death, and so we shall never solve our literary problems at all.[28]

27 Shangri-La is the name of a Utopian Tibetan lamassery that first appeared in *Lost Horizon* (1933), a novel by English author James Hilton (1900–1954).
28 The Reformation is the name for the revolution that arose out of the challenges to the Catholic Church, beginning in the early sixteenth century with such figures as Martin Luther and John Calvin; it led to the establishment of Protestantism. The Black Death was a pandemic that lasted from 1347 to 1351, wiping out a large proportion of Europe's population.

Religious Art[1]

One cannot defend a set of religious paintings on the ground that they are "conventional," or attack them because they are "unconventional." These are terms with a vast complex of meanings, and a whole history of aesthetic debate lies behind them. What does conventional mean in practice, is the question.

There are pleasant and there are unpleasant conventions, and a great many religious and religious-art conventions might be held to be quite unpleasant. In Spain if it is not exactly a convention it is certainly not regarded as unconventional to depict the Crucifixion with what we would consider a hideous exaggeration of torture and bleeding; and we may dislike those conventional Italian Virgins dressed in not always clean, in fact sometimes dirty and tattered, lace, pink and blue satin, glass beads, gaudy tinsel, strings of Woolworth-Upim pears and perhaps carrying an old basket in which are piled lire notes.[2]

1 "Religious Art" appeared in *The Bell* 16, no. 4 (January 1951): 39–42. The essay was preceded by the following statement:
  Recently a set of Stations of the Cross were criticised in the Press on the ground of their conventionality. The painter was defended on the ground that religious art is intended to edify, that this is the prime consideration, and that the people are accustomed to a certain type of conventional treatment from which, because of this need for edification, it would be fatal to depart.
  Stations of the Cross are a series of fourteen images portraying the events of the Passion of Christ, beginning with the judgment by Pontius Pilate and ending with Christ being placed in His tomb.
2 Upim is a department store chain in Italy that is roughly the equivalent of the former F.W. Woolworth chain, which would have been well known to O'Faolain's readers.

Yet, they presumably edify? Ergo: no more is to be said? But, surely, much more is to be said. On this basis of edification must all religious art be graded to the level of the unsophisticated? On that basis we would never have had any religious art at all. It would not have worked, certainly, in the trecento and the quattrocento.³ Then an aristocracy imposed its taste on the populace. Democracy has since dragged those standards down and down. In Eire our churchmen are our only effective aristocracy. It cannot be necessary to labour the obvious implication.

Are we, in fact, reared in a convention of religious art? I think the essential fault one may find with religious art in Eire is that it is in no convention at all. We are mostly brought up on sentimental German prints which are the almost total debasement of a once noble, largely Italian, convention. Time was when we had a conventional religious art. We may see it in the entrance-hall of the National Museum, in ruined churches throughout the country.⁴ It presumably once edified?

The question, then, is not only one of edification, but of the level on which the edification occurs. Perhaps it may be said that it doesn't matter on what level it occurs, so long as it occurs. A dozen heresies might be quoted as illustrations to the contrary. But the real objection to this theory is that it is based on the implicit notion that there is one religion for the simple and another for the sophisticated. The Church, it is implied, has to keep the masses in order with sentimental slushery from the commercial-religious-art shops, but to be sure it knows better, and does better for the better-educated groups. The better-educated might reasonably conclude that the same thing can be said of sermons; that most of these are intended for the masses, but that there is, of course, an inner circle that knows better and where you can get a better commodity: e.g., a Redemptorist for the mob but a Ronny Knox for the nob.⁵ And the same would gradually apply to all sorts of other things, such as miracles, to be handed out to the mob in a crudely simple form, but to be interpreted, subtilised, metaphysicised

3 The Trecento and the Quattrocento are cultural periods in Italy that correspond to and are named for the 1300s and 1400s, respectively.
4 The National Museum of Ireland was founded in 1877 as The Museum of Science and Art, Dublin, but its name was changed in 1921 to reflect the country's independence. Its building on Kildare Street was designed by Thomas Newenham Deane (1828–1899) and opened in 1920. It incorporates Irish and continental influences, including in the design of its entrance hall, the Rotunda as it is called.
5 Ronald Knox (1888–1957) was an English theologian, novelist, and translator of the Bible. The nob is slang for those who are wealthy.

and abraded away for the others. The next step would be the difficult dogma, like the Assumption, which one country priest was heard to handle with a direct, unassailable *foi de charbonnier* as the lifting up of the Virgin "holus-bolus-body-and-bones into heaven";[6] while a subtle Dominican descanted on the theme of "What, after all, is Death?" Well, it may be said, in a way isn't that how it works, has always worked, always will work, in secular matters as in religious? But is it? As long as we had an obedient mob, perhaps yes: a totally unlettered mob; a mob which only mixed with mob; a mob which did not mix with sceptical mobs, cynical mobs, rationalist mobs, argumentative mobs, socialist mobs, even communist mobs. But now? An English bishop pointed out some time ago to Maynooth that if all the Irish whom we have exported to Britain had remained Catholic there would now be millions more Catholics in Britain than there actually are. This theory of the two circles, outer and inner, loses to the Church large proportions of both outer and inner, and lowers the total morale.

It is accompanied here by the theory of protection for the simple: they must not hear of the wicked world: they must not read anything, for example, but the most innocuous and simple-minded and unchallenging books. The result is frightening on every count. For it means that we export boys and girls with minds quite unprepared; and those we retain are insulated, isolated, and smug. It is not so elsewhere. The Italian masses, for example, may be unlettered, but the pressure of the world outside, and of the world inside through various relentlessly-challenging groups leaves no room for smugness. You *might* argue that, in Italy, it is better to cultivate a fervent mob than to cultivate religious art, or high religious thinking; you *might* there ignore the educated classes, set the Christian masses against the other masses, if you thought it a good tactic, because you would at least know that your Christian masses would fight. But here – remote from the maelstrom – the result of catering for simplicity is willy-nilly, to cater also for ignorance, mental torpor, indifference to the way of the world and a highly ambiguous morality, to produce, in short, a mob which does not want to do anything at all but be ... "edified?" Edified for what purpose? To get to the next world safely? Without

6 The Assumption is the doctrine that Mary, the mother of Jesus Christ, ascended – or was assumed – into heaven in body as well as spirit at the end of her earthly life; it is fêted on 15 August. To have *la foi de charbonnier*, which directly translated from French means "the faith of a collier," is to be absolutely convinced of something.

more than the minimum reference to this one? It sounds mighty like Plymouth Brethrenism to me.[7]

The point is that the pattern of a country's life is interwoven. You cannot chop it up. It isn't several patterns. It is one. You say, "Oh! Religious *Art*! That's not important. Edification is what's important." And you have thereby cut out a hole from pattern. The whole blessed pattern would soon be moth-holed if we went on like this. A country's life is tested here, there and everywhere. It's not really important to dress well? To make our houses look good? To eat interesting food? To be formal in our behaviour? To wash or to shave in the morning? To keep appointments? To do this, that and the other? The same applies to a Church. Why not say, "It's not important to pay your dues? It's not important if the Holy Water font looks like Dollymount at low-tide?[8] It's not important if nuns talk balderdash about the Inquisition to their classes? It's not important if Bishops' pastorals are boring? It's not important if ..."

What then *is* important? The answer is that everything is important, including Religious Art. If the religious art of a country is of a low standard you may safely conclude that the intellectual vitality of that country – and of that Church – is also of a low standard. One may be quite certain that any parish priest who decks his church without taste will give a sermon without intelligence; he will no doubt be a good man; but he is not likely to raise the standards of his church; and is it likely that he will raise the standards of his people?

7 The Plymouth Brethren are members of an Evangelical movement that began in Ireland but was founded in Plymouth, England, in 1831.
8 Dollymount Strand is the five kilometre eastern beach of Bull Island, located in the north of Dublin Bay.

Autoantiamericanism[1]

Recently, an article[2] in *The Irish Times*, about I.D.A.- E.C.A. plans for co-operation between Irish industrialists and American industrialist experts to help, by consultation, advice and suggestions, to step-up Irish productivity and improve Irish markets had one unforeseen effect on productivity.[3] It produced the following I'll-curdle-yer-blooming-blood letter from Miss Louie Bennett, who is founder of the Irish Women

---

1 "Autoantiamericanism" appeared in *The Bell* 16, no. 6 (March 1951): 7–18. The essay touched off considerable controversy, drawing four published responses by Hubert Butler, Brigid Lalor, D. Sevitt, and Louie Bennett. It was a letter from Bennett to the press, quoted by O'Faolain in this essay, that had provoked him to write the piece. *The Bell* prepared its readers for controversy by appending a footnote to the essay: "The commentary on O'Faolain's AUTOANTIAMERICANISM will appear in our May issue." The responses were collected under the title "Autoantiamericanism: Four Comments," *The Bell* 17, no. 2 (May 1951): 8–28. O'Faolain responded in kind with "Autoantiamericanism," *The Bell* 17, no. 3 (June 1951): 57–9.

2 *O'Faolain's note:* "Pin-pointing Politics" by Aknefton. January 20, 1951. [*Editor's note:* Aknefton was reputedly the pseudonym for three authors: Chris Ferguson of the Worker's Union of Ireland; Sheila Greene, the former editor of the *Irish People*; and Michael McInerney, the political correspondent of *The Irish Times*.]

3 The I.D.A. is Ireland's Industrial Development Agency, formed in 1949 as part of the Department of Industry and Commerce. The E.C.A. is the United States' Economic Cooperation Administration, a governmental agency created in 1948 to administer the Marshall Plan and expand direct trade. The Marshall Plan, which was implemented from 1948 to 1951, was meant to provide economic assistance to western and southern European countries in order to combat the poverty and unemployment that were making communist parties more attractive to their citizens.

Workers' Union and one time President of the Trades Union Congress.[4]
She circulated it to all the Dublin papers. I quote it from *The Irish Press*
of January 23rd:

Dear Sir,
   Our newspapers have failed to give big headlines to the information that the I.D.A. and E.C.A. have jointly evolved a large-scale
plan for the expansion of existing Irish industries and the establishment of new ones. Apparently this plan will be carried out under
American direction and according to American methods. We might
query the wisdom of the attempt to Americanise our Irish economy
from many aspects. But for those of us who view with anxiety the
subtle over-all "penetration" of Ireland by the E.C.A. the primary
question that arises is, what does America hope to gain from the
development of Irish industry?
   The American government is not more purely altruistic than any
other Government. They look for returns in some form from their
investments. Their interest in us at the moment must inevitably be
coloured by their Defence campaign. War-preparations are now the
all-absorbing and dominant interest of ruling authorities in America.
This far-reaching plan now emerging from the I.D.A. and the E.C.A.
should therefore make us pause to consider whether we wish to be
entangled in America's international policy, and perhaps used for her
particular purposes in the event of another world war.
   Are we drifting into such entanglements, or is it the deliberate policy
of our government to link Ireland with the U.S.A. in external affairs?
We are made aware that we are outside the Atlantic Pact only because
of partition.[5] But America can provide a back door to the Pact.
   It seems a long step from an innocent plan for industrial development to co-operation with the Atlantic Pact group. But the spectre of
war makes some of us think, "Whither now?" on every new evidence
of peaceful penetration which the E.C.A. have initiated here.
                                        Yours sincerely,
                                        LOUIE BENNETT

4 Louie Bennett (1870–1956) was president of the Irish Trades Union Congress,
founded in 1894. The Irish Women Workers' Union was founded in 1911.
5 The Atlantic pact is better known as the North Atlantic Treaty Organization, or
NATO, which was established in 1949. The United Kingdom is an original member,
but Ireland has never joined.

The version sent to *The Irish Times* concluded gratefully with the quotation: "*Timeo Danaos et dona ferentes.*"[6] I fear the Greeks even when they are bringing gifts. It was cut out of the *Irish Press* version. This presumably refers to the generous gift (not loan) of $16,000,000 which America has given to Ireland. Now, I have a great respect and regard for Louie Bennett who has spent a lifetime in devoted service to various humanitarian and liberal causes, but I can only see in this outburst an example of what I call Auto-anti-ism, which is short for Autoantiamericanism. It is unreasoned. Not one fact is produced. It is a purely emotional reaction. I propose to use this letter as a peg on which to hang an article on Antiamericanism, with apologies, if they are needed, to an old neighbour and friend.

What are the sources, motives or unconscious origins of Anti-Americanism? First, I would put *British Influences.* Secondly, *General Loss of Belief.* Leading to, thirdly, *Suspiciousness*, directed against America in particular. Lastly I will take *Patriotism*, however misapplied.

1. BRITISH INFLUENCES. Mainly from the Old Guard, but by no means only. That it should exist there is only natural, and that it should start immediately the Marshall Plan was mooted. It cannot be nice for Britain to have to descend from being a Class I Power, and the world's Banker, to the role of a Class II Power taking loans from America, now in a position to be a world-leader. The British would not be human if they had liked it, or if they did not begin to feel suspicious, critical, a bit sore and even a bit sour. Some sections became and have remained very sour indeed, and go on being sour. Evelyn Waugh once called their sourness "the snarl of the under-dog at his benefactor."[7] That was in the pages of *The New Statesman.*[8] I suppose no English paper better represents the extreme anti-Americanism in Britain: and, as it happens, no paper has as much influence on our own periodical-reading public. It is the organ of genuine Socialists. It contains very good literary articles. It is also the British Bible of every washed-up Liberal, soured Conservative, lapsed Catholic, half-baked Grammar School intellectual, the new technical school boys whose knowing twang you hear on every bus, every manic-depressive Orwellite,

6 This quote, which O'Faolain translates in the following sentence, appears in Book II, line 49, of Virgil's *Aeneid*. The phrase is uttered by Laocoön when he warns the people not to accept the gift of the Trojan horse. It has come to be better known in English as "Beware of Greeks bearing gifts."
7 English novelist Evelyn Waugh (1903–1966).
8 *New Statesman* is a weekly political and literary magazine that was founded by Sidney and Beatrice Webb in 1913.

fissurated Koestlerite, pre-historic Fabian, antique Keir Hardyite,[9] flaming anti-Roman Catholic, like Mr. Trevor-Roper or the editor himself, Mr. Kingsley Martin, and every other unhappy misfit, pink and pacifist whose sole prophylactic against despair, if not suicide is a weekly injection of Kingsley Martin's Bottled Bellyache.[10] Other papers are more polite, or not so outspoken. The *Daily Herald* recently published a "Low" cartoon which summed up the midway attitude of most Britishers to America. One half of the cartoon showed an Englishman looking at a wild Elk, Moose, or other flannel-mouthed American, carrying a tomahawk and in an Indian head-dress, howling bloody-murder into a microphone, with a little Englishman saying, "What a headache sometimes to be with America!" The other half of the cartoon showed Stalin with a sack and a rope smilingly beckoning the same little Englishman to come into his bag, and the Englishman is saying now, "But to be without America – O Lor!" The fact is, the Americans have learned the sad truth that the only people in this universe to whom you can give, or even lend something without humiliating them are the poor, who have always lived on favours, and the rich, who take favours as their due. You could have made a gift of all Africa to Queen Victoria and she would have simply said "Thank you." But give a gift of sixteen million dollars to Ireland and see what you get!

Well, where do we get our world-news and world-views from? Work it out for yourself. Oh, yes! We are *very* independent-minded! But you cannot prevent it from seeping in, especially if you are at all inclined that way.

2. UNBELIEF. It is the phenomenon of our time that nobody any longer believes in anybody. Time was when the Munster Fusiliers went off from the Glanmire Station to fight Kruger or the Czar with a song on their lips.[11] "And the Rooshians shall not have Constantinople … "[12] The world has opened up, or closed in, since then. Nobody then told us that the Cross

9 J. Keir Hardie (1856–1915) was a British labour leader. Hugh Trevor-Roper (1914–2003) was a British historian.
10 English journalist Kingsley Martin (1897–1969) edited the *New Statesman* from 1930 to 1960.
11 The Royal Munster Fusiliers was a British army infantry brigade that was formed in 1881 with the amalgamation of the 101st Regiment of Foot (Royal Bengal Fusiliers) and the 104th Regiment of Foot (Bengal Fusiliers), both of which were founded in 1756; it was disbanded when the Irish state declared its independence in 1922.
12 Constantinople is the former name of Istanbul, Turkey, from its foundation in 330 to 1930. It was named for its founder, the Roman Emperor Constantine I (280–337), also known as Constantine the Great.

and the Crescent were on the same flag. We believed that "it was all right." All over the world, since then, men have been going off to fight wars with less and less certainty that it is "all right." Now, only the Russians and the Americans seem to believe firmly that anything is worth fighting for. The French? Frustrated, exhausted, and cynical. Would anybody have believed five or six years ago that France would ever agree to the re-arming of Germany? And the Germans? They don't want to re-arm. They are terrified as well they might be. The Italians? Weighted down by the cynical selfishness of the middle-classes on whom De Gasperi and the Christian Democrats have only now begun to turn the screw, driven to it by the pressure of the Communists on one side and by the pressure of the Americans on the other.[13] The British? How *can* these poor devils want to fight, when they have hardly enough to eat?

And, everywhere, the old *trahison des clercs* is with us again.[14] These sceptical, clever gentlemen having once believed in the millennium – have we forgotten the Lefty poets of the 'twenties? – now believe in nothing, neither in Capitalism nor Communism in their own country nor in any other country: they mock the past and they moan over the future, they don't believe that anything is wrong or right, good or bad, worth living for or dying for. They moan feebly, "World in a perfectly rotten way, old chap!" "La guerre? Quelle blague!"[15] "Che sciocchezza!"[16] Not that there is anything new in this. Anybody who knew England at the time of Dunkirk knows that when those brainy boys were saying in every elegant restaurant, "I'm afraid, old man, we're finished!" a very wicked old man with a cigar was calling on the brainless Bills of England in every local to pull up their trousers, with or without a blasphemy and go out and fight Nazism with pitchforks.[17]

13 Alcide De Gasperi (1881–1954) was the leader of the Christian Democratic Party and prime minister of Italy from 1945 to 1953.

14 In *La Trahison des clercs* (1927), translated from the French as *The Treason of the Intellectuals*, by Julien Benda (1867–1956), a leading French philosopher, denounces those who betray truth and justice for political and economic gain. The phrase became well-known after the book's publication.

15 "La guerre? Quelle blague!" translates from the French as "The war? What a joke!"

16 "Che sciocchezza!" translates from the Italian as "What foolishness!"

17 From 26 May to 4 June 1940, over 300,000 British, French, and Belgian troops were saved from the advancing German army when they were evacuated from the northern French seaport of Dunkirk to England.

Unbelief has been creeping slowly over us all for a hundred and fifty years, ever since Benthamism started asking about everything – not, I must agree in honesty, always without justification – "What is the use of it?"[18] The Marxist rationalist dialectic of our day has further infected every one of us whether we know it or not, killing all the poetry and mystery of life. There is not a single item in current life or in history that we do not tend to explain by this cynical dialectic. There are many who if they saw a rich man giving a sixpence to a blind man would at once explain it in terms of economic self-interest. I suppose that when they read that John Howard spent his life trying to reform the prison system, or that William Wilberforce persuaded the British tax-payers to cough up 20,000,000 pounds for the abolition of slavery they have the cynical answer all pat and ready.[19] Howard did it, I suppose, for gain? And Wilberforce did it for gain?

Would it not be more just, instead of cynically believing that everybody is in everything for anything they can get out of it, to make some effort to find out whether the Americans are in fact doing anything for Europe?

This October-November I went down into the wilds of Calabria to see for myself what they are doing in one corner of Europe.[20] If you want to know what "wilds" mean, and the hard life that goes with them, with which *nothing* in the poorest western farm here is comparable, go up into the Great Sila: a bare – that is to say *bare* – plateau of rolling, leonine clay, without schools, without houses, without telephones, without roads (except the main road), without enough water to drink, without a shrub or a tree;[21] where, for ever since the days of Norman feudalism the land

18 Jeremy Bentham (1748–1832) was the earliest and chief proponent of utilitarianism, the doctrine that humans should be driven by the desire to assure the greatest happiness for the greatest number of people.
19 When he became the high sheriff of Bedfordshire in 1773, John Howard (1726–1790) was so shocked at prison conditions that he worked towards persuading the House of Commons to reform the penal system and the treatment of prisoners in two acts in 1774. William Wilberforce (1759–1833) was a British politician who from 1787 was a prominent leader in the struggle to abolish the slave trade and slavery.
20 Calabria is a region in southern Italy, the "toe" of the "boot." O'Faolain writes of his experiences in the region in his travel book *An Autumn in Italy* (1953).
21 O'Faolain speaks of the leonine clay in *An Autumn in Italy*. Of his experience in the village of Crotone, he writes: "I had only been here three days and already the bare Ethopian beauty of this Southwest was stealing slowly into my senses. It is like falling in love with the desert. It creeps into one like its own peculiar smell; that hot Calabrian smell that is like half-remembered music, a poignant blend of growing spring and dying autumn, less a scent than a musk. It comes from the

has been owned by big landlords living in comfort far away from it all; where 90% of the peasants don't own a square inch of soil; where they live not on the land – hence the bareness – but in remote, stinking, villages suppurating with men, women, children, hens and pigs, sometimes ten to a room, and I have seen them *twenty* to a room, without light and without sanitation: a land scourged by malaria in the past, as it is blasted by wind to-day and worn by erosion because the landlords don't give a tinker's damn so long as they have enough lire to play baccarat in Monte Carlo.[22]

Into that worn-out land the Americans have poured millions upon millions upon millions of lire – I can give the figures; but any figure above seven-and-sixpence means nothing to me – to reclaim the exhausted soil; to recreate and establish on it a peasant life that has been almost crushed out by the most putrefied landlordism in the world; all the time pushing and pushing at the Government until at last the land is being expropriated, on payment, and given to the people. I am not ashamed to say the tears often blinded me, and I have seen many another as moved, to see old men, who might be my grandfather, or your's, getting at last the amazing gift of liberty for their children and their children's children. They hardly believe it when it happens. I have heard one old man saying, "I *won't* believe it! Not until I take up the clay in my fist and say, *It is mine!*"

It is all exactly as if America came here in the 1840s and took England by the back of the neck, and poured money into our soil, and made the landlords share the land, and ploughed and enriched the land and saved us from Famine and the miseries of revolution. There are, to be sure, plenty of Italians who are protesting. The Fascist Old Guard are squealing like mad. But you don't hear the peasants squealing, and Communism is wilting there before your eyes.

Well? If some sceptic went down there would he say, "Ha, ha! But what is the u.s.a. getting *out* of it?" I suppose he would. He would look for the catch rather than for the faith. I will tell you what the u.s.a. is putting *into* it. The whole of Marshall Aid to the end of 1950 has cost every crude,

---

dried cistus. On a warm night it swoons. This bare beauty conquers us as gently as its single colour changes, this omnipresent leonine dusty or sodden clay, wavering into a dozen shades under the passing clouds" (176).

22 The lira (lire in the plural) was the currency of Italy until 2002, when the Euro took its place. Baccarat is a casino card game. Monte Carlo is a luxurious resort located in the principality of Monaco; it lies on the French Mediterranean coast near the Italian border, and is famous for its glamorous casino, which was opened in 1861.

rude, grasping, vulgar, selfish, racketeering American fifteen shillings a week out of his back-pocket. All those billions are a free grant to Italy.

You have never seen the town of Matera in Lucania?[23] A pity. It's worth seeing. The entire poor quarter consists of holes dug out of a mighty cliff face, honeycombed with them, with one wall of mud or stones closing the opening, and in this wall a door – the only ingress for light and air and the only egress for smoke; housing father, mother, children, grandchildren, the mule, the hens, and maybe a pig. No sanitation whatever. These truly wretched people had to wait until far-off Americans came to build houses and sewers for them. I could mention half a dozen such examples, the burning memory of which makes me just wonder whether the people who believe America has only selfish aims in Europe are not the meanest, most ungrateful abortions on earth.

3. SUSPICION. Here the Auto-anti cries, "I suspect the Yanks. The Yanks cannot be doing all this for nothing! They are just preserving capitalism." What a discovery! I have no doubt that in the process of preserving other things they *are* preserving capitalism. And why not? Aren't *we* preserving capitalism? Or, perhaps, dear reader, you say you are a socialist? You want to preserve State Capitalism? That is, you wish to wipe out private ownership completely – England has not and doesn't wish to? You wish to replace every individual employer in Ireland by a State Board? Oh, perhaps, you are a Communist? In which case I can at least respect your honesty. For I can understand a man honestly being anticapitalist and anti-American; I can understand a man being pro-capitalist and pro-American, but I can have no patience with the man who is so fissurated and addled as to be on principle a pro-Capitalist and an anti-American. He may on this subject or that disagree with American methods. That is another matter.

But we must ask just why does the auto-anti use this word Capitalism at all? Is there nobody else in what we call Democracy but capitalists? Does the auto-anti want to whittle down Democracy to the pounds, the francs, the lire and dollars in the employers' pockets? If so, is this not part of that cynical materialist-dialectic I have just mentioned? Here is the opening paragraph of the Agreement we have signed with America – the words are taken from the opening of the Master Act of Congress to whose purposes and policies our Government has expressed complete adherence:

23 Matera is a city in the Basilicata region of Italy. Lucania is an ancient territorial division of southern Italy.

Recognising that the restoration or maintenance in European countries of principles of individual liberty, free institutions and genuine
independence rests largely upon the establishment of sound economic conditions, stable international economic relationships and
the achievement by the countries of Europe of a healthy economy
independent of extraordinary outside assistance ... the respective representatives (in our case Mr. Sean MacBride and the American
Minister) have signed the present Agreement.[24]

If that is what you mean by "preserving Captialism," then the Americans
have said, and *we* have said, over and over again, that we are doing precisely what you say. Have you, dear reader, anything against it?

"Oh! well!" our suspicious friend persists. "What I *really* mean is that
the Americans have simply organised the Marshall Plan to sell their own
goods over here. The whole thing is a racket. They *have* to have world-
markets! It's as plain as a pikestaff!" Is it? Perhaps we had better have a
few cold figures. (Our suspicious anti is, after all, merely saying what
Miss Bennett said: "What does America hope to gain from the development of Irish industry?")

The gross National Productivity of the United States in 1948, in round
figures of dollars, was 262,000 millions. In that year the entire world
outside the U.S.A. took from her 5% of her total products. In 1949 she
produced 257,000 millions. The entire world took in that year 4.8% of
her total products. Last year she produced 278,000 millions. The entire
world took from her only 3.6% of her total products.

Let's see how much of her total products she off-loaded on to Ireland.
In 1948 we took of her total 0.00175%. In 1948 we took 0.00328%.
Last year we took 0.00212%. It does not look, does it, as if the U.S.A.
would die without us – or the world? If the Marshall Plan was a plan
invented to sell America's goods abroad it has been a total wash-out.

Mind you, 5% or even 3.6%, is not to be sniffed at. It meant that in
1948 the U.S.A. exported 13,000 million dollars' worth. On the other
hand she imported 8,000 million dollars' worth. It meant that last year
she exported 10,000 million dollars' worth (estimated). But, then, she

24 Seán MacBride (1904–1988), son of Irish revolutionaries Maud Gonne
(1866–1953) and John MacBride (1865–1916), was Ireland's minister for external
affairs from 1948 to 1951; he was awarded the Nobel Peace Prize in 1974 for his
humanitarian work, most notably as founding chairman of Amnesty International
from 1961 to 1975.

imported (estimated) 9,000 millions worth. The "gap" was closing. It is of some interest that since 1947 her total exports have dropped from 15,000 millions to 10,000 millions, while her total imports have gone up between '47 and '50 from 6,000 millions to 9,000 millions. So that, once again, the Marshall Plan as a clever salesman's plan does not seem to have worked out very well?[25]

By the same token we Irish quadrupled our exports to the United States between 1947 and 1950. We went from one million to four million. Between 1947 and 1950, the same years, American exports to Ireland *dropped* from 118 millions to 59 millions. You can, if you think so, say we are importing far too much, and that our gap is closing very, very slowly indeed, but you *cannot* say that the Marshall Plan is selling us more goods.

I am bound to say that these figures have all been kindly supplied to me, at my request, by E.C.A.

4. PATRIOTISM. Here we come to the motive which probably interests most people. They are not anti-American, they are not anti-Democracy (or anti-Capitalist, if you prefer that word). They fear two things: (1) that their country may be "Americanised"; and (2) that Ireland may be, in Miss Bennett's words, "entangled in America's international policy, and perhaps used for her particular purposes in the event of another war."

Now, take Americanisation. I, for one, do not want to see Ireland Americanised, or Anglicised, or Gallicised, or "ised" by any country, least of all Russianised. But let us be objective about this "isation," and admit that, in fact, in practice, in history, we have been submitted over a very, very long period to a process of Anglicisation; and agree that, unless we are to acknowledge that we have been and now are Anglicised, we seem to have a normal power of resistance. I think, myself, that if America conquered and ruled us, as the British did, they would, over a course of time, leave a powerful mark. Does the reader seriously think it likely otherwise?

Ironically, the Americans are far less anxious to change us than the British ever were or are. To the British mind we are still, even still, a colony. They look at us with colonial minds. They find this absurd and that absurd because it isn't the way they do it themselves. Very often, of course, they think it charming, quaint and very funny. And the Lord knows "it" is often funny – or, to put it another way, to an Irishman crazy and exasperating! But they find it so, always, by comparison with Britain: we by comparison with our dreams. The American attitude to Europe is quite different. It is much more open. The reason is that they are all descended

25 O'Faolain again uses a question mark after a statement for rhetorical purposes.

from Europeans: ultimately their ancestral roots, their atavistic memories are in some village in Lucania or Limerick, some field in Poland or Hungary, and when they go back there they want to find it the way it always was. But human nature being contradictory they do also want it to be efficient and comfortable. Personally, to that sort of Americanisation I have no objection.

So, do not be frightened, my little ones! Nobody really wants to ise you. Unless, maybe, dear Mother Russia might like to ise us? And if they did they would be pretty ruthless about it! If we have a way-of-life of our own E.C.A. is not going to stop us from living it. All the Americans would like us to do is what they are trying to make the Calabrese do – to go and live our own lives decently. And if that rises any Irishman's dander so that he says to America, "Thank you very much, mister, we are very well able to do that for ourselves," the first cheer will come from the throats of E.C.A. who will eagerly pack their grips and hasten off home to the little old farm near Oshkosh or to a hot jam-session (God help them!) at Jimmy Ryan's place on 52nd Street.[26] For, though Americans "adore" Europe, and are very glad to work in – and, saving our haughty presence – for Europe, I hope nobody thinks they want to live in this damn continent? And, anyway, who brought 'em over in the first place? So, as far as all that is concerned, Miss Bennett has just been having a little nightmare.

America's international policy. Here is the anti-American's last ditch. Or, perhaps, by this he will have tactfully dropped the anti-Americanism and say, "I am not! But I am pro-Independence!" Well, that is fine! I am all for Independence ... To be Free ... Who does not want it? Who would not die for it? But "free" to do what? To sit on our hunkers and be walked-over? Free to go to sleep in the middle of the traffic? The world of to-day is an Either-Or world. In a global war between Communism and democracy (or, again, call it Capitalism if you will) any country that could use-fully take sides and does not will thereby, in fact, take sides. Nobody is free to dither indefinitely.

We do not have to sell ourselves to anybody. We can agree or disagree with other nations on a hundred questions. Thus, if we were in U.N.O. to-day there is nothing on earth to stop us from lining up with, say, India on the problem – now the crucial problem for Peace – of Asia. (Have you read Nehru's speech at the Commonwealth Conference? It was

26 Oshkosh is a city in Wisconsin. Jimmy Ryan's was a popular jazz club in New York City.

magnificent.)²⁷ There is nothing to stop us from being absolutely objective about America's aims and methods, her policies and her techniques. The one thing we cannot do, that it would be base for us to try to do, is to wash our hands, Pilate-like, over the urgent questions of our time and, then, to hide our weak withdrawal from these problems of peace and war under the mask of a faked-up anti-Americanism. On this, it is a profound tragedy for us that we are not in U.N.O.: if we were we would now be forced to take a considered stand on these questions there, and that stand would have to be hammered out in the Dáil and in the Press: and the whole country, instead of wavering along from day to day inarticulately as it now is, would be forced to make crucial definitions and clear distinctions – *a thing we Irish are very prone not to do.* While we shirk this job we can only blunder about in a fog of doubt, fear, ignorance, and suspicion, the end of which can only be that, if war should break out, we will be caught unprepared in every sense, confused and bewildered without wills, minds, or beliefs of our own, and wake up to find, to our astonishment, that we have, in practice, taken sides or been forced to take sides without any say in the matter. And where then would be our Freedom? Or our Pride?

I think our auto-anti is by this time out of his last ditch and digging himself madly into a foxhole, over the edge of which he screams, "I don't want to be pushed about by America. I don't want to be dragged by America into a line-up against Communism!" The answer to that is simple. "Why not do it of your own free-will? Because you do want to take that position anyway, do you? *Or don't you?*" It is difficult to understand people who say that the U.S.A. is hoping to make use of this country or that in the event of a global anti-Communist war. Of course she is. What else would she be hoping to do? Just like Russia. Look at the map of Europe from Finland to Greece. "America is bellicose!" from the foxhole. "So is Russia." The voice over the fox-hole sobs: "I don't want to be in any war!" One can only approach poor Sweetie Pie with a saucer of milk, and, making soothing noises, say: "Look, son. Neither do I. When I

27 Jawaharlal Nehru (1889–1964) was the first prime minister of India, from 1847 to 1964. The speech to which O'Faolain refers was likely made at the Commonwealth Prime Ministers' Conference in London on 27 April 1949, where it was decided that India could remain within the Commonwealth while becoming the first member nation to refuse to profess allegiance to the Crown, as long as it accepted the King as the symbol and Head of the Commonwealth. Fittingly, Nehru visited Ireland the next day, where he was welcomed as the first person from outside permitted on the floor of the Dáil while was it was in session.

hear an air-raid siren I shiver in my britches. And in any Middle Western farm, in any cabin in the Ukraine, every Joe and every Ivan feels just the same as you and me." At which you and I may weep the tears of all humanity, and ask: "Then who is making wars?" The only truthful answer possible is: "Nobody knows." Then you and I walk along together, and we say: "Can't we do anything about it? We Irishmen?" And, at that point, we will have at last arrived at the doorstep of reality.

I put it to readers of this article that before we start to pick holes in America we should first examine our own conscience. What is *our* foreign policy? *Our* contribution? I put it to you that our policy is a mean one. We are slipping into the attitude that our hands are too lily-white, our souls too pure, to touch the muck of the world; that we just *hope* nothing will happen; that we are remote from it all; ready to be protected again by American G.I.'s, Dutch flyers, British sailors, French, Belgian or Italian blood, with nothing of our own but a joke army, a joke navy and a joke air force – all manned, agreed, by gallant men; together with geography, geology, and God's special regard for his chosen people.[28] In short, we are snoring gently behind the Green curtain that we have been rigging up for the last thirty years – Thought-proof, World-proof, Life-proof. The only people *we* are ready to fight for are the angels. For we keep on saying we will fight, if needs be, for Christ, that is against Communism; but, then, we add, only on terms! If they give us our Six Counties we will fight for Christ. Not otherwise. "Who will buy Christ?" we cry. "Going for a song! Just for half a dozen bits of mortal soil!" Or, if you like to put it in another way – Ireland is on the market ...

Is that an honourable policy? Is it a contribution to anything?

It seems to me to be no more than one more clever dodge to manoeuvre our people into a cowardly neutrality, which will be then paraded as a "robust patriotism."

---

28 A G.I. is an enlisted member of the American armed forces; it was an acronym for "government issue," which referred to the equipment that was designed for and used by soldiers.

The Death of Nationalism[1]

It is the essence of nationalism that as soon as it has achieved its object it dies as a force. Until its object is achieved it seems inexhaustible. While it is still striving for its object its creatures, patriots by the tens of thousands, may die, and seem to fail; the force thrives. But, ultimately, nationalism is not inexhaustible. We know from Irish history that this is true as for the power of failure to succeed. "They went forth to battle and they always fell"; and the urge that drove them to their death flourished by their deaths. But we have not yet learned the truth of Dean Inge's epigram that "Nothing fails like success";[2] although the experience is under our eyes if we only wish to see it. Nationalism now blocks our road like a broken-down car. We have driven it to death.

Nationalism as a force did not come into Ireland until the 19th century. The very *idea* had no effective existence until the 17th century, and then its effectiveness was limited. This does not mean that the idea of "Ireland," and of racial distinctiveness, did not exist long before the 18th century; but it does mean that the idea of unity did not exist in any effective form, and, obviously, without the idea of unity there cannot be an idea of a nation. The city-states of mediaeval and Renaissance Italy did not develop the idea of nationalism until the French invasion of Charles VIII – which, by challenge, evoked the promise of a coherent response: a national resistance.[3] Alexander Borgia's efforts to form a League against the French was one

1 "The Death of Nationalism" appeared in *The Bell* 17, no. 2 (May 1951): 44–53.
2 William Ralph Inge (1860–1954) was dean of St. Paul's Cathedral in London and known for his pessimistic views.
3 Charles VIII (1470–1498) invaded Italy in 1494.

such effort.[4] The vigour of his son, Caesar Borgia, was another;[5] and, we remember, it evoked the ardent admiration of the first Italian – Niccolo Machiavelli – to formulate a technique of government, for this very purpose of saving not Florence, his own city-state, but *Italy*. Here in Ireland, faced by the cohesion of the new English State born out of the Wars of the Roses, our fissurated and disparate society failed miserably to respond in kind.[6] That great man, the Earl of Tyrone, attempted to reply in kind by becoming, in effect, a central Irish king.[7] But the petty chiefs, too long accustomed to their patriarchal ways, too long accustomed to think themselves immune, too long conditioned to the life of the border-raider and to its purely local techniques, foiled all his efforts to turn what was to all intents and purposes a rabble into a nation, and, as a result, as we know, he and they alike went down in the Battle of Kinsale.[8] Nationalism as a creative urge to unification did not therefore arrive here, and then unsuccessfully, until the 17th century. The point of interest to us, in view of the fact that we owe the existence of modern Ireland to the rise of Nationalism, is that its rise was frustrated by a stubborn, short-sighted policy of clinging to an outmoded, antique past which, to-day, we actually idolise!

But it is one of the most common follies of nationalism, as Toynbee has pointed out, with many historical illustrations, to idolise an ephemeral self, ephemeral institutions, and ephemeral techniques: and indeed the sum of what I have to say about nationalism is that, in all its most dangerous aspects, it is, in effect, a form of idolatry. That is, it tends to create idols, and to put those dead idols between the intelligence of a people and their proper object.

To follow the history of Ireland into the 17th and 18th centuries is to meet this idolatry again and again: as when in reading the Gaelic poets we find all their thoughts and hopes bound up with a past that could never be recalled, with a caste-system, and a way of life, and notions of government long discredited. No theme, for instance, is so common with theses relicts

---

4 Rodrigo Borgia (1431–1503), also known as Pope Alexander VI.

5 Cesare (spelled Caesar by O'Faolain) Borgia (c. 1475/6–1507) was a Renaissance captain who tried to establish his own principality; his policies inspired Machiavelli to refer to him as the new "Prince."

6 The Wars of the Roses (1455–85) were a series of English dynastic wars fought between the Houses of Lancaster and York.

7 Hugh O'Neill.

8 The Battle of Kinsale was fought between the Irish and English forces in County Cork in December 1601. The victory resulted in England's conquest of Ireland.

of the old Gaelic world than the return of the Stuart kings, who will free Ireland.[9] Once again, it is part of the folly of our present policy of idolising the Past that our children are encouraged to take inspiration from these political and literary anachronisms of the 17th and 18th centuries.

Nationalism did not become a really effective force here until the 19th century when a great man arose amongst us with enough vigour of intellect to observe that the days of kings and princes were over and that two great revolutionary forces had come into the world to replace them, Democracy and Industrialism. O'Connell saw that if Irishmen wished to take their place among the free peoples of this modern world they would first have to fashion themselves into a modern democracy, and take over from the world of the Industrial Revolution its political techniques, as well, indeed, as something of its ruthless, utilitarian philosophy. O'Connell is our first successful nationalist of major size precisely because, in his realism, he accepted the principle of change. He refused to be dominated by any historical mystique, he cut away the past, he adapted himself to his own times, he never allowed any idol to tyrannise over him. In the sense that O'Connell was an European we might say that while serving the Irish people day and night he refused to allow "Ireland" to tyrannise over him. Yet, once again, we do not revere O'Connell to-day for these his real powers, and his real achievement: we associate him almost solely with Catholic Emancipation and minimise the fact that he emancipated us from parochialism. We do this because our once-urgent nationalism has receded back into Berdyaev's definition of Nationalism as "an aggressive parochialism in space."[10]

In our own time nationalism came to its zenith and to its final achievement. Most unfortunately its elements have never been submitted to an objective analysis. The mystique which always accompanies a fervent period of nationalism, and which is its outward symptom rather than its inward impetus, has been mistaken for its impetus. We have never, for example, sufficiently appraised the force of the crude economic impetus behind Sinn Féin, although we are, now, fully aware that the Land League was the driving force in Parnellism: we know, that is, that the Parnellite

9 The House of Stuart was the royal house of Scotland from 1371 and of England from 1603. With the exception of the establishment of the Commonwealth from 1649 to 1660, its reign ended in 1714 when the House of Hanover acceded to the Crown.

10 Russian philosopher Nikolay Aleksandrovich Berdyayev (spelled Berdyaev by O'Faolain) (1874–1948).

movement was largely a peasant movement. But we have never acknowledged that behind its outward mystique Sinn Féin was basically an artisan movement: that the peasant hunger for land in the nineteenth century
was matched in the twentieth by a hunger just as powerful among the
grandsons and sons of those peasants who emigrated into the towns. For
whereas the peasants had won their land and were fast changing from
peasants to yeoman farmers, what future lay before their children in the
towns and cities? The social aspect of the 1916–1922 revolutionary
movement has not been realised. Or is only being very slowly realised
now that we can plainly see the effects of the revolution in the rise to
power of a bourgeoisie composed of men who, thirty years ago, had not
one penny to rattle against another. We sold the revolution to the world
as a romantic thing. It was, behind that facade, a very realistic thing. That
was why it succeeded.

The type who best illustrates the revolution illustrates its causes and its
impetus: its most active leader, Collins, the son of a farmer, obliged to
work in London at a modest salary, with no prospects commensurate
with his abilities, and, were he to marry, with no prospects for his children
but to live either in exile or as the family of a modestly-paid official. He
was what one might call a typical member of the urban, intellectual Irish
proletariat. All his colleagues conform more or less to the same pattern.
However we may glorify and worship the ancient rural Gaelic tradition
the revolution of 1916–1922 did *not* originate in that quarter. Efforts
have, of course, been made to suggest the contrary: as when some significance is alleged to attach to the fact that a professor of Celtic, and a member of the Gaelic League, originated the Irish Volunteers; but we now
know that he was merely a figure-head or puppet being pulled by the
wires of the purely urban Irish Republican Brotherhood, and that the
driving force behind the scenes the whole time was this secret society
which had as much to do with antiquity as a Mills bomb.[11] One might
draw a comparison between this urban movement, equally fostered in
London and semi-Anglicised Dublin, led by men of such mixed blood or
foreign experiences as Pearse, Griffith, de Valera, Collins, Burgess or
Childers and the Italian Risorgimento, led by a sailor born across the Alps
in Nice, travelling the world, picking up his ideas in the cosmopolitan
port of Genoa, collaborating with a French-speaking statesman, Cavour,
and a trans-Alpine monarchy, and owing nothing whatsoever to the

11 A Mills bomb is a hand grenade.

"great Italian past."[12] But it seems that the past never gives birth to revolution. (The past is always dead.) Its effects in modern life do. The point is that modern nationalism here succeeded because it had a modern and realistic impetus. To-day's idolisation of antiquity, over the head of all that originated that movement and brought it to success, is another sign that Irish nationalism, having achieved its object, is a spent force. Old men always bore us with their memories. The present, doubtless inevitably, has no interest for them. "This is no country for old men … " What country is?

This is the central evil of nationalism: that, sooner or later, it ossifies the mind. In automobile language it chugs along splendidly for ten or twenty thousand miles, and then we hear the *pink-pink*. A good engineer, a good statesman, does a job of decarbonising, and we chug along again; but before long we have to get a new car, and it is, by then, also a new model. To be sure, one meets the type of man who says, "I wouldn't give up that old car for anything. It carried me here and it carried me there, and my heart is stuck in it." He ends up in a ditch, having been passed-out all along the road for years by amused racers. Or he may even store the old crock away and bring it out once a year on Saint Patrick's Day for the Old Crocks' Race.[13] And, yet, in his day he was a great man and it was a great car.

Toynbee, in his study of the causes for the disintegrations of civilisations, or their abortion, has a good phrase for this: "The Nemesis of Creativity." By this he means that there is a limit to the creative power of any party. This is what Dean Inge meant by "Nothing fails like success." As Toynbee sees it, all leadership – that is the example of a pioneer minority, whether a minority inside a country or inside a continent; leading a country or leading a continent – has the power of responding to one challenge, but rarely to two. They become slaves of the machine they create and of the philosophy they have established. Hence becomes the adoration of the "ephemeral self."

He gives examples of this idolatry of the ephemeral self, ephemeral institutions and ephemeral techniques: the vain-glory of Athens, the sterility of

12 The Risorgimento is the nineteenth-century movement for Italian unification that resulted in the foundation of the Kingdom of Italy in 1861; the process was completed with the annexation of Venetia in 1866 and Rome in 1870. Guiseppe Mazzini, the Italian revolutionary, is the sailor to whom O'Faolain refers. Camillo Benso (1810–1861), Count of Cavour, was the first prime minister of the Kingdom of Italy.

13 Here, a "crock" is an old vehicle, usually a vintage car.

Italy after her great hey-day, the contrast between the ossification of South Carolina, caught by the spell of her past, and the initiative and inventiveness of North Carolina, the prolonged sterility of the East Roman Empire, clinging to the idea of Rome's past greatness, the conservatism of the British Parliamentary system (an "institutional idol"), which makes him gravely doubt that the new political leadership of this changing world can possibly come from that quarter, the manner in which British industry has clung too long to obsolescent techniques, the overthrow in war of old techniques by new, as in the debacle of the French army against the German in 1870.[14] I have heard men here in Ireland, so spell-bound by their admiration of their own deeds as guerilla fighters against Britain thirty golden years ago that they still believe that they could contain an invasion of Ireland by the same methods. If they are a tragic joke there is this to be said for them that the history of civilisation provides many examples of similar tragedies due to the same cause.

One of the most tragic examples of this idol-worship is in Education. It would take too long to develop the history of popular education in Britain, which began in the 1800s with the facile Liberal fancy of universal uplift and which has so far arrived at universal vulgarisation, involving among other things, as the present state of the House of Commons shews, the virtual destruction of Liberalism: though it is to be added, however, that the story is not ended, and that by various inventive devices the British are attempting to cope with this immense problem of universal literacy. It will be simpler to refer to our own case.

Here, our now-decrepit nationalism has based our educational policy on Past-worship and on a principle of Immunisation. We have failed to observe that side by side with the political revolution we have undergone a social revolution as a result of which we have created a new proletariat and a new bourgeoisie with enormously increased ambitions; that these have developed desires for standards of living based not on our own experience but on the only other experience we have – that of life in modern Britain and, to a lesser degree life in the United States; and that we are physically unable to provide ourselves with the needs and luxuries of these ambitions. One evident result of popular education has been much publicised from time to time, our colossal imports of reading-matter. The effect is that we are teaching our children to read in order that they may read papers, periodicals and books – I make no mention of the cinema or

14 The Franco-Prussian War of 1870–71 led to the end of France as the dominant power in continental Europe and the unification of Germany.

the radio – whose total influence is to make a joke of the educational principle of Past-worship and Immunisation. To this our chauvinists have no reply but to ask for more and more censorship disguised, in this case, as penal tariffs.

This passing mention of the idea of censorship brings me to a last example of the evil effects of a decayed nationalism: the effect on the arts. The theory of and practice of censorship in modern Ireland is part and parcel of the idolatry of nationalism: that is, it has arisen out of Past-worship as a futile effort at immunisation. Nowhere, of course, is there less of Past-worship than in a living literature. The past is utilised, exploited, may even inspire, but we have only to compare the persistent development in the work of Yeats with the stasis, or mimesis, of his many imitators, whom he well compared to a dog's fleas, and who thought that anybody could become a Celtic poet by playing with a bunch of clichés – fairies, leprachauns, clurachauns, bog-pools, Irish names all wrapped up in a moony mist – to realise that a truly creative writer never allows his material to become his master.[15] Nationalism, while still struggling towards its object, was enormously inspiring between 1900 and 1922. A great change came over Irish letters after 1922, seen clearly in Sean O'Casey's fury at the cruelty of idealism; and with him may be put almost every Irish writer of distinction since. The Past Worshippers were aghast at O'Casey and riots broke out in the theatre. Outside the theatre we got a virulent Censorship of books. The theory of all these people was that the new writers were assailing the old traditions and, if allowed a free run, would break them down. The truth is quite the opposite. Men never abandon old techniques, old ways of looking at life, old values until these things have all broken down already. To say that the writers by abandoning the old roads are weakening the old country is as absurd as if somebody suggested that the abandonment of the old Roman roads helped to weaken the Roman Empire. The grass on the Appian Way grew from seeds of the wild grass on the Capitoline Hill.[16]

Irish writers since 1922 are not one whit less patriotic than Irish writers before 1922, or than anybody else. But they do not measure patriotism by the same standards as in 1916–22 – because to-day a living

15 Leprachauns and clurachauns – also spelled leprechauns and clurichauns – are small sprites or fairies in Irish folklore.
16 The Appian Way is the most famous of ancient Roman roads, running south from Rome to Brindisi on the Adriatic Sea. The Capitoline Hill was the fortress of ancient Rome.

patriotism does not measure itself by the same standards. In this they are not clearer-headed than other people, they are merely responding instinctively to the changed life which they are aware of intuitively. Moreover, the writers tend to be aware of life in a broader way than others: life in the world at large. They see that the parochialism of nationalism-in-decay bears no relation to the world at large. They therefore become aware more acutely, and quickly, than others do of this parochialism and its futility and spit on it.

Moreover, all literary development is a process of a swing between "Tradition and Revolt" – read John Livingstone Lowes' book of that title; and the value of writers in any country is that they do revolt against a tradition, by instinct, as soon as it is exhausted.[17] But the mechanical nationalists – for the old clockwork still ticks over, even while it is running down – stuck in the grove of 1916–22 can only measure patriotism by the old ways and the old days, and feel betrayed, and in their egocentricity think that this means that "Ireland" is betrayed by men of letters who know that that is all over and done with, and want to write about a modern Ireland in a modern world.

But here is the dilemma of modern Irish writing; here is why the Theatre, for example, is dead as a door-nail in Ireland to-day; namely, that the politicians – the Old-Men-of-the-Sea on our backs – are thinking in terms of thirty years ago, and so are the churchmen, and they will not *allow*, or help to create, a modern Ireland in a modern world. So: (1) your writers get angry, and say angry things; and we have the amazing spectacle of a Government Department deliberately smearing the writers of its own country abroad; and (2) your writers have nothing to write about that is living and urgent. The present decay of Irish writing is due solely to the Old Men of the Sea who refuse to move with the times – politicians and churchmen alike. And the Devil of the piece is our rotting Nationalism.

Unhappily even when nationalism is dead or dying as a creative force it can go on being a profitable force. In fact true nationalism never pays – one pays for it; but chauvinism and jingoism, which are nationalism rotting, do pay. Every Irish businessman to-day is a patriot. If he wants a tariff he will want it not for his own sake but for Ireland's sake. But this is not peculiar to Ireland. We are dealing with universal laws. There is no kind of nationalism so aggressive as economic nationalism, and, by the way, no kind of nationalism is so prolific in wars, and, at that, in the

17 The book is not *Tradition and Revolt*, but *Convention and Revolt in Poetry* (1919), by American scholar John Livingstone Lowes (1867–1945).

bitterest of wars. No wars up to the Industrial Revolution were fought as bitterly – I am not saying as destructively – as wars since then. Laurence Sterne went to the continent completely forgetting that England and France were at war (it was during the Seven Years War),[18] and when taken into custody by an official was, with very little difficulty, allowed to go on his way. When Napoleon interned British residents and travellers Wellington said he was no gentleman. Our methods of total war naturally go hand in hand with economic nationalism. But when this economic nationalism, based on the theory of self-sufficiency, shakes hands with the theory of Immunisation – here the sole, lazy and negative policy of the Catholic Church – businessmen become not merely super-patriots but super-churchmen. Under this cloak of a desire for patriotic and religious unity they develop an internal kind of totalitarianism. This naturally results in anti-liberalism, anti-Semitism, anti-individualism, the most disgusting kind of vain-glory, isolationism, neutralism, antiquarianism, all defended as Nationalism. It is not nationalism. It is simply exhaustion and jingoism.

To conclude, let me not be thought for one moment to be advocating internationalism. That also is an abstraction. It does not suggest any sort of individual existence. It does not suggest the normal life of any man – except perhaps that of a newspaper correspondent or a wagon-lit attendant or a Cook's guide.[19] To me the ultimate evil of nationalism (and most other *isms*) is this threat to the creative individual by the tyranny arising from the idolisation of an abstraction. For after nationalism has achieved its aim it is no more than that, a tyranny of the mind. Here, one of the best recent examples of an exhausted nationalism was Clann na Poblachta, the belated offspring of 1916 and all that.[20] It had one social thinker, and having fired him, it must inevitably die.

What replaces nationalism? Dr. Browne answered that.[21] And the "profitable force," which I have described above, answered him. That is

18 The Seven Years War, which involved most European powers, lasted from 1756 to 1763.
19 "Wagon-lit" is a French term for a sleeping coach on a train. A Cook's guide is someone who works for Thomas Cook and Son, a world-wide travel agency.
20 Clann na Poblachta, which translated from the Irish means "Party of the Republic," was an Irish social democratic political party founded by Seán MacBride in 1946; its last contested election was in 1965.
21 Noël Browne (1915–1997) was a medical doctor and a long-serving TD for several political parties, including Clann na Poblachta. He was the minister for

the struggle of forces that is going on to-day in Ireland, and if it has any vitality we are all right. If it has not, we are sunk

Health from 1948 to 1951, when the Mother and Child Scheme collapsed. The Mother and Child Scheme was an attempt to bring a form of socialised medicine to Ireland. Its failure resulted in Browne's political downfall. See the next essay, "The Dáil and the Bishops," for more on the matter.

The Dáil and the Bishops[1]

Now that the excitement aroused by the sudden demise of the Mother and Child Scheme has died away, and we can detach our emotions and our thoughts from the accidents and personalities involved, the issue becomes a bit easier to define. The issue is that no country can be ruled "democratically" by two parliaments; or at least not as the world understands that word.

Here in the Republic, as this crisis has revealed to us, we have two parliaments: a parliament at Maynooth and a parliament in Dublin.[2] I do not know whether a country can be ruled *satisfactorily* by two parliaments. Ours has – as this crisis has suddenly revealed – been so ruled since it was founded. It is for the people of the Republic to decide whether they consider it a satisfactory system. It is certainly not an entirely democratic one. Personally, I am not sure that I much care about its not being entirely democratic, but I suspect that I am in a minority.

∼

Some Catholics have been trying to obscure this issue; or, perhaps, as is more likely, they have not seen it. For example – it is an extreme example – Lord Killanin wrote in the *Irish Times* of April 25th a letter in which he referred to "the principle of the right of those qualified to comment on moral issues to do so."[3] And, by way of enforcing this principle he drew

---

1 "The Dáil and the Bishops" appeared in *The Bell* 17, no. 3 (June 1951): 5–13.
2 O'Faolain uses Maynooth, the site of the renowned seminary, as a metonym for the Catholic Hierarchy.
3 Michael Morris (1914–1999), 3rd Baron Killanin, was a London-born Irish author and president of the International Olympic Committee from 1972 to 1980.

our attention to the powers of the Church of England, saying: "When the Church of the majority gives advice it is immediately acceptable." On giving due and patient consideration to this magnificently silly statement all one can reasonably say about it is that either Lord Killanin was very good at games when he was at school, or his teachers and tutors at Eton and Magdalene succeeded in concealing from him the unpleasant historical fact of the Reformation, and the entire history of the relationship of Church and State in England ever since: a relationship whose upshot has been that the Church of the majority in England knows better now than to risk a snub by giving advice except on the most rare and safe occasions.[4] However, I may be doing Michael Killanin an injustice: it may have been his sly intention to hold up an admirable model to the Irish Hierarchy.

But it is when he speaks (and others have spoken in a like manner), of "the principle of the right of those qualified to comment on moral issues to do so," that he really conceals – by a master-piece of understatement – the essential issue involved. What does he mean by "comment"? It is, evidently, a little more than a "comment" when the Prime Minister of a country is invited to hear the decision of the Hierarchy on a piece of legislation which Parliament has not discussed?[5] It is surely more than a "comment" when the result is that the Prime Minister of that country agrees to the dismissal of the Minister responsible, and when he then withdraws the proposed legislation without more ado, and without giving the Parliament of his country an opportunity to speak on behalf of the people whom it represents.

Nobody, so far as I have observed, has denied the right of the Catholic bishops to "comment"; or to give "advice" on proposed legislation; or to enunciate the official attitude of the Roman Catholic Church to proposed legislation. That principle is fully and wholeheartedly admitted. I believe that not even the most ashen-jawed, beetle-browed, black-bowler-hatted Orangeman in Portadown could reasonably object to that principle.[6] I doubt if anybody, north or south, could even object to the Hierarchy publicly condemning any proposed piece of legislation, provided that, in the end, it is the Parliament which freely decides. I doubt if there is a

---

4 The University of Cambridge's Magdalene College was founded in 1542.
5 O'Faolain again uses a question mark to close a combative statement, one that is supposed to be "evident" in this case.
6 Portadown, County Armagh, Northern Ireland, has long been the site of sectarian conflicts, many of which are directly related to the traditional Orange Order parades that march through Catholic neighbourhoods.

single Bishop in the Republic, or in all Christendom, who would wish to contravert this. In practice, the Hierarchy does much more than "comment" or "advise." It commands.

∾

There has been a lot of talk about the rights of institutions to advise, comment and consult and so on. If we accept this principle, and I do not see why not, should we not also give the same rights to, say, the Protestant Hierarchy; or to the Presbyterian Synod; or to the Worshipful Company of Masons; or to the Trades Union Congress; or to any other representative institution?[7]

But how can we? Nobody *can* give those other institutions the same rights for the simple reason that nobody can give them the same power.

The Maynooth Parliament holds a weapon which none of the other institutions mentioned holds: the weapon of the Sacraments. The Church of England cannot wield the power of the Catholic Church because it does not hold this weapon. If a Prime Minister in England were informed by the Archbishop of Canterbury that a proposed law would be condemned by the Church of England, he would deplore it, but he would not be afraid of any effects other than political effects.[8] If our Taoiseach were informed thus by the Protestant Archbishop of Dublin he would measure the effects in the same way. And likewise with most other institutions, religious or secular. But when the Catholic Church, through its representatives, speaks, he realises, and the Roman Catholic public realises, that if they disobey they may draw on themselves this weapon whose touch means death. (Most of us feel, I think, that it is unfair to use this weapon on political occasions: and that is putting it mildly.)

There is, therefore, no use in talking blandly about "comment," or "advice." The lightest word from this quarter is tantamount to the raising of the sword. That is why it is just to speak of two Parliaments. The Dáil proposes; Maynooth disposes. The Dáil had, when up against the Second Parliament, only one right of decision: the right to surrender.

---

7 The Presbyterian Synod is the ruling body for the Presbyterian Church in Ireland. The Worshipful Company of Masons was founded in London in 1356 to regulate the craft of stonemasonry and still functions today; it is unrelated to the Free and Accepted Masons.
8 The Archbishop of Canterbury is the primate of all England in the Church of England.

That is what made the Browne affair so interesting and so dramatic. It revealed to the people of the Republic that if this is a Democracy it is a form of Democracy unlike any other in the world. That is to say: the supreme power is not here, in practice – which is what matters – vested in the people's Parliament. It is vested in the Second Parliament.

∼

What then do we do about all this?

We must define our position. Then and then only can we handle it. I suggest that there are three essential points:

(1) This is an unusual Democracy. Our ideology might perhaps be defined as that of Christian Democrats. It would be more accurate to say Catholic Democrats, because that part of the Constitution which gives equal liberty to *all* religions is poppycock. What use is liberty without political power? Our Parliament can legislate only as a Roman Catholic parliament. One may say that this is as it should be since this is a Catholic country. But, of course, the Republic is not a Catholic country even under its own Constitution. There is, in fact, no such thing in the world as a Catholic country. The only historical example of a state where the secular power and the religious power ever were coterminous is the example of the Papal States: and nobody, except some lunatic Catholic Actionists, would wish to restore that state of affairs anywhere to-day.[9] A Catholic country is a country where the Church has both the power *and* the responsibility. Here the Church, through the Second Parliament, has enormous power but very little responsibility: the Dáil has all the responsibility and, as we see, a limited amount of power. I speak, of course, of social responsibility.

(2) If, as I suppose it is safe to say, nobody wishes and hopes to get rid of the Second Parliament, we must all agree to accept this curious marriage of divided power, i.e., the root principle of Irish democracy is the Principle of the Second Parliament.

(3) This division of power is the crux. Nobody has ever defined the just limits of the Church's power in politics; nobody ever will. *The relation of Church and State is, must be, and should be one of constant tussle.* That is the essence of the whole matter.

∼

9 Catholic Action is the work of the laity performed under the direction of the Church Hierarchy.

We can see how this would work by imagining how the Dáil and the Taoiseach would have acted in this recent crisis, if they had had any historical sense of this problem, or had studied to define their position *vis-à-vis* the Church. Mr. Costello faced by this clerical opposition to a piece of legislation which he and his cabinet, on behalf of the Government, on behalf of the people, were proposing, should have strongly and stubbornly resisted the Bishops to the limit.[10] He should have been scrupulously careful to avoid all "secret diplomacy," behind the back of the Parliament. (It is, really, this whispering behind curtains which has done most to upset the people.) He should have kept the Parliament fully informed. He should have asked the Hierarchy to come out in the open. Mr. de Valera, who had earlier met the same opposition, should have done likewise. Instead, as the Editor has pointed out, both these Leaders acted in the old conspiratorial tradition which is our inheritance from I.R.A and I.R.B. and Fenianism and '16 and '48 and '67 and '98 and all that. Had these men told the Bishops that the Dáil would have to thrash out the whole matter in public, and that they would not accept the decision of the Hierarchy unless that decision was publicly conveyed to the Dáil as a command then, at least, the minimal principle of our special democratic ideology would have been preserved. More than that, I believe that the Hierarchy would have acted far more prudently if they had been met in this sturdy way. It is quite clear that this is what Dr. Browne was trying to do – as he was fully entitled to do, and as any democrat should do. His colleagues preferred to sell him, and the Dáil, down the river.

All this procedure would have been fully within the rights of any loyal Catholic. No other procedure would have reconciled the two loyalties in Irish life – the loyalty owed to the People's Parliament by patriotic Irishmen, and the loyalty owed to the Second Parliament by Catholics.

The relationship between Church and State always has been, and always must be, a healthy struggle, in which the Church will properly, *but always prudently* fight for power, and the State will always try to restrain that power within due limits. There is no other way in which the thing can work. There is no other way in which it has ever worked. The whole history of the Italian city-states – the whole life-story of Dante – illustrates this: shews us that if that prudence on the one hand, and that restraint on

10 John A. Costello (1891–1976), leader of Fine Gael, was taoiseach from 1948 to 1951 and 1954 to 1957.

the other are not effective you get a condition in which the laity has responsibility without due power and the Church has undue power without responsibility. In that state of affairs the Church will be blamed, and rightly blamed, for such things as infant mortality, slums, and poverty, and the State will be hamstrung. Then you really would have the tragedy of a so-called "Catholic country."

Moreover, it is the duty of Parliament, as Catholics, as Christians of any denomination, to resist the Church for its own sake. For more and more the Church here is approaching near to this point of undue power without due responsibility, and the more she approaches this dreadful position the more will the people lay at her doors the blame for human misery. Do we desire a state of affairs to arise here wherein a form of bitter anti-clericalism may develop, and wherein people like, let us say, Dr. Browne, find themselves in the miserable position of defending the Church in a bitter internecine struggle against the super-loutish revolution of an unthinking and maddened mob?

Is this a fantastic picture: something that "could not happen here"? It has happened elsewhere, in countries as religious-minded as Ireland. I need only mention Spain in our own day. There is, one agrees, no comparison – at this moment: but that is the way things came slowly to a head there, and sooner or later, if undue intervention by the Church is not resisted by the State, must be the way things happen in every country, including this.

Some will say that when the bishops have spoken it is enough. It *is* enough for obedience. But a Church is an army, and must have a good morale. And the Catholic Church is not merely composed of priests and bishops. The Catholic Church is one mystical body including (has it to be said?) the laity; and the laity are not only part of the army, they are the vastly largest part of the army.

I am afraid too often our clergy do not realise that, as John Henry Newman was so fond of insisting, "it is the whole man that moves." If you shatter a man's pride – by, for example, shattering his belief that he is worthy of trust – you shatter his personality as a Christian: for as a Christian he is a whole man or he is nothing. If people are treated as children, and all that is asked of them is that they go here, go there, do this, do that, and are never left to act as whole Christians, why, then, you are left with children and a childish morale. Nor can you insist that obedience to a Church is, in actual life, more important than loyalty to a country. In theory, in some abstract sort of existence, it may be so. God before Country: but in life as it is lived man cannot be chopped up like that – and the Catholic Church, being universal, has always recognised this, and has wisely and prudently refused, for example, to take sides in wars, or in civil wars. I may be quite wrong in my impression, but my impression is that this imprudent intervention of our Second Parliament has roused feelings of the most agonised dismay, and even exacerbation of feeling, to whose force churchmen seem to be quite blind.

The whole affair has done harm to the morale of the Republic and of the Catholic Church in the Republic. The people must feel that there is a wide gap between Theology and Humanity. They must feel themselves distrusted by their own clergy: for, if this Scheme had gone through who would have worked it almost wholly but a Catholic Government, Catholic doctors, Catholic civil servants, the ordinary Catholic laymen? This almost total distrust of the laity is, to be sure, an old thing. When Newman was here he found it so and protested manfully against it. It is humiliating to Catholics, and must sometimes infuriate them, to find that, let us say, they are trusted and praised when they gladly subscribe thousands upon thousands of pounds to keep Maynooth alive, but that, as soon as something like this comes along, they are at once told from Maynooth that they cannot be trusted for a moment. The people, henceforth, must distrust their own government and in wondering what else has been kept, or is being kept from Parliament fall into a state of disrespect for the whole parliamentary institution. The Dáil has suffered a blow to its prestige which cannot but react on the morale of the whole country.

∼

Some may also say, some also said that the Church has no interest in politics and is only concerned with morality. Certainly, in an absolute way of speech, we may suppose that no Church is concerned about the secular affairs of a nation. But, here at any rate, in a divided country, politics and religion are inseparable in practice. And the recent decision of the Hierarchy has, in practice, had a pulverising political effect. I refer, of course, to Partition. We must presume that their Lordships, being farseeing men, weighed it all up, and came to their decision that the unification of Ireland must be sacrificed to higher considerations. And this, evidently, is one other thing which we must accept henceforth as a fact in Irish life. To adapt Pitt's famous remark, we can now roll up the map of Ireland: it will not be wanted for a hundred years.[11]

11 William Pitt the Younger (1759–1806) was twice British prime minister (1783–1801 and 1804–06). A distraught Pitt made the remark in reference to a map of

The North, however, has been both ingenuous and disingenuous about the whole affair. On the one hand it is not likely that State Socialism – of which Dr. Browne's Scheme was felt to be the thin end of the wedge – would be madly popular with the North. Therefore they should, in honesty, have given three cheers for the bishops. On the other hand the old cry that Home Rule means Rome Rule is unsophisticated to the last degree. For who would object – except the sort of fanatic whose comment on the proverb "Rome was not built in a day" was, "It should never have been built!" – who would object if the Vatican stood where Maynooth stands; with all its ancient culture, its human wisdom, its political intelligence, its immense tolerance, its rich traditions, its prestige and its panoply? Would, indeed, a thousand times over that Home Rule meant Rome Rule! And since our only concern now, at this stage, is to see coldly and unsentimentally, what we really are, and where we may be going – and to avoid deluding ourselves that we are something which we are not – we must, I suggest, see this as the dim outline of the best possible future: to wit, a Church humanised and sophisticated, with a world-outlook and a universal culture, in about the same relation to the secular Parliament of Eire as the Vatican bears to the Parliament of Italy. Give us that and what a happy country we should be!

It seems, the Browne affair has closed a whole volume of Irish history. The so-called Republican tradition and all the bye-echoes of that tradition – in so far as they ever really clarified themselves – are washed-up: 1916 and Fenianism, '67 and '48, Wolfe Tone and the French Revolution. Out of the nineteenth century only one man – O'Connell – remains, and if any statue is to be put up outside the Dáil to replace Queen Victoria it should be to O'Connell. All our latter-day political alignments that do not go back to him have become meaningless. Fianna Fail, and Fine Gael and Clann na Poblachta, and any others after them will be just as meaningless unless they stem in some fashion from O'Connellism. For his concept of democracy is the only one that has lasted: and not only, and not least because he worked with the Church but because when occasion demanded it could, and did, resist to the limit in the name of the struggling poor whom, like a Vulcan manufacturing thousands, he hammered into the shape of a

---

Europe after Napoleon defeated Russia and Austria, England's allies, in the Battle of Austerlitz (1805). In Pitt's version, he said that the map would not be needed for ten years, not a hundred.

nation.[12] Republicanism, we see at last, never did work. It gradually became verbiage and was, in our time, finally subjected in the Dáil, on a famous occasion, to the fit if shameful tests of the Oxford Dictionary. It broke in de Valera's hands. Costello and MacBride gave it decent burial. The only possible triumphant movement of the future will, whatever it calls itself, be far removed from all that. It will be a Christian Radical Movement; which, allowing much for his times and personal limitations, was what O'Connell tried gropingly to adumbrate for Ireland and the world. It is extraordinary that Ireland, so famous for its religion and its rebels, should have so far shown no signs of that movement, except one, rash, brilliant young man, whose appearance in public life instantaneously produces a universal shout of *Masks on, God Save Ireland,* and *Sauve qui peut.*[13]

12 Vulcan is the Roman god of fire and the forge.
13 *Sauve qui peut* is French for "every man for himself."

On a Recent Incident at the International Affairs Association[1]

In the October of 1952 an unfortunate incident occurred at a meeting of the International Affairs Association in Dublin. At the conclusion of a paper on "The Pattern of Persecution in Yugoslavia," read by Mr. Peter O'Curry of *The Standard*, the usual discussion began.[2] The first speaker did not get very far. He was Mr. Hubert Butler, a guest of Dr. Owen Sheehy-Skeffington, who is a member.[3] He had uttered a very few words to express the opinion that Archbishop Stepinac had, during the German occupation of Yugoslavia, been duped or deceived by the Quisling, Pavelic, when the discussion was peremptorily stopped by the Chairman.[4] It was stopped because His Excellency, the Papal Nuncio, who was present, had risen from his seat and walked out in protest against Mr. Butler's opinion. The next day two members of the Committee called on the Nuncio to apologise to him. Subsequently, Mr. Butler was forced to resign from his honorary post as Secretary of the Kilkenny Archaeological Society. Later, under obscure circumstances, but with the greatest publicity, Dr.

1 "On a Recent Incident at the International Affairs Association" appeared in *The Bell* 18, no. 9 (February 1953): 517–27. Hubert Butler provides an account of the evening, the politics around it, and its fallout in his most renowned essay "The Sub-Prefect Should Have Held His Tongue" (1956).
2 Peter O'Curry was the long-time editor of *The Standard*.
3 Owen Sheehy-Skeffington (1909–1970) was a lecturer in French at Trinity College Dublin; he became a senator in 1954.
4 Archbishop Alojzije Stepinac (1898–1960). A "quisling" is a person who collaborates with an occupying enemy force; the term alludes to Vidkun Quisling (1887–1945), a Norwegian army officer who collaborated with the German occupation of Norway during World War II. In 1941, after the conquest of Yugoslavia, Ante Pavelić (1889–1959) was installed by the Axis forces as the fascist leader of Croatia.

Sheehy-Skeffington was banned from a public debate in Dublin – controlled, or controllable by the Dublin Vocational Committee.[5] The subject of the debate, ironically enough, was "Can the Individual Survive?" A heated controversy immediately started, and at the moment of writing, still goes on in the Dublin Press.

At a remove from the passions of the arena, and several months after the incident, it ought to be possible to elicit some of the principles involved in the unfortunate affair.

~

It has to be admitted, I think, that the International Affairs Association blundered. They blundered when they asked the Editor of *The Standard*, which describes itself as "Catholic Ireland's National Weekly," to speak on "The Pattern of Persecution in Yugoslavia." Mr. Peter O'Curry was, and is, obviously, bound hand and foot in discussing such a matter. He could, indeed, be objective, but only on one side of the question. Even if the Rules of the Association did not demand it, the choice of such a speaker made a discussion inevitable. The Association, with incredible tactlessness, blundered when it invited His Excellency, the Papal Nuncio, to be present at such a discussion – of its nature controversial.[6] We do not know whether the Association's officers (forgetful of, or in spite of, their own Rules) told the Nuncio that there would be no discussion, but it is most likely that they did, for it would otherwise be difficult to understand why His Excellency attended: in which case they blundered exceedingly. It is well-known that other Diplomats would like to attend these meetings, but, in practice, tactfully remain away; for if any Diplomat does attend, and takes umbrage at some reference to the State he represents, he is bound by protocol to indicate his disagreement and displeasure at once, either by speaking, or, if he prefers, by leaving.

The Association's officers should know this. The only thing they could maintain on this score in their defence is that since His Excellency the Papal Nuncio represents not Yugoslavia but the Vatican State he was not compelled by protocol to take formal notice of any references to the affairs of Yugoslavia, such as the activities of Archbishop Stepinac. Had, for example, some blunt reference been made to Cardinal Segura of Seville,

5 Under the terms of the Vocational Education Act, Vocational Education Committees were created in 1930 to oversee training in trade schools.
6 A nuncio is a papal ambassador; at the time, Gerald Patrick Aloysius O'Hara (1895–1963) was the papal nuncio to Ireland, a position he held from 1951 to 1954.

whose intensive persecution of Spanish Protestants has caused considerable embarrassment to many Catholics (including American Catholics, who have spoken out very bluntly indeed) His Excellency would not have felt compelled to take formal notice, and doubtless would not have done so.[7] Finally, members were left unaware of the presence of the Nuncio, which, in the circumstances, it would have been proper for the Association to have announced to those present. It seems to me that the Association did well to apologise to His Excellency. But they should have apologised for their own gaffes, rather than have made Mr. Butler their whipping-boy.

Of course, we all see quite clearly why His Excellency and other Catholics have been deeply moved by the statement that Archbishop Stepinac was duped. Loyalties were involved. The antagonists are not seen as Marshal Tito and Archbishop Stepinac; they are seen as Satan and Christ.[8] So, although no Catholic is in the least degree bound to believe that the Archbishop behaved with impeccable wisdom and patriotism during the German occupation of his country – and, as we know, Catholics have constantly, and with good reason, disbelieved in the wisdom and patriotism of quite a number of priests, bishops, archbishops, cardinals and even Popes in history – they very naturally feel that Marshal Tito has, since the war, behaved in a manner beyond all tolerance; so that they cannot understand why, if there is to be any public criticism of anybody in Yugoslavia, it should not be of Tito, whose crimes cry out to heaven, rather than an Archbishop who must, beside him, seem an unspotted angel. Loyalty, however – it has been one of the more profound observations of Mr. Graham Greene – is one of the worst possible guides to Truth: wherefore he maintains that it is the duty of writers to be disloyal – meaning that once a writer commits himself irrevocably to any party-line he must, sooner or later, commit a sin against the truth. Which is one reason why politicians, and I suppose Churchmen, are not particularly enamoured of writers, or anybody else who puts Truth before Loyalty. In Russia they bump them off or buy them off. In the West they suffer them uncomfortably. In Ireland we ostracise them.

7 Pedro Segura y Sáenz (1880–1957) was appointed Cardinal in 1927.
8 Communist leader Josip Broz Tito (1892–1980) was marshal (1943–80), premier (1945–53), and president (1953–80) of Yugoslavia. Yugoslavia was a country from 1929 to 2003; it was composed of present-day Serbia, Montenegro, Bosnia and Herzegovina, Croatia, Macedonia, and Slovenia.

Now, may I say that I believe, I certainly hope, that His Excellency the Papal Nuncio had not, up to the incident I am discussing, fully appreciated just how severe the penalties are in this country for people who, like Mr. Butler and Dr. Sheehy-Skeffington, appear to put Truth before Loyalty. It would, at any rate, be entirely understandable that he would not have foreseen the sequels his protest would evoke. In America, certainly, had an Archbishop walked out of a public discussion there would have been no such sequel. Indeed, the discussion would not have been interrupted. In the Irish Republic it is sufficient for any Churchman to utter a whisper, not only to stop all discussion, but to produce the subsequent fury of the laity against the offender. The reason for the contrast is obvious: in the United States the Catholic Church is in a minority; in our island it is all powerful. Moreover, the saddest effect of His Excellency's protest has been one with which he can surely have no sympathy – the throwing of yet another stone on the cairn erected, stone by stone, over the last twenty-five years, on the grave of an adult, informed, intellectual, Catholic conscience. Such a conscience can only live where full liberty of discussion is permitted to the laity, whose fundamental Loyalty to their Church and Faith must otherwise be as useless as the Loyalty of an ignorant, untrained and unarmed army of mercenaries, unfitted to defend the Truth.

~

For there is not, in fact, an utter chasm between Truth and Loyalty, at least in the domain of religious belief. If there were it would mean that that to which we are Loyal is not the Truth. But two conditions are involved: the first is that we will distinguish between an office and a man; the second, that we do not trade in short-term loyalties for those which we believe to be eternal: in other words, we do not play politics in the name of religion, or subserve religion to some passing tactical advantage. Churchmen and laymen have done that before now; and the Church has paid dearly for it. I will refer to one of the simplest examples – the corruptions which at one period attended the distribution of Indulgences, at various times employed to promote wars against the Hussites, the Albigensians, the Turks; bought and sold in the Temple; ultimately reformed by the Council of Trent.[9]

9 In the Catholic Church, an indulgence is a full or partial remission of penance or punishment by a member of the hierarchy for a sin that has been committed by an individual; they were granted in medieval times for those who undertook military campaigns against non-Catholic lands, an example of which was the Crusades. Hussites were followers of the religious reformer Jan Hus (c. 1370–1415). The

(Would "Loyalty" have demanded before then that Catholics should not discuss such matters, or condemn such practices?) The historical examples are numerous, but a contemporary problem is to hand. I have mentioned the Cardinal of Seville. His activity in persecuting Protestants in Spain is a test case.[10] Is it Religion or is it Politics? It is open to anybody who so wishes to argue that those American Catholics who roundly condemn this churchman for pursuing Spanish Protestants are doing so because it does not suit *their* political book: because, that is, they have had too much trouble already in living down the Inquisition, or because they realise that Catholics are in a minority in the United States (as Protestants are in Spain);[11] or they fear that other Americans will use the Cardinal Archbishop as a stick to beat them with, saying, "Aha! That is what you Catholics would do to us if you had the same power." It is equally open to anybody who wishes to do so to praise these same American Catholics for asserting that Catholicism and Intolerance are two mutually exclusive things; that the honest individual conscience has rights which must be respected, with all the logical conclusions that follow therefrom, such as that the Church must not coerce others; or that a Censorship, imposed by clerical influence, is to be deplored; or that the Church must not – as Cardinal Segura would – employ the State to enforce its wishes on minorities, or even on majorities; or that the Church and the State has each its own sphere of influence – and, in fact, if any Irish Catholic cares to read that excellent weekly American Catholic layman's paper, *The Commonweal*, he will find that many intelligent American Catholics lean very much in all those directions. (It is only right to say that they are in turn hotly pursued by their less liberal co-religionists. The term "A Commonweal Catholic" is used in the United States as a term of derision by the die-hard right-handers.)

Albigensians, also known as the Cathari, were dualists who lived in southern France; the paradoxically named Pope Innocent III (1160/1–1216) launched a murderous crusade against the Albigensians that lasted from 1209 to 1229. The Council of Trent (1545–63) issued many reforms and clarified the doctrine of the Catholic Church against Protestant challenges.

10 *O'Faolain's note:* Some remarkable statements have been attributed to Cardinal Segura: e.g., in a Pastoral last year: "Protestant proselytism having broken the dikes of tolerance is not hesitating to advance on the open field towards religious freedom in our country."

11 The Inquisition, which occurred in Spain from 1478 to 1834 but was part of a larger exercise of the Catholic Church in all territories, was a judicial inquiry that attempted to expunge heresy. It led to hundreds of thousands of expulsions and the torture and execution of untold numbers.

I think the reader will see my point. It is that whatever view we may form of *the reasons* why the Cardinal Archbishop of Seville is condemned by these American Catholics those reasons must inevitably affect our opinion of the rights and wrongs of their decision. If they are moved by reasons of tactics or politics – call them Church-politics if you will – we will obviously have difficulty in believing that they were simultaneously motivated by pure principle. If we feel that they have been moved solely by principle we may still disagree with them, but we will not, at any rate, charge them with lack of loyalty. On the contrary, we may be inclined to believe that by sticking to long-term principles and by distinguishing between the Office and the man, they are serving their cause far better than if, for the sake of a short-term tactic, or a short-term loyalty, they stuck to the Cardinal Archbishop of Seville.[12]

And another point is inherent in this: namely, that it is not always easy to decide whether men are motivated by politics or by principle. Sometimes the two things coincide. Here in Ireland, for example, I have heard people say about the attitude of the Hierarchy towards the famous Browne Scheme that it was motivated by the politics of power, i.e., a clerical desire for power.[13] But, put side by side with this cynical interpretation the fact that it cannot have been motivated by the politics of power *if one takes Northern Ireland into account*; since, on the contrary, few things have done so much to bang the door against all hope of ever persuading our Northern fellow-countrymen to join us. Again, when Catholics living in a region where Catholicism is in a minority – e.g., Northern Ireland or the U.S.A. – plead for Tolerance must we at once suspect selfish political motives? We must, therefore, when we return to the case before us, be both careful and charitable.

≈

I, for one, do not doubt for a moment that those Catholics in Kilkenny and Dublin who have been pursuing Mr. Hubert Butler and Dr. Owen

12 *O'Faolain's note:* Here is a comment from another American quarter, the official newspaper of the Archdiocese of Indianapolis: "We feel it is past time for American Catholics to be relieved from the oppressive burden of our Spanish brethren. We have spent weary hours cleaning up the blood the Spaniards overzealously spilled in the Inquisition. If they wish to call the cops on the Protestants four centuries later they can take the blame themselves. Let them fend for themselves against the slings and arrows of world opinion … "

13 For more on this matter, see the previous essay, "The Dáil and the Bishops."

Sheehy-Skeffington were, in their own feelings, genuinely moved by a desire to demonstrate their loyalty to their Church and their Faith, and by no other motive. Why then do I go on to say that I am satisfied that they were, nevertheless, playing an unwise and shameful political game? First: because "feelings" are not enough; one must have concrete proof of the intelligence and worth of this loyalty. Secondly: because everything we observe about us in Ireland proves the contrary – it is an empty, unthinking loyalty which is in the long run of no positive value to any cause. Politics and principle do not here coincide. Does anybody, really and truly, believe when Irishmen get up and utter loud phrases against Communism and then sit down satisfied that they have demonstrated their "loyalty," does anybody believe that one iota of the slightest permanent value has been thereby contributed to anything whatsoever?[14] Here, too, we may learn from Catholicism elsewhere: in France, Italy, Britain, or the United States. For example, there are, I know, people in Italy – and possibly in Ireland also – who do not think that Signor De Gasperi is as good a Catholic as he should be. But who has really been fighting Communism, by his handling, for example, of the Land Question? Who is it that has realised that social unrest arises solely out of social injustice? Anybody who has read *Esprit*, or *Témoignage Chrétien*, or read about the priest-workers of France, or remembers such a gallant statement as that of Cardinal Gerlier's auxiliary, Monsignor Ancel, that the reason men become Communists is because they have "no longer any hope," or (to balance Cardinal Segura) has read of the constructive, concrete social reform policy of Don Angelo Herrera, the Bishop of Malaga, or is at all in any way aware of practical Catholic anti-communism elsewhere – must ask himself: "What are *we* doing?"[15]

14 *O'Faolain's note:* Everyone respects a declaration of faith. Though we will remember a sentence about faith without good works, which in this context seems particularly pertinent as what follows may indicate. It is such a soft option to declare one's faith in Ireland. [*Editor's note:* James 2: 14–26 discusses the necessary relationship between faith and good deeds. O'Faolain's reference is likely to verse 26: "For as the body without the spirit is dead, so faith without works is dead also."]
15 *Esprit*, which translates as "Spirit," and *Témoignage Chrétien*, which translates as "Christian Witness," are French magazines founded in 1932 and 1941, respectively. Pierre-Marie Paul Gerlier (1880–1965), Archbishop of Lyon, was elevated to Cardinal in 1937. Alfred-Jean-Félix Ancel (1898–1984) was appointed Auxiliary Bishop of Lyon in 1947. Ángel Herrera Oria (1886–1968) was appointed the Bishop of Malaga in 1947.

Do those well-meaning, good-hearted, decent chaps down in Kilkenny
– your potential friends and mine; men we might drink a glass with, or
kneel beside at Mass – really think that by ejecting Mr. Butler from the
Secretaryship of an Archæological Society they have struck a tremendous
blow for Christ? Here in Dublin, do the same sort of men – you might be
standing up beside one of them in The Pearl Bar any night, or putting on
a bet at the dogs, or stuck with one of them in a bus-queue – really think
they have served their Church nobly by preventing a University lecturer
from talking about The Freedom of the Individual? Are they serving anything by that sort of behaviour? Or disserving it? Is that true Loyalty? Or
is it just an outburst of that sort of self-kidding emotionalism for which
we Irish are famous?

I wrote the following paragraph in this magazine in 1951; and it is still
true. (I was talking about noble-minded people here who sneer at America's
foreign policy):

I put it to readers that before we start to pick holes in America we
should first examine our own conscience. What is *our* foreign policy?
Our contribution? I put it to you that our policy is a mean one. We
are slipping into the attitude that our hands are too lily-white, our
souls too pure, to touch the muck of the world; that we just *hope*
nothing will happen; that we are remote from it all; ready to be protected again by American G.I.'s, Dutch flyers, British sailors, French,
Belgian or Italian blood, with nothing of our own but a joke army, a
joke navy and a joke air force – all manned, agreed, by gallant men;
together with geography, geology, and God's special regard for His
chosen people. In short, we are snoring gently behind the Green
Curtain that we have been rigging up for the last thirty years –
Thought-proof, World-proof, Life-proof. The only people *we* are
ready to fight for are the angels. For we keep on saying we will fight,
if needs be, for Christ, that is against Communism; but, then, we
add, only on terms! If they give us our Six Counties we will fight for
Christ. Not otherwise! "Who will buy Christ?" we cry. "Going for a
song! Just for half a dozen bits of mortal soil!" Or, if you like to put
it in another way – Ireland's soul is on the market ...

Is that an honourable policy? Is it a contribution to anything?[16]

---

16 This is an excerpt from "Autoantiamericanism." It is provocative that O'Faolain
cites this essay, one that was roundly though sympathetically criticised by Butler,
in defending Butler in this later instance; yet it also testifies to his ability to accept
criticism in debate and to defend that adversary when a principle is at stake.

That was almost two years ago. Since then Ireland's practical contribution to the fight for Christianity versus Communism has been a vote by the Trades Union Congress in favour of Neutrality in any forthcoming war; the gallant disposition of a Protestant country gentleman from an Archæological Society in Kilkenny; and a public insult to the son of a patriotic father shot by the English, and a mother whose life was one long record of selfless devotion to her people.[17] I really think these three things should be registered by U.N.O. as Ireland's proof of her boundless loyalty to Faith and Freedom.[18] These good men in Kilkenny and Dublin need not, however, think that I am suggesting that they should apologise to Mr. Butler or to Dr. Sheehy-Skeffington. They can decide for themselves whether they might care to apologise to their Country and their God.

It is no disloyalty to God, or to any Institution, to believe that Archbishop Stepinac behaved unwisely. I do not know whether he did or not. I have not gone into the question. But I could quite understand that he might, for reasons of Loyalty – to his flock. And here, I wonder whether those Catholics who have been so offended by the suggestion that he did behave unwisely really know what he is charged with having done. It was the simplest thing and it could have happened to any of us. Suppose (to get a dimly analogous picture) the Germans had successfully invaded this island in the early 1940s. Resisted by the existing government, which would have had to flee to the hills at about ten minutes' notice, they would have invited a dozen reputable Catholic gentlemen to set up some sort of Standing Government to "carry on." (Pétainism.)[19] The men who would so act would be, again, decent fellows, your potential friends and mine. They would be motivated by the best principles. Marshal Pétain had the highest principles. In this sad state of affairs – the country wasted, under a foreign heel, its prosperity ruined, without hope, half-starving – is it difficult to imagine that some Bishop down the country, moved by the misery of his flock, might say: "These fellows up in the hills can do no good for us. These good gentlemen of the Standing Government up in the

17 This is a reference to Owen Sheehy-Skeffington, his father Francis, and his mother Hanna Sheehy-Skeffington (1877–1946), who was a renowned Irish suffragette and activist for several republican and workers' causes.
18 The United Nations organisation was founded in 1945.
19 Pétainism refers to the policy of Philippe Pétain (1856–1951), a French general who served as the head of the collaborationist French government during World War II.

capital are good Catholic men. Let us co-operate with them." This is the
first thing that Archbishop Stepinac is charged with having done.
Co-operation: i.e., "collaboration."

Now move over to the Balkans: a land of mixed races, mixed religions;
a land torn for centuries by the most savage internecine feuds; a land
where life has been for periods like a prolonged Belfast Pogrom; a land of
the fiercest and most revengeful passions.[20] The "good gentlemen up in
the capital" are here neither particularly good nor gentle. Their Balkan
methods are as savage as their Balkan memories, and finding themselves
in the saddle they start to spill Balkan blood. Our poor "Bishop down the
country" finds himself in anything but good company and some of the
spatter of the bloodshed falls on his innocent robe. (In Yugoslavia the
bloodshed was pretty terrible. For is it not rather terrifying to think of a
church being packed with non-Catholics and set on fire? Or Protestants
being forced under dire threats to become Catholics? The Archbishop
protested manfully against such conversions: but by then, as with Pétain,
it was too late.) When Mr. Butler said it was the "Bishop down the country" (Stepinac) had been duped by the fellows up in the capital (Pavelic)
it was, it seems to me, as much a defence as a charge.

It is always a great danger for the Church to come too close to the State.
The State is of this world. The Church is not. Far too much in the political
field is, I am convinced, always being asked of the Church and it is always
to her loss – and our's – if she yields to our persuasions and cajoleries to
enter into it. Let me digress to give an urgent topical example. Take all this
about Social Justice. When I spoke, a few pages back, of other countries'
efforts to right social injustice I spoke chiefly of laymen, for I do not see
that the Church has anything directly to say to Social Reform. In such matters she may be a referee. She cannot be a legislator. I do not even believe – I
hope I am allowed not to believe so – that Christ ever had anything directly
to say about Social Reform. I find nothing about that sort of justice either
in the Old or the New Testament, where all references to justice are to
Divine justice, or to justice within the existing system, or to justice in the
sense of justification. "Justice and judgment are the habitation of Thy
throne; mercy and truth shall go before Thy face."[21] It is true that Moses
brought down from Sinai many more specific ordinances than the Ten
Commandments: but the whole of Christ's teaching is a dematerialisation
of those old Mosaic laws. The whole force and quality of the Sermon on
the Mount is spiritual, not economic! It is either men of more goodwill

20 A pogrom is an organised massacre aimed at the destruction of a people.
21 Psalms 89:14.

than sense, or rationalists, who see Christ as a divine Tom Paine. Social justice, as we understand this modern term, is touched on by Christ only on the lofty ground of: "Lay not up for yourselves treasures upon earth where moth and rust doth corrupt";[22] a ground where social injustice will cease to exist, when greed ceases to exist, when we begin to do to others only what we would that men should do to us. Since that day, it is true, we have all become super-organised. Christ is now heard in committee. And everything is now put to the ruthless practical test of: "How does this, or this, or this, fit in with His teaching?" But can a Church be expected to legislate on these multitudinous questions? And how else can she be free of the blame of the laity in such questions but by insisting that though she may have much to say to the actions of the State, the Church and the State are not one. Which is something on which everybody should (but doubtless won't) be glad to agree, Catholics and non-Catholics, Christians and non-Christians; for those who are not of the Church should be glad to have it admitted that the domain of the Church and the domain of the State are disparate; and those who are of the Church should be glad that the blame for every small and large political matter should not be lobbed on the shoulders of a Church which could not possibly have controlled these problems either in their origins or their climax. But look about you! To-day every organised Body, from doctors to teachers, is trying to gang-up the Church behind them! And, unless she is careful, they sometimes succeed.

I fail to see why, in the field of international politics, the Church should be held to be involved every time a churchman makes a political mistake. A few months ago, when a distinguished Jesuit, in Rome, went over neck and crop to Communism, was the Church to blame? From all of which it follows that we may well ask why, if Archbishop Stepinac did, in fact, get unwisely involved in internecine Yugoslav politics, every Catholic must consider himself obliged to take up his fight? It is rather, it seems to me, a case where our Loyalties as Catholics must get on to higher ground and move in longer span, with far longer perspective than any temporal, tactical, political or personal ground or time-span. It ought not be necessary for me to say since the reader can look back over these pages and see for himself, that I am making no charge whatever against Archbishop Stepinac. All I am saying is that we should not only be allowed but *encouraged* to discuss the matter freely, on the ground of that Higher Loyalty where the Truth and all lesser Loyalties become, or should become, magnificently one.

22 Matthew 6:19.

The Irish and the Latins[1]

It is impossible to talk about "the Latin countries" as if they could all be bottled in one set of generalisations. The Catholicism of Italy is not quite the same thing as the Catholicism of France; the Italian approach to sex is not the same as the French; the lack of social conscience in Spain must astonish a Frenchman; there is anti-clericalism in every Latin country that I know about, but it takes a somewhat different form in each; each has an unique cultural pattern and way of life.

To an Irishman I think the only thing which is equally and blissfully true of them all is that they are not Anglo-Saxon. For there is a lot of truth in Salvador de Madariaga's speculation that the Irish are really a Mediterranean people, and even more truth in his sly suggestion that much of our racial sourness comes from the secret knowledge that we are far more anglicised than we ever care to admit, and can do nothing about it.[2] I know that whenever I cross the Italian frontier I feel I have come home, and that among the hundreds of uncomfortable inhibitions that fall from me is the domination of that English way of life which we Irish call Irish. In Italy I have often felt: "Why, oh why weren't we conquered by the Italians (or the French, or even the Spanish) and given their way of life, instead of this second-hand Saxon suit that fits us like one!"

This is, surely, the core of it all: that every race, like every man, has a nuclear instinct or concept of life personal to itself, and that nine-tenths of its job is to fashion an elaborate vessel to hold and display this instinctive attitude – a vessel that, when fashioned, we will call a racial cultural pattern, a racial art of living. We Irish have not done this. We took over

---

1 "The Irish and the Latins" appeared in *The Commonweal* (13 March 1953): 571–3.
2 Salvador de Madariaga y Rojo (1886–1978) was a Spanish writer and diplomat.

from England its laws, language, food, dress, architecture, games, even its literary tradition, almost everything except its religion. We adapted these things as much as we could, but we had to have them because the English had stripped us of everything of our own, and they are our veneer now; tough, hard, useful, sourly cherished because useful. But scratch an Irishman and you find an Irishman. The unfulfilled atavistic instinct is there all the time, though overtly we are so anglicised that Englishmen are sometimes taken aback to find beneath the familiar exterior the irredeemable Celt. Land any one of us in Italy and we go all native; back to the womb. Italy is the nearest thing to what we might have been and still would like to be.

It takes us quite a while to find out that we are not Italians. At first we are enchanted by the Catholicism of Italy. The essential things of life seem to us to be ordered there by the right philosophy. It is with an enormous relief that we notice that nobody is going about wearing aggressive, pious emblems. (Modern Ireland is painfully aggressive, touchy, fearful about its religion.) It is with dismay that we discover the existence of a political movement called *Azione Cattolica*.[3] We had thought or hoped that we had left all that behind us. And how can one need Catholic Action in a Catholic country? In Ireland we have Catholic Boy Scouts, Catholic Seamen, Catholic Young Men's Societies, Catholic Young Women's Societies, a Catholic Stage Guild, Catholic Commercial Travelers … Even there the adjective seemed redundant … But in Italy!

Our joy in being Catholics in Italy is like the joy of breathing, something one does not think about at all. And then, just as we have been feeling flawlessly happy in the company of a people simultaneously radiant with the joy of this good Life that is, and a deep faith in an even more joyous Life to come, we find ourselves hit by a sudden squall of squeamishness. Those miracles, for example! For while we also believe in miracles we cannot wander about Italy for very long without deciding that we do not believe in miracles all that much! I have never asked any other Irishman what he felt at the liquefaction of the blood of Saint Januarius; all I can say is that I beheld the frenzied scenes that accompanied it with a fascinated horror.[4]

3 *Azione Cattolica* translates as "Catholic Action."
4 A vial containing what is believed to be the blood of Saint Januarius (died c. 305) is kept in the Cathedral of Naples. Normally solid in substance, the blood reputedly liquefies eighteen times each year.

On such occasions an Irishman might well feel a tremor of fear. Could it, he may think, by any chance, be a small portion of English Puritanism that has, all unbeknownst, accompanied him to Italy like a mouse in his suitcase? And yet, old civilisations do breed corruption as well as grace. Wines can be kept too long. I prefer the Catholicism of France. I believe Frenchmen know more about religion, and wine.

It is on such occasions that we do well to remember the differences between the Latin races. The French look crookedly enough at the more orgiastic forms of Italian and Spanish religiosity. The Spanish and the Italians look just as askance at the more frank manifestations of the French attitude to Woman. It is not only a puritanical Englishman, or an infected Irishman, who feels that stiffening of the spine which goes with the feeling of being shocked when he beholds a row of men and women in a Paris café clinched in passionate embrace.

Only twice have I seen public love-making in Italy, though, of course, one sees plenty of playful courtship. Educated Italians are always envying the free way in which boys and girls mingle in Britain and America; no Italian boy dares, for instance, see a girl home unless he wishes to be instantaneously known as her exclusive choice; which is awkward in a country where a girl's one protection against unwelcome attentions is to be known as *fidanzata* – nobody else would ask her out afterwards.[5]

The Italians have a great dignity about sex. They treat it as a serious business, a grave business, a business, as we Irish do, except that they rejoice in this serious business and we are terrified of it. But if we would only be as natural about it as they are, this, I feel, is how we too would behave. We would frankly admire, as we probably secretly do, the sort of women they admire and whose rich, procreative beauty they love to display at every opportunity. We like their animal adoration of children. It is splendid to see the pride of a pregnant Italian, arrogant and honoured as an army with banners. It is sad that Irish women are not particularly proud when they are big with child. They are almost as embarrassed as English women.

Italy takes Ireland farther. We boast that we have no respect for the Law; a hang-over from our rebelly days, a poor and timid self-compensation for having, in fact, taken over Lor an' Order holus-bolus.[6] For what

5 *Fidanzata* translates from the Italian as "fiancée."
6 Holus-bolus means all at once.

is our timid dodgery compared with an Italian's magnificently total contempt for all rules and regulations without exception! And is there anything so foolish as the legend which the English have profitably propagated
amongst us and about us – the myth that we love fighting? (We enjoy
quarreling, a totally different thing.)

With what relief this priggish load of nonsense falls from our shoulders
when we observe the cold-blooded, unenthusiastic and generally cantankerous attitude of the French to all war; the utter dismay with which the
Italian faces it, and the delighted agility with which he drops it. We no
more like fighting than Shaw's Bluntschli did; in *Arms and the Man*, which
the English – for whom war is, or was, of necessity, a great and glorious
adventure – at once scornfully turned into a musical comedy, *The
Chocolate Soldier*.[7] It seems to me that the Italians and the Spanish are
civilised in that they kill with pleasure only for passion and cash.

The Latin spirit throws a deep light into our souls; it exposes our own
truth to us. It makes us, for instance, admit with the relief of confession
that we are not truthful at all. Have you ever seen Goldoni's play *The
Liar*?[8] It could be about Ireland. We are a cynical people, but we are
half-afraid to be cynical until we mingle with the Italians.

We are, I truly believe, an artistic people, a people who like colour; but
have you ever seen an Irish soldier, an Irish policeman? They are slavish
copies of the English pattern. Our sailors dare to carry a red bob on top
of their caps. It is the one solitary touch of colour in all our non-fighting
forces. Land us on the Continent and we drink up its colour as a thirsty
plant drinks water.

What has happened elsewhere to this splendid naturalness of the Latins?
An Italian peasant will suckle her child in public; so far as I know the
only other women who behave in this civilised fashion are savages. But it
is not naturalness in the sense of being uncultivated. Their spontaneous
response to nature is part of their whole convention of living, so that it is
the essence of their achievement to have clothed the nakedness of nature

7 Bluntschli is the pragmatic soldier in *Arms and the Man* (1894), by Bernard Shaw.
The Chocolate Soldier (1908) is an operetta by the Austrian composer Oscar Straus
(1870–1954); it was originally written in German under the title *Der tapfere Soldat*
and was only later translated into English.
8 *The Liar* (1750–51), by Italian dramatist Carlo Goldoni (1707–1793).

with a garment of grace that never becomes, as it too often does with other races, a strait jacket; a discipline near to a tyranny.

Compare the Latin idea of the gentleman with the northern idea. That, too, is a very fine idea, sometimes a noble ideal – one thinks of Sir Philip Sidney; but the core of it, when all is said and done, is property, position, the hierarchical outlook *de haute en bas*.⁹ It is a revelation to move about Italy with an Italian nobleman – a hereditary noble, not one of those half-million *conti*, and *dei conti* and late-comers to the purple with political or purchased titles.¹⁰ Such a man – he may be by the sea in summer, dressed in old blue jeans and rope sandals – will talk to the fishermen in the *trattoria* with absolute simplicity, both completely at their ease, and though it will be evident to everybody that he is a Somebody neither side will give the least sign of their awareness of the practical distinctions between them.¹¹ And this is quite different from the rather aggressive friendliness, that assertive egalitarianism which is not egalitarian at all, adopted by other races towards poorer foreigners. It is an art, so old now as to be second-nature, so instinctive now that it might be mistaken for Arcadian innocence.¹² It is only when we turn from Latin life – to which I have deliberately confined myself – to Latin painting or architecture, that we realise how deliberate it all is.

But here, at last, one comes up against the one unacceptable anomaly in the Latin way of life. I approach it via the one generalisation which holds true for all the Latin countries: that anti-clericalism is rife in all of them. This is not just that sort of sparring that goes on in every army between the rankers and the brass hats, and which sensible Catholics, priests and laity, take for granted, perhaps even welcome as a healthy sign of intellectual independence. There must be something terribly wrong when priests evoke a hatred so terrible that it can only be satisfied, as it was in Spain, by the murder of thousands upon thousands of clerics. It would be a foolish evasion to refer these horrors merely to Communist influence; for why should Communism thrive in countries historically rooted in Catholicism, and wilt in a country like England, now basically Protestant?

9 Sir Philip Sidney (1554–1586) was an English courtier and poet. *De haute en bas* translates from the French as "from top to bottom"; it refers to one who regards another condescendingly or with an air of contempt.
10 A *conte*, which O'Faolain spells "conti," is the noble title "count" in Italian.
11 A *trattoria* is a restaurant.
12 Arcadia is a region in Greece long-noted for its pastoral character and isolation; it has come to represent an earthly paradise.

At this thought everything one may otherwise say in praise of the Italian concept of the Gentleman seems to fall into pieces; their art of living suddenly seems hollow and rotten at the core; when one remembers the misery of southern Italy and Sicily one wonders how far Catholicism there has failed itself by letting injustice feed into social and religious revolt. And it is a sardonic thought that those cancerous injustices would never have been met and treated clinically, as they now are being treated (ever since the winter of 1949–50), without the financial assistance of the United States, paid for the most part by non-Catholics, even by anti-Catholics, anxious to repair an injury that Catholic Italy has allowed to fester for a thousand years.[13]

It is at this point, too, that one begins to think that, after all, one may have to turn back sadly from the warmth, indifference, ruthlessness and indiscipline of the South to the intellect and the conscience of Catholic France. For while Italy welcomes, France challenges; which is not quite so comfortable.

Italy takes our pleasures farther; France takes our problems farther, the one Latin country in which there is a vital Catholic intellect. Italy may be a joy to Irishmen; she is also a warning to us. And so, we go from one to another, and wish we could make a synthesis of them all: a restlessness that is, I suppose, in the nature of life, part of Adam's curse.[14]

13 See the earlier essay "Autoantiamericanism."
14 Adam's curse is the life of labour to which God condemned humankind after the Fall in the Garden of Eden.

Love Among the Irish[1]

Ever since the Black Forties of the 19th Century we Irish have been flying from our homeland. And I am using the right word, for that wholesale Irish Diaspora of the 19th Century was nothing but a wild, terrified flight from hunger. The net result of that stampede has been that in 100 years the population of southern Ireland has dwindled from between six and seven million to under three million.

We always maintained in Ireland that this national loss of blood – I might call it a racial hemophilia – was entirely due to foreign misrule. We

1 "Love Among the Irish" appeared in *Life* (16 March 1953): 140–57. The essay was prefaced with the following editorial passage:

Some months ago the distinguished Irishman of letters Sean O'Faolain was asked by Father John O'Brien of Notre Dame University to contribute to a symposium entitled "The Vanishing Irish," to be published in book form by McGraw-Hill next fall. Mr. O'Faolain did so and subsequently adapted his contribution for publication in LIFE. This article, in which he describes himself as "an Irishman and a Catholic," is the result. Mr. O'Faolain, as novelist, historian, biographer, critic and playwright, has over the past 20 years made his name as one of the foremost in the long list of Irish writers with international reputations. He lives at Knockaderry in County Dublin.

The essay caused an uproar of sorts in Ireland, with an article in the *Irish Press* on 27 March 1953 taking O'Faolain to task. O'Faolain's critical response was published in the *Irish Press* on 2 April 1953, along with a rebuttal of it by one of the paper's correspondents. For the better part of a month, letters on the subject appeared in the paper. Peadar O'Donnell offered a sober postscript commentary on the controversy in "The *Irish Press* and O'Faolain," *The Bell* 18, no. 11 (May 1953): 5–7.

promised ourselves and the world that once we got a native government we would soon put a stop to all that.

In 1946, after a quarter of a century of native rule, we looked at the ledger and we got a bad shock. Census figures showed that we were still on the downgrade. We had to face the bitter truth that something more than foreign misrule is involved. We had to pick rock salt out of our sores when we discovered simultaneously that while our own people were vanishing from Ireland the English were coming back to it in droves: in full flight from the austerities of Socialist England, they were buying up houses and farms in every part of the country. To discourage what became known as England's Reconquest by Checkbook we promptly clapped a tax on all alien purchasers of land and property. But, seven years after, we are still ruefully scratching our heads over the essential problem of our own racial decay.

It is a poor consolation to tell ourselves that we are never likely to disappear from the earth. That is merely to say that we are performing a graceful and gradual diminuendo into insignificance. It would give us even less consolation to observe that at the rate of recent years our population will not drop below the two-million mark for at least five generations, if then. A land so under-populated could neither feed itself, clothe itself nor defend itself. We would be like a scattering of chaste rabbits nibbling around the coastline of Australia. In the Black Forties of the 19th Century we were hungry because we were so many.[2] In the Black Forties of the next century will we be hungry because we are too few?

What explanations do we usually offer for this persistent withering away of the Celt?

Emigration is the first explanation. Now it is chiefly to Great Britain. It is a convenient safety valve for unemployment at home. But should there be, at any time, serious unemployment in Great Britain the thousands upon thousands we have been sending over there for years past will come stampeding back to us to queue at our labour exchanges for a weekly dole. A bottling-up like that could easily produce a social explosion and shake our economy to its foundations.

The second explanation is a brutal one. It is that old Irishmen never die, they merely fade away at ages of such fantastic antiquity that their offspring are by then too old to start fruitful lives of their own. The commonest example of this adamantine refusal to surrender is the aging

---

2 The Black Forties refers to the 1840s. In the latter half of the decade, Ireland was stricken by the Great Famine, which resulted from repeated failures of the potato crop.

farmer who will not hand over his farm to his sons.[3] When one of these old Irish farmers refers to his "boy" it is 10-to-one that the "boy" is hitting 50. A while ago when two brothers, aged about 60 and 65, came before the courts for riotous and wanton behaviour it developed that they were two "boys" who had been having their first real taste of liberty and liquor on the night of their father's unlooked-for demise at the early age of 92.

The results of this old *v.* young tussle are late marriages, a slow birth rate and a declining population, not to mention poor productivity from the older age groups.

This is where we bump up against the most disturbing explanation of all. For the surprising fact is that even in our towns and cities, where the boys and girls can earn enough money to be independent of the old, they still refuse to marry young. The state appeals to them to wed. The Church appeals to them to multiply. In the blunt language of Shaw's Miss Eliza Doolittle they reply with one voice, "Not bloody likely!"[4] This is the core of the whole thing. It is a human resistance that defies statesmen, churchmen and statisticians. "Why," we all ask, "why, ye young divils, why in the name of God and nature won't ye marry one another?"

Well, here are their own replies, chosen from scores which came to me through the mail some time ago when I happened to be writing articles for a popular newspaper about this very question of late marriages in Ireland.

To begin with let us see what the young men have to say about the girls. Two plaints are made by the young men. The first: what they want from their girls is not love, not romance, not passion, not beauty, not companionship, not charm, not wit, not intelligence – but simply the plain, homespun qualities of housekeeper and mother. The second: they are extremely sceptical about the capacity of the modern young Irishwoman to fill either of these two very simple requirements.

Here is how one young Irishman approaches wedlock. One might think that he is not so much approaching woman as stalking her:

> I am a bachelor, aged 38. I am in no hurry to get married. Next September, or the September after, I will take a holiday with an object at Lisdoonvarna, County Clare.[5] I will inform some of the priests on holiday that I am on the lookout, and that I am a bachelor

3 Adamantine means hard or unbreakable.
4 From *Pygmalion* (1913), by Bernard Shaw.
5 The Lisdoonvarna Matchmaking Festival has run every September for over 150 years.

of some substance who requires a wife with a dowry of a certain minimum figure. The good priests will pass the word around. In due course a girl will be selected and the wooing will proceed on a sane plane. At Christmas [this eager lover continues] my people will visit her people, and her people will investigate my background, credentials and relatives. I will meet the young lady again on some such occasion as the Rugby International in Dublin during the following Easter. In due course the nuptials will take place. If I marry at 40 on the lines I have indicated I will guarantee that at 60 my wife and myself will be fonder of one another than any couple of the same age who married in their youth for what Hollywood miscalls love, but which is in fact *lustful infatuation* ...

There are, in this letter, two points of some anthropological interest to anybody investigating the problem of love among the Irish. This man wants his bride to bear him a dowry. He also considers that he is young enough to marry at 40 but does not mention the desirable age for his bride. If he is prepared to allow her the same slow-motion approach to marriage as himself it is evident that there could not be a very large family – if any! But in practice our hairy old Irish bachelors seek out young brides – and they seem to get them. It is to be remembered that there are more men than women in Ireland, one of the very few countries in the world of which this is true. Besides, as one of them shrewdly remarked to me, "A young woman can take a chance on marriage. She must, because she cannot wait. If she waits her good looks will fade. But we men *can* wait!"

But there is often an implicit objection to young wives. Harken, ye tender virgins of Eire, to another of your potential husbands:

The average, modern Irish girl is a painted, powdered, padded, puffed parrot, except for her nails which are hawk's claws. Their adoration of film actors has reached a STATE OF IMBECILITY! It is often said that slow horses and fast women would ruin any man, but we don't need the horses, the women would do it alone. How could any man in his sane senses, for whom marriage means a family and responsibility, contemplate a life spent with one of these lassies? The sight alone of one of them swigging expensive liquors in lounge bars at a rate that would knock out a navvy in half the time is enough to deter any man from taking the plunge. Marriage is a hell of a serious business. It is not a business for flighty flibbertigibbets like these. It is a business for grown men and women with their eyes open. The modern Irish girl seems to be quite unaware of this fact. I will not jump headlong into matrimony. I will look carefully around me. I will wait and bide my time, and choose with careful circumspection. Marriage is for ever. It is a sobering thought for any man ...

Unreliable, extravagant, spoiled: such, according to the men, are modern Irish girls. They say it over and over again, in various ways:

I am a bachelor, and so far as I can see I am likely to remain so for some years to come unless God is especially kind to me. How could any man expect the girls that are going nowadays to cook and wash for him, to rear his children and to keep his home, with their heads full of all sorts of nonsense from morning to night? And they have no more sense of the value of money than if they were John D. Rockefeller himself.[6]

Recently I was rather inclined to be interested in a young woman. I went out with her one night, accompanied by another lady. The first thing was I found myself in a lounge bar, and I felt it was up to me to invite the two ladies to have some refreshment, with no thought in my head but that they would ask for a soft drink, or at the most a sherry. I was much astonished when the young woman I was attracted to asked for a "gin and it," and her friend demanded nothing less if you please than a Pimms Number One.[7] Now, I am a mechanic by trade, earning around £7.10.0 ($21) per week. How could I keep up that rate of going? And it is a poor preparation for matrimony. If the girls are not married it is their own fault by the example they give beforehand ...

What pleases me most about these letters is their splendidly hoary smell. That last chap is not a modern Irishman at all, except in the sense that every modern Irishman is a mediaeval European. All these attacks on women are part of that ancient and undying battle of the sexes on which

6 John D. Rockefeller (1839–1937) was an American industrialist and philanthropist. He was the father of John D. Rockefeller, Jr. (1874–1960), grandfather of John D. Rockefeller III (1906–1978), and great-grandfather of John D. Rockefeller IV (b. 1937). The reference was likely not meant to be to any one of these four men, but rather to use the Rockefeller name as a metonym for an extremely wealthy man.

7 Pimms No. 1 Cup is a liqueur that was created in 1823.

we come with such glee in the scabrous antifeminist pages of Rabelais or Jean de Meung.[8]

When we turn to the girls' opinions of the men we find almost precisely the same charges. In their belief the men are cagey, spiritless, selfish and spoiled by their mothers.

> I have been reading what the men are alleged to think of the women. In my experience modern Irishmen are nothing but a race of male cuckoos, beer sharks and boogie-woogie fanatics. This is a land made for the male – card playing, horse racing, coursing, fishing. It is a paradise for the male. It is not that the young man in modern Ireland cannot afford to get married. It is that he cannot get married and still afford his car, his club, his betting, his poker, his golf and his holidays. So the young man remains single ...

On the overmothered Irishman:

> The men of today are mammy's darlings. They have everything at home so why should they leave it? Their mothers slave for them and they expect that their wives will slave for them in the same way. Gosh! Haven't men got away with a lot! It is no wonder they used to marry early long ago when they even expected their wives to polish their boots for them. But we women now want marriage on a 50-50 basis, so the darlings have slowed up. Look at the way a man can drink Lough Erne dry and it is only called a binge, but if a poor woman gets a cold she is told to cure it with buttermilk boiled with onions. There is no doubt either that parents do influence their sons to wait a little longer, and you know what that means – 10 or 15 years maybe. The odd thing is that these mothers are more than anxious to find other mothers' sons to marry their own daughters. The sum of it all is, mother is an Irishman's landlady – without pay.

What has happened to the legendary wild Irish lover? Another letter:

> I used to think Irishmen ideal. After meeting Englishmen and men of other nationalities I soon found that he has feet of clay. He may be brave on the battlefield but when it comes to love he is the greatest

8 Jean de Meung (c. 1240–c. 1305), also spelled de Meun, was a French poet who wrote of courtly love and was renowned for his satire.

coward in the world. And the conceit of the creatures! Quite laugh-
able to the Latin races who are so busy adoring women that they can
sometimes forget themselves. I used to think of all Irishmen as dashing, romantic fellows ...

But now? Did you ever read the 'get-together' columns in the
newspapers? *Young man, teetotaller, no means, wishes to meet girl,
same, with means.* Emphasis on the means. How blooming romantic!
It should read, *Young man, adventurous and enterprising, wishes to
meet beautiful girl and have a whale of a time.* Instead, how often do
we hear, "He's after marrying £5,000." The truth is our eligible bachelors are quaking bundles of inhibitions. You will find the answer to
the whole thing in Arland Ussher's *The Face and Mind of Ireland.*[9]
He states that Irishmen have hardly enough sex to perpetuate their
own cantankerous species ...

After reading such outbursts as these – however we may laugh at them,
whatever may lie behind them – we can hardly be surprised to discover
that, according to the last census, only one person out of 100 marries
each year.

How do they manage it? How can any normally sexed man (for I refuse
to believe that Arland Ussher's opinion is the right one) wait as patiently
and as dangerously as these Irish near-celibates do for the joys of love and
marriage? And we must remember that there are no irregular safety
valves in Catholic Ireland. In the whole country there is not one brothel.[10] Prostitution is exceedingly rare, sordid and furtive. There is a certain amount of illegitimacy, but no reliable statistics are available because
there are so many loopholes – emigration before the birth, marriage after
conception and so on. Some believe that homosexuality is on the increase.
There are no proper figures for venereal disease but its incidence is large
enough to be taken seriously by church and state. If there were an atmosphere of free and frank discussion, as there is not, we might get a better
general picture.

I have heard only four plausible explanations for Irish continence: that
sexual desire is either sublimated by religion, exhausted by sport, drugged

9 *The Face and Mind of Ireland* (1949), by Arland Ussher (1899–1980).
10 This is a questionable claim. See Diarmaid Ferriter's *Occasions of Sin: Sex &
Society in Modern Ireland* (2009) for a useful account of the subject and Kate
O'Brien's *Pray for the Wanderer* (1938) for a literary work that attests to the
presence of brothels in post-independence Ireland.

by drink or deflected by either an innate or an inculcated Puritanism. The fact stands that Irishmen can and do wait longer than any other race in the world for the joys of love.

What lies behind those angry letters I have quoted? How seriously should we take all such sparrings between young Irishmen and young Irishwomen? I think that we have to take them quite seriously but it would be a mistake to take them quite literally.

Irishmen, for example, are undoubtedly much more calculating in love than a foreigner might think if he based his notions on the reckless and dashing characters of Anglo-Irish fiction. Those gallant rakes were bred in the big houses of a minority landlord class. The mass of the people were hard-pressed peasants for whom love had to take a second place before the essential tie of blood and economy. Today this basic, rural class is dominant in Ireland and they have brought into the towns and cities the traditions and techniques of the country. Furthermore, matriarchal power still counts for a good deal. Prudence and respect for family authority can easily become misinterpreted as caginess and Momism.[11] When the girls, grown wiser in their generation, respond to what they consider caginess with a bit of dash – and Irishwomen have far more "go" in them than Irishmen – the boys react by calling them extravagant, spoiled, unreliable. Mutual irritation has set in.

The young people are angry: there is no denying that. But it is a transferred anger. I am satisfied that these young people are dying to throw their arms around one another, human nature being the same the world over. But because, for one reason or another, they cannot make the grade they foolishly turn on one another all the anger and frustration that – if they had more courage – they would turn on the conditions that are denying them a natural sex life.

What are the conditions that keep them apart? Poverty? Nonsense! And here is the proof of it: when most of our people were living on the lowest subsistence level, a hundred years ago, 57% of the younger people normally got married between the ages of 23 and 34. Today, when the standard of living is incomparably higher – though by no means as yet high enough – only 25% marry before the age of 34.

What is creating the psychological block here is something far nearer to the opposite of poverty. All our young people are developing a proper concept of what constitutes decent living conditions and until they get them they are on strike against marriage. We are rearing generations in

11 Momism is matriarchal domination or excessive allegiance to one's mother.

Ireland that have ten times more pride and ambition than their parents ever had, and good luck to them for it. As one young woman put it to me in two sentences: "I saw what my mother went through. Not for me, thank you!"

Naturally the young folk do not fully realise what they are doing: theirs is an instinctive reaction. For the first time in our history they have begun to taste, though still only to taste, the rewards of a full life, and they very naturally want more of them. Nor is it likely that our young celibates will be any more objective when, at last, no longer quite so young, they cease to be celibates. Then they will tell us that they are entering the happiest years of their lives, forgetting that they waited for them – dangerously, painfully and prudently – until they had first collected every possible cushion against their hardships and risks. And no doubt when they become fathers themselves they will, in their turn, wonder why their children do not marry young, and proceed simultaneously to excuse, uphold and consolidate all those discouraging living conditions which had been responsible for their own procrastination.

What are these discouraging conditions?

To begin with, no form of birth control is permitted by Church or state. The sale and advertisement of contraceptives is forbidden by law. Books and periodicals which advocate or even refer to the use of contraceptives are regularly banned by the state and seized by customs officials. Even that form of control of, or limitation on, conception known as "rhythm," or the use of the so-called "safe period," is frowned upon by Church and state.

It will be obvious that any youth obedient to his Church (or at any rate to its local representatives) and submissive to the state will in these circumstances foresee marriage as a very heavy responsibility indeed.

No divorce. This restriction is unlikely to deter any man from marriage unless he is a very cold-blooded and calculating fish indeed. But it does underline the gravity of the step.

Social services are not generous in Ireland. A children's allowance grants 17 shillings 6 pence (about $2.44) per month for every child after the second. There is no comprehensive maternity-grant system. The children of the destitute are delivered free of charge, the poor pay whatever they can afford to pay. Nursing homes for middle-class mothers are expensive. There are no comprehensive state schemes for prenatal or postnatal advice.

In 1951 when the then minister for health, Dr. Noel Browne, wished to introduce a mother-and-child scheme of a comprehensive nature, with pre- and postnatal advice, free medical attention without a means test and other such benefits, the Catholic hierarchy condemned the scheme, the government obeyed without question and the scheme fell through.[12] It is only proper to add that the Irish medical profession opposed the scheme root and branch.

The fact stands that marriage can be a costly business in Ireland and our provident young men foresee this.

Housing is dear and often difficult to come by. An average worker, say a bus driver or a garage mechanic, who will draw a pay packet of between £7 and £8 (about $21) a week will pay about a third of his wages for a couple of rooms and may have to wait for years before he can rent a small house or an apartment worthy of the name. For those couple of rooms are not what any American wife would call an apartment: they are simply a couple of rooms in a house, with a makeshift kitchenette, one shared lavatory and bathroom for a whole houseful of families. Why should any young man be expected to take his young bride into a couple of rooms of this type? It is right to say that our government has done a great deal of work to provide housing for the workers, but the leeway yet to be made up is great.

Rural living conditions are enough to drive any young man of spirit to emigration or to drink. All the small towns and villages are dwindling for this reason. Before the cinema came these places offered virtually no means of entertainment in the winter other than the public house or the free pleasure of standing with one's back to a damp wall surveying the falling rain. And those of us who visit and revel in the Irish countryside during the brief summer months must not forget that our winter lasts long, that the high spirits which are turned on for social occasions die down as quickly as they flare up and remain down for a long solstice. The natural instinct of any young man or woman born into such places cannot be to marry and sink deeper into their Nile mud but to get out and marry elsewhere; and so they do, via the larger centres to England.

But the term "living conditions" involves far more than physical limitations. The whole question of sex in Ireland is dominated also by profound psychological repressions. To explain this I have kept to this point one extract from a letter by a young man who has been very honest and percipient about these limitations. He writes: "We Irishmen have been conditioned into a state of sexual frigidity and repression because for generations we have clothed the sublimity of love in shrouds of taboo,

---

12 For more on this, see the earlier essay "The Dáil and the Bishops."

false prudery and an attitude of Victorian Puritanism that has given to the act of sexual union the blasphemous nature of something offensive."

If this attitude has been – and I am afraid it has been – fostered by the Church in Ireland in our time, it has not been fostered consciously and deliberately. How could it be? It is the doctrine of the Catholic Church that to seek satisfaction of bodily desire in sexual union, that is in marriage, is one of the most virtuous functions of mankind, a holy act in which God and man must take constant joy and delight. It has been fostered, most unhappily, because the young people will not marry young and the clergy fear that the result must be a relaxation of sexual morality. The stage is set for conflict and an impasse. The Church thunders against the dangers of sex. The young men, obedient up to the point of marriage, at which they balk, are inevitably conditioned into a frustrated terror of woman.

I am an Irishman and a Catholic. I live in Ireland. I am bringing up my children in Ireland as Catholics. I fully acknowledge the right of the Catholic clergy in Ireland to adopt any attitude they think fit to the problems of young love. I am simply objecting that the position I see adopted by Church and state in Ireland is short-sighted, inhuman, unwise and may be fatal to both.

Since my boyhood I have heard my elders fulminating about company keeping, night courting, dancing at the crossroads, V-necks, silk stockings, late dances, drinking at dances, mixed bathing, advertisements for feminine underwear, jitterbugging, girls who take part in immodest sports (such as jumping or hurdling), English and American books and magazines, short frocks, Bikinis, cycling shorts and even waltzing, which I have heard elegantly described as "belly to belly dancing." Perhaps the most extreme example of this kind of thing was to hear woman described from a pulpit to a mixed congregation as "the unclean vessel."

Our censorship of books and publications, instigated by the clergy and submitted to, willy-nilly, by everybody, is a symbol of this fear of sex. Some years ago Dr. Halliday Sutherland, the well-known Catholic apologist, published an essay on the "safe period" form of birth control in a book entitled *The Laws of Life*. Although one edition of this book bore the *Permissu Superiorum* (by permission of superiors) of the English Archdiocese of Westminster, the permission was not considered good enough for Ireland. (Catholicism in Ireland and Catholicism in England and elsewhere have apparently different standards.) All editions of that book were banned as "indecent and obscene" by the Irish Censorship Board and they still remain banned. When a debate took place on the banning of this book in the Irish Senate the following exchange took place:

SENATOR JOHNSTON: What does the law of the state say about the safe period with regard to birth control?

THE MINISTER FOR JUSTICE: I am not prepared to go into the law of the state. Whether the [Censorship] Board was technically and legally correct, whether the book was in its general tendency indecent and obscene may be open to question. But on the grounds that it was calculated to do untold harm I was perfectly satisfied it should be banned.[13]

In the 150 close-packed pages of the official register of books and periodicals banned by the Irish Censorship Board we find the name of almost every single Irish writer of note, some for one book, some for several. The banning is done in secret. There is no appeal to the courts of law, apart from a possible indictment of the Minister for Justice on the grounds of unconstitutional behaviour, a process beyond the means of any writer and not very likely, in the present state of public opinion, to be fruitful. After 20 years of agitation, headed originally by such writers as the late Æ and W.B. Yeats, an appeal board was established, also giving its decisions in secret conclave, and without right of appeal therefrom to the courts of law. It has debanned a minute fraction of banned books and periodicals, by which time the books are often out of print and the writer's name irretrievably smeared.

Among authors who, for one book or several, have been considered indecent and obscene are George Bernard Shaw, William Faulkner, Hervey Allen, Graham Greene, F. Scott Fitzgerald, Eric Linklater, Lucius Apuleius, Ernest Hemingway, Erskine Caldwell, Thomas Wolfe, John Dos Passos, Somerset Maugham, Aldous Huxley, James T. Farrell, Jean Paul Sartre, Albert Camus, Arthur Koestler, André Malraux, Charles Morgan, Anatole France, John Steinbeck, Joyce Cary, Sean O'Casey, Liam O'Flaherty, Frank O'Connor, George Moore, Sinclair Lewis ... [14] Really, the roster is so lengthy with its thousands of names, that one might be done with it by

13 This exchange, between Joseph Johnston and Gerald Boland (1885–1973) (Fianna Fáil), occurred on 18 November 1942. The parenthetical addition is O'Faolain's.
14 Americans William Faulkner (1897–1962), Hervey Allen (1889–1949), Thomas Wolfe (1900–1938), John Dos Passos, and James T. Farrell (1904–1979); Britons Somerset Maugham (1874–1965), Aldous Huxley (1894–1963), and Charles Langbridge Morgan (1894–1958); Roman philosopher Lucius Apuleius (c. 124–c. 70 BCE); Frenchmen Jean-Paul Sartre (1905–1980), Albert Camus (1913–1960), André Malraux (1901–1976), and Anatole France; and Northern Irishman Joyce Cary (1888–1957).

saying that the motto of the Censorship Board could be, "If it's good we've got it!"

Nor is this all. Under the influence of this official censorship a widespread censorship-rabies has developed throughout the country. If any old woman, of either sex, utters an objection to a library book (as they do early and often) the librarian must withdraw it from his shelves unless he is prepared to live like a hunted beast for the rest of his life. I have before me several private lists, exchanged between librarians, of books considered unsuitable within their bailiwicks. A list issued by the Dublin County Libraries Committee, headed "Books Considered Unsuitable for General Circulation," includes among other astonishing titles: George Borrow's *Lavengro*, Thomas Hardy's *Tess of the D'Urbervilles*, Fyodor Dostoevsky's *Crime and Punishment*, Leo Tolstoy's *Anna Karenina*, Victor Hugo's *The Hunchback of Notre Dame*, Willa Cather's *Death Comes for the Archbishop* and the complete works of John Galsworthy.[15]

Any reader with a gram of imagination will be able to imagine that young people in a country which sees dangers to chastity in *Death Comes for the Archbishop* are not living in an atmosphere favourable to a sane or healthy attitude to sex. The only ray of light is that of farce. Some time ago a priest objected to a performance of *Othello*. And when O'Casey's *The Shadow of a Gunman* visited Cork the local dean decided to do some censoring. (He has since gone to his reward where all men and women are angels and Irish men and women, of course, the most angelic angels of the lot.) In this play a volley of shots evokes from one of the characters the terrified cry, "Jesus, Mary an' Joseph!" The line was cut on the ground that no proper Irish person would utter such a cry. The play went on, and the shots went off, evoking a terrified cry of "Jesus, Mary an' Joseph!" in the first row of the pit – from a lady.

One novel banned as indecent was written – the censors discovered too late – over a pen name by Count Michael de la Bédoyère, the respected editor of *The Catholic Herald*.

Enough. What we need, surely, is the lifting of an unclean cloud. For a picture of a saner attitude to woman go into any southern city of Europe. There the God-given beauty of woman is almost adored. Courtship is frank and fair. The youths discuss the charms of their girls openly and with enthusiasm. Their songs are of love; their thoughts are of love; their blood is at natural blood heat. They marry young. While the population

15 *Lavengro* (1851), by George Borrow (1803–1881); *Anna Karenina* (1875–77); *The Hunchback of Notre Dame* (1831), by Victor Hugo (1802–1885); and *Death Comes for the Archbishop* (1927).

of Ireland is dwindling the population of Italy is soaring. And yet the young Italian hardly ever goes to church, except for his First Communion, his marriage, his christenings, his annual confession and to lie on his catafalque. His priest is not his policeman. He hardly ever thinks of his priest. Yet that good man should be well and truly content because God's lovely life is being lived naturally and sweetly by His children.

If I were an Irish priest I would take Italy for my model. Instead, for example, of pleading for stricter licensing laws, I would plead for the importation of wine by the million-gallon, scatter licenses broadcast for ale-and-wine shops, allow them to open and close at their own sweet will, and I would say to my children: "Go to the wineshop! Take your girl, take your wife, take your daughter! Drink and be happy! Young man, embrace your girl, come to me and I will bless your love, and after that may God look down on you, do the best you can. God made woman, not the devil. Don't be shy of looking at those lovely pictures of women by Botticelli or Giorgione or Titian.[16] Look at them! Revel in the thought that you have a woman just as beautiful as the *Primavera*.[17] Bring me your child that I may offer it to the true God of beauty. What are you afraid of? If you have health, love and wine you will have the vigour and courage to break down and live down every obstacle to your happiness."

But while I said that, as a priest to my flock, I would also storm the gates of the government to make this Ireland a country fit for my children to live in and to love in.

Is this dual revolution likely to occur in Holy Ireland? If it does not, what is happening will go on happening. The more cautious will marry late in life. The more spirited will go on emigrating to get out from under the cloud. And the saddest fact of all is denied by nobody: that when they do emigrate they fall away from their religion in large numbers, so that both the nation and the church loses them. If some such revolution does not take place it can only mean that that impalpable thing we know as the Irish nature is shrivelling and hardening into selfishness, is growing less and less attractive in its smug blindness to the unhappiness of this generation and the threat to the generations of the future. In that sense the Irish whom the world has known, and admired, may indeed vanish from the earth; and I am still proud enough of my race to think that their disappearance would be the world's loss.

16 Italian painters Sandro Botticelli (1445–1510); Giorgione (c. 1477/8–1510), né Giorgio da Castelfranco; and Titian (c. 1488/90–1576), né Tiziano Vecellio.
17 *Primavera* (c. 1477–82), which translates as "Spring" or "Springtime," is a painting by Botticelli.

Fifty Years of Irish Writing[1]

When the editor of *Studies* kindly invited me to write an article on the fortunes of Irish literature over the past fifty years I presumed that the main interest of anything I might have to say would lie in the fact that I am an Irish writer who was born in 1900, which implies, I suppose, that, within the limitations of my personal oddities and idiosyncrasies, what I here say cannot fail to be, at any rate to some degree, representative of the views of the generation after Yeats. In other words I am, very happily, presenting myself and my views as a type-specimen. I feel obliged to say this at the outset, to give myself full freedom of expression by making it quite clear to my readers, especially to readers outside Ireland, that some of the things I have to say must be displeasing to my host. I might otherwise seem to be taking an unfair advantage of his hospitality.

I do not propose to say much about the earlier part of the last fifty years. What was written in that period, say 1910–1921, is well known and has been much discussed. It was the hey-day of the Abbey Theatre. The riots over *The Playboy* were over and the battle won – the play was now being produced without opposition, largely through the tough courage of Yeats and the gallant support of his players. Prose was flourishing – Moore, Stephens, Canon Sheehan, Somerville and Ross, lesser entertainers like George Birmingham, and, to move on a bit in years but still within the general "period," Eimar O'Duffy, Shan Bullock, Conal O'Riordan and others.[2] I am aware that to move on outside date-brackets is always tricky

1 "Fifty Years of Irish Writing" appeared in *Studies: An Irish Quarterly Review* 51, no. 201 (Spring 1962): 93–105. An earlier version of this article appeared as "Ireland After Yeats," *The Bell* 18, no. 11 (May 1953): 37–48.
2 George A. Birmingham (the *nom de plume* of Canon James Owen Hannay) (1865–1950) and Eimar O'Duffy (1893–1935).

in dealing with a literary period, but, in the first place, dates and "periods" rarely coincide in literary history. (For example, the eighteenth century period in English literature did not end with the year 1800.) And, the second, and for our purposes, more important point here is that the whole story of latter-day developments in Anglo-Irish letters is very much a story of pioneering and overlapping. (Joyce's *Dubliners*, for example, appeared in 1914 but he is alien to most of our literary traditions before him, though he was fully contemporaneous with Yeats as a young Dubliner.) Poetry, too, in the opening ten years of our chosen fifty was flourishing – Yeats, Clarke, Higgins, Campbell, Seamus O'Sullivan;[3] though here again I am over-leaping dates, to keep the sense of period. Clarke and Higgins both were born in 1896. Clarke did not publish his first book *The Vengeance* of *Fionn* until 1917.

The general mood of that period, before the establishment of the Irish Free State, was romantic, nationalist, fervid, critical of others, especially of one's political opponents, whether native or foreign, but not very critical of ourselves – apart from the sort of rather superficial satire one got from plays like William Boyle's *The Eloquent Dempsey* – and it was quite uncritical in matters literary, historical and what would nowadays be called sociological.[4] This absence of a deep-cutting critical objectivity was, I think, the great weakness of the so-called Irish Literary Movement. It made it, as some of us at the time kept on saying worriedly, without being able to do anything about it, a movement of feeling rather than of thought. As one looks back over the prose of the period one sometimes wonders whether our writers ever took off their green glasses. Exceptions will, no doubt, be offered, such as O'Duffy and O'Riordan, yet, on re-opening such novels as *The Wasted Island* or *Adam of Dublin* I, for one, still feel that nothing in them is at all as tough and clearsighted as, say, *The Real Charlotte* (Somerville and Ross) or *A Drama in Muslin*.[5] This last, and to most readers I feel sure, unexpected title, may make my point clear.

George Moore was a flippant Bohemian; the novel is not a good novel; it is melodramatic, often absurd, even penny-noveletteish; yet to what other novel of that time can one go for such a clear observation of the formative social factors behind, and responsible for, the grimness of Dublin life as depicted, but never explained – it was not his interest – by

3 Joseph Campbell (1879–1944).
4 *The Eloquent Dempsey* (1907), by William Boyle (1853–1923).
5 *The Wasted Island* (1919), by Eimar O'Duffy; *Adam of Dublin* (1920), by Conal O'Riordan; *The Real Charlotte* (1894); *A Drama in Muslin* (1886), by George Moore.

Joyce in the *Portrait* and *Ulysses*? Moore, trained by Zola and Flaubert, saw, displayed and eviscerated – an amazing feat for a man normally without an iota of responsibility in his composition – the real forces, social and economic, which had infected Ireland with the state of spiritual paralysis that so disgusted Joyce and produced in contemporary Irish writing so much verse that if not actually a form of compensatory escapism is dangerously close to it. To the Irish Literary Movement, taken by and large, the evil enemy was England, holding down and frustrating all that was lovely and worth while in the Holy Land of Ireland whose beauty the poets endlessly chanted. Moore, whose relations with Ireland were consistently those of *odi et amo* – with at times an almost psychopathic stress on the *odi* – saw that the real source of infection was the native middle-classes, and – religion apart – all their tawdry, snobbish, and provincial, social values.[6] Events were to support Moore's contention to the full.

This leads me to explain why, as I see things, the story of Irish writing since 1900 falls into two parts: growth and decline.

Though nobody could have observed it at the time, the causes for this decline began to operate immediately the Irish Free State was founded, in 1921. Their effects were, however, held at bay for a time by the continuing momentum of nationalist excitement persisting after the revolution was over. Sean O'Casey's plays illustrate this. His *Juno and the Paycock* was staged in 1924, and his *The Plough and the Stars* in 1926, both of them dealing with the revolutionary period which was finished and done with. It is true that there was a theatre-riot over the latter play, but nobody attached any special significance to it. If anything one took it for a good omen. It was like the old days of the *Playboy* riots. It promised a continuity of tradition. "*Plus ça change,*" we said. But we were wrong. It was not *la même chose.*[7] There was a fundamental difference between the circumstances surrounding O'Casey and those surrounding Synge. One might build on the two riots a parable of the reasons for the later decline in Irish writing.

In the old days – to keep, for the moment, to the example of the Theatre – an élite had been in the saddle. The whole of Yeats's outlook had been aristocratic though nationalist, just as he had always been both European

6 *Odi et amo* is Latin for "I hate and I love."

7 O'Faolain refers here to the French phrase *plus ça change, plus c'est la même chose*, whose English equivalent and near direct translation is "the more things change, the more they stay the same."

and Irish, as excited by the *Axël* of Villiers de L'Isle Adam as by the peasant folktales of Biddy Early. He had said several times that his sort of theatre should be as hard to get into as a secret society. He liked small audiences. The poetic drama he admired could never have become popular, and in so far as the Abbey Theatre did become a popular or people's theatre, he felt that he had failed to create what he set out to create. So, he had always struggled against the popular taste for so-called "realistic" drama. In spite of every inevitable concession to that taste he dominated his ambiguous creation as a poet with a poet's ideals. This all began to change immediately a native government was established. The type of people who had, long ago, protested against Synge's *Playboy* had had no political power. The people who objected to O'Casey had political power. (It is to be remembered that the new Irish Government decided to subsidise the Abbey Theatre; which, at the time, seemed to us all a splendid gesture – disillusion was to come slowly with the gradual realisation that when governments give money they receive influence in exchange.)[8]

Moreover, in those "old days" the Catholic Church had had only a limited amount of political power because the government had been an alien and non-Catholic government, and the foreign Gallio, like all proconsuls, had kept the ring with the tolerance of total indifference.[9] Now the Church could wield almost unlimited power because the native government was composed of men who respected, loved, and feared it. It is evident that the new intellectual atmosphere depended on the sophistication, cultivation, and tolerance of both the native Government and the Church, the new élite. Unfortunately, centuries of depression had bred in both not only a passionate desire for liberty – each with its own interpretation and its own aims – but the antithesis of that natural desire. It had induced a nervy, sensitive, touchy, defensive-aggressive, on-guard mentality as a result of which patriotism became infected by chauvinism and true religious feeling by what most Irish writers after 1921 tended to call "puritanism." I imagine that I am describing something which happens commonly in all countries which have emerged from a revolutionary phase, and that it does not involve any special criticism of Ireland or

---

8 It is interesting to read this parenthetical comment in light of the arguments in "Autoantiamericanism" and the criticisms that the essay provoked.

9 Junius Gallio (c. 5 BCE–65 CE), né Lucius Annaeus Novatus. The Spanish-born Gallio rose to become a highly placed Roman official; he famously dismissed charges brought against the apostle Paul in an attempt to keep Rome unaligned in the struggles between the Jews and the nascent Christian religion.

the Irish nature. (An intellectual Jew in contemporary Palestine, an intellectual Cypriot in Cyprus, would probably nod his head in understanding and sympathy if he were to read my summary.)

The simplest illustration of what happened was the establishment of a severe Literary Censorship, in 1929. Its aim was, and its aim no doubt still is, a blending of the moral and the patriotic: the desire to protect from corruption this infant nation born out of so much hardship. Within twenty years thousands of books were banned as indecent or obscene. It will be noted that the reason for banning was not political and it was social (and religious) only in so far as books and periodicals were and still are banned if they advocate, or advertise, contraception, abortion, or the artificial insemination of humans. Within recent years this early fervour for banning has been much abated, thanks to the nomination of intelligent censors, following prolonged protests by writers and the general public. Most of the books now banned are ephemeral and their absence from the public libraries and bookshops is no loss. This may be acknowledged and welcomed as a sign of a growing sophistication in contemporary Ireland.

But there have been two particularly bad results for Irish literature; within a few years there was scarcely an Irish writer of distinction who had not, at least once, been declared the author of obscenity, and he was – and still is – denied recourse to the courts of the land in self-defence. But the worst feature of the Censorship has been that with it there arose a private censorship all over the country in the form of a witch-hunt which no librarian or bookseller could dare to resist by stocking books objected to by these un-official censors. Demos was in the saddle.[10]

10 O'Faolain's note: I take, at random, from my files a typical list of Banned Books as published in February 1952. Eighty-nine books were banned. The greater number included cheap American importations of a popular nature, thrillers with sexy titles on the lines of Make Mine a Virgin. One Irish novelist was listed, Francis Stuart, for Good Friday's Daughter. The list also included: John Steinbeck's Tortilla Flat, Anita Loos's A Mouse Is Born, André Gide's Les Nourritures terrestres, Carson McCuller's Reflections in a Golden Eye. There has been, for some years, an Appeal Board which has unbanned a small proportion of books. They are usually out-of-print by the time they are unbanned. The Censorship Board is immune from legal action. In any case, writers have no money for prolonged action against the State. Today one still, but rarely now, finds a worth while book on the lists. [Editor's note: Make Mine a Virgin (1949), by Michael Storm (n.d.); Good Friday's Daughter (1952); Tortilla Flat (1935); A Mouse Is Born (1951), by Anita Loos (c. 1893–1981); Les Nourritures terrestres (1897); Reflections in a Golden Eye (1941), by Carson McCullers (1917–1967). Demos is Greek for "the common people."]

To form a just picture of this new intellectual atmosphere it is essential to grasp one other point. The revolution of 1916–21 had been a social revolution. This fact lifts the history of Irish writing over the past twenty-five years out of its apparently local setting and puts it in its proper place as part of a general world-tendency. The idealists who inspired the people to rise against British rule were – as I have said – unaware of the social forces they were working with and releasing. In the nineteenth century these forces had been personified by the impoverished farming community in the Land League's fight for decent conditions of land-tenure. In our day the social forces behind the last stage of the Irish Revolution were personified by the sons and daughters of those farmers – surplus children squeezed into the towns and cities, and finding there that all the power and most of the wealth was in the hands of people of a different religion, racial origin, or political loyalty. Sean O'Casey's plays are thus an exactly true statement of the Irish Revolution whose flag, he dearly felt, should be, not the tricolour, but the plough-and-the-stars flag of the urban labouring classes.

We must, finally, understand that the class that came to power and influence was not a labouring class; the more able among them were *petit bourgeois*, middle-men, importers, small manufacturers – the modern counterpart of Moore's nineteenth-century middle-classes – forming a new twentieth-century middle-class to fill the vacuum created by the departure or depression of the earlier alien middle-class. These men, naturally, had had very little education and could have only a slight interest in the intellectuals' fight for liberty of expression. They were ordinary, decent, kindly, self-seeking men who had no intention of jeopardising their newfound prosperity by gratuitous displays of moral courage. In any case, since they were rising to sudden wealth behind protective tariff-walls they had a vested interest in nationalism and even in isolationism. The upshot of it was an alliance between the Church, the new businessmen, and the politicians, all three nationalist-isolationist for, respectively, moral reasons, commercial reasons, and politico-patriotic reasons, in themselves all perfectly sound reasons. The effect on letters was not good. The intellectuals became a depressed group. Possibly they were also infected by the atmosphere around them.

For completeness let us try to look sympathetically on the other side of the picture. Ireland is not a publishing country. All but a number of books, so few that it would be an exaggeration to call them a handful, are published abroad, apart from all primary school texts and most secondary school texts. Practically all our mental food is therefore imported: good food but not native. If there is such a thing as a racial Irish quality of life it is very difficult for it to resist almost overwhelming external influences, since this local way-of-life is not equipped intellectually to support it. The intellectuals cried out for a bold, adventurous, and thoroughly modern system of popular education, but both the Church and the State feared the results. It is to be said that the Irish way-of-life, though poor, indeed impoverished as to institutions fit to represent it – e.g. publishing houses, periodicals, rich universities – is atavistically powerful, spiritually obstinate, strongly resistant, in a great many ways appealing; it represents precious and lovable qualities, and is eminently worth preservation, provided it expresses itself in achievement and not merely in emotional declaration. The intellectuals' position is that it cannot and will not preserve itself by negative methods, and that it is, in practice, now as in the past, being undermined and corrupted by a lack of moral and intellectual courage.

We can now look at Irish writing against this social, political, and religious background. First, the Theatre:

As we look back over the plays produced in the Abbey Theatre since the First World War we find that the Theatre was still lively almost up to 1932. (This suggests that the momentum of the revolutionary stimulus went on for some ten years.) The lists include first productions of plays by Lady Gregory, Brinsley MacNamara, Padraic Colum, Daniel Corkery, Shaw, Lord Dunsany, Lennox Robinson, George Shiels, Sean O'Casey, T.C. Murray, Yeats, Wilde, Rutherford Mayne, Teresa Deevy, Denis Johnston, and Paul Vincent Carroll.[11] Lady Gregory died in 1932. From then onward two or three plays of distinction were produced but no outstanding name is added to the list. In 1935 Yeats, who was ageing and ailing, felt that the theatre needed younger men. His friend, the poet Frederick Robert Higgins, was appointed Director; so was Frank O'Connor; and a significant name also appeared among the directors, an ex-Cabinet Minister, Mr. Ernest Blythe. Mr. Hugh Hunt, now producer at the Old Vic Theatre, London, was brought in as producer, and from 1935 to 1938, the combination of Higgins, O'Connor and Hunt gave the theatre a new and exciting spurt.[12] It is of interest that in those three years the Abbey produced several non-Irish plays – including plays by Shakespeare,

---

11 George Shiels (1886–1949); Rutherford Mayne (the *nom de plume* of Samuel John Waddell) (1878–1967); and Teresa Deevy (1894–1963).
12 Hugh Hunt (1911–1993). He returned as the artistic director of the Abbey Theatre from 1969 to 1971. The Old Vic Theatre was opened in 1818 and now forms a part of the National Theatre.

Flecker, Toller, Shaw, André Obey.[13] Yeats died in 1939. O'Connor, feeling unable to cope with influences of which he disapproved, resigned in 1939. Higgins died in 1941. Mr. Blythe became Managing Director. Thus, there remained on the Board, to represent old tradition, only Mr. Lennox Robinson. Otherwise the bridge with the past was down.

Unless we imagine that literature exists in a vacuum we must see what sort of official influences played on the Theatre at this period. I will give two examples. In 1932 when the Abbey Theatre visited the United States the usual hyper-patriotic societies there protested against some of the plays, including O'Casey's, and at home Deputies were prompted to ask awkward questions in the Dáil. In reply to one questioner on this issue, Mr. de Valera said (26 April 1933) that the Government had made indirect representations to the Abbey Theatre, and that it was hoped that if the Company visited America again plays of the kind objected to by the American-Irish would not be produced. In that year the official subsidy was reduced. In 1934 a similar angry question received a similar reply, de Valera then saying that such plays damage the good name of Ireland. Yeats stood his ground, and was attacked bitterly by the popular press.

The second significant incident occurred in 1938 when the Board of the Theatre decided that plays in the Irish language should henceforth become a regular feature of the work of the Theatre. This, I hold, was a retrograde step artistically, however laudable from the patriotic point of view, since there happened to be no Gaelic-writing playwrights worth mentioning and most of the trained actors could not speak Gaelic. The result showed itself in 1942 when the Government again intervened to ask the Theatre to take over the work of an existing company of Gaelic players called "An Comhar Drámuíochta" (The Drama Co-operative). After this, so far as I know, no junior players were employed unless they could speak Gaelic, an accomplishment which had as much to do with acting as if they could dance the *cancan*.[14] I record this incident solely to give the reader my impression of the lowering of intellectual standards after Yeats.

Let us now try to define the precise effect on the arts. Fundamentally what had happened was that a social concept of the function of literature was beginning to replace the "individualist" concept. Compare Yeats, taking him as representative of the first twenty-five years of the Anglo-Irish revival. Yeats had loved all art that was remote and uncommon, "distinguished and lonely." He had seen the element of nobility in the simplest

13 British author James Elroy Flecker (1884–1915).
14 The *cancan* is a risqué stage dance performed by women.

people but he had never permitted his affection for familiar life to be confused with a preoccupation with the common or the popular.[15] Thus, writing of the Theatre he had said:

> The modern author, if he be a man of genius, is a solitary, he does not know the everchanging public well enough to be its servant. He cannot learn their convention; they must learn his. All that is greatest in modern literature is soliloquy, or, at most, words addressed to a few friends.[16]

This dislike of "realism" had always been with him. He sought always to sublimate reality, and it was in that search for a dissolvent of the flesh that he had formed the distinction between Character, that is, the social, public, moral thing, formed by and for the purposes of organised society, and Personality, which is what appears in all the great moments of drama when this social, functional thing drops away and a man's spirit burns with the "pure gem-like flame." So, he had found inspiration in the ancient mind of his people, but it was not a political mind, or a social mind, but a mystical memory, linking man to those ages when life was still a unity, before he became fissured by rationalism and splintered by what we nowadays call psychological analysis.

One could easily demur at much of this. The Theatre, after all, is the most sociable of all the arts. And, as I have indicated in my opening remarks, there was already too much of this withdrawal-from-life in the first period of the Irish Literary Movement. At any rate our new, ambitious, hardfaced democracy understood none of this aristocratic concept. It understood only "realistic plays," political plays, representationalism, characterisation, explanations, social comedies and tragedies. It is to the credit of some Irish playwrights resident in Ireland that they took the risks of some sort of criticism and satire, and it is to the credit of the Abbey Theatre, even in its decline, that it staged some of these plays. But what we have had even of

15 O'Faolain's note: So brief a summary is inadequate even to suggest the complexity of Yeats's thought. I put the word *individualist* in inverted commas solely to indicate its inadequacy. See Yeats's attack on the popular idea of "individualism" in his own record of his famous meeting with The Young Joyce in: *The Identity of Yeats*, by Richard Ellmann, p. 86 foll. [*Editor's note: The Identity of Yeats* (1954), by the American scholar Richard Ellmann (1918–1987).]
16 From a letter in the *Providence Sunday Journal*, 10 February 1889. Yeats was discussing *The Banshee and other Poems* (1888) by John Todhunter (1839–1916).

this "some sort of criticism and satire" has been so feeble as to extinguish the value of the terms I have used ("realistic," "political," "representational," "social") to describe the sort of plays the new public wanted. Because the new audiences did not really want any of those things; they wanted those things in an *ersatz* form: plays that merely gave the illusion of being political, realistic, social, critical, and so on. They were ready to laugh at plays dealing with the surface of things. They were not ready for plays that opposed what might be called, for short, the new synthetic orthodoxy, or at any rate diverged radically from it, let alone that denied it or rejected it. No social-realistic drama – whether comic or tragic – can thrive in this atmosphere. Mr. Brendan Behan, for instance, whether good, bad or indifferent, could not have broken through in Dublin.[17] He first had to break through in London or New York.[18]

But there are even greater and deeper dangers in the writers' battle for honesty. The danger of becoming embittered, or twisted, threatens creativity itself, and here we come to the real battle-ground of contemporary Irish writing. For the first time Irish writers have had to *think* themselves into personal release. Disillusion is also a form of revelation. There is no longer any question of dishing up local colour. (The Noble Peasant is as dead as the Noble Savage. Poems about fairies and leprechauns, about misted lakes, old symbols of national longing, are over and done with.) We need to explore Irish life with an objectivity never hitherto applied to it – and in this Joyce rather than Yeats is our inspiration. But to see clearly is not to write passionately. An artist must, in some fashion, love his material, and his material must, in some fashion, co-operate with him. It is not enough for an artist to be clinically interested in life: he must take fire from it. This has been the great rub in Ireland for some thirty years. It is not confined to Ireland. Everywhere to-day, as I see it, literature is facing the same problem: How to transmute into permanent forms a life that one sees critically rather than lovingly.

If this really is an universal problem, why is it so? I think it is so because writers everywhere feel that life no longer has any sense of Pattern and Destination. The argosies set out.[19] They forget why. To give the most naïve example possible of Pattern and Destination: time was when novelists

17 Irish author Brendan Behan (1923–1964).
18 The success of *The Hostage* (1958) in both London and New York turned Behan into a celebrity, although his earlier play *The Quare Fellow* (1954) was a hit when it opened at Dublin's Pike Theatre.
19 Argosies are large merchant vessels.

moved their men and women, with a sense of completion, towards a home and a family, in love and marriage. Countless is the number of novels and plays shaped about the thwarting of this journey. All the hypocrisy of the Victorian novel, its sentimental, evangelical piety, its evasiveness exposed itself in this "Destination" which everybody knows to-day is only a starting point, another challenge, another problem. No writer dares to play this old tune to-day. The result is that men of genius have been writing as the matador kills bulls, by virtuosity or by savagery – Joyce, Hemingway, Anouilh, Aymé, Bazin, Julien Green, Mailer, all the writers of the *roman nouveau*; or they impose Pattern and Destination by sheer force – Lagerkvist by his symbolism, Malraux by his mysticism, Sartre by his Existentialism, Bernanos, Greene, or Mauriac by their Catholicism, the later O'Casey by his Communism.[20] One may be lost in admiration of this forcible handling of intractable material, though one does sometimes wonder whether humanity has not emerged from their work literally man-handled, moulded to shape, intellectualised, not men but puppets. The regionalists are in the happier position. Faulkner may still find Pattern and Destination about him, or imagine he can find it.

An Irish writer might expect to find old patterns persisting in his region also. But the dilemma has here taken a particularly sardonic form. My countrymen are so satisfied with their sentimental Pattern that they have no interest in Destination. Everything having been solved they have no further to go – except to Heaven. They are frustrated by the illusory completeness of their own conventions. The novel elsewhere may be frustrated by the certainties of men lost; here it is frustrated by the certainties of men saved. We read with an excited absorption the work of Catholic novelists elsewhere – that is, novelists who work within the frame of the struggle between God and the Devil, rather than the struggle of man with material evil or impersonal misfortune – and we observe that they deal with characters who are wilful, rebellious, passionate, arrogant, conscious, persistent, reckless – men who put theology to the test of experience, either to uphold it or not as their experiences prompt. We turn,

---

20 French authors Jean Anouilh (1910–1987) and Hervé Bazin (1911–1996); American authors Julien Green (1900–1998) and Norman Mailer (1923–2007). The *nouveau roman*, meaning "new novel" in French and also referred to as the "anti-novel," took shape in France in the 1950s; it is marked by an avant-gardist rejection or marginalising of such traditional generic conventions as plot, linear narrative, and dialogue. Swedish author and Nobel laureate Pär Lagerkvist (1891–1974); French writer Georges Bernanos (1888–1948).

hopefully, to the potential material of Irish novels on the lines of Bernanos or Mauriac. We discover to our dismay that no error has been so great as the popular conception of the Irishman as rebellious, passionate, reckless, wilful, and so on. We are, in effect, very much in the same position as Hawthorne who just managed to squeeze one novel – and it is not really as fine a novel as the professors say; he lacked courage to push his concept of life to its end – out of equally unmalleable material, in a society where, also, sin was furtive, convention rigid, courage slight and honesty scant.

One of the most striking effects of all this on Irish letters in the period before us is the comparative failure of the modern Irish Novel. If one were to exclude Joyce – which is like saying if one were to exclude Everest – and Liam O'Flaherty how little is left! We have, of course, plenty of honourable efforts (perhaps, I might suggest, like my own efforts) but of anything like top-notchers (Joyce's *Portrait* aside) how many others would the really serious critic want to put beside, say, Elizabeth Bowen's Irish novel *The Last September* or whichever one, two or three of O'Flaherty's he would choose for this test? My explanation for this I have already given – that Irish life in our period does not supply the *dramatis personae*, ready for the hard conflicts, the readiness to take anything *jusqu'au bout* in either full or at least some awareness of what is at stake, without which dramatic themes for the novel are missing.[21] We produce spurts of spirit. They end in laughter (the great national vice and virtue) or exile.

This may be why, on the other hand, the Short Story has thriven in the meantime, and this is probably the best product of our period. The successes here have been so numerous that I need not even mention names. They have been wise to choose the smaller, yet revealing themes in the absence of the larger, more dramatic ones.

The Irish novelist who has been most persistent in mining for revolt and passion has been Liam O'Flaherty. He has found his passionate creatures in the west of Ireland and in the Revolution. His best-known novels *The Informer* (1925), *The Assassin* (1928), *The Martyr* (1933) are in the middle of our period. Each deals with the revolutionary upheaval, which was a godsend to all Irish writers until, as in the Theatre, the vein became exhausted around 1932, ten years after the Revolution ended. In that year O'Flaherty wrote *The Puritan*, a study of the new Irish rigorism, and thereafter he chose, with one exception, which was a failure, historical

---

21 *Dramatis personae* translates from the Latin as "persons of a drama" and is used to refer to the characters of a play. *Jusqu'au bout* translates from the French as "to the end."

subjects. It is most revealing that all of O'Flaherty's work is shot through by a wild romanticism – to put it crudely, the romanticism of the Noble Savage. He had to write in this way to gear himself and his characters to action. Since he is so much a Romantic one should not expect intellectual as well as emotional rewards from his work. I regret their absence – as I do in Hemingway: it is an equally pointless regret.

I think my reader will begin to realise the difficulties of writing in a country where the policeman and the priest are in a perpetual glow of satisfaction. He must, however, also see that, to a real extent, Irish novelists have failed to solve a problem. I will illustrate this problem by quoting the comment of an intelligent American critic on his first visit to Ireland. He said: "This seems to be a very prosperous, comfortable, well-to-do country. We do not get that picture from your writers. Why not?" His comment was not wholly fair. He ignored Emigration, to make but one point, and other things that do not immediately strike the eye. Still, I have failed to present an intelligible picture of contemporary Irish society – acquisitive, bourgeois, unsophisticated, intellectually conservative and unadventurous, rigidly controlled on every side – if the answer to that "Why not?" is not apparent. I will underline it only by pointing out that the change-over from a stratified society – ranging from aristocrat to outcast – to a one-class society, where there are not native aristocrats and no outcasts (except the writers?), and where the hard, traditional core is in a farming population, rarely induces a fertile awareness either among people or writers. And awareness in literature is an essential. Even before the Revolution Irish writers – Joyce, Shaw, Wilde, dozens besides – felt this, in so far as our awareness was then (as they saw it) all going down the drain of politics and nationalism. They left Ireland for the more interesting life of the island next door. Unawareness itself is, it may be added, not a theme for any writer: it is a negative; it eliminates the element of self-conflict, which alone gives meaning to any theme.

One other obstacle, and of all perhaps the most difficult to surmount, has come between the Irish writer, whether poet, dramatist, or novelist, and his normal material in Irish life. It may be expressed in the words of the poet, Robert Greacen, in a poem significantly entitled "Written on the Sense of Isolation in Contemporary Ireland."[22] Having called up the

22 "Written on the Sense of Isolation in Contemporary Ireland" (1944), by Robert Greacen (1920–2008).

"unfettered great in heart and mind who gave no inch to fate" – Swift, Burke, Sheridan, Congreve, Goldsmith, Moore and Yeats – he says:[23]

Yet all of these the world for subject took
And wed the fearless thesis to their book.

We are, it would seem, only just beginning to learn how to be, as Yeats was, European though nationalist. Hitherto, Irish writers, still tuning-in, as writers always do, to the intellectual stations of the world did so almost like men in an occupied country listening to forbidden voices. The writer who had the feel of the world rose, hitherto, from his grapevine, excited by the sense of the world, then turned to his page to write as he felt ... But with what? With whom? What characters would think and speak for him, in his poem, play, or novel? As I have said, the *dramatis personae* were otherwise engaged. Perhaps this is now changing?

I feel profoundly that Greacen's point has much to say about the last thirty years of Irish poetry. There is no loss of technical skill – if anything a far greater verbal sophistication has arrived in Irish poetry over the last thirty years than existed previously. There is no decline in receptiveness. The later work of Austin Clarke, Patrick Kavanagh, Padraic Fallon, Valentin Iremonger, Thomas Kinsella, Robert Farren, to name only a few, show poetry just as much on tiptoe, ready for flight, as it ever was.[24] All that is lacking is not significant subject, but width of personal vision – and one rarely hears a modern idiom, a modern speech. The voltage of poetry (of any art) must do more than illuminate the local, or bring the barque of the mind happily home. Poetry is a lighthouse calling us to far seas. Clarke, for all his intense nationalism and smoored piety, often speaks with a far-echoing voice, as understandable to any part of the world as to us. I have always felt that Denis Devlin was a great loss to us: he wrote with a full response to the fulness of life everywhere.[25] So, frequently, does Iremonger.

This need for a larger vision shows itself most poignantly in modern Irish poetry in the Irish language. Within my knowledge I am aware of only three Gaelic poets who are not utterly lost in the Gaelic Mist, trying

23 Irish politician and political thinker Edmund Burke (1729–1797) and Irish playwright and politician Richard Brinsley Sheridan (1751–1816).
24 Padraic Fallon (1905–1974); Valentin Iremonger (1918–1991); Thomas Kinsella (b. 1928); Robert Farren is also known as Roibeárd Ó Faracháin (1909–1984).
25 Denis Devlin (1908–1959).

to extract ore from long-exhausted mines, symbols worn threadbare by the first phase of the Irish Literary Movement. Those three are Máire Mhac an tSaoi (now Mrs. Conor Cruise O'Brien), Tomás Tóibín, but above all the Seán O'Riordáin of *Eireaball Spideóige*, a delightfully fresh-minded poet irrespective of place or language.[26] Here, again, it is not the subject or theme (as with the novelist) which is important; it is the freedom and scope of the imagination, dealing with any subject. For where the novelist is contained by character the poet is not – he is his own character, his own subject. This O'Riordáin has instinctively grasped and is thereby liberated at once from the old trap of writing *about* Ireland.

The lesson of our time is that Irish writers cannot any longer go on writing about Ireland, or for Ireland within the narrow confines of the traditional Irish life-concept; it is too slack, too cosy, too evasive, too untense. They must, or perish as regionalists, take, as writers everywhere do, the local (since they know its detail most intimately) and universalise it, as Joyce did – as Kavanagh can do it even when he is writing about a potato-field or O'Riordáin about a hospital-nurse. It is a matter of bravely and clearsightedly accepting the tensions of one's own being, or relentlessly challenging the life about one with their sharpest questions, of looking, then, far and wide, in time and place, for others who have been in some like conflict – a Stendhal, Balzac, Hawthorne, Forster, Joyce, Trollope, Yeats, Frost, Hardy, Lampedusa, Lorca, Cavafy, Zhivago, whoever it may be anywhere at any time who, one feels, might ironically sympathise – saying to them, "That was how it seemed to you! Here is how it strikes me," and seize one's pen, *for them* and one's self.[27]

Men of genius accelerate the processes of time for their country, *if* (which is a challenging, and often the most dismaying conjecture) they can cope with their country. The problem is up to the writers themselves. Nobody outside can help them; nobody inside will help them. They will not evade it by exile – Ibsen did not, and did not wish to. (He had other reasons for his exile.) Nobody need pity them either, since by the grace of God and the savagery of Oliver Cromwell their language is now the English language and if they have anything worth saying that they can say well, the periodicals

26 Máire Mhac an tSaoi (b. 1922) was married to Conor Cruise O'Brien (1917–2008); Tomás Tóibín (b. 1920); Seán Ó Ríordáin (1916–1977) was the author of *Eireaball Spideoige* (1952).
27 Robert Frost (1874–1963); Guiseppe Tomasi di Lampedusa (1896–1957); Federico García Lorca (1898–1936); Constantine P. Cavafy (1863–1933); and *Doctor Zhivago* (1957), by Boris Pasternak (1890–1960).

and publishers of Britain and America are waiting for them with open arms and purses.[28] If they feel that exile is absolutely necessary, they may, alone among the writers of the small countries of the world, emigrate freely. What they have to cope with either way is complex enough. But was there ever a writer whose life and work was plain sailing? Their main worry must be that their worst enemies are impalpable and insinuating: self-pity, bitterness, sentimentality, cynicism, their own unsophistication, barren rage, even their love of country, their love of friends. (It was Ibsen who said that he had to leave Norway because friendship was too expensive: meaning that, for friendship's sake, one refrained from saying things that should be said.) It is improper for any critic to probe into these struggles. They are delicate, intimate, and fearful.

28 Oliver Cromwell (1599–1658) was the leader of the parliamentary forces during the English Civil War, lord protector of the republican Commonwealth from 1653 to 1658, and ruthless coloniser of the Irish.

A Portrait of the Artist as an Old Man[1]

You ask for a self-portrait? Very well. In that case I must ask you to imagine me at this moment standing in front of a painter's easel, my right hand poised to make the first charcoal outline on the bare canvas. And you must also imagine that I am looking into a mirror placed a little to my left, because what I am about to execute is *A Portrait of the Artist as an Old Man*. I need hardly say that when I present myself to you as a portrait painter, I am using a metaphor. I am really a portrait writer, a very different person indeed, if only in so far as a painter of self-portraits is always the same age as his sitter, whereas a portrait writer is always older, always remembering, always looking back. And since I am now seventy-six, I can look back quite a long way.

Now if my self-portrait does not appear before you at once, with the speed of what used to be called in my boyhood "a lightning artist", the reason is that what I see in my mirror is not at all to my liking. I see there an old boy with two very blue eyes that at worst look terrified, at best troubled; at worst cynical, at best quizzical; at worst mocking, at best ironical. "Can *you*", I ask myself in my mirror, "possibly be in the right frame of mind to make what used to be called in your childhood "a good confession"? Could you, in fact, ever be in the right frame of mind to recall without equivocation any part of your seventy-odd years?" Since, as some of you may know, I actually published a whole volume of autobiography several years ago, you may think it rather late in the day for me to be asking myself such questions now; but when I was writing that volume I did frequently ask myself whether it is ever possible for a man of letters

1 "A Portrait of the Artist as an Old Man" appeared in *Irish University Review* 6, no. 1 (Spring 1976): 10–18.

to write a completely unequivocal autobiography, and the answer that came to my lips was always, No!

This is not because writers are an untruthful profession but because every artist, of his nature, always wants to discover some sort of personal pattern in the apparently formless chaos of his life. Unfortunately there is no such consistent pattern in any man's life. Man is not a roll of wall-paper. He is not homogeneous. He is a multitude of particles, full of those contradictions, inconsistencies and incompatibilities that are our efforts to adapt to change, to chance, to fate, to unforeseen experiences, to new discoveries and to our own manifold mistakes. Some of the most famous autobiographies in literature prove it. *The Confessions of Saint Augustine* are largely fiction. Rousseau's *Confessions* are riddled with proven lies.[2] Yeats's autobiographies are about as useful to his biographer as the words of a dreamer trying to recall a dream. Stendhal, who is of all the novelists in the world the one I most adore, has been justifiably called a rhapsodic liar but on at least one occasion he told the truth about himself. He did it in a note that he scribbled on the margin of one of his travel books about Naples. It reads, "I was in Naples at the same time as M. de Stendhal and he is a great liar." One may be equally sceptical about Tolstoy, Benjamin Constant, De Quincey, Benvenuto Cellini, Goethe, Baudelaire, George Moore, Sean O'Casey, Paustovsky or Charlie Chaplin.[3] And what is one's personal memory anyway but a scattered jigsaw, most of whose more revealing bits we have deliberately mislaid? Certainly, from what is left of my jigsaw, all I can make out is an intermittent struggle to free myself from the effects of Chance or Fate.

Let me begin with the primal interference in my life by Fate, Chance, the gods, God, the Life Force, the Evolutionary Process, or whatever you like to call it. I was born in 1900 in a place that did not exist. That is to say I was born in Ireland, which then was, politically, culturally and psycho-logically just not there. All that was there was a bastard piece of the British Empire, and I in it as much a subject of the Crown as any contemporary in Jamaica or the Barbadoes, India or Africa, Trinidad or Malta, or, to mention a closer analogy, the Channel Islands or Wales. I had, in short, no consciousness of my country as a separate cultural entity inside the

2 Jean-Jacques Rousseau, *Les Confessions de J.J. Rousseau* (1782).

3 Benjamin Constant (1767–1830); Thomas De Quincey (1785–1859); Benvenuto Cellini (1500–1571); and Konstantin Georgiyevich Paustovsky (1892–1968). All of the people that O'Faolain lists here wrote major autobiographical works, including O'Faolain with his *Vive Moi!* (1963).

Empire. Not that this bothered me in the least. On the contrary, I was tremendously proud of belonging to the Empire, as were at that time most Irishmen. I gloried in all its trappings, Kings, Queens, dukes, duchesses, generals, admirals, soldiers, sailors, colonists, and conquerors, the lot.

And then, in the April of 1916, the date of the last Irish rebellion, I suffered the greatest trauma of my entire life. I had the upsetting experience of being suddenly presented with a country whose birth was supposed to wipe out all those social values that I had so contentedly lived by for my first sixteen years: G.A. Henty, Gordon of Khartoum, the Relief of Lucknow, the Charge of the Light Brigade, Irish-born Wellington, the Munster Fusiliers, the glory of the flag, the belly stirring rumble of the preliminary drum roll of *God Save the King*, Lord Kitchener, the Angels at Mons, but above all the dream of every well-bred imperial boy of one day becoming A Gentleman.[4] It was like being given a blank cheque for a completely new way of life, a new culture that would instantaneously replace everything British down to the last bit of fish-and-chips in the frying pan, the last damp bit of toad-in-the-hole in the larder, my last Wild Woodbine cigarette behind my ear, and what was I going to do without Lottie Collins, George Robey, Little Titch and Harry Lauder, and the smutty pictures in *London Life*, and the *Gem*, the *Magnet*, *Chums*, and the *Boys Own Paper*, and Sexton Blake, Tinker and Pedro, in fact the whole treasure chest of English literature from Goldsmith to Shaw, from Joseph Conrad to Israel Zangwill, from W.W. Jacobs to H.G. Wells?[5]

4 English writer and celebrator of empire G.A. Henty (1832–1902). British general Charles George Gordon (1833–1885) and his troops were slaughtered in Khartoum, Sudan, by Muslim forces after a ten-month siege. The siege of Lucknow, India, began with the Indian Mutiny in 1857 and was relieved after several months by British troops. "The Charge of the Light Brigade" (1855), a poem by Alfred, Lord Tennyson, celebrates the courageous and ill-fated charge of British soldiers during the Battle of Balaklava (1854). Horatio Herbert Kitchener (1850–1916), 1st Earl of Kitchener, vanquished Gordon's rivals in the Battle of Omdurman (1898), was commander of British forces in the Boer War from 1899–1902, and was secretary of state for war during World War I. It is legend that angels interceded on the side of British forces to help them to retreat despite being heavily outnumbered by German soldiers during the Battle of Mons (1914), in Belgium, the first major conflict between the two countries in World War I.

5 English actress, singer, and dancer Lottie Collins (1865–1910). Music hall comedians George Robey (1869–1954), né George Edward Wade, Little Titch (1867–1928), né Harry Relph, and Harry Lauder (1870–1950). Fictional comic strip detective Sexton Blake, his assistant Tinker, and his bloodhound dog Pedro. English authors Israel Zangwill (1864–1926) and W.W. Jacobs (1863–1943).

That hit me hard, I may tell you, in 1916 because it was thereabouts that I had begun to discover Thomas Hardy, and *Lavengro*, and English nature poetry, and R.L.S., and Conrad, and a novel that I then thought the loveliest thing ever written, Theodore Watts Dunton's *Aylwyn*, which had the same effect on me as when, a quarter of a century later, I came on the work of Isak Dinesen and Alain Fournier and fifty years later the magical novels of Theodor Fontane.[6]

Oh, well ... All that is a familiar problem to-day when, ever since the forties, hosts of youngsters have been wondering what to believe in, what to live by now that the old ways of life have been discredited. It is, I take it, a problem of personal identity and it must be as old as the history of imperialism. I am sure that if we had the lost chronicles of Cassiodorus recording the daily life of Rome after the Goths came in, we would find it there among the empire's disinterested hippies.[7] The Greeks, as we might expect, had a word for it. They called it *anomos*. Meaning, life without a code. That was my problem after 1916: "What gods do I live by now?" Everything I have thought and written since then has probably had that modest question at the root of it.

At this point I observe that the face in my mirror is looking at me very sardonically. It knows what is coming next. "After the accident of Fatherland," my face smiles, "was there not the accident of Faith? Surely, your inherited religion," one of those blue eyes winks at me, "must have supplied you with a complete and most detailed set of rules, codes and values to guide you through the labyrinthine ways?" The answer to this is that it depends on what Faith one is accidentally born into – Buddhist, Mississippi Baptist, Belfast Presbyterian, Oxford Anglican, Irish Catholic? I was reared a pious, a very pious Irish Catholic boy and of this quaint religion I have two things to say. The first is to inform the people who sell detergents that there is one dye, one pigment, one stain, scar or mark that no soap in the world can wholly eradicate, and this is the experience of being filled from the age of four onward with – in the words of John Henry Newman – a profound mistrust of the reality of material phenomena; an early fear that all life may be a dream and all this physical world a

6 R.L.S. refers to Robert Louis Stevenson; *Aylwyn* (1898), by Theodore Watts-Dunton (1832–1914); Danish author Isak Dinesen (1885–1962), née Karen Christence Dinesen, Baroness Blixen-Finecke; French writer Alain-Fournier (1886–1914), né Henri-Alban Fournier; and German writer Theodor Fontane (1819–1898).

7 Cassiodorus (490–c. 585), né Flavius Magnus Aurelius Cassiodorus, was a historian who helped preserve the culture of Rome against invading barbarians by collecting manuscripts and having monks copy the writings of many ancient authors.

deception. The second thing is that while this mesmeric power is by no means the monopoly of any one religion, I do not think that any western church revels so perfervidly as the Irish Catholic church does, or at any rate did when I was a boy, in the liquefaction of common life, the vaporisation of the mortal into the mystical, the veiling of the natural in the fumes of the supernatural, always at the expense of failing to develop the character of men as social animals. So, then, far from providing me with codes, values or rules for living in this pragmatical pig of a world, as Yeats calls it, all that, so far as I could see, the Faith into which I was born offered me was a useful set of formalities, rather like a passport stamped with a lot of visas, guaranteed to get me as quickly as possible through this unpleasant world to my happy destination in the next. Since I was fated to become a writer concerned with the character and behaviour of men and women, I could not but feel that this kind of mystical contempt for common actuality was something that would have to be put severely in its place if I ever hoped to write one truthful word about the human condition. Of course as a child I did not think like this but I did begin to feel this way as soon as I began to write, which was from about the age of seventeen on. I was in fact exactly forty-six years old before I finally abandoned the faith of my fathers, and, under the life-loving example of Italy, became converted to Roman Catholicism. It took me another ten years to see how sadly even those Roman institutions had deteriorated over the centuries, constantly forcing millions of men and women all over the world to put the old wine into new bottles. Since then, without losing touch completely with the old Roman vineyard, I too have had to do my own bottling.

As well as these Grecian gifts of Faith and Fatherland, I got a third birthday gift from the fates: my Family; unless this was not so much a gift from the gods as a human mistake on my part. I mean, every artist should, at birth, have the wit to choose a wealthy and generous father who will in due course subsidise him in his chosen profession. When I came to the age of reason, I discovered that I had chosen as my father a policeman, an Irish cop, rank of constable, a member of the old Royal Irish Constabulary, as fine, decent, honest and kindly a man as ever trod the peaceful pavements of Cork city; as a father, a man with only one flaw – his salary was only 30 bob a week, worth, as I discovered recently on examining his discharge papers, a pension of exactly £40 10 shillings and 8 pence a year. Nevertheless he had such a respect both for education and for social position that with this tiny salary, and the help of my mother who took in lodgers, he managed to make his eldest son a priest, his second son a higher civil servant (British of course), and pushed me through University

College Cork, an odd but very pleasant institution where I passed the four happiest years of my life; read voraciously, and learned nothing, not even the facts of life. All of which explains why, in later years when I did become a freelance writer, I had to spend half my working life beating the pavement between one lamp-post and another like a tart, trying to earn enough money to support my beautiful goldenhaired mistress, my beloved duck and darling, my exigent Muse. In other words, out of my forty years devoted exclusively to writing, I had, having inherited no private income, to spend some twenty years between life and letters, that is to say hack journalism, in order to earn twenty years to spend in the service of pure literature. You may say that twenty years is a lot of time for literature. And so it is if you are a genius. My admired Stendhal, for example, was able to write his supreme masterpiece, *The Charterhouse of Parma*, in an astounding outburst of energy lasting some six weeks. People of talent, like myself, cannot perform miracles like that. It is only the happy few who strike the rock like Moses.

So far, then, Fatherland, Faith and Family, and with them my last gift, come from God knows where, a talent for writing imaginative prose for which I deserve no credit whatsoever apart from the fact that I worked hard to perfect it and that I had the courage to let it have its head from the start, and I doubt if I had any alternative even in that, for what else can any artist do but say whatever is in him to say. For, as I see it, all art is no more than a mode of speech whereby the imaginative man dramatises life according to his own personal way of seeing it.

So when anybody asks me now when, how and why I began writing, I answer that I began writing (as distinct from scribbling) as soon as I had been given enough mortal shocks to shatter those three refracting lenses, Family, Fatherland and Faith, that up to that moment of time prevented me from seeing with my own eyes at least some little bit of the nature of life as it is really lived. Those three lenses had to be shattered because they amounted to other people's clotted thought-filters, composed of received opinions, social conventions, political ideas, inherited prejudices. Those ways of seeing or thinking were in many cases admirably suited to those who held them. But they were not my discoveries. And youth always wants to discover for itself. And every artist must. For years I obediently held those inherited views. Then very slowly, painfully, even unwillingly, and not at all heroically, I inched myself out of them. I reckon that it took me about forty years to get free.

As for the various shocks that began my de-illusion, I think one of the reasons why I keep on thinking of Stendhal while composing this outline of a self-portrait is that they were not at all unlike the shocks that liberated him. He however, being French, or Franco-Italian, and a great genius, began much earlier; my shocks did not begin until I was about eighteen. He was unable to contain his joy at the age of seven when he heard that Louis xvi had been guillotined;[8] he was an enthusiastic revolutionary at the age of nine; he fell on his knees with gratitude at the age of eleven when the Terror visited his native town of Grenoble and, to his immense delight, put his father on the list of Royalist suspects; after which he adored the risen people, despised the fallen aristocracy, and gave his total admiration to one man alone, Napoleon. What a deep fellow feeling he inspires in me when he records that he duly found the risen people a most scruffy lot, damp, dingy and dirty, horribly vulgar and endowed with such disgusting habits that he was to write, "I detest all oppressors, I love my people, but it would be torture for me to have to live with them for one day." I feel even more deeply for him when he comes to think of Napoleon as a tyrant depriving France of its liberty. I entirely understand what he means when he, who was a dragoon and took part in the retreat from Moscow, describes the Emperor's soldiers and generals as heroes on the field of battle, as a mob of grovelling Jesuits when off it. Saddest of all, he was to find that his most agreeable companions came from the upper classes.

The French Revolution and the Irish Troubles bear little comparison with one another in point of bloodshed, military glory, foreign conquest, ecclesiastical reform, the curtailment of the aristocracy, and financial bankruptcy. However, in such matters size is purely a matter of digestion, and I am sure that between 1800 and the fall of Napoleon no dragoon in the Grande Armée consumed more emotion than I did as a private in the Irish Republican Army between 1918 and 1924. It was one of the most ecstatic periods of my life, during which all moral problems vanished in the fire of patriotism, and death and destruction, bloodshed and brutality became dear alike to God, Ireland and the British cabinet. During those heavenly years I dreamed of liberty, equality, fraternity. I adored without reservation the risen people. Every month I discovered a new Napoleon in yet another political or military leader. At the age of twenty-four I was awakened from my feelings of rapture by that famous "pistol shot during a concert" which is my adored Stendhal's definition of practical politics intruding on political theory.

8 Louis xvi (1754–1793) was the last king of France; he was executed by guillotine, as was his queen consort Marie-Antoinette (1755–1793).

I really have been one of the most fortunate of men, for hereabouts, when I had suffered the mild penance for my youthful Republican idealism, of having to teach school for a year in the wilds of County Clare, an actual real living Republic, the United States of America, flung its arms, and its purse wide open to me. I got a fellowship which enabled me to spend three years in Harvard University. I have been accused of legerdemain in pulling off this miracle and certainly it does savour of prestidigitation that a private of the IRA should shake the hand of Edward VIII in Saint James's Palace, London – he was patron of the Fellowship – before taking off for the only English-speaking republic in the world. I got this chance only because I was recommended by Lennox Robinson, a most kind man to all young people, and by George W. Russell, the poet and good friend of Yeats, better known by his pseudonym Æ, given to me purely on the strength of a few things I had been writing to fend off despair and suicide while in the service of those kindly and innocent men who somewhat invidiously call themselves the *Christian* brothers.[9]

America and Harvard between them did a great deal to fill some of the larger gaps left in my education by Ireland, University College Cork, and my first ingenuous adventures in war and politics. Harvard did it within sixty seconds when my professor of philology gently intimated (or perhaps the better word is conveyed) that it is impolite for anybody to make a statement which he cannot prove. In Ireland I had been under the impression that it is boring to make any statement that one can prove. As for America, I had not been there a week before it became plain that a country may be a powerful and prosperous republic while being inhabited by millions of citizens who either are or have every intention of becoming exploiting capitalists. In Ireland I had thought in my innocence that a republic meant equality as well as liberty and fraternity. Thereafter I knew that a republic always means not a state of government but a state of mind, and that it is for that reason as indefinable as such forces as love or truth. America did one other thing for me or to me. It made me dream agonisingly of all that I had crossed 3000 miles of water to escape – Fatherland, Family and Faith. Against the assault of that trident I had no defence except to write, and write, and write like a man drilling for oil, or panning for gold, or a physicist searching for an equation to explain some hitherto inexplicable natural phenomenon. After all, the only weapon that the fates had given me are those twenty-six letters on the keyboard

9 The Christian Brothers was first founded in France in 1684. A separate Irish group was founded in 1802 to serve the educational needs of poor Catholic boys.

of my typewriter, so many black dots on a white page that merge into shapes, acts, conflicts, and characters, as my imagination creates a small world of my own as if I were a god creating life.

Looking back at the books that I have written, I perceive that, certainly at the beginning, I was not very intelligent about my job for the simple reason that I clung too long to too many loyalties. And as I have since said, over and over again, all any artist should ask of his country is his freedom, and all he should promise it in return is his disloyalty. If he achieves both, he will serve his country well.

I returned finally to Ireland in 1933 with my wife, whom I had married in Boston, having fathered our first child, and published my first book of stories, called *Midsummer Night Madness*.[10] With it I broke through to the world of literature. It is still, forty years after, on the list of books that my country's government proclaims as "indecent and obscene" to whatever part of the world knows of me as a reputable writer.[11] Why on earth did I return to live in a country that at that time was doing this sort of thing to practically every one of its writers, as well as to thousands of other writers from all over the world? Was my return an act of folly, or of faith? When I was leaving Harvard I had been invited to go to Peking to teach there.[12] I have never understood why I did not go there rather than to a country run by a cowardly, priest-bullied, ignorant, bigoted mob of bourgeois, gom-been-men and – What was this that Stendhal called *his* risen people? Ah, yes! – "grovelling Jesuits." I shall never know whether what I did was wrong or right. One would have to live twice over to know the answer to such might-have-beens. After all, if I had stayed in America, what awful things might have happened to me? I might have become a professional Irishman. I think of what they used to do to Willy Yeats when he used to lecture there: he was never allowed to leave a platform without once again going through the agony of reciting "The Lake Isle of Innisfree."[13] It is like

10 *Midsummer Night Madness and Other Stories* was published by Jonathan Cape in 1932.

11 *Midsummer Night Madness* was no longer banned at the time that O'Faolain wrote this essay. Its prohibition order was revoked almost a decade earlier under the terms of the Censorship of Publications Act of 1967 that set a twelve-year limit on all bannings; therefore, all works that had been censored prior to 1955 were immediately free to circulate.

12 Peking was the more common way to refer to Beijing, China's capital city, at the time O'Faolain was writing.

13 Yeats's "The Lake Isle of Innisfree" (1890).

the way they always make Marlene Dietrich sing "Falling in Love Again ... " At her age![14]

Well, that is all forty years ago and my face in the mirror says to me: "And here you still are, in your green Elba, still just as stupidly romantic as when you were sixteen, still wondering why men betray their better selves, still refusing to learn the facts of life, still full of admiration for the arrogant reply of Joyce's mouthpiece in *Exiles* to the man who said that such and such is the law of nature."[15] "The law of nature." Joyce replies coldly, "Did I vote for it?"

My only reply to my mirror is that I have changed in one way. To me, now, Ireland is worth my attention only when it is the world. I have no least speck of local patriotism left in me. I believe only that the dignity of man should never be diminished anywhere: in India, Johannesburg, Salisbury, Belfast, Mexico, Venezuela, Hungary, Czechoslovakia, or Great Britain. I don't give a tinker's curse who rules any one of these places so long as every man there is given parity of social, economic and cultural opportunity to be himself, and, at that, without interfering with the right of the man at his side to be himself in a completely opposite way. If this is childishness, I can only say that I have never understood why Saint Paul's grown man should put away the ways of a child.[16] Indeed, when they come to bury me, my only hope is that somebody will say something like, "But this coffin is as light as if it contained a boy."

14 German-American actress Marlene Dietrich (1901–1992); she sang "Falling in Love Again" (1930), which later became her signature song, in the film *Der blaue Engel* (*The Blue Angel*) (1930).

15 James Joyce's play *Exiles* (1918).

16 In 1 Corinthians 13, verse 11, St. Paul says: "When I was a child, I spake as a child, I understood as a child, I thought as a child: but when I became a man, I put away childish things."

Index